THE NEW TESTAMENT AND OTHER EARLY CHRISTIAN WRITINGS

A READER

Bart D. Ehrman

New York   Oxford
OXFORD UNIVERSITY PRESS
1998

Oxford University Press

Oxford   New York
Athens Auckland Bangkok Bogotá Bombay Buenos Aires
Calcutta Cape Town Dar es Salaam Delhi Florence Hong Kong
Istanbul Karachi Kuala Lumpur Madras Madrid Melbourne
Mexico City Nairobi Paris Singapore Taipei Tokyo Toronto

and associated companies in
Berlin Ibadan

Library of Congress Cataloging-in-Publication Data
Ehrman, Bart D.
The New Testament and other early Christian writings : a reader /
Bart D. Ehrman.
p.   cm.
ISBN 0-19-511192-3 (pbk. : alk. paper)
1. Bible. N.T.—Introductions.   2. Christian literature, Early—
History and criticism.   3. Church history—Primitive and early
church, ca. 30-600.   I. Title.
BS2330.2.E355   1998
270.1—dc20   96-43600

The publishers of the original translations used in this collection are hereby gratefully acknowledged:
    The books of the New Testament are from the New Revised Standard Version Bible, © 1989 by the Division of
Christian Education of the National Council of the Churches of Christ in the U.S.A. All rights reserved. Used by permission.
    "The Gospel of Thomas," from *The Nag Hammadi Library in English,* 3d. ed., by James M. Robinson, General Edi-
tor. © 1988 by E. J. Brill, Leiden, The Netherlands. Reprinted by permission of HarperCollins, New York.
    "The Gospel of Peter" and "The Infancy Gospel of Thomas," from *Documents for the Study of the Gospels,* edited
by David R. Cartlidge and David L. Dungan. © 1980 by David R. Cartlidge and David L. Dungan. Reprinted by permission
of Augsburg Fortress Press, Minneapolis.
    "The Letters of Ignatius," "The Letter of Polycarp to the Philippians," "The Letter of 1 Clement," and "The Di-
dache" from *Early Christian Fathers,* edited by Cyril D. Richardson (Library of Christian Classics Series). © 1953 by Westminster Press. Reprinted by permission of the Westminster Press/John Knox Press, Louisville.
    "The Gospel According to the Hebrews," "The Gospel of the Nazareans," "The Gospel of the Ebionites," "The
Preaching of Peter," "Papyrus Egerton 2," "The Secret Gospel of Mark," "The Acts of Paul and Thecla," "The Third Letter
to the Corinthians," and "The Apocalypse of Peter," from *The Apocryphal New Testament,* translated by J. K. Elliott, ©
1993 by Oxford University Press. Reprinted by permission.
    The "Fragments of Papias," translated by J. B. Lightfoot and J. R. Harmer, from *The Apostolic Fathers,* 2d ed., by
Michael W. Holmes. © 1989 by Baker Book House.
    "The Shepherd of Hermas," translated by Graydon F. Snyder, from *The Apostolic Fathers,* edited by Jack N.
Sparks. © 1978 by Thomas Nelson, Inc. Reprinted by permission.
    "The Letter of Barnabas," translated by Robert Kraft, from *The Apostolic Fathers,* edited by Jack N. Sparks. ©
1978 by Thomas Nelson, Inc. Reprinted by permission.

1 3 5 7 9 8 6 4 2

Printed in the United States of America
on acid-free paper.

Contents

Preface

The impetus for this collection of the earliest Christian writings came from my classroom experience. Even though my undergraduate class on the New Testament focuses, naturally enough, on the twenty-seven books that Christians eventually came to regard as canonical Scripture, it also considers other Christian books written at approximately the same time but not included, for a variety of reasons, in the Christian canon, books like the Gospels of *Peter* and *Thomas* and the letters of Ignatius and Barnabas. Many of these books were at one time or another considered Scripture by various Christians, and they are absolutely critical for any full understanding of the history and literature of early Christianity. But until now they have not been available in one volume, so that students wanting to own them have had to buy not only a New Testament, but also collections of the "Apostolic Fathers" (for such books as the letters of Ignatius and the *Epistle of Barnabas*), of the "New Testament Apocrypha" (e.g., for the *Gospel* and *Apocalypse of Peter*), and of the newly discovered "Nag Hammadi Library" (e.g., for the *Gospel of Thomas*).

It occurred to me, then, that it would make sense to have an inexpensive collection of *all* of the earliest Christian writings from the ancient world. Moreover, it seemed reasonable to assume that this collection would also appeal to readers outside the classroom setting, to anyone, in fact, interested in the earliest Christian church, its history, beliefs, practices, and literature. And so, as explained in the general introduction, this volume presents in clear and readable English translations every surviving document produced by a Christian during the first hundred years of the church, that is, from the time of Jesus' death (ca. 30 C.E.) through the first third of the second century (ca. 130 C.E.). Each document is provided with a brief introduction; the collection is preceded by a general introduction to the writings of the early Christians and to the question of how some of these writings came to be collected into the canon of Scripture.

Here I would like to acknowledge several people who assisted me in making this collection and, especially, in writing the introductions: Elizabeth Parker, my friend and former student, whose perspicacity exceeds her years; my good friends since graduate days, E. Elizabeth Johnson, Dale Martin, and Jeffrey Siker, themselves keen scholars and superb teachers; and Robert Miller, my exceptionally clearheaded editor at Oxford.

General Introduction

In the judgment of most scholars, the earliest New Testament book is 1 Thessalonians, written sometime around 50 C.E.; the latest is probably 2 Peter, written around 120 C.E. The seventy years separating these two works saw the appearance of scores of other Christian documents, some of them later canonized as parts of the New Testament, others of them not. Around 95 C.E., for example, the Christian congregation in Rome produced the letter called 1 Clement. Some fifteen or twenty years later Ignatius of Antioch wrote his surviving seven letters. At about the same time, the *Gospel of Thomas* appeared, as did the church manual called the *Didache* and the apocalypse known as *The Shepherd* of Hermas. These other works were not included among the books of the New Testament when the canon came to be fixed in the fourth and fifth centuries. Yet they also represent writings of the early Christians. And many of them, at one time or another, were considered sacred Scripture.

The purpose of the present work is to collect all of the earliest surviving Christian writings in one volume. For purposes of convenience, the term "earliest" refers to the first century of Christianity, 30 C.E. (the approximate year of Jesus' death) to 130 C.E., or thereabouts. The volume includes every work thought to have been produced by a Christian from this period, books that made it into the New Testament and those that did not, books later judged to be orthodox and those condemned as heretical, books that survive complete and books that survive only in fragments.

The collection does not, of course, include all of the literature actually *produced* during Christianity's first hundred years. On the contrary, we know of numerous texts from the period that, for one reason or another, no longer survive. Just from the writings of the New Testament, for example, we learn of a letter that Paul sent to the Christians of Corinth *before* he wrote 1 Corinthians (1 Cor 5:9), a letter that some of the Corinthians had sent to him (1 Cor 7:1), a letter forged in Paul's name to the Thessalonians (2 Thess 2:2), and a letter sent in his name to the church of Laodicea (Col 4:16). Moreover, the author of the Gospel of Luke indicates that "many" authors before him had written accounts of Jesus' life (1:1). Scholars are reasonably sure that the Gospel of Mark was one of these predecessors, but what of the others? At least one of them, the source of Jesus' sayings that scholars have called Q (from the German *Quelle,* "source," which was also used by Matthew), can probably be reconstructed to some extent. But this is a hypothetical undertaking.

The historical reality is that most of the noncanonical books mentioned in our early surviving sources have been lost. Some were destroyed when Christian leaders found their teachings dangerous. Others simply disappeared out of general disinterest: no one bothered to reproduce them for posterity. The books that do survive were copied through the Middle Ages by Christian scribes intent on preserving their sacred texts, or they were hidden for one reason or another in antiquity, only to be turned up in modern times by professional archaeologists or rummaging bedouin. In any event, most of the writings that survive from early Christianity have come down to us in the New Testament itself.

THE CANON OF THE NEW TESTAMENT

One of the major breakthroughs in biblical scholarship over the past century—a break-through whose roots lie in the Reformation—is the recognition that even the twenty-seven books of the New Testament evidence a considerable degree of diversity among themselves. These writings were produced by at least seventeen different authors living in various countries. These authors addressed different audiences for different reasons; in some instances, they express fundamentally different perspectives on fundamentally significant issues. When the early literature that was *not* included in the New Testament is thrown into the mix, the rich and wide diversity of the early Christian movement becomes even more apparent.

This, then, raises the question of why some books were chosen to be included in the New Testament while others were excluded. Full-length studies of this question are readily available; for the purposes of this introduction, a basic sketch of the situation will suffice.[1]

From the very beginning, Christianity was deeply rooted both in oral traditions about its founder and in written texts that it had inherited from Judaism. Jesus himself, as a Jewish teacher and prophet, discussed, explained, and debated the Hebrew Scriptures; his followers eventually came to understand him to be the Messiah sent from God in fulfillment of these Scriptures. As the early Christians told stories about what he said and did, the Scriptures were never far removed from their thoughts; indeed the oral traditions about Jesus, especially in the formative period of the religion, were closely informed by Christian understandings of the Law, the Psalms, and the prophets. Soon after Jesus' death, his followers interpreted his life in light of these writings; they eventually saw themselves as the true heirs of the traditions they contained, even when their own communities were comprised, by and large, of Gentiles rather than Jews.

We do not know which Christian was the first to write a book, but the earliest surviving works are by the apostle Paul, who some twenty years after Jesus' death began to write letters to churches that he had founded in the northeastern Mediterranean. Soon thereafter a flood of literature appeared: letters urging certain beliefs and lifestyles on their Christian addressees; accounts of the life, death, and resurrection of Jesus; apocalyptic portrayals of the end time. Eventually there appeared histories of the Christian church, sermons delivered to Christian congregations, manuals for conducting Christian rituals, and accounts of the deaths of early Christian martyrs.

Early Christianity became a remarkably literary movement. Apart from Judaism, there was nothing quite like it in the entire Greco-Roman world, where literary texts typically had very little to do with religion per se. In part, of course, the literary impulse came from the Jewish religion from which the Christian church emerged, but in part it came from the universalistic thrust of the new religion itself. Many Christians believed that in fulfillment of the promises made to the Jewish patriarchs, Jesus had come as a savior of the entire world, not just Israel. As different communities came to be established throughout the Roman Empire, Christians everywhere had a sense that they *belonged* together, that they were part of something larger than their own small communities, that the church was not merely a local congregation but a worldwide movement through which God was bringing salvation to all people.

---

[1]For a brief sketch, see Bart D. Ehrman, *The New Testament: A Historical Introduction to the Early Christian Writings* (New York: Oxford, 1996) chap. 1. For a fuller, article-length discussion, see Harry Gamble, "Canon: New Testament," in the *Anchor Bible Dictionary,* vol. 1 (New York: Doubleday, 1992) pp. 852–61. A nice, concise, book-length treatment can be found in H. Gamble, *The New Testament Canon: Its Making and Meaning,* Guides to Biblical Scholarship (Philadelphia: Fortress, 1985). For a full and authoritative discussion, see Bruce M. Metzger, *The Canon of the New Testament* (New York: Oxford, 1987).

The literature that was produced by early Christians served to bind the various Christian communities together. Leaders and groups from one congregation wrote to others; books written in one place for one purpose were taken to another place, copied there, and read by Christians completely unknown to the author and his or her own community. This earliest Christian literature thus provided spiritual, intellectual, and emotional cohesion for communities that were geographically separated.

Already by the middle of the first century C.E., many Christians considered the words of Jesus to be as authoritative as the words of Scripture found in the Hebrew Bible; by the end of the century, some Christian writings were being granted comparable authority. The process is already evident in works that made it into the New Testament: 1 Timothy 5:18, for example, places a saying of Jesus on a par with the Jewish Bible, and 2 Peter 3:16 numbers Paul's letters among the Scriptures. Even at this relatively early stage, then, two kinds of Christian authority had begun to emerge: traditions about Jesus and writings by his apostles. The Christian canon that eventually developed reflects this bipartite structure, comprising Gospels and other apostolic books.

A good deal of the early Christian literature responded to the needs of the various local congregations. Leaders of the churches were concerned that their followers understood what to believe (doctrine), how to live (ethics), and how to engage in Christian worship and ritual (practice). As might be expected of congregations scattered throughout vast tracts of the Roman empire, individuals coming from richly varied backgrounds—in terms of cultural heritage, social class, economic position, religious upbringing, educational opportunity, and so forth—had widely diverse views about almost everything Christian. The written texts produced by these individuals reflect their range of opinions.

This kind of diversity soon became a problem for Christian leaders intent on the unity of the religion, who saw Christianity as *one* thing rather than lots of *different* things, who understood the gospel of Christ as having a single meaning to be professed and practiced by all Christians in the same way everywhere. The diversity of the movement came to be especially evident around the middle of the second century, just after the period covered in the present volume. Forceful and charismatic Christians came forward, advocating beliefs and practices that were seen by others as totally unacceptable. Battle lines were drawn, with each side claiming to represent the authentic Christian tradition passed down from Jesus himself to the disciples.

In the debates that ensued, nothing proved more important than the Christian literature that had been produced earlier. Christians of various stripe put forth their own "authoritative" texts, claiming that books written by apostles were normative for what Christians should believe and how they should live. The side that won these debates decided the contours of the canon that was to be passed down to Christian posterity. We have the results of this victory in the writings of the New Testament. Even for ancient readers, when these books were taken individually outside of their canonical contexts they could be thought to represent a wide range of Christian perspective; but when they were grouped together into *one* book, the New Testament canon, they were understood to present a unified theological and practical perspective that was acceptable to the majority of Christians involved in the selection process.

The decisions concerning which books should be considered Scripture did not come immediately to an end at the close of the second century. On the contrary, the debates continued for centuries. To be sure, already by 200 C.E. many churches accepted most of the books that eventually made it into the canon. But not all churches agreed. We know of some second- and third-century Christian communities, for example, that accepted only one of our canonical Gospels as authoritative (e.g., only Matthew or only Luke or only John); other communities that accepted none of the four individually, but used a much fuller Gospel created around 170 C.E., a harmonization of our four books into one megagospel (the so-called *Diatesseron,* which no longer survives intact); and other communities that had their own favorites, including Gospels that did not come to be included in the New Testament (e.g., the *Gospel of Peter* or the *Gospel of Thomas*). During this same period, some Christian communities saw the Apostle Paul as the only final authority for faith and practice, while other communities saw him as an arch-heretic and enemy of God. There were some communities that accepted the Apocalypse of John as a divine revelation of the future course of events, and other communities that rejected the book as naive and nonapostolic. And there were some communities that accepted the *Letter of 1 Clement, The Shepherd* of Hermas, and the *Letter of Barnabas* as Scripture, while other communities did not.

Christians involved in the disputes over the canon of Scripture typically invoked several considerations. Generally it was thought that, to be included, a book needed to be ancient (close to the time of Jesus), apostolic (written by an apostle or one of their companions), orthodox (affirming the "right" belief, whatever that was judged to be), and catholic (widely used throughout the church). The debates were sometimes harsh; by all counts, they were long and drawn out. Strikingly enough, it was not until 367 C.E.—nearly 250 years after the last of the canonical books was actually written—that any Christian author listed the twenty-seven books of our New Testament, and only these books, as belonging to the Christian Scriptures. The author was Athanasius, the bishop of Alexandria, who penned his list precisely because so many people in his community and elsewhere disagreed.

In sum, it is important for modern readers to realize that the book we call the New Testament is actually a *collection* of books, put together by persons living much later than the actual authors. When "Matthew" wrote his Gospel, he had no idea that someone would eventually combine his book with three others that were more or less like it to form the first section of a canon of Scripture, a canon that was to include a history of the Christian movement, personal letters sent by other early Christians, and an apocalyptic narrative of the end time. The New Testament, in other words, is a historical construct, not a "given." It comprises twenty-seven diverse books brought together under one cover for particular religious reasons and under specific historical circumstances. It is not fully representative of the views and writings of the early Christians.

On the other hand, and somewhat unfortunately, *no* collection of Christian books can be fully representative of these early Christians, precisely because so much of their literature has been lost. The present collection at least provides the best cross-sampling possible, in that it gives all of the earliest Christian literature that has come down to us, both the books that came to form part of the New Testament and those that did not.

By way of conclusion, it may be worthwhile to say a brief word concerning the collection itself.

LIMITATIONS OF THE COLLECTION

This collection includes the early Christian writings that appear to have been composed by the first third of the second century. These writings survive either in manuscript form (i.e., as copied by scribes) or in direct quotations by other authors. The collection does not include texts that do not actually survive, such as the Q source of Jesus' sayings that appears to lie behind Matthew and Luke. Nor does it include paraphrases of early Christian writings found in later sources. As a matter of convenience, several highly fragmentary texts have been excluded, such as the one-sentence statement drawn from the Apology of Quadratus by the fourth-century church father Eusebius (*Ecclesiastical History* 4.3).

There are some texts that other scholars would include among the literature of this period, such as the *Apocryphon of James* and the *Gospel of the Egyptians,* that have been excluded here simply because, in the opinion of the present editor, they cannot be reliably dated to the first hundred years of the Christian movement (30–130 C.E.). These two particular examples, in any event, happen to be gospel texts, of which enough other samples survive to provide a good sense of the materials that were being produced and read in the period.

TEXTS

All of the texts are given in previously published and well-established English translations, with full permission of their original publishers. Translations have been chosen on the grounds of accuracy and, especially, readability. The New Revised Standard Version of the New Testament will be familiar to many readers; the other texts are also readily available. Alterations have been kept to a minimum and been made with permission; these involve such things as the standardization of spelling, capitalization, and punctuation and the occasional modernization of language (e.g., *thee's* and *thou's* and jarring instances of non-inclusive language).

Cross-references are provided for explicit or clear citations of the Hebrew Bible and other sacred texts (including earlier Christian writings cited by later authors; these earlier writings are themselves, of course, also presented in full). No attempt has been made to identify scriptural allusions or distant echoes.

The complete text of each book or surviving fragment has been included, except in the cases of *The Shepherd* of Hermas and the *Apocalypse of Peter.* These are unusually long documents; the selections provided here should give an adequate idea of their content and style.

STRUCTURE

There is no completely satisfactory way to arrange these materials. It is impossible to give them chronologically, since so many of them can be dated with only proximate accuracy. And because so many of them cover a variety of topics, a thematic arrangement is likewise out of the question. For the sake of convenience, therefore, the collection follows the structure provided by the New Testament itself, with books arranged more or less by genre: Gospels (written accounts of the words and/or deeds of Jesus), Acts (narratives of the history of the church and/or the activities of the apostles), Pauline epistles (letters sent by Paul and other early Christians in his name), other writings (a mixture of genres, including other letters, a sermon, a persuasive essay, and a church manual), and apocalypses (narrative visions of the heavenly realities that explain earthly existence).

INTRODUCTIONS

Each of the texts is provided with a concise introduction that highlights its important features and supplies essential background information. The collection as a whole was originally designed to accompany the fuller introduction to this literature in Bart D. Ehrman, *The New Testament: A Historical Introduction to the Early Christian Writings* (New York: Oxford University Press, 1997). Anyone interested in learning more about these texts can turn to that volume or to any other historical introduction to the New Testament and other early Christian writings.

EARLY CHRISTIAN GOSPELS

The Gospel According to Matthew

Matthew was awarded pride of place as the first Gospel of the New Testament, not because it was the first to be written, but probably because it was the most widely used by early Christians interested in knowing about the birth, life, death, and resurrection of Jesus. Indeed, stories found in Matthew but in none of our other Gospels continue to be among the best known and most popular accounts for readers of the New Testament today. Only here do we read of the visit of the magi to the infant Jesus and of the flight to Egypt; here alone does Jesus deliver his Sermon on the Mount with its memorable form of the Beatitudes ("Blessed are the poor in spirit" . . .), Antitheses ("You have heard that it was said, 'An eye for an eye and a tooth for a tooth,' But I say to you . . ."), and other inspirational sayings ("Store up for yourselves treasures in heaven," "No one can serve two masters," "Do not worry about tomorrow, for tomorrow will bring worries of its own").

Christian writers of the second century ascribed the book to Matthew, the tax collector called by Jesus to be his disciple (see Matt 9:9). The actual author of the book, however, did not disclose his name. Scholars today generally think that he was a Greek-speaking Christian writing in the second half of the first century, perhaps around 80–85 C.E., probably outside of Palestine, possibly, in the opinion of some, in Antioch of Syria. The author's insistence that Jesus' followers adhere closely to the Jewish law (Matt 7:17–20) may suggest that he was himself a Jewish Christian; at the same time, his claim that Gentiles who accepted Jesus would enter into God's kingdom while many Jews would remain outside (8:10–12) may indicate that his own Christian community was comprised of both Jews and Gentiles.

It appears that Matthew's accounts were drawn from written and oral sources, including the Gospel of Mark and a collection of Jesus' sayings that scholars have designated Q (from the German word for "source," *Quelle*), a lost Gospel that was also available to the author of Luke. "Matthew" used these sources to create a distinctive portrayal of Jesus as a new Moses who provides the authoritative interpretation of the Jewish law (e.g., 5:1–48). His followers are to adhere to this law in all its particulars, and to do so even better than the Jewish leaders, the scribes and Pharisees who throughout this Gospel are condemned as self-serving hypocrites (see chap. 23).

These leaders fail to be convinced of Jesus' identity, despite his many miraculous deeds; as his opponents, they ultimately arrange to have him executed (chaps. 26–27). But this death is according to God's plan, for through it Jesus "saves his people from their sins" (1:21). On the third day, Jesus is raised from the dead and appears to his disciples, commissioning them to spread his "good news" throughout the entire world, teaching their converts to observe all that Jesus commanded, until he returns (28:19–20).

From the New Revised Standard Version Bible, © 1989.

1 An account of the genealogy[a] of Jesus the Messiah,[b] the son of David, the son of Abraham.

2 Abraham was the father of Isaac, and Isaac the father of Jacob, and Jacob the father of Judah and his brothers, 3 and Judah the father of Perez and Zerah by Tamar, and Perez the father of Hezron, and Hezron the father of Aram, 4 and Aram the father of Aminadab, and Aminadab the father of Nahshon, and Nahshon the father of Salmon, 5 and Salmon the father of Boaz by Rahab, and Boaz the father of Obed by Ruth, and Obed the father of Jesse, 6 and Jesse the father of King David.

And David was the father of Solomon by the wife of Uriah, 7 and Solomon the father of Rehoboam, and Rehoboam the father of Abijah, and Abijah the father of Asaph,[c] 8 and Asaph[c] the father of Jehoshaphat, and Jehoshaphat the father of Joram, and Joram the father of Uzziah, 9 and Uzziah the father of Jotham, and Jotham the father of Ahaz, and Ahaz the father of Hezekiah, 10 and Hezekiah the father of Manasseh, and Manasseh the father of Amos,[d] and Amos[d] the father of Josiah, 11 and Josiah the father of Jechoniah and his brothers, at the time of the deportation to Babylon.

12 And after the deportation to Babylon: Jechoniah was the father of Salathiel, and Salathiel the father of Zerubbabel, 13 and Zerubbabel the father of Abiud, and Abiud the father of Eliakim, and Eliakim the father of Azor, 14 and Azor the father of Zadok, and Zadok the father of Achim, and Achim the father of Eliud, 15 and Eliud the father of Eleazar, and Eleazar the father of Matthan, and Matthan the father of Jacob, 16 and Jacob the father of Joseph the husband of Mary, of whom Jesus was born, who is called the Messiah.[e]

17 So all the generations from Abraham to David are fourteen generations; and from David to the deportation to Babylon, fourteen generations; and from the deportation to Babylon to the Messiah,[e] fourteen generations.

18 Now the birth of Jesus the Messiah[b] took place in this way. When his mother Mary had been engaged to Joseph, but before they lived together, she was found to be with child from the Holy Spirit. 19 Her husband Joseph, being a righteous man and unwilling to expose her to public disgrace, planned to dismiss her quietly. 20 But just when

he had resolved to do this, an angel of the Lord appeared to him in a dream and said, "Joseph, son of David, do not be afraid to take Mary as your wife, for the child conceived in her is from the Holy Spirit. 21 She will bear a son, and you are to name him Jesus, for he will save his people from their sins." 22 All this took place to fulfill what had been spoken by the Lord through the prophet:

23   "Look, the virgin shall conceive
              and bear a son,
          and they shall name him
              Emmanuel,"[1]

which means, "God is with us."[2] 24 When Joseph awoke from sleep, he did as the angel of the Lord commanded him; he took her as his wife, 25 but had no marital relations with her until she had borne a son;[f] and he named him Jesus.

2 In the time of King Herod, after Jesus was born in Bethlehem of Judea, wise men[g] from the East came to Jerusalem, 2 asking, "Where is the child who has been born king of the Jews? For we observed his star at its rising,[i] and have come to pay him homage." 3 When King Herod heard this, he was frightened, and all Jerusalem with him; 4 and calling together all the chief priests and scribes of the people, he inquired of them where the Messiah[e] was to be born. 5 They told him, "In Bethlehem of Judea; for so it has been written by the prophet:

6   'And you, Bethlehem, in the land
              of Judah,
          are by no means least among
              the rulers of Judah;
          for from you shall come a ruler
          who is to shepherd[j] my people
              Israel.'"[3]

7 Then Herod secretly called for the wise men[g] and learned from them the exact time when the star had appeared. 8 Then he sent them to Bethlehem, saying, "Go and search diligently for the child; and when you have found him, bring me word so

---

[a]Or birth   [b]Or Jesus Christ   [c]Other ancient authorities read Asa
[d]Other ancient authorities read Amon   [e]Or the Christ   [f]Or rule
[g]Or astrologers; Gk magi   [h]Other ancient authorities read her firstborn son   [i]Or in the East   [j]Or rule

---

[1]Isa 7:14   [2]Isa 8:8, 10   [3]Mic 5:2; 2 Sam 5:2

that I may also go and pay him homage." 9 When they had heard the king, they set out; and there, ahead of them, went the star that they had seen at its rising,[k] until it stopped over the place where the child was. 10 When they saw that the star had stopped,[l] they were overwhelmed with joy. 11 On entering the house, they saw the child with Mary his mother; and they knelt down and paid him homage. Then, opening their treasure chests, they offered him gifts of gold, frankincense, and myrrh. 12 And having been warned in a dream not to return to Herod, they left for their own country by another road.

13 Now after they had left, an angel of the Lord appeared to Joseph in a dream and said, "Get up, take the child and his mother, and flee to Egypt, and remain there until I tell you; for Herod is about to search for the child, to destroy him." 14 Then Joseph[m] got up, took the child and his mother by night, and went to Egypt, 15 and remained there until the death of Herod. This was to fulfill what had been spoken by the Lord through the prophet, "Out of Egypt I have called my son."[4]

16 When Herod saw that he had been tricked by the wise men,[n] he was infuriated, and he sent and killed all the children in and around Bethlehem who were two years old or under, according to the time that he had learned from the wise men.[n] 17 Then was fulfilled what had been spoken through the prophet Jeremiah:

18 "A voice was heard in Ramah,
       wailing and loud lamentation,
     Rachel weeping for her children;
       she refused to be consoled,
         because they are no more."[5]

19 When Herod died, an angel of the Lord suddenly appeared in a dream to Joseph in Egypt and said, 20 "Get up, take the child and his mother, and go to the land of Israel, for those who were seeking the child's life are dead." 21 Then Joseph[m] got up, took the child and his mother, and went to the land of Israel. 22 But when he heard that Archelaus was ruling over Judea in place of his father Herod, he was afraid to go there. And after being warned in a dream, he went away to the district of Galilee. 23 There he made his home in a town called Nazareth, so that what had been spoken through the prophets might be fulfilled, "He will be called a Nazorean."[6]

3 In those days John the Baptist appeared in the wilderness of Judea, proclaiming, 2 "Repent, for the kingdom of heaven has come near."[o] 3 This is the one of whom the prophet Isaiah spoke when he said,

       "The voice of one crying out in
         the wilderness:
       'Prepare the way of the Lord,
         make his paths straight.'"[7]

4 Now John wore clothing of camel's hair with a leather belt around his waist, and his food was locusts and wild honey. 5 Then the people of Jerusalem and all Judea were going out to him, and all the region along the Jordan, 6 and they were baptized by him in the river Jordan, confessing their sins.

7 But when he saw many Pharisees and Sadducees coming for baptism, he said to them, "You brood of vipers! Who warned you to flee from the wrath to come? 8 Bear fruit worthy of repentance. 9 Do not presume to say to yourselves, 'We have Abraham as our ancestor'; for I tell you, God is able from these stones to raise up children to Abraham. 10 Even now the ax is lying at the root of the trees; every tree therefore that does not bear good fruit is cut down and thrown into the fire.

11 "I baptize you with[p] water for repentance, but one who is more powerful than I is coming after me; I am not worthy to carry his sandals. He will baptize you with[p] the Holy Spirit and fire. 12 His winnowing fork is in his hand, and he will clear his threshing floor and will gather his wheat into the granary; but the chaff he will burn with unquenchable fire."

13 Then Jesus came from Galilee to John at the Jordan, to be baptized by him. 14 John would have prevented him, saying, "I need to be baptized by you, and do you come to me?" 15 But Jesus answered him, "Let it be so now; for it is proper for us in this way to fulfill all righteousness." Then he consented. 16 And when Jesus had been baptized, just as he came up from the water, suddenly the heavens were opened to him and he saw the Spirit of God descending like a dove and alighting on

---

[k]Or *in the East* [l]Gk *saw the star* [m]Gk *he* [n]Or *astrologers*; Gk *magi* [o]Or *is at hand* [p]Or *in*

---

[4]Hos 11:1 [5]Jer 31:15 [6]Isa 11:1(?) [7]Isa 40:3

him. 17 And a voice from heaven said, "This is my Son, the Beloved,[q] with whom I am well pleased."

4 Then Jesus was led up by the Spirit into the wilderness to be tempted by the devil. 2 He fasted forty days and forty nights, and afterwards he was famished. 3 The tempter came and said to him, "If you are the Son of God, command these stones to become loaves of bread." 4 But he answered, "It is written,

'One does not live by bread alone,
 but by every word that comes
  from the mouth of God.'"[8]

5 Then the devil took him to the holy city and placed him on the pinnacle of the temple, 6 saying to him, "If you are the Son of God, throw yourself down; for it is written,

'He will command his angels
 concerning you,'
and 'On their hands they will
 bear you up,
so that you will not dash your
 foot against a stone.'"[9]

7 Jesus said to him, "Again it is written, 'Do not put the Lord your God to the test.'"[10]

8 Again, the devil took him to a very high mountain and showed him all the kingdoms of the world and their splendor; 9 and he said to him, "All these I will give you, if you will fall down and worship me." 10 Jesus said to him, "Away with you, Satan! for it is written,

'Worship the Lord your God,
 and serve only him.'"[11]

11 Then the devil left him, and suddenly angels came and waited on him.

12 Now when Jesus[r] heard that John had been arrested, he withdrew to Galilee. 13 He left Nazareth and made his home in Capernaum by the sea, in the territory of Zebulun and Naphtali, 14 so that what had been spoken through the prophet Isaiah might be fulfilled:

15   "Land of Zebulun, land of
       Naphtali,
     on the road by the sea, across
       the Jordan, Galilee of the
       Gentiles—
16   the people who sat in darkness
       have seen a great light,
     and for those who sat in

the region and shadow of death
 light has dawned."[12]

17 From that time Jesus began to proclaim, "Repent, for the kingdom of heaven has come near."[s]

18 As he walked by the Sea of Galilee, he saw two brothers, Simon, who is called Peter, and Andrew his brother, casting a net into the sea—for they were fishermen. 19 And he said to them, "Follow me, and I will make you fish for people." 20 Immediately they left their nets and followed him. 21 As he went from there, he saw two other brothers, James son of Zebedee and his brother John, in the boat with their father Zebedee, mending their nets, and he called them. 22 Immediately they left the boat and their father, and followed him.

23 Jesus[r] went throughout Galilee, teaching in their synagogues and proclaiming the good news[t] of the kingdom and curing every disease and every sickness among the people. 24 So his fame spread throughout all Syria, and they brought to him all the sick, those who were afflicted with various diseases and pains, demoniacs, epileptics, and paralytics, and he cured them. 25 And great crowds followed him from Galilee, the Decapolis, Jerusalem, Judea, and from beyond the Jordan.

5 When Jesus[r] saw the crowds, he went up the mountain; and after he sat down, his disciples came to him. 2 Then he began to speak, and taught them, saying:

3 "Blessed are the poor in spirit, for theirs is the kingdom of heaven.

4 "Blessed are those who mourn, for they will be comforted.

5 "Blessed are the meek, for they will inherit the earth.

6 "Blessed are those who hunger and thirst for righteousness, for they will be filled.

7 "Blessed are the merciful, for they will receive mercy.

8 "Blessed are the pure in heart, for they will see God.

9 "Blessed are the peacemakers, for they will be called children of God.

---

[q]Or *my beloved Son*   [r]Gk *he*   [s]Or *is at hand*   [t]Gk *gospel*

[8]Deut 8:3   [9]Ps 91:11–12   [10]Deut 6:16   [11]Deut 6:13   [12]Isa 9:1–2

10 "Blessed are those who are persecuted for righteousness' sake, for theirs is the kingdom of heaven.

11 "Blessed are you when people revile you and persecute you and utter all kinds of evil against you falsely[u] on my account. 12 Rejoice and be glad, for your reward is great in heaven, for in the same way they persecuted the prophets who were before you.

13 "You are the salt of the earth; but if salt has lost its taste, how can its saltiness be restored? It is no longer good for anything, but is thrown out and trampled under foot.

14 "You are the light of the world. A city built on a hill cannot be hid. 15 No one after lighting a lamp puts it under the bushel basket, but on the lampstand, and it gives light to all in the house. 16 In the same way, let your light shine before others, so that they may see your good works and give glory to your Father in heaven.

17 "Do not think that I have come to abolish the law or the prophets; I have come not to abolish but to fulfill. 18 For truly I tell you, until heaven and earth pass away, not one letter,[v] not one stroke of a letter, will pass from the law until all is accomplished. 19 Therefore, whoever breaks[w] one of the least of these commandments, and teaches others to do the same, will be called least in the kingdom of heaven; but whoever does them and teaches them will be called great in the kingdom of heaven. 20 For I tell you, unless your righteousness exceeds that of the scribes and Pharisees, you will never enter the kingdom of heaven.

21 "You have heard that it was said to those of ancient times, 'You shall not murder';[13] and 'whoever murders shall be liable to judgment.' 22 But I say to you that if you are angry with a brother or sister,[x] you will be liable to judgment; and if you insult[y] a brother or sister,[z] you will be liable to the council; and if you say, 'You fool,' you will be liable to the hell[a] of fire. 23 So when you are offering your gift at the altar, if you remember that your brother or sister[b] has something against you, 24 leave your gift there before the altar and go; first be reconciled to your brother or sister,[b] and then come and offer your gift. 25 Come to terms quickly with your accuser while you are on the way to court[c] with him, or your accuser may hand you over to the judge, and the judge to the guard, and you will be thrown into prison. 26 Truly I tell you, you will never get out until you have paid the last penny.

27 "You have heard that it was said, 'You shall not commit adultery.'[14] 28 But I say to you that everyone who looks at a woman with lust has already committed adultery with her in his heart. 29 If your right eye causes you to sin, tear it out and throw it away; it is better for you to lose one of your members than for your whole body to be thrown into hell.[a] 30 And if your right hand causes you to sin, cut it off and throw it away; it is better for you to lose one of your members than for your whole body to go into hell.[a]

31 "It was also said, 'Whoever divorces his wife, let him give her a certificate of divorce.'[15] 32 But I say to you that anyone who divorces his wife, except on the ground of unchastity, causes her to commit adultery; and whoever marries a divorced woman commits adultery.

33 "Again, you have heard that it was said to those of ancient times, 'You shall not swear falsely, but carry out the vows you have made to the Lord.'[16] 34 But I say to you, Do not swear at all, either by heaven, for it is the throne of God, 35 or by the earth, for it is his footstool, or by Jerusalem, for it is the city of the great King. 36 And do not swear by your head, for you cannot make one hair white or black. 37 Let your word be 'Yes, Yes' or 'No, No'; anything more than this comes from the evil one.[d]

38 "You have heard that it was said, 'An eye for an eye and a tooth for a tooth.'[17] 39 But I say to you, Do not resist an evildoer. But if anyone strikes you on the right cheek, turn the other also; 40 and if anyone wants to sue you and take your coat, give your cloak as well; 41 and if anyone forces you to go one mile, go also the second mile. 42 Give to everyone who begs from you, and do not refuse anyone who wants to borrow from you.

43 "You have heard that it was said, 'You shall love your neighbor and hate your enemy.'[18]

---

[u]Other ancient authorities lack *falsely*   [v]Gk *one iota*   [w]Or *annuls*
[x]Gk *a brother*; other ancient authorities add *without cause*   [y]Gk *say Raca to* (an obscure term of abuse)   [z]Gk *a brother*   [a]Gk *Gehenna*
[b]Gk *your brother*   [c]Gk lacks *to court*   [d]Or *evil*

[13]Exod 20:13; Deut 5:17   [14]Exod 20:14; Deut 5:18   [15]Deut 24:1
[16]Exod 20:7; Lev 19:12; Num 30:2; Deut 23:21   [17]Exod 21:24; Lev 24:20; Deut 19:21   [18]Lev 19:18

44 But I say to you, Love your enemies and pray for those who persecute you, 45 so that you may be children of your Father in heaven; for he makes his sun rise on the evil and on the good, and sends rain on the righteous and on the unrighteous. 46 For if you love those who love you, what reward do you have? Do not even the tax collectors do the same? 47 And if you greet only your brothers and sisters,[e] what more are you doing than others? Do not even the Gentiles do the same? 48 Be perfect, therefore, as your heavenly Father is perfect.

6 "Beware of practicing your piety before others in order to be seen by them; for then you have no reward from your Father in heaven.

2 "So whenever you give alms, do not sound a trumpet before you, as the hypocrites do in the synagogues and in the streets, so that they may be praised by others. Truly I tell you, they have received their reward. 3 But when you give alms, do not let your left hand know what your right hand is doing, 4 so that your alms may be done in secret; and your Father who sees in secret will reward you.[f]

5 "And whenever you pray, do not be like the hypocrites; for they love to stand and pray in the synagogues and at the street corners, so that they may be seen by others. Truly I tell you, they have received their reward. 6 But whenever you pray, go into your room and shut the door and pray to your Father who is in secret; and your Father who sees in secret will reward you.[f]

7 "When you are praying, do not heap up empty phrases as the Gentiles do; for they think that they will be heard because of their many words. 8 Do not be like them, for your Father knows what you need before you ask him.

9 "Pray then in this way:
Our Father in heaven,
    hallowed be your name.
10   Your kingdom come.
    Your will be done,
      on earth as it is in heaven.
11   Give us this day our daily
      bread.[g]
12   And forgive us our debts,
      as we also have forgiven our
      debtors.

13   And do not bring us to the time
      of trial,[h]
    but rescue us from the evil
      one.[i]

14 For if you forgive others their trespasses, your heavenly Father will also forgive you; 15 but if you do not forgive others, neither will your Father forgive your trespasses.

16 "And whenever you fast, do not look dismal, like the hypocrites, for they disfigure their faces so as to show others that they are fasting. Truly I tell you, they have received their reward. 17 But when you fast, put oil on your head and wash your face, 18 so that your fasting may be seen not by others but by your Father who is in secret; and your Father who sees in secret will reward you.[f]

19 "Do not store up for yourselves treasures on earth, where moth and rust[j] consume and where thieves break in and steal; 20 but store up for yourselves treasures in heaven, where neither moth nor rust[j] consumes and where thieves do not break in and steal. 21 For where your treasure is, there your heart will be also.

22 "The eye is the lamp of the body. So, if your eye is healthy, your whole body will be full of light; 23 but if your eye is unhealthy, your whole body will be full of darkness. If then the light in you is darkness, how great is the darkness!

24 "No one can serve two masters; for a slave will either hate the one and love the other, or be devoted to the one and despise the other. You cannot serve God and wealth.[k]

25 "Therefore I tell you, do not worry about your life, what you will eat or what you will drink,[l] or about your body, what you will wear. Is not life more than food, and the body more than clothing? 26 Look at the birds of the air; they neither sow nor reap nor gather into barns, and yet your heavenly Father feeds them. Are you not of more value than they? 27 And can any of you by worrying add a single hour to your span of life?[m] 28 And why do you worry about clothing? Consider the lilies of

---

[e]Gk your brothers   [f]Other ancient authorities add openly   [g]Or our bread for tomorrow   [h]Or us into temptation   [i]Or from evil. Other ancient authorities add, in some form, For the kingdom and the power and the glory are yours forever. Amen.   [j]Gk eating   [k]Gk mammon [l]Other ancient authorities lack or what you will drink   [m]Or add one cubit to your height

the field, how they grow; they neither toil nor spin, 29 yet I tell you, even Solomon in all his glory was not clothed like one of these. 30 But if God so clothes the grass of the field, which is alive today and tomorrow is thrown into the oven, will he not much more clothe you—you of little faith? 31 Therefore do not worry, saying, 'What will we eat?' or 'What will we drink?' or 'What will we wear?' 32 For it is the Gentiles who strive for all these things; and indeed your heavenly Father knows that you need all these things. 33 But strive first for the kingdom of God[n] and his[o] righteousness, and all these things will be given to you as well.

34 "So do not worry about tomorrow, for tomorrow will bring worries of its own. Today's trouble is enough for today.

7 "Do not judge, so that you may not be judged. 2 For with the judgment you make you will be judged, and the measure you give will be the measure you get. 3 Why do you see the speck in your neighbor's[p] eye, but do not notice the log in your own eye? 4 Or how can you say to your neighbor,[q] 'Let me take the speck out of your eye,' while the log is in your own eye? 5 You hypocrite, first take the log out of your own eye, and then you will see clearly to take the speck out of your neighbor's[p] eye.

6 "Do not give what is holy to dogs; and do not throw your pearls before swine, or they will trample them under foot and turn and maul you.

7 "Ask, and it will be given you; search, and you will find; knock, and the door will be opened for you. 8 For everyone who asks receives, and everyone who searches finds, and for everyone who knocks, the door will be opened. 9 Is there anyone among you who, if your child asks for bread, will give a stone? 10 Or if the child asks for a fish, will give a snake? 11 If you then, who are evil, know how to give good gifts to your children, how much more will your Father in heaven give good things to those who ask him!

12 "In everything do to others as you would have them do to you; for this is the law and the prophets.

13 "Enter through the narrow gate; for the gate is wide and the road is easy[r] that leads to destruction, and there are many who take it. 14 For the gate is narrow and the road is hard that leads to life, and there are few who find it.

15 "Beware of false prophets, who come to you in sheep's clothing but inwardly are ravenous wolves. 16 You will know them by their fruits. Are grapes gathered from thorns, or figs from thistles? 17 In the same way, every good tree bears good fruit, but the bad tree bears bad fruit. 18 A good tree cannot bear bad fruit, nor can a bad tree bear good fruit. 19 Every tree that does not bear good fruit is cut down and thrown into the fire. 20 Thus you will know them by their fruits.

21 "Not everyone who says to me, 'Lord, Lord,' will enter the kingdom of heaven, but only the one who does the will of my Father in heaven. 22 On that day many will say to me, 'Lord, Lord, did we not prophesy in your name, and cast out demons in your name, and do many deeds of power in your name?' 23 Then I will declare to them, 'I never knew you; go away from me, you evildoers.'

24 "Everyone then who hears these words of mine and acts on them will be like a wise man who built his house on rock. 25 The rain fell, the floods came, and the winds blew and beat on that house, but it did not fall, because it had been founded on rock. 26 And everyone who hears these words of mine and does not act on them will be like a foolish man who built his house on sand. 27 The rain fell, and the floods came, and the winds blew and beat against that house, and it fell—and great was its fall!"

28 Now when Jesus had finished saying these things, the crowds were astounded at his teaching, 29 for he taught them as one having authority, and not as their scribes.

8 When Jesus[s] had come down from the mountain, great crowds followed him; 2 and there was a leper[t] who came to him and knelt before him, saying, "Lord, if you choose, you can make me clean." 3 He stretched out his hand and touched him, saying, "I do choose. Be made clean!" Immediately his leprosy[t] was cleansed. 4 Then Jesus said to him, "See that you say noth-

---

[n]Other ancient authorities lack *of God*   [o]Or *its*   [p]Gk *brother's*
[q]Gk *brother*   [r]Other ancient authorities read *for the road is wide and easy*   [s]Gk *he*   [t]The terms *leper* and *leprosy* can refer to several diseases

ing to anyone; but go, show yourself to the priest, and offer the gift that Moses commanded, as a testimony to them."

5 When he entered Capernaum, a centurion came to him, appealing to him 6 and saying, "Lord, my servant is lying at home paralyzed, in terrible distress." 7 And he said to him, "I will come and cure him." 8 The centurion answered, "Lord, I am not worthy to have you come under my roof; but only speak the word, and my servant will be healed. 9 For I also am a man under authority, with soldiers under me; and I say to one, 'Go,' and he goes, and to another, 'Come,' and he comes, and to my slave, 'Do this,' and the slave does it." 10 When Jesus heard him, he was amazed and said to those who followed him, "Truly I tell you, in no one[u] in Israel have I found such faith. 11 I tell you, many will come from east and west and will eat with Abraham and Isaac and Jacob in the kingdom of heaven, 12 while the heirs of the kingdom will be thrown into the outer darkness, where there will be weeping and gnashing of teeth." 13 And to the centurion Jesus said, "Go; let it be done for you according to your faith." And the servant was healed in that hour.

14 When Jesus entered Peter's house, he saw his mother-in-law lying in bed with a fever; 15 he touched her hand, and the fever left her, and she got up and began to serve him. 16 That evening they brought to him many who were possessed with demons; and he cast out the spirits with a word, and cured all who were sick. 17 This was to fulfill what had been spoken through the prophet Isaiah, "He took our infirmities and bore our diseases."[19]

18 Now when Jesus saw great crowds around him, he gave orders to go over to the other side. 19 A scribe then approached and said, "Teacher, I will follow you wherever you go." 20 And Jesus said to him, "Foxes have holes, and birds of the air have nests; but the Son of Man has nowhere to lay his head." 21 Another of his disciples said to him, "Lord, first let me go and bury my father." 22 But Jesus said to him, "Follow me, and let the dead bury their own dead."

23 And when he got into the boat, his disciples followed him. 24 A windstorm arose on the sea, so great that the boat was being swamped by the waves; but he was asleep. 25 And they went and woke him up, saying, "Lord, save us! We are perishing!" 26 And he said to them, "Why are you afraid, you of little faith?" Then he got up and rebuked the winds and the sea; and there was a dead calm. 27 They were amazed, saying, "What sort of man is this, that even the winds and the sea obey him?"

28 When he came to the other side, to the country of the Gadarenes,[v] two demoniacs coming out of the tombs met him. They were so fierce that no one could pass that way. 29 Suddenly they shouted, "What have you to do with us, Son of God? Have you come here to torment us before the time?" 30 Now a large herd of swine was feeding at some distance from them. 31 The demons begged him, "If you cast us out, send us into the herd of swine." 32 And he said to them, "Go!" So they came out and entered the swine; and suddenly, the whole herd rushed down the steep bank into the sea and perished in the water. 33 The swineherds ran off, and on going into the town, they told the whole story about what had happened to the demoniacs. 34 Then the whole town came out to meet Jesus; and when they saw him, they begged him to leave their neighborhood.

9 And after getting into a boat he crossed the sea and came to his own town.

2 And just then some people were carrying a paralyzed man lying on a bed. When Jesus saw their faith, he said to the paralytic, "Take heart, son; your sins are forgiven." 3 Then some of the scribes said to themselves, "This man is blaspheming." 4 But Jesus, perceiving their thoughts, said, "Why do you think evil in your hearts? 5 For which is easier, to say, 'Your sins are forgiven,' or to say, 'Stand up and walk'? 6 But so that you may know that the Son of Man has authority on earth to forgive sins"—he then said to the paralytic—"Stand up, take your bed and go to your home." 7 And he stood up and went to his home. 8 When the crowds saw it, they were filled with awe, and they glorified God, who had given such authority to human beings.

9 As Jesus was walking along, he saw a man called Matthew sitting at the tax booth; and he said

[u]Other ancient authorities read *Truly I tell you, not even*   [v]Other ancient authorities read *Gergesenes*; others, *Gerasenes*

[19]Isa 53:4

to him, "Follow me." And he got up and followed him.

10 And as he sat at dinner[w] in the house, many tax collectors and sinners came and were sitting[x] with him and his disciples. 11 When the Pharisees saw this, they said to his disciples, "Why does your teacher eat with tax collectors and sinners?" 12 But when he heard this, he said, "Those who are well have no need of a physician, but those who are sick. 13 Go and learn what this means, 'I desire mercy, not sacrifice.'[20] For I have come to call not the righteous but sinners."

14 Then the disciples of John came to him, saying, "Why do we and the Pharisees fast often,[y] but your disciples do not fast?" 15 And Jesus said to them, "The wedding guests cannot mourn as long as the bridegroom is with them, can they? The days will come when the bridegroom is taken away from them, and then they will fast. 16 No one sews a piece of unshrunk cloth on an old cloak, for the patch pulls away from the cloak, and a worse tear is made. 17 Neither is new wine put into old wineskins; otherwise, the skins burst, and the wine is spilled, and the skins are destroyed; but new wine is put into fresh wineskins, and so both are preserved."

18 While he was saying these things to them, suddenly a leader of the synagogue[z] came in and knelt before him, saying, "My daughter has just died; but come and lay your hand on her, and she will live." 19 And Jesus got up and followed him, with his disciples. 20 Then suddenly a woman who had been suffering from hemorrhages for twelve years came up behind him and touched the fringe of his cloak, 21 for she said to herself, "If I only touch his cloak, I will be made well." 22 Jesus turned, and seeing her he said, "Take heart, daughter; your faith has made you well." And instantly the woman was made well. 23 When Jesus came to the leader's house and saw the flute players and the crowd making a commotion, 24 he said, "Go away; for the girl is not dead but sleeping." And they laughed at him. 25 But when the crowd had been put outside, he went in and took her by the hand, and the girl got up. 26 And the report of this spread throughout that district.

27 As Jesus went on from there, two blind men followed him, crying loudly, "Have mercy on us, Son of David!" 28 When he entered the house, the blind men came to him; and Jesus said to them, "Do you believe that I am able to do this?" They said to him, "Yes, Lord." 29 Then he touched their eyes and said, "According to your faith let it be done to you." 30 And their eyes were opened. Then Jesus sternly ordered them, "See that no one knows of this." 31 But they went away and spread the news about him throughout that district.

32 After they had gone away, a demoniac who was mute was brought to him. 33 And when the demon had been cast out, the one who had been mute spoke; and the crowds were amazed and said, "Never has anything like this been seen in Israel." 34 But the Pharisees said, "By the ruler of the demons he casts out the demons."[a]

35 Then Jesus went about all the cities and villages, teaching in their synagogues, and proclaiming the good news of the kingdom, and curing every disease and every sickness. 36 When he saw the crowds, he had compassion for them, because they were harassed and helpless, like sheep without a shepherd. 37 Then he said to his disciples, "The harvest is plentiful, but the laborers are few; 38 therefore ask the Lord of the harvest to send out laborers into his harvest."

10 Then Jesus[b] summoned his twelve disciples and gave them authority over unclean spirits, to cast them out, and to cure every disease and every sickness. 2 These are the names of the twelve apostles: first, Simon, also known as Peter, and his brother Andrew; James son of Zebedee, and his brother John; 3 Philip and Bartholomew; Thomas and Matthew the tax collector; James son of Alphaeus, and Thaddaeus;[c] 4 Simon the Cananaean, and Judas Iscariot, the one who betrayed him.

5 These twelve Jesus sent out with the following instructions: "Go nowhere among the Gentiles, and enter no town of the Samaritans, 6 but go rather to the lost sheep of the house of Israel. 7 As you go, proclaim the good news, 'The kingdom of heaven has come near.'[d] 8 Cure the sick,

---

[w]Gk *reclined* [x]Gk *were reclining* [y]Other ancient authorities lack *often* [z]Gk lacks *of the synagogue* [a]Other ancient authorities lack this verse [b]Gk *he* [c]Other ancient authorities read *Lebbaeus,* or *Lebbaeus called Thaddaeus* [d]Or *is at hand*

---

[20]Hos 6:6

raise the dead, cleanse the lepers,[e] cast out demons. You received without payment; give without payment. 9 Take no gold, or silver, or copper in your belts, 10 no bag for your journey, or two tunics, or sandals, or a staff; for laborers deserve their food. 11 Whatever town or village you enter, find out who in it is worthy, and stay there until you leave. 12 As you enter the house, greet it. 13 If the house is worthy, let your peace come upon it; but if it is not worthy, let your peace return to you. 14 If anyone will not welcome you or listen to your words, shake off the dust from your feet as you leave that house or town. 15 Truly I tell you, it will be more tolerable for the land of Sodom and Gomorrah on the day of judgment than for that town.

16 "See, I am sending you out like sheep into the midst of wolves; so be wise as serpents and innocent as doves. 17 Beware of them, for they will hand you over to councils and flog you in their synagogues; 18 and you will be dragged before governors and kings because of me, as a testimony to them and the Gentiles. 19 When they hand you over, do not worry about how you are to speak or what you are to say; for what you are to say will be given to you at that time; 20 for it is not you who speak, but the Spirit of your Father speaking through you. 21 Brother will betray brother to death, and a father his child, and children will rise against parents and have them put to death; 22 and you will be hated by all because of my name. But the one who endures to the end will be saved. 23 When they persecute you in one town, flee to the next; for truly I tell you, you will not have gone through all the towns of Israel before the Son of Man comes.

24 "A disciple is not above the teacher, nor a slave above the master; 25 it is enough for the disciple to be like the teacher, and the slave like the master. If they have called the master of the house Beelzebul, how much more will they malign those of his household!

26 "So have no fear of them; for nothing is covered up that will not be uncovered, and nothing secret that will not become known. 27 What I say to you in the dark, tell in the light; and what you hear whispered, proclaim from the housetops. 28 Do not fear those who kill the body but cannot kill the soul; rather fear him who can destroy both soul and body in hell.[f] 29 Are not two sparrows sold for a penny? Yet not one of them will fall to the ground apart from your Father. 30 And even the hairs of your head are all counted. 31 So do not be afraid; you are of more value than many sparrows.

32 "Everyone therefore who acknowledges me before others, I also will acknowledge before my Father in heaven; 33 but whoever denies me before others, I also will deny before my Father in heaven.

34 "Do not think that I have come to bring peace to the earth; I have not come to bring peace, but a sword.

35   For I have come to set a man
          against his father,
       and a daughter against her
          mother,
       and a daughter-in-law against her
          mother-in-law;
36   and one's foes will be members of
          one's own household.[21]

37 Whoever loves father or mother more than me is not worthy of me; and whoever loves son or daughter more than me is not worthy of me; 38 and whoever does not take up the cross and follow me is not worthy of me. 39 Those who find their life will lose it, and those who lose their life for my sake will find it.

40 "Whoever welcomes you welcomes me, and whoever welcomes me welcomes the one who sent me. 41 Whoever welcomes a prophet in the name of a prophet will receive a prophet's reward; and whoever welcomes a righteous person in the name of a righteous person will receive the reward of the righteous; 42 and whoever gives even a cup of cold water to one of these little ones in the name of a disciple—truly I tell you, none of these will lose their reward."

11 Now when Jesus had finished instructing his twelve disciples, he went on from there to teach and proclaim his message in their cities.

2 When John heard in prison what the Messiah[g] was doing, he sent word by his[h] disciples 3 and

---

[e]The terms *leper* and *leprosy* can refer to several diseases   [f]Gk *Gehenna*   [g]Or *the Christ*   [h]Other ancient authorities read *two of his*

[21]Mic 7:6

said to him, "Are you the one who is to come, or are we to wait for another?" 4 Jesus answered them, "Go and tell John what you hear and see: 5 the blind receive their sight, the lame walk, the lepers[i] are cleansed, the deaf hear, the dead are raised, and the poor have good news brought to them. 6 And blessed is anyone who takes no offense at me."

7 As they went away, Jesus began to speak to the crowds about John: "What did you go out into the wilderness to look at? A reed shaken by the wind? 8 What then did you go out to see? Someone[j] dressed in soft robes? Look, those who wear soft robes are in royal palaces. 9 What then did you go out to see? A prophet?[k] Yes, I tell you, and more than a prophet. 10 This is the one about whom it is written,

> 'See, I am sending my messenger
>   ahead of you,
>   who will prepare your way
>   before you.'[22]

11 Truly I tell you, among those born of women no one has arisen greater than John the Baptist; yet the least in the kingdom of heaven is greater than he. 12 From the days of John the Baptist until now the kingdom of heaven has suffered violence,[l] and the violent take it by force. 13 For all the prophets and the law prophesied until John came; 14 and if you are willing to accept it, he is Elijah who is to come. 15 Let anyone with ears[m] listen!

16 "But to what will I compare this generation? It is like children sitting in the marketplaces and calling to one another,

> 17   'We played the flute for you, and
>   you did not dance;
>   we wailed, and you did not
>   mourn.'

18 For John came neither eating nor drinking, and they say, 'He has a demon'; 19 the Son of Man came eating and drinking, and they say, 'Look, a glutton and a drunkard, a friend of tax collectors and sinners!' Yet wisdom is vindicated by her deeds."[n]

20 Then he began to reproach the cities in which most of his deeds of power had been done, because they did not repent. 21 "Woe to you, Chorazin! Woe to you, Bethsaida! For if the deeds of power done in you had been done in Tyre and Sidon, they would have repented long ago in sackcloth and

ashes. 22 But I tell you, on the day of judgment it will be more tolerable for Tyre and Sidon than for you. 23 And you, Capernaum,

> will you be exalted to heaven?
>   No, you will be brought down
>   to Hades.

For if the deeds of power done in you had been done in Sodom, it would have remained until this day. 24 But I tell you that on the day of judgment it will be more tolerable for the land of Sodom than for you."

25 At that time Jesus said, "I thank[o] you, Father, Lord of heaven and earth, because you have hidden these things from the wise and the intelligent and have revealed them to infants; 26 yes, Father, for such was your gracious will.[p] 27 All things have been handed over to me by my Father; and no one knows the Son except the Father, and no one knows the Father except the Son and anyone to whom the Son chooses to reveal him.

28 "Come to me, all you that are weary and are carrying heavy burdens, and I will give you rest. 29 Take my yoke upon you, and learn from me; for I am gentle and humble in heart, and you will find rest for your souls. 30 For my yoke is easy, and my burden is light."

12 At that time Jesus went through the grainfields on the sabbath; his disciples were hungry, and they began to pluck heads of grain and to eat. 2 When the Pharisees saw it, they said to him, "Look, your disciples are doing what is not lawful to do on the sabbath." 3 He said to them, "Have you not read what David did when he and his companions were hungry? 4 He entered the house of God and ate the bread of the Presence, which it was not lawful for him or his companions to eat, but only for the priests. 5 Or have you not read in the law that on the sabbath the priests in the temple break the sabbath and yet are guiltless? 6 I tell you, something greater than the temple is here. 7 But if you had known what this means, 'I desire mercy and not sacrifice,'[23] you would not have

---

[i] The terms *leper* and *leprosy* can refer to several diseases   [j] Or *Why then did you go out? To see someone*   [k] Other ancient authorities read *Why then did you go out? To see a prophet?*   [l] Or *has been coming violently*   [m] Other ancient authorities add *to hear*   [n] Other ancient authorities read *children*   [o] Or *praise*   [p] Or *for so it was well-pleasing in your sight*

[22] Mal 3:1   [23] Hos 6:6

condemned the guiltless. 8 For the Son of Man is lord of the sabbath."

9 He left that place and entered their synagogue; 10 a man was there with a withered hand, and they asked him, "Is it lawful to cure on the sabbath?" so that they might accuse him. 11 He said to them, "Suppose one of you has only one sheep and it falls into a pit on the sabbath; will you not lay hold of it and lift it out? 12 How much more valuable is a human being than a sheep! So it is lawful to do good on the sabbath." 13 Then he said to the man, "Stretch out your hand." He stretched it out, and it was restored, as sound as the other. 14 But the Pharisees went out and conspired against him, how to destroy him.

15 When Jesus became aware of this, he departed. Many crowds[q] followed him, and he cured all of them, 16 and he ordered them not to make him known. 17 This was to fulfill what had been spoken through the prophet Isaiah:

18   "Here is my servant, whom I have
              chosen,
          my beloved, with whom my soul
              is well pleased.
      I will put my Spirit upon him,
          and he will proclaim justice to
              the Gentiles.
19   He will not wrangle or cry aloud,
          nor will anyone hear his voice
              in the streets.
20   He will not break a bruised reed
          or quench a smoldering wick
          until he brings justice to victory.
21   And in his name the Gentiles
              will hope."[24]

22 Then they brought to him a demoniac who was blind and mute; and he cured him, so that the one who had been mute could speak and see. 23 All the crowds were amazed and said, "Can this be the Son of David?" 24 But when the Pharisees heard it, they said, "It is only by Beelzebul, the ruler of the demons, that this fellow casts out the demons." 25 He knew what they were thinking and said to them, "Every kingdom divided against itself is laid waste, and no city or house divided against itself will stand. 26 If Satan casts out Satan, he is divided against himself; how then will his kingdom stand? 27 If I cast out demons by Beelzebul, by whom do your own exorcists[r] cast

them out? Therefore they will be your judges. 28 But if it is by the Spirit of God that I cast out demons, then the kingdom of God has come to you. 29 Or how can one enter a strong man's house and plunder his property, without first tying up the strong man? Then indeed the house can be plundered. 30 Whoever is not with me is against me, and whoever does not gather with me scatters. 31 Therefore I tell you, people will be forgiven for every sin and blasphemy, but blasphemy against the Spirit will not be forgiven. 32 Whoever speaks a word against the Son of Man will be forgiven, but whoever speaks against the Holy Spirit will not be forgiven, either in this age or in the age to come.

33 "Either make the tree good, and its fruit good; or make the tree bad, and its fruit bad; for the tree is known by its fruit. 34 You brood of vipers! How can you speak good things, when you are evil? For out of the abundance of the heart the mouth speaks. 35 The good person brings good things out of a good treasure, and the evil person brings evil things out of an evil treasure. 36 I tell you, on the day of judgment you will have to give an account for every careless word you utter; 37 for by your words you will be justified, and by your words you will be condemned."

38 Then some of the scribes and Pharisees said to him, "Teacher, we wish to see a sign from you." 39 But he answered them, "An evil and adulterous generation asks for a sign, but no sign will be given to it except the sign of the prophet Jonah. 40 For just as Jonah was three days and three nights in the belly of the sea monster, so for three days and three nights the Son of Man will be in the heart of the earth. 41 The people of Nineveh will rise up at the judgment with this generation and condemn it, because they repented at the proclamation of Jonah, and see, something greater than Jonah is here! 42 The queen of the South will rise up at the judgment with this generation and condemn it, because she came from the ends of the earth to listen to the wisdom of Solomon, and see, something greater than Solomon is here!

43 "When the unclean spirit has gone out of a person, it wanders through waterless regions look-

---

[q]Other ancient authorities lack *crowds*   [r]Gk *sons*

[24]Isa 42:1–4

ing for a resting place, but it finds none. 44 Then it says, 'I will return to my house from which I came.' When it comes, it finds it empty, swept, and put in order. 45 Then it goes and brings along seven other spirits more evil than itself, and they enter and live there; and the last state of that person is worse than the first. So will it be also with this evil generation."

46 While he was still speaking to the crowds, his mother and his brothers were standing outside, wanting to speak to him. 47 Someone told him, "Look, your mother and your brothers are standing outside, wanting to speak to you."ˢ 48 But to the one who had told him this, Jesusᵗ replied, "Who is my mother, and who are my brothers?" 49 And pointing to his disciples, he said, "Here are my mother and my brothers! 50 For whoever does the will of my Father in heaven is my brother and sister and mother."

13 That same day Jesus went out of the house and sat beside the sea. 2 Such great crowds gathered around him that he got into a boat and sat there, while the whole crowd stood on the beach. 3 And he told them many things in parables, saying: "Listen! A sower went out to sow. 4 And as he sowed, some seeds fell on the path, and the birds came and ate them up. 5 Other seeds fell on rocky ground, where they did not have much soil, and they sprang up quickly, since they had no depth of soil. 6 But when the sun rose, they were scorched; and since they had no root, they withered away. 7 Other seeds fell among thorns, and the thorns grew up and choked them. 8 Other seeds fell on good soil and brought forth grain, some a hundredfold, some sixty, some thirty. 9 Let anyone with earsᵘ listen!"

10 Then the disciples came and asked him, "Why do you speak to them in parables?" 11 He answered, "To you it has been given to know the secretsᵛ of the kingdom of heaven, but to them it has not been given. 12 For to those who have, more will be given, and they will have an abundance; but from those who have nothing, even what they have will be taken away. 13 The reason I speak to them in parables is that 'seeing they do not perceive, and hearing they do not listen, nor do they understand.' 14 With them indeed is fulfilled the prophecy of Isaiah that says:

'You will indeed listen, but never
    understand,
  and you will indeed look, but
    never perceive.
15 For this people's heart has grown
    dull,
  and their ears are hard of
    hearing,
    and they have shut their eyes;
      so that they might not look
        with their eyes,
    and listen with their ears,
  and understand with their heart
    and turn—
  and I would heal them.'²⁵

16 But blessed are your eyes, for they see, and your ears, for they hear. 17 Truly I tell you, many prophets and righteous people longed to see what you see, but did not see it, and to hear what you hear, but did not hear it.

18 "Hear then the parable of the sower. 19 When anyone hears the word of the kingdom and does not understand it, the evil one comes and snatches away what is sown in the heart; this is what was sown on the path. 20 As for what was sown on rocky ground, this is the one who hears the word and immediately receives it with joy; 21 yet such a person has no root, but endures only for a while, and when trouble or persecution arises on account of the word, that person immediately falls away.ʷ 22 As for what was sown among thorns, this is the one who hears the word, but the cares of the world and the lure of wealth choke the word, and it yields nothing. 23 But as for what was sown on good soil, this is the one who hears the word and understands it, who indeed bears fruit and yields, in one case a hundredfold, in another sixty, and in another thirty."

24 He put before them another parable: "The kingdom of heaven may be compared to someone who sowed good seed in his field; 25 but while everybody was asleep, an enemy came and sowed weeds among the wheat, and then went away. 26 So when the plants came up and bore grain, then the weeds appeared as well. 27 And the

---

ˢOther ancient authorities lack verse 47   ᵗGk he   ᵘOther ancient authorities add to hear   ᵛOr mysteries   ʷGk stumbles

---

²⁵Isa 6:9–10

slaves of the householder came and said to him, 'Master, did you not sow good seed in your field? Where, then, did these weeds come from?' 28 He answered, 'An enemy has done this.' The slaves said to him, 'Then do you want us to go and gather them?' 29 But he replied, 'No; for in gathering the weeds you would uproot the wheat along with them. 30 Let both of them grow together until the harvest; and at harvest time I will tell the reapers, Collect the weeds first and bind them in bundles to be burned, but gather the wheat into my barn.'"

31 He put before them another parable: "The kingdom of heaven is like a mustard seed that someone took and sowed in his field; 32 it is the smallest of all the seeds, but when it has grown it is the greatest of shrubs and becomes a tree, so that the birds of the air come and make nests in its branches."

33 He told them another parable: "The kingdom of heaven is like yeast that a woman took and mixed in with[x] three measures of flour until all of it was leavened."

34 Jesus told the crowds all these things in parables; without a parable he told them nothing. 35 This was to fulfill what had been spoken through the prophet:[y]

> "I will open my mouth to speak
> in parables;
> I will proclaim what has been
> hidden from the foundation
> of the world."[z][26]

36 Then he left the crowds and went into the house. And his disciples approached him, saying, "Explain to us the parable of the weeds of the field." 37 He answered, "The one who sows the good seed is the Son of Man; 38 the field is the world, and the good seed are the children of the kingdom; the weeds are the children of the evil one, 39 and the enemy who sowed them is the devil; the harvest is the end of the age, and the reapers are angels. 40 Just as the weeds are collected and burned up with fire, so will it be at the end of the age. 41 The Son of Man will send his angels, and they will collect out of his kingdom all causes of sin and all evildoers, 42 and they will throw them into the furnace of fire, where there will be weeping and gnashing of teeth. 43 Then the righteous will shine like the sun in the kingdom of their Father. Let anyone with ears[a] listen!

44 "The kingdom of heaven is like treasure hidden in a field, which someone found and hid; then in his joy he goes and sells all that he has and buys that field.

45 "Again, the kingdom of heaven is like a merchant in search of fine pearls; 46 on finding one pearl of great value, he went and sold all that he had and bought it.

47 "Again, the kingdom of heaven is like a net that was thrown into the sea and caught fish of every kind; 48 when it was full, they drew it ashore, sat down, and put the good into baskets but threw out the bad. 49 So it will be at the end of the age. The angels will come out and separate the evil from the righteous 50 and throw them into the furnace of fire, where there will be weeping and gnashing of teeth.

51 "Have you understood all this?" They answered, "Yes." 52 And he said to them, "Therefore every scribe who has been trained for the kingdom of heaven is like the master of a household who brings out of his treasure what is new and what is old." 53 When Jesus had finished these parables, he left that place.

54 He came to his hometown and began to teach the people[b] in their synagogue, so that they were astounded and said, "Where did this man get this wisdom and these deeds of power? 55 Is not this the carpenter's son? Is not his mother called Mary? And are not his brothers James and Joseph and Simon and Judas? 56 And are not all his sisters with us? Where then did this man get all this?" 57 And they took offense at him. But Jesus said to them, "Prophets are not without honor except in their own country and in their own house." 58 And he did not do many deeds of power there, because of their unbelief.

14 At that time Herod the ruler[c] heard reports about Jesus; 2 and he said to his servants, "This is John the Baptist; he has been raised from the dead, and for this reason these powers are at work in him." 3 For Herod had arrested John, bound him, and put him in prison on account of Herodias, his brother Philip's wife,[d]

---

[x]Gk *hid in*   [y]Other ancient authorities read *the prophet Isaiah*   [z]Other ancient authorities lack *of the world*   [a]Other ancient authorities add *to hear*   [b]Gk *them*   [c]Gk *tetrarch*   [d]Other ancient authorities read *his brother's wife*

[26]Ps 78:2

4 because John had been telling him, "It is not lawful for you to have her." 5 Though Herod[e] wanted to put him to death, he feared the crowd, because they regarded him as a prophet. 6 But when Herod's birthday came, the daughter of Herodias danced before the company, and she pleased Herod 7 so much that he promised on oath to grant her whatever she might ask. 8 Prompted by her mother, she said, "Give me the head of John the Baptist here on a platter." 9 The king was grieved, yet out of regard for his oaths and for the guests, he commanded it to be given; 10 he sent and had John beheaded in the prison. 11 The head was brought on a platter and given to the girl, who brought it to her mother. 12 His disciples came and took the body and buried it; then they went and told Jesus.

13 Now when Jesus heard this, he withdrew from there in a boat to a deserted place by himself. But when the crowds heard it, they followed him on foot from the towns. 14 When he went ashore, he saw a great crowd; and he had compassion for them and cured their sick. 15 When it was evening, the disciples came to him and said, "This is a deserted place, and the hour is now late; send the crowds away so that they may go into the villages and buy food for themselves." 16 Jesus said to them, "They need not go away; you give them something to eat." 17 They replied, "We have nothing here but five loaves and two fish." 18 And he said, "Bring them here to me." 19 Then he ordered the crowds to sit down on the grass. Taking the five loaves and the two fish, he looked up to heaven, and blessed and broke the loaves, and gave them to the disciples, and the disciples gave them to the crowds. 20 And all ate and were filled; and they took up what was left over of the broken pieces, twelve baskets full. 21 And those who ate were about five thousand men, besides women and children.

22 Immediately he made the disciples get into the boat and go on ahead to the other side, while he dismissed the crowds. 23 And after he had dismissed the crowds, he went up the mountain by himself to pray. When evening came, he was there alone, 24 but by this time the boat, battered by the waves, was far from the land,[f] for the wind was against them. 25 And early in the morning he came walking toward them on the sea. 26 But when the disciples saw him walking on the sea, they were terrified, saying, "It is a ghost!" And they cried out in fear. 27 But immediately Jesus spoke to them and said, "Take heart, it is I; do not be afraid."

28 Peter answered him, "Lord, if it is you, command me to come to you on the water." 29 He said, "Come." So Peter got out of the boat, started walking on the water, and came toward Jesus. 30 But when he noticed the strong wind,[g] he became frightened, and beginning to sink, he cried out, "Lord, save me!" 31 Jesus immediately reached out his hand and caught him, saying to him, "You of little faith, why did you doubt?" 32 When they got into the boat, the wind ceased. 33 And those in the boat worshiped him, saying, "Truly you are the Son of God."

34 When they had crossed over, they came to land at Gennesaret. 35 After the people of that place recognized him, they sent word throughout the region and brought all who were sick to him, 36 and begged him that they might touch even the fringe of his cloak; and all who touched it were healed.

15 Then Pharisees and scribes came to Jesus from Jerusalem and said, 2 "Why do your disciples break the tradition of the elders? For they do not wash their hands before they eat." 3 He answered them, "And why do you break the commandment of God for the sake of your tradition? 4 For God said,[h] 'Honor your father and your mother,'[27] and, 'Whoever speaks evil of father or mother must surely die.'[28] 5 But you say that whoever tells father or mother, 'Whatever support you might have had from me is given to God,'[i] then that person need not honor the father.[j] 6 So, for the sake of your tradition, you make void the word[k] of God. 7 You hypocrites! Isaiah prophesied rightly about you when he said:

8   'This people honors me with their
            lips,
        but their hearts are far from me;

---

[e]Gk *he*   [f]Other ancient authorities read *was out on the sea*   [g]Other ancient authorities read *the wind*   [h]Other ancient authorities read *commanded, saying*   [i]Or *is an offering*   [j]Other ancient authorities add *or the mother*   [k]Other ancient authorities read *law*; others, *commandment*

[27]Exod 20:12; Deut 5:16   [28]Exod 21:17; Lev 20:9

9   in vain do they worship me,
              teaching human precepts as
                    doctrines.'"[29]

10 Then he called the crowd to him and said to them, "Listen and understand: 11 it is not what goes into the mouth that defiles a person, but it is what comes out of the mouth that defiles." 12 Then the disciples approached and said to him, "Do you know that the Pharisees took offense when they heard what you said?" 13 He answered, "Every plant that my heavenly Father has not planted will be uprooted. 14 Let them alone; they are blind guides of the blind.[l] And if one blind person guides another, both will fall into a pit." 15 But Peter said to him, "Explain this parable to us." 16 Then he said, "Are you also still without understanding? 17 Do you not see that whatever goes into the mouth enters the stomach, and goes out into the sewer? 18 But what comes out of the mouth proceeds from the heart, and this is what defiles. 19 For out of the heart come evil intentions, murder, adultery, fornication, theft, false witness, slander. 20 These are what defile a person, but to eat with unwashed hands does not defile."

21 Jesus left that place and went away to the district of Tyre and Sidon. 22 Just then a Canaanite woman from that region came out and started shouting, "Have mercy on me, Lord, Son of David; my daughter is tormented by a demon." 23 But he did not answer her at all. And his disciples came and urged him, saying, "Send her away, for she keeps shouting after us." 24 He answered, "I was sent only to the lost sheep of the house of Israel." 25 But she came and knelt before him, saying, "Lord, help me." 26 He answered, "It is not fair to take the children's food and throw it to the dogs." 27 She said, "Yes, Lord, yet even the dogs eat the crumbs that fall from their masters' table." 28 Then Jesus answered her, "Woman, great is your faith! Let it be done for you as you wish." And her daughter was healed instantly.

29 After Jesus had left that place, he passed along the Sea of Galilee, and he went up the mountain, where he sat down. 30 Great crowds came to him, bringing with them the lame, the maimed, the blind, the mute, and many others. They put them at his feet, and he cured them, 31 so that the crowd was amazed when they saw the mute speaking, the maimed whole, the lame walking, and the blind seeing. And they praised the God of Israel.

32 Then Jesus called his disciples to him and said, "I have compassion for the crowd, because they have been with me now for three days and have nothing to eat; and I do not want to send them away hungry, for they might faint on the way." 33 The disciples said to him, "Where are we to get enough bread in the desert to feed so great a crowd?" 34 Jesus asked them, "How many loaves have you?" They said, "Seven, and a few small fish." 35 Then ordering the crowd to sit down on the ground, 36 he took the seven loaves and the fish; and after giving thanks he broke them and gave them to the disciples, and the disciples gave them to the crowds. 37 And all of them ate and were filled; and they took up the broken pieces left over, seven baskets full. 38 Those who had eaten were four thousand men, besides women and children. 39 After sending away the crowds, he got into the boat and went to the region of Magadan.[m]

16 The Pharisees and Sadducees came, and to test Jesus[n] they asked him to show them a sign from heaven. 2 He answered them, "When it is evening, you say, 'It will be fair weather, for the sky is red.' 3 And in the morning, 'It will be stormy today, for the sky is red and threatening.' You know how to interpret the appearance of the sky, but you cannot interpret the signs of the times.[o] 4 An evil and adulterous generation asks for a sign, but no sign will be given to it except the sign of Jonah." Then he left them and went away.

5 When the disciples reached the other side, they had forgotten to bring any bread. 6 Jesus said to them, "Watch out, and beware of the yeast of the Pharisees and Sadducees." 7 They said to one another, "It is because we have brought no bread." 8 And becoming aware of it, Jesus said, "You of little faith, why are you talking about having no bread? 9 Do you still not perceive? Do you not remember the five loaves for the five thousand, and how many baskets you gathered? 10 Or the seven loaves for the four thousand, and how many bas-

[l]Other ancient authorities lack *of the blind*   [m]Other ancient authorities read *Magdala* or *Magdalan*   [n]Gk *him*   [o]Other ancient authorities lack 2*When it is . . . of the times*

[29]Isa 29:13

kets you gathered? 11 How could you fail to perceive that I was not speaking about bread? Beware
of the yeast of the Pharisees and Sadducees!"
12 Then they understood that he had not told them
to beware of the yeast of bread, but of the teaching of the Pharisees and Sadducees.

13 Now when Jesus came into the district of
Caesarea Philippi, he asked his disciples, "Who do
people say that the Son of Man is?" 14 And they
said, "Some say John the Baptist, but others
Elijah, and still others Jeremiah or one of the
prophets." 15 He said to them, "But who do you
say that I am?" 16 Simon Peter answered, "You
are the Messiah,[p] the Son of the living God."
17 And Jesus answered him, "Blessed are you,
Simon son of Jonah! For flesh and blood has
not revealed this to you, but my Father in heaven.
18 And I tell you, you are Peter,[q] and on this
rock[r] I will build my church, and the gates of
Hades will not prevail against it. 19 I will give
you the keys of the kingdom of heaven, and whatever you bind on earth will be bound in heaven,
and whatever you loose on earth will be loosed in
heaven." 20 Then he sternly ordered the disciples
not to tell anyone that he was[s] the Messiah.[p]

21 From that time on, Jesus began to show his
disciples that he must go to Jerusalem and undergo great suffering at the hands of the elders and
chief priests and scribes, and be killed, and on the
third day be raised. 22 And Peter took him aside
and began to rebuke him, saying, "God forbid it,
Lord! This must never happen to you." 23 But he
turned and said to Peter, "Get behind me, Satan!
You are a stumbling block to me; for you are setting your mind not on divine things but on human
things."

24 Then Jesus told his disciples, "If any want to
become my followers, let them deny themselves
and take up their cross and follow me. 25 For
those who want to save their life will lose it, and
those who lose their life for my sake will find it.
26 For what will it profit them if they gain the
whole world but forfeit their life? Or what will
they give in return for their life?

27 "For the Son of Man is to come with his angels in the glory of his Father, and then he will repay everyone for what has been done. 28 Truly I
tell you, there are some standing here who will not
taste death before they see the Son of Man coming
in his kingdom."

17 Six days later, Jesus took with him Peter
and James and his brother John and led
them up a high mountain, by themselves. 2 And
he was transfigured before them, and his face
shone like the sun, and his clothes became dazzling white. 3 Suddenly there appeared to them
Moses and Elijah, talking with him. 4 Then Peter
said to Jesus, "Lord, it is good for us to be here; if
you wish, I[t] will make three dwellings[u] here, one
for you, one for Moses, and one for Elijah."
5 While he was still speaking, suddenly a bright
cloud overshadowed them, and from the cloud a
voice said, "This is my Son, the Beloved;[v] with
him I am well pleased; listen to him!" 6 When the
disciples heard this, they fell to the ground and
were overcome by fear. 7 But Jesus came and
touched them, saying, "Get up and do not be
afraid." 8 And when they looked up, they saw no
one except Jesus himself alone.

9 As they were coming down the mountain, Jesus ordered them, "Tell no one about the vision until after the Son of Man has been raised from the
dead." 10 And the disciples asked him, "Why,
then, do the scribes say that Elijah must come
first?" 11 He replied, "Elijah is indeed coming
and will restore all things; 12 but I tell you that
Elijah has already come, and they did not recognize him, but they did to him whatever they
pleased. So also the Son of Man is about to suffer
at their hands." 13 Then the disciples understood
that he was speaking to them about John the
Baptist.

14 When they came to the crowd, a man came
to him, knelt before him, 15 and said, "Lord, have
mercy on my son, for he is an epileptic and he suffers terribly; he often falls into the fire and often
into the water. 16 And I brought him to your disciples, but they could not cure him." 17 Jesus answered, "You faithless and perverse generation,
how much longer must I be with you? How much
longer must I put up with you? Bring him here to
me." 18 And Jesus rebuked the demon,[w] and it[x]
came out of him, and the boy was cured instantly.
19 Then the disciples came to Jesus privately and

[p]Or *the Christ* [q]Gk *Petros* [r]Gk *petra* [s]Other ancient authorities add *Jesus* [t]Other ancient authorities read *we* [u]Or *tents* [v]Or *my beloved Son* [w]Gk *it* or *him* [x]Gk *the demon*

said, "Why could we not cast it out?" 20 He said to them, "Because of your little faith. For truly I tell you, if you have faith the size of a[y] mustard seed, you will say to this mountain, 'Move from here to there,' and it will move; and nothing will be impossible for you."[z]

22 As they were gathering[a] in Galilee, Jesus said to them, "The Son of Man is going to be betrayed into human hands, 23 and they will kill him, and on the third day he will be raised." And they were greatly distressed.

24 When they reached Capernaum, the collectors of the temple tax[b] came to Peter and said, "Does your teacher not pay the temple tax?"[b] 25 He said, "Yes, he does." And when he came home, Jesus spoke of it first, asking, "What do you think, Simon? From whom do kings of the earth take toll or tribute? From their children or from others?" 26 When Peter[c] said, "From others," Jesus said to him, "Then the children are free. 27 However, so that we do not give offense to them, go to the sea and cast a hook; take the first fish that comes up; and when you open its mouth, you will find a coin;[d] take that and give it to them for you and me."

18

At that time the disciples came to Jesus and asked, "Who is the greatest in the kingdom of heaven?" 2 He called a child, whom he put among them, 3 and said, "Truly I tell you, unless you change and become like children, you will never enter the kingdom of heaven. 4 Whoever becomes humble like this child is the greatest in the kingdom of heaven. 5 Whoever welcomes one such child in my name welcomes me.

6 "If any of you put a stumbling block before one of these little ones who believe in me, it would be better for you if a great millstone were fastened around your neck and you were drowned in the depth of the sea. 7 Woe to the world because of stumbling blocks! Occasions for stumbling are bound to come, but woe to the one by whom the stumbling block comes!

8 "If your hand or your foot causes you to stumble, cut it off and throw it away; it is better for you to enter life maimed or lame than to have two hands or two feet and to be thrown into the eternal fire. 9 And if your eye causes you to stumble, tear it out and throw it away; it is better for you to en-

ter life with one eye than to have two eyes and to be thrown into the hell[e] of fire.

10 "Take care that you do not despise one of these little ones; for, I tell you, in heaven their angels continually see the face of my Father in heaven.[f] 12 What do you think? If a shepherd has a hundred sheep, and one of them has gone astray, does he not leave the ninety-nine on the mountains and go in search of the one that went astray? 13 And if he finds it, truly I tell you, he rejoices over it more than over the ninety-nine that never went astray. 14 So it is not the will of your[g] Father in heaven that one of these little ones should be lost.

15 "If another member of the church[h] sins against you,[i] go and point out the fault when the two of you are alone. If the member listens to you, you have regained that one.[j] 16 But if you are not listened to, take one or two others along with you, so that every word may be confirmed by the evidence of two or three witnesses. 17 If the member refuses to listen to them, tell it to the church; and if the offender refuses to listen even to the church, let such a one be to you as a Gentile and a tax collector. 18 Truly I tell you, whatever you bind on earth will be bound in heaven, and whatever you loose on earth will be loosed in heaven. 19 Again, truly I tell you, if two of you agree on earth about anything you ask, it will be done for you by my Father in heaven. 20 For where two or three are gathered in my name, I am there among them."

21 Then Peter came and said to him, "Lord, if another member of the church[k] sins against me, how often should I forgive? As many as seven times?" 22 Jesus said to him, "Not seven times, but, I tell you, seventy-seven[l] times.

23 "For this reason the kingdom of heaven may be compared to a king who wished to settle accounts with his slaves. 24 When he began the reckoning, one who owed him ten thousand talents[m] was brought to him; 25 and, as he could not

---

[y]Gk *faith as a grain of*   [z]Other ancient authorities add verse 21, *But this kind does not come out except by prayer and fasting*   [a]Other ancient authorities read *living*   [b]Gk *didrachma*   [c]Gk *he*   [d]Gk *stater*; the stater was worth two didrachmas   [e]Gk *Gehenna*   [f]Other ancient authorities add verse 11, *For the Son of Man came to save the lost*   [g]Other ancient authorities read *my*   [h]Gk *If your brother*   [i]Other ancient authorities lack *against you*   [j]Gk *the brother*   [k]Gk *if my brother*   [l]Or *seventy times seven*   [m]A talent was worth more than fifteen years' wages of a laborer

pay, his lord ordered him to be sold, together with his wife and children and all his possessions, and payment to be made. 26 So the slave fell on his knees before him, saying, 'Have patience with me, and I will pay you everything.' 27 And out of pity for him, the lord of that slave released him and forgave him the debt. 28 But that same slave, as he went out, came upon one of his fellow slaves who owed him a hundred denarii;[n] and seizing him by the throat, he said, 'Pay what you owe.' 29 Then his fellow slave fell down and pleaded with him, 'Have patience with me, and I will pay you.' 30 But he refused; then he went and threw him into prison until he would pay the debt. 31 When his fellow slaves saw what had happened, they were greatly distressed, and they went and reported to their lord all that had taken place. 32 Then his lord summoned him and said to him, 'You wicked slave! I forgave you all that debt because you pleaded with me. 33 Should you not have had mercy on your fellow slave, as I had mercy on you?' 34 And in anger his lord handed him over to be tortured until he would pay his entire debt. 35 So my heavenly Father will also do to every one of you, if you do not forgive your brother or sister[o] from your heart.''

19 When Jesus had finished saying these things, he left Galilee and went to the region of Judea beyond the Jordan. 2 Large crowds followed him, and he cured them there.

3 Some Pharisees came to him, and to test him they asked, "Is it lawful for a man to divorce his wife for any cause?" 4 He answered, "Have you not read that the one who made them at the beginning 'made them male and female,'[30] 5 and said, 'For this reason a man shall leave his father and mother and be joined to his wife, and the two shall become one flesh'?[31] 6 So they are no longer two, but one flesh. Therefore what God has joined together, let no one separate." 7 They said to him, "Why then did Moses command us to give a certificate of dismissal and to divorce her?"[32] 8 He said to them, "It was because you were so hardhearted that Moses allowed you to divorce your wives, but from the beginning it was not so. 9 And I say to you, whoever divorces his wife, except for unchastity, and marries another commits adultery."[p]

10 His disciples said to him, "If such is the case of a man with his wife, it is better not to marry." 11 But he said to them, "Not everyone can accept this teaching, but only those to whom it is given. 12 For there are eunuchs who have been so from birth, and there are eunuchs who have been made eunuchs by others, and there are eunuchs who have made themselves eunuchs for the sake of the kingdom of heaven. Let anyone accept this who can."

13 Then little children were being brought to him in order that he might lay his hands on them and pray. The disciples spoke sternly to those who brought them; 14 but Jesus said, "Let the little children come to me, and do not stop them; for it is to such as these that the kingdom of heaven belongs." 15 And he laid his hands on them and went on his way.

16 Then someone came to him and said, "Teacher, what good deed must I do to have eternal life?" 17 And he said to him, "Why do you ask me about what is good? There is only one who is good. If you wish to enter into life, keep the commandments." 18 He said to him, "Which ones?" And Jesus said, "You shall not murder; You shall not commit adultery; You shall not steal; You shall not bear false witness; 19 Honor your father and mother;[33] also, You shall love your neighbor as yourself."[34] 20 The young man said to him, "I have kept all these;[q] what do I still lack?" 21 Jesus said to him, "If you wish to be perfect, go, sell your possessions, and give the money[r] to the poor, and you will have treasure in heaven; then come, follow me." 22 When the young man heard this word, he went away grieving, for he had many possessions.

23 Then Jesus said to his disciples, "Truly I tell you, it will be hard for a rich person to enter the kingdom of heaven. 24 Again I tell you, it is easier for a camel to go through the eye of a needle than for someone who is rich to enter the kingdom of God." 25 When the disciples heard this, they

---

[n]The denarius was the usual day's wage for a laborer   [o]Gk *brother*
[p]Other ancient authorities read *except on the ground of unchastity, causes her to commit adultery*; others add at the end of the verse *and he who marries a divorced woman commits adultery*   [q]Other ancient authorities add *from my youth*   [r]Gk lacks *the money*

[30]Gen 1:27   [31]Gen 2:24   [32]Deut 24:1   [33]Exod 20:12–16; Deut 5:16–20   [34]Lev 19:18

were greatly astounded and said, "Then who can be saved?" 26 But Jesus looked at them and said, "For mortals it is impossible, but for God all things are possible."

27 Then Peter said in reply, "Look, we have left everything and followed you. What then will we have?" 28 Jesus said to them, "Truly I tell you, at the renewal of all things, when the Son of Man is seated on the throne of his glory, you who have followed me will also sit on twelve thrones, judging the twelve tribes of Israel. 29 And everyone who has left houses or brothers or sisters or father or mother or children or fields, for my name's sake, will receive a hundredfold,ˢ and will inherit eternal life. 30 But many who are first will be last, and the last will be first.

20 "For the kingdom of heaven is like a landowner who went out early in the morning to hire laborers for his vineyard. 2 After agreeing with the laborers for the usual daily wage,ᵗ he sent them into his vineyard. 3 When he went out about nine o'clock, he saw others standing idle in the marketplace; 4 and he said to them, 'You also go into the vineyard, and I will pay you whatever is right.' So they went. 5 When he went out again about noon and about three o'clock, he did the same. 6 And about five o'clock he went out and found others standing around; and he said to them, 'Why are you standing here idle all day?' 7 They said to him, 'Because no one has hired us.' He said to them, 'You also go into the vineyard.' 8 When evening came, the owner of the vineyard said to his manager, 'Call the laborers and give them their pay, beginning with the last and then going to the first.' 9 When those hired about five o'clock came, each of them received the usual daily wage.ᵗ 10 Now when the first came, they thought they would receive more; but each of them also received the usual daily wage.ᵗ 11 And when they received it, they grumbled against the landowner, 12 saying, 'These last worked only one hour, and you have made them equal to us who have borne the burden of the day and the scorching heat.' 13 But he replied to one of them, 'Friend, I am doing you no wrong; did you not agree with me for the usual daily wage?ᵗ 14 Take what belongs to you and go; I choose to give to this last the same as I give to you. 15 Am I not allowed to do what I choose with what

belongs to me? Or are you envious because I am generous?'ᵘ 16 So the last will be first, and the first will be last."ᵛ

17 While Jesus was going up to Jerusalem, he took the twelve disciples aside by themselves, and said to them on the way, 18 "See, we are going up to Jerusalem, and the Son of Man will be handed over to the chief priests and scribes, and they will condemn him to death; 19 then they will hand him over to the Gentiles to be mocked and flogged and crucified; and on the third day he will be raised."

20 Then the mother of the sons of Zebedee came to him with her sons, and kneeling before him, she asked a favor of him. 21 And he said to her, "What do you want?" She said to him, "Declare that these two sons of mine will sit, one at your right hand and one at your left, in your kingdom." 22 But Jesus answered, "You do not know what you are asking. Are you able to drink the cup that I am about to drink?"ʷ They said to him, "We are able." 23 He said to them, "You will indeed drink my cup, but to sit at my right hand and at my left, this is not mine to grant, but it is for those for whom it has been prepared by my Father."

24 When the ten heard it, they were angry with the two brothers. 25 But Jesus called them to him and said, "You know that the rulers of the Gentiles lord it over them, and their great ones are tyrants over them. 26 It will not be so among you; but whoever wishes to be great among you must be your servant, 27 and whoever wishes to be first among you must be your slave; 28 just as the Son of Man came not to be served but to serve, and to give his life a ransom for many."

29 As they were leaving Jericho, a large crowd followed him. 30 There were two blind men sitting by the roadside. When they heard that Jesus was passing by, they shouted, "Lord,ˣ have mercy on us, Son of David!" 31 The crowd sternly ordered them to be quiet; but they shouted even more loudly, "Have mercy on us, Lord, Son of David!" 32 Jesus stood still and called them, saying, "What do you want me to do for you?" 33 They said to

ˢOther ancient authorities read *manifold*   ᵗGk *a denarius*   ᵘGk *is your eye evil because I am good?*   ᵛOther ancient authorities add *for many are called but few are chosen*   ʷOther ancient authorities add *or to be baptized with the baptism that I am baptized with?*   ˣOther ancient authorities lack *Lord*

him, "Lord, let our eyes be opened." 34 Moved with compassion, Jesus touched their eyes. Immediately they regained their sight and followed him.

21 When they had come near Jerusalem and had reached Bethphage, at the Mount of Olives, Jesus sent two disciples, 2 saying to them, "Go into the village ahead of you, and immediately you will find a donkey tied, and a colt with her; untie them and bring them to me. 3 If anyone says anything to you, just say this, 'The Lord needs them.' And he will send them immediately.^{y}"
4 This took place to fulfill what had been spoken through the prophet, saying,

5   "Tell the daughter of Zion,
       Look, your king is coming to
              you,
         humble, and mounted on a
              donkey,
           and on a colt, the foal of a
              donkey."^{35}

6 The disciples went and did as Jesus had directed them; 7 they brought the donkey and the colt, and put their cloaks on them, and he sat on them. 8 A very large crowd^z spread their cloaks on the road, and others cut branches from the trees and spread them on the road. 9 The crowds that went ahead of him and that followed were shouting,

       "Hosanna to the Son of David!
         Blessed is the one who comes in
              the name of the Lord!^{36}
         Hosanna in the highest heaven!"

10 When he entered Jerusalem, the whole city was in turmoil, asking, "Who is this?" 11 The crowds were saying, "This is the prophet Jesus from Nazareth in Galilee."

12 Then Jesus entered the temple^a and drove out all who were selling and buying in the temple, and he overturned the tables of the money changers and the seats of those who sold doves. 13 He said to them, "It is written,

       'My house shall be called a house
              of prayer';
         but you are making it a den of
              robbers."^{37}

14 The blind and the lame came to him in the temple, and he cured them. 15 But when the chief priests and the scribes saw the amazing things that he did, and heard^b the children crying out in the

temple, "Hosanna to the Son of David," they became angry 16 and said to him, "Do you hear what these are saying?" Jesus said to them, "Yes; have you never read,

       'Out of the mouths of infants and
              nursing babies
         you have prepared praise for
              yourself'?"^{38}

17 He left them, went out of the city to Bethany, and spent the night there.

18 In the morning, when he returned to the city, he was hungry. 19 And seeing a fig tree by the side of the road, he went to it and found nothing at all on it but leaves. Then he said to it, "May no fruit ever come from you again!" And the fig tree withered at once. 20 When the disciples saw it, they were amazed, saying, "How did the fig tree wither at once?" 21 Jesus answered them, "Truly I tell you, if you have faith and do not doubt, not only will you do what has been done to the fig tree, but even if you say to this mountain, 'Be lifted up and thrown into the sea,' it will be done. 22 Whatever you ask for in prayer with faith, you will receive."

23 When he entered the temple, the chief priests and the elders of the people came to him as he was teaching, and said, "By what authority are you doing these things, and who gave you this authority?" 24 Jesus said to them, "I will also ask you one question; if you tell me the answer, then I will also tell you by what authority I do these things. 25 Did the baptism of John come from heaven, or was it of human origin?" And they argued with one another, "If we say, 'From heaven,' he will say to us, 'Why then did you not believe him?' 26 But if we say, 'Of human origin,' we are afraid of the crowd; for all regard John as a prophet." 27 So they answered Jesus, "We do not know." And he said to them, "Neither will I tell you by what authority I am doing these things.

28 "What do you think? A man had two sons; he went to the first and said, 'Son, go and work in the vineyard today.' 29 He answered, 'I will not'; but later he changed his mind and went. 30 The father^c went to the second and said the same; and he

^{y}Or *'The Lord needs them and will send them back immediately.'*
^{z}Or *Most of the crowd* ^{a}Other ancient authorities add *of God*
^{b}Gk lacks *heard* ^{c}Gk *He*

^{35}Isa 62:11; Zech 9:9 ^{36}Ps 118:25–26 ^{37}Isa 56:7; Jer 7:11 ^{38}Ps 8:3

answered, 'I go, sir'; but he did not go. 31 Which of the two did the will of his father?" They said, "The first." Jesus said to them, "Truly I tell you, the tax collectors and the prostitutes are going into the kingdom of God ahead of you. 32 For John came to you in the way of righteousness and you did not believe him, but the tax collectors and the prostitutes believed him; and even after you saw it, you did not change your minds and believe him.

33 "Listen to another parable. There was a landowner who planted a vineyard, put a fence around it, dug a wine press in it, and built a watchtower. Then he leased it to tenants and went to another country. 34 When the harvest time had come, he sent his slaves to the tenants to collect his produce. 35 But the tenants seized his slaves and beat one, killed another, and stoned another. 36 Again he sent other slaves, more than the first; and they treated them in the same way. 37 Finally he sent his son to them, saying, 'They will respect my son.' 38 But when the tenants saw the son, they said to themselves, 'This is the heir; come, let us kill him and get his inheritance.' 39 So they seized him, threw him out of the vineyard, and killed him. 40 Now when the owner of the vineyard comes, what will he do to those tenants?" 41 They said to him, "He will put those wretches to a miserable death, and lease the vineyard to other tenants who will give him the produce at the harvest time."

42 Jesus said to them, "Have you never read in the scriptures:

'The stone that the builders
        rejected
    has become the cornerstone;[d]
this was the Lord's doing,
    and it is amazing in our eyes'?[39]

43 Therefore I tell you, the kingdom of God will be taken away from you and given to a people that produces the fruits of the kingdom.[e] 44 The one who falls on this stone will be broken to pieces; and it will crush anyone on whom it falls."[f]

45 When the chief priests and the Pharisees heard his parables, they realized that he was speaking about them. 46 They wanted to arrest him, but they feared the crowds, because they regarded him as a prophet.

22

Once more Jesus spoke to them in parables, saying: 2 "The kingdom of heaven may be compared to a king who gave a wedding banquet for his son. 3 He sent his slaves to call those who had been invited to the wedding banquet, but they would not come. 4 Again he sent other slaves, saying, 'Tell those who have been invited: Look, I have prepared my dinner, my oxen and my fat calves have been slaughtered, and everything is ready; come to the wedding banquet.' 5 But they made light of it and went away, one to his farm, another to his business, 6 while the rest seized his slaves, mistreated them, and killed them. 7 The king was enraged. He sent his troops, destroyed those murderers, and burned their city. 8 Then he said to his slaves, 'The wedding is ready, but those invited were not worthy. 9 Go therefore into the main streets, and invite everyone you find to the wedding banquet.' 10 Those slaves went out into the streets and gathered all whom they found, both good and bad; so the wedding hall was filled with guests.

11 "But when the king came in to see the guests, he noticed a man there who was not wearing a wedding robe, 12 and he said to him, 'Friend, how did you get in here without a wedding robe?' And he was speechless. 13 Then the king said to the attendants, 'Bind him hand and foot, and throw him into the outer darkness, where there will be weeping and gnashing of teeth.' 14 For many are called, but few are chosen."

15 Then the Pharisees went and plotted to entrap him in what he said. 16 So they sent their disciples to him, along with the Herodians, saying, "Teacher, we know that you are sincere, and teach the way of God in accordance with truth, and show deference to no one; for you do not regard people with partiality. 17 Tell us, then, what you think. Is it lawful to pay taxes to the emperor, or not?" 18 But Jesus, aware of their malice, said, "Why are you putting me to the test, you hypocrites? 19 Show me the coin used for the tax." And they brought him a denarius. 20 Then he said to them, "Whose head is this, and whose title?" 21 They answered, "The emperor's." Then he said to them, "Give therefore to the emperor the things that are the emperor's, and to God the things that are

---

[d]Or *keystone*   [e]Gk *the fruits of it*   [f]Other ancient authorities lack verse 44

[39]Ps 118:22–23

God's." 22 When they heard this, they were amazed; and they left him and went away.

23 The same day some Sadducees came to him, saying there is no resurrection;[g] and they asked him a question, saying, 24 "Teacher, Moses said, 'If a man dies childless, his brother shall marry the widow, and raise up children for his brother.'[40] 25 Now there were seven brothers among us; the first married, and died childless, leaving the widow to his brother. 26 The second did the same, so also the third, down to the seventh. 27 Last of all, the woman herself died. 28 In the resurrection, then, whose wife of the seven will she be? For all of them had married her."

29 Jesus answered them, "You are wrong, because you know neither the scriptures nor the power of God. 30 For in the resurrection they neither marry nor are given in marriage, but are like angels[h] in heaven. 31 And as for the resurrection of the dead, have you not read what was said to you by God, 32 'I am the God of Abraham, the God of Isaac, and the God of Jacob'? He is God not of the dead, but of the living."[41] 33 And when the crowd heard it, they were astounded at his teaching.

34 When the Pharisees heard that he had silenced the Sadducees, they gathered together, 35 and one of them, a lawyer, asked him a question to test him. 36 "Teacher, which commandment in the law is the greatest?" 37 He said to him, "'You shall love the Lord your God with all your heart, and with all your soul, and with all your mind.'[42] 38 This is the greatest and first commandment. 39 And a second is like it: 'You shall love your neighbor as yourself.'[43] 40 On these two commandments hang all the law and the prophets."

41 Now while the Pharisees were gathered together, Jesus asked them this question: 42 "What do you think of the Messiah?[i] Whose son is he?" They said to him, "The son of David." 43 He said to them, "How is it then that David by the Spirit[j] calls him Lord, saying,

44   'The Lord said to my Lord,
          "Sit at my right hand,
              until I put your enemies under
                  your feet"'?[44]

45 If David thus calls him Lord, how can he be his son?" 46 No one was able to give him an answer, nor from that day did anyone dare to ask him any more questions.

23 Then Jesus said to the crowds and to his disciples, 2 "The scribes and the Pharisees sit on Moses' seat; 3 therefore, do whatever they teach you and follow it; but do not do as they do, for they do not practice what they teach. 4 They tie up heavy burdens, hard to bear,[k] and lay them on the shoulders of others; but they themselves are unwilling to lift a finger to move them. 5 They do all their deeds to be seen by others; for they make their phylacteries broad and their fringes long. 6 They love to have the place of honor at banquets and the best seats in the synagogues, 7 and to be greeted with respect in the marketplaces, and to have people call them rabbi. 8 But you are not to be called rabbi, for you have one teacher, and you are all students.[l] 9 And call no one your father on earth, for you have one Father—the one in heaven. 10 Nor are you to be called instructors, for you have one instructor, the Messiah.[m] 11 The greatest among you will be your servant. 12 All who exalt themselves will be humbled, and all who humble themselves will be exalted.

13 "But woe to you, scribes and Pharisees, hypocrites! For you lock people out of the kingdom of heaven. For you do not go in yourselves, and when others are going in, you stop them.[n] 15 Woe to you, scribes and Pharisees, hypocrites! For you cross sea and land to make a single convert, and you make the new convert twice as much a child of hell[o] as yourselves.

16 "Woe to you, blind guides, who say, 'Whoever swears by the sanctuary is bound by nothing, but whoever swears by the gold of the sanctuary is bound by the oath.' 17 You blind fools! For which is greater, the gold or the sanctuary that has made the gold sacred? 18 And you say, 'Whoever swears by the altar is bound by nothing, but whoever swears by the gift that is on the altar is bound by the oath.' 19 How blind you are! For which is

---

[g]Other ancient authorities read *who say that there is no resurrection* [h]Other ancient authorities add *of God* [i]Or *Christ* [j]Gk *in spirit* [k]Other ancient authorities lack *hard to bear* [l]Gk *brothers* [m]Or *the Christ* [n]Other authorities add here (or after verse 12) verse 14, *Woe to you, scribes and Pharisees, hypocrites! For you devour widows' houses and for the sake of appearance you make long prayers; therefore you will receive the greater condemnation* [o]Gk *Gehenna*

[40]Deut 25:5; Gen 38:8   [41]Exod 3:6,15   [42]Deut 6:5   [43]Lev 19:18 [44]Ps 110:1

greater, the gift or the altar that makes the gift sacred? 20 So whoever swears by the altar, swears by it and by everything on it; 21 and whoever swears by the sanctuary, swears by it and by the one who dwells in it; 22 and whoever swears by heaven, swears by the throne of God and by the one who is seated upon it.

23 "Woe to you, scribes and Pharisees, hypocrites! For you tithe mint, dill, and cummin, and have neglected the weightier matters of the law: justice and mercy and faith. It is these you ought to have practiced without neglecting the others. 24 You blind guides! You strain out a gnat but swallow a camel!

25 "Woe to you, scribes and Pharisees, hypocrites! For you clean the outside of the cup and of the plate, but inside they are full of greed and self-indulgence. 26 You blind Pharisee! First clean the inside of the cup,[p] so that the outside also may become clean.

27 "Woe to you, scribes and Pharisees, hypocrites! For you are like whitewashed tombs, which on the outside look beautiful, but inside they are full of the bones of the dead and of all kinds of filth. 28 So you also on the outside look righteous to others, but inside you are full of hypocrisy and lawlessness.

29 "Woe to you, scribes and Pharisees, hypocrites! For you build the tombs of the prophets and decorate the graves of the righteous, 30 and you say, 'If we had lived in the days of our ancestors, we would not have taken part with them in shedding the blood of the prophets.' 31 Thus you testify against yourselves that you are descendants of those who murdered the prophets. 32 Fill up, then, the measure of your ancestors. 33 You snakes, you brood of vipers! How can you escape being sentenced to hell?[q] 34 Therefore I send you prophets, sages, and scribes, some of whom you will kill and crucify, and some you will flog in your synagogues and pursue from town to town, 35 so that upon you may come all the righteous blood shed on earth, from the blood of righteous Abel to the blood of Zechariah son of Barachiah, whom you murdered between the sanctuary and the altar. 36 Truly I tell you, all this will come upon this generation.

37 "Jerusalem, Jerusalem, the city that kills the prophets and stones those who are sent to it! How often have I desired to gather your children together as a hen gathers her brood under her wings, and you were not willing! 38 See, your house is left to you, desolate.[r] 39 For I tell you, you will not see me again until you say, 'Blessed is the one who comes in the name of the Lord.'"[45]

24 As Jesus came out of the temple and was going away, his disciples came to point out to him the buildings of the temple. 2 Then he asked them, "You see all these, do you not? Truly I tell you, not one stone will be left here upon another; all will be thrown down."

3 When he was sitting on the Mount of Olives, the disciples came to him privately, saying, "Tell us, when will this be, and what will be the sign of your coming and of the end of the age?" 4 Jesus answered them, "Beware that no one leads you astray. 5 For many will come in my name, saying, 'I am the Messiah!'[s] and they will lead many astray. 6 And you will hear of wars and rumors of wars; see that you are not alarmed; for this must take place, but the end is not yet. 7 For nation will rise against nation, and kingdom against kingdom, and there will be famines[t] and earthquakes in various places: 8 all this is but the beginning of the birth pangs.

9 "Then they will hand you over to be tortured and will put you to death, and you will be hated by all nations because of my name. 10 Then many will fall away,[u] and they will betray one another and hate one another. 11 And many false prophets will arise and lead many astray. 12 And because of the increase of lawlessness, the love of many will grow cold. 13 But the one who endures to the end will be saved. 14 And this good news[v] of the kingdom will be proclaimed throughout the world, as a testimony to all the nations; and then the end will come.

15 "So when you see the desolating sacrilege standing in the holy place, as was spoken of by the prophet Daniel (let the reader understand), 16 then those in Judea must flee to the mountains; 17 the one on the housetop must not go down to

[p]Other ancient authorities add *and of the plate* [q]Gk *Gehenna* [r]Other ancient authorities lack *desolate* [s]Or *the Christ* [t]Other ancient authorities add *and pestilences* [u]Or *stumble* [v]Or *gospel*

---

[45]Ps 118:26

take what is in the house; 18 the one in the field must not turn back to get a coat. 19 Woe to those who are pregnant and to those who are nursing infants in those days! 20 Pray that your flight may not be in winter or on a sabbath. 21 For at that time there will be great suffering, such as has not been from the beginning of the world until now, no, and never will be. 22 And if those days had not been cut short, no one would be saved; but for the sake of the elect those days will be cut short. 23 Then if anyone says to you, 'Look! Here is the Messiah!'ʷ or 'There he is!'—do not believe it. 24 For false messiahsˣ and false prophets will appear and produce great signs and omens, to lead astray, if possible, even the elect. 25 Take note, I have told you beforehand. 26 So, if they say to you, 'Look! He is in the wilderness,' do not go out. If they say, 'Look! He is in the inner rooms,' do not believe it. 27 For as the lightning comes from the east and flashes as far as the west, so will be the coming of the Son of Man. 28 Wherever the corpse is, there the vultures will gather.

29 "Immediately after the suffering of those days
the sun will be darkened,
and the moon will not give its
light;
the stars will fall from heaven,
and the powers of heaven will
be shaken.

30 Then the sign of the Son of Man will appear in heaven, and then all the tribes of the earth will mourn, and they will see 'the Son of Man coming on the clouds of heaven'⁴⁶ with power and great glory. 31 And he will send out his angels with a loud trumpet call, and they will gather his elect from the four winds, from one end of heaven to the other.

32 "From the fig tree learn its lesson: as soon as its branch becomes tender and puts forth its leaves, you know that summer is near. 33 So also, when you see all these things, you know that heʸ is near, at the very gates. 34 Truly I tell you, this generation will not pass away until all these things have taken place. 35 Heaven and earth will pass away, but my words will not pass away.

36 "But about that day and hour no one knows, neither the angels of heaven, nor the Son,ᶻ but only the Father. 37 For as the days of Noah were, so will be the coming of the Son of Man. 38 For as

in those days before the flood they were eating and drinking, marrying and giving in marriage, until the day Noah entered the ark, 39 and they knew nothing until the flood came and swept them all away, so too will be the coming of the Son of Man. 40 Then two will be in the field; one will be taken and one will be left. 41 Two women will be grinding meal together; one will be taken and one will be left. 42 Keep awake therefore, for you do not know on what dayᵃ your Lord is coming. 43 But understand this: if the owner of the house had known in what part of the night the thief was coming, he would have stayed awake and would not have let his house be broken into. 44 Therefore you also must be ready, for the Son of Man is coming at an unexpected hour.

45 "Who then is the faithful and wise slave, whom his master has put in charge of his household, to give the other slavesᵇ their allowance of food at the proper time? 46 Blessed is that slave whom his master will find at work when he arrives. 47 Truly I tell you, he will put that one in charge of all his possessions. 48 But if that wicked slave says to himself, 'My master is delayed,' 49 and he begins to beat his fellow slaves, and eats and drinks with drunkards, 50 the master of that slave will come on a day when he does not expect him and at an hour that he does not know. 51 He will cut him in piecesᶜ and put him with the hypocrites, where there will be weeping and gnashing of teeth.

25 "Then the kingdom of heaven will be like this. Ten bridesmaidsᵈ took their lamps and went to meet the bridegroom.ᵉ 2 Five of them were foolish, and five were wise. 3 When the foolish took their lamps, they took no oil with them; 4 but the wise took flasks of oil with their lamps. 5 As the bridegroom was delayed, all of them became drowsy and slept. 6 But at midnight there was a shout, 'Look! Here is the bridegroom! Come out to meet him.' 7 Then all those bridesmaidsᵈ got up and trimmed their lamps. 8 The foolish said to the wise, 'Give us some of your oil,

ʷOr *the Christ* ˣOr *christs* ʸOr *it* ᶻOther ancient authorities lack *nor the Son* ᵃOther ancient authorities read *at what hour* ᵇGk *to give them* ᶜOr *cut him off* ᵈGk *virgins* ᵉOther ancient authorities add *and the bride*

⁴⁶Dan 7:13

for our lamps are going out.' 9 But the wise replied, 'No! there will not be enough for you and for us; you had better go to the dealers and buy some for yourselves.' 10 And while they went to buy it, the bridegroom came, and those who were ready went with him into the wedding banquet; and the door was shut. 11 Later the other brides-maids[f] came also, saying, 'Lord, lord, open to us.' 12 But he replied, 'Truly I tell you, I do not know you.' 13 Keep awake therefore, for you know neither the day nor the hour.[g]

14 "For it is as if a man, going on a journey, summoned his slaves and entrusted his property to them; 15 to one he gave five talents,[h] to another two, to another one, to each according to his ability. Then he went away. 16 The one who had received the five talents went off at once and traded with them, and made five more talents. 17 In the same way, the one who had the two talents made two more talents. 18 But the one who had received the one talent went off and dug a hole in the ground and hid his master's money. 19 After a long time the master of those slaves came and settled accounts with them. 20 Then the one who received the five talents came forward, bringing five more talents, saying, 'Master, you handed over to me five talents; see, I have made five more talents.' 21 His master said to him, 'Well done, good and trustworthy slave; you have been trustworthy in a few things, I will put you in charge of many things; enter into the joy of your master.' 22 And the one with the two talents also came forward, saying, 'Master, you handed over to me two talents; see, I have made two more talents.' 23 His master said to him, 'Well done, good and trustworthy slave; you have been trustworthy in a few things, I will put you in charge of many things; enter into the joy of your master.' 24 Then the one who had received the one talent also came forward, saying, 'Master, I knew that you were a harsh man, reaping where you did not sow, and gathering where you did not scatter seed; 25 so I was afraid, and I went and hid your talent in the ground. Here you have what is yours.' 26 But his master replied, 'You wicked and lazy slave! You knew, did you, that I reap where I did not sow, and gather where I did not scatter? 27 Then you ought to have invested my money with the bankers, and on my return I would have received what was my

own with interest. 28 So take the talent from him, and give it to the one with the ten talents. 29 For to all those who have, more will be given, and they will have an abundance; but from those who have nothing, even what they have will be taken away. 30 As for this worthless slave, throw him into the outer darkness, where there will be weeping and gnashing of teeth.'

31 "When the Son of Man comes in his glory, and all the angels with him, then he will sit on the throne of his glory. 32 All the nations will be gathered before him, and he will separate people one from another as a shepherd separates the sheep from the goats, 33 and he will put the sheep at his right hand and the goats at the left. 34 Then the king will say to those at his right hand, 'Come, you that are blessed by my Father, inherit the kingdom prepared for you from the foundation of the world; 35 for I was hungry and you gave me food, I was thirsty and you gave me something to drink, I was a stranger and you welcomed me, 36 I was naked and you gave me clothing, I was sick and you took care of me, I was in prison and you visited me.' 37 Then the righteous will answer him, 'Lord, when was it that we saw you hungry and gave you food, or thirsty and gave you something to drink? 38 And when was it that we saw you a stranger and welcomed you, or naked and gave you clothing? 39 And when was it that we saw you sick or in prison and visited you?' 40 And the king will answer them, 'Truly I tell you, just as you did it to one of the least of these who are members of my family,[i] you did it to me.' 41 Then he will say to those at his left hand, 'You that are accursed, depart from me into the eternal fire prepared for the devil and his angels; 42 for I was hungry and you gave me no food, I was thirsty and you gave me nothing to drink, 43 I was a stranger and you did not welcome me, naked and you did not give me clothing, sick and in prison and you did not visit me.' 44 Then they also will answer, 'Lord, when was it that we saw you hungry or thirsty or a stranger or naked or sick or in prison, and did not take care of you?' 45 Then he will answer them, 'Truly I tell you, just as you did not do it to one of the least of these, you did not do it to me.' 46 And

[f]Gk *virgins*   [g]Other ancient authorities add *in which the Son of Man is coming*   [h]A talent was worth more than fifteen years' wages of a laborer   [i]Gk *these my brothers*

these will go away into eternal punishment, but the righteous into eternal life."

26

When Jesus had finished saying all these things, he said to his disciples, 2 "You know that after two days the Passover is coming, and the Son of Man will be handed over to be crucified."

3 Then the chief priests and the elders of the people gathered in the palace of the high priest, who was called Caiaphas, 4 and they conspired to arrest Jesus by stealth and kill him. 5 But they said, "Not during the festival, or there may be a riot among the people."

6 Now while Jesus was at Bethany in the house of Simon the leper,[j] 7 a woman came to him with an alabaster jar of very costly ointment, and she poured it on his head as he sat at the table. 8 But when the disciples saw it, they were angry and said, "Why this waste? 9 For this ointment could have been sold for a large sum, and the money given to the poor." 10 But Jesus, aware of this, said to them, "Why do you trouble the woman? She has performed a good service for me. 11 For you always have the poor with you, but you will not always have me. 12 By pouring this ointment on my body she has prepared me for burial. 13 Truly I tell you, wherever this good news[k] is proclaimed in the whole world, what she has done will be told in remembrance of her."

14 Then one of the twelve, who was called Judas Iscariot, went to the chief priests 15 and said, "What will you give me if I betray him to you?" They paid him thirty pieces of silver. 16 And from that moment he began to look for an opportunity to betray him.

17 On the first day of Unleavened Bread the disciples came to Jesus, saying, "Where do you want us to make the preparations for you to eat the Passover?" 18 He said, "Go into the city to a certain man, and say to him, 'The Teacher says, My time is near; I will keep the Passover at your house with my disciples.'" 19 So the disciples did as Jesus had directed them, and they prepared the Passover meal.

20 When it was evening, he took his place with the twelve;[l] 21 and while they were eating, he said, "Truly I tell you, one of you will betray me." 22 And they became greatly distressed and began to say to him one after another, "Surely not I, Lord?" 23 He answered, "The one who has dipped his hand into the bowl with me will betray me. 24 The Son of Man goes as it is written of him, but woe to that one by whom the Son of Man is betrayed! It would have been better for that one not to have been born." 25 Judas, who betrayed him, said, "Surely not I, Rabbi?" He replied, "You have said so."

26 While they were eating, Jesus took a loaf of bread, and after blessing it he broke it, gave it to the disciples, and said, "Take, eat; this is my body." 27 Then he took a cup, and after giving thanks he gave it to them, saying, "Drink from it, all of you; 28 for this is my blood of the[m] covenant, which is poured out for many for the forgiveness of sins. 29 I tell you, I will never again drink of this fruit of the vine until that day when I drink it new with you in my Father's kingdom."

30 When they had sung the hymn, they went out to the Mount of Olives.

31 Then Jesus said to them, "You will all become deserters because of me this night; for it is written,

'I will strike the shepherd,
    and the sheep of the flock will
        be scattered.'[47]

32 But after I am raised up, I will go ahead of you to Galilee." 33 Peter said to him, "Though all become deserters because of you, I will never desert you." 34 Jesus said to him, "Truly I tell you, this very night, before the cock crows, you will deny me three times." 35 Peter said to him, "Even though I must die with you, I will not deny you." And so said all the disciples.

36 Then Jesus went with them to a place called Gethsemane; and he said to his disciples, "Sit here while I go over there and pray." 37 He took with him Peter and the two sons of Zebedee, and began to be grieved and agitated. 38 Then he said to them, "I am deeply grieved, even to death; remain here, and stay awake with me." 39 And going a little farther, he threw himself on the ground and

---

[j]The terms *leper* and *leprosy* can refer to several diseases   [k]Or *gospel*   [l]Other ancient authorities add *disciples*   [m]Other ancient authorities add *new*

[47]Zech 13:7

prayed, "My Father, if it is possible, let this cup pass from me; yet not what I want but what you want." 40 Then he came to the disciples and found them sleeping; and he said to Peter, "So, could you not stay awake with me one hour? 41 Stay awake and pray that you may not come into the time of trial;[n] the spirit indeed is willing, but the flesh is weak." 42 Again he went away for the second time and prayed, "My Father, if this cannot pass unless I drink it, your will be done." 43 Again he came and found them sleeping, for their eyes were heavy. 44 So leaving them again, he went away and prayed for the third time, saying the same words. 45 Then he came to the disciples and said to them, "Are you still sleeping and taking your rest? See, the hour is at hand, and the Son of Man is betrayed into the hands of sinners. 46 Get up, let us be going. See, my betrayer is at hand."

47 While he was still speaking, Judas, one of the twelve, arrived; with him was a large crowd with swords and clubs, from the chief priests and the elders of the people. 48 Now the betrayer had given them a sign, saying, "The one I will kiss is the man; arrest him." 49 At once he came up to Jesus and said, "Greetings, Rabbi!" and kissed him. 50 Jesus said to him, "Friend, do what you are here to do." Then they came and laid hands on Jesus and arrested him. 51 Suddenly, one of those with Jesus put his hand on his sword, drew it, and struck the slave of the high priest, cutting off his ear. 52 Then Jesus said to him, "Put your sword back into its place; for all who take the sword will perish by the sword. 53 Do you think that I cannot appeal to my Father, and he will at once send me more than twelve legions of angels? 54 But how then would the scriptures be fulfilled, which say it must happen in this way?" 55 At that hour Jesus said to the crowds, "Have you come out with swords and clubs to arrest me as though I were a bandit? Day after day I sat in the temple teaching, and you did not arrest me. 56 But all this has taken place, so that the scriptures of the prophets may be fulfilled." Then all the disciples deserted him and fled.

57 Those who had arrested Jesus took him to Caiaphas the high priest, in whose house the scribes and the elders had gathered. 58 But Peter was following him at a distance, as far as the courtyard of the high priest; and going inside, he sat with the guards in order to see how this would end. 59 Now the chief priests and the whole council were looking for false testimony against Jesus so that they might put him to death, 60 but they found none, though many false witnesses came forward. At last two came forward 61 and said, "This fellow said, 'I am able to destroy the temple of God and to build it in three days.'" 62 The high priest stood up and said, "Have you no answer? What is it that they testify against you?" 63 But Jesus was silent. Then the high priest said to him, "I put you under oath before the living God, tell us if you are the Messiah,[o] the Son of God." 64 Jesus said to him, "You have said so. But I tell you,

> From now on you will see
>> the Son of Man
>>> seated at the right hand of
>>>> Power
>>> and coming on the clouds of
>>>> heaven."[48]

65 Then the high priest tore his clothes and said, "He has blasphemed! Why do we still need witnesses? You have now heard his blasphemy. 66 What is your verdict?" They answered, "He deserves death." 67 Then they spat in his face and struck him; and some slapped him, 68 saying, "Prophesy to us, you Messiah![o] Who is it that struck you?"

69 Now Peter was sitting outside in the courtyard. A servant-girl came to him and said, "You also were with Jesus the Galilean." 70 But he denied it before all of them, saying, "I do not know what you are talking about." 71 When he went out to the porch, another servant-girl saw him, and she said to the bystanders, "This man was with Jesus of Nazareth."[p] 72 Again he denied it with an oath, "I do not know the man." 73 After a little while the bystanders came up and said to Peter, "Certainly you are also one of them, for your accent betrays you." 74 Then he began to curse, and he swore an oath, "I do not know the man!" At that moment the cock crowed. 75 Then Peter remembered what Jesus had said: "Before the cock crows, you will deny me three times." And he went out and wept bitterly.

[n]Or *into temptation*   [o]Or *Christ*   [p]Gk *the Nazorean*

[48]Ps 110:1; Dan 7:13

27 When morning came, all the chief priests and the elders of the people conferred together against Jesus in order to bring about his death. 2 They bound him, led him away, and handed him over to Pilate the governor.

3 When Judas, his betrayer, saw that Jesus[q] was condemned, he repented and brought back the thirty pieces of silver to the chief priests and the elders. 4 He said, "I have sinned by betraying innocent[r] blood." But they said, "What is that to us? See to it yourself." 5 Throwing down the pieces of silver in the temple, he departed; and he went and hanged himself. 6 But the chief priests, taking the pieces of silver, said, "It is not lawful to put them into the treasury, since they are blood money." 7 After conferring together, they used them to buy the potter's field as a place to bury foreigners. 8 For this reason that field has been called the Field of Blood to this day. 9 Then was fulfilled what had been spoken through the prophet Jeremiah,[s] "And they took[t] the thirty pieces of silver, the price of the one on whom a price had been set,[u] on whom some of the people of Israel had set a price, 10 and they gave[v] them for the potter's field, as the Lord commanded me."[49]

11 Now Jesus stood before the governor; and the governor asked him, "Are you the King of the Jews?" Jesus said, "You say so." 12 But when he was accused by the chief priests and elders, he did not answer. 13 Then Pilate said to him, "Do you not hear how many accusations they make against you?" 14 But he gave him no answer, not even to a single charge, so that the governor was greatly amazed.

15 Now at the festival the governor was accustomed to release a prisoner for the crowd, anyone whom they wanted. 16 At that time they had a notorious prisoner, called Jesus[w] Barabbas. 17 So after they had gathered, Pilate said to them, "Whom do you want me to release for you, Jesus[w] Barabbas or Jesus who is called the Messiah?"[x] 18 For he realized that it was out of jealousy that they had handed him over. 19 While he was sitting on the judgment seat, his wife sent word to him, "Have nothing to do with that innocent man, for today I have suffered a great deal because of a dream about him." 20 Now the chief priests and the elders persuaded the crowds to ask for Barabbas and to have Jesus killed. 21 The governor again said to them, "Which of the two do you want me to release for you?" And they said, "Barabbas." 22 Pilate said to them, "Then what should I do with Jesus who is called the Messiah?"[x] All of them said, "Let him be crucified!" 23 Then he asked, "Why, what evil has he done?" But they shouted all the more, "Let him be crucified!"

24 So when Pilate saw that he could do nothing, but rather that a riot was beginning, he took some water and washed his hands before the crowd, saying, "I am innocent of this man's blood;[y] see to it yourselves." 25 Then the people as a whole answered, "His blood be on us and on our children!" 26 So he released Barabbas for them; and after flogging Jesus, he handed him over to be crucified.

27 Then the soldiers of the governor took Jesus into the governor's headquarters,[z] and they gathered the whole cohort around him. 28 They stripped him and put a scarlet robe on him, 29 and after twisting some thorns into a crown, they put it on his head. They put a reed in his right hand and knelt before him and mocked him, saying, "Hail, King of the Jews!" 30 They spat on him, and took the reed and struck him on the head. 31 After mocking him, they stripped him of the robe and put his own clothes on him. Then they led him away to crucify him.

32 As they went out, they came upon a man from Cyrene named Simon; they compelled this man to carry his cross. 33 And when they came to a place called Golgotha (which means Place of a Skull), 34 they offered him wine to drink, mixed with gall; but when he tasted it, he would not drink it. 35 And when they had crucified him, they divided his clothes among themselves by casting lots;[a] 36 then they sat down there and kept watch over him. 37 Over his head they put the charge against him, which read, "This is Jesus, the King of the Jews."

38 Then two bandits were crucified with him,

---

[q]Gk *he*   [r]Other ancient authorities read *righteous*   [s]Other ancient authorities read *Zechariah* or *Isaiah*   [t]Or *I took*   [u]Or *the price of the precious One*   [v]Other ancient authorities read *I gave*   [w]Other ancient authorities lack *Jesus*   [x]Or *the Christ*   [y]Other ancient authorities read *this righteous blood*, or *this righteous man's blood*   [z]Gk *the praetorium*   [a]Other ancient authorities add *in order that what had been spoken through the prophet might be fulfilled, "They divided my clothes among themselves, and for my clothing they cast lots."*

---

[49]Zech 11:12–13; Jer 32:6–9

one on his right and one on his left. 39 Those who passed by derided[b] him, shaking their heads 40 and saying, "You who would destroy the temple and build it in three days, save yourself! If you are the Son of God, come down from the cross." 41 In the same way the chief priests also, along with the scribes and elders, were mocking him, saying, 42 "He saved others; he cannot save himself.[c] He is the King of Israel; let him come down from the cross now, and we will believe in him. 43 He trusts in God; let God deliver him now, if he wants to; for he said, 'I am God's Son.'" 44 The bandits who were crucified with him also taunted him in the same way.

45 From noon on, darkness came over the whole land[d] until three in the afternoon. 46 And about three o'clock Jesus cried with a loud voice, "Eli, Eli, lema sabachthani?" that is, "My God, my God, why have you forsaken me?"[50] 47 When some of the bystanders heard it, they said, "This man is calling for Elijah." 48 At once one of them ran and got a sponge, filled it with sour wine, put it on a stick, and gave it to him to drink. 49 But the others said, "Wait, let us see whether Elijah will come to save him."[e] 50 Then Jesus cried again with a loud voice and breathed his last.[f] 51 At that moment the curtain of the temple was torn in two, from top to bottom. The earth shook, and the rocks were split. 52 The tombs also were opened, and many bodies of the saints who had fallen asleep were raised. 53 After his resurrection they came out of the tombs and entered the holy city and appeared to many. 54 Now when the centurion and those with him, who were keeping watch over Jesus, saw the earthquake and what took place, they were terrified and said, "Truly this man was God's Son!"[g]

55 Many women were also there, looking on from a distance; they had followed Jesus from Galilee and had provided for him. 56 Among them were Mary Magdalene, and Mary the mother of James and Joseph, and the mother of the sons of Zebedee.

57 When it was evening, there came a rich man from Arimathea, named Joseph, who was also a disciple of Jesus. 58 He went to Pilate and asked for the body of Jesus; then Pilate ordered it to be given to him. 59 So Joseph took the body and wrapped it in a clean linen cloth 60 and laid it in his own new tomb, which he had hewn in the rock.

He then rolled a great stone to the door of the tomb and went away. 61 Mary Magdalene and the other Mary were there, sitting opposite the tomb.

62 The next day, that is, after the day of Preparation, the chief priests and the Pharisees gathered before Pilate 63 and said, "Sir, we remember what that impostor said while he was still alive, 'After three days I will rise again.' 64 Therefore command the tomb to be made secure until the third day; otherwise his disciples may go and steal him away, and tell the people, 'He has been raised from the dead,' and the last deception would be worse than the first." 65 Pilate said to them, "You have a guard[h] of soldiers; go, make it as secure as you can."[i] 66 So they went with the guard and made the tomb secure by sealing the stone.

28 After the sabbath, as the first day of the week was dawning, Mary Magdalene and the other Mary went to see the tomb. 2 And suddenly there was a great earthquake; for an angel of the Lord, descending from heaven, came and rolled back the stone and sat on it. 3 His appearance was like lightning, and his clothing white as snow. 4 For fear of him the guards shook and became like dead men. 5 But the angel said to the women, "Do not be afraid; I know that you are looking for Jesus who was crucified. 6 He is not here; for he has been raised, as he said. Come, see the place where he[j] lay. 7 Then go quickly and tell his disciples, 'He has been raised from the dead,[k] and indeed he is going ahead of you to Galilee; there you will see him.' This is my message for you." 8 So they left the tomb quickly with fear and great joy, and ran to tell his disciples. 9 Suddenly Jesus met them and said, "Greetings!" And they came to him, took hold of his feet, and worshiped him. 10 Then Jesus said to them, "Do not be afraid; go and tell my brothers to go to Galilee; there they will see me."

11 While they were going, some of the guard went into the city and told the chief priests everything that had happened. 12 After the priests[l]

---

[b]Or *blasphemed*   [c]Or *is he unable to save himself?*   [d]Or *earth*
[e]Other ancient authorities add *And another took a spear and pierced his side, and out came water and blood*   [f]Or *gave up his spirit*
[g]Or *a son of God*   [h]Or *Take a guard*   [i]Gk *you know how*   [j]Other ancient authorities read *the Lord*   [k]Other ancient authorities lack *from the dead*   [l]Gk *they*

[50]Ps 22:1

had assembled with the elders, they devised a plan to give a large sum of money to the soldiers, 13 telling them, "You must say, 'His disciples came by night and stole him away while we were asleep.' 14 If this comes to the governor's ears, we will satisfy him and keep you out of trouble." 15 So they took the money and did as they were directed. And this story is still told among the Jews to this day.

16 Now the eleven disciples went to Galilee, to the mountain to which Jesus had directed them. 17 When they saw him, they worshiped him; but some doubted. 18 And Jesus came and said to them, "All authority in heaven and on earth has been given to me. 19 Go therefore and make disciples of all nations, baptizing them in the name of the Father and of the Son and of the Holy Spirit, 20 and teaching them to obey everything that I have commanded you. And remember, I am with you always, to the end of the age."[m]

[m]Other ancient authorities add *Amen*

The Gospel According to Mark

Mark is the shortest of the New Testament Gospels, and, in the opinion of most scholars, it was the first to be written. Although traditionally ascribed to John Mark, the companion of the apostle Peter, its author chose to remain anonymous. Most scholars think that the book was composed thirty or forty years after Jesus' death, possibly during the early years of the Jewish uprising against Rome that culminated in the destruction of the Jerusalem Temple in 70 C.E. Its author was a Greek-speaking Christian who had heard, and possibly read, accounts of Jesus' life and death and created a kind of biographical account of his own in order to proclaim the "good news of Jesus, the Christ, the Son of God." (1:1).

Jesus is declared to be the Son of God by God himself at the outset of the narrative (1:11) and is proclaimed the Son of God during his ministry by the evil spirits that he casts out (3:11). One of the striking features of this Gospel, however, is that no one else seems to understand who Jesus is. Despite the fact that his teachings astound his listeners (1:22) and that his miracles cause his fame to spread far and wide (1:28, 45), his family thinks that he has gone out of his mind (3:21), the Jewish leaders claim that he is inspired by the devil (3:22), the people from his hometown do not accept him (6:1–5), and, worst of all, his own disciples do not understand who he is (6:51–52; 8:21).

It is not until halfway through the Gospel that the disciples begin to have an inkling of Jesus' identity (8:27–30). Even then, their understanding is partial at best (8:31–33). They recognize that he is the Messiah, but appear to share the traditional Jewish notion that the Messiah would be a great and powerful figure who would bring salvation through his mighty deeds against God's enemies. They do not understand that Jesus, as God's Son, must suffer humiliation and death (9:30–31; 10:32–34).

For this author, however, this is precisely Jesus' destiny. At the end of his life Jesus makes a pilgrimage to Jerusalem for Passover, where he is arrested, tried, and executed (chaps. 11–15). For Mark, this death is not a simple miscarriage of justice; it is a death for the sake of others in fulfillment of God's will (10:45). God's definitive vindication of Jesus on the one hand and his followers' continuing inability to understand on the other are decisively shown in the concluding scene of the narrative. For on the third day, three women go to Jesus' tomb to anoint his body, only to find that he is not there but has been raised from the dead. They flee the tomb, not saying anything to anybody, "for they were afraid" (16:1–18).

From the New Revised Standard Version Bible, © 1989.

1

The beginning of the good news[a] of Jesus Christ, the Son of God.[b]

2 As it is written in the prophet Isaiah,[c]

"See, I am sending my messenger
    ahead of you,[d]
who will prepare your way;[1]
3   the voice of one crying out in the
        wilderness:
    'Prepare the way of the Lord,
    make his paths straight,'"[2]

4 John the baptizer appeared[e] in the wilderness, proclaiming a baptism of repentance for the forgiveness of sins. 5 And people from the whole Judean countryside and all the people of Jerusalem were going out to him, and were baptized by him in the river Jordan, confessing their sins. 6 Now John was clothed with camel's hair, with a leather belt around his waist, and he ate locusts and wild honey. 7 He proclaimed, "The one who is more powerful than I is coming after me; I am not worthy to stoop down and untie the thong of his sandals. 8 I have baptized you with[f] water; but he will baptize you with[f] the Holy Spirit."

9 In those days Jesus came from Nazareth of Galilee and was baptized by John in the Jordan. 10 And just as he was coming up out of the water, he saw the heavens torn apart and the Spirit descending like a dove on him. 11 And a voice came from heaven, "You are my Son, the Beloved;[g] with you I am well pleased."

12 And the Spirit immediately drove him out into the wilderness. 13 He was in the wilderness forty days, tempted by Satan; and he was with the wild beasts; and the angels waited on him.

14 Now after John was arrested, Jesus came to Galilee, proclaiming the good news[a] of God,[h] 15 and saying, "The time is fulfilled, and the kingdom of God has come near;[i] repent, and believe in the good news."[a]

16 As Jesus passed along the Sea of Galilee, he saw Simon and his brother Andrew casting a net into the sea—for they were fishermen. 17 And Jesus said to them, "Follow me and I will make you fish for people." 18 And immediately they left their nets and followed him. 19 As he went a little farther, he saw James son of Zebedee and his brother John, who were in their boat mending the nets. 20 Immediately he called them; and they left their father Zebedee in the boat with the hired men, and followed him.

21 They went to Capernaum; and when the sabbath came, he entered the synagogue and taught. 22 They were astounded at his teaching, for he taught them as one having authority, and not as the scribes. 23 Just then there was in their synagogue a man with an unclean spirit, 24 and he cried out, "What have you to do with us, Jesus of Nazareth? Have you come to destroy us? I know who you are, the Holy One of God." 25 But Jesus rebuked him, saying, "Be silent, and come out of him!" 26 And the unclean spirit, convulsing him and crying with a loud voice, came out of him. 27 They were all amazed, and they kept on asking one another, "What is this? A new teaching—with authority! He[j] commands even the unclean spirits, and they obey him." 28 At once his fame began to spread throughout the surrounding region of Galilee.

29 As soon as they[k] left the synagogue, they entered the house of Simon and Andrew, with James and John. 30 Now Simon's mother-in-law was in bed with a fever, and they told him about her at once. 31 He came and took her by the hand and lifted her up. Then the fever left her, and she began to serve them.

32 That evening, at sundown, they brought to him all who were sick or possessed with demons. 33 And the whole city was gathered around the door. 34 And he cured many who were sick with various diseases, and cast out many demons; and he would not permit the demons to speak, because they knew him.

35 In the morning, while it was still very dark, he got up and went out to a deserted place, and there he prayed. 36 And Simon and his companions hunted for him. 37 When they found him, they said to him, "Everyone is searching for you." 38 He answered, "Let us go on to the neighboring towns, so that I may proclaim the message there also; for that is what I came out to do." 39 And he went throughout Galilee, proclaiming the message in their synagogues and casting out demons.

40 A leper[l] came to him begging him, and

[j]Or *A new teaching! With authority he*   [k]Other ancient authorities read *he*   [l]The terms *leper* and *leprosy* can refer to several diseases

[1]Mal 3:1   [2]Isa 40:3

kneeling[m] he said to him, "If you choose, you can make me clean." 41 Moved with pity,[n] Jesus[o] stretched out his hand and touched him, and said to him, "I do choose. Be made clean!" 42 Immediately the leprosy[p] left him, and he was made clean. 43 After sternly warning him he sent him away at once, 44 saying to him, "See that you say nothing to anyone; but go, show yourself to the priest, and offer for your cleansing what Moses commanded, as a testimony to them." 45 But he went out and began to proclaim it freely, and to spread the word, so that Jesus[o] could no longer go into a town openly, but stayed out in the country; and people came to him from every quarter.

2 When he returned to Capernaum after some days, it was reported that he was at home. 2 So many gathered around that there was no longer room for them, not even in front of the door; and he was speaking the word to them. 3 Then some people[q] came, bringing to him a paralyzed man, carried by four of them. 4 And when they could not bring him to Jesus because of the crowd, they removed the roof above him; and after having dug through it, they let down the mat on which the paralytic lay. 5 When Jesus saw their faith, he said to the paralytic, "Son, your sins are forgiven." 6 Now some of the scribes were sitting there, questioning in their hearts, 7 "Why does this fellow speak in this way? It is blasphemy! Who can forgive sins but God alone?" 8 At once Jesus perceived in his spirit that they were discussing these questions among themselves; and he said to them, "Why do you raise such questions in your hearts? 9 Which is easier, to say to the paralytic, 'Your sins are forgiven,' or to say, 'Stand up and take your mat and walk'? 10 But so that you may know that the Son of Man has authority on earth to forgive sins"—he said to the paralytic— 11 "I say to you, stand up, take your mat and go to your home." 12 And he stood up, and immediately took the mat and went out before all of them; so that they were all amazed and glorified God, saying, "We have never seen anything like this!"

13 Jesus[r] went out again beside the sea; the whole crowd gathered around him, and he taught them. 14 As he was walking along, he saw Levi son of Alphaeus sitting at the tax booth, and he said to him, "Follow me." And he got up and followed him.

15 And as he sat at dinner[s] in Levi's[t] house, many tax collectors and sinners were also sitting[u] with Jesus and his disciples—for there were many who followed him. 16 When the scribes of [v] the Pharisees saw that he was eating with sinners and tax collectors, they said to his disciples, "Why does he eat[w] with tax collectors and sinners?" 17 When Jesus heard this, he said to them, "Those who are well have no need of a physician, but those who are sick; I have come to call not the righteous but sinners."

18 Now John's disciples and the Pharisees were fasting; and people[x] came and said to him, "Why do John's disciples and the disciples of the Pharisees fast, but your disciples do not fast?" 19 Jesus said to them, "The wedding guests cannot fast while the bridegroom is with them, can they? As long as they have the bridegroom with them, they cannot fast. 20 The days will come when the bridegroom is taken away from them, and then they will fast on that day.

21 "No one sews a piece of unshrunk cloth on an old cloak; otherwise, the patch pulls away from it, the new from the old, and a worse tear is made. 22 And no one puts new wine into old wineskins; otherwise, the wine will burst the skins, and the wine is lost, and so are the skins; but one puts new wine into fresh wineskins." [y]

23 One sabbath he was going through the grainfields; and as they made their way his disciples began to pluck heads of grain. 24 The Pharisees said to him, "Look, why are they doing what is not lawful on the sabbath?" 25 And he said to them, "Have you never read what David did when he and his companions were hungry and in need of food? 26 He entered the house of God, when Abiathar was high priest, and ate the bread of the Presence, which it is not lawful for any but the priests to eat, and he gave some to his companions." 27 Then he said to them, "The sabbath was made for humankind, and not humankind for the sabbath; 28 so the Son of Man is lord even of the sabbath."

[m]Other ancient authorities lack *kneeling* [n]Other ancient authorities read *anger* [o]Gk *he* [p]The terms *leper* and *leprosy* can refer to several diseases [q]Gk *they* [r]Gk *He* [s]Gk *reclined* [t]Gk *his* [u]Gk *reclining* [v]Other ancient authorities read *and* [w]Other ancient authorities add *and drink* [x]Gk *they* [y]Other ancient authorities lack *but one puts new wine into fresh wineskins*

3 Again he entered the synagogue, and a man was there who had a withered hand. 2 They watched him to see whether he would cure him on the sabbath, so that they might accuse him. 3 And he said to the man who had the withered hand, "Come forward." 4 Then he said to them, "Is it lawful to do good or to do harm on the sabbath, to save life or to kill?" But they were silent. 5 He looked around at them with anger; he was grieved at their hardness of heart and said to the man, "Stretch out your hand." He stretched it out, and his hand was restored. 6 The Pharisees went out and immediately conspired with the Herodians against him, how to destroy him.

7 Jesus departed with his disciples to the sea, and a great multitude from Galilee followed him; 8 hearing all that he was doing, they came to him in great numbers from Judea, Jerusalem, Idumea, beyond the Jordan, and the region around Tyre and Sidon. 9 He told his disciples to have a boat ready for him because of the crowd, so that they would not crush him; 10 for he had cured many, so that all who had diseases pressed upon him to touch him. 11 Whenever the unclean spirits saw him, they fell down before him and shouted, "You are the Son of God!" 12 But he sternly ordered them not to make him known.

13 He went up the mountain and called to him those whom he wanted, and they came to him. 14 And he appointed twelve, whom he also named apostles,[z] to be with him, and to be sent out to proclaim the message, 15 and to have authority to cast out demons. 16 So he appointed the twelve:[a] Simon (to whom he gave the name Peter); 17 James son of Zebedee and John the brother of James (to whom he gave the name Boanerges, that is, Sons of Thunder); 18 and Andrew, and Philip, and Bartholomew, and Matthew, and Thomas, and James son of Alphaeus, and Thaddaeus, and Simon the Cananaean, 19 and Judas Iscariot, who betrayed him.

Then he went home; 20 and the crowd came together again, so that they could not even eat. 21 When his family heard it, they went out to restrain him, for people were saying, "He has gone out of his mind." 22 And the scribes who came down from Jerusalem said, "He has Beelzebul, and by the ruler of the demons he casts out demons." 23 And he called them to him, and spoke to them in parables, "How can Satan cast out Satan? 24 If a kingdom is divided against itself, that kingdom cannot stand. 25 And if a house is divided against itself, that house will not be able to stand. 26 And if Satan has risen up against himself and is divided, he cannot stand, but his end has come. 27 But no one can enter a strong man's house and plunder his property without first tying up the strong man; then indeed the house can be plundered.

28 "Truly I tell you, people will be forgiven for their sins and whatever blasphemies they utter; 29 but whoever blasphemes against the Holy Spirit can never have forgiveness, but is guilty of an eternal sin"— 30 for they had said, "He has an unclean spirit."

31 Then his mother and his brothers came; and standing outside, they sent to him and called him. 32 A crowd was sitting around him; and they said to him, "Your mother and your brothers and sisters[b] are outside, asking for you." 33 And he replied, "Who are my mother and my brothers?" 34 And looking at those who sat around him, he said, "Here are my mother and my brothers! 35 Whoever does the will of God is my brother and sister and mother."

4 Again he began to teach beside the sea. Such a very large crowd gathered around him that he got into a boat on the sea and sat there, while the whole crowd was beside the sea on the land. 2 He began to teach them many things in parables, and in his teaching he said to them: 3 "Listen! A sower went out to sow. 4 And as he sowed, some seed fell on the path, and the birds came and ate it up. 5 Other seed fell on rocky ground, where it did not have much soil, and it sprang up quickly, since it had no depth of soil. 6 And when the sun rose, it was scorched; and since it had no root, it withered away. 7 Other seed fell among thorns, and the thorns grew up and choked it, and it yielded no grain. 8 Other seed fell into good soil and brought forth grain, growing up and increasing and yielding thirty and sixty and a hundredfold." 9 And he said, "Let anyone with ears to hear listen!"

[z]Other ancient authorities lack *whom he also named apostles*   [a]Other ancient authorities lack *So he appointed the twelve*   [b]Other ancient authorities lack *and sisters*

10 When he was alone, those who were around him along with the twelve asked him about the parables. 11 And he said to them, "To you has been given the secret[c] of the kingdom of God, but for those outside, everything comes in parables; 12 in order that

> 'they may indeed look, but not
> perceive,
>   and may indeed listen, but not
> understand;
> so that they may not turn again
>   and be forgiven.'"[3]

13 And he said to them, "Do you not understand this parable? Then how will you understand all the parables? 14 The sower sows the word. 15 These are the ones on the path where the word is sown: when they hear, Satan immediately comes and takes away the word that is sown in them. 16 And these are the ones sown on rocky ground: when they hear the word, they immediately receive it with joy. 17 But they have no root, and endure only for a while; then, when trouble or persecution arises on account of the word, immediately they fall away.[d] 18 And others are those sown among the thorns: these are the ones who hear the word, 19 but the cares of the world, and the lure of wealth, and the desire for other things come in and choke the word, and it yields nothing. 20 And these are the ones sown on the good soil: they hear the word and accept it and bear fruit, thirty and sixty and a hundredfold."

21 He said to them, "Is a lamp brought in to be put under the bushel basket, or under the bed, and not on the lampstand? 22 For there is nothing hidden, except to be disclosed; nor is anything secret, except to come to light. 23 Let anyone with ears to hear listen!" 24 And he said to them, "Pay attention to what you hear; the measure you give will be the measure you get, and still more will be given you. 25 For to those who have, more will be given; and from those who have nothing, even what they have will be taken away."

26 He also said, "The kingdom of God is as if someone would scatter seed on the ground, 27 and would sleep and rise night and day, and the seed would sprout and grow, he does not know how. 28 The earth produces of itself, first the stalk, then the head, then the full grain in the head. 29 But when the grain is ripe, at once he goes in with his sickle, because the harvest has come."

30 He also said, "With what can we compare the kingdom of God, or what parable will we use for it? 31 It is like a mustard seed, which, when sown upon the ground, is the smallest of all the seeds on earth; 32 yet when it is sown it grows up and becomes the greatest of all shrubs, and puts forth large branches, so that the birds of the air can make nests in its shade."

33 With many such parables he spoke the word to them, as they were able to hear it; 34 he did not speak to them except in parables, but he explained everything in private to his disciples.

35 On that day, when evening had come, he said to them, "Let us go across to the other side." 36 And leaving the crowd behind, they took him with them in the boat, just as he was. Other boats were with him. 37 A great windstorm arose, and the waves beat into the boat, so that the boat was already being swamped. 38 But he was in the stern, asleep on the cushion; and they woke him up and said to him, "Teacher, do you not care that we are perishing?" 39 He woke up and rebuked the wind, and said to the sea, "Peace! Be still!" Then the wind ceased, and there was a dead calm. 40 He said to them, "Why are you afraid? Have you still no faith?" 41 And they were filled with great awe and said to one another, "Who then is this, that even the wind and the sea obey him?"

5 They came to the other side of the sea, to the country of the Gerasenes.[e] 2 And when he had stepped out of the boat, immediately a man out of the tombs with an unclean spirit met him. 3 He lived among the tombs; and no one could restrain him any more, even with a chain; 4 for he had often been restrained with shackles and chains, but the chains he wrenched apart, and the shackles he broke in pieces; and no one had the strength to subdue him. 5 Night and day among the tombs and on the mountains he was always howling and bruising himself with stones. 6 When he saw Jesus from a distance, he ran and bowed down before him; 7 and he shouted at the top of his voice,

---

[c]Or *mystery*   [d]Or *stumble*   [e]Other ancient authorities read *Gergesenes*; others, *Gadarenes*

---

[3]Isa 6:9–10

"What have you to do with me, Jesus, Son of the Most High God? I adjure you by God, do not torment me." 8 For he had said to him, "Come out of the man, you unclean spirit!" 9 Then Jesus[f] asked him, "What is your name?" He replied, "My name is Legion; for we are many." 10 He begged him earnestly not to send them out of the country. 11 Now there on the hillside a great herd of swine was feeding; 12 and the unclean spirits[g] begged him, "Send us into the swine; let us enter them." 13 So he gave them permission. And the unclean spirits came out and entered the swine; and the herd, numbering about two thousand, rushed down the steep bank into the sea, and were drowned in the sea.

14 The swineherds ran off and told it in the city and in the country. Then people came to see what it was that had happened. 15 They came to Jesus and saw the demoniac sitting there, clothed and in his right mind, the very man who had had the legion; and they were afraid. 16 Those who had seen what had happened to the demoniac and to the swine reported it. 17 Then they began to beg Jesus[h] to leave their neighborhood. 18 As he was getting into the boat, the man who had been possessed by demons begged him that he might be with him. 19 But Jesus[f] refused, and said to him, "Go home to your friends, and tell them how much the Lord has done for you, and what mercy he has shown you." 20 And he went away and began to proclaim in the Decapolis how much Jesus had done for him; and everyone was amazed.

21 When Jesus had crossed again in the boat[i] to the other side, a great crowd gathered around him; and he was by the sea. 22 Then one of the leaders of the synagogue named Jairus came and, when he saw him, fell at his feet 23 and begged him repeatedly, "My little daughter is at the point of death. Come and lay your hands on her, so that she may be made well, and live." 24 So he went with him.

And a large crowd followed him and pressed in on him. 25 Now there was a woman who had been suffering from hemorrhages for twelve years. 26 She had endured much under many physicians, and had spent all that she had; and she was no better, but rather grew worse. 27 She had heard about Jesus, and came up behind him in the crowd and touched his cloak, 28 for she said, "If I but touch his clothes, I will be made well." 29 Immediately her hemorrhage stopped; and she felt in her body that she was healed of her disease. 30 Immediately aware that power had gone forth from him, Jesus turned about in the crowd and said, "Who touched my clothes?" 31 And his disciples said to him, "You see the crowd pressing in on you; how can you say, 'Who touched me?'" 32 He looked all around to see who had done it. 33 But the woman, knowing what had happened to her, came in fear and trembling, fell down before him, and told him the whole truth. 34 He said to her, "Daughter, your faith has made you well; go in peace, and be healed of your disease."

35 While he was still speaking, some people came from the leader's house to say, "Your daughter is dead. Why trouble the teacher any further?" 36 But overhearing[j] what they said, Jesus said to the leader of the synagogue, "Do not fear, only believe." 37 He allowed no one to follow him except Peter, James, and John, the brother of James. 38 When they came to the house of the leader of the synagogue, he saw a commotion, people weeping and wailing loudly. 39 When he had entered, he said to them, "Why do you make a commotion and weep? The child is not dead but sleeping." 40 And they laughed at him. Then he put them all outside, and took the child's father and mother and those who were with him, and went in where the child was. 41 He took her by the hand and said to her, "Talitha cum," which means, "Little girl, get up!" 42 And immediately the girl got up and began to walk about (she was twelve years of age). At this they were overcome with amazement. 43 He strictly ordered them that no one should know this, and told them to give her something to eat.

6 He left that place and came to his hometown, and his disciples followed him. 2 On the sabbath he began to teach in the synagogue, and many who heard him were astounded. They said, "Where did this man get all this? What is this wisdom that has been given to him? What deeds of power are being done by his hands! 3 Is not this the carpenter, the son of Mary[k] and brother of James and Joses and Judas and Simon, and are not

[f]Gk he [g]Gk they [h]Gk him [i]Other ancient authorities lack in the boat [j]Or ignoring; other ancient authorities read hearing [k]Other ancient authorities read son of the carpenter and of Mary

his sisters here with us?" And they took offense[l] at him. 4 Then Jesus said to them, "Prophets are not without honor, except in their hometown, and among their own kin, and in their own house." 5 And he could do no deed of power there, except that he laid his hands on a few sick people and cured them. 6 And he was amazed at their unbelief.

Then he went about among the villages teaching. 7 He called the twelve and began to send them out two by two, and gave them authority over the unclean spirits. 8 He ordered them to take nothing for their journey except a staff; no bread, no bag, no money in their belts; 9 but to wear sandals and not to put on two tunics. 10 He said to them, "Wherever you enter a house, stay there until you leave the place. 11 If any place will not welcome you and they refuse to hear you, as you leave, shake off the dust that is on your feet as a testimony against them." 12 So they went out and proclaimed that all should repent. 13 They cast out many demons, and anointed with oil many who were sick and cured them.

14 King Herod heard of it, for Jesus'[m] name had become known. Some were[n] saying, "John the baptizer has been raised from the dead; and for this reason these powers are at work in him." 15 But others said, "It is Elijah." And others said, "It is a prophet, like one of the prophets of old." 16 But when Herod heard of it, he said, "John, whom I beheaded, has been raised."

17 For Herod himself had sent men who arrested John, bound him, and put him in prison on account of Herodias, his brother Philip's wife, because Herod[o] had married her. 18 For John had been telling Herod, "It is not lawful for you to have your brother's wife." 19 And Herodias had a grudge against him, and wanted to kill him. But she could not, 20 for Herod feared John, knowing that he was a righteous and holy man, and he protected him. When he heard him, he was greatly perplexed;[p] and yet he liked to listen to him. 21 But an opportunity came when Herod on his birthday gave a banquet for his courtiers and officers and for the leaders of Galilee. 22 When his daughter Herodias[q] came in and danced, she pleased Herod and his guests; and the king said to the girl, "Ask me for whatever you wish, and I will give it." 23 And he solemnly swore to her, "Whatever you ask me, I will give you, even half of my kingdom." 24 She went out and said to her mother, "What should I ask for?" She replied, "The head of John the baptizer." 25 Immediately she rushed back to the king and requested, "I want you to give me at once the head of John the Baptist on a platter." 26 The king was deeply grieved; yet out of regard for his oaths and for the guests, he did not want to refuse her. 27 Immediately the king sent a soldier of the guard with orders to bring John's[m] head. He went and beheaded him in the prison, 28 brought his head on a platter, and gave it to the girl. Then the girl gave it to her mother. 29 When his disciples heard about it, they came and took his body, and laid it in a tomb.

30 The apostles gathered around Jesus, and told him all that they had done and taught. 31 He said to them, "Come away to a deserted place all by yourselves and rest a while." For many were coming and going, and they had no leisure even to eat. 32 And they went away in the boat to a deserted place by themselves. 33 Now many saw them going and recognized them, and they hurried there on foot from all the towns and arrived ahead of them. 34 As he went ashore, he saw a great crowd; and he had compassion for them, because they were like sheep without a shepherd; and he began to teach them many things. 35 When it grew late, his disciples came to him and said, "This is a deserted place, and the hour is now very late; 36 send them away so that they may go into the surrounding country and villages and buy something for themselves to eat." 37 But he answered them, "You give them something to eat." They said to him, "Are we to go and buy two hundred denarii[r] worth of bread, and give it to them to eat?" 38 And he said to them, "How many loaves have you? Go and see." When they had found out, they said, "Five, and two fish." 39 Then he ordered them to get all the people to sit down in groups on the green grass. 40 So they sat down in groups of hundreds and of fifties. 41 Taking the five loaves and the two fish, he looked up to heaven, and

---

[l]Or *stumbled*　[m]Gk *his*　[n]Other ancient authorities read *He was*
[o]Gk *he*　[p]Other ancient authorities read *he did many things*　[q]Other ancient authorities read *the daughter of Herodias herself*
[r]The denarius was the usual day's wage for a laborer

blessed and broke the loaves, and gave them to his disciples to set before the people; and he divided the two fish among them all. 42 And all ate and were filled; 43 and they took up twelve baskets full of broken pieces and of the fish. 44 Those who had eaten the loaves numbered five thousand men.

45 Immediately he made his disciples get into the boat and go on ahead to the other side, to Bethsaida, while he dismissed the crowd. 46 After saying farewell to them, he went up on the mountain to pray.

47 When evening came, the boat was out on the sea, and he was alone on the land. 48 When he saw that they were straining at the oars against an adverse wind, he came towards them early in the morning, walking on the sea. He intended to pass them by. 49 But when they saw him walking on the sea, they thought it was a ghost and cried out; 50 for they all saw him and were terrified. But immediately he spoke to them and said, "Take heart, it is I; do not be afraid." 51 Then he got into the boat with them and the wind ceased. And they were utterly astounded, 52 for they did not understand about the loaves, but their hearts were hardened.

53 When they had crossed over, they came to land at Gennesaret and moored the boat. 54 When they got out of the boat, people at once recognized him, 55 and rushed about that whole region and began to bring the sick on mats to wherever they heard he was. 56 And wherever he went, into villages or cities or farms, they laid the sick in the marketplaces, and begged him that they might touch even the fringe of his cloak; and all who touched it were healed.

7 Now when the Pharisees and some of the scribes who had come from Jerusalem gathered around him, 2 they noticed that some of his disciples were eating with defiled hands, that is, without washing them. 3 (For the Pharisees, and all the Jews, do not eat unless they thoroughly wash their hands,[s] thus observing the tradition of the elders; 4 and they do not eat anything from the market unless they wash it;[t] and there are also many other traditions that they observe, the washing of cups, pots, and bronze kettles.[u]) 5 So the Pharisees and the scribes asked him, "Why do your disciples not live[v] according to the tradition of the elders, but eat with defiled hands?" 6 He

said to them, "Isaiah prophesied rightly about you hypocrites, as it is written,

'This people honors me with their
        lips,
    but their hearts are far from me;
7   in vain do they worship me,
        teaching human precepts as
            doctrines.'[4]

8 You abandon the commandment of God and hold to human tradition."

9 Then he said to them, "You have a fine way of rejecting the commandment of God in order to keep your tradition! 10 For Moses said, 'Honor your father and your mother';[5] and, 'Whoever speaks evil of father or mother must surely die.'[6] 11 But you say that if anyone tells father or mother, 'Whatever support you might have had from me is Corban' (that is, an offering to God[w])— 12 then you no longer permit doing anything for a father or mother, 13 thus making void the word of God through your tradition that you have handed on. And you do many things like this."

14 Then he called the crowd again and said to them, "Listen to me, all of you, and understand: 15 there is nothing outside a person that by going in can defile, but the things that come out are what defile."[x]

17 When he had left the crowd and entered the house, his disciples asked him about the parable. 18 He said to them, "Then do you also fail to understand? Do you not see that whatever goes into a person from outside cannot defile, 19 since it enters, not the heart but the stomach, and goes out into the sewer?" (Thus he declared all foods clean.) 20 And he said, "It is what comes out of a person that defiles. 21 For it is from within, from the human heart, that evil intentions come: fornication, theft, murder, 22 adultery, avarice, wickedness, deceit, licentiousness, envy, slander, pride, folly. 23 All these evil things come from within, and they defile a person."

24 From there he set out and went away to the region of Tyre.[y] He entered a house and did not

---

[w]Gk lacks *to God*   [x]Other ancient authorities add verse 16, *"Let anyone with ears to hear listen"*   [y]Other ancient authorities add *and Sidon*

[4]Isa 29:13   [5]Exod 20:12; Deut 5:16   [6]Exod 21:17; Lev 20:9

want anyone to know he was there. Yet he could not escape notice, 25 but a woman whose little daughter had an unclean spirit immediately heard about him, and she came and bowed down at his feet. 26 Now the woman was a Gentile, of Syrophoenician origin. She begged him to cast the demon out of her daughter. 27 He said to her, "Let the children be fed first, for it is not fair to take the children's food and throw it to the dogs." 28 But she answered him, "Sir,[z] even the dogs under the table eat the children's crumbs." 29 Then he said to her, "For saying that, you may go—the demon has left your daughter." 30 So she went home, found the child lying on the bed, and the demon gone.

31 Then he returned from the region of Tyre, and went by way of Sidon towards the Sea of Galilee, in the region of the Decapolis. 32 They brought to him a deaf man who had an impediment in his speech; and they begged him to lay his hand on him. 33 He took him aside in private, away from the crowd, and put his fingers into his ears, and he spat and touched his tongue. 34 Then looking up to heaven, he sighed and said to him, "Ephphatha," that is, "Be opened." 35 And immediately his ears were opened, his tongue was released, and he spoke plainly. 36 Then Jesus[a] ordered them to tell no one; but the more he ordered them, the more zealously they proclaimed it. 37 They were astounded beyond measure, saying, "He has done everything well; he even makes the deaf to hear and the mute to speak."

8 In those days when there was again a great crowd without anything to eat, he called his disciples and said to them, 2 "I have compassion for the crowd, because they have been with me now for three days and have nothing to eat. 3 If I send them away hungry to their homes, they will faint on the way—and some of them have come from a great distance." 4 His disciples replied, "How can one feed these people with bread here in the desert?" 5 He asked them, "How many loaves do you have?" They said, "Seven." 6 Then he ordered the crowd to sit down on the ground; and he took the seven loaves, and after giving thanks he broke them and gave them to his disciples to distribute; and they distributed them to the crowd. 7 They had also a few small fish; and after blessing them, he ordered that these too should be distributed. 8 They ate and were filled; and

they took up the broken pieces left over, seven baskets full. 9 Now there were about four thousand people. And he sent them away. 10 And immediately he got into the boat with his disciples and went to the district of Dalmanutha.[b]

11 The Pharisees came and began to argue with him, asking him for a sign from heaven, to test him. 12 And he sighed deeply in his spirit and said, "Why does this generation ask for a sign? Truly I tell you, no sign will be given to this generation." 13 And he left them, and getting into the boat again, he went across to the other side.

14 Now the disciples[c] had forgotten to bring any bread; and they had only one loaf with them in the boat. 15 And he cautioned them, saying, "Watch out—beware of the yeast of the Pharisees and the yeast of Herod."[d] 16 They said to one another, "It is because we have no bread." 17 And becoming aware of it, Jesus said to them, "Why are you talking about having no bread? Do you still not perceive or understand? Are your hearts hardened? 18 Do you have eyes, and fail to see? Do you have ears, and fail to hear? And do you not remember? 19 When I broke the five loaves for the five thousand, how many baskets full of broken pieces did you collect?" They said to him, "Twelve." 20 "And the seven for the four thousand, how many baskets full of broken pieces did you collect?" And they said to him, "Seven." 21 Then he said to them, "Do you not yet understand?"

22 They came to Bethsaida. Some people[e] brought a blind man to him and begged him to touch him. 23 He took the blind man by the hand and led him out of the village; and when he had put saliva on his eyes and laid his hands on him, he asked him, "Can you see anything?" 24 And the man[a] looked up and said, "I can see people, but they look like trees, walking." 25 Then Jesus[a] laid his hands on his eyes again; and he looked intently and his sight was restored, and he saw everything clearly. 26 Then he sent him away to his home, saying, "Do not even go into the village."[f]

[z]Or *Lord*; other ancient authorities prefix *Yes* [a]Gk *he* [b]Other ancient authorities read *Mageda* or *Magdala* [c]Gk *they* [d]Other ancient authorities read *the Herodians* [e]Gk *They* [f]Other ancient authorities add *or tell anyone in the village*

27 Jesus went on with his disciples to the villages of Caesarea Philippi; and on the way he asked his disciples, "Who do people say that I am?" 28 And they answered him, "John the Baptist; and others, Elijah; and still others, one of the prophets." 29 He asked them, "But who do you say that I am?" Peter answered him, "You are the Messiah."[g] 30 And he sternly ordered them not to tell anyone about him.

31 Then he began to teach them that the Son of Man must undergo great suffering, and be rejected by the elders, the chief priests, and the scribes, and be killed, and after three days rise again. 32 He said all this quite openly. And Peter took him aside and began to rebuke him. 33 But turning and looking at his disciples, he rebuked Peter and said, "Get behind me, Satan! For you are setting your mind not on divine things but on human things."

34 He called the crowd with his disciples, and said to them, "If any want to become my followers, let them deny themselves and take up their cross and follow me. 35 For those who want to save their life will lose it, and those who lose their life for my sake, and for the sake of the gospel,[h] will save it. 36 For what will it profit them to gain the whole world and forfeit their life? 37 Indeed, what can they give in return for their life? 38 Those who are ashamed of me and of my words[i] in this adulterous and sinful generation, of them the Son of Man will also be ashamed when he comes in the glory of his Father with the holy angels."

9 And he said to them, "Truly I tell you, there are some standing here who will not taste death until they see that the kingdom of God has come with[j] power."

2 Six days later, Jesus took with him Peter and James and John, and led them up a high mountain apart, by themselves. And he was transfigured before them, 3 and his clothes became dazzling white, such as no one[k] on earth could bleach them. 4 And there appeared to them Elijah with Moses, who were talking with Jesus. 5 Then Peter said to Jesus, "Rabbi, it is good for us to be here; let us make three dwellings,[l] one for you, one for Moses, and one for Elijah." 6 He did not know what to say, for they were terrified. 7 Then a cloud overshadowed them, and from the cloud there came a voice, "This is my Son, the Beloved;[m] listen to him!" 8 Suddenly when they looked around, they saw no one with them any more, but only Jesus.

9 As they were coming down the mountain, he ordered them to tell no one about what they had seen, until after the Son of Man had risen from the dead. 10 So they kept the matter to themselves, questioning what this rising from the dead could mean. 11 Then they asked him, "Why do the scribes say that Elijah must come first?" 12 He said to them, "Elijah is indeed coming first to restore all things. How then is it written about the Son of Man, that he is to go through many sufferings and be treated with contempt? 13 But I tell you that Elijah has come, and they did to him whatever they pleased, as it is written about him."

14 When they came to the disciples, they saw a great crowd around them, and some scribes arguing with them. 15 When the whole crowd saw him, they were immediately overcome with awe, and they ran forward to greet him. 16 He asked them, "What are you arguing about with them?" 17 Someone from the crowd answered him, "Teacher, I brought you my son; he has a spirit that makes him unable to speak; 18 and whenever it seizes him, it dashes him down; and he foams and grinds his teeth and becomes rigid; and I asked your disciples to cast it out, but they could not do so." 19 He answered them, "You faithless generation, how much longer must I be among you? How much longer must I put up with you? Bring him to me." 20 And they brought the boy[n] to him. When the spirit saw him, immediately it convulsed the boy,[n] and he fell on the ground and rolled about, foaming at the mouth. 21 Jesus[o] asked the father, "How long has this been happening to him?" And he said, "From childhood. 22 It has often cast him into the fire and into the water, to destroy him; but if you are able to do anything, have pity on us and help us." 23 Jesus said to him, "If you are able!—All things can be done for the one who believes." 24 Immediately the father of the child cried out,[p] "I believe; help my unbelief!" 25 When Jesus saw that a crowd came running together, he rebuked the unclean spirit, saying to it,

---

[g]Or *the Christ* [h]Other ancient authorities read *lose their life for the sake of the gospel* [i]Other ancient authorities read *and of mine* [j]Or *in* [k]Gk *no fuller* [l]Or *tents* [m]Or *my beloved Son* [n]Gk *him* [o]Gk *He* [p]Other ancient authorities add *with tears*

"You spirit that keeps this boy from speaking and hearing, I command you, come out of him, and never enter him again!" 26 After crying out and convulsing him terribly, it came out, and the boy was like a corpse, so that most of them said, "He is dead." 27 But Jesus took him by the hand and lifted him up, and he was able to stand. 28 When he had entered the house, his disciples asked him privately, "Why could we not cast it out?" 29 He said to them, "This kind can come out only through prayer."q

30 They went on from there and passed through Galilee. He did not want anyone to know it; 31 for he was teaching his disciples, saying to them, "The Son of Man is to be betrayed into human hands, and they will kill him, and three days after being killed, he will rise again." 32 But they did not understand what he was saying and were afraid to ask him.

33 Then they came to Capernaum; and when he was in the house he asked them, "What were you arguing about on the way?" 34 But they were silent, for on the way they had argued with one another who was the greatest. 35 He sat down, called the twelve, and said to them, "Whoever wants to be first must be last of all and servant of all." 36 Then he took a little child and put it among them; and taking it in his arms, he said to them, 37 "Whoever welcomes one such child in my name welcomes me, and whoever welcomes me welcomes not me but the one who sent me."

38 John said to him, "Teacher, we saw some-oner casting out demons in your name, and we tried to stop him, because he was not following us." 39 But Jesus said, "Do not stop him; for no one who does a deed of power in my name will be able soon afterward to speak evil of me. 40 Whoever is not against us is for us. 41 For truly I tell you, whoever gives you a cup of water to drink because you bear the name of Christ will by no means lose the reward.

42 "If any of you put a stumbling block before one of these little ones who believe in me,s it would be better for you if a great millstone were hung around your neck and you were thrown into the sea. 43 If your hand causes you to stumble, cut it off; it is better for you to enter life maimed than to have two hands and to go to hell,t to the un-

quenchable fire.u 45 And if your foot causes you to stumble, cut it off; it is better for you to enter life lame than to have two feet and to be thrown into hell.t, u 47 And if your eye causes you to stumble, tear it out; it is better for you to enter the kingdom of God with one eye than to have two eyes and to be thrown into hell,t 48 where their worm never dies, and the fire is never quenched.

49 "For everyone will be salted with fire.v 50 Salt is good; but if salt has lost its saltiness, how can you season it?w Have salt in yourselves, and be at peace with one another."

10 He left that place and went to the region of Judea andx beyond the Jordan. And crowds again gathered around him; and, as was his custom, he again taught them.

2 Some Pharisees came, and to test him they asked, "Is it lawful for a man to divorce his wife?" 3 He answered them, "What did Moses command you?" 4 They said, "Moses allowed a man to write a certificate of dismissal and to divorce her."7 5 But Jesus said to them, "Because of your hardness of heart he wrote this commandment for you. 6 But from the beginning of creation, 'God made them male and female.'8 7 'For this reason a man shall leave his father and mother and be joined to his wife,y 8 and the two shall become one flesh.'9 So they are no longer two, but one flesh. 9 Therefore what God has joined together, let no one separate."

10 Then in the house the disciples asked him again about this matter. 11 He said to them, "Whoever divorces his wife and marries another commits adultery against her; 12 and if she divorces her husband and marries another, she commits adultery."

13 People were bringing little children to him in order that he might touch them; and the disciples spoke sternly to them. 14 But when Jesus saw this, he was indignant and said to them, "Let the little children come to me; do not stop them; for it

---

qOther ancient authorities add *and fasting* rOther ancient authorities add *who does not follow us* sOther ancient authorities lack *in me* tGk *Gehenna* uVerses 44 and 46 (which are identical with verse 48) are lacking in the best ancient authorities vOther ancient authorities either add or substitute *and every sacrifice will be salted with salt* wOr *how can you restore its saltiness?* xOther ancient authorities lack *and* yOther ancient authorities lack *and be joined to his wife*

7Deut 24:1 8Gen 1:27 9Gen 2:24

is to such as these that the kingdom of God belongs. 15 Truly I tell you, whoever does not receive the kingdom of God as a little child will never enter it." 16 And he took them up in his arms, laid his hands on them, and blessed them.

17 As he was setting out on a journey, a man ran up and knelt before him, and asked him, "Good Teacher, what must I do to inherit eternal life?" 18 Jesus said to him, "Why do you call me good? No one is good but God alone. 19 You know the commandments: 'You shall not murder; You shall not commit adultery; You shall not steal; You shall not bear false witness; You shall not defraud; Honor your father and mother.'"[10] 20 He said to him, "Teacher, I have kept all these since my youth." 21 Jesus, looking at him, loved him and said, "You lack one thing; go, sell what you own, and give the money[z] to the poor, and you will have treasure in heaven; then come, follow me." 22 When he heard this, he was shocked and went away grieving, for he had many possessions.

23 Then Jesus looked around and said to his disciples, "How hard it will be for those who have wealth to enter the kingdom of God!" 24 And the disciples were perplexed at these words. But Jesus said to them again, "Children, how hard it is[a] to enter the kingdom of God! 25 It is easier for a camel to go through the eye of a needle than for someone who is rich to enter the kingdom of God." 26 They were greatly astounded and said to one another,[b] "Then who can be saved?" 27 Jesus looked at them and said, "For mortals it is impossible, but not for God; for God all things are possible."

28 Peter began to say to him, "Look, we have left everything and followed you." 29 Jesus said, "Truly I tell you, there is no one who has left house or brothers or sisters or mother or father or children or fields, for my sake and for the sake of the good news,[c] 30 who will not receive a hundredfold now in this age—houses, brothers and sisters, mothers and children, and fields, with persecutions—and in the age to come eternal life. 31 But many who are first will be last, and the last will be first."

32 They were on the road, going up to Jerusalem, and Jesus was walking ahead of them; they were amazed, and those who followed were afraid.

He took the twelve aside again and began to tell them what was to happen to him, 33 saying, "See, we are going up to Jerusalem, and the Son of Man will be handed over to the chief priests and the scribes, and they will condemn him to death; then they will hand him over to the Gentiles; 34 they will mock him, and spit upon him, and flog him, and kill him; and after three days he will rise again."

35 James and John, the sons of Zebedee, came forward to him and said to him, "Teacher, we want you to do for us whatever we ask of you." 36 And he said to them, "What is it you want me to do for you?" 37 And they said to him, "Grant us to sit, one at your right hand and one at your left, in your glory." 38 But Jesus said to them, "You do not know what you are asking. Are you able to drink the cup that I drink, or be baptized with the baptism that I am baptized with?" 39 They replied, "We are able." Then Jesus said to them, "The cup that I drink you will drink; and with the baptism with which I am baptized, you will be baptized; 40 but to sit at my right hand or at my left is not mine to grant, but it is for those for whom it has been prepared."

41 When the ten heard this, they began to be angry with James and John. 42 So Jesus called them and said to them, "You know that among the Gentiles those whom they recognize as their rulers lord it over them, and their great ones are tyrants over them. 43 But it is not so among you; but whoever wishes to become great among you must be your servant, 44 and whoever wishes to be first among you must be slave of all. 45 For the Son of Man came not to be served but to serve, and to give his life a ransom for many."

46 They came to Jericho. As he and his disciples and a large crowd were leaving Jericho, Bartimaeus son of Timaeus, a blind beggar, was sitting by the roadside. 47 When he heard that it was Jesus of Nazareth, he began to shout out and say, "Jesus, Son of David, have mercy on me!" 48 Many sternly ordered him to be quiet, but he cried out even more loudly, "Son of David, have mercy on

---

[z]Gk lacks *the money*   [a]Other ancient authorities add *for those who trust in riches*   [b]Other ancient authorities read *to him*   [c]Or *gospel*

[10]Exod 20:12–16; Deut 5:16–20

me!" 49 Jesus stood still and said, "Call him here." And they called the blind man, saying to him, "Take heart; get up, he is calling you." 50 So throwing off his cloak, he sprang up and came to Jesus. 51 Then Jesus said to him, "What do you want me to do for you?" The blind man said to him, "My teacher,[d] let me see again." 52 Jesus said to him, "Go; your faith has made you well." Immediately he regained his sight and followed him on the way.

11

When they were approaching Jerusalem, at Bethphage and Bethany, near the Mount of Olives, he sent two of his disciples 2 and said to them, "Go into the village ahead of you, and immediately as you enter it, you will find tied there a colt that has never been ridden; untie it and bring it. 3 If anyone says to you, 'Why are you doing this?' just say this, 'The Lord needs it and will send it back here immediately.'" 4 They went away and found a colt tied near a door, outside in the street. As they were untying it, 5 some of the bystanders said to them, "What are you doing, untying the colt?" 6 They told them what Jesus had said; and they allowed them to take it. 7 Then they brought the colt to Jesus and threw their cloaks on it; and he sat on it. 8 Many people spread their cloaks on the road, and others spread leafy branches that they had cut in the fields. 9 Then those who went ahead and those who followed were shouting,

> "Hosanna!
>> Blessed is the one who comes in
>> the name of the Lord![11]
> 10   Blessed is the coming kingdom
>>   of our ancestor David!
> Hosanna in the highest heaven!"

11 Then he entered Jerusalem and went into the temple; and when he had looked around at everything, as it was already late, he went out to Bethany with the twelve.

12 On the following day, when they came from Bethany, he was hungry. 13 Seeing in the distance a fig tree in leaf, he went to see whether perhaps he would find anything on it. When he came to it, he found nothing but leaves, for it was not the season for figs. 14 He said to it, "May no one ever eat fruit from you again." And his disciples heard it.

15 Then they came to Jerusalem. And he entered the temple and began to drive out those who were selling and those who were buying in the temple, and he overturned the tables of the money changers and the seats of those who sold doves; 16 and he would not allow anyone to carry anything through the temple. 17 He was teaching and saying, "Is it not written,

> 'My house shall be called a house
>> of prayer for all the
>> nations'?
>> But you have made it a den of
>> robbers.'"[12]

18 And when the chief priests and the scribes heard it, they kept looking for a way to kill him; for they were afraid of him, because the whole crowd was spellbound by his teaching. 19 And when evening came, Jesus and his disciples[e] went out of the city.

20 In the morning as they passed by, they saw the fig tree withered away to its roots. 21 Then Peter remembered and said to him, "Rabbi, look! The fig tree that you cursed has withered." 22 Jesus answered them, "Have[f] faith in God. 23 Truly I tell you, if you say to this mountain, 'Be taken up and thrown into the sea,' and if you do not doubt in your heart, but believe that what you say will come to pass, it will be done for you. 24 So I tell you, whatever you ask for in prayer, believe that you have received[g] it, and it will be yours.

25 "Whenever you stand praying, forgive, if you have anything against anyone; so that your Father in heaven may also forgive you your trespasses."[h]

27 Again they came to Jerusalem. As he was walking in the temple, the chief priests, the scribes, and the elders came to him 28 and said, "By what authority are you doing these things? Who gave you this authority to do them?" 29 Jesus said to them, "I will ask you one question; answer me, and I will tell you by what authority I do these things. 30 Did the baptism of John come from heaven, or was it of human origin? Answer

---

[d]Aramaic *Rabbouni*   [e]Gk *they*: other ancient authorities read *he*
[f]Other ancient authorities read *"If you have*   [g]Other ancient authorities read *are receiving*   [h]Other ancient authorities add verse 26, *"But if you do not forgive, neither will your Father in heaven forgive your trespasses."*

---

[11]Ps 118:25–26   [12]Isa 56:7; Jer 7:11

me." 31 They argued with one another, "If we say, 'From heaven,' he will say, 'Why then did you not believe him?' 32 But shall we say, 'Of human origin'?"—they were afraid of the crowd, for all regarded John as truly a prophet. 33 So they answered Jesus, "We do not know." And Jesus said to them, "Neither will I tell you by what authority I am doing these things."

12 Then he began to speak to them in parables. "A man planted a vineyard, put a fence around it, dug a pit for the wine press, and built a watchtower; then he leased it to tenants and went to another country. 2 When the season came, he sent a slave to the tenants to collect from them his share of the produce of the vineyard. 3 But they seized him, and beat him, and sent him away empty-handed. 4 And again he sent another slave to them; this one they beat over the head and insulted. 5 Then he sent another, and that one they killed. And so it was with many others; some they beat, and others they killed. 6 He had still one other, a beloved son. Finally he sent him to them, saying, 'They will respect my son.' 7 But those tenants said to one another, 'This is the heir; come, let us kill him, and the inheritance will be ours.' 8 So they seized him, killed him, and threw him out of the vineyard. 9 What then will the owner of the vineyard do? He will come and destroy the tenants and give the vineyard to others. 10 Have you not read this scripture:

'The stone that the builders
    rejected
    has become the cornerstone;[i]
11   this was the Lord's doing,
    and it is amazing in our eyes'?"[13]

12 When they realized that he had told this parable against them, they wanted to arrest him, but they feared the crowd. So they left him and went away.

13 Then they sent to him some Pharisees and some Herodians to trap him in what he said. 14 And they came and said to him, "Teacher, we know that you are sincere, and show deference to no one; for you do not regard people with partiality, but teach the way of God in accordance with truth. Is it lawful to pay taxes to the emperor, or not? 15 Should we pay them, or should we not?" But knowing their hypocrisy, he said to them, "Why are you putting me to the test? Bring me a denarius and let me see it." 16 And they brought one. Then he said to them, "Whose head is this, and whose title?" They answered, "The emperor's." 17 Jesus said to them, "Give to the emperor the things that are the emperor's, and to God the things that are God's." And they were utterly amazed at him.

18 Some Sadducees, who say there is no resurrection, came to him and asked him a question, saying, 19 "Teacher, Moses wrote for us that if a man's brother dies, leaving a wife but no child, the man[j] shall marry the widow and raise up children for his brother.[14] 20 There were seven brothers; the first married and, when he died, left no children; 21 and the second married her and died, leaving no children; and the third likewise; 22 none of the seven left children. Last of all the woman herself died. 23 In the resurrection[k] whose wife will she be? For the seven had married her."

24 Jesus said to them, "Is not this the reason you are wrong, that you know neither the scriptures nor the power of God? 25 For when they rise from the dead, they neither marry nor are given in marriage, but are like angels in heaven. 26 And as for the dead being raised, have you not read in the book of Moses, in the story about the bush, how God said to him, 'I am the God of Abraham, the God of Isaac, and the God of Jacob'?[15] 27 He is God not of the dead, but of the living; you are quite wrong."

28 One of the scribes came near and heard them disputing with one another, and seeing that he answered them well, he asked him, "Which commandment is the first of all?" 29 Jesus answered, "The first is, 'Hear, O Israel: the Lord our God, the Lord is one; 30 you shall love the Lord your God with all your heart, and with all your soul, and with all your mind, and with all your strength.'[16] 31 The second is this, 'You shall love your neighbor as yourself.'[17] There is no other commandment greater than these." 32 Then the scribe said to him, "You are right, Teacher; you have truly said that 'he is one, and besides him there is no

---

[i]Or *keystone*   [j]Gk *his brother*   [k]Other ancient authorities add *when they rise*

---

[13]Ps 118:22–23   [14]Deut 25:5; Gen 38:8   [15]Exod 3:6, 15   [16]Deut 6:4–5   [17]Lev 19:18

other';[18] 33 and 'to love him with all the heart, and with all the understanding, and with all the strength,'[19] and 'to love one's neighbor as oneself,'[20]—this is much more important than all whole burnt offerings and sacrifices." 34 When Jesus saw that he answered wisely, he said to him, "You are not far from the kingdom of God." After that no one dared to ask him any question.

35 While Jesus was teaching in the temple, he said, "How can the scribes say that the Messiah[l] is the son of David? 36 David himself, by the Holy Spirit, declared,

> 'The Lord said to my Lord,
>   "Sit at my right hand,
>   until I put your enemies under
>   your feet."'[21]

37 David himself calls him Lord; so how can he be his son?" And the large crowd was listening to him with delight.

38 As he taught, he said, "Beware of the scribes, who like to walk around in long robes, and to be greeted with respect in the marketplaces, 39 and to have the best seats in the synagogues and places of honor at banquets! 40 They devour widows' houses and for the sake of appearance say long prayers. They will receive the greater condemnation."

41 He sat down opposite the treasury, and watched the crowd putting money into the treasury. Many rich people put in large sums. 42 A poor widow came and put in two small copper coins, which are worth a penny. 43 Then he called his disciples and said to them, "Truly I tell you, this poor widow has put in more than all those who are contributing to the treasury. 44 For all of them have contributed out of their abundance; but she out of her poverty has put in everything she had, all she had to live on."

13 As he came out of the temple, one of his disciples said to him, "Look, Teacher, what large stones and what large buildings!" 2 Then Jesus asked him, "Do you see these great buildings? Not one stone will be left here upon another; all will be thrown down."

3 When he was sitting on the Mount of Olives opposite the temple, Peter, James, John, and Andrew asked him privately, 4 "Tell us, when will this be, and what will be the sign that all these things are about to be accomplished?" 5 Then Jesus began to say to them, "Beware that no one leads you astray. 6 Many will come in my name and say, 'I am he!'[m] and they will lead many astray. 7 When you hear of wars and rumors of wars, do not be alarmed; this must take place, but the end is still to come. 8 For nation will rise against nation, and kingdom against kingdom; there will be earthquakes in various places; there will be famines. This is but the beginning of the birth pangs.

9 "As for yourselves, beware; for they will hand you over to councils; and you will be beaten in synagogues; and you will stand before governors and kings because of me, as a testimony to them. 10 And the good news[n] must first be proclaimed to all nations. 11 When they bring you to trial and hand you over, do not worry beforehand about what you are to say; but say whatever is given you at that time, for it is not you who speak, but the Holy Spirit. 12 Brother will betray brother to death, and a father his child, and children will rise against parents and have them put to death; 13 and you will be hated by all because of my name. But the one who endures to the end will be saved.

14 "But when you see the desolating sacrilege set up where it ought not to be (let the reader understand), then those in Judea must flee to the mountains; 15 the one on the housetop must not go down or enter the house to take anything away; 16 the one in the field must not turn back to get a coat. 17 Woe to those who are pregnant and to those who are nursing infants in those days! 18 Pray that it may not be in winter. 19 For in those days there will be suffering, such as has not been from the beginning of the creation that God created until now, no, and never will be. 20 And if the Lord had not cut short those days, no one would be saved; but for the sake of the elect, whom he chose, he has cut short those days. 21 And if anyone says to you at that time, 'Look! Here is the Messiah!'[o] or 'Look! There he is!'— do not believe it. 22 False messiahs[p] and false prophets will appear and produce signs and omens, to lead astray, if possible, the elect. 23 But be alert; I have already told you everything.

24 "But in those days, after that suffering,
the sun will be darkened,
and the moon will not give its
light,
25 and the stars will be falling from
heaven,
and the powers in the heavens
will be shaken.

26 Then they will see 'the Son of Man coming in clouds'[22] with great power and glory. 27 Then he will send out the angels, and gather his elect from the four winds, from the ends of the earth to the ends of heaven.

28 "From the fig tree learn its lesson: as soon as its branch becomes tender and puts forth its leaves, you know that summer is near. 29 So also, when you see these things taking place, you know that he[q] is near, at the very gates. 30 Truly I tell you, this generation will not pass away until all these things have taken place. 31 Heaven and earth will pass away, but my words will not pass away.

32 "But about that day or hour no one knows, neither the angels in heaven, nor the Son, but only the Father. 33 Beware, keep alert;[r] for you do not know when the time will come. 34 It is like a man going on a journey, when he leaves home and puts his slaves in charge, each with his work, and commands the doorkeeper to be on the watch. 35 Therefore, keep awake—for you do not know when the master of the house will come, in the evening, or at midnight, or at cockcrow, or at dawn, 36 or else he may find you asleep when he comes suddenly. 37 And what I say to you I say to all: Keep awake."

14 It was two days before the Passover and the festival of Unleavened Bread. The chief priests and the scribes were looking for a way to arrest Jesus[s] by stealth and kill him; 2 for they said, "Not during the festival, or there may be a riot among the people."

3 While he was at Bethany in the house of Simon the leper,[t] as he sat at the table, a woman came with an alabaster jar of very costly ointment of nard, and she broke open the jar and poured the ointment on his head. 4 But some were there who said to one another in anger, "Why was the ointment wasted in this way? 5 For this ointment could have been sold for more than three hundred denarii,[u] and the money given to the poor." And they scolded her. 6 But Jesus said, "Let her alone; why do you trouble her? She has performed a good service for me. 7 For you always have the poor with you, and you can show kindness to them whenever you wish; but you will not always have me. 8 She has done what she could; she has anointed my body beforehand for its burial. 9 Truly I tell you, wherever the good news[v] is proclaimed in the whole world, what she has done will be told in remembrance of her."

10 Then Judas Iscariot, who was one of the twelve, went to the chief priests in order to betray him to them. 11 When they heard it, they were greatly pleased, and promised to give him money. So he began to look for an opportunity to betray him.

12 On the first day of Unleavened Bread, when the Passover lamb is sacrificed, his disciples said to him, "Where do you want us to go and make the preparations for you to eat the Passover?" 13 So he sent two of his disciples, saying to them, "Go into the city, and a man carrying a jar of water will meet you; follow him, 14 and wherever he enters, say to the owner of the house, 'The Teacher asks, Where is my guest room where I may eat the Passover with my disciples?' 15 He will show you a large room upstairs, furnished and ready. Make preparations for us there." 16 So the disciples set out and went to the city, and found everything as he had told them; and they prepared the Passover meal.

17 When it was evening, he came with the twelve. 18 And when they had taken their places and were eating, Jesus said, "Truly I tell you, one of you will betray me, one who is eating with me." 19 They began to be distressed and to say to him one after another, "Surely, not I?" 20 He said to them, "It is one of the twelve, one who is dipping bread[w] into the bowl[x] with me. 21 For the Son of Man goes as it is written of him, but woe to that one by whom the Son of Man is betrayed! It would have been better for that one not to have been born."

---

qOr *it* rOther ancient authorities add *and pray* sGk *him*
tThe terms *leper* and *leprosy* can refer to several diseases
uThe denarius was the usual day's wage for a laborer vOr *gospel*
wGk lacks *bread* xOther ancient authorities read *same bowl*

22Dan 7:13

22 While they were eating, he took a loaf of bread, and after blessing it he broke it, gave it to them, and said, "Take; this is my body." 23 Then he took a cup, and after giving thanks he gave it to them, and all of them drank from it. 24 He said to them, "This is my blood of the[y] covenant, which is poured out for many. 25 Truly I tell you, I will never again drink of the fruit of the vine until that day when I drink it new in the kingdom of God."

26 When they had sung the hymn, they went out to the Mount of Olives. 27 And Jesus said to them, "You will all become deserters; for it is written,

'I will strike the shepherd,
    and the sheep will be scattered.'[23]

28 But after I am raised up, I will go before you to Galilee." 29 Peter said to him, "Even though all become deserters, I will not." 30 Jesus said to him, "Truly I tell you, this day, this very night, before the cock crows twice, you will deny me three times." 31 But he said vehemently, "Even though I must die with you, I will not deny you." And all of them said the same.

32 They went to a place called Gethsemane; and he said to his disciples, "Sit here while I pray." 33 He took with him Peter and James and John, and began to be distressed and agitated. 34 And he said to them, "I am deeply grieved, even to death; remain here, and keep awake." 35 And going a little farther, he threw himself on the ground and prayed that, if it were possible, the hour might pass from him. 36 He said, "Abba,[z] Father, for you all things are possible; remove this cup from me; yet, not what I want, but what you want." 37 He came and found them sleeping; and he said to Peter, "Simon, are you asleep? Could you not keep awake one hour? 38 Keep awake and pray that you may not come into the time of trial;[a] the spirit indeed is willing, but the flesh is weak." 39 And again he went away and prayed, saying the same words. 40 And once more he came and found them sleeping, for their eyes were very heavy; and they did not know what to say to him. 41 He came a third time and said to them, "Are you still sleeping and taking your rest? Enough! The hour has come; the Son of Man is betrayed into the hands of sinners. 42 Get up, let us be going. See, my betrayer is at hand."

43 Immediately, while he was still speaking, Judas, one of the twelve, arrived; and with him there was a crowd with swords and clubs, from the chief priests, the scribes, and the elders. 44 Now the betrayer had given them a sign, saying, "The one I will kiss is the man; arrest him and lead him away under guard." 45 So when he came, he went up to him at once and said, "Rabbi!" and kissed him. 46 Then they laid hands on him and arrested him. 47 But one of those who stood near drew his sword and struck the slave of the high priest, cutting off his ear. 48 Then Jesus said to them, "Have you come out with swords and clubs to arrest me as though I were a bandit? 49 Day after day I was with you in the temple teaching, and you did not arrest me. But let the scriptures be fulfilled." 50 All of them deserted him and fled.

51 A certain young man was following him, wearing nothing but a linen cloth. They caught hold of him, 52 but he left the linen cloth and ran off naked.

53 They took Jesus to the high priest; and all the chief priests, the elders, and the scribes were assembled. 54 Peter had followed him at a distance, right into the courtyard of the high priest; and he was sitting with the guards, warming himself at the fire. 55 Now the chief priests and the whole council were looking for testimony against Jesus to put him to death; but they found none. 56 For many gave false testimony against him, and their testimony did not agree. 57 Some stood up and gave false testimony against him, saying, 58 "We heard him say, 'I will destroy this temple that is made with hands, and in three days I will build another, not made with hands.'" 59 But even on this point their testimony did not agree. 60 Then the high priest stood up before them and asked Jesus, "Have you no answer? What is it that they testify against you?" 61 But he was silent and did not answer. Again the high priest asked him, "Are you the Messiah,[b] the Son of the Blessed One?" 62 Jesus said, "I am; and

'you will see the Son of Man
    seated at the right hand of the
        Power,'
and 'coming with the clouds of
        heaven.'"[24]

[y]Other ancient authorities add *new*   [z]Aramaic for *Father*   [a]Or *into temptation*   [b]Or *the Christ*

[23]Zech 13:7   [24]Ps 110:1; Dan 7:13

63 Then the high priest tore his clothes and said, "Why do we still need witnesses? 64 You have heard his blasphemy! What is your decision?" All of them condemned him as deserving death. 65 Some began to spit on him, to blindfold him, and to strike him, saying to him, "Prophesy!" The guards also took him over and beat him.

66 While Peter was below in the courtyard, one of the servant-girls of the high priest came by. 67 When she saw Peter warming himself, she stared at him and said, "You also were with Jesus, the man from Nazareth." 68 But he denied it, saying, "I do not know or understand what you are talking about." And he went out into the forecourt.[c] Then the cock crowed.[d] 69 And the servant-girl, on seeing him, began again to say to the bystanders, "This man is one of them." 70 But again he denied it. Then after a little while the bystanders again said to Peter, "Certainly you are one of them; for you are a Galilean." 71 But he began to curse, and he swore an oath, "I do not know this man you are talking about." 72 At that moment the cock crowed for the second time. Then Peter remembered that Jesus had said to him, "Before the cock crows twice, you will deny me three times." And he broke down and wept.

15 As soon as it was morning, the chief priests held a consultation with the elders and scribes and the whole council. They bound Jesus, led him away, and handed him over to Pilate. 2 Pilate asked him, "Are you the King of the Jews?" He answered him, "You say so." 3 Then the chief priests accused him of many things. 4 Pilate asked him again, "Have you no answer? See how many charges they bring against you." 5 But Jesus made no further reply, so that Pilate was amazed.

6 Now at the festival he used to release a prisoner for them, anyone for whom they asked. 7 Now a man called Barabbas was in prison with the rebels who had committed murder during the insurrection. 8 So the crowd came and began to ask Pilate to do for them according to his custom. 9 Then he answered them, "Do you want me to release for you the King of the Jews?" 10 For he realized that it was out of jealousy that the chief priests had handed him over. 11 But the chief priests stirred up the crowd to have him release Barabbas for them instead. 12 Pilate spoke to

them again, "Then what do you wish me to do[e] with the man you call[f] the King of the Jews?" 13 They shouted back, "Crucify him!" 14 Pilate asked them, "Why, what evil has he done?" But they shouted all the more, "Crucify him!" 15 So Pilate, wishing to satisfy the crowd, released Barabbas for them; and after flogging Jesus, he handed him over to be crucified.

16 Then the soldiers led him into the courtyard of the palace (that is, the governor's headquarters[g]); and they called together the whole cohort. 17 And they clothed him in a purple cloak; and after twisting some thorns into a crown, they put it on him. 18 And they began saluting him, "Hail, King of the Jews!" 19 They struck his head with a reed, spat upon him, and knelt down in homage to him. 20 After mocking him, they stripped him of the purple cloak and put his own clothes on him. Then they led him out to crucify him.

21 They compelled a passer-by, who was coming in from the country, to carry his cross; it was Simon of Cyrene, the father of Alexander and Rufus. 22 Then they brought Jesus[h] to the place called Golgotha (which means the place of a skull). 23 And they offered him wine mixed with myrrh; but he did not take it. 24 And they crucified him, and divided his clothes among them, casting lots to decide what each should take.

25 It was nine o'clock in the morning when they crucified him. 26 The inscription of the charge against him read, "The King of the Jews." 27 And with him they crucified two bandits, one on his right and one on his left.[i] 29 Those who passed by derided[j] him, shaking their heads and saying, "Aha! You who would destroy the temple and build it in three days, 30 save yourself, and come down from the cross!" 31 In the same way the chief priests, along with the scribes, were also mocking him among themselves and saying, "He saved others; he cannot save himself. 32 Let the Messiah,[k] the King of Israel, come down from the cross now, so that we may see and believe." Those who were crucified with him also taunted him.

33 When it was noon, darkness came over the

---

[c]Or *gateway*   [d]Other ancient authorities lack *Then the cock crowed*
[e]Other ancient authorities read *what should I do*   [f]Other ancient authorities lack *the man you call*   [g]Gk *the praetorium*   [h]Gk *him*
[i]Other ancient authorities add verse 28, *And the scripture was fulfilled that says, "And he was counted among the lawless."*
[j]Or *blasphemed*   [k]Or *the Christ*

whole land[l] until three in the afternoon. 34 At three o'clock Jesus cried out with a loud voice, "Eloi, Eloi, lema sabachthani?" which means, "My God, my God, why have you forsaken me?"[m][25] 35 When some of the bystanders heard it, they said, "Listen, he is calling for Elijah." 36 And someone ran, filled a sponge with sour wine, put it on a stick, and gave it to him to drink, saying, "Wait, let us see whether Elijah will come to take him down." 37 Then Jesus gave a loud cry and breathed his last. 38 And the curtain of the temple was torn in two, from top to bottom. 39 Now when the centurion, who stood facing him, saw that in this way he[n] breathed his last, he said, "Truly this man was God's Son!"[o]

40 There were also women looking on from a distance; among them were Mary Magdalene, and Mary the mother of James the younger and of Joses, and Salome. 41 These used to follow him and provided for him when he was in Galilee; and there were many other women who had come up with him to Jerusalem.

42 When evening had come, and since it was the day of Preparation, that is, the day before the sabbath, 43 Joseph of Arimathea, a respected member of the council, who was also himself waiting expectantly for the kingdom of God, went boldly to Pilate and asked for the body of Jesus. 44 Then Pilate wondered if he were already dead; and summoning the centurion, he asked him whether he had been dead for some time. 45 When he learned from the centurion that he was dead, he granted the body to Joseph. 46 Then Joseph[p] bought a linen cloth, and taking down the body,[q] wrapped it in the linen cloth, and laid it in a tomb that had been hewn out of the rock. He then rolled a stone against the door of the tomb. 47 Mary Magdalene and Mary the mother of Joses saw where the body[q] was laid.

16 When the sabbath was over, Mary Magdalene, and Mary the mother of James, and Salome bought spices, so that they might go and anoint him. 2 And very early on the first day of the week, when the sun had risen, they went to the tomb. 3 They had been saying to one another, "Who will roll away the stone for us from the entrance to the tomb?" 4 When they looked up, they saw that the stone, which was very large, had al-

ready been rolled back. 5 As they entered the tomb, they saw a young man, dressed in a white robe, sitting on the right side; and they were alarmed. 6 But he said to them, "Do not be alarmed; you are looking for Jesus of Nazareth, who was crucified. He has been raised; he is not here. Look, there is the place they laid him. 7 But go, tell his disciples and Peter that he is going ahead of you to Galilee; there you will see him, just as he told you." 8 So they went out and fled from the tomb, for terror and amazement had seized them; and they said nothing to anyone, for they were afraid.[r]

THE SHORTER ENDING OF MARK

[And all that had been commanded them they told briefly to those around Peter. And afterward Jesus himself sent out through them, from east to west, the sacred and imperishable proclamation of eternal salvation.[s]]

THE LONGER ENDING OF MARK

9 [Now after he rose early on the first day of the week, he appeared first to Mary Magdalene, from whom he had cast out seven demons. 10 She went out and told those who had been with him, while they were mourning and weeping. 11 But when they heard that he was alive and had been seen by her, they would not believe it.

12 After this he appeared in another form to two of them, as they were walking into the country. 13 And they went back and told the rest, but they did not believe them.

14 Later he appeared to the eleven themselves as they were sitting at the table; and he upbraided them for their lack of faith and stubbornness, because they had not believed those who saw him af-

---

[l]Or *earth*   [m]Other ancient authorities read *made me a reproach*
[n]Other ancient authorities add *cried out and*   [o]Or *a son of God*
[p]Gk *he*   [q]Gk *it*   [r]Some of the most ancient authorities bring the book to a close at the end of verse 8. One authority concludes the book with the shorter ending; others include the shorter ending and then continue with verses 9-20. In most authorities verses 9-20 follow immediately after verse 8, though in some of these authorities the passage is marked as being doubtful.   [s]Other ancient authorities add *Amen*

[25]Ps 22:1

ter he had risen.ᵗ 15 And he said to them, "Go into all the world and proclaim the good newsᵘ to the whole creation. 16 The one who believes and is baptized will be saved; but the one who does not believe will be condemned. 17 And these signs will accompany those who believe: by using my name they will cast out demons; they will speak in new tongues; 18 they will pick up snakes in their hands,ᵛ and if they drink any deadly thing, it will not hurt them; they will lay their hands on the sick, and they will recover."

19 So then the Lord Jesus, after he had spoken to them, was taken up into heaven and sat down at the right hand of God. 20 And they went out and proclaimed the good news everywhere, while the Lord worked with them and confirmed the message by the signs that accompanied it.ʷ]

ᵗOther ancient authorities add, in whole or in part, *And they excused themselves, saying, "This age of lawlessness and unbelief is under Satan, who does not allow the truth and power of God to prevail over the unclean things of the spirits. Therefore reveal your righteousness now"—thus they spoke to Christ. And Christ replied to them, "The term of years of Satan's power has been fulfilled, but other terrible things draw near. And for those who have sinned I was handed over to death, that they may return to the truth and sin no more, that they may inherit the spiritual and imperishable glory of righteousness that is in heaven."* ᵘOr *gospel* ᵛOther ancient authorities lack *in their hands* ʷOther ancient authorities add *Amen*

The Gospel According to Luke

Luke is the only surviving Gospel whose author also produced a sequel, the Book of Acts. Whereas the Gospel records the birth, life, death, and resurrection of Jesus, the Book of Acts records the spread of Christianity after Jesus' resurrection and ascension to heaven. Taken together, these two books comprise over one-fourth of the entire New Testament.

Traditionally the author has been identified as Luke, the Gentile traveling companion of Paul; but as is the case with the other Gospels, the author does not actually disclose his identity. Whoever he was, he appears to have been writing in the final quarter of the first century, possibly around 80 or 85 C.E. He addresses his book to someone called "most excellent Theophilus" (1:3), whom some scholars take to be a non-Christian Roman official. If they are right, then Luke may have written his books to persuade Theophilus that Jesus and the religion he founded were morally admirable and socially innocuous (see, e.g., 23:47). Other scholars, however, think that the addressee's name is symbolic: it literally means "beloved of God" and may simply refer to the Christian community that the author addresses.

Like the author of Matthew, "Luke" appears to have had access to both the Gospel of Mark and the lost collection of sayings designated Q (from the German for "source," *Quelle*); from these and other sources (see 1:1–4) he constructed his own distinctive portrayal of Jesus. The basic story line of this Gospel is similar to those of Matthew and Mark; here, too, Jesus is the Son of God, who delivers inspired teachings and does astounding miracles; he is rejected by the leaders of his people and executed by the Romans for claiming to be the king of the Jews; but he is then raised by God from the dead.

More than the other Gospels, however, Luke is intent on showing that Jesus is God's special "prophet," or spokesperson, sent to his people. Thus, in stories found only in Luke, Jesus' birth is reminiscent of the prophet Samuel's (compare 1:46–56 with 1 Sam 2:1–10); he is anointed as a prophet (4:18), preaches as a prophet (4:20–30), does miracles as a prophet (7:11–17), and dies as a prophet (13:33–34). As God's prophet, Jesus not only proclaims God's will, but his entire life and the outcome of his death also conform to God's will, as found in the writings of the Jewish Scriptures (24:44).

As God's prophet, Jesus is rejected by his own people (13:33–34). This too, however, is according to the plan of God. For Jesus' rejection in Jerusalem allows his message to be taken outside of Israel, to the nations of the Gentiles (24:44–49). The spread of the good news of Jesus' salvation will then be recounted in Luke's second volume, the Book of Acts.

1 Since many have undertaken to set down an orderly account of the events that have been fulfilled among us, 2 just as they were handed on to us by those who from the beginning were eyewitnesses and servants of the word, 3 I too decided, after investigating everything carefully from the very first,[a] to write an orderly account for you, most excellent Theophilus, 4 so that you may

[a] Or *for a long time*

From the New Revised Standard Version Bible, © 1989.

know the truth concerning the things about which you have been instructed.

5 In the days of King Herod of Judea, there was a priest named Zechariah, who belonged to the priestly order of Abijah. His wife was a descendant of Aaron, and her name was Elizabeth. 6 Both of them were righteous before God, living blamelessly according to all the commandments and regulations of the Lord. 7 But they had no children, because Elizabeth was barren, and both were getting on in years.

8 Once when he was serving as priest before God and his section was on duty, 9 he was chosen by lot, according to the custom of the priesthood, to enter the sanctuary of the Lord and offer incense. 10 Now at the time of the incense offering, the whole assembly of the people was praying outside. 11 Then there appeared to him an angel of the Lord, standing at the right side of the altar of incense. 12 When Zechariah saw him, he was terrified; and fear overwhelmed him. 13 But the angel said to him, "Do not be afraid, Zechariah, for your prayer has been heard. Your wife Elizabeth will bear you a son, and you will name him John. 14 You will have joy and gladness, and many will rejoice at his birth, 15 for he will be great in the sight of the Lord. He must never drink wine or strong drink; even before his birth he will be filled with the Holy Spirit. 16 He will turn many of the people of Israel to the Lord their God. 17 With the spirit and power of Elijah he will go before him, to turn the hearts of parents to their children, and the disobedient to the wisdom of the righteous, to make ready a people prepared for the Lord." 18 Zechariah said to the angel, "How will I know that this is so? For I am an old man, and my wife is getting on in years." 19 The angel replied, "I am Gabriel. I stand in the presence of God, and I have been sent to speak to you and to bring you this good news. 20 But now, because you did not believe my words, which will be fulfilled in their time, you will become mute, unable to speak, until the day these things occur."

21 Meanwhile the people were waiting for Zechariah, and wondered at his delay in the sanctuary. 22 When he did come out, he could not speak to them, and they realized that he had seen a vision in the sanctuary. He kept motioning to them and remained unable to speak. 23 When his time of service was ended, he went to his home.

24 After those days his wife Elizabeth conceived, and for five months she remained in seclusion. She said, 25 "This is what the Lord has done for me when he looked favorably on me and took away the disgrace I have endured among my people."

26 In the sixth month the angel Gabriel was sent by God to a town in Galilee called Nazareth, 27 to a virgin engaged to a man whose name was Joseph, of the house of David. The virgin's name was Mary. 28 And he came to her and said, "Greetings, favored one! The Lord is with you."[b] 29 But she was much perplexed by his words and pondered what sort of greeting this might be. 30 The angel said to her, "Do not be afraid, Mary, for you have found favor with God. 31 And now, you will conceive in your womb and bear a son, and you will name him Jesus. 32 He will be great, and will be called the Son of the Most High, and the Lord God will give to him the throne of his ancestor David. 33 He will reign over the house of Jacob forever, and of his kingdom there will be no end." 34 Mary said to the angel, "How can this be, since I am a virgin?"[c] 35 The angel said to her, "The Holy Spirit will come upon you, and the power of the Most High will overshadow you; therefore the child to be born[d] will be holy; he will be called Son of God. 36 And now, your relative Elizabeth in her old age has also conceived a son; and this is the sixth month for her who was said to be barren. 37 For nothing will be impossible with God." 38 Then Mary said, "Here am I, the servant of the Lord; let it be with me according to your word." Then the angel departed from her.

39 In those days Mary set out and went with haste to a Judean town in the hill country, 40 where she entered the house of Zechariah and greeted Elizabeth. 41 When Elizabeth heard Mary's greeting, the child leaped in her womb. And Elizabeth was filled with the Holy Spirit 42 and exclaimed with a loud cry, "Blessed are you among women, and blessed is the fruit of your womb. 43 And why has this happened to me, that

---

[b]Other ancient authorities add *Blessed are you among women*   [c]Gk *I do not know a man*   [d]Other ancient authorities add *of you*

the mother of my Lord comes to me? 44 For as soon as I heard the sound of your greeting, the child in my womb leaped for joy. 45 And blessed is she who believed that there would be[e] a fulfillment of what was spoken to her by the Lord."

46 And Mary[f] said,

> "My soul magnifies the Lord,
> 47 and my spirit rejoices in God my Savior,
> 48 for he has looked with favor on the lowliness of his servant.
> Surely, from now on all generations will call me blessed;
> 49 for the Mighty One has done great things for me, and holy is his name.
> 50 His mercy is for those who fear him from generation to generation.
> 51 He has shown strength with his arm;
> he has scattered the proud in the thoughts of their hearts.
> 52 He has brought down the powerful from their thrones,
> and lifted up the lowly;
> 53 he has filled the hungry with good things,
> and sent the rich away empty.
> 54 He has helped his servant Israel, in remembrance of his mercy,
> 55 according to the promise he made to our ancestors,
> to Abraham and to his descendants forever."

56 And Mary remained with her about three months and then returned to her home.

57 Now the time came for Elizabeth to give birth, and she bore a son. 58 Her neighbors and relatives heard that the Lord had shown his great mercy to her, and they rejoiced with her.

59 On the eighth day they came to circumcise the child, and they were going to name him Zechariah after his father. 60 But his mother said, "No; he is to be called John." 61 They said to her, "None of your relatives has this name." 62 Then they began motioning to his father to find out what name he wanted to give him. 63 He asked for a writing tablet and wrote, "His name is John." And all of them were amazed. 64 Immediately his mouth was opened and his tongue freed, and he began to speak, praising God. 65 Fear came over all their neighbors, and all these things were talked about throughout the entire hill country of Judea. 66 All who heard them pondered them and said, "What then will this child become?" For, indeed, the hand of the Lord was with him.

67 Then his father Zechariah was filled with the Holy Spirit and spoke this prophecy:

> 68 "Blessed be the Lord God of Israel,
> for he has looked favorably on his people and redeemed them.
> 69 He has raised up a mighty savior[g] for us
> in the house of his servant David,
> 70 as he spoke through the mouth of his holy prophets from of old,
> 71 that we would be saved from our enemies and from the hand of all who hate us.
> 72 Thus he has shown the mercy promised to our ancestors,
> and has remembered his holy covenant,
> 73 the oath that he swore to our ancestor Abraham,
> to grant us 74 that we, being rescued from the hands of our enemies,
> might serve him without fear, 75 in holiness and righteousness before him all our days.
> 76 And you, child, will be called the prophet of the Most High;
> for you will go before the Lord to prepare his ways,
> 77 to give knowledge of salvation to his people
> by the forgiveness of their sins.

[e]Or believed, for there will be [f]Other ancient authorities read Elizabeth [g]Gk a horn of salvation

78   By the tender mercy of our God,
         the dawn from on high will
            break upon[h] us,
79   to give light to those who sit in
            darkness and in the shadow
               of death,
         to guide our feet into the way
            of peace."

80 The child grew and became strong in spirit, and he was in the wilderness until the day he appeared publicly to Israel.

2 In those days a decree went out from Emperor Augustus that all the world should be registered. 2 This was the first registration and was taken while Quirinius was governor of Syria. 3 All went to their own towns to be registered. 4 Joseph also went from the town of Nazareth in Galilee to Judea, to the city of David called Bethlehem, because he was descended from the house and family of David. 5 He went to be registered with Mary, to whom he was engaged and who was expecting a child. 6 While they were there, the time came for her to deliver her child. 7 And she gave birth to her firstborn son and wrapped him in bands of cloth, and laid him in a manger, because there was no place for them in the inn.

8 In that region there were shepherds living in the fields, keeping watch over their flock by night. 9 Then an angel of the Lord stood before them, and the glory of the Lord shone around them, and they were terrified. 10 But the angel said to them, "Do not be afraid; for see—I am bringing you good news of great joy for all the people: 11 to you is born this day in the city of David a Savior, who is the Messiah,[i] the Lord. 12 This will be a sign for you: you will find a child wrapped in bands of cloth and lying in a manger." 13 And suddenly there was with the angel a multitude of the heavenly host,[j] praising God and saying,
14   "Glory to God in the highest
            heaven,
         and on earth peace among those
            whom he favors!"[k]

15 When the angels had left them and gone into heaven, the shepherds said to one another, "Let us go now to Bethlehem and see this thing that has taken place, which the Lord has made known to us." 16 So they went with haste and found Mary and Joseph, and the child lying in the manger. 17 When they saw this, they made known what had been told them about this child; 18 and all who heard it were amazed at what the shepherds told them. 19 But Mary treasured all these words and pondered them in her heart. 20 The shepherds returned, glorifying and praising God for all they had heard and seen, as it had been told them.

21 After eight days had passed, it was time to circumcise the child; and he was called Jesus, the name given by the angel before he was conceived in the womb.

22 When the time came for their purification according to the law of Moses, they brought him up to Jerusalem to present him to the Lord 23 (as it is written in the law of the Lord, "Every firstborn male shall be designated as holy to the Lord"[1]), 24 and they offered a sacrifice according to what is stated in the law of the Lord, "a pair of turtledoves or two young pigeons."[2]

25 Now there was a man in Jerusalem whose name was Simeon;[l] this man was righteous and devout, looking forward to the consolation of Israel, and the Holy Spirit rested on him. 26 It had been revealed to him by the Holy Spirit that he would not see death before he had seen the Lord's Messiah.[m] 27 Guided by the Spirit, Simeon[n] came into the temple; and when the parents brought in the child Jesus, to do for him what was customary under the law, 28 Simeon[o] took him in his arms and praised God, saying,

29   "Master, now you are dismissing
            your servant[p] in peace,
         according to your word;
30   for my eyes have seen your
            salvation,
31   which you have prepared in the
            presence of all peoples,
32   a light for revelation to the
            Gentiles
         and for glory to your people
            Israel."

33 And the child's father and mother were

---

[h]Other ancient authorities read *has broken upon*   [i]Or *the Christ*
[j]Gk *army*   [k]Other ancient authorities read *peace, goodwill among people*   [l]Gk *Symeon*   [m]Or *the Lord's Christ*   [n]Gk *In the Spirit, he*
[o]Gk *he*   [p]Gk *slave*

[1]Exod 13:2   [2]Lev 12:8

amazed at what was being said about him. 34 Then Simeon[q] blessed them and said to his mother Mary, "This child is destined for the falling and the rising of many in Israel, and to be a sign that will be opposed 35 so that the inner thoughts of many will be revealed—and a sword will pierce your own soul too."

36 There was also a prophet, Anna[r] the daughter of Phanuel, of the tribe of Asher. She was of a great age, having lived with her husband seven years after her marriage, 37 then as a widow to the age of eighty-four. She never left the temple but worshiped there with fasting and prayer night and day. 38 At that moment she came, and began to praise God and to speak about the child[s] to all who were looking for the redemption of Jerusalem.

39 When they had finished everything required by the law of the Lord, they returned to Galilee, to their own town of Nazareth. 40 The child grew and became strong, filled with wisdom; and the favor of God was upon him.

41 Now every year his parents went to Jerusalem for the festival of the Passover. 42 And when he was twelve years old, they went up as usual for the festival. 43 When the festival was ended and they started to return, the boy Jesus stayed behind in Jerusalem, but his parents did not know it. 44 Assuming that he was in the group of travelers, they went a day's journey. Then they started to look for him among their relatives and friends. 45 When they did not find him, they returned to Jerusalem to search for him. 46 After three days they found him in the temple, sitting among the teachers, listening to them and asking them questions. 47 And all who heard him were amazed at his understanding and his answers. 48 When his parents[t] saw him they were astonished; and his mother said to him, "Child, why have you treated us like this? Look, your father and I have been searching for you in great anxiety." 49 He said to them, "Why were you searching for me? Did you not know that I must be in my Father's house?"[u] 50 But they did not understand what he said to them. 51 Then he went down with them and came to Nazareth, and was obedient to them. His mother treasured all these things in her heart.

52 And Jesus increased in wisdom and in years,[v] and in divine and human favor.

3 In the fifteenth year of the reign of Emperor Tiberius, when Pontius Pilate was governor of Judea, and Herod was ruler[w] of Galilee, and his brother Philip ruler[w] of the region of Ituraea and Trachonitis, and Lysanias ruler[w] of Abilene, 2 during the high priesthood of Annas and Caiaphas, the word of God came to John son of Zechariah in the wilderness. 3 He went into all the region around the Jordan, proclaiming a baptism of repentance for the forgiveness of sins, 4 as it is written in the book of the words of the prophet Isaiah,

"The voice of one crying out in
      the wilderness:
'Prepare the way of the Lord,
      make his paths straight.
5   Every valley shall be filled,
      and every mountain and hill
            shall be made low,
and the crooked shall be made
            straight,
      and the rough ways made
            smooth;
6   and all flesh shall see the salvation
            of God.'"[3]

7 John said to the crowds that came out to be baptized by him, "You brood of vipers! Who warned you to flee from the wrath to come? 8 Bear fruits worthy of repentance. Do not begin to say to yourselves, 'We have Abraham as our ancestor'; for I tell you, God is able from these stones to raise up children to Abraham. 9 Even now the ax is lying at the root of the trees; every tree therefore that does not bear good fruit is cut down and thrown into the fire."

10 And the crowds asked him, "What then should we do?" 11 In reply he said to them, "Whoever has two coats must share with anyone who has none; and whoever has food must do likewise." 12 Even tax collectors came to be baptized, and they asked him, "Teacher, what should we do?" 13 He said to them, "Collect no more than the amount prescribed for you." 14 Soldiers also asked him, "And we, what should we do?" He said to them, "Do not extort money from anyone by

[q]Gk Symeon [r]Gk Hanna [s]Gk him [t]Gk they [u]Or be about my Father's interests? [v]Or in stature [w]Gk tetrarch

[3]Isa 40:3–5

threats or false accusation, and be satisfied with your wages."

15 As the people were filled with expectation, and all were questioning in their hearts concerning John, whether he might be the Messiah,[x]16 John answered all of them by saying, "I baptize you with water; but one who is more powerful than I is coming; I am not worthy to untie the thong of his sandals. He will baptize you with[y] the Holy Spirit and fire. 17 His winnowing fork is in his hand, to clear his threshing floor and to gather the wheat into his granary; but the chaff he will burn with unquenchable fire."

18 So, with many other exhortations, he proclaimed the good news to the people. 19 But Herod the ruler,[z] who had been rebuked by him because of Herodias, his brother's wife, and because of all the evil things that Herod had done, 20 added to them all by shutting up John in prison.

21 Now when all the people were baptized, and when Jesus also had been baptized and was praying, the heaven was opened, 22 and the Holy Spirit descended upon him in bodily form like a dove. And a voice came from heaven, "You are my Son, the Beloved;[a] with you I am well pleased."[b]

23 Jesus was about thirty years old when he began his work. He was the son (as was thought) of Joseph son of Heli, 24 son of Matthat, son of Levi, son of Melchi, son of Jannai, son of Joseph, 25 son of Mattathias, son of Amos, son of Nahum, son of Esli, son of Naggai, 26 son of Maath, son of Mattathias, son of Semein, son of Josech, son of Joda, 27 son of Joanan, son of Rhesa, son of Zerubbabel, son of Shealtiel,[c] son of Neri, 28 son of Melchi, son of Addi, son of Cosam, son of Elmadam, son of Er, 29 son of Joshua, son of Eliezer, son of Jorim, son of Matthat, son of Levi, 30 son of Simeon, son of Judah, son of Joseph, son of Jonam, son of Eliakim, 31 son of Melea, son of Menna, son of Mattatha, son of Nathan, son of David, 32 son of Jesse, son of Obed, son of Boaz, son of Sala,[d] son of Nahshon, 33 son of Amminadab, son of Admin, son of Arni,[e] son of Hezron, son of Perez, son of Judah, 34 son of Jacob, son of Isaac, son of Abraham, son of Terah, son of Nahor, 35 son of Serug, son of Reu, son of Peleg, son of Eber, son of Shelah, 36 son of Cainan, son of Arphaxad, son of Shem, son of Noah, son of Lamech, 37 son of Methuselah, son of Enoch, son of Jared, son of Mahalaleel, son of Cainan, 38 son of Enos, son of Seth, son of Adam, son of God.

4 Jesus, full of the Holy Spirit, returned from the Jordan and was led by the Spirit in the wilderness, 2 where for forty days he was tempted by the devil. He ate nothing at all during those days, and when they were over, he was famished. 3 The devil said to him, "If you are the Son of God, command this stone to become a loaf of bread." 4 Jesus answered him, "It is written, 'One does not live by bread alone.'"[4]

5 Then the devil[f] led him up and showed him in an instant all the kingdoms of the world. 6 And the devil[f] said to him, "To you I will give their glory and all this authority; for it has been given over to me, and I give it to anyone I please. 7 If you, then, will worship me, it will all be yours." 8 Jesus answered him, "It is written,

'Worship the Lord your God,
    and serve only him.'"[5]

9 Then the devil[f] took him to Jerusalem, and placed him on the pinnacle of the temple, saying to him, "If you are the Son of God, throw yourself down from here, 10 for it is written,

'He will command his angels
    concerning you,
    to protect you,'

11 and

'On their hands they will bear you
    up,
    so that you will not dash your
    foot against a stone.'"[6]

12 Jesus answered him, "It is said, 'Do not put the Lord your God to the test.'"[7] 13 When the devil had finished every test, he departed from him until an opportune time.

14 Then Jesus, filled with the power of the Spirit, returned to Galilee, and a report about him spread through all the surrounding country. 15 He

[x]Or *the Christ* [y]Or *in* [z]Gk *tetrarch* [a]Or *my beloved Son* [b]Other ancient authorities read *You are my Son, today I have begotten you* [c]Gk *Salathiel* [d]Other ancient authorities read *Salmon* [e]Other ancient authorities read *Amminadab, son of Aram*; others vary widely [f]Gk *he*

[4]Deut 8:3   [5]Deut 6:13   [6]Ps 91:11–12   [7]Deut 6:16

began to teach in their synagogues and was praised by everyone.

16 When he came to Nazareth, where he had been brought up, he went to the synagogue on the sabbath day, as was his custom. He stood up to read, 17 and the scroll of the prophet Isaiah was given to him. He unrolled the scroll and found the place where it was written:

18   "The Spirit of the Lord is upon
                me,
             because he has anointed me
                to bring good news to the
                   poor.
             He has sent me to proclaim release
                to the captives
             and recovery of sight to the
                blind,
                to let the oppressed go
                   free,
19   to proclaim the year of the Lord's
                favor."[8]

20 And he rolled up the scroll, gave it back to the attendant, and sat down. The eyes of all in the synagogue were fixed on him. 21 Then he began to say to them, "Today this scripture has been fulfilled in your hearing." 22 All spoke well of him and were amazed at the gracious words that came from his mouth. They said, "Is not this Joseph's son?" 23 He said to them, "Doubtless you will quote to me this proverb, 'Doctor, cure yourself!' And you will say, 'Do here also in your hometown the things that we have heard you did at Capernaum.'" 24 And he said, "Truly I tell you, no prophet is accepted in the prophet's hometown. 25 But the truth is, there were many widows in Israel in the time of Elijah, when the heaven was shut up three years and six months, and there was a severe famine over all the land; 26 yet Elijah was sent to none of them except to a widow at Zarephath in Sidon. 27 There were also many lepers[g] in Israel in the time of the prophet Elisha, and none of them was cleansed except Naaman the Syrian." 28 When they heard this, all in the synagogue were filled with rage. 29 They got up, drove him out of the town, and led him to the brow of the hill on which their town was built, so that they might hurl him off the cliff. 30 But he passed through the midst of them and went on his way.

31 He went down to Capernaum, a city in Galilee, and was teaching them on the sabbath. 32 They were astounded at his teaching, because he spoke with authority. 33 In the synagogue there was a man who had the spirit of an unclean demon, and he cried out with a loud voice, 34 "Let us alone! What have you to do with us, Jesus of Nazareth? Have you come to destroy us? I know who you are, the Holy One of God." 35 But Jesus rebuked him, saying, "Be silent, and come out of him!" When the demon had thrown him down before them, he came out of him without having done him any harm. 36 They were all amazed and kept saying to one another, "What kind of utterance is this? For with authority and power he commands the unclean spirits, and out they come!" 37 And a report about him began to reach every place in the region.

38 After leaving the synagogue he entered Simon's house. Now Simon's mother-in-law was suffering from a high fever, and they asked him about her. 39 Then he stood over her and rebuked the fever, and it left her. Immediately she got up and began to serve them.

40 As the sun was setting, all those who had any who were sick with various kinds of diseases brought them to him; and he laid his hands on each of them and cured them. 41 Demons also came out of many, shouting, "You are the Son of God!" But he rebuked them and would not allow them to speak, because they knew that he was the Messiah.[h]

42 At daybreak he departed and went into a deserted place. And the crowds were looking for him; and when they reached him, they wanted to prevent him from leaving them. 43 But he said to them, "I must proclaim the good news of the kingdom of God to the other cities also; for I was sent for this purpose." 44 So he continued proclaiming the message in the synagogues of Judea.[i]

5 Once while Jesus[j] was standing beside the lake of Gennesaret, and the crowd was pressing in on him to hear the word of God, 2 he saw two boats there at the shore of the lake; the fishermen had gone out of them and were washing their nets. 3 He got into one of the boats, the one

---

gThe terms *leper* and *leprosy* can refer to several diseases   hOr *the Christ*   iOther ancient authorities read *Galilee*   jGk *he*

8Isa 61:1–2; 58:6

belonging to Simon, and asked him to put out a little way from the shore. Then he sat down and taught the crowds from the boat. 4 When he had finished speaking, he said to Simon, "Put out into the deep water and let down your nets for a catch." 5 Simon answered, "Master, we have worked all night long but have caught nothing. Yet if you say so, I will let down the nets." 6 When they had done this, they caught so many fish that their nets were beginning to break. 7 So they signaled their partners in the other boat to come and help them. And they came and filled both boats, so that they began to sink. 8 But when Simon Peter saw it, he fell down at Jesus' knees, saying, "Go away from me, Lord, for I am a sinful man!" 9 For he and all who were with him were amazed at the catch of fish that they had taken; 10 and so also were James and John, sons of Zebedee, who were partners with Simon. Then Jesus said to Simon, "Do not be afraid; from now on you will be catching people." 11 When they had brought their boats to shore, they left everything and followed him.

12 Once, when he was in one of the cities, there was a man covered with leprosy.[k] When he saw Jesus, he bowed with his face to the ground and begged him, "Lord, if you choose, you can make me clean." 13 Then Jesus[l] stretched out his hand, touched him, and said, "I do choose. Be made clean." Immediately the leprosy[k] left him. 14 And he ordered him to tell no one. "Go," he said, "and show yourself to the priest, and, as Moses commanded, make an offering for your cleansing, for a testimony to them." 15 But now more than ever the word about Jesus[m] spread abroad; many crowds would gather to hear him and to be cured of their diseases. 16 But he would withdraw to deserted places and pray.

17 One day, while he was teaching, Pharisees and teachers of the law were sitting near by (they had come from every village of Galilee and Judea and from Jerusalem); and the power of the Lord was with him to heal.[n] 18 Just then some men came, carrying a paralyzed man on a bed. They were trying to bring him in and lay him before Jesus;[m] 19 but finding no way to bring him in because of the crowd, they went up on the roof and let him down with his bed through the tiles into the middle of the crowd[o] in front of Jesus. 20 When he saw their faith, he said, "Friend,[p] your sins are forgiven you." 21 Then the scribes and the Pharisees began to question, "Who is this who is speaking blasphemies? Who can forgive sins but God alone?" 22 When Jesus perceived their questionings, he answered them, "Why do you raise such questions in your hearts? 23 Which is easier, to say, 'Your sins are forgiven you,' or to say, 'Stand up and walk'? 24 But so that you may know that the Son of Man has authority on earth to forgive sins"—he said to the one who was paralyzed—"I say to you, stand up and take your bed and go to your home." 25 Immediately he stood up before them, took what he had been lying on, and went to his home, glorifying God. 26 Amazement seized all of them, and they glorified God and were filled with awe, saying, "We have seen strange things today."

27 After this he went out and saw a tax collector named Levi, sitting at the tax booth; and he said to him, "Follow me." 28 And he got up, left everything, and followed him.

29 Then Levi gave a great banquet for him in his house; and there was a large crowd of tax collectors and others sitting at the table[q] with them. 30 The Pharisees and their scribes were complaining to his disciples, saying, "Why do you eat and drink with tax collectors and sinners?" 31 Jesus answered, "Those who are well have no need of a physician, but those who are sick; 32 I have come to call not the righteous but sinners to repentance."

33 Then they said to him, "John's disciples, like the disciples of the Pharisees, frequently fast and pray, but your disciples eat and drink." 34 Jesus said to them, "You cannot make wedding guests fast while the bridegroom is with them, can you? 35 The days will come when the bridegroom will be taken away from them, and then they will fast in those days." 36 He also told them a parable: "No one tears a piece from a new garment and sews it on an old garment; otherwise the new will be torn, and the piece from the new will not match the old. 37 And no one puts new wine into old wineskins; otherwise the new wine will burst the skins and will be spilled, and the skins will be destroyed. 38 But new wine must be put into fresh wineskins. 39 And no one after drink-

[k]The terms *leper* and *leprosy* can refer to several diseases   [l]Gk *he*   [m]Gk *him*   [n]Other ancient authorities read *was present to heal them*   [o]Gk *into the midst*   [p]Gk *Man*   [q]Gk *reclining*

ing old wine desires new wine, but says, 'The old is good.'"[r]

6 One sabbath[s] while Jesus[t] was going through the grainfields, his disciples plucked some heads of grain, rubbed them in their hands, and ate them. 2 But some of the Pharisees said, "Why are you doing what is not lawful[u] on the sabbath?" 3 Jesus answered, "Have you not read what David did when he and his companions were hungry? 4 He entered the house of God and took and ate the bread of the Presence, which it is not lawful for any but the priests to eat, and gave some to his companions?" 5 Then he said to them, "The Son of Man is lord of the sabbath."

6 On another sabbath he entered the synagogue and taught, and there was a man there whose right hand was withered. 7 The scribes and the Pharisees watched him to see whether he would cure on the sabbath, so that they might find an accusation against him. 8 Even though he knew what they were thinking, he said to the man who had the withered hand, "Come and stand here." He got up and stood there. 9 Then Jesus said to them, "I ask you, is it lawful to do good or to do harm on the sabbath, to save life or to destroy it?" 10 After looking around at all of them, he said to him, "Stretch out your hand." He did so, and his hand was restored. 11 But they were filled with fury and discussed with one another what they might do to Jesus.

12 Now during those days he went out to the mountain to pray; and he spent the night in prayer to God. 13 And when day came, he called his disciples and chose twelve of them, whom he also named apostles: 14 Simon, whom he named Peter, and his brother Andrew, and James, and John, and Philip, and Bartholomew, 15 and Matthew, and Thomas, and James son of Alphaeus, and Simon, who was called the Zealot, 16 and Judas son of James, and Judas Iscariot, who became a traitor.

17 He came down with them and stood on a level place, with a great crowd of his disciples and a great multitude of people from all Judea, Jerusalem, and the coast of Tyre and Sidon. 18 They had come to hear him and to be healed of their diseases; and those who were troubled with unclean spirits were cured. 19 And all in the crowd were trying to touch him, for power came out from him and healed all of them.

20 Then he looked up at his disciples and said:
"Blessed are you who are poor,
   for yours is the kingdom of
      God.
21   "Blessed are you who are hungry
         now,
      for you will be filled.
   "Blessed are you who weep now,
      for you will laugh.

22 "Blessed are you when people hate you, and when they exclude you, revile you, and defame you[v] on account of the Son of Man. 23 Rejoice in that day and leap for joy, for surely your reward is great in heaven; for that is what their ancestors did to the prophets.

24   "But woe to you who are rich,
         for you have received your
            consolation.
25   "Woe to you who are full now,
         for you will be hungry.
      "Woe to you who are laughing
         now,
         for you will mourn and weep.

26 "Woe to you when all speak well of you, for that is what their ancestors did to the false prophets.

27 "But I say to you that listen, Love your enemies, do good to those who hate you, 28 bless those who curse you, pray for those who abuse you. 29 If anyone strikes you on the cheek, offer the other also; and from anyone who takes away your coat do not withhold even your shirt. 30 Give to everyone who begs from you; and if anyone takes away your goods, do not ask for them again. 31 Do to others as you would have them do to you.

32 "If you love those who love you, what credit is that to you? For even sinners love those who love them. 33 If you do good to those who do good to you, what credit is that to you? For even sinners do the same. 34 If you lend to those from whom you hope to receive, what credit is that to you? Even sinners lend to sinners, to receive as much again. 35 But love your enemies, do good, and lend, expecting nothing in return.[w] Your re-

[r]Other ancient authorities read *better*; others lack verse 39   [s]Other ancient authorities read *On the second first sabbath*   [t]Gk *he*   [u]Other ancient authorities add *to do*   [v]Gk *cast out your name as evil*   [w]Other ancient authorities read *despairing of no one*

ward will be great, and you will be children of the Most High; for he is kind to the ungrateful and the wicked. 36 Be merciful, just as your Father is merciful.

37 "Do not judge, and you will not be judged; do not condemn, and you will not be condemned. Forgive, and you will be forgiven; 38 give, and it will be given to you. A good measure, pressed down, shaken together, running over, will be put into your lap; for the measure you give will be the measure you get back."

39 He also told them a parable: "Can a blind person guide a blind person? Will not both fall into a pit? 40 A disciple is not above the teacher, but everyone who is fully qualified will be like the teacher. 41 Why do you see the speck in your neighbor's[x] eye, but do not notice the log in your own eye? 42 Or how can you say to your neighbor,[y] 'Friend,[y] let me take out the speck in your eye,' when you yourself do not see the log in your own eye? You hypocrite, first take the log out of your own eye, and then you will see clearly to take the speck out of your neighbor's[x] eye.

43 "No good tree bears bad fruit, nor again does a bad tree bear good fruit; 44 for each tree is known by its own fruit. Figs are not gathered from thorns, nor are grapes picked from a bramble bush. 45 The good person out of the good treasure of the heart produces good, and the evil person out of evil treasure produces evil; for it is out of the abundance of the heart that the mouth speaks.

46 "Why do you call me 'Lord, Lord,' and do not do what I tell you? 47 I will show you what someone is like who comes to me, hears my words, and acts on them. 48 That one is like a man building a house, who dug deeply and laid the foundation on rock; when a flood arose, the river burst against that house but could not shake it, because it had been well built.[z] 49 But the one who hears and does not act is like a man who built a house on the ground without a foundation. When the river burst against it, immediately it fell, and great was the ruin of that house."

7 After Jesus[a] had finished all his sayings in the hearing of the people, he entered Capernaum. 2 A centurion there had a slave whom he valued highly, and who was ill and close to death. 3 When he heard about Jesus, he sent some Jewish elders to him, asking him to come and heal his slave. 4 When they came to Jesus, they appealed to him earnestly, saying, "He is worthy of having you do this for him, 5 for he loves our people, and it is he who built our synagogue for us." 6 And Jesus went with them, but when he was not far from the house, the centurion sent friends to say to him, "Lord, do not trouble yourself, for I am not worthy to have you come under my roof; 7 therefore I did not presume to come to you. But only speak the word, and let my servant be healed. 8 For I also am a man set under authority, with soldiers under me; and I say to one, 'Go,' and he goes, and to another, 'Come,' and he comes, and to my slave, 'Do this,' and the slave does it." 9 When Jesus heard this he was amazed at him, and turning to the crowd that followed him, he said, "I tell you, not even in Israel have I found such faith." 10 When those who had been sent returned to the house, they found the slave in good health.

11 Soon afterwards[b] he went to a town called Nain, and his disciples and a large crowd went with him. 12 As he approached the gate of the town, a man who had died was being carried out. He was his mother's only son, and she was a widow; and with her was a large crowd from the town. 13 When the Lord saw her, he had compassion for her and said to her, "Do not weep." 14 Then he came forward and touched the bier, and the bearers stood still. And he said, "Young man, I say to you, rise!" 15 The dead man sat up and began to speak, and Jesus[a] gave him to his mother. 16 Fear seized all of them; and they glorified God, saying, "A great prophet has risen among us!" and "God has looked favorably on his people!" 17 This word about him spread throughout Judea and all the surrounding country.

18 The disciples of John reported all these things to him. So John summoned two of his disciples 19 and sent them to the Lord to ask, "Are you the one who is to come, or are we to wait for another?" 20 When the men had come to him, they said, "John the Baptist has sent us to you to ask, 'Are you the one who is to come, or are we to wait for another?'" 21 Jesus[c] had just then cured many people of diseases, plagues, and evil spirits,

[x]Gk brother's [y]Gk brother [z]Other ancient authorities read founded upon the rock [a]Gk he [b]Other ancient authorities read Next day [c]Gk He

and had given sight to many who were blind. 22 And he answered them, "Go and tell John what you have seen and heard: the blind receive their sight, the lame walk, the lepers[d] are cleansed, the deaf hear, the dead are raised, the poor have good news brought to them. 23 And blessed is anyone who takes no offense at me."

24 When John's messengers had gone, Jesus[e] began to speak to the crowds about John:[f] "What did you go out into the wilderness to look at? A reed shaken by the wind? 25 What then did you go out to see? Someone[g] dressed in soft robes? Look, those who put on fine clothing and live in luxury are in royal palaces. 26 What then did you go out to see? A prophet? Yes, I tell you, and more than a prophet. 27 This is the one about whom it is written,

> 'See, I am sending my messenger
> ahead of you,
> who will prepare your way
> before you.'[9]

28 I tell you, among those born of women no one is greater than John; yet the least in the kingdom of God is greater than he." 29 (And all the people who heard this, including the tax collectors, acknowledged the justice of God,[h] because they had been baptized with John's baptism. 30 But by refusing to be baptized by him, the Pharisees and the lawyers rejected God's purpose for themselves.)

31 "To what then will I compare the people of this generation, and what are they like? 32 They are like children sitting in the marketplace and calling to one another,

> 'We played the flute for you, and
> you did not dance;
> we wailed, and you did not
> weep.'

33 For John the Baptist has come eating no bread and drinking no wine, and you say, 'He has a demon'; 34 the Son of Man has come eating and drinking, and you say, 'Look, a glutton and a drunkard, a friend of tax collectors and sinners!' 35 Nevertheless, wisdom is vindicated by all her children."

36 One of the Pharisees asked Jesus[i] to eat with him, and he went into the Pharisee's house and took his place at the table. 37 And a woman in the city, who was a sinner, having learned that he was eating in the Pharisee's house, brought an al-

abaster jar of ointment. 38 She stood behind him at his feet, weeping, and began to bathe his feet with her tears and to dry them with her hair. Then she continued kissing his feet and anointing them with the ointment. 39 Now when the Pharisee who had invited him saw it, he said to himself, "If this man were a prophet, he would have known who and what kind of woman this is who is touching him—that she is a sinner." 40 Jesus spoke up and said to him, "Simon, I have something to say to you." "Teacher," he replied, "speak." 41 "A certain creditor had two debtors; one owed five hundred denarii,[j] and the other fifty. 42 When they could not pay, he canceled the debts for both of them. Now which of them will love him more?" 43 Simon answered, "I suppose the one for whom he canceled the greater debt." And Jesus[e] said to him, "You have judged rightly." 44 Then turning toward the woman, he said to Simon, "Do you see this woman? I entered your house; you gave me no water for my feet, but she has bathed my feet with her tears and dried them with her hair. 45 You gave me no kiss, but from the time I came in she has not stopped kissing my feet. 46 You did not anoint my head with oil, but she has anointed my feet with ointment. 47 Therefore, I tell you, her sins, which were many, have been forgiven; hence she has shown great love. But the one to whom little is forgiven, loves little." 48 Then he said to her, "Your sins are forgiven." 49 But those who were at the table with him began to say among themselves, "Who is this who even forgives sins?" 50 And he said to the woman, "Your faith has saved you; go in peace."

8 Soon afterwards he went on through cities and villages, proclaiming and bringing the good news of the kingdom of God. The twelve were with him, 2 as well as some women who had been cured of evil spirits and infirmities: Mary, called Magdalene, from whom seven demons had gone out, 3 and Joanna, the wife of Herod's steward Chuza, and Susanna, and many others, who provided for them[k] out of their resources.

---

[d]The terms *leper* and *leprosy* can refer to several diseases [e]Gk *he*
[f]Gk *him* [g]Or *Why then did you go out? To see someone*
[h]Or *praised God* [i]Gk *him* [j]The denarius was the usual day's wage for a laborer [k]Other ancient authorities read *him*

---

[9]Mal 3:1

4 When a great crowd gathered and people from town after town came to him, he said in a parable: 5 "A sower went out to sow his seed; and as he sowed, some fell on the path and was trampled on, and the birds of the air ate it up. 6 Some fell on the rock; and as it grew up, it withered for lack of moisture. 7 Some fell among thorns, and the thorns grew with it and choked it. 8 Some fell into good soil, and when it grew, it produced a hundredfold." As he said this, he called out, "Let anyone with ears to hear listen!"

9 Then his disciples asked him what this parable meant. 10 He said, "To you it has been given to know the secrets[1] of the kingdom of God; but to others I speak[m] in parables, so that

'looking they may not perceive,
   and listening they may not
        understand.'[10]

11 "Now the parable is this: The seed is the word of God. 12 The ones on the path are those who have heard; then the devil comes and takes away the word from their hearts, so that they may not believe and be saved. 13 The ones on the rock are those who, when they hear the word, receive it with joy. But these have no root; they believe only for a while and in a time of testing fall away. 14 As for what fell among the thorns, these are the ones who hear; but as they go on their way, they are choked by the cares and riches and pleasures of life, and their fruit does not mature. 15 But as for that in the good soil, these are the ones who, when they hear the word, hold it fast in an honest and good heart, and bear fruit with patient endurance.

16 "No one after lighting a lamp hides it under a jar, or puts it under a bed, but puts it on a lampstand, so that those who enter may see the light. 17 For nothing is hidden that will not be disclosed, nor is anything secret that will not become known and come to light. 18 Then pay attention to how you listen; for to those who have, more will be given; and from those who do not have, even what they seem to have will be taken away."

19 Then his mother and his brothers came to him, but they could not reach him because of the crowd. 20 And he was told, "Your mother and your brothers are standing outside, wanting to see you." 21 But he said to them, "My mother and my brothers are those who hear the word of God and do it."

22 One day he got into a boat with his disciples, and he said to them, "Let us go across to the other side of the lake." So they put out, 23 and while they were sailing he fell asleep. A windstorm swept down on the lake, and the boat was filling with water, and they were in danger. 24 They went to him and woke him up, shouting, "Master, Master, we are perishing!" And he woke up and rebuked the wind and the raging waves; they ceased, and there was a calm. 25 He said to them, "Where is your faith?" They were afraid and amazed, and said to one another, "Who then is this, that he commands even the winds and the water, and they obey him?"

26 Then they arrived at the country of the Gerasenes,[n] which is opposite Galilee. 27 As he stepped out on land, a man of the city who had demons met him. For a long time he had worn[o] no clothes, and he did not live in a house but in the tombs. 28 When he saw Jesus, he fell down before him and shouted at the top of his voice, "What have you to do with me, Jesus, Son of the Most High God? I beg you, do not torment me"— 29 for Jesus[p] had commanded the unclean spirit to come out of the man. (For many times it had seized him; he was kept under guard and bound with chains and shackles, but he would break the bonds and be driven by the demon into the wilds.) 30 Jesus then asked him, "What is your name?" He said, "Legion"; for many demons had entered him. 31 They begged him not to order them to go back into the abyss.

32 Now there on the hillside a large herd of swine was feeding; and the demons[q] begged Jesus[r] to let them enter these. So he gave them permission. 33 Then the demons came out of the man and entered the swine, and the herd rushed down the steep bank into the lake and was drowned.

34 When the swineherds saw what had happened, they ran off and told it in the city and in the country. 35 Then people came out to see what had happened, and when they came to Jesus, they found the man from whom the demons had gone

---

[1]Or *mysteries*   [m]Gk lacks *I speak*   [n]Other ancient authorities read *Gadarenes*; others, *Gergesenes*   [o]Other ancient authorities read *a man of the city who had had demons for a long time met him. He wore*   [p]Gk *he*   [q]Gk *they*   [r]Gk *him*

[10]Isa 6:9

sitting at the feet of Jesus, clothed and in his right mind. And they were afraid. 36 Those who had seen it told them how the one who had been possessed by demons had been healed. 37 Then all the people of the surrounding country of the Gerasenes[s] asked Jesus[t] to leave them; for they were seized with great fear. So he got into the boat and returned. 38 The man from whom the demons had gone begged that he might be with him; but Jesus[u] sent him away, saying, 39 "Return to your home, and declare how much God has done for you." So he went away, proclaiming throughout the city how much Jesus had done for him.

40 Now when Jesus returned, the crowd welcomed him, for they were all waiting for him. 41 Just then there came a man named Jairus, a leader of the synagogue. He fell at Jesus' feet and begged him to come to his house, 42 for he had an only daughter, about twelve years old, who was dying.

As he went, the crowds pressed in on him. 43 Now there was a woman who had been suffering from hemorrhages for twelve years; and though she had spent all she had on physicians,[v] no one could cure her. 44 She came up behind him and touched the fringe of his clothes, and immediately her hemorrhage stopped. 45 Then Jesus asked, "Who touched me?" When all denied it, Peter[w] said, "Master, the crowds surround you and press in on you." 46 But Jesus said, "Someone touched me; for I noticed that power had gone out from me." 47 When the woman saw that she could not remain hidden, she came trembling; and falling down before him, she declared in the presence of all the people why she had touched him, and how she had been immediately healed. 48 He said to her, "Daughter, your faith has made you well; go in peace."

49 While he was still speaking, someone came from the leader's house to say, "Your daughter is dead; do not trouble the teacher any longer." 50 When Jesus heard this, he replied, "Do not fear. Only believe, and she will be saved." 51 When he came to the house, he did not allow anyone to enter with him, except Peter, John, and James, and the child's father and mother. 52 They were all weeping and wailing for her; but he said, "Do not weep; for she is not dead but sleeping." 53 And they laughed at him, knowing that she was dead.

54 But he took her by the hand and called out, "Child, get up!" 55 Her spirit returned, and she got up at once. Then he directed them to give her something to eat. 56 Her parents were astounded; but he ordered them to tell no one what had happened.

9 Then Jesus[u] called the twelve together and gave them power and authority over all demons and to cure diseases, 2 and he sent them out to proclaim the kingdom of God and to heal. 3 He said to them, "Take nothing for your journey, no staff, nor bag, nor bread, nor money—not even an extra tunic. 4 Whatever house you enter, stay there, and leave from there. 5 Wherever they do not welcome you, as you are leaving that town shake the dust off your feet as a testimony against them." 6 They departed and went through the villages, bringing the good news and curing diseases everywhere.

7 Now Herod the ruler[x] heard about all that had taken place, and he was perplexed, because it was said by some that John had been raised from the dead, 8 by some that Elijah had appeared, and by others that one of the ancient prophets had arisen. 9 Herod said, "John I beheaded; but who is this about whom I hear such things?" And he tried to see him.

10 On their return the apostles told Jesus[t] all they had done. He took them with him and withdrew privately to a city called Bethsaida. 11 When the crowds found out about it, they followed him; and he welcomed them, and spoke to them about the kingdom of God, and healed those who needed to be cured.

12 The day was drawing to a close, and the twelve came to him and said, "Send the crowd away, so that they may go into the surrounding villages and countryside, to lodge and get provisions; for we are here in a deserted place." 13 But he said to them, "You give them something to eat." They said, "We have no more than five loaves and two fish—unless we are to go and buy food for all these people." 14 For there were about five thousand men. And he said to his disciples, "Make

---

[s]Other ancient authorities read *Gadarenes*; others, *Gergesenes*
[t]Gk *him*   [u]Gk *he*   [v]Other ancient authorities lack *and though she had spent all she had on physicians*   [w]Other ancient authorities add *and those who were with him*   [x]Gk *tetrarch*

them sit down in groups of about fifty each." 15 They did so and made them all sit down. 16 And taking the five loaves and the two fish, he looked up to heaven, and blessed and broke them, and gave them to the disciples to set before the crowd. 17 And all ate and were filled. What was left over was gathered up, twelve baskets of broken pieces.

18 Once when Jesus[y] was praying alone, with only the disciples near him, he asked them, "Who do the crowds say that I am?" 19 They answered, "John the Baptist; but others, Elijah; and still others, that one of the ancient prophets has arisen." 20 He said to them, "But who do you say that I am?" Peter answered, "The Messiah[z] of God."

21 He sternly ordered and commanded them not to tell anyone, 22 saying, "The Son of Man must undergo great suffering, and be rejected by the elders, chief priests, and scribes, and be killed, and on the third day be raised."

23 Then he said to them all, "If any want to become my followers, let them deny themselves and take up their cross daily and follow me. 24 For those who want to save their life will lose it, and those who lose their life for my sake will save it. 25 What does it profit them if they gain the whole world, but lose or forfeit themselves? 26 Those who are ashamed of me and of my words, of them the Son of Man will be ashamed when he comes in his glory and the glory of the Father and of the holy angels. 27 But truly I tell you, there are some standing here who will not taste death before they see the kingdom of God."

28 Now about eight days after these sayings Jesus[y] took with him Peter and John and James, and went up on the mountain to pray. 29 And while he was praying, the appearance of his face changed, and his clothes became dazzling white. 30 Suddenly they saw two men, Moses and Elijah, talking to him. 31 They appeared in glory and were speaking of his departure, which he was about to accomplish at Jerusalem. 32 Now Peter and his companions were weighed down with sleep; but since they had stayed awake,[a] they saw his glory and the two men who stood with him. 33 Just as they were leaving him, Peter said to Jesus, "Master, it is good for us to be here; let us make three dwellings,[b] one for you, one for Moses, and one for Elijah"—not knowing what he said. 34 While

he was saying this, a cloud came and overshadowed them; and they were terrified as they entered the cloud. 35 Then from the cloud came a voice that said, "This is my Son, my Chosen;[c] listen to him!" 36 When the voice had spoken, Jesus was found alone. And they kept silent and in those days told no one any of the things they had seen.

37 On the next day, when they had come down from the mountain, a great crowd met him. 38 Just then a man from the crowd shouted, "Teacher, I beg you to look at my son; he is my only child. 39 Suddenly a spirit seizes him, and all at once he[d] shrieks. It convulses him until he foams at the mouth; it mauls him and will scarcely leave him. 40 I begged your disciples to cast it out, but they could not." 41 Jesus answered, "You faithless and perverse generation, how much longer must I be with you and bear with you? Bring your son here." 42 While he was coming, the demon dashed him to the ground in convulsions. But Jesus rebuked the unclean spirit, healed the boy, and gave him back to his father. 43 And all were astounded at the greatness of God.

While everyone was amazed at all that he was doing, he said to his disciples, 44 "Let these words sink into your ears: The Son of Man is going to be betrayed into human hands." 45 But they did not understand this saying; its meaning was concealed from them, so that they could not perceive it. And they were afraid to ask him about this saying.

46 An argument arose among them as to which one of them was the greatest. 47 But Jesus, aware of their inner thoughts, took a little child and put it by his side, 48 and said to them, "Whoever welcomes this child in my name welcomes me, and whoever welcomes me welcomes the one who sent me; for the least among all of you is the greatest."

49 John answered, "Master, we saw someone casting out demons in your name, and we tried to stop him, because he does not follow with us." 50 But Jesus said to him, "Do not stop him; for whoever is not against you is for you."

51 When the days drew near for him to be taken up, he set his face to go to Jerusalem. 52 And

[y]Gk he [z]Or The Christ [a]Or but when they were fully awake
[b]Or tents [c]Other ancient authorities read my Beloved [d]Or it

he sent messengers ahead of him. On their way they entered a village of the Samaritans to make ready for him; 53 but they did not receive him, because his face was set toward Jerusalem. 54 When his disciples James and John saw it, they said, "Lord, do you want us to command fire to come down from heaven and consume them?"[e] 55 But he turned and rebuked them. 56 Then[f] they went on to another village.

57 As they were going along the road, someone said to him, "I will follow you wherever you go." 58 And Jesus said to him, "Foxes have holes, and birds of the air have nests; but the Son of Man has nowhere to lay his head." 59 To another he said, "Follow me." But he said, "Lord, first let me go and bury my father." 60 But Jesus[g] said to him, "Let the dead bury their own dead; but as for you, go and proclaim the kingdom of God." 61 Another said, "I will follow you, Lord; but let me first say farewell to those at my home." 62 Jesus said to him, "No one who puts a hand to the plow and looks back is fit for the kingdom of God."

10 After this the Lord appointed seventy[h] others and sent them on ahead of him in pairs to every town and place where he himself intended to go. 2 He said to them, "The harvest is plentiful, but the laborers are few; therefore ask the Lord of the harvest to send out laborers into his harvest. 3 Go on your way. See, I am sending you out like lambs into the midst of wolves. 4 Carry no purse, no bag, no sandals; and greet no one on the road. 5 Whatever house you enter, first say, 'Peace to this house!' 6 And if anyone is there who shares in peace, your peace will rest on that person; but if not, it will return to you. 7 Remain in the same house, eating and drinking whatever they provide, for the laborer deserves to be paid. Do not move about from house to house. 8 Whenever you enter a town and its people welcome you, eat what is set before you; 9 cure the sick who are there, and say to them, 'The kingdom of God has come near to you.'[i] 10 But whenever you enter a town and they do not welcome you, go out into its streets and say, 11 'Even the dust of your town that clings to our feet, we wipe off in protest against you. Yet know this: the kingdom of God has come near.'[j] 12 I tell you, on that day it will be more tolerable for Sodom than for that town.

13 "Woe to you, Chorazin! Woe to you, Beth-

saida! For if the deeds of power done in you had been done in Tyre and Sidon, they would have repented long ago, sitting in sackcloth and ashes. 14 But at the judgment it will be more tolerable for Tyre and Sidon than for you. 15 And you, Capernaum,

> will you be exalted to heaven?
> No, you will be brought down
> to Hades."

16 "Whoever listens to you listens to me, and whoever rejects you rejects me, and whoever rejects me rejects the one who sent me."

17 The seventy[k] returned with joy, saying, "Lord, in your name even the demons submit to us!" 18 He said to them, "I watched Satan fall from heaven like a flash of lightning. 19 See, I have given you authority to tread on snakes and scorpions, and over all the power of the enemy; and nothing will hurt you. 20 Nevertheless, do not rejoice at this, that the spirits submit to you, but rejoice that your names are written in heaven."

21 At that same hour Jesus[l] rejoiced in the Holy Spirit[m] and said, "I thank[n] you, Father, Lord of heaven and earth, because you have hidden these things from the wise and the intelligent and have revealed them to infants; yes, Father, for such was your gracious will.[o] 22 All things have been handed over to me by my Father; and no one knows who the Son is except the Father, or who the Father is except the Son and anyone to whom the Son chooses to reveal him."

23 Then turning to the disciples, Jesus[p] said to them privately, "Blessed are the eyes that see what you see! 24 For I tell you that many prophets and kings desired to see what you see, but did not see it, and to hear what you hear, but did not hear it."

25 Just then a lawyer stood up to test Jesus.[q] "Teacher," he said, "what must I do to inherit eternal life?" 26 He said to him, "What is written in the law? What do you read there?" 27 He answered, "You shall love the Lord your God with all your heart, and with all your soul, and with all

---

[e]Other ancient authorities add *as Elijah did*   [f]Other ancient authorities read *rebuked them, and said, "You do not know what spirit you are of,* 56*for the Son of Man has not come to destroy the lives of human beings but to save them." Then*   [g]Gk *he*   [h]Other ancient authorities read *seventy-two*   [i]Or *is at hand for you*   [j]Or *is at hand*   [k]Other ancient authorities read *seventy-two*   [l]Gk *he*   [m]Other authorities read *in the spirit*   [n]Or *praise*   [o]Or *for so it was well-pleasing in your sight*   [p]Gk *he*   [q]Gk *him*

your strength, and with all your mind; and your neighbor as yourself."[11] 28 And he said to him, "You have given the right answer; do this, and you will live."

29 But wanting to justify himself, he asked Jesus, "And who is my neighbor?" 30 Jesus replied, "A man was going down from Jerusalem to Jericho, and fell into the hands of robbers, who stripped him, beat him, and went away, leaving him half dead. 31 Now by chance a priest was going down that road; and when he saw him, he passed by on the other side. 32 So likewise a Levite, when he came to the place and saw him, passed by on the other side. 33 But a Samaritan while traveling came near him; and when he saw him, he was moved with pity. 34 He went to him and bandaged his wounds, having poured oil and wine on them. Then he put him on his own animal, brought him to an inn, and took care of him. 35 The next day he took out two denarii,[r] gave them to the innkeeper, and said, 'Take care of him; and when I come back, I will repay you whatever more you spend.' 36 Which of these three, do you think, was a neighbor to the man who fell into the hands of the robbers?" 37 He said, "The one who showed him mercy." Jesus said to him, "Go and do likewise."

38 Now as they went on their way, he entered a certain village, where a woman named Martha welcomed him into her home. 39 She had a sister named Mary, who sat at the Lord's feet and listened to what he was saying. 40 But Martha was distracted by her many tasks; so she came to him and asked, "Lord, do you not care that my sister has left me to do all the work by myself? Tell her then to help me." 41 But the Lord answered her, "Martha, Martha, you are worried and distracted by many things; 42 there is need of only one thing.[s] Mary has chosen the better part, which will not be taken away from her."

11 He was praying in a certain place, and after he had finished, one of his disciples said to him, "Lord, teach us to pray, as John taught his disciples." 2 He said to them, "When you pray, say:

Father,[t] hallowed be your name.
Your kingdom come.[u]
3   Give us each day our daily
          bread.[v]

4   And forgive us our sins,
          for we ourselves forgive
                everyone indebted to us.
     And do not bring us to the time
          of trial."[w]

5 And he said to them, "Suppose one of you has a friend, and you go to him at midnight and say to him, 'Friend, lend me three loaves of bread; 6 for a friend of mine has arrived, and I have nothing to set before him.' 7 And he answers from within, 'Do not bother me; the door has already been locked, and my children are with me in bed; I cannot get up and give you anything.' 8 I tell you, even though he will not get up and give him anything because he is his friend, at least because of his persistence he will get up and give him whatever he needs.

9 "So I say to you, Ask, and it will be given you; search, and you will find; knock, and the door will be opened for you. 10 For everyone who asks receives, and everyone who searches finds, and for everyone who knocks, the door will be opened. 11 Is there anyone among you who, if your child asks for[x] a fish, will give a snake instead of a fish? 12 Or if the child asks for an egg, will give a scorpion? 13 If you then, who are evil, know how to give good gifts to your children, how much more will the heavenly Father give the Holy Spirit[y] to those who ask him!"

14 Now he was casting out a demon that was mute; when the demon had gone out, the one who had been mute spoke, and the crowds were amazed. 15 But some of them said, "He casts out demons by Beelzebul, the ruler of the demons." 16 Others, to test him, kept demanding from him a sign from heaven. 17 But he knew what they were thinking and said to them, "Every kingdom divided against itself becomes a desert, and house falls on house. 18 If Satan also is divided against himself, how will his kingdom stand? —for you say

---

[r]The denarius was the usual day's wage for a laborer   [s]Other ancient authorities read *few things are necessary, or only one*   [t]Other ancient authorities read *Our Father in heaven*   [u]Other ancient authorities read *Our Father in heaven*   [v]Or *our bread for tomorrow*   [w]Or *us into temptation*. Other ancient authorities add *but rescue us from the evil one* (or *from evil*)   [x]Other ancient authorities add *bread, will give a stone; or if your child asks for*   [y]Other ancient authorities read *the Father give the Holy Spirit from heaven*

---

[11]Deut 6:5; Lev 19:18

that I cast out the demons by Beelzebul. 19 Now if I cast out the demons by Beelzebul, by whom do your exorcists[z] cast them out? Therefore they will be your judges. 20 But if it is by the finger of God that I cast out the demons, then the kingdom of God has come to you. 21 When a strong man, fully armed, guards his castle, his property is safe. 22 But when one stronger than he attacks him and overpowers him, he takes away his armor in which he trusted and divides his plunder. 23 Whoever is not with me is against me, and whoever does not gather with me scatters.

24 "When the unclean spirit has gone out of a person, it wanders through waterless regions looking for a resting place, but not finding any, it says, 'I will return to my house from which I came.' 25 When it comes, it finds it swept and put in order. 26 Then it goes and brings seven other spirits more evil than itself, and they enter and live there; and the last state of that person is worse than the first."

27 While he was saying this, a woman in the crowd raised her voice and said to him, "Blessed is the womb that bore you and the breasts that nursed you!" 28 But he said, "Blessed rather are those who hear the word of God and obey it!"

29 When the crowds were increasing, he began to say, "This generation is an evil generation; it asks for a sign, but no sign will be given to it except the sign of Jonah. 30 For just as Jonah became a sign to the people of Nineveh, so the Son of Man will be to this generation. 31 The queen of the South will rise at the judgment with the people of this generation and condemn them, because she came from the ends of the earth to listen to the wisdom of Solomon, and see, something greater than Solomon is here! 32 The people of Nineveh will rise up at the judgment with this generation and condemn it, because they repented at the proclamation of Jonah, and see, something greater than Jonah is here!

33 "No one after lighting a lamp puts it in a cellar,[a] but on the lampstand so that those who enter may see the light. 34 Your eye is the lamp of your body. If your eye is healthy, your whole body is full of light; but if it is not healthy, your body is full of darkness. 35 Therefore consider whether the light in you is not darkness. 36 If then your whole body is full of light, with no part of it in darkness, it will be as full of light as when a lamp gives you light with its rays."

37 While he was speaking, a Pharisee invited him to dine with him; so he went in and took his place at the table. 38 The Pharisee was amazed to see that he did not first wash before dinner. 39 Then the Lord said to him, "Now you Pharisees clean the outside of the cup and of the dish, but inside you are full of greed and wickedness. 40 You fools! Did not the one who made the outside make the inside also? 41 So give for alms those things that are within; and see, everything will be clean for you.

42 "But woe to you Pharisees! For you tithe mint and rue and herbs of all kinds, and neglect justice and the love of God; it is these you ought to have practiced, without neglecting the others. 43 Woe to you Pharisees! For you love to have the seat of honor in the synagogues and to be greeted with respect in the marketplaces. 44 Woe to you! For you are like unmarked graves, and people walk over them without realizing it."

45 One of the lawyers answered him, "Teacher, when you say these things, you insult us too." 46 And he said, "Woe also to you lawyers! For you load people with burdens hard to bear, and you yourselves do not lift a finger to ease them. 47 Woe to you! For you build the tombs of the prophets whom your ancestors killed. 48 So you are witnesses and approve of the deeds of your ancestors; for they killed them, and you build their tombs. 49 Therefore also the Wisdom of God said, 'I will send them prophets and apostles, some of whom they will kill and persecute,' 50 so that this generation may be charged with the blood of all the prophets shed since the foundation of the world, 51 from the blood of Abel to the blood of Zechariah, who perished between the altar and the sanctuary. Yes, I tell you, it will be charged against this generation. 52 Woe to you lawyers! For you have taken away the key of knowledge; you did not enter yourselves, and you hindered those who were entering."

53 When he went outside, the scribes and the Pharisees began to be very hostile toward him and to cross-examine him about many things, 54 lying in wait for him, to catch him in something he might say.

---

[z]Gk *sons*   [a]Other ancient authorities add *or under the bushel basket*

12 Meanwhile, when the crowd gathered by the thousands, so that they trampled on one another, he began to speak first to his disciples, "Beware of the yeast of the Pharisees, that is, their hypocrisy. 2 Nothing is covered up that will not be uncovered, and nothing secret that will not become known. 3 Therefore whatever you have said in the dark will be heard in the light, and what you have whispered behind closed doors will be proclaimed from the housetops.

4 "I tell you, my friends, do not fear those who kill the body, and after that can do nothing more. 5 But I will warn you whom to fear: fear him who, after he has killed, has authority[b] to cast into hell.[c] Yes, I tell you, fear him! 6 Are not five sparrows sold for two pennies? Yet not one of them is forgotten in God's sight. 7 But even the hairs of your head are all counted. Do not be afraid; you are of more value than many sparrows.

8 "And I tell you, everyone who acknowledges me before others, the Son of Man also will acknowledge before the angels of God; 9 but whoever denies me before others will be denied before the angels of God. 10 And everyone who speaks a word against the Son of Man will be forgiven; but whoever blasphemes against the Holy Spirit will not be forgiven. 11 When they bring you before the synagogues, the rulers, and the authorities, do not worry about how[d] you are to defend yourselves or what you are to say; 12 for the Holy Spirit will teach you at that very hour what you ought to say."

13 Someone in the crowd said to him, "Teacher, tell my brother to divide the family inheritance with me." 14 But he said to him, "Friend, who set me to be a judge or arbitrator over you?" 15 And he said to them, "Take care! Be on your guard against all kinds of greed; for one's life does not consist in the abundance of possessions." 16 Then he told them a parable: "The land of a rich man produced abundantly. 17 And he thought to himself, 'What should I do, for I have no place to store my crops?' 18 Then he said, 'I will do this: I will pull down my barns and build larger ones, and there I will store all my grain and my goods. 19 And I will say to my soul, Soul, you have ample goods laid up for many years; relax, eat, drink, be merry.' 20 But God said to him, 'You fool! This very night your life is being demanded of you. And the things you have prepared, whose will they be?' 21 So it is with those who store up treasures for themselves but are not rich toward God."

22 He said to his disciples, "Therefore I tell you, do not worry about your life, what you will eat, or about your body, what you will wear. 23 For life is more than food, and the body more than clothing. 24 Consider the ravens: they neither sow nor reap, they have neither storehouse nor barn, and yet God feeds them. Of how much more value are you than the birds! 25 And can any of you by worrying add a single hour to your span of life?[e] 26 If then you are not able to do so small a thing as that, why do you worry about the rest? 27 Consider the lilies, how they grow: they neither toil nor spin;[f] yet I tell you, even Solomon in all his glory was not clothed like one of these. 28 But if God so clothes the grass of the field, which is alive today and tomorrow is thrown into the oven, how much more will he clothe you—you of little faith! 29 And do not keep striving for what you are to eat and what you are to drink, and do not keep worrying. 30 For it is the nations of the world that strive after all these things, and your Father knows that you need them. 31 Instead, strive for his[g] kingdom, and these things will be given to you as well.

32 "Do not be afraid, little flock, for it is your Father's good pleasure to give you the kingdom. 33 Sell your possessions, and give alms. Make purses for yourselves that do not wear out, an unfailing treasure in heaven, where no thief comes near and no moth destroys. 34 For where your treasure is, there your heart will be also.

35 "Be dressed for action and have your lamps lit; 36 be like those who are waiting for their master to return from the wedding banquet, so that they may open the door for him as soon as he comes and knocks. 37 Blessed are those slaves whom the master finds alert when he comes; truly I tell you, he will fasten his belt and have them sit down to eat, and he will come and serve them. 38 If he comes during the middle of the night, or near dawn, and finds them so, blessed are those slaves.

39 "But know this: if the owner of the house had

---

[b]Or *power* [c]Gk *Gehenna* [d]Other ancient authorities add *or what* [e]Or *add a cubit to your stature* [f]Other ancient authorities read *Consider the lilies; they neither spin nor weave* [g]Other ancient authorities read *God's*

known at what hour the thief was coming, he[h] would not have let his house be broken into. 40 You also must be ready, for the Son of Man is coming at an unexpected hour."

41 Peter said, "Lord, are you telling this parable for us or for everyone?" 42 And the Lord said, "Who then is the faithful and prudent manager whom his master will put in charge of his slaves, to give them their allowance of food at the proper time? 43 Blessed is that slave whom his master will find at work when he arrives. 44 Truly I tell you, he will put that one in charge of all his possessions. 45 But if that slave says to himself, 'My master is delayed in coming,' and if he begins to beat the other slaves, men and women, and to eat and drink and get drunk, 46 the master of that slave will come on a day when he does not expect him and at an hour that he does not know, and will cut him in pieces,[i] and put him with the unfaithful. 47 That slave who knew what his master wanted, but did not prepare himself or do what was wanted, will receive a severe beating. 48 But the one who did not know and did what deserved a beating will receive a light beating. From everyone to whom much has been given, much will be required; and from the one to whom much has been entrusted, even more will be demanded.

49 "I came to bring fire to the earth, and how I wish it were already kindled! 50 I have a baptism with which to be baptized, and what stress I am under until it is completed! 51 Do you think that I have come to bring peace to the earth? No, I tell you, but rather division! 52 From now on five in one household will be divided, three against two and two against three; 53 they will be divided:

> father against son
>   and son against father,
> mother against daughter
>   and daughter against mother,
> mother-in-law against her
>   daughter-in-law
>   and daughter-in-law against
>   mother-in-law."

54 He also said to the crowds, "When you see a cloud rising in the west, you immediately say, 'It is going to rain'; and so it happens. 55 And when you see the south wind blowing, you say, 'There will be scorching heat'; and it happens. 56 You hypocrites! You know how to interpret the ap-

pearance of earth and sky, but why do you not know how to interpret the present time?

57 "And why do you not judge for yourselves what is right? 58 Thus, when you go with your accuser before a magistrate, on the way make an effort to settle the case,[j] or you may be dragged before the judge, and the judge hand you over to the officer, and the officer throw you in prison. 59 I tell you, you will never get out until you have paid the very last penny."

13 At that very time there were some present who told him about the Galileans whose blood Pilate had mingled with their sacrifices. 2 He asked them, "Do you think that because these Galileans suffered in this way they were worse sinners than all other Galileans? 3 No, I tell you; but unless you repent, you will all perish as they did. 4 Or those eighteen who were killed when the tower of Siloam fell on them—do you think that they were worse offenders than all the others living in Jerusalem? 5 No, I tell you; but unless you repent, you will all perish just as they did."

6 Then he told this parable: "A man had a fig tree planted in his vineyard; and he came looking for fruit on it and found none. 7 So he said to the gardener, 'See here! For three years I have come looking for fruit on this fig tree, and still I find none. Cut it down! Why should it be wasting the soil?' 8 He replied, 'Sir, let it alone for one more year, until I dig around it and put manure on it. 9 If it bears fruit next year, well and good; but if not, you can cut it down.'"

10 Now he was teaching in one of the synagogues on the sabbath. 11 And just then there appeared a woman with a spirit that had crippled her for eighteen years. She was bent over and was quite unable to stand up straight. 12 When Jesus saw her, he called her over and said, "Woman, you are set free from your ailment." 13 When he laid his hands on her, immediately she stood up straight and began praising God. 14 But the leader of the synagogue, indignant because Jesus had cured on the sabbath, kept saying to the crowd, "There are six days on which work ought to be done; come on those days and be cured, and not on the sabbath day." 15 But the Lord answered him

---

[h]Other ancient authorities add *would have watched and*   [i]Or *cut him off*   [j]Gk *settle with him*

and said, "You hypocrites! Does not each of you on the sabbath untie his ox or his donkey from the manger, and lead it away to give it water? 16 And ought not this woman, a daughter of Abraham whom Satan bound for eighteen long years, be set free from this bondage on the sabbath day?" 17 When he said this, all his opponents were put to shame; and the entire crowd was rejoicing at all the wonderful things that he was doing.

18 He said therefore, "What is the kingdom of God like? And to what should I compare it? 19 It is like a mustard seed that someone took and sowed in the garden; it grew and became a tree, and the birds of the air made nests in its branches."

20 And again he said, "To what should I compare the kingdom of God? 21 It is like yeast that a woman took and mixed in with[k] three measures of flour until all of it was leavened."

22 Jesus[l] went through one town and village after another, teaching as he made his way to Jerusalem. 23 Someone asked him, "Lord, will only a few be saved?" He said to them, 24 "Strive to enter through the narrow door; for many, I tell you, will try to enter and will not be able. 25 When once the owner of the house has got up and shut the door, and you begin to stand outside and to knock at the door, saying, 'Lord, open to us,' then in reply he will say to you, 'I do not know where you come from.' 26 Then you will begin to say, 'We ate and drank with you, and you taught in our streets.' 27 But he will say, 'I do not know where you come from; go away from me, all you evildoers!' 28 There will be weeping and gnashing of teeth when you see Abraham and Isaac and Jacob and all the prophets in the kingdom of God, and you yourselves thrown out. 29 Then people will come from east and west, from north and south, and will eat in the kingdom of God. 30 Indeed, some are last who will be first, and some are first who will be last."

31 At that very hour some Pharisees came and said to him, "Get away from here, for Herod wants to kill you." 32 He said to them, "Go and tell that fox for me,[m] 'Listen, I am casting out demons and performing cures today and tomorrow, and on the third day I finish my work. 33 Yet today, tomorrow, and the next day I must be on my way, because it is impossible for a prophet to be killed outside of Jerusalem.' 34 Jerusalem, Jerusalem, the city that kills the prophets and stones those who are sent to it! How often have I desired to gather your children together as a hen gathers her brood under her wings, and you were not willing! 35 See, your house is left to you. And I tell you, you will not see me until the time comes when[n] you say, 'Blessed is the one who comes in the name of the Lord.'"[12]

14 On one occasion when Jesus[o] was going to the house of a leader of the Pharisees to eat a meal on the sabbath, they were watching him closely. 2 Just then, in front of him, there was a man who had dropsy. 3 And Jesus asked the lawyers and Pharisees, "Is it lawful to cure people on the sabbath, or not?" 4 But they were silent. So Jesus[o] took him and healed him, and sent him away. 5 Then he said to them, "If one of you has a child[p] or an ox that has fallen into a well, will you not immediately pull it out on a sabbath day?" 6 And they could not reply to this.

7 When he noticed how the guests chose the places of honor, he told them a parable. 8 "When you are invited by someone to a wedding banquet, do not sit down at the place of honor, in case someone more distinguished than you has been invited by your host; 9 and the host who invited both of you may come and say to you, 'Give this person your place,' and then in disgrace you would start to take the lowest place. 10 But when you are invited, go and sit down at the lowest place, so that when your host comes, he may say to you, 'Friend, move up higher'; then you will be honored in the presence of all who sit at the table with you. 11 For all who exalt themselves will be humbled, and those who humble themselves will be exalted."

12 He said also to the one who had invited him, "When you give a luncheon or a dinner, do not invite your friends or your brothers or your relatives or rich neighbors, in case they may invite you in return, and you would be repaid. 13 But when you give a banquet, invite the poor, the crippled, the lame, and the blind. 14 And you will be blessed, because they cannot repay you, for you will be repaid at the resurrection of the righteous."

---

[k]Gk *hid in*   [l]Gk *He*   [m]Gk lacks *for me*   [n]Other ancient authorities lack *the time comes when*   [o]Gk *he*   [p]Other ancient authorities read *a donkey*

[12]Ps 118:26

15 One of the dinner guests, on hearing this, said to him, "Blessed is anyone who will eat bread in the kingdom of God!" 16 Then Jesus[q] said to him, "Someone gave a great dinner and invited many. 17 At the time for the dinner he sent his slave to say to those who had been invited, 'Come; for everything is ready now.' 18 But they all alike began to make excuses. The first said to him, 'I have bought a piece of land, and I must go out and see it; please accept my regrets.' 19 Another said, 'I have bought five yoke of oxen, and I am going to try them out; please accept my regrets.' 20 Another said, 'I have just been married, and therefore I cannot come.' 21 So the slave returned and reported this to his master. Then the owner of the house became angry and said to his slave, 'Go out at once into the streets and lanes of the town and bring in the poor, the crippled, the blind, and the lame.' 22 And the slave said, 'Sir, what you ordered has been done, and there is still room.' 23 Then the master said to the slave, 'Go out into the roads and lanes, and compel people to come in, so that my house may be filled. 24 For I tell you,[r] none of those who were invited will taste my dinner.'"

25 Now large crowds were traveling with him; and he turned and said to them, 26 "Whoever comes to me and does not hate father and mother, wife and children, brothers and sisters, yes, and even life itself, cannot be my disciple. 27 Whoever does not carry the cross and follow me cannot be my disciple. 28 For which of you, intending to build a tower, does not first sit down and estimate the cost, to see whether he has enough to complete it? 29 Otherwise, when he has laid a foundation and is not able to finish, all who see it will begin to ridicule him, 30 saying, 'This fellow began to build and was not able to finish.' 31 Or what king, going out to wage war against another king, will not sit down first and consider whether he is able with ten thousand to oppose the one who comes against him with twenty thousand? 32 If he cannot, then, while the other is still far away, he sends a delegation and asks for the terms of peace. 33 So therefore, none of you can become my disciple if you do not give up all your possessions.

34 "Salt is good; but if salt has lost its taste, how can its saltiness be restored?[s] 35 It is fit neither for the soil nor for the manure pile; they throw it away. Let anyone with ears to hear listen!"

15 Now all the tax collectors and sinners were coming near to listen to him. 2 And the Pharisees and the scribes were grumbling and saying, "This fellow welcomes sinners and eats with them."

3 So he told them this parable: 4 "Which one of you, having a hundred sheep and losing one of them, does not leave the ninety-nine in the wilderness and go after the one that is lost until he finds it? 5 When he has found it, he lays it on his shoulders and rejoices. 6 And when he comes home, he calls together his friends and neighbors, saying to them, 'Rejoice with me, for I have found my sheep that was lost.' 7 Just so, I tell you, there will be more joy in heaven over one sinner who repents than over ninety-nine righteous persons who need no repentance.

8 "Or what woman having ten silver coins,[t] if she loses one of them, does not light a lamp, sweep the house, and search carefully until she finds it? 9 When she has found it, she calls together her friends and neighbors, saying, 'Rejoice with me, for I have found the coin that I had lost.' 10 Just so, I tell you, there is joy in the presence of the angels of God over one sinner who repents."

11 Then Jesus[u] said, "There was a man who had two sons. 12 The younger of them said to his father, 'Father, give me the share of the property that will belong to me.' So he divided his property between them. 13 A few days later the younger son gathered all he had and traveled to a distant country, and there he squandered his property in dissolute living. 14 When he had spent everything, a severe famine took place throughout that country, and he began to be in need. 15 So he went and hired himself out to one of the citizens of that country, who sent him to his fields to feed the pigs. 16 He would gladly have filled himself with[v] the pods that the pigs were eating; and no one gave him anything. 17 But when he came to himself he said, 'How many of my father's hired hands have bread enough and to spare, but here I am dying of

---

[q]Gk *he*   [r]The Greek word for *you* here is plural   [s]Or *how can it be used for seasoning?*   [t]Gk *drachmas*, each worth about a day's wage for a laborer   [u]Gk *he*   [v]Other ancient authorities read *filled his stomach with*

hunger! 18 I will get up and go to my father, and I will say to him, "Father, I have sinned against heaven and before you; 19 I am no longer worthy to be called your son; treat me like one of your hired hands."' 20 So he set off and went to his father. But while he was still far off, his father saw him and was filled with compassion; he ran and put his arms around him and kissed him. 21 Then the son said to him, 'Father, I have sinned against heaven and before you; I am no longer worthy to be called your son.'ᵂ 22 But the father said to his slaves, 'Quickly, bring out a robe—the best one—and put it on him; put a ring on his finger and sandals on his feet. 23 And get the fatted calf and kill it, and let us eat and celebrate; 24 for this son of mine was dead and is alive again; he was lost and is found!' And they began to celebrate.

25 "Now his elder son was in the field; and when he came and approached the house, he heard music and dancing. 26 He called one of the slaves and asked what was going on. 27 He replied, 'Your brother has come, and your father has killed the fatted calf, because he has got him back safe and sound.' 28 Then he became angry and refused to go in. His father came out and began to plead with him. 29 But he answered his father, 'Listen! For all these years I have been working like a slave for you, and I have never disobeyed your command; yet you have never given me even a young goat so that I might celebrate with my friends. 30 But when this son of yours came back, who has devoured your property with prostitutes, you killed the fatted calf for him!' 31 Then the fatherˣ said to him, 'Son, you are always with me, and all that is mine is yours. 32 But we had to celebrate and rejoice, because this brother of yours was dead and has come to life; he was lost and has been found.'"

16 Then Jesusˣ said to the disciples, "There was a rich man who had a manager, and charges were brought to him that this man was squandering his property. 2 So he summoned him and said to him, 'What is this that I hear about you? Give me an accounting of your management, because you cannot be my manager any longer.' 3 Then the manager said to himself, 'What will I do, now that my master is taking the position away from me? I am not strong enough to dig, and I am ashamed to beg. 4 I have decided what to do so that, when I am dismissed as manager, people may welcome me into their homes.' 5 So, summoning his master's debtors one by one, he asked the first, 'How much do you owe my master?' 6 He answered, 'A hundred jugs of olive oil.' He said to him, 'Take your bill, sit down quickly, and make it fifty.' 7 Then he asked another, 'And how much do you owe?' He replied, 'A hundred containers of wheat.' He said to him, 'Take your bill and make it eighty.' 8 And his master commended the dishonest manager because he had acted shrewdly; for the children of this age are more shrewd in dealing with their own generation than are the children of light. 9 And I tell you, make friends for yourselves by means of dishonest wealthᵛ so that when it is gone, they may welcome you into the eternal homes.ᶻ

10 "Whoever is faithful in a very little is faithful also in much; and whoever is dishonest in a very little is dishonest also in much. 11 If then you have not been faithful with the dishonest wealth,ᵛ who will entrust to you the true riches? 12 And if you have not been faithful with what belongs to another, who will give you what is your own? 13 No slave can serve two masters; for a slave will either hate the one and love the other, or be devoted to the one and despise the other. You cannot serve God and wealth."ᵛ

14 The Pharisees, who were lovers of money, heard all this, and they ridiculed him. 15 So he said to them, "You are those who justify yourselves in the sight of others; but God knows your hearts; for what is prized by human beings is an abomination in the sight of God.

16 "The law and the prophets were in effect until John came; since then the good news of the kingdom of God is proclaimed, and everyone tries to enter it by force.ᵃ 17 But it is easier for heaven and earth to pass away, than for one stroke of a letter in the law to be dropped.

18 "Anyone who divorces his wife and marries another commits adultery, and whoever marries a woman divorced from her husband commits adultery.

ᵂOther ancient authorities add *Treat me like one of your hired servants* ˣGk *he* ʸGk *mammon* ᶻGk *tents* ᵃOr *everyone is strongly urged to enter it*

19 "There was a rich man who was dressed in purple and fine linen and who feasted sumptuously every day. 20 And at his gate lay a poor man named Lazarus, covered with sores, 21 who longed to satisfy his hunger with what fell from the rich man's table; even the dogs would come and lick his sores. 22 The poor man died and was carried away by the angels to be with Abraham.[b] The rich man also died and was buried. 23 In Hades, where he was being tormented, he looked up and saw Abraham far away with Lazarus by his side.[c] 24 He called out, 'Father Abraham, have mercy on me, and send Lazarus to dip the tip of his finger in water and cool my tongue; for I am in agony in these flames.' 25 But Abraham said, 'Child, remember that during your lifetime you received your good things, and Lazarus in like manner evil things; but now he is comforted here, and you are in agony. 26 Besides all this, between you and us a great chasm has been fixed, so that those who might want to pass from here to you cannot do so, and no one can cross from there to us.' 27 He said, 'Then, father, I beg you to send him to my father's house— 28 for I have five brothers—that he may warn them, so that they will not also come into this place of torment.' 29 Abraham replied, 'They have Moses and the prophets; they should listen to them.' 30 He said, 'No, father Abraham; but if someone goes to them from the dead, they will repent.' 31 He said to him, 'If they do not listen to Moses and the prophets, neither will they be convinced even if someone rises from the dead.'"

17 Jesus[d] said to his disciples, "Occasions for stumbling are bound to come, but woe to anyone by whom they come! 2 It would be better for you if a millstone were hung around your neck and you were thrown into the sea than for you to cause one of these little ones to stumble. 3 Be on your guard! If another disciple[e] sins, you must rebuke the offender, and if there is repentance, you must forgive. 4 And if the same person sins against you seven times a day, and turns back to you seven times and says, 'I repent,' you must forgive."

5 The apostles said to the Lord, "Increase our faith!" 6 The Lord replied, "If you had faith the size of a[f] mustard seed, you could say to this mulberry tree, 'Be uprooted and planted in the sea,' and it would obey you.

7 "Who among you would say to your slave who has just come in from plowing or tending sheep in the field, 'Come here at once and take your place at the table'? 8 Would you not rather say to him, 'Prepare supper for me, put on your apron and serve me while I eat and drink; later you may eat and drink'? 9 Do you thank the slave for doing what was commanded? 10 So you also, when you have done all that you were ordered to do, say, 'We are worthless slaves; we have done only what we ought to have done!'"

11 On the way to Jerusalem Jesus[g] was going through the region between Samaria and Galilee. 12 As he entered a village, ten lepers[h] approached him. Keeping their distance, 13 they called out, saying, "Jesus, Master, have mercy on us!" 14 When he saw them, he said to them, "Go and show yourselves to the priests." And as they went, they were made clean. 15 Then one of them, when he saw that he was healed, turned back, praising God with a loud voice. 16 He prostrated himself at Jesus'[i] feet and thanked him. And he was a Samaritan. 17 Then Jesus asked, "Were not ten made clean? But the other nine, where are they? 18 Was none of them found to return and give praise to God except this foreigner?" 19 Then he said to him, "Get up and go on your way; your faith has made you well."

20 Once Jesus[g] was asked by the Pharisees when the kingdom of God was coming, and he answered, "The kingdom of God is not coming with things that can be observed; 21 nor will they say, 'Look, here it is!' or 'There it is!' For, in fact, the kingdom of God is among[j] you."

22 Then he said to the disciples, "The days are coming when you will long to see one of the days of the Son of Man, and you will not see it. 23 They will say to you, 'Look there!' or 'Look here!' Do not go, do not set off in pursuit. 24 For as the lightning flashes and lights up the sky from one side to the other, so will the Son of Man be in his day.[k] 25 But first he must endure much suffering and be rejected by this generation. 26 Just as it was in the days of Noah, so too it will be in the days of the Son of Man. 27 They were eating and drinking,

[b]Gk *to Abraham's bosom*   [c]Gk *in his bosom*   [d]Gk *He*   [e]Gk *your brother*   [f]Gk *faith as a grain of*   [g]Gk *he*   [h]The terms *leper* and *leprosy* can refer to several diseases   [i]Gk *his*   [j]Or *within*   [k]Other ancient authorities lack *in his day*

and marrying and being given in marriage, until the day Noah entered the ark, and the flood came and destroyed all of them. 28 Likewise, just as it was in the days of Lot: they were eating and drinking, buying and selling, planting and building, 29 but on the day that Lot left Sodom, it rained fire and sulfur from heaven and destroyed all of them 30 —it will be like that on the day that the Son of Man is revealed. 31 On that day, anyone on the housetop who has belongings in the house must not come down to take them away; and likewise anyone in the field must not turn back. 32 Remember Lot's wife. 33 Those who try to make their life secure will lose it, but those who lose their life will keep it. 34 I tell you, on that night there will be two in one bed; one will be taken and the other left. 35 There will be two women grinding meal together; one will be taken and the other left."[1] 37 Then they asked him, "Where, Lord?" He said to them, "Where the corpse is, there the vultures will gather."

18 Then Jesus[m] told them a parable about their need to pray always and not to lose heart. 2 He said, "In a certain city there was a judge who neither feared God nor had respect for people. 3 In that city there was a widow who kept coming to him and saying, 'Grant me justice against my opponent.' 4 For a while he refused; but later he said to himself, 'Though I have no fear of God and no respect for anyone, 5 yet because this widow keeps bothering me, I will grant her justice, so that she may not wear me out by continually coming.'"[n] 6 And the Lord said, "Listen to what the unjust judge says. 7 And will not God grant justice to his chosen ones who cry to him day and night? Will he delay long in helping them? 8 I tell you, he will quickly grant justice to them. And yet, when the Son of Man comes, will he find faith on earth?"

9 He also told this parable to some who trusted in themselves that they were righteous and regarded others with contempt: 10 "Two men went up to the temple to pray, one a Pharisee and the other a tax collector. 11 The Pharisee, standing by himself, was praying thus, 'God, I thank you that I am not like other people: thieves, rogues, adulterers, or even like this tax collector. 12 I fast twice a week; I give a tenth of all my income.' 13 But the tax collector, standing far off, would not

even look up to heaven, but was beating his breast and saying, 'God, be merciful to me, a sinner!' 14 I tell you, this man went down to his home justified rather than the other; for all who exalt themselves will be humbled, but all who humble themselves will be exalted."

15 People were bringing even infants to him that he might touch them; and when the disciples saw it, they sternly ordered them not to do it. 16 But Jesus called for them and said, "Let the little children come to me, and do not stop them; for it is to such as these that the kingdom of God belongs. 17 Truly I tell you, whoever does not receive the kingdom of God as a little child will never enter it."

18 A certain ruler asked him, "Good Teacher, what must I do to inherit eternal life?" 19 Jesus said to him, "Why do you call me good? No one is good but God alone. 20 You know the commandments: 'You shall not commit adultery; You shall not murder; You shall not steal; You shall not bear false witness; Honor your father and mother.'"[13] 21 He replied, "I have kept all these since my youth." 22 When Jesus heard this, he said to him, "There is still one thing lacking. Sell all that you own and distribute the money[o] to the poor, and you will have treasure in heaven; then come, follow me." 23 But when he heard this, he became sad; for he was very rich. 24 Jesus looked at him and said, "How hard it is for those who have wealth to enter the kingdom of God! 25 Indeed, it is easier for a camel to go through the eye of a needle than for someone who is rich to enter the kingdom of God."

26 Those who heard it said, "Then who can be saved?" 27 He replied, "What is impossible for mortals is possible for God."

28 Then Peter said, "Look, we have left our homes and followed you." 29 And he said to them, "Truly I tell you, there is no one who has left house or wife or brothers or parents or children, for the sake of the kingdom of God, 30 who will not get back very much more in this age, and in the age to come eternal life."

---

[1]Other ancient authorities add verse 36, *"Two will be in the field; one will be taken and the other left."*   [m]Gk *he*   [n]Or *so that she may not finally come and slap me in the face*   [o]Gk lacks *the money*

[13]Exod 20:12–16; Deut 5:16–20

31 Then he took the twelve aside and said to them, "See, we are going up to Jerusalem, and everything that is written about the Son of Man by the prophets will be accomplished. 32 For he will be handed over to the Gentiles; and he will be mocked and insulted and spat upon. 33 After they have flogged him, they will kill him, and on the third day he will rise again." 34 But they understood nothing about all these things; in fact, what he said was hidden from them, and they did not grasp what was said.

35 As he approached Jericho, a blind man was sitting by the roadside begging. 36 When he heard a crowd going by, he asked what was happening. 37 They told him, "Jesus of Nazareth[p] is passing by." 38 Then he shouted, "Jesus, Son of David, have mercy on me!" 39 Those who were in front sternly ordered him to be quiet; but he shouted even more loudly, "Son of David, have mercy on me!" 40 Jesus stood still and ordered the man to be brought to him; and when he came near, he asked him, 41 "What do you want me to do for you?" He said, "Lord, let me see again." 42 Jesus said to him, "Receive your sight; your faith has saved you." 43 Immediately he regained his sight and followed him, glorifying God; and all the people, when they saw it, praised God.

19 He entered Jericho and was passing through it. 2 A man was there named Zacchaeus; he was a chief tax collector and was rich. 3 He was trying to see who Jesus was, but on account of the crowd he could not, because he was short in stature. 4 So he ran ahead and climbed a sycamore tree to see him, because he was going to pass that way. 5 When Jesus came to the place, he looked up and said to him, "Zacchaeus, hurry and come down; for I must stay at your house today." 6 So he hurried down and was happy to welcome him. 7 All who saw it began to grumble and said, "He has gone to be the guest of one who is a sinner." 8 Zacchaeus stood there and said to the Lord, "Look, half of my possessions, Lord, I will give to the poor; and if I have defrauded anyone of anything, I will pay back four times as much." 9 Then Jesus said to him, "Today salvation has come to this house, because he too is a son of Abraham. 10 For the Son of Man came to seek out and to save the lost."

11 As they were listening to this, he went on to tell a parable, because he was near Jerusalem, and because they supposed that the kingdom of God was to appear immediately. 12 So he said, "A nobleman went to a distant country to get royal power for himself and then return. 13 He summoned ten of his slaves, and gave them ten pounds,[q] and said to them, 'Do business with these until I come back.' 14 But the citizens of his country hated him and sent a delegation after him, saying, 'We do not want this man to rule over us.' 15 When he returned, having received royal power, he ordered these slaves, to whom he had given the money, to be summoned so that he might find out what they had gained by trading. 16 The first came forward and said, 'Lord, your pound has made ten more pounds.' 17 He said to him, 'Well done, good slave! Because you have been trustworthy in a very small thing, take charge of ten cities.' 18 Then the second came, saying, 'Lord, your pound has made five pounds.' 19 He said to him, 'And you, rule over five cities.' 20 Then the other came, saying, 'Lord, here is your pound. I wrapped it up in a piece of cloth, 21 for I was afraid of you, because you are a harsh man; you take what you did not deposit, and reap what you did not sow.' 22 He said to him, 'I will judge you by your own words, you wicked slave! You knew, did you, that I was a harsh man, taking what I did not deposit and reaping what I did not sow? 23 Why then did you not put my money into the bank? Then when I returned, I could have collected it with interest.' 24 He said to the bystanders, 'Take the pound from him and give it to the one who has ten pounds.' 25 (And they said to him, 'Lord, he has ten pounds!') 26 'I tell you, to all those who have, more will be given; but from those who have nothing, even what they have will be taken away. 27 But as for these enemies of mine who did not want me to be king over them— bring them here and slaughter them in my presence.'"

28 After he had said this, he went on ahead, going up to Jerusalem.

29 When he had come near Bethphage and Bethany, at the place called the Mount of Olives, he sent two of the disciples, 30 saying, "Go into

---

[p]Gk *the Nazorean*   [q]The mina, rendered here by *pound,* was about three months' wages for a laborer

the village ahead of you, and as you enter it you will find tied there a colt that has never been ridden. Untie it and bring it here. 31 If anyone asks you, 'Why are you untying it?' just say this, 'The Lord needs it.'" 32 So those who were sent departed and found it as he had told them. 33 As they were untying the colt, its owners asked them, "Why are you untying the colt?" 34 They said, "The Lord needs it." 35 Then they brought it to Jesus; and after throwing their cloaks on the colt, they set Jesus on it. 36 As he rode along, people kept spreading their cloaks on the road. 37 As he was now approaching the path down from the Mount of Olives, the whole multitude of the disciples began to praise God joyfully with a loud voice for all the deeds of power that they had seen, 38 saying,

> "Blessed is the king
>> who comes in the name of the
>> Lord!"[14]
> Peace in heaven,
>> and glory in the highest
>> heaven!"

39 Some of the Pharisees in the crowd said to him, "Teacher, order your disciples to stop." 40 He answered, "I tell you, if these were silent, the stones would shout out."

41 As he came near and saw the city, he wept over it, 42 saying, "If you, even you, had only recognized on this day the things that make for peace! But now they are hidden from your eyes. 43 Indeed, the days will come upon you, when your enemies will set up ramparts around you and surround you, and hem you in on every side. 44 They will crush you to the ground, you and your children within you, and they will not leave within you one stone upon another; because you did not recognize the time of your visitation from God."[r]

45 Then he entered the temple and began to drive out those who were selling things there; 46 and he said, "It is written,

> 'My house shall be a house of
>> prayer';
>> but you have made it a den of
>> robbers.'"[15]

47 Every day he was teaching in the temple. The chief priests, the scribes, and the leaders of the people kept looking for a way to kill him; 48 but they did not find anything they could do,

for all the people were spellbound by what they heard.

20 One day, as he was teaching the people in the temple and telling the good news, the chief priests and the scribes came with the elders 2 and said to him, "Tell us, by what authority are you doing these things? Who is it who gave you this authority?" 3 He answered them, "I will also ask you a question, and you tell me: 4 Did the baptism of John come from heaven, or was it of human origin?" 5 They discussed it with one another, saying, "If we say, 'From heaven,' he will say, 'Why did you not believe him?' 6 But if we say, 'Of human origin,' all the people will stone us; for they are convinced that John was a prophet." 7 So they answered that they did not know where it came from. 8 Then Jesus said to them, "Neither will I tell you by what authority I am doing these things."

9 He began to tell the people this parable: "A man planted a vineyard, and leased it to tenants, and went to another country for a long time. 10 When the season came, he sent a slave to the tenants in order that they might give him his share of the produce of the vineyard; but the tenants beat him and sent him away empty-handed. 11 Next he sent another slave; that one also they beat and insulted and sent away empty-handed. 12 And he sent still a third; this one also they wounded and threw out. 13 Then the owner of the vineyard said, 'What shall I do? I will send my beloved son; perhaps they will respect him.' 14 But when the tenants saw him, they discussed it among themselves and said, 'This is the heir; let us kill him so that the inheritance may be ours.' 15 So they threw him out of the vineyard and killed him. What then will the owner of the vineyard do to them? 16 He will come and destroy those tenants and give the vineyard to others." When they heard this, they said, "Heaven forbid!" 17 But he looked at them and said, "What then does this text mean:

> 'The stone that the builders
>> rejected
>> has become the cornerstone'?[s][16]

18 Everyone who falls on that stone will be broken to pieces; and it will crush anyone on whom it

---

[r]Gk lacks *from God*   [s]Or *keystone*

[14]Ps 118:26   [15]Isa 56:7; Jer 7:11   [16]Ps 118:22

falls." 19 When the scribes and chief priests realized that he had told this parable against them, they wanted to lay hands on him at that very hour, but they feared the people.

20 So they watched him and sent spies who pretended to be honest, in order to trap him by what he said, so as to hand him over to the jurisdiction and authority of the governor. 21 So they asked him, "Teacher, we know that you are right in what you say and teach, and you show deference to no one, but teach the way of God in accordance with truth. 22 Is it lawful for us to pay taxes to the emperor, or not?" 23 But he perceived their craftiness and said to them, 24 "Show me a denarius. Whose head and whose title does it bear?" They said, "The emperor's." 25 He said to them, "Then give to the emperor the things that are the emperor's, and to God the things that are God's." 26 And they were not able in the presence of the people to trap him by what he said; and being amazed by his answer, they became silent.

27 Some Sadducees, those who say there is no resurrection, came to him 28 and asked him a question, "Teacher, Moses wrote for us that if a man's brother dies, leaving a wife but no children, the man[t] shall marry the widow and raise up children for his brother.[17] 29 Now there were seven brothers; the first married, and died childless; 30 then the second 31 and the third married her, and so in the same way all seven died childless. 32 Finally the woman also died. 33 In the resurrection, therefore, whose wife will the woman be? For the seven had married her."

34 Jesus said to them, "Those who belong to this age marry and are given in marriage; 35 but those who are considered worthy of a place in that age and in the resurrection from the dead neither marry nor are given in marriage. 36 Indeed they cannot die anymore, because they are like angels and are children of God, being children of the resurrection. 37 And the fact that the dead are raised Moses himself showed, in the story about the bush, where he speaks of the Lord as the God of Abraham, the God of Isaac, and the God of Jacob.[18] 38 Now he is God not of the dead, but of the living; for to him all of them are alive." 39 Then some of the scribes answered, "Teacher, you have spoken well." 40 For they no longer dared to ask him another question.

41 Then he said to them, "How can they say that the Messiah[u] is David's son? 42 For David himself says in the book of Psalms,

'The Lord said to my Lord,
    "Sit at my right hand,
43   until I make your enemies your
                footstool."'[19]

44 David thus calls him Lord; so how can he be his son?"

45 In the hearing of all the people he said to the[v] disciples, 46 "Beware of the scribes, who like to walk around in long robes, and love to be greeted with respect in the marketplaces, and to have the best seats in the synagogues and places of honor at banquets. 47 They devour widows' houses and for the sake of appearance say long prayers. They will receive the greater condemnation."

21 He looked up and saw rich people putting their gifts into the treasury; 2 he also saw a poor widow put in two small copper coins. 3 He said, "Truly I tell you, this poor widow has put in more than all of them; 4 for all of them have contributed out of their abundance, but she out of her poverty has put in all she had to live on."

5 When some were speaking about the temple, how it was adorned with beautiful stones and gifts dedicated to God, he said, 6 "As for these things that you see, the days will come when not one stone will be left upon another; all will be thrown down."

7 They asked him, "Teacher, when will this be, and what will be the sign that this is about to take place?" 8 And he said, "Beware that you are not led astray; for many will come in my name and say, 'I am he!'[w] and, 'The time is near!'[x] Do not go after them.

9 "When you hear of wars and insurrections, do not be terrified; for these things must take place first, but the end will not follow immediately." 10 Then he said to them, "Nation will rise against nation, and kingdom against kingdom; 11 there will be great earthquakes, and in various places famines and plagues; and there will be dreadful portents and great signs from heaven.

12 "But before all this occurs, they will arrest you and persecute you; they will hand you over to

[t]Gk *his brother*   [u]Or *the Christ*   [v]Other ancient authorities read *his*
[w]Gk *I am*   [x]Or *at hand*

---

[17]Deut 25:5; Gen 38:8   [18]Exod 3:6, 15   [19]Ps 110:1

synagogues and prisons, and you will be brought before kings and governors because of my name. 13 This will give you an opportunity to testify. 14 So make up your minds not to prepare your defense in advance; 15 for I will give you words[y] and a wisdom that none of your opponents will be able to withstand or contradict. 16 You will be betrayed even by parents and brothers, by relatives and friends; and they will put some of you to death. 17 You will be hated by all because of my name. 18 But not a hair of your head will perish. 19 By your endurance you will gain your souls.

20 "When you see Jerusalem surrounded by armies, then know that its desolation has come near.[z] 21 Then those in Judea must flee to the mountains, and those inside the city must leave it, and those out in the country must not enter it; 22 for these are days of vengeance, as a fulfillment of all that is written. 23 Woe to those who are pregnant and to those who are nursing infants in those days! For there will be great distress on the earth and wrath against this people; 24 they will fall by the edge of the sword and be taken away as captives among all nations; and Jerusalem will be trampled on by the Gentiles, until the times of the Gentiles are fulfilled.

25 "There will be signs in the sun, the moon, and the stars, and on the earth distress among nations confused by the roaring of the sea and the waves. 26 People will faint from fear and foreboding of what is coming upon the world, for the powers of the heavens will be shaken. 27 Then they will see 'the Son of Man coming in a cloud' with power and great glory. 28 Now when these things begin to take place, stand up and raise your heads, because your redemption is drawing near."

29 Then he told them a parable: "Look at the fig tree and all the trees; 30 as soon as they sprout leaves you can see for yourselves and know that summer is already near. 31 So also, when you see these things taking place, you know that the kingdom of God is near. 32 Truly I tell you, this generation will not pass away until all things have taken place. 33 Heaven and earth will pass away, but my words will not pass away.

34 "Be on guard so that your hearts are not weighed down with dissipation and drunkenness and the worries of this life, and that day does not catch you unexpectedly, 35 like a trap. For it will come upon all who live on the face of the whole earth. 36 Be alert at all times, praying that you may have the strength to escape all these things that will take place, and to stand before the Son of Man."

37 Every day he was teaching in the temple, and at night he would go out and spend the night on the Mount of Olives, as it was called. 38 And all the people would get up early in the morning to listen to him in the temple.

22 Now the festival of Unleavened Bread, which is called the Passover, was near. 2 The chief priests and the scribes were looking for a way to put Jesus[a] to death, for they were afraid of the people.

3 Then Satan entered into Judas called Iscariot, who was one of the twelve; 4 he went away and conferred with the chief priests and officers of the temple police about how he might betray him to them. 5 They were greatly pleased and agreed to give him money. 6 So he consented and began to look for an opportunity to betray him to them when no crowd was present.

7 Then came the day of Unleavened Bread, on which the Passover lamb had to be sacrificed. 8 So Jesus[b] sent Peter and John, saying, "Go and prepare the Passover meal for us that we may eat it." 9 They asked him, "Where do you want us to make preparations for it?" 10 "Listen," he said to them, "when you have entered the city, a man carrying a jar of water will meet you; follow him into the house he enters 11 and say to the owner of the house, 'The teacher asks you, "Where is the guest room, where I may eat the Passover with my disciples?"' 12 He will show you a large room upstairs, already furnished. Make preparations for us there." 13 So they went and found everything as he had told them; and they prepared the Passover meal.

14 When the hour came, he took his place at the table, and the apostles with him. 15 He said to them, "I have eagerly desired to eat this Passover with you before I suffer; 16 for I tell you, I will not eat it[c] until it is fulfilled in the kingdom of God." 17 Then he took a cup, and after giving thanks he

---

[y]Gk *a mouth* [z]Or *is at hand* [a]Gk *him* [b]Gk *he* [c]Other ancient authorities read *never eat it again*

said, "Take this and divide it among yourselves; 18 for I tell you that from now on I will not drink of the fruit of the vine until the kingdom of God comes." 19 Then he took a loaf of bread, and when he had given thanks, he broke it and gave it to them, saying, "This is my body, which is given for you. Do this in remembrance of me." 20 And he did the same with the cup after supper, saying, "This cup that is poured out for you is the new covenant in my blood.ᵈ 21 But see, the one who betrays me is with me, and his hand is on the table. 22 For the Son of Man is going as it has been determined, but woe to that one by whom he is betrayed!" 23 Then they began to ask one another which one of them it could be who would do this.

24 A dispute also arose among them as to which one of them was to be regarded as the greatest. 25 But he said to them, "The kings of the Gentiles lord it over them; and those in authority over them are called benefactors. 26 But not so with you; rather the greatest among you must become like the youngest, and the leader like one who serves. 27 For who is greater, the one who is at the table or the one who serves? Is it not the one at the table? But I am among you as one who serves.

28 "You are those who have stood by me in my trials; 29 and I confer on you, just as my Father has conferred on me, a kingdom, 30 so that you may eat and drink at my table in my kingdom, and you will sit on thrones judging the twelve tribes of Israel.

31 "Simon, Simon, listen! Satan has demandedᵉ to sift all of you like wheat, 32 but I have prayed for you that your own faith may not fail; and you, when once you have turned back, strengthen your brothers." 33 And he said to him, "Lord, I am ready to go with you to prison and to death!" 34 Jesusᶠ said, "I tell you, Peter, the cock will not crow this day, until you have denied three times that you know me."

35 He said to them, "When I sent you out without a purse, bag, or sandals, did you lack anything?" They said, "No, not a thing." 36 He said to them, "But now, the one who has a purse must take it, and likewise a bag. And the one who has no sword must sell his cloak and buy one. 37 For I tell you, this scripture must be fulfilled in me, 'And he was counted among the lawless';²⁰ and indeed what is written about me is being fulfilled."

38 They said, "Lord, look, here are two swords." He replied, "It is enough."

39 He came out and went, as was his custom, to the Mount of Olives; and the disciples followed him. 40 When he reached the place, he said to them, "Pray that you may not come into the time of trial."ᵍ 41 Then he withdrew from them about a stone's throw, knelt down, and prayed, 42 "Father, if you are willing, remove this cup from me; yet, not my will but yours be done." [43 Then an angel from heaven appeared to him and gave him strength. 44 In his anguish he prayed more earnestly, and his sweat became like great drops of blood falling down on the ground.]ʰ 45 When he got up from prayer, he came to the disciples and found them sleeping because of grief, 46 and he said to them, "Why are you sleeping? Get up and pray that you may not come into the time of trial."ᵍ

47 While he was still speaking, suddenly a crowd came, and the one called Judas, one of the twelve, was leading them. He approached Jesus to kiss him; 48 but Jesus said to him, "Judas, is it with a kiss that you are betraying the Son of Man?" 49 When those who were around him saw what was coming, they asked, "Lord, should we strike with the sword?" 50 Then one of them struck the slave of the high priest and cut off his right ear. 51 But Jesus said, "No more of this!" And he touched his ear and healed him. 52 Then Jesus said to the chief priests, the officers of the temple police, and the elders who had come for him, "Have you come out with swords and clubs as if I were a bandit? 53 When I was with you day after day in the temple, you did not lay hands on me. But this is your hour, and the power of darkness!"

54 Then they seized him and led him away, bringing him into the high priest's house. But Peter was following at a distance. 55 When they had kindled a fire in the middle of the courtyard and sat down together, Peter sat among them. 56 Then a servant-girl, seeing him in the firelight, stared at him and said, "This man also was with him." 57 But he denied it, saying, "Woman, I do not

---

ᵈOther ancient authorities lack, in whole or in part, verses 19b-20 (*which is given . . . in my blood*)   ᵉOr *has obtained permission*
ᶠGk *He*   ᵍOr *into temptation*   ʰOther ancient authorities lack verses 43 and 44

²⁰Isa 53:12

know him." 58 A little later someone else, on seeing him, said, "You also are one of them." But Peter said, "Man, I am not!" 59 Then about an hour later still another kept insisting, "Surely this man also was with him; for he is a Galilean." 60 But Peter said, "Man, I do not know what you are talking about!" At that moment, while he was still speaking, the cock crowed. 61 The Lord turned and looked at Peter. Then Peter remembered the word of the Lord, how he had said to him, "Before the cock crows today, you will deny me three times." 62 And he went out and wept bitterly.

63 Now the men who were holding Jesus began to mock him and beat him; 64 they also blindfolded him and kept asking him, "Prophesy! Who is it that struck you?" 65 They kept heaping many other insults on him.

66 When day came, the assembly of the elders of the people, both chief priests and scribes, gathered together, and they brought him to their council. 67 They said, "If you are the Messiah,[i] tell us." He replied, "If I tell you, you will not believe; 68 and if I question you, you will not answer. 69 But from now on the Son of Man will be seated at the right hand of the power of God."[21] 70 All of them asked, "Are you, then, the Son of God?" He said to them, "You say that I am." 71 Then they said, "What further testimony do we need? We have heard it ourselves from his own lips!"

23 Then the assembly rose as a body and brought Jesus[j] before Pilate. 2 They began to accuse him, saying, "We found this man perverting our nation, forbidding us to pay taxes to the emperor, and saying that he himself is the Messiah, a king."[k] 3 Then Pilate asked him, "Are you the king of the Jews?" He answered, "You say so." 4 Then Pilate said to the chief priests and the crowds, "I find no basis for an accusation against this man." 5 But they were insistent and said, "He stirs up the people by teaching throughout all Judea, from Galilee where he began even to this place."

6 When Pilate heard this, he asked whether the man was a Galilean. 7 And when he learned that he was under Herod's jurisdiction, he sent him off to Herod, who was himself in Jerusalem at that time. 8 When Herod saw Jesus, he was very glad, for he had been wanting to see him for a long time, because he had heard about him and was hoping to see him perform some sign. 9 He questioned him at some length, but Jesus[l] gave him no answer. 10 The chief priests and the scribes stood by, vehemently accusing him. 11 Even Herod with his soldiers treated him with contempt and mocked him; then he put an elegant robe on him, and sent him back to Pilate. 12 That same day Herod and Pilate became friends with each other; before this they had been enemies.

13 Pilate then called together the chief priests, the leaders, and the people, 14 and said to them, "You brought me this man as one who was perverting the people; and here I have examined him in your presence and have not found this man guilty of any of your charges against him. 15 Neither has Herod, for he sent him back to us. Indeed, he has done nothing to deserve death. 16 I will therefore have him flogged and release him."[m]

18 Then they all shouted out together, "Away with this fellow! Release Barabbas for us!" 19 (This was a man who had been put in prison for an insurrection that had taken place in the city, and for murder.) 20 Pilate, wanting to release Jesus, addressed them again; 21 but they kept shouting, "Crucify, crucify him!" 22 A third time he said to them, "Why, what evil has he done? I have found in him no ground for the sentence of death; I will therefore have him flogged and then release him." 23 But they kept urgently demanding with loud shouts that he should be crucified; and their voices prevailed. 24 So Pilate gave his verdict that their demand should be granted. 25 He released the man they asked for, the one who had been put in prison for insurrection and murder, and he handed Jesus over as they wished.

26 As they led him away, they seized a man, Simon of Cyrene, who was coming from the country, and they laid the cross on him, and made him carry it behind Jesus. 27 A great number of the people followed him, and among them were women who were beating their breasts and wailing for him. 28 But Jesus turned to them and said, "Daughters of Jerusalem, do not weep for me, but weep for yourselves and for your children. 29 For

---

[i] Or *the Christ* [j] Gk *him* [k] Or *is an anointed king* [l] Gk *he* [m] Here, or after verse 19, other ancient authorities add verse 17, *Now he was obliged to release someone for them at the festival*

---

[21] Ps 110:1; Dan 7:13

the days are surely coming when they will say, 'Blessed are the barren, and the wombs that never bore, and the breasts that never nursed.' 30 Then they will begin to say to the mountains, 'Fall on us'; and to the hills, 'Cover us.'[22] 31 For if they do this when the wood is green, what will happen when it is dry?"

32 Two others also, who were criminals, were led away to be put to death with him. 33 When they came to the place that is called The Skull, they crucified Jesus[n] there with the criminals, one on his right and one on his left. [34 Then Jesus said, "Father, forgive them; for they do not know what they are doing."][o] And they cast lots to divide his clothing. 35 And the people stood by, watching; but the leaders scoffed at him, saying, "He saved others; let him save himself if he is the Messiah[p] of God, his chosen one!" 36 The soldiers also mocked him, coming up and offering him sour wine, 37 and saying, "If you are the King of the Jews, save yourself!" 38 There was also an inscription over him,[q] "This is the King of the Jews."

39 One of the criminals who were hanged there kept deriding[r] him and saying, "Are you not the Messiah?[s] Save yourself and us!" 40 But the other rebuked him, saying, "Do you not fear God, since you are under the same sentence of condemnation? 41 And we indeed have been condemned justly, for we are getting what we deserve for our deeds, but this man has done nothing wrong." 42 Then he said, "Jesus, remember me when you come into[t] your kingdom." 43 He replied, "Truly I tell you, today you will be with me in Paradise."

44 It was now about noon, and darkness came over the whole land[u] until three in the afternoon, 45 while the sun's light failed;[v] and the curtain of the temple was torn in two. 46 Then Jesus, crying with a loud voice, said, "Father, into your hands I commend my spirit."[23] Having said this, he breathed his last. 47 When the centurion saw what had taken place, he praised God and said, "Certainly this man was innocent."[w] 48 And when all the crowds who had gathered there for this spectacle saw what had taken place, they returned home, beating their breasts. 49 But all his acquaintances, including the women who had followed him from Galilee, stood at a distance, watching these things.

50 Now there was a good and righteous man named Joseph, who, though a member of the council, 51 had not agreed to their plan and action. He came from the Jewish town of Arimathea, and he was waiting expectantly for the kingdom of God. 52 This man went to Pilate and asked for the body of Jesus. 53 Then he took it down, wrapped it in a linen cloth, and laid it in a rock-hewn tomb where no one had ever been laid. 54 It was the day of Preparation, and the sabbath was beginning.[x] 55 The women who had come with him from Galilee followed, and they saw the tomb and how his body was laid. 56 Then they returned, and prepared spices and ointments.

On the sabbath they rested according to the commandment.

24 But on the first day of the week, at early dawn, they came to the tomb, taking the spices that they had prepared. 2 They found the stone rolled away from the tomb, 3 but when they went in, they did not find the body.[y] 4 While they were perplexed about this, suddenly two men in dazzling clothes stood beside them. 5 The women[z] were terrified and bowed their faces to the ground, but the men[a] said to them, "Why do you look for the living among the dead? He is not here, but has risen.[b] 6 Remember how he told you, while he was still in Galilee, 7 that the Son of Man must be handed over to sinners, and be crucified, and on the third day rise again." 8 Then they remembered his words, 9 and returning from the tomb, they told all this to the eleven and to all the rest. 10 Now it was Mary Magdalene, Joanna, Mary the mother of James, and the other women with them who told this to the apostles. 11 But these words seemed to them an idle tale, and they did not believe them. 12 But Peter got up and ran to the tomb; stooping and looking in, he saw the linen cloths by themselves; then he went home, amazed at what had happened.[c]

13 Now on that same day two of them were go-

---

[n]Gk him   [o]Other ancient authorities lack the sentence *Then Jesus . . . what they are doing*   [p]Or *the Christ*   [q]Other ancient authorities add *written in Greek and Latin and Hebrew* (that is, *Aramaic*)   [r]Or *blaspheming*   [s]Or *the Christ*   [t]Other ancient authorities read *in*   [u]Or *earth*   [v]Or *the sun was eclipsed.* Other ancient authorities read *the sun was darkened*   [w]Or *righteous*   [x]Gk *was dawning*   [y]Other ancient authorities add *of the Lord Jesus*   [z]Gk *They*   [a]Gk *but they*   [b]Other ancient authorities lack *He is not here, but has risen*   [c]Other ancient authorities lack verse 12

[22]Hos 10:8   [23]Ps 31:5

ing to a village called Emmaus, about seven miles[d] from Jerusalem, 14 and talking with each other about all these things that had happened. 15 While they were talking and discussing, Jesus himself came near and went with them, 16 but their eyes were kept from recognizing him. 17 And he said to them, "What are you discussing with each other while you walk along?" They stood still, looking sad.[e] 18 Then one of them, whose name was Cleopas, answered him, "Are you the only stranger in Jerusalem who does not know the things that have taken place there in these days?" 19 He asked them, "What things?" They replied, "The things about Jesus of Nazareth,[f] who was a prophet mighty in deed and word before God and all the people, 20 and how our chief priests and leaders handed him over to be condemned to death and crucified him. 21 But we had hoped that he was the one to redeem Israel.[g] Yes, and besides all this, it is now the third day since these things took place. 22 Moreover, some women of our group astounded us. They were at the tomb early this morning, 23 and when they did not find his body there, they came back and told us that they had indeed seen a vision of angels who said that he was alive. 24 Some of those who were with us went to the tomb and found it just as the women had said; but they did not see him." 25 Then he said to them, "Oh, how foolish you are, and how slow of heart to believe all that the prophets have declared! 26 Was it not necessary that the Messiah[h] should suffer these things and then enter into his glory?" 27 Then beginning with Moses and all the prophets, he interpreted to them the things about himself in all the scriptures.

28 As they came near the village to which they were going, he walked ahead as if he were going on. 29 But they urged him strongly, saying, "Stay with us, because it is almost evening and the day is now nearly over." So he went in to stay with them. 30 When he was at the table with them, he took bread, blessed and broke it, and gave it to them. 31 Then their eyes were opened, and they recognized him; and he vanished from their sight. 32 They said to each other, "Were not our hearts burning within us[i] while he was talking to us on the road, while he was opening the scriptures to us?" 33 That same hour they got up and returned to Jerusalem; and they found the eleven and their companions gathered together. 34 They were saying, "The Lord has risen indeed, and he has appeared to Simon!" 35 Then they told what had happened on the road, and how he had been made known to them in the breaking of the bread.

36 While they were talking about this, Jesus himself stood among them and said to them, "Peace be with you."[j] 37 They were startled and terrified, and thought that they were seeing a ghost. 38 He said to them, "Why are you frightened, and why do doubts arise in your hearts? 39 Look at my hands and my feet; see that it is I myself. Touch me and see; for a ghost does not have flesh and bones as you see that I have." 40 And when he had said this, he showed them his hands and his feet.[k] 41 While in their joy they were disbelieving and still wondering, he said to them, "Have you anything here to eat?" 42 They gave him a piece of broiled fish, 43 and he took it and ate in their presence.

44 Then he said to them, "These are my words that I spoke to you while I was still with you—that everything written about me in the law of Moses, the prophets, and the psalms must be fulfilled." 45 Then he opened their minds to understand the scriptures, 46 and he said to them, "Thus it is written, that the Messiah[h] is to suffer and to rise from the dead on the third day, 47 and that repentance and forgiveness of sins is to be proclaimed in his name to all nations, beginning from Jerusalem. 48 You are witnesses[l] of these things. 49 And see, I am sending upon you what my Father promised; so stay here in the city until you have been clothed with power from on high."

50 Then he led them out as far as Bethany, and, lifting up his hands, he blessed them. 51 While he was blessing them, he withdrew from them and was carried up into heaven.[m] 52 And they worshiped him, and[n] returned to Jerusalem with great joy; 53 and they were continually in the temple blessing God.[o]

---

[d]Gk *sixty stadia;* other ancient authorities read *a hundred sixty stadia* [e]Other ancient authorities read *walk along, looking sad?"* [f]Other ancient authorities read *Jesus the Nazorean* [g]Or *to set Israel free* [h]Or *the Christ* [i]Other ancient authorities lack *within us* [j]Other ancient authorities lack *and said to them, "Peace be with you."* [k]Other ancient authorities lack verse 40 [l]Or *nations. Beginning from Jerusalem* [48]*you are witnesses* [m]Other ancient authorities lack *and was carried up into heaven* [n]Other ancient authorities lack *worshiped him, and* [o]Other ancient authorities add *Amen*

The Gospel According to John

Perennially one of the most beloved writings of the New Testament, the Gospel of John has always been recognized for its distinctive portrayal of Jesus. Here alone do we find Jesus turning the water into wine, raising Lazarus from the dead, and washing his disciples' feet. Here alone do we hear Jesus proclaim "I am the Light of the World," "I am the Bread of Life," "Before Abraham was, I am," and "I and the Father are one." Whereas in the other New Testament Gospels Jesus refuses to prove his identity by performing miraculous signs, here that is precisely what he does: his signs are performed and narrated to reveal his identity so that others might believe (cf. 2:10; 4:48; 20:30–31). Similarly, whereas in the other Gospels Jesus proclaims the coming kingdom of God but rarely speaks about himself, in this Gospel he proclaims almost nothing but himself and scarcely mentions the kingdom.

The Gospel has been traditionally ascribed to John, the son of Zebedee (a person never named in the narrative); as with the other New Testament Gospels, however, the book itself is anonymous. The author was clearly a Greek-speaking Christian; he evidently lived outside of Palestine. As one of his sources for his accounts, he claims to have used the testimony of one of Jesus' closest followers (19:35; 21:24), whom he never names but calls the "disciple whom Jesus loved" (21:7).

Scholars today widely recognize that the author utilized several written sources, including (a) a written account of Jesus' signs that may have been composed, originally, to convince Jews that Jesus was the Messiah (see, e.g., 2:1–10; 20:30–31); (b) one or more collections of Jesus' long speeches, including the "Farewell Discourse" that comprises all of chapters 14–17; and (c) the introductory hymn to Christ that serves as the Gospel's prologue (1:1–18).

These various sources arose within the author's own community, which evidently began as a group of Jews who came to believe in Jesus as the Messiah and eventually were expelled from their synagogue as a result of their belief, leading them to form a worshipping community of their own (see 9:22; 16:2). The community's various conflicts stimulated their theological reflections about the meaning and importance of Jesus, reflections that came to be embodied within the Gospel when it was written sometime near the end of the first century (ca. 90–95 C.E.).

As in the other Gospels, here Jesus continues to be portrayed as a Jewish rabbi, a great prophet, and a messiah sent from God to die for the sins of the world. But he is also far more. For here Jesus is said to be the one who reveals God; he is the embodiment of God's very Word, through which the world was made and by which all things have life (1:1–18). Those who see Jesus have seen the Father, those who believe in him have eternal life, those who reject him are subject to the wrathful judgment of God (3:36; 14:9). In short, for this Gospel, Jesus is God's very presence on earth, the one who came from the Father to reveal his identity and who at his death and exaltation returned to heaven to prepare a place for his people (14:2).

1

In the beginning was the Word, and the Word was with God, and the Word was God. 2 He was in the beginning with God. 3 All things came into being through him, and without him not one thing came into being. What has come into being 4 in him was life,[a] and the life was the light of all people. 5 The light shines in the darkness, and the darkness did not overcome it.

6 There was a man sent from God, whose name was John. 7 He came as a witness to testify to the light, so that all might believe through him. 8 He himself was not the light, but he came to testify to the light. 9 The true light, which enlightens everyone, was coming into the world.[b]

10 He was in the world, and the world came into being through him; yet the world did not know him. 11 He came to what was his own,[c] and his own people did not accept him. 12 But to all who received him, who believed in his name, he gave power to become children of God, 13 who were born, not of blood or of the will of the flesh or of the will of man, but of God.

14 And the Word became flesh and lived among us, and we have seen his glory, the glory as of a father's only son,[d] full of grace and truth. 15 (John testified to him and cried out, "This was he of whom I said, 'He who comes after me ranks ahead of me because he was before me.'") 16 From his fullness we have all received, grace upon grace. 17 The law indeed was given through Moses; grace and truth came through Jesus Christ. 18 No one has ever seen God. It is God the only Son,[e] who is close to the Father's heart,[f] who has made him known.

19 This is the testimony given by John when the Jews sent priests and Levites from Jerusalem to ask him, "Who are you?" 20 He confessed and did not deny it, but confessed, "I am not the Messiah."[g] 21 And they asked him, "What then? Are you Elijah?" He said, "I am not." "Are you the prophet?" He answered, "No." 22 Then they said to him, "Who are you? Let us have an answer for those who sent us. What do you say about yourself?" 23 He said,

"I am the voice of one crying out
    in the wilderness,
'Make straight the way of the
    Lord,'"[1]

as the prophet Isaiah said.

24 Now they had been sent from the Pharisees. 25 They asked him, "Why then are you baptizing if you are neither the Messiah,[g] nor Elijah, nor the prophet?" 26 John answered them, "I baptize with water. Among you stands one whom you do not know, 27 the one who is coming after me; I am not worthy to untie the thong of his sandal." 28 This took place in Bethany across the Jordan where John was baptizing.

29 The next day he saw Jesus coming toward him and declared, "Here is the Lamb of God who takes away the sin of the world! 30 This is he of whom I said, 'After me comes a man who ranks ahead of me because he was before me.' 31 I myself did not know him; but I came baptizing with water for this reason, that he might be revealed to Israel." 32 And John testified, "I saw the Spirit descending from heaven like a dove, and it remained on him. 33 I myself did not know him, but the one who sent me to baptize with water said to me, 'He on whom you see the Spirit descend and remain is the one who baptizes with the Holy Spirit.' 34 And I myself have seen and have testified that this is the Son of God."[h]

35 The next day John again was standing with two of his disciples, 36 and as he watched Jesus walk by, he exclaimed, "Look, here is the Lamb of God!" 37 The two disciples heard him say this, and they followed Jesus. 38 When Jesus turned and saw them following, he said to them, "What are you looking for?" They said to him, "Rabbi" (which translated means Teacher), "where are you staying?" 39 He said to them, "Come and see." They came and saw where he was staying, and they remained with him that day. It was about four o'clock in the afternoon. 40 One of the two who heard John speak and followed him was Andrew, Simon Peter's brother. 41 He first found his brother Simon and said to him, "We have found the Messiah" (which is translated Anointed [i]). 42 He brought Simon[j] to Jesus, who looked at him and

---

[a]Or [3]through him. And without him not one thing came into being that has come into being. [4]In him was life   [b]Or He was the true light that enlightens everyone coming into the world   [c]Or to his own home [d]Or the Father's only Son   [e]Other ancient authorities read It is an only Son, God, or It is the only Son   [f]Gk bosom [g]Or the Christ [h]Other ancient authorities read is God's chosen one   [i]Or Christ [j]Gk him

[1]Isa 40:3

said, "You are Simon son of John. You are to be called Cephas" (which is translated Peter[k]).

43 The next day Jesus decided to go to Galilee. He found Philip and said to him, "Follow me." 44 Now Philip was from Bethsaida, the city of Andrew and Peter. 45 Philip found Nathanael and said to him, "We have found him about whom Moses in the law and also the prophets wrote, Jesus son of Joseph from Nazareth." 46 Nathanael said to him, "Can anything good come out of Nazareth?" Philip said to him, "Come and see." 47 When Jesus saw Nathanael coming toward him, he said of him, "Here is truly an Israelite in whom there is no deceit!" 48 Nathanael asked him, "Where did you get to know me?" Jesus answered, "I saw you under the fig tree before Philip called you." 49 Nathanael replied, "Rabbi, you are the Son of God! You are the King of Israel!" 50 Jesus answered, "Do you believe because I told you that I saw you under the fig tree? You will see greater things than these." 51 And he said to him, "Very truly, I tell you,[l] you will see heaven opened and the angels of God ascending and descending upon the Son of Man."

2 On the third day there was a wedding in Cana of Galilee, and the mother of Jesus was there. 2 Jesus and his disciples had also been invited to the wedding. 3 When the wine gave out, the mother of Jesus said to him, "They have no wine." 4 And Jesus said to her, "Woman, what concern is that to you and to me? My hour has not yet come." 5 His mother said to the servants, "Do whatever he tells you." 6 Now standing there were six stone water jars for the Jewish rites of purification, each holding twenty or thirty gallons. 7 Jesus said to them, "Fill the jars with water." And they filled them up to the brim. 8 He said to them, "Now draw some out, and take it to the chief steward." So they took it. 9 When the steward tasted the water that had become wine, and did not know where it came from (though the servants who had drawn the water knew), the steward called the bridegroom 10 and said to him, "Everyone serves the good wine first, and then the inferior wine after the guests have become drunk. But you have kept the good wine until now." 11 Jesus did this, the first of his signs, in Cana of Galilee, and revealed his glory; and his disciples believed in him.

12 After this he went down to Capernaum with his mother, his brothers, and his disciples; and they remained there a few days.

13 The Passover of the Jews was near, and Jesus went up to Jerusalem. 14 In the temple he found people selling cattle, sheep, and doves, and the money changers seated at their tables. 15 Making a whip of cords, he drove all of them out of the temple, both the sheep and the cattle. He also poured out the coins of the money changers and overturned their tables. 16 He told those who were selling the doves, "Take these things out of here! Stop making my Father's house a marketplace!" 17 His disciples remembered that it was written, "Zeal for your house will consume me."[2] 18 The Jews then said to him, "What sign can you show us for doing this?" 19 Jesus answered them, "Destroy this temple, and in three days I will raise it up." 20 The Jews then said, "This temple has been under construction for forty-six years, and will you raise it up in three days?" 21 But he was speaking of the temple of his body. 22 After he was raised from the dead, his disciples remembered that he had said this; and they believed the scripture and the word that Jesus had spoken.

23 When he was in Jerusalem during the Passover festival, many believed in his name because they saw the signs that he was doing. 24 But Jesus on his part would not entrust himself to them, because he knew all people 25 and needed no one to testify about anyone; for he himself knew what was in everyone.

3 Now there was a Pharisee named Nicodemus, a leader of the Jews. 2 He came to Jesus[m] by night and said to him, "Rabbi, we know that you are a teacher who has come from God; for no one can do these signs that you do apart from the presence of God." 3 Jesus answered him, "Very truly, I tell you, no one can see the kingdom of God without being born from above."[n] 4 Nicodemus said to him, "How can anyone be born after having grown old? Can one enter a second time into the mother's womb and be born?" 5 Jesus answered, "Very truly, I tell you, no one can enter the kingdom of God without being born

---

[k]From the word for *rock* in Aramaic (*kepha*) and Greek (*petra*), respectively   [l]Both instances of the Greek word for *you* in this verse are plural   [m]Gk *him*   [n]Or *born anew*

[2]Ps 69:9

of water and Spirit. 6 What is born of the flesh is flesh, and what is born of the Spirit is spirit.º 7 Do not be astonished that I said to you, 'Youᵖ must be born from above.'ᑫ 8 The windº blows where it chooses, and you hear the sound of it, but you do not know where it comes from or where it goes. So it is with everyone who is born of the Spirit." 9 Nicodemus said to him, "How can these things be?" 10 Jesus answered him, "Are you a teacher of Israel, and yet you do not understand these things?

11 "Very truly, I tell you, we speak of what we know and testify to what we have seen; yet youʳ do not receive our testimony. 12 If I have told you about earthly things and you do not believe, how can you believe if I tell you about heavenly things? 13 No one has ascended into heaven except the one who descended from heaven, the Son of Man.ˢ 14 And just as Moses lifted up the serpent in the wilderness, so must the Son of Man be lifted up, 15 that whoever believes in him may have eternal life.ᵗ

16 "For God so loved the world that he gave his only Son, so that everyone who believes in him may not perish but may have eternal life.

17 "Indeed, God did not send the Son into the world to condemn the world, but in order that the world might be saved through him. 18 Those who believe in him are not condemned; but those who do not believe are condemned already, because they have not believed in the name of the only Son of God. 19 And this is the judgment, that the light has come into the world, and people loved darkness rather than light because their deeds were evil. 20 For all who do evil hate the light and do not come to the light, so that their deeds may not be exposed. 21 But those who do what is true come to the light, so that it may be clearly seen that their deeds have been done in God."ᵗ

22 After this Jesus and his disciples went into the Judean countryside, and he spent some time there with them and baptized. 23 John also was baptizing at Aenon near Salim because water was abundant there; and people kept coming and were being baptized 24 —John, of course, had not yet been thrown into prison.

25 Now a discussion about purification arose between John's disciples and a Jew.ᵘ 26 They came to John and said to him, "Rabbi, the one who was with you across the Jordan, to whom you testified, here he is baptizing, and all are going to him." 27 John answered, "No one can receive anything except what has been given from heaven. 28 You yourselves are my witnesses that I said, 'I am not the Messiah,ᵛ but I have been sent ahead of him.' 29 He who has the bride is the bridegroom. The friend of the bridegroom, who stands and hears him, rejoices greatly at the bridegroom's voice. For this reason my joy has been fulfilled. 30 He must increase, but I must decrease."ʷ

31 The one who comes from above is above all; the one who is of the earth belongs to the earth and speaks about earthly things. The one who comes from heaven is above all. 32 He testifies to what he has seen and heard, yet no one accepts his testimony. 33 Whoever has accepted his testimony has certifiedˣ this, that God is true. 34 He whom God has sent speaks the words of God, for he gives the Spirit without measure. 35 The Father loves the Son and has placed all things in his hands. 36 Whoever believes in the Son has eternal life; whoever disobeys the Son will not see life, but must endure God's wrath.

4 Now when Jesusʸ learned that the Pharisees had heard, "Jesus is making and baptizing more disciples than John" 2 —although it was not Jesus himself but his disciples who baptized— 3 he left Judea and started back to Galilee. 4 But he had to go through Samaria. 5 So he came to a Samaritan city called Sychar, near the plot of ground that Jacob had given to his son Joseph. 6 Jacob's well was there, and Jesus, tired out by his journey, was sitting by the well. It was about noon.

7 A Samaritan woman came to draw water, and Jesus said to her, "Give me a drink." 8 (His disciples had gone to the city to buy food.) 9 The Samaritan woman said to him, "How is it that you, a Jew, ask a drink of me, a woman of Samaria?" (Jews do not share things in common with Samaritans.)ᶻ 10 Jesus answered her, "If you knew the

---

ºThe same Greek word means both *wind* and *spirit* ᵖThe Greek word for *you* here is plural ᑫOr *anew* ʳThe Greek word for *you* here and in verse 12 is plural ˢOther ancient authorities add *who is in heaven* ᵗSome interpreters hold that the quotation concludes with verse 15 ᵘOther ancient authorities read *the Jews* ᵛOr *the Christ* ʷSome interpreters hold that the quotation continues through verse 36 ˣGk *set a seal to* ʸOther ancient authorities read *the Lord* ᶻOther ancient authorities lack this sentence

gift of God, and who it is that is saying to you, 'Give me a drink,' you would have asked him, and he would have given you living water." 11 The woman said to him, "Sir, you have no bucket, and the well is deep. Where do you get that living water? 12 Are you greater than our ancestor Jacob, who gave us the well, and with his sons and his flocks drank from it?" 13 Jesus said to her, "Everyone who drinks of this water will be thirsty again, 14 but those who drink of the water that I will give them will never be thirsty. The water that I will give will become in them a spring of water gushing up to eternal life." 15 The woman said to him, "Sir, give me this water, so that I may never be thirsty or have to keep coming here to draw water."

16 Jesus said to her, "Go, call your husband, and come back." 17 The woman answered him, "I have no husband." Jesus said to her, "You are right in saying, 'I have no husband'; 18 for you have had five husbands, and the one you have now is not your husband. What you have said is true!" 19 The woman said to him, "Sir, I see that you are a prophet. 20 Our ancestors worshiped on this mountain, but you[a] say that the place where people must worship is in Jerusalem." 21 Jesus said to her, "Woman, believe me, the hour is coming when you will worship the Father neither on this mountain nor in Jerusalem. 22 You worship what you do not know; we worship what we know, for salvation is from the Jews. 23 But the hour is coming, and is now here, when the true worshipers will worship the Father in spirit and truth, for the Father seeks such as these to worship him. 24 God is spirit, and those who worship him must worship in spirit and truth." 25 The woman said to him, "I know that Messiah is coming" (who is called Christ). "When he comes, he will proclaim all things to us." 26 Jesus said to her, "I am he,[b] the one who is speaking to you."

27 Just then his disciples came. They were astonished that he was speaking with a woman, but no one said, "What do you want?" or, "Why are you speaking with her?" 28 Then the woman left her water jar and went back to the city. She said to the people, 29 "Come and see a man who told me everything I have ever done! He cannot be the Messiah,[c] can he?" 30 They left the city and were on their way to him.

31 Meanwhile the disciples were urging him, "Rabbi, eat something." 32 But he said to them, "I have food to eat that you do not know about." 33 So the disciples said to one another, "Surely no one has brought him something to eat?" 34 Jesus said to them, "My food is to do the will of him who sent me and to complete his work. 35 Do you not say, 'Four months more, then comes the harvest'? But I tell you, look around you, and see how the fields are ripe for harvesting. 36 The reaper is already receiving[d] wages and is gathering fruit for eternal life, so that sower and reaper may rejoice together. 37 For here the saying holds true, 'One sows and another reaps.' 38 I sent you to reap that for which you did not labor. Others have labored, and you have entered into their labor."

39 Many Samaritans from that city believed in him because of the woman's testimony, "He told me everything I have ever done." 40 So when the Samaritans came to him, they asked him to stay with them; and he stayed there two days. 41 And many more believed because of his word. 42 They said to the woman, "It is no longer because of what you said that we believe, for we have heard for ourselves, and we know that this is truly the Savior of the world."

43 When the two days were over, he went from that place to Galilee 44 (for Jesus himself had testified that a prophet has no honor in the prophet's own country). 45 When he came to Galilee, the Galileans welcomed him, since they had seen all that he had done in Jerusalem at the festival; for they too had gone to the festival.

46 Then he came again to Cana in Galilee where he had changed the water into wine. Now there was a royal official whose son lay ill in Capernaum. 47 When he heard that Jesus had come from Judea to Galilee, he went and begged him to come down and heal his son, for he was at the point of death. 48 Then Jesus said to him, "Unless you[e] see signs and wonders you will not believe." 49 The official said to him, "Sir, come down before my little boy dies." 50 Jesus said to him, "Go; your son will live." The man believed the word that Jesus spoke to him and started on his way.

[a]The Greek word for *you* here and in verses 21 and 22 is plural
[b]Gk *I am*   [c]Or *the Christ*   [d]Or [35]. . . *the fields are already ripe for harvesting.* [36]*The reaper is receiving*   [e]Both instances of the Greek word for *you* in this verse are plural

51 As he was going down, his slaves met him and told him that his child was alive. 52 So he asked them the hour when he began to recover, and they said to him, "Yesterday at one in the afternoon the fever left him." 53 The father realized that this was the hour when Jesus had said to him, "Your son will live." So he himself believed, along with his whole household. 54 Now this was the second sign that Jesus did after coming from Judea to Galilee.

5 After this there was a festival of the Jews, and Jesus went up to Jerusalem.

2 Now in Jerusalem by the Sheep Gate there is a pool, called in Hebrew[f] Beth-zatha,[g] which has five porticoes. 3 In these lay many invalids— blind, lame, and paralyzed.[h] 5 One man was there who had been ill for thirty-eight years. 6 When Jesus saw him lying there and knew that he had been there a long time, he said to him, "Do you want to be made well?" 7 The sick man answered him, "Sir, I have no one to put me into the pool when the water is stirred up; and while I am making my way, someone else steps down ahead of me." 8 Jesus said to him, "Stand up, take your mat and walk." 9 At once the man was made well, and he took up his mat and began to walk.

Now that day was a sabbath. 10 So the Jews said to the man who had been cured, "It is the sabbath; it is not lawful for you to carry your mat." 11 But he answered them, "The man who made me well said to me, 'Take up your mat and walk.'" 12 They asked him, "Who is the man who said to you, 'Take it up and walk'?" 13 Now the man who had been healed did not know who it was, for Jesus had disappeared in[i] the crowd that was there. 14 Later Jesus found him in the temple and said to him, "See, you have been made well! Do not sin any more, so that nothing worse happens to you." 15 The man went away and told the Jews that it was Jesus who had made him well. 16 Therefore the Jews started persecuting Jesus, because he was doing such things on the sabbath. 17 But Jesus answered them, "My Father is still working, and I also am working." 18 For this reason the Jews were seeking all the more to kill him, because he was not only breaking the sabbath, but was also calling God his own Father, thereby making himself equal to God.

19 Jesus said to them, "Very truly, I tell you, the Son can do nothing on his own, but only what he sees the Father doing; for whatever the Father[j] does, the Son does likewise. 20 The Father loves the Son and shows him all that he himself is doing; and he will show him greater works than these, so that you will be astonished. 21 Indeed, just as the Father raises the dead and gives them life, so also the Son gives life to whomever he wishes. 22 The Father judges no one but has given all judgment to the Son, 23 so that all may honor the Son just as they honor the Father. Anyone who does not honor the Son does not honor the Father who sent him. 24 Very truly, I tell you, anyone who hears my word and believes him who sent me has eternal life, and does not come under judgment, but has passed from death to life.

25 "Very truly, I tell you, the hour is coming, and is now here, when the dead will hear the voice of the Son of God, and those who hear will live. 26 For just as the Father has life in himself, so he has granted the Son also to have life in himself; 27 and he has given him authority to execute judgment, because he is the Son of Man. 28 Do not be astonished at this; for the hour is coming when all who are in their graves will hear his voice 29 and will come out—those who have done good, to the resurrection of life, and those who have done evil, to the resurrection of condemnation.

30 "I can do nothing on my own. As I hear, I judge; and my judgment is just, because I seek to do not my own will but the will of him who sent me.

31 "If I testify about myself, my testimony is not true. 32 There is another who testifies on my behalf, and I know that his testimony to me is true. 33 You sent messengers to John, and he testified to the truth. 34 Not that I accept such human testimony, but I say these things so that you may be saved. 35 He was a burning and shining lamp, and you were willing to rejoice for a while in his light. 36 But I have a testimony greater than John's. The works that the Father has given me to complete,

[f]That is, *Aramaic*   [g]Other ancient authorities read *Bethesda*, others *Bethsaida*   [h]Other ancient authorities add, wholly or in part, *waiting for the stirring of the water; [4]for an angel of the Lord went down at certain seasons into the pool, and stirred up the water; whoever stepped in first after the stirring of the water was made well from whatever disease that person had.*   [i]Or *had left because of*   [j]Gk *that one*

the very works that I am doing, testify on my behalf that the Father has sent me. 37 And the Father who sent me has himself testified on my behalf. You have never heard his voice or seen his form, 38 and you do not have his word abiding in you, because you do not believe him whom he has sent.

39 "You search the scriptures because you think that in them you have eternal life; and it is they that testify on my behalf. 40 Yet you refuse to come to me to have life. 41 I do not accept glory from human beings. 42 But I know that you do not have the love of God in[k] you. 43 I have come in my Father's name, and you do not accept me; if another comes in his own name, you will accept him. 44 How can you believe when you accept glory from one another and do not seek the glory that comes from the one who alone is God? 45 Do not think that I will accuse you before the Father; your accuser is Moses, on whom you have set your hope. 46 If you believed Moses, you would believe me, for he wrote about me. 47 But if you do not believe what he wrote, how will you believe what I say?"

6 After this Jesus went to the other side of the Sea of Galilee, also called the Sea of Tiberias.[l] 2 A large crowd kept following him, because they saw the signs that he was doing for the sick. 3 Jesus went up the mountain and sat down there with his disciples. 4 Now the Passover, the festival of the Jews, was near. 5 When he looked up and saw a large crowd coming toward him, Jesus said to Philip, "Where are we to buy bread for these people to eat?" 6 He said this to test him, for he himself knew what he was going to do. 7 Philip answered him, "Six months' wages[m] would not buy enough bread for each of them to get a little." 8 One of his disciples, Andrew, Simon Peter's brother, said to him, 9 "There is a boy here who has five barley loaves and two fish. But what are they among so many people?" 10 Jesus said, "Make the people sit down." Now there was a great deal of grass in the place; so they[n] sat down, about five thousand in all. 11 Then Jesus took the loaves, and when he had given thanks, he distributed them to those who were seated; so also the fish, as much as they wanted. 12 When they were satisfied, he told his disciples, "Gather up the fragments left over, so that

nothing may be lost." 13 So they gathered them up, and from the fragments of the five barley loaves, left by those who had eaten, they filled twelve baskets. 14 When the people saw the sign that he had done, they began to say, "This is indeed the prophet who is to come into the world."

15 When Jesus realized that they were about to come and take him by force to make him king, he withdrew again to the mountain by himself.

16 When evening came, his disciples went down to the sea, 17 got into a boat, and started across the sea to Capernaum. It was now dark, and Jesus had not yet come to them. 18 The sea became rough because a strong wind was blowing. 19 When they had rowed about three or four miles,[o] they saw Jesus walking on the sea and coming near the boat, and they were terrified. 20 But he said to them, "It is I;[p] do not be afraid." 21 Then they wanted to take him into the boat, and immediately the boat reached the land toward which they were going.

22 The next day the crowd that had stayed on the other side of the sea saw that there had been only one boat there. They also saw that Jesus had not got into the boat with his disciples, but that his disciples had gone away alone. 23 Then some boats from Tiberias came near the place where they had eaten the bread after the Lord had given thanks.[q] 24 So when the crowd saw that neither Jesus nor his disciples were there, they themselves got into the boats and went to Capernaum looking for Jesus.

25 When they found him on the other side of the sea, they said to him, "Rabbi, when did you come here?" 26 Jesus answered them, "Very truly, I tell you, you are looking for me, not because you saw signs, but because you ate your fill of the loaves. 27 Do not work for the food that perishes, but for the food that endures for eternal life, which the Son of Man will give you. For it is on him that God the Father has set his seal." 28 Then they said to him, "What must we do to perform the works of God?" 29 Jesus answered them, "This is the work of God, that you believe in him whom he has sent." 30 So they said to him, "What sign are you going to give us then, so that we may see it and believe

[k]Or *among*   [l]Gk *of Galilee of Tiberias*   [m]Gk *Two hundred denarii*; the denarius was the usual day's wage for a laborer   [n]Gk *the men* [o]Gk *about twenty-five or thirty stadia*   [p]Gk *I am*   [q]Other ancient authorities lack *after the Lord had given thanks*

you? What work are you performing? 31 Our ancestors ate the manna in the wilderness; as it is written, 'He gave them bread from heaven to eat.'"[3] 32 Then Jesus said to them, "Very truly, I tell you, it was not Moses who gave you the bread from heaven, but it is my Father who gives you the true bread from heaven. 33 For the bread of God is that which[r] comes down from heaven and gives life to the world." 34 They said to him, "Sir, give us this bread always."

35 Jesus said to them, "I am the bread of life. Whoever comes to me will never be hungry, and whoever believes in me will never be thirsty. 36 But I said to you that you have seen me and yet do not believe. 37 Everything that the Father gives me will come to me, and anyone who comes to me I will never drive away; 38 for I have come down from heaven, not to do my own will, but the will of him who sent me. 39 And this is the will of him who sent me, that I should lose nothing of all that he has given me, but raise it up on the last day. 40 This is indeed the will of my Father, that all who see the Son and believe in him may have eternal life; and I will raise them up on the last day."

41 Then the Jews began to complain about him because he said, "I am the bread that came down from heaven." 42 They were saying, "Is not this Jesus, the son of Joseph, whose father and mother we know? How can he now say, 'I have come down from heaven'?" 43 Jesus answered them, "Do not complain among yourselves. 44 No one can come to me unless drawn by the Father who sent me; and I will raise that person up on the last day. 45 It is written in the prophets, 'And they shall all be taught by God.'[4] Everyone who has heard and learned from the Father comes to me. 46 Not that anyone has seen the Father except the one who is from God; he has seen the Father. 47 Very truly, I tell you, whoever believes has eternal life. 48 I am the bread of life. 49 Your ancestors ate the manna in the wilderness, and they died. 50 This is the bread that comes down from heaven, so that one may eat of it and not die. 51 I am the living bread that came down from heaven. Whoever eats of this bread will live forever; and the bread that I will give for the life of the world is my flesh."

52 The Jews then disputed among themselves, saying, "How can this man give us his flesh to eat?" 53 So Jesus said to them, "Very truly, I tell you, unless you eat the flesh of the Son of Man and drink his blood, you have no life in you. 54 Those who eat my flesh and drink my blood have eternal life, and I will raise them up on the last day; 55 for my flesh is true food and my blood is true drink. 56 Those who eat my flesh and drink my blood abide in me, and I in them. 57 Just as the living Father sent me, and I live because of the Father, so whoever eats me will live because of me. 58 This is the bread that came down from heaven, not like that which your ancestors ate, and they died. But the one who eats this bread will live forever." 59 He said these things while he was teaching in the synagogue at Capernaum.

60 When many of his disciples heard it, they said, "This teaching is difficult; who can accept it?" 61 But Jesus, being aware that his disciples were complaining about it, said to them, "Does this offend you? 62 Then what if you were to see the Son of Man ascending to where he was before? 63 It is the spirit that gives life; the flesh is useless. The words that I have spoken to you are spirit and life. 64 But among you there are some who do not believe." For Jesus knew from the first who were the ones that did not believe, and who was the one that would betray him. 65 And he said, "For this reason I have told you that no one can come to me unless it is granted by the Father."

66 Because of this many of his disciples turned back and no longer went about with him. 67 So Jesus asked the twelve, "Do you also wish to go away?" 68 Simon Peter answered him, "Lord, to whom can we go? You have the words of eternal life. 69 We have come to believe and know that you are the Holy One of God."[s] 70 Jesus answered them, "Did I not choose you, the twelve? Yet one of you is a devil." 71 He was speaking of Judas son of Simon Iscariot,[t] for he, though one of the twelve, was going to betray him.

7 After this Jesus went about in Galilee. He did not wish[u] to go about in Judea because

---

[r] Or *he who* [s] Other ancient authorities read *the Christ, the Son of the living God* [t] Other ancient authorities read *Judas Iscariot son of Simon;* others, *Judas son of Simon from Karyot* (Kerioth) [u] Other ancient authorities read *was not at liberty*

[3] Ps 78:24 [4] Isa 54:13

the Jews were looking for an opportunity to kill him. 2 Now the Jewish festival of Booths[v] was near. 3 So his brothers said to him, "Leave here and go to Judea so that your disciples also may see the works you are doing; 4 for no one who wants[w] to be widely known acts in secret. If you do these things, show yourself to the world." 5 (For not even his brothers believed in him.) 6 Jesus said to them, "My time has not yet come, but your time is always here. 7 The world cannot hate you, but it hates me because I testify against it that its works are evil. 8 Go to the festival yourselves. I am not[x] going to this festival, for my time has not yet fully come." 9 After saying this, he remained in Galilee.

10 But after his brothers had gone to the festival, then he also went, not publicly but as it were[y] in secret. 11 The Jews were looking for him at the festival and saying, "Where is he?" 12 And there was considerable complaining about him among the crowds. While some were saying, "He is a good man," others were saying, "No, he is deceiving the crowd." 13 Yet no one would speak openly about him for fear of the Jews.

14 About the middle of the festival Jesus went up into the temple and began to teach. 15 The Jews were astonished at it, saying, "How does this man have such learning,[z] when he has never been taught?" 16 Then Jesus answered them, "My teaching is not mine but his who sent me. 17 Anyone who resolves to do the will of God will know whether the teaching is from God or whether I am speaking on my own. 18 Those who speak on their own seek their own glory; but the one who seeks the glory of him who sent him is true, and there is nothing false in him.

19 "Did not Moses give you the law? Yet none of you keeps the law. Why are you looking for an opportunity to kill me?" 20 The crowd answered, "You have a demon! Who is trying to kill you?" 21 Jesus answered them, "I performed one work, and all of you are astonished. 22 Moses gave you circumcision (it is, of course, not from Moses, but from the patriarchs), and you circumcise a man on the sabbath. 23 If a man receives circumcision on the sabbath in order that the law of Moses may not be broken, are you angry with me because I healed a man's whole body on the sabbath? 24 Do

not judge by appearances, but judge with right judgment."

25 Now some of the people of Jerusalem were saying, "Is not this the man whom they are trying to kill? 26 And here he is, speaking openly, but they say nothing to him! Can it be that the authorities really know that this is the Messiah?[a] 27 Yet we know where this man is from; but when the Messiah[a] comes, no one will know where he is from." 28 Then Jesus cried out as he was teaching in the temple, "You know me, and you know where I am from. I have not come on my own. But the one who sent me is true, and you do not know him. 29 I know him, because I am from him, and he sent me." 30 Then they tried to arrest him, but no one laid hands on him, because his hour had not yet come. 31 Yet many in the crowd believed in him and were saying, "When the Messiah[a] comes, will he do more signs than this man has done?"[b]

32 The Pharisees heard the crowd muttering such things about him, and the chief priests and Pharisees sent temple police to arrest him. 33 Jesus then said, "I will be with you a little while longer, and then I am going to him who sent me. 34 You will search for me, but you will not find me; and where I am, you cannot come." 35 The Jews said to one another, "Where does this man intend to go that we will not find him? Does he intend to go to the Dispersion among the Greeks and teach the Greeks? 36 What does he mean by saying, 'You will search for me and you will not find me' and 'Where I am, you cannot come'?"

37 On the last day of the festival, the great day, while Jesus was standing there, he cried out, "Let anyone who is thirsty come to me, 38 and let the one who believes in me drink. As[c] the scripture has said, 'Out of the believer's heart[d] shall flow rivers of living water.'" 39 Now he said this about the Spirit, which believers in him were to receive; for as yet there was no Spirit,[e] because Jesus was not yet glorified.

40 When they heard these words, some in the

[v]Or *Tabernacles* [w]Other ancient authorities read *wants i* [x]Other ancient authorities add *yet* [y]Other ancient authorities lack *as it were* [z]Or *this man know his letters* [a]Or *the Christ* [b]Other ancient authorities read *is doing* [c]Or *come to me and drink.* [38]*The one who believes in me, as* [d]Gk *out of his belly* [e]Other ancient authorities read *for as yet the Spirit* (others, *Holy Spirit*) *had not been given*

crowd said, "This is really the prophet." 41 Others said, "This is the Messiah."[f] But some asked, "Surely the Messiah[f] does not come from Galilee, does he? 42 Has not the scripture said that the Messiah[f] is descended from David and comes from Bethlehem, the village where David lived?" 43 So there was a division in the crowd because of him. 44 Some of them wanted to arrest him, but no one laid hands on him.

45 Then the temple police went back to the chief priests and Pharisees, who asked them, "Why did you not arrest him?" 46 The police answered, "Never has anyone spoken like this!" 47 Then the Pharisees replied, "Surely you have not been deceived too, have you? 48 Has any one of the authorities or of the Pharisees believed in him? 49 But this crowd, which does not know the law—they are accursed." 50 Nicodemus, who had gone to Jesus[g] before, and who was one of them, asked, 51 "Our law does not judge people without first giving them a hearing to find out what they are doing, does it?" 52 They replied, "Surely you are not also from Galilee, are you? Search and you will see that no prophet is to arise from Galilee."

8 [53 Then each of them went home, 1 while Jesus went to the Mount of Olives. 2 Early in the morning he came again to the temple. All the people came to him and he sat down and began to teach them. 3 The scribes and the Pharisees brought a woman who had been caught in adultery; and making her stand before all of them, 4 they said to him, "Teacher, this woman was caught in the very act of committing adultery. 5 Now in the law Moses commanded us to stone such women. Now what do you say?" 6 They said this to test him, so that they might have some charge to bring against him. Jesus bent down and wrote with his finger on the ground. 7 When they kept on questioning him, he straightened up and said to them, "Let anyone among you who is without sin be the first to throw a stone at her." 8 And once again he bent down and wrote on the ground.[h] 9 When they heard it, they went away, one by one, beginning with the elders; and Jesus was left alone with the woman standing before him. 10 Jesus straightened up and said to her, "Woman, where are they? Has no one condemned you?" 11 She said, "No one, sir."[i] And Jesus said, "Neither do I condemn you. Go your way, and from now on do not sin again."][j]

12 Again Jesus spoke to them, saying, "I am the light of the world. Whoever follows me will never walk in darkness but will have the light of life." 13 Then the Pharisees said to him, "You are testifying on your own behalf; your testimony is not valid." 14 Jesus answered, "Even if I testify on my own behalf, my testimony is valid because I know where I have come from and where I am going, but you do not know where I come from or where I am going. 15 You judge by human standards;[k] I judge no one. 16 Yet even if I do judge, my judgment is valid; for it is not I alone who judge, but I and the Father[l] who sent me. 17 In your law it is written that the testimony of two witnesses is valid. 18 I testify on my own behalf, and the Father who sent me testifies on my behalf." 19 Then they said to him, "Where is your Father?" Jesus answered, "You know neither me nor my Father. If you knew me, you would know my Father also." 20 He spoke these words while he was teaching in the treasury of the temple, but no one arrested him, because his hour had not yet come.

21 Again he said to them, "I am going away, and you will search for me, but you will die in your sin. Where I am going, you cannot come." 22 Then the Jews said, "Is he going to kill himself? Is that what he means by saying, 'Where I am going, you cannot come'?" 23 He said to them, "You are from below, I am from above; you are of this world, I am not of this world. 24 I told you that you would die in your sins, for you will die in your sins unless you believe that I am he."[m] 25 They said to him, "Who are you?" Jesus said to them, "Why do I speak to you at all?[n] 26 I have much to say about you and much to condemn; but the one who sent me is true, and I declare to the world what I have heard from him." 27 They did not understand that he was speaking to them about the Father. 28 So Jesus said, "When you have lifted up

[f] Or *the Christ*   [g] Gk *him*   [h] Other ancient authorities add *the sins of each of them*   [i] Or *Lord*   [j] The most ancient authorities lack 7.53— 8.11; other authorities add the passage here or after 7.36 or after 21.25 or after Luke 21.38, with variations of text; some mark the passage as doubtful.   [k] Gk *according to the flesh*   [l] Other ancient authorities read *he*   [m] Gk *I am*   [n] Or *What I have told you from the beginning*

the Son of Man, then you will realize that I am he,[o] and that I do nothing on my own, but I speak these things as the Father instructed me. 29 And the one who sent me is with me; he has not left me alone, for I always do what is pleasing to him." 30 As he was saying these things, many believed in him.

31 Then Jesus said to the Jews who had believed in him, "If you continue in my word, you are truly my disciples; 32 and you will know the truth, and the truth will make you free." 33 They answered him, "We are descendants of Abraham and have never been slaves to anyone. What do you mean by saying, 'You will be made free'?"

34 Jesus answered them, "Very truly, I tell you, everyone who commits sin is a slave to sin. 35 The slave does not have a permanent place in the household; the son has a place there forever. 36 So if the Son makes you free, you will be free indeed. 37 I know that you are descendants of Abraham; yet you look for an opportunity to kill me, because there is no place in you for my word. 38 I declare what I have seen in the Father's presence; as for you, you should do what you have heard from the Father."[p]

39 They answered him, "Abraham is our father." Jesus said to them, "If you were Abraham's children, you would be doing[q] what Abraham did, 40 but now you are trying to kill me, a man who has told you the truth that I heard from God. This is not what Abraham did. 41 You are indeed doing what your father does." They said to him, "We are not illegitimate children; we have one father, God himself." 42 Jesus said to them, "If God were your Father, you would love me, for I came from God and now I am here. I did not come on my own, but he sent me. 43 Why do you not understand what I say? It is because you cannot accept my word. 44 You are from your father the devil, and you choose to do your father's desires. He was a murderer from the beginning and does not stand in the truth, because there is no truth in him. When he lies, he speaks according to his own nature, for he is a liar and the father of lies. 45 But because I tell the truth, you do not believe me. 46 Which of you convicts me of sin? If I tell the truth, why do you not believe me? 47 Whoever is from God hears the words of God. The reason you do not hear them is that you are not from God."

48 The Jews answered him, "Are we not right in saying that you are a Samaritan and have a demon?" 49 Jesus answered, "I do not have a demon; but I honor my Father, and you dishonor me. 50 Yet I do not seek my own glory; there is one who seeks it and he is the judge. 51 Very truly, I tell you, whoever keeps my word will never see death." 52 The Jews said to him, "Now we know that you have a demon. Abraham died, and so did the prophets; yet you say, 'Whoever keeps my word will never taste death.' 53 Are you greater than our father Abraham, who died? The prophets also died. Who do you claim to be?" 54 Jesus answered, "If I glorify myself, my glory is nothing. It is my Father who glorifies me, he of whom you say, 'He is our God,' 55 though you do not know him. But I know him; if I would say that I do not know him, I would be a liar like you. But I do know him and I keep his word. 56 Your ancestor Abraham rejoiced that he would see my day; he saw it and was glad." 57 Then the Jews said to him, "You are not yet fifty years old, and have you seen Abraham?"[r] 58 Jesus said to them, "Very truly, I tell you, before Abraham was, I am." 59 So they picked up stones to throw at him, but Jesus hid himself and went out of the temple.

9 As he walked along, he saw a man blind from birth. 2 His disciples asked him, "Rabbi, who sinned, this man or his parents, that he was born blind?" 3 Jesus answered, "Neither this man nor his parents sinned; he was born blind so that God's works might be revealed in him. 4 We[s] must work the works of him who sent me[t] while it is day; night is coming when no one can work. 5 As long as I am in the world, I am the light of the world." 6 When he had said this, he spat on the ground and made mud with the saliva and spread the mud on the man's eyes, 7 saying to him, "Go, wash in the pool of Siloam" (which means Sent). Then he went and washed and came back able to see. 8 The neighbors and those who had seen him before as a beggar began to ask, "Is this not the man who used to sit and beg?" 9 Some were say-

---

[o]Gk *I am* [p]Other ancient authorities read *you do what you have heard from your father* [q]Other ancient authorities read *If you are Abraham's children, then do* [r]Other ancient authorities read *has Abraham seen you?* [s]Other ancient authorities read *I* [t]Other ancient authorities read *us*

ing, "It is he." Others were saying, "No, but it is someone like him." He kept saying, "I am the man." 10 But they kept asking him, "Then how were your eyes opened?" 11 He answered, "The man called Jesus made mud, spread it on my eyes, and said to me, 'Go to Siloam and wash.' Then I went and washed and received my sight." 12 They said to him, "Where is he?" He said, "I do not know."

13 They brought to the Pharisees the man who had formerly been blind. 14 Now it was a sabbath day when Jesus made the mud and opened his eyes. 15 Then the Pharisees also began to ask him how he had received his sight. He said to them, "He put mud on my eyes. Then I washed, and now I see." 16 Some of the Pharisees said, "This man is not from God, for he does not observe the sabbath." But others said, "How can a man who is a sinner perform such signs?" And they were divided. 17 So they said again to the blind man, "What do you say about him? It was your eyes he opened." He said, "He is a prophet."

18 The Jews did not believe that he had been blind and had received his sight until they called the parents of the man who had received his sight 19 and asked them, "Is this your son, who you say was born blind? How then does he now see?" 20 His parents answered, "We know that this is our son, and that he was born blind; 21 but we do not know how it is that now he sees, nor do we know who opened his eyes. Ask him; he is of age. He will speak for himself." 22 His parents said this because they were afraid of the Jews; for the Jews had already agreed that anyone who confessed Jesus[u] to be the Messiah[v] would be put out of the synagogue. 23 Therefore his parents said, "He is of age; ask him."

24 So for the second time they called the man who had been blind, and they said to him, "Give glory to God! We know that this man is a sinner." 25 He answered, "I do not know whether he is a sinner. One thing I do know, that though I was blind, now I see." 26 They said to him, "What did he do to you? How did he open your eyes?" 27 He answered them, "I have told you already, and you would not listen. Why do you want to hear it again? Do you also want to become his disciples?" 28 Then they reviled him, saying, "You are his dis-

ciple, but we are disciples of Moses. 29 We know that God has spoken to Moses, but as for this man, we do not know where he comes from." 30 The man answered, "Here is an astonishing thing! You do not know where he comes from, and yet he opened my eyes. 31 We know that God does not listen to sinners, but he does listen to one who worships him and obeys his will. 32 Never since the world began has it been heard that anyone opened the eyes of a person born blind. 33 If this man were not from God, he could do nothing." 34 They answered him, "You were born entirely in sins, and are you trying to teach us?" And they drove him out.

35 Jesus heard that they had driven him out, and when he found him, he said, "Do you believe in the Son of Man?"[w] 36 He answered, "And who is he, sir?[x] Tell me, so that I may believe in him." 37 Jesus said to him, "You have seen him, and the one speaking with you is he." 38 He said, "Lord,[x] I believe." And he worshiped him. 39 Jesus said, "I came into this world for judgment so that those who do not see may see, and those who do see may become blind." 40 Some of the Pharisees near him heard this and said to him, "Surely we are not blind, are we?" 41 Jesus said to them, "If you were blind, you would not have sin. But now that you say, 'We see,' your sin remains.

10 "Very truly, I tell you, anyone who does not enter the sheepfold by the gate but climbs in by another way is a thief and a bandit. 2 The one who enters by the gate is the shepherd of the sheep. 3 The gatekeeper opens the gate for him, and the sheep hear his voice. He calls his own sheep by name and leads them out. 4 When he has brought out all his own, he goes ahead of them, and the sheep follow him because they know his voice. 5 They will not follow a stranger, but they will run from him because they do not know the voice of strangers." 6 Jesus used this figure of speech with them, but they did not understand what he was saying to them.

7 So again Jesus said to them, "Very truly, I tell you, I am the gate for the sheep. 8 All who came before me are thieves and bandits; but the sheep

---

[u]Gk *him* [v]Or *the Christ* [w]Other ancient authorities read *the Son of God* [x]*Sir* and *Lord* translate the same Greek word

did not listen to them. 9 I am the gate. Whoever enters by me will be saved, and will come in and go out and find pasture. 10 The thief comes only to steal and kill and destroy. I came that they may have life, and have it abundantly.

11 "I am the good shepherd. The good shepherd lays down his life for the sheep. 12 The hired hand, who is not the shepherd and does not own the sheep, sees the wolf coming and leaves the sheep and runs away—and the wolf snatches them and scatters them. 13 The hired hand runs away because a hired hand does not care for the sheep. 14 I am the good shepherd. I know my own and my own know me, 15 just as the Father knows me and I know the Father. And I lay down my life for the sheep. 16 I have other sheep that do not belong to this fold. I must bring them also, and they will listen to my voice. So there will be one flock, one shepherd. 17 For this reason the Father loves me, because I lay down my life in order to take it up again. 18 No one takes[y] it from me, but I lay it down of my own accord. I have power to lay it down, and I have power to take it up again. I have received this command from my Father."

19 Again the Jews were divided because of these words. 20 Many of them were saying, "He has a demon and is out of his mind. Why listen to him?" 21 Others were saying, "These are not the words of one who has a demon. Can a demon open the eyes of the blind?"

22 At that time the festival of the Dedication took place in Jerusalem. It was winter, 23 and Jesus was walking in the temple, in the portico of Solomon. 24 So the Jews gathered around him and said to him, "How long will you keep us in suspense? If you are the Messiah,[z] tell us plainly." 25 Jesus answered, "I have told you, and you do not believe. The works that I do in my Father's name testify to me; 26 but you do not believe, because you do not belong to my sheep. 27 My sheep hear my voice. I know them, and they follow me. 28 I give them eternal life, and they will never perish. No one will snatch them out of my hand. 29 What my Father has given me is greater than all else, and no one can snatch it out of the Father's hand.[a] 30 The Father and I are one."

31 The Jews took up stones again to stone him. 32 Jesus replied, "I have shown you many good works from the Father. For which of these are you going to stone me?" 33 The Jews answered, "It is not for a good work that we are going to stone you, but for blasphemy, because you, though only a human being, are making yourself God." 34 Jesus answered, "Is it not written in your law,[b] 'I said, you are gods'?[5] 35 If those to whom the word of God came were called 'gods'—and the scripture cannot be annulled— 36 can you say that the one whom the Father has sanctified and sent into the world is blaspheming because I said, 'I am God's Son'? 37 If I am not doing the works of my Father, then do not believe me. 38 But if I do them, even though you do not believe me, believe the works, so that you may know and understand[c] that the Father is in me and I am in the Father." 39 Then they tried to arrest him again, but he escaped from their hands.

40 He went away again across the Jordan to the place where John had been baptizing earlier, and he remained there. 41 Many came to him, and they were saying, "John performed no sign, but everything that John said about this man was true." 42 And many believed in him there.

11 Now a certain man was ill, Lazarus of Bethany, the village of Mary and her sister Martha. 2 Mary was the one who anointed the Lord with perfume and wiped his feet with her hair; her brother Lazarus was ill. 3 So the sisters sent a message to Jesus,[d] "Lord, he whom you love is ill." 4 But when Jesus heard it, he said, "This illness does not lead to death; rather it is for God's glory, so that the Son of God may be glorified through it." 5 Accordingly, though Jesus loved Martha and her sister and Lazarus, 6 after having heard that Lazarus[e] was ill, he stayed two days longer in the place where he was.

7 Then after this he said to the disciples, "Let us go to Judea again." 8 The disciples said to him, "Rabbi, the Jews were just now trying to stone you, and are you going there again?" 9 Jesus answered, "Are there not twelve hours of daylight? Those who walk during the day do not stumble,

---

[y]Other ancient authorities read *has taken* [z]Or *the Christ* [a]Other ancient authorities read *My Father who has given them to me is greater than all, and no one can snatch them out of the Father's hand* [b]Other ancient authorities read *in the law* [c]Other ancient authorities lack *and understand*; others read *and believe* [d]Gk *him* [e]Gk *he*

[5]Ps 82:6

because they see the light of this world. 10 But those who walk at night stumble, because the light is not in them." 11 After saying this, he told them, "Our friend Lazarus has fallen asleep, but I am going there to awaken him." 12 The disciples said to him, "Lord, if he has fallen asleep, he will be all right." 13 Jesus, however, had been speaking about his death, but they thought that he was referring merely to sleep. 14 Then Jesus told them plainly, "Lazarus is dead. 15 For your sake I am glad I was not there, so that you may believe. But let us go to him." 16 Thomas, who was called the Twin,[f] said to his fellow disciples, "Let us also go, that we may die with him."

17 When Jesus arrived, he found that Lazarus-[g]had already been in the tomb four days. 18 Now Bethany was near Jerusalem, some two miles[h] away, 19 and many of the Jews had come to Martha and Mary to console them about their brother. 20 When Martha heard that Jesus was coming, she went and met him, while Mary stayed at home. 21 Martha said to Jesus, "Lord, if you had been here, my brother would not have died. 22 But even now I know that God will give you whatever you ask of him." 23 Jesus said to her, "Your brother will rise again." 24 Martha said to him, "I know that he will rise again in the resurrection on the last day." 25 Jesus said to her, "I am the resurrection and the life.[i] Those who believe in me, even though they die, will live, 26 and everyone who lives and believes in me will never die. Do you believe this?" 27 She said to him, "Yes, Lord, I believe that you are the Messiah,[j] the Son of God, the one coming into the world."

28 When she had said this, she went back and called her sister Mary, and told her privately, "The Teacher is here and is calling for you." 29 And when she heard it, she got up quickly and went to him. 30 Now Jesus had not yet come to the village, but was still at the place where Martha had met him. 31 The Jews who were with her in the house, consoling her, saw Mary get up quickly and go out. They followed her because they thought that she was going to the tomb to weep there. 32 When Mary came where Jesus was and saw him, she knelt at his feet and said to him, "Lord, if you had been here, my brother would not have died." 33 When Jesus saw her weeping, and the Jews who came with her also weeping, he was

greatly disturbed in spirit and deeply moved. 34 He said, "Where have you laid him?" They said to him, "Lord, come and see." 35 Jesus began to weep. 36 So the Jews said, "See how he loved him!" 37 But some of them said, "Could not he who opened the eyes of the blind man have kept this man from dying?"

38 Then Jesus, again greatly disturbed, came to the tomb. It was a cave, and a stone was lying against it. 39 Jesus said, "Take away the stone." Martha, the sister of the dead man, said to him, "Lord, already there is a stench because he has been dead four days." 40 Jesus said to her, "Did I not tell you that if you believed, you would see the glory of God?" 41 So they took away the stone. And Jesus looked upward and said, "Father, I thank you for having heard me. 42 I knew that you always hear me, but I have said this for the sake of the crowd standing here, so that they may believe that you sent me." 43 When he had said this, he cried with a loud voice, "Lazarus, come out!" 44 The dead man came out, his hands and feet bound with strips of cloth, and his face wrapped in a cloth. Jesus said to them, "Unbind him, and let him go."

45 Many of the Jews therefore, who had come with Mary and had seen what Jesus did, believed in him. 46 But some of them went to the Pharisees and told them what he had done. 47 So the chief priests and the Pharisees called a meeting of the council, and said, "What are we to do? This man is performing many signs. 48 If we let him go on like this, everyone will believe in him, and the Romans will come and destroy both our holy place[k] and our nation." 49 But one of them, Caiaphas, who was high priest that year, said to them, "You know nothing at all! 50 You do not understand that it is better for you to have one man die for the people than to have the whole nation destroyed." 51 He did not say this on his own, but being high priest that year he prophesied that Jesus was about to die for the nation, 52 and not for the nation only, but to gather into one the dispersed children of God. 53 So from that day on they planned to put him to death.

54 Jesus therefore no longer walked about open-

---

[f]Gk *Didymus*   [g]Gk *he*   [h]Gk *fifteen stadia*   [i]Other ancient authorities lack *and the life*   [j]Or *the Christ*   [k]Or *our temple*; Greek *our place*

ly among the Jews, but went from there to a town called Ephraim in the region near the wilderness; and he remained there with the disciples.

55 Now the Passover of the Jews was near, and many went up from the country to Jerusalem before the Passover to purify themselves. 56 They were looking for Jesus and were asking one another as they stood in the temple, "What do you think? Surely he will not come to the festival, will he?" 57 Now the chief priests and the Pharisees had given orders that anyone who knew where Jesus[l] was should let them know, so that they might arrest him.

12 Six days before the Passover Jesus came to Bethany, the home of Lazarus, whom he had raised from the dead. 2 There they gave a dinner for him. Martha served, and Lazarus was one of those at the table with him. 3 Mary took a pound of costly perfume made of pure nard, anointed Jesus' feet, and wiped them[m] with her hair. The house was filled with the fragrance of the perfume. 4 But Judas Iscariot, one of his disciples (the one who was about to betray him), said, 5 "Why was this perfume not sold for three hundred denarii[n] and the money given to the poor?" 6 (He said this not because he cared about the poor, but because he was a thief; he kept the common purse and used to steal what was put into it.) 7 Jesus said, "Leave her alone. She bought it[o] so that she might keep it for the day of my burial. 8 You always have the poor with you, but you do not always have me."

9 When the great crowd of the Jews learned that he was there, they came not only because of Jesus but also to see Lazarus, whom he had raised from the dead. 10 So the chief priests planned to put Lazarus to death as well, 11 since it was on account of him that many of the Jews were deserting and were believing in Jesus.

12 The next day the great crowd that had come to the festival heard that Jesus was coming to Jerusalem. 13 So they took branches of palm trees and went out to meet him, shouting,

"Hosanna!
    Blessed is the one who comes in
        the name of the Lord—[6]
    the King of Israel!"

14 Jesus found a young donkey and sat on it; as it is written:

15   "Do not be afraid, daughter of
            Zion.
        Look, your king is coming,
            sitting on a donkey's colt!"[7]

16 His disciples did not understand these things at first; but when Jesus was glorified, then they remembered that these things had been written of him and had been done to him. 17 So the crowd that had been with him when he called Lazarus out of the tomb and raised him from the dead continued to testify.[p] 18 It was also because they heard that he had performed this sign that the crowd went to meet him. 19 The Pharisees then said to one another, "You see, you can do nothing. Look, the world has gone after him!"

20 Now among those who went up to worship at the festival were some Greeks. 21 They came to Philip, who was from Bethsaida in Galilee, and said to him, "Sir, we wish to see Jesus." 22 Philip went and told Andrew; then Andrew and Philip went and told Jesus. 23 Jesus answered them, "The hour has come for the Son of Man to be glorified. 24 Very truly, I tell you, unless a grain of wheat falls into the earth and dies, it remains just a single grain; but if it dies, it bears much fruit. 25 Those who love their life lose it, and those who hate their life in this world will keep it for eternal life. 26 Whoever serves me must follow me, and where I am, there will my servant be also. Whoever serves me, the Father will honor.

27 "Now my soul is troubled. And what should I say—'Father, save me from this hour'? No, it is for this reason that I have come to this hour. 28 Father, glorify your name." Then a voice came from heaven, "I have glorified it, and I will glorify it again." 29 The crowd standing there heard it and said that it was thunder. Others said, "An angel has spoken to him." 30 Jesus answered, "This voice has come for your sake, not for mine. 31 Now is the judgment of this world; now the ruler of this world will be driven out. 32 And I, when I am lifted up from the earth, will draw all people[q] to myself." 33 He said this to indicate the

---

[l]Gk *he*   [m]Gk *his feet*   [n]Three hundred denarii would be nearly a year's wages for a laborer   [o]Gk lacks *She bought it*   [p]Other ancient authorities read *with him began to testify that he had called. . .from the dead*   [q]Other ancient authorities read *all things*

[6]Ps 118:26   [7]Zech 9:9

kind of death he was to die. 34 The crowd answered him, "We have heard from the law that the Messiah[r] remains forever. How can you say that the Son of Man must be lifted up? Who is this Son of Man?" 35 Jesus said to them, "The light is with you for a little longer. Walk while you have the light, so that the darkness may not overtake you. If you walk in the darkness, you do not know where you are going. 36 While you have the light, believe in the light, so that you may become children of light."

After Jesus had said this, he departed and hid from them. 37 Although he had performed so many signs in their presence, they did not believe in him. 38 This was to fulfill the word spoken by the prophet Isaiah:

> "Lord, who has believed our
>   message,
> and to whom has the arm of the
>   Lord been revealed?"[8]

39 And so they could not believe, because Isaiah also said,

40   "He has blinded their eyes
>   and hardened their heart,
> so that they might not look with
>   their eyes,
> and understand with their heart
>   and turn—
> and I would heal them."[9]

41 Isaiah said this because[s] he saw his glory and spoke about him. 42 Nevertheless many, even of the authorities, believed in him. But because of the Pharisees they did not confess it, for fear that they would be put out of the synagogue; 43 for they loved human glory more than the glory that comes from God.

44 Then Jesus cried aloud: "Whoever believes in me believes not in me but in him who sent me. 45 And whoever sees me sees him who sent me. 46 I have come as light into the world, so that everyone who believes in me should not remain in the darkness. 47 I do not judge anyone who hears my words and does not keep them, for I came not to judge the world, but to save the world. 48 The one who rejects me and does not receive my word has a judge; on the last day the word that I have spoken will serve as judge, 49 for I have not spoken on my own, but the Father who sent me has himself given me a commandment about what to say and what to speak. 50 And I know that his commandment is eternal life. What I speak, therefore, I speak just as the Father has told me."

13 Now before the festival of the Passover, Jesus knew that his hour had come to depart from this world and go to the Father. Having loved his own who were in the world, he loved them to the end. 2 The devil had already put it into the heart of Judas son of Simon Iscariot to betray him. And during supper 3 Jesus, knowing that the Father had given all things into his hands, and that he had come from God and was going to God, 4 got up from the table,[t] took off his outer robe, and tied a towel around himself. 5 Then he poured water into a basin and began to wash the disciples' feet and to wipe them with the towel that was tied around him. 6 He came to Simon Peter, who said to him, "Lord, are you going to wash my feet?" 7 Jesus answered, "You do not know now what I am doing, but later you will understand." 8 Peter said to him, "You will never wash my feet." Jesus answered, "Unless I wash you, you have no share with me." 9 Simon Peter said to him, "Lord, not my feet only but also my hands and my head!" 10 Jesus said to him, "One who has bathed does not need to wash, except for the feet,[u] but is entirely clean. And you[v] are clean, though not all of you." 11 For he knew who was to betray him; for this reason he said, "Not all of you are clean."

12 After he had washed their feet, had put on his robe, and had returned to the table, he said to them, "Do you know what I have done to you? 13 You call me Teacher and Lord—and you are right, for that is what I am. 14 So if I, your Lord and Teacher, have washed your feet, you also ought to wash one another's feet. 15 For I have set you an example, that you also should do as I have done to you. 16 Very truly, I tell you, servants[w] are not greater than their master, nor are messengers greater than the one who sent them. 17 If you know these things, you are blessed if you do them. 18 I am not speaking of all of you; I know whom I have chosen. But it is to fulfill the scripture, 'The

---

[r]Or the Christ [s]Other ancient witnesses read when [t]Gk from supper [u]Other ancient authorities lack except for the feet [v]The Greek word for you here is plural [w]Gk slaves

[8]Isa 53:1 [9]Isa 6:10

one who ate my bread[x] has lifted his heel against me.'[10] 19 I tell you this now, before it occurs, so that when it does occur, you may believe that I am he.[y] 20 Very truly, I tell you, whoever receives one whom I send receives me; and whoever receives me receives him who sent me."

21 After saying this Jesus was troubled in spirit, and declared, "Very truly, I tell you, one of you will betray me." 22 The disciples looked at one another, uncertain of whom he was speaking. 23 One of his disciples—the one whom Jesus loved—was reclining next to him; 24 Simon Peter therefore motioned to him to ask Jesus of whom he was speaking. 25 So while reclining next to Jesus, he asked him, "Lord, who is it?" 26 Jesus answered, "It is the one to whom I give this piece of bread when I have dipped it in the dish."[z] So when he had dipped the piece of bread, he gave it to Judas son of Simon Iscariot.[a] 27 After he received the piece of bread,[b] Satan entered into him. Jesus said to him, "Do quickly what you are going to do." 28 Now no one at the table knew why he said this to him. 29 Some thought that, because Judas had the common purse, Jesus was telling him, "Buy what we need for the festival"; or, that he should give something to the poor. 30 So, after receiving the piece of bread, he immediately went out. And it was night.

31 When he had gone out, Jesus said, "Now the Son of Man has been glorified, and God has been glorified in him. 32 If God has been glorified in him,[c] God will also glorify him in himself and will glorify him at once. 33 Little children, I am with you only a little longer. You will look for me; and as I said to the Jews so now I say to you, 'Where I am going, you cannot come.' 34 I give you a new commandment, that you love one another. Just as I have loved you, you also should love one another. 35 By this everyone will know that you are my disciples, if you have love for one another."

36 Simon Peter said to him, "Lord, where are you going?" Jesus answered, "Where I am going, you cannot follow me now; but you will follow afterward." 37 Peter said to him, "Lord, why can I not follow you now? I will lay down my life for you." 38 Jesus answered, "Will you lay down your life for me? Very truly, I tell you, before the cock crows, you will have denied me three times.

14 "Do not let your hearts be troubled. Believe[d] in God, believe also in me. 2 In my Father's house there are many dwelling places. If it were not so, would I have told you that I go to prepare a place for you?[e] 3 And if I go and prepare a place for you, I will come again and will take you to myself, so that where I am, there you may be also. 4 And you know the way to the place where I am going."[f] 5 Thomas said to him, "Lord, we do not know where you are going. How can we know the way?" 6 Jesus said to him, "I am the way, and the truth, and the life. No one comes to the Father except through me. 7 If you know me, you will know[g] my Father also. From now on you do know him and have seen him."

8 Philip said to him, "Lord, show us the Father, and we will be satisfied." 9 Jesus said to him, "Have I been with you all this time, Philip, and you still do not know me? Whoever has seen me has seen the Father. How can you say, 'Show us the Father'? 10 Do you not believe that I am in the Father and the Father is in me? The words that I say to you I do not speak on my own; but the Father who dwells in me does his works. 11 Believe me that I am in the Father and the Father is in me; but if you do not, then believe me because of the works themselves. 12 Very truly, I tell you, the one who believes in me will also do the works that I do and, in fact, will do greater works than these, because I am going to the Father. 13 I will do whatever you ask in my name, so that the Father may be glorified in the Son. 14 If in my name you ask me[h] for anything, I will do it.

15 "If you love me, you will keep[i] my commandments. 16 And I will ask the Father, and he will give you another Advocate,[j] to be with you forever. 17 This is the Spirit of truth, whom the world cannot receive, because it neither sees him

[x]Other ancient authorities read *ate bread with me*   [y]Gk *I am*
[z]Gk *dipped it*   [a]Other ancient authorities read *Judas Iscariot son of Simon*; others, *Judas son of Simon from Karyot* (Kerioth)   [b]Gk *After the piece of bread*   [c]Other ancient authorities lack *If God has been glorified in him*   [d]Or *You believe*   [e]Or *If it were not so, I would have told you; for I go to prepare a place for you*   [f]Other ancient authorities read *Where I am going you know, and the way you know*   [g]Other ancient authorities read *If you had known me, you would have known*   [h]Other ancient authorities lack *me*   [i]Other ancient authorities read *me, keep*   [j]Or *Helper*

[10]Ps 41:9

nor knows him. You know him, because he abides with you, and he will be in[k] you.

18 "I will not leave you orphaned; I am coming to you. 19 In a little while the world will no longer see me, but you will see me; because I live, you also will live. 20 On that day you will know that I am in my Father, and you in me, and I in you. 21 They who have my commandments and keep them are those who love me; and those who love me will be loved by my Father, and I will love them and reveal myself to them." 22 Judas (not Iscariot) said to him, "Lord, how is it that you will reveal yourself to us, and not to the world?" 23 Jesus answered him, "Those who love me will keep my word, and my Father will love them, and we will come to them and make our home with them. 24 Whoever does not love me does not keep my words; and the word that you hear is not mine, but is from the Father who sent me.

25 "I have said these things to you while I am still with you. 26 But the Advocate,[l] the Holy Spirit, whom the Father will send in my name, will teach you everything, and remind you of all that I have said to you. 27 Peace I leave with you; my peace I give to you. I do not give to you as the world gives. Do not let your hearts be troubled, and do not let them be afraid. 28 You heard me say to you, 'I am going away, and I am coming to you.' If you loved me, you would rejoice that I am going to the Father, because the Father is greater than I. 29 And now I have told you this before it occurs, so that when it does occur, you may believe. 30 I will no longer talk much with you, for the ruler of this world is coming. He has no power over me; 31 but I do as the Father has commanded me, so that the world may know that I love the Father. Rise, let us be on our way.

15 "I am the true vine, and my Father is the vinegrower. 2 He removes every branch in me that bears no fruit. Every branch that bears fruit he prunes[m] to make it bear more fruit. 3 You have already been cleansed[m] by the word that I have spoken to you. 4 Abide in me as I abide in you. Just as the branch cannot bear fruit by itself unless it abides in the vine, neither can you unless you abide in me. 5 I am the vine, you are the branches. Those who abide in me and I in them bear much fruit, because apart from me you can do nothing. 6 Whoever does not abide in me is thrown away like a branch and withers; such branches are gathered, thrown into the fire, and burned. 7 If you abide in me, and my words abide in you, ask for whatever you wish, and it will be done for you. 8 My Father is glorified by this, that you bear much fruit and become[n] my disciples. 9 As the Father has loved me, so I have loved you; abide in my love. 10 If you keep my commandments, you will abide in my love, just as I have kept my Father's commandments and abide in his love. 11 I have said these things to you so that my joy may be in you, and that your joy may be complete.

12 "This is my commandment, that you love one another as I have loved you. 13 No one has greater love than this, to lay down one's life for one's friends. 14 You are my friends if you do what I command you. 15 I do not call you servants[o] any longer, because the servant[p] does not know what the master is doing; but I have called you friends, because I have made known to you everything that I have heard from my Father. 16 You did not choose me but I chose you. And I appointed you to go and bear fruit, fruit that will last, so that the Father will give you what ever you ask him in my name. 17 I am giving you these commands so that you may love one another.

18 "If the world hates you, be aware that it hated me before it hated you. 19 If you belonged to the world,[q] the world would love you as its own. Because you do not belong to the world, but I have chosen you out of the world—therefore the world hates you. 20 Remember the word that I said to you, 'Servants[r] are not greater than their master.' If they persecuted me, they will persecute you; if they kept my word, they will keep yours also. 21 But they will do all these things to you on account of my name, because they do not know him who sent me. 22 If I had not come and spoken to them, they would not have sin; but now they have no excuse for their sin. 23 Whoever hates me hates my Father also. 24 If I had not done among them the works that no one else did, they would not have sin. But now they have seen and hated both me and my Father. 25 It was to fulfill the

[k]Or among [l]Or Helper [m]The same Greek root refers to pruning and cleansing [n]Or be [o]Gk slaves [p]Gk slave [q]Gk were of the world [r]Gk Slaves

word that is written in their law, 'They hated me without a cause.'[11]

26 "When the Advocate[s] comes, whom I will send to you from the Father, the Spirit of truth who comes from the Father, he will testify on my behalf. 27 You also are to testify because you have been with me from the beginning.

16 "I have said these things to you to keep you from stumbling. 2 They will put you out of the synagogues. Indeed, an hour is coming when those who kill you will think that by doing so they are offering worship to God. 3 And they will do this because they have not known the Father or me. 4 But I have said these things to you so that when their hour comes you may remember that I told you about them.

"I did not say these things to you from the beginning, because I was with you. 5 But now I am going to him who sent me; yet none of you asks me, 'Where are you going?' 6 But because I have said these things to you, sorrow has filled your hearts. 7 Nevertheless I tell you the truth: it is to your advantage that I go away, for if I do not go away, the Advocate[r] will not come to you; but if I go, I will send him to you. 8 And when he comes, he will prove the world wrong about[t] sin and righteousness and judgment: 9 about sin, because they do not believe in me; 10 about righteousness, because I am going to the Father and you will see me no longer; 11 about judgment, because the ruler of this world has been condemned.

12 "I still have many things to say to you, but you cannot bear them now. 13 When the Spirit of truth comes, he will guide you into all the truth; for he will not speak on his own, but will speak whatever he hears, and he will declare to you the things that are to come. 14 He will glorify me, because he will take what is mine and declare it to you. 15 All that the Father has is mine. For this reason I said that he will take what is mine and declare it to you.

16 "A little while, and you will no longer see me, and again a little while, and you will see me." 17 Then some of his disciples said to one another, "What does he mean by saying to us, 'A little while, and you will no longer see me, and again a little while, and you will see me'; and 'Because I am going to the Father'?" 18 They said, "What does he mean by this 'a little while'? We do not know what he is talking about." 19 Jesus knew

that they wanted to ask him, so he said to them, "Are you discussing among yourselves what I meant when I said, 'A little while, and you will no longer see me, and again a little while, and you will see me'? 20 Very truly, I tell you, you will weep and mourn, but the world will rejoice; you will have pain, but your pain will turn into joy. 21 When a woman is in labor, she has pain, because her hour has come. But when her child is born, she no longer remembers the anguish because of the joy of having brought a human being into the world. 22 So you have pain now; but I will see you again, and your hearts will rejoice, and no one will take your joy from you. 23 On that day you will ask nothing of me.[u] Very truly, I tell you, if you ask anything of the Father in my name, he will give it to you.[v] 24 Until now you have not asked for anything in my name. Ask and you will receive, so that your joy may be complete.

25 "I have said these things to you in figures of speech. The hour is coming when I will no longer speak to you in figures, but will tell you plainly of the Father. 26 On that day you will ask in my name. I do not say to you that I will ask the Father on your behalf; 27 for the Father himself loves you, because you have loved me and have believed that I came from God.[w] 28 I came from the Father and have come into the world; again, I am leaving the world and am going to the Father."

29 His disciples said, "Yes, now you are speaking plainly, not in any figure of speech! 30 Now we know that you know all things, and do not need to have anyone question you; by this we believe that you came from God." 31 Jesus answered them, "Do you now believe? 32 The hour is coming, indeed it has come, when you will be scattered, each one to his home, and you will leave me alone. Yet I am not alone because the Father is with me. 33 I have said this to you, so that in me you may have peace. In the world you face persecution. But take courage; I have conquered the world!"

17 After Jesus had spoken these words, he looked up to heaven and said, "Father, the hour has come; glorify your Son so that the Son

[s]Or *Helper* [t]Or *convict the world of* [u]Or *will ask me no question* [v]Other ancient authorities read *Father, he will give it to you in my name* [w]Other ancient authorities read *the Father*

[11]Ps 35:19; 69:4

may glorify you, 2 since you have given him authority over all people,[x] to give eternal life to all whom you have given him. 3 And this is eternal life, that they may know you, the only true God, and Jesus Christ whom you have sent. 4 I glorified you on earth by finishing the work that you gave me to do. 5 So now, Father, glorify me in your own presence with the glory that I had in your presence before the world existed.

6 "I have made your name known to those whom you gave me from the world. They were yours, and you gave them to me, and they have kept your word. 7 Now they know that everything you have given me is from you; 8 for the words that you gave to me I have given to them, and they have received them and know in truth that I came from you; and they have believed that you sent me. 9 I am asking on their behalf; I am not asking on behalf of the world, but on behalf of those whom you gave me, because they are yours. 10 All mine are yours, and yours are mine; and I have been glorified in them. 11 And now I am no longer in the world, but they are in the world, and I am coming to you. Holy Father, protect them in your name that you have given me, so that they may be one, as we are one. 12 While I was with them, I protected them in your name that[y] you have given me. I guarded them, and not one of them was lost except the one destined to be lost,[z] so that the scripture might be fulfilled. 13 But now I am coming to you, and I speak these things in the world so that they may have my joy made complete in themselves.[a] 14 I have given them your word, and the world has hated them because they do not belong to the world, just as I do not belong to the world. 15 I am not asking you to take them out of the world, but I ask you to protect them from the evil one.[b] 16 They do not belong to the world, just as I do not belong to the world. 17 Sanctify them in the truth; your word is truth. 18 As you have sent me into the world, so I have sent them into the world. 19 And for their sakes I sanctify myself, so that they also may be sanctified in truth.

20 "I ask not only on behalf of these, but also on behalf of those who will believe in me through their word, 21 that they may all be one. As you, Father, are in me and I am in you, may they also be in us,[c] so that the world may believe that you have sent me. 22 The glory that you have given me I have given them, so that they may be one, as we are one, 23 I in them and you in me, that they may become completely one, so that the world may know that you have sent me and have loved them even as you have loved me. 24 Father, I desire that those also, whom you have given me, may be with me where I am, to see my glory, which you have given me because you loved me before the foundation of the world.

25 "Righteous Father, the world does not know you, but I know you; and these know that you have sent me. 26 I made your name known to them, and I will make it known, so that the love with which you have loved me may be in them, and I in them."

18 After Jesus had spoken these words, he went out with his disciples across the Kidron valley to a place where there was a garden, which he and his disciples entered. 2 Now Judas, who betrayed him, also knew the place, because Jesus often met there with his disciples. 3 So Judas brought a detachment of soldiers together with police from the chief priests and the Pharisees, and they came there with lanterns and torches and weapons. 4 Then Jesus, knowing all that was to happen to him, came forward and asked them, "Whom are you looking for?" 5 They answered, "Jesus of Nazareth."[d] Jesus replied, "I am he."[e] Judas, who betrayed him, was standing with them. 6 When Jesus[f] said to them, "I am he,"[e] they stepped back and fell to the ground. 7 Again he asked them, "Whom are you looking for?" And they said, "Jesus of Nazareth."[d] 8 Jesus answered, "I told you that I am he.[e] So if you are looking for me, let these men go." 9 This was to fulfill the word that he had spoken, "I did not lose a single one of those whom you gave me." 10 Then Simon Peter, who had a sword, drew it, struck the high priest's slave, and cut off his right ear. The slave's name was Malchus. 11 Jesus said to Peter, "Put your sword back into its sheath. Am I not to drink the cup that the Father has given me?"

12 So the soldiers, their officer, and the Jewish police arrested Jesus and bound him. 13 First they took him to Annas, who was the father-in-law of

[x]Gk *flesh*   [y]Other ancient authorities read *protected in your name those whom*   [z]Gk *except the son of destruction*   [a]Or *among themselves*   [b]Or *from evil*   [c]Other ancient authorities read *be one in us*   [d]Gk *the Nazorean*   [e]Gk *I am*   [f]Gk *he*

Caiaphas, the high priest that year. 14 Caiaphas was the one who had advised the Jews that it was better to have one person die for the people.

15 Simon Peter and another disciple followed Jesus. Since that disciple was known to the high priest, he went with Jesus into the courtyard of the high priest, 16 but Peter was standing outside at the gate. So the other disciple, who was known to the high priest, went out, spoke to the woman who guarded the gate, and brought Peter in. 17 The woman said to Peter, "You are not also one of this man's disciples, are you?" He said, "I am not." 18 Now the slaves and the police had made a charcoal fire because it was cold, and they were standing around it and warming themselves. Peter also was standing with them and warming himself.

19 Then the high priest questioned Jesus about his disciples and about his teaching. 20 Jesus answered, "I have spoken openly to the world; I have always taught in synagogues and in the temple, where all the Jews come together. I have said nothing in secret. 21 Why do you ask me? Ask those who heard what I said to them; they know what I said." 22 When he had said this, one of the police standing nearby struck Jesus on the face, saying, "Is that how you answer the high priest?" 23 Jesus answered, "If I have spoken wrongly, testify to the wrong. But if I have spoken rightly, why do you strike me?" 24 Then Annas sent him bound to Caiaphas the high priest.

25 Now Simon Peter was standing and warming himself. They asked him, "You are not also one of his disciples, are you?" He denied it and said, "I am not." 26 One of the slaves of the high priest, a relative of the man whose ear Peter had cut off, asked, "Did I not see you in the garden with him?" 27 Again Peter denied it, and at that moment the cock crowed.

28 Then they took Jesus from Caiaphas to Pilate's headquarters.ᵍ It was early in the morning. They themselves did not enter the headquarters,ᶠ so as to avoid ritual defilement and to be able to eat the Passover. 29 So Pilate went out to them and said, "What accusation do you bring against this man?" 30 They answered, "If this man were not a criminal, we would not have handed him over to you." 31 Pilate said to them, "Take him yourselves and judge him according to your law." The Jews replied, "We are not permitted to put

anyone to death." 32 (This was to fulfill what Jesus had said when he indicated the kind of death he was to die.)

33 Then Pilate entered the headquartersᵍ again, summoned Jesus, and asked him, "Are you the King of the Jews?" 34 Jesus answered, "Do you ask this on your own, or did others tell you about me?" 35 Pilate replied, "I am not a Jew, am I? Your own nation and the chief priests have handed you over to me. What have you done?" 36 Jesus answered, "My kingdom is not from this world. If my kingdom were from this world, my followers would be fighting to keep me from being handed over to the Jews. But as it is, my kingdom is not from here." 37 Pilate asked him, "So you are a king?" Jesus answered, "You say that I am a king. For this I was born, and for this I came into the world, to testify to the truth. Everyone who belongs to the truth listens to my voice." 38 Pilate asked him, "What is truth?"

After he had said this, he went out to the Jews again and told them, "I find no case against him. 39 But you have a custom that I release someone for you at the Passover. Do you want me to release for you the King of the Jews?" 40 They shouted in reply, "Not this man, but Barabbas!" Now Barabbas was a bandit.

19 Then Pilate took Jesus and had him flogged. 2 And the soldiers wove a crown of thorns and put it on his head, and they dressed him in a purple robe. 3 They kept coming up to him, saying, "Hail, King of the Jews!" and striking him on the face. 4 Pilate went out again and said to them, "Look, I am bringing him out to you to let you know that I find no case against him." 5 So Jesus came out, wearing the crown of thorns and the purple robe. Pilate said to them, "Here is the man!" 6 When the chief priests and the police saw him, they shouted, "Crucify him! Crucify him!" Pilate said to them, "Take him yourselves and crucify him; I find no case against him." 7 The Jews answered him, "We have a law, and according to that law he ought to die because he has claimed to be the Son of God."

8 Now when Pilate heard this, he was more afraid than ever. 9 He entered his headquartersᵍ again and asked Jesus, "Where are you from?" But

ᵍGk the praetorium

Jesus gave him no answer. 10 Pilate therefore said to him, "Do you refuse to speak to me? Do you not know that I have power to release you, and power to crucify you?" 11 Jesus answered him, "You would have no power over me unless it had been given you from above; therefore the one who handed me over to you is guilty of a greater sin." 12 From then on Pilate tried to release him, but the Jews cried out, "If you release this man, you are no friend of the emperor. Everyone who claims to be a king sets himself against the emperor."

13 When Pilate heard these words, he brought Jesus outside and sat[h] on the judge's bench at a place called The Stone Pavement, or in Hebrew[i] Gabbatha. 14 Now it was the day of Preparation for the Passover; and it was about noon. He said to the Jews, "Here is your King!" 15 They cried out, "Away with him! Away with him! Crucify him!" Pilate asked them, "Shall I crucify your King?" The chief priests answered, "We have no king but the emperor." 16 Then he handed him over to them to be crucified.

So they took Jesus; 17 and carrying the cross by himself, he went out to what is called The Place of the Skull, which in Hebrew[i] is called Golgotha. 18 There they crucified him, and with him two others, one on either side, with Jesus between them. 19 Pilate also had an inscription written and put on the cross. It read, "Jesus of Nazareth,[j] the King of the Jews." 20 Many of the Jews read this inscription, because the place where Jesus was crucified was near the city; and it was written in Hebrew,[i] in Latin, and in Greek. 21 Then the chief priests of the Jews said to Pilate, "Do not write, 'The King of the Jews,' but, 'This man said, I am King of the Jews.'" 22 Pilate answered, "What I have written I have written." 23 When the soldiers had crucified Jesus, they took his clothes and divided them into four parts, one for each soldier. They also took his tunic; now the tunic was seamless, woven in one piece from the top. 24 So they said to one another, "Let us not tear it, but cast lots for it to see who will get it." This was to fulfill what the scripture says,

> "They divided my clothes among
> themselves,
> and for my clothing they cast
> lots."[12]

25 And that is what the soldiers did.

Meanwhile, standing near the cross of Jesus were his mother, and his mother's sister, Mary the wife of Clopas, and Mary Magdalene. 26 When Jesus saw his mother and the disciple whom he loved standing beside her, he said to his mother, "Woman, here is your son." 27 Then he said to the disciple, "Here is your mother." And from that hour the disciple took her into his own home.

28 After this, when Jesus knew that all was now finished, he said (in order to fulfill the scripture), "I am thirsty." 29 A jar full of sour wine was standing there. So they put a sponge full of the wine on a branch of hyssop and held it to his mouth. 30 When Jesus had received the wine, he said, "It is finished." Then he bowed his head and gave up his spirit.

31 Since it was the day of Preparation, the Jews did not want the bodies left on the cross during the sabbath, especially because that sabbath was a day of great solemnity. So they asked Pilate to have the legs of the crucified men broken and the bodies removed. 32 Then the soldiers came and broke the legs of the first and of the other who had been crucified with him. 33 But when they came to Jesus and saw that he was already dead, they did not break his legs. 34 Instead, one of the soldiers pierced his side with a spear, and at once blood and water came out. 35 (He who saw this has testified so that you also may believe. His testimony is true, and he knows[k] that he tells the truth.) 36 These things occurred so that the scripture might be fulfilled, "None of his bones shall be broken."[13] 37 And again another passage of scripture says, "They will look on the one whom they have pierced."[14]

38 After these things, Joseph of Arimathea, who was a disciple of Jesus, though a secret one because of his fear of the Jews, asked Pilate to let him take away the body of Jesus. Pilate gave him permission; so he came and removed his body. 39 Nicodemus, who had at first come to Jesus by night, also came, bringing a mixture of myrrh and aloes, weighing about a hundred pounds. 40 They took the body of Jesus and wrapped it with the spices in linen cloths, according to the burial custom of the Jews. 41 Now there was a garden in the

---

[h]Or *seated him* [i]That is, *Aramaic* [j]Gk *the Nazorean* [k]Or *there is one who knows*

[12]Ps 22:18   [13]Ps 34:20; Exod 12:46; Num 9:12   [14]Zech 12:10

place where he was crucified, and in the garden there was a new tomb in which no one had ever been laid. 42 And so, because it was the Jewish day of Preparation, and the tomb was nearby, they laid Jesus there.

20 Early on the first day of the week, while it was still dark, Mary Magdalene came to the tomb and saw that the stone had been removed from the tomb. 2 So she ran and went to Simon Peter and the other disciple, the one whom Jesus loved, and said to them, "They have taken the Lord out of the tomb, and we do not know where they have laid him." 3 Then Peter and the other disciple set out and went toward the tomb. 4 The two were running together, but the other disciple outran Peter and reached the tomb first. 5 He bent down to look in and saw the linen wrappings lying there, but he did not go in. 6 Then Simon Peter came, following him, and went into the tomb. He saw the linen wrappings lying there, 7 and the cloth that had been on Jesus' head, not lying with the linen wrappings but rolled up in a place by itself. 8 Then the other disciple, who reached the tomb first, also went in, and he saw and believed; 9 for as yet they did not understand the scripture, that he must rise from the dead. 10 Then the disciples returned to their homes.

11 But Mary stood weeping outside the tomb. As she wept, she bent over to look[l] into the tomb; 12 and she saw two angels in white, sitting where the body of Jesus had been lying, one at the head and the other at the feet. 13 They said to her, "Woman, why are you weeping?" She said to them, "They have taken away my Lord, and I do not know where they have laid him." 14 When she had said this, she turned around and saw Jesus standing there, but she did not know that it was Jesus. 15 Jesus said to her, "Woman, why are you weeping? Whom are you looking for?" Supposing him to be the gardener, she said to him, "Sir, if you have carried him away, tell me where you have laid him, and I will take him away." 16 Jesus said to her, "Mary!" She turned and said to him in Hebrew,[m] "Rabbouni!" (which means Teacher). 17 Jesus said to her, "Do not hold on to me, because I have not yet ascended to the Father. But go to my brothers and say to them, 'I am ascending to my Father and your Father, to my God and your God.'" 18 Mary Magdalene went and announced

to the disciples, "I have seen the Lord"; and she told them that he had said these things to her.

19 When it was evening on that day, the first day of the week, and the doors of the house where the disciples had met were locked for fear of the Jews, Jesus came and stood among them and said, "Peace be with you." 20 After he said this, he showed them his hands and his side. Then the disciples rejoiced when they saw the Lord. 21 Jesus said to them again, "Peace be with you. As the Father has sent me, so I send you." 22 When he had said this, he breathed on them and said to them, "Receive the Holy Spirit. 23 If you forgive the sins of any, they are forgiven them; if you retain the sins of any, they are retained."

24 But Thomas (who was called the Twin[n]), one of the twelve, was not with them when Jesus came. 25 So the other disciples told him, "We have seen the Lord." But he said to them, "Unless I see the mark of the nails in his hands, and put my finger in the mark of the nails and my hand in his side, I will not believe."

26 A week later his disciples were again in the house, and Thomas was with them. Although the doors were shut, Jesus came and stood among them and said, "Peace be with you." 27 Then he said to Thomas, "Put your finger here and see my hands. Reach out your hand and put it in my side. Do not doubt but believe." 28 Thomas answered him, "My Lord and my God!" 29 Jesus said to him, "Have you believed because you have seen me? Blessed are those who have not seen and yet have come to believe."

30 Now Jesus did many other signs in the presence of his disciples, which are not written in this book. 31 But these are written so that you may come to believe[o] that Jesus is the Messiah,[p] the Son of God, and that through believing you may have life in his name.

21 After these things Jesus showed himself again to the disciples by the Sea of Tiberias; and he showed himself in this way. 2 Gathered there together were Simon Peter, Thomas called the Twin,[n] Nathanael of Cana in Galilee, the sons of Zebedee, and two others of his

---

[l]Gk lacks *to look*   [m]That is, *Aramaic*   [n]Gk *Didymus*   [o]Other ancient authorities read *may continue to believe*   [p]Or *the Christ*

disciples. 3 Simon Peter said to them, "I am going fishing." They said to him, "We will go with you." They went out and got into the boat, but that night they caught nothing.

4 Just after daybreak, Jesus stood on the beach; but the disciples did not know that it was Jesus. 5 Jesus said to them, "Children, you have no fish, have you?" They answered him, "No." 6 He said to them, "Cast the net to the right side of the boat, and you will find some." So they cast it, and now they were not able to haul it in because there were so many fish. 7 That disciple whom Jesus loved said to Peter, "It is the Lord!" When Simon Peter heard that it was the Lord, he put on some clothes, for he was naked, and jumped into the sea. 8 But the other disciples came in the boat, dragging the net full of fish, for they were not far from the land, only about a hundred yards[q] off.

9 When they had gone ashore, they saw a charcoal fire there, with fish on it, and bread. 10 Jesus said to them, "Bring some of the fish that you have just caught." 11 So Simon Peter went aboard and hauled the net ashore, full of large fish, a hundred fifty-three of them; and though there were so many, the net was not torn. 12 Jesus said to them, "Come and have breakfast." Now none of the disciples dared to ask him, "Who are you?" because they knew it was the Lord. 13 Jesus came and took the bread and gave it to them, and did the same with the fish. 14 This was now the third time that Jesus appeared to the disciples after he was raised from the dead.

15 When they had finished breakfast, Jesus said to Simon Peter, "Simon son of John, do you love me more than these?" He said to him, "Yes, Lord; you know that I love you." Jesus said to him, "Feed my lambs." 16 A second time he said to him, "Simon son of John, do you love me?" He said to him, "Yes, Lord; you know that I love you." Jesus said to him, "Tend my sheep." 17 He said to him the third time, "Simon son of John, do you love me?" Peter felt hurt because he said to him the third time, "Do you love me?" And he said to him, "Lord, you know everything; you know that I love you." Jesus said to him, "Feed my sheep. 18 Very truly, I tell you, when you were younger, you used to fasten your own belt and to go wherever you wished. But when you grow old, you will stretch out your hands, and someone else will fasten a belt around you and take you where you do not wish to go." 19 (He said this to indicate the kind of death by which he would glorify God.) After this he said to him, "Follow me."

20 Peter turned and saw the disciple whom Jesus loved following them; he was the one who had reclined next to Jesus at the supper and had said, "Lord, who is it that is going to betray you?" 21 When Peter saw him, he said to Jesus, "Lord, what about him?" 22 Jesus said to him, "If it is my will that he remain until I come, what is that to you? Follow me!" 23 So the rumor spread in the community[r] that this disciple would not die. Yet Jesus did not say to him that he would not die, but, "If it is my will that he remain until I come, what is that to you?"[s]

24 This is the disciple who is testifying to these things and has written them, and we know that his testimony is true. 25 But there are also many other things that Jesus did; if every one of them were written down, I suppose that the world itself could not contain the books that would be written.

[q]Gk *two hundred cubits*   [r]Gk *among the brothers*   [s]Other ancient authorities lack *what is that to you*

The Gospel of Thomas

The *Gospel of Thomas* was one of the most sensational archaeological discoveries of the twentieth century. The document was unknown except by name before 1945, when a peasant digging for fertilizer near the village of Nag Hammadi, Egypt, accidentally uncovered a jar containing thirteen leather-bound manuscripts buried sometime in the late fourth century. When the manuscripts came to the attention of scholars of antiquity, their significance was almost immediately recognized: they contained fifty-two tractates that, by and large, represented "heretical" writings of Gnostic Christians. Although originally composed in Greek, the writings were in Coptic (ancient Egyptian) translation. Many of them had been previously known by title only.

None of the fifty-two tractates has attracted more attention than the *Gospel of Thomas.* For this is a book of Jesus' sayings that claims to have been written by Didymos Judas Thomas. According to some early Christian legends, Thomas was Jesus' twin brother.

The book records 114 "secret teachings" of Jesus. It includes no other material: no miracles, no passion narrative, no stories of any kind. In this it appears to resemble that lost collection of sayings that scholars have designated Q (from the German word *Quelle,* "source"), which was used by Matthew and Luke for their Gospels. What ultimately mattered for the author of Thomas was evidently not Jesus' death and resurrection (which he does not narrate or discuss), but the mysterious teachings that he delivered. Indeed, the Gospel begins by stating that anyone who learns the interpretation of these words will have eternal life.

Many of the sayings will sound familiar to readers already conversant with the Gospels of Matthew, Mark, and Luke. For example, here one finds, in slightly different wording, the warning against the "blind leading the blind" and the parables of the sower and of the mustard seed (sayings 9, 20, 34). Other sayings, however, are quite different and appear to presuppose a gnostic point of view, in which people are understood to be spirits who have fallen from the divine realm and become entrapped in matter (i.e., in the prisons of their material bodies). Salvation, according to this perspective, comes to those who learn the truth of their plight and so are enabled to escape this impoverished material existence by acquiring the knowledge necessary for salvation (e.g., sayings 11, 22, 29, 37, and 80). Jesus is the one who conveys this knowledge.

Some scholars have maintained that the sayings of Thomas may be closer to what Jesus actually taught than what we find in the New Testament; others, however, have pointed out that the theology implicit in the more gnostic teachings cannot be dated with confidence prior to the beginning of the second century. Thus, while some of these sayings may be quite old—may, in fact, go back to Jesus himself—the document as a whole probably came to be written sometime after the New Testament Gospels (though perhaps independently of them), perhaps in the early second century.

These are the secret sayings which the living Jesus spoke and which Didymos Judas Thomas wrote down.

1 And he said, "Whoever finds the interpretation of these sayings will not experience death."

2 Jesus said, "Let him who seeks continue seeking until he finds. When he finds, he will become troubled. When he becomes troubled, he will be astonished, and he will rule over the all."

3 Jesus said, "If those who lead you say to you, 'See the kingdom is in the sky,' then the birds of the sky will precede you. If they say to you, 'It is in the sea,' then the fish will precede you. Rather, the kingdom is inside of you, and it is outside of you. When you come to know yourselves, then you will become known, and you will realize that it is you who are the sons of the living father. But if you will not know yourselves, you dwell in poverty and it is you who are that poverty."

4 Jesus said, "The man old in days will not hesitate to ask a small child seven days old about the place of life, and he will live. For many who are first will become last, and they will become one and the same."

5 Jesus said, "Recognize what is in your (sing.) sight, and that which is hidden from you (sing.) will become plain to you (sing.). For there is nothing hidden which will not become manifest."

6 His disciples questioned him and said to him, "Do you want us to fast? How shall we pray? Shall we give alms? What diet shall we observe?"

Jesus said, "Do not tell lies,' and do not do what you hate, for all things are plain in the sight of heaven. For nothing hidden will not become manifest, and nothing covered will remain without being uncovered."

7 Jesus said, "Blessed is the lion which becomes man when consumed by man; and cursed is the man whom the lion consumes, and the lion becomes man."

8 And he said, "The man is like a wise fisherman who cast his net into the sea and drew it up from the sea full of small fish. Among them the wise fisherman found a fine large fish. He threw all the small fish back into the sea and chose the large fish without difficulty. Whoever has ears to hear, let him hear."

9 Jesus said, "Now the sower went out, took a handful (of seeds), and scattered them. Some fell on the road; the birds came and gathered them up. Others fell on rock, did not take root in the soil, and did not produce ears. And others fell on thorns; they choked the seed(s) and worms ate them. And others fell on the good soil and it produced good fruit: it bore sixty per measure and a hundred and twenty per measure."

10 Jesus said, "I have cast fire upon the world, and see, I am guarding it until it blazes."

11 Jesus said, "This heaven will pass away, and the one above it will pass away. The dead are not alive, and the living will not die. In the days when you consumed what is dead, you made it what is alive. When you come to dwell in the light, what will you do? On the day when you were one you became two. But when you become two, what will you do?"

12 The disciples said to Jesus, "We know that you will depart from us. Who is to be our leader?"

Jesus said to them, "Wherever you are, you are to go to James the righteous, for whose sake heaven and earth came into being."

13 Jesus said to his disciples, "Compare me to someone and tell me whom I am like."

Simon Peter said to him, "You are like a righteous angel."

Matthew said to him, "You are like a wise philosopher."

Thomas said to him, "Master, my mouth is wholly incapable of saying whom you are like."

Jesus said, "I am not your (sing.) master. Because you (sing.) have drunk, you (sing.) have become intoxicated from the bubbling spring which I have measured out."

And he took him and withdrew and told him three things. When Thomas returned to his companions, they asked him, "What did Jesus say to you?"

Thomas said to them, "If I tell you one of the things which he told me, you will pick up stones and throw them at me; a fire will come out of the stones and burn you up."

14 Jesus said to them, "If you fast, you will give rise to sin for yourselves; and if you pray, you will be condemned; and if you give alms, you will do harm to your spirits. When you go into any land and walk about in the districts, if they receive you, eat what they will set before you, and heal the sick among them. For what goes into your mouth will not defile you, but that which issues from your mouth—it is that which will defile you."

15 Jesus said, "When you see one who was not born of woman, prostrate yourselves on your faces and worship him. That one is your father."

16 Jesus said, "Men think, perhaps, that it is peace which I have come to cast upon the world. They do not know that it is dissension which I have come to cast upon the earth: fire, sword, and war. For there will be five in a house: three will be against two, and two against three, the father against the son, and the son against the father. And they will stand solitary."

17 Jesus said, "I shall give you what no eye has seen and what no ear has heard and what no hand has touched and what has never occurred to the human mind."

18 The disciples said to Jesus, "Tell us how our end will be."

Jesus said, "Have you discovered, then, the beginning, that you look for the end? For where the beginning is, there will the end be. Blessed is he who will take his place in the beginning; he will know the end and will not experience death."

19 Jesus said, "Blessed is he who came into being before he came into being. If you become my disciples and listen to my words, these stones will minister to you. For there are five trees for you in Paradise which remain undisturbed summer and winter and whose leaves do not fall. Whoever be-

comes acquainted with them will not experience death."

20 The disciples said to Jesus, "Tell us what the kingdom of heaven is like."

He said to them, "It is like a mustard seed. It is the smallest of all seeds. But when it falls on tilled soil, it produces a great plant and becomes a shelter for birds of the sky."

21 Mary said to Jesus, "Whom are your disciples like?"

He said, "They are like children who have settled in a field which is not theirs. When the owners of the field come, they will say, 'Let us have back our field.' They (will) undress in their presence in order to let them have back their field and to give it back to them. Therefore I say, if the owner of a house knows that the thief is coming, he will begin his vigil before he comes and will not let him dig through into his house of his domain to carry away his goods. You (pl.), then, be on your guard against the world. Arm yourselves with great strength lest the robbers find a way to come to you, for the difficulty which you expect will (surely) materialize. Let there be among you a man of understanding. When the grain ripened, he came quickly with his sickle in his hand and reaped it. Whoever has ears to hear, let him hear."

22 Jesus saw infants being suckled. He said to his disciples, "These infants being suckled are like those who enter the kingdom."

They said to him, "Shall we then, as children, enter the kingdom?"

Jesus said to them, "When you make the two one, and when you make the inside like the outside and the outside like the inside, and the above like the below, and when you make the male and the female one and the same, so that the male not be male nor the female female; and when you fashion eyes in place of an eye, and a hand in place of a hand, and a foot in place of a foot, and a likeness in place of a likeness; then will you enter [the kingdom]."

23 Jesus said, "I shall choose you, one out of a thousand, and two out of ten thousand, and they shall stand as a single one."

24 His disciples said to him, "Show us the place where you are, since it is necessary for us to seek it."

He said to them, "Whoever has ears, let him hear. There is light within a man of light, and he lights up the whole world. If he does not shine, he is darkness."

25 Jesus said, "Love your (sing.) brother like your soul, guard him like the pupil of your eye."

26 Jesus said, "You (sing.) see the mote in your brother's eye, but you do not see the beam in your own eye. When you cast the beam out of your own eye, then you will see clearly to cast the mote from your brother's eye."

27 [Jesus said,] "If you do not fast as regards the world, you will not find the kingdom. If you do not observe the Sabbath as a Sabbath, you will not see the father."

28 Jesus said, "I took my place in the midst of the world, and I appeared to them in flesh. I found all of them intoxicated; I found none of them thirsty. And my soul became afflicted for the sons of men, because they are blind in their hearts and do not have sight; for empty they came into the world, and empty too they seek to leave the world. But for the moment they are intoxicated. When they shake off their wine, then they will repent."

29 Jesus said, "If the flesh came into being because of spirit, it is a wonder. But if spirit came into being because of the body, it is a wonder of wonders. Indeed, I am amazed at how this great wealth has made its home in this poverty."

30 Jesus said, "Where there are three gods, they are gods. Where there are two or one, I am with him."

31 Jesus said, "No prophet is accepted in his own village; no physician heals those who know him."

32 Jesus said, "A city being built on a high mountain and fortified cannot fall, nor can it be hidden."

33 Jesus said, "Preach from your (pl.) housetops that which you (sing.) will hear in your (sing.) ear. For no one lights a lamp and puts it under a bushel, nor does he put it in a hidden place, but rather he sets it on a lampstand so that everyone who enters and leaves will see its light."

34 Jesus said, "If a blind man leads a blind man, they will both fall into a pit."

35 Jesus said, "It is not possible for anyone to enter the house of a strong man and take it by force unless he binds his hands; then he will (be able to) ransack his house."

36 Jesus said, "Do not be concerned from morning until evening and from evening until morning about what you will wear."

37 His disciples said, "When will you become revealed to us and when shall we see you?"

Jesus said, "When you disrobe without being ashamed and take up your garments and place them under your feet like little children and tread on them, then [will you see] the son of the living one, and you will not be afraid."

38 Jesus said, "Many times have you desired to hear these words which I am saying to you, and you have no one else to hear them from. There will be days when you will look for me and will not find me."

39 Jesus said, "The pharisees and the scribes have taken the keys of knowledge (gnosis) and hidden them. They themselves have not entered, nor have they allowed to enter those who wish to. You, however, be as wise as serpents and as innocent as doves."

40 Jesus said, "A grapevine has been planted outside of the father, but being unsound, it will be pulled up by its roots and destroyed."

41 Jesus said, "Whoever has something in his hand will receive more, and whoever has nothing will be deprived of even the little he has."

42 Jesus said, "Become passers-by."

43 His disciples said to him, "Who are you, that you should say these things to us?"

[Jesus said to them,] "You do not realize who I am from what I say to you, but you have become like the Jews, for they (either) love the tree and hate its fruit (or) love the fruit and hate the tree."

44 Jesus said, "Whoever blasphemes against the father will be forgiven, and whoever blasphemes against the son will be forgiven, but whoever blasphemes against the holy spirit will not be forgiven either on earth or in heaven."

45 Jesus said, "Grapes are not harvested from thorns, nor are figs gathered from thistles, for they do not produce fruit. A good man brings forth good from his storehouse; an evil man brings forth evil things from his evil storehouse, which is in his heart, and says evil things. For out

of the abundance of the heart he brings forth evil things."

46 Jesus said, "Among those born of women, from Adam until John the Baptist, there is no one so superior to John the Baptist that his eyes should not be lowered (before him). Yet I have said, whichever one of you comes to be a child will be acquainted with the kingdom and will become superior to John."

47 Jesus said, "It is impossible for a man to mount two horses or to stretch two bows. And it is impossible for a servant to serve two masters; otherwise, he will honor the one and treat the other contemptuously. No man drinks old wine and immediately desires to drink new wine. And new wine is not put into old wineskins, lest they burst; nor is old wine put into a new wineskin, lest it spoil it. An old patch is not sewn into a new garment, because a tear would result."

48 Jesus said, "If two make peace with each other in this one house, they will say to the mountain, 'Move away,' and it will move away."

49 Jesus said, "Blessed are the solitary and elect, for you will find the kingdom. For you are from it, and to it you will return."

50 Jesus said, "If they say to you, 'Where did you come from?', say to them, "We came from the light, the place where the light came into being on its own accord and established [itself] and became manifest through their image.' If they say to you, 'Is it you?', say, 'We are its children, and we are the elect of the living father.' If they ask you, 'What is the sign of your father in you?', say to them, 'It is movement and repose.'"

51 His disciples said to him, "When will the repose of the dead come about, and when will the new world come?"

He said to them, "What you look forward to has already come, but you do not recognize it."

52 His disciples said to him, "Twenty-four prophets spoke in Israel, and all of them spoke in you."

He said to them, "You have omitted the one living in your presence and have spoken (only) of the dead."

53 His disciples said to him, "Is circumcision beneficial or not?"

He said to them, "If it were beneficial, their father would beget them already circumcised from their mother. Rather, the true circumcision in spirit has become completely profitable."

54 Jesus said, "Blessed are the poor, for yours is the kingdom of heaven."

55 Jesus said, "Whoever does not hate his father and his mother cannot become a disciple to me. And whoever does not hate his brothers and sisters and take up his cross in my way will not be worthy of me."

56 Jesus said, "Whoever has come to understand the world has found (only) a corpse, and whoever has found a corpse is superior to the world."

57 Jesus said, "The kingdom of the father is like a man who had [good] seed. His enemy came by night and sowed weeds among the good seed. The man did not allow them to pull up the weeds; he said to them, 'I am afraid that you will go intending to pull up the weeds and pull up the wheat along with them.' For on the day of the harvest the weeds will be plainly visible, and they will be pulled up and burned."

58 Jesus said, "Blessed is the man who has suffered and found life."

59 Jesus said, "Take heed of the living one while you are alive, lest you die and seek to see him and be unable to do so."

60 [They saw] a Samaritan carrying a lamb on his way to Judea. He said to his disciples, "That man is round about the lamb."

They said to him, "So that he may kill it and eat it."

He said to them, "While it is alive, he will not eat it, but only when he has killed it and it has become a corpse."

They said to him, "He cannot do so otherwise."

He said to them, "You too, look for a place for yourselves within repose, lest you become a corpse and be eaten."

61 Jesus said, "Two will rest on a bed: the one will die, and the other will live."

Salome said, "Who are you, man, that you . . . have come up on my couch and eaten from my table?"

Jesus said to her, "I am he who exists from the undivided. I was given some of the things of my father."

[. . .] "I am your disciple."

[. . .] "Therefore I say, if he is destroyed he will

be filled with light, but if he is divided, he will be filled with darkness."

62 Jesus said, "It is to those [who are worthy of my] mysteries that I tell my mysteries. Do not let your (sing.) left hand know what your (sing.) right hand is doing."

63 Jesus said, There was a rich man who had much money. He said, 'I shall put my money to use so that I may sow, reap, plant, and fill my storehouse with produce, with the result that I shall lack nothing.' Such were his intentions, but that same night he died. Let him who has ears hear."

64 Jesus said, "A man had received visitors. And when he had prepared the dinner, he sent his servant to invite the guests. He went to the first one and said to him, 'My master invites you.' He said, 'I have claims against some merchants. They are coming to me this evening. I must go and give them my orders. I ask to be excused from the dinner.' He went to another and said to him, 'My master has invited you.' He said to him, 'I have just bought a house and am required for the day. I shall not have any spare time.' He went to another and said to him, 'My master invites you.' He said to him, 'My friend is going to get married, and I am to prepare the banquet. I shall not be able to come. I ask to be excused from the dinner.' He went to another and said to him, 'My master invites you.' He said to him, 'I have just bought a farm, and I am on my way to collect the rent. I shall not be able to come. I ask to be excused.' The servant returned and said to his master, 'Those whom you invited to the dinner have asked to be excused.' The master said to his servant, 'Go outside to the streets and bring back those whom you happen to meet, so that they may dine.' Businessmen and merchants [will] not enter the places of my father."

65 He said, "There was a good man who owned a vineyard. He leased it to tenant farmers so that they might work it and he might collect the produce from them. He sent his servant so that the tenants might give him the produce of the vineyard. They seized his servant and beat him, all but killing him. The servant went back and told his master. The master said, 'Perhaps he did not recognize them.' He sent another servant. The tenants beat this one was well. Then the owner sent his son and said, 'Perhaps they will show respect to my son.' Because the tenants knew that it was he who

was the heir to the vineyard, they seized him and killed him. Let him who has ears hear."

66 Jesus said, "Show me the stone which the builders have rejected. That one is the cornerstone."

67 Jesus said, "If one who knows the all still feels a personal deficiency, he is completely deficient."

68 Jesus said, "Blessed are you when you are hated and persecuted. Wherever you have been persecuted they will find no place."

69 Jesus said, "Blessed are they who have been persecuted within themselves. It is they who have truly come to know the father. Blessed are the hungry, for the belly of him who desires will be filled."

70 Jesus said, "That which you have will save you if you bring it forth from yourselves. That which you do not have within you [will] kill you if you do not have it within you."

71 Jesus said, "I shall [destroy this] house, and no one will be able to build it [. . .]"

72 [A man said] to him, "Tell my brothers to divide my father's possessions with me."

He said to him, "O man, who has made me a divider?"

He turned to his disciples and said to them, "I am not a divider, am I?"

73 Jesus said, "The harvest is great but the laborers are few. Beseech the lord, therefore, to send out laborers to the harvest."

74 He said, "O lord, there are many around the drinking trough, but there is nothing in the cistern."

75 Jesus said, "Many are standing at the door, but it is the solitary who will enter the bridal chamber."

76 Jesus said, "The kingdom of the father is like a merchant who had a consignment of merchandise and who discovered a pearl. That merchant was shrewd. He sold the merchandise and bought the pearl alone for himself. You too, seek his unfailing and enduring treasure where no moth comes near to devour and no worm destroys."

77 Jesus said, "It is I who am the light which is above them all. It is I who am the all. From me did the all come forth, and unto me did the all extend. Split a piece of wood, and I am there. Lift up the stone, and you will find me there."

78 Jesus said, "Why have you come out into the desert? To see a reed shaken by the wind? And to see a man clothed in fine garments [like your] kings and your great men? Upon them are the fine garments, and they are unable to discern the truth."

79 A woman from the crowd said to him, "Blessed are the womb which bore you and the breasts which nourished you."

He said to [her], "Blessed are those who have heard the word of the father and have truly kept it. For there will be days when you (pl.) will say, 'Blessed are the womb which has not conceived and the breasts which have not given milk.'"

80 Jesus said, "He who has recognized the world has found the body, but he who has found the body is superior to the world."

81 Jesus said, "Let him who has grown rich be king, and let him who possesses power renounce it."

82 Jesus said, "He who is near me is near the fire, and he who is far from me is far from the kingdom."

83 Jesus said, "The images are manifest to man, but the light in them remains concealed in the image of the light of the father. He will become manifest, but his image will remain concealed by his light."

84 Jesus said, "When you see your likeness, you rejoice. But when you see your images which came into being before you, and which neither die nor become manifest, how much you will have to bear!"

85 Jesus said, "Adam came into being from a great power and a great wealth, but he did not become worthy of you. For had he been worthy, [he would] not [have experienced] death."

86 Jesus said, "[The foxes have their holes] and the birds have their nests, but the son of man has no place to lay his head and rest."

87 Jesus said, "Wretched is the body that is dependent upon a body, and wretched is the soul that is dependent on these two."

88 Jesus said, "The angels and the prophets will come to you and give to you those things you (already) have. And you too, give them those things which you have, and say to yourselves, 'When will they come and take what is theirs?'"

89 Jesus said, "Why do you wash the outside of the cup? Do you not realize that he who made the inside is the same one who made the outside?"

90 Jesus said, "Come unto me, for my yoke is easy and my lordship is mild, and you will find repose for yourselves."

91 They said to him, "Tell us who you are so that we may believe in you."

He said to them, "You read the face of the sky and of the earth, but you have not recognized the one who is before you, and you do not know how to read this moment."

92 Jesus said, "Seek and you will find. Yet, what you asked me about in former times and which I did not tell you then, now I do desire to tell, but you do not inquire after it."

93 [Jesus said] "Do not give what is holy to dogs, lest they throw them on the dung heap. Do not throw the pearls [to] swine, lest they . . . it [. . .]."

94 Jesus [said], "He who seeks will find, and [he who knocks] will be let in."

95 [Jesus said], "If you have money, do not lend it at interest, but give [it] to one from whom you will not get it back."

96 Jesus said, "The kingdom of the father is like [a certain] woman. She took a little leaven, [concealed] it in some dough, and made it into large loaves. Let him who has ears hear."

97 Jesus said, "The kingdom of the [father] is like a certain woman who was carrying a [jar] full of meal. While she was walking [on the] road, still some distance from home, the handle of the jar broke and the meal emptied out behind her [on] the road. She did not realize it; she had noticed no accident. When she reached her house, she set the jar down and found it empty."

98 Jesus said, "The kingdom of the father is like a certain man who wanted to kill a powerful man. In his own house he drew his sword and stuck it into the wall in order to find out whether his hand could carry through. Then he slew the powerful man."

99 The disciples said to him, "Your brothers and your mother are standing outside."

He said to them, "Those here who do the will of my father are my brothers and my mother. It is they who will enter the kingdom of my father."

100 They showed Jesus a gold coin and said to him, "Caesar's men demand taxes from us."

He said to them, "Give Caesar what belongs to Caesar, give God what belongs to God, and give me what is mine."

101 [Jesus said] "Whoever does not hate his [father] and his mother as I do cannot become a [disciple] to me. And whoever does [not] love his [father and] his mother as I do cannot become a [disciple to] me. For my mother [. . .], but [my] true [mother] gave me life."

102 Jesus said, "Woe to the pharisees, for they are like a dog sleeping in the manger of oxen, for neither does he eat nor does he [let] the oxen eat."

103 Jesus said, "Fortunate is the man who knows where the brigands will enter, so that [he] may get up, muster his domain, and arm himself before they invade."

104 They said to Jesus, "Come, let us pray today and let us fast."

Jesus said, "What is the sin that I have committed, or wherein have I been defeated? But when the bridegroom leaves the bridal chamber then let them fast and pray."

105 Jesus said, "He who knows the father and the mother will be called the son of a harlot."

106 Jesus said, "When you make the two one, you will become the sons of man, and when you say, 'Mountain, move away,' it will move away."

107 Jesus said, "The kingdom is like a shepherd who had a hundred sheep. One of them, the largest, went astray. He left the ninety-nine and looked for that one until he found it. When he had gone to such trouble, he said to the sheep, 'I care for you more than the ninety-nine.'"

108 Jesus said, "He who will drink from my mouth will become like me. I myself shall become

he, and the things that are hidden will be revealed to him."

109 Jesus said, "The kingdom is like a man who had a [hidden] treasure in his field without knowing it. And [after] he died, he left it to his [son]. The son [did] not know (about the treasure). He inherited the field and sold [it]. And the one who bought it went plowing and [found] the treasure. He began to lend money at interest to whomever he wished."

110 Jesus said, "Whoever finds the world and becomes rich, let him renounce the world."

111 Jesus said, "The heavens and the earth will be rolled up in your presence. And the one who lives from the living one will not see death." Does not Jesus say, "Whoever finds himself is superior to the world"?

112 Jesus said, "Woe to the flesh that depends on the soul; woe to the soul that depends on the flesh."

113 His disciples said to him, "When will the kingdom come?"

[Jesus said] "It will not come by waiting for it. It will not be a matter of saying 'here it is' or 'there it is'. Rather, the kingdom of the father is spread out upon the earth, and men do not see it."

114 Simon Peter said to them, "Let Mary leave us, for women are not worthy of life."

Jesus said, "I myself shall lead her in order to make her male, so that she too may become a living spirit resembling you males. For every woman who will make herself male will enter the kingdom of heaven."

The Gospel of Peter

The *Gospel of Peter* was known and used as Scripture in some parts of the Christian church in the second century. Its use was eventually disallowed by church leaders, however, who considered some of its teachings heretical and who claimed, as a consequence, that it could not have been written by its imputed author, Simon Peter. Having fallen out of circulation, it was practically forgotten in all but name until a fragment of its text was discovered near the end of the nineteenth century in the tomb of a Christian monk in Egypt.

The fragment narrates the events of Jesus' passion and resurrection; it begins in mid-sentence by describing Pilate's washing of his hands at Jesus' trial. The narrative that follows bears a close relationship with the accounts found in the New Testament Gospels, especially Matthew, including descriptions of Jesus' crucifixion, his burial, the posting of a guard, and the events surrounding the resurrection. Some of the details here, however, are strikingly different. During the crucifixion, for example, Jesus is said to have been "silent as if he had no pain" (v. 10). In addition, some of the stories found here occur nowhere else among our early Christian Gospels. Most significantly, the Gospel narrates an account of Jesus' emergence from his tomb. He is supported by two gigantic angels whose heads reach up to heaven; his own head reaches above the heavens. Behind them emerges the cross. A voice then speaks from heaven, "Have you preached to those who are sleeping?" The cross replies, "Yes" (vv. 39–42).

At the conclusion of the narrative the story breaks off in the middle of a sentence in which the author reveals his name: "But I, Simon Peter, and Andrew my brother, took our nets and went to the sea . . ." (v. 60).

It is impossible to know whether the complete *Gospel of Peter* contained only a passion narrative or, like the New Testament Gospels, simply ended with one. Some scholars maintain that its pseudonymous author (no one actually thinks it was Peter) derived his stories from the New Testament Gospels and modified them according to his own theological perspective; others think that he is depending on *other* sources than the canonical Gospels or that all five Gospels derived their stories from the same sources, but independently of one another.

In any event, it is clear that one of this Gospel's principal concerns is to incriminate Jews for the death of Jesus. Here, for instance, after Jesus' crucifixion, the Jewish people bewail their guilt and lament the certain fate of their beloved sacred city Jerusalem, which God will now destroy as retribution for their disobedience (v. 25). This anti-Judaic slant can perhaps be used to help date the Gospel in its final form, for such themes became common among Christian authors in the second century. The author was possibly writing at the beginning of the century, utilizing traditions from oral and written sources that were themselves much older.

"The Gospel of Peter," from *Documents for the Study of the Gospels,* by David R. Cartlidge and David L. Dungan. © 1980 by David R. Cartlidge and David L. Dungan. Reprinted by permission of Augsburg Fortress.

1 . . . None of the Jews washed his hands, neither did Herod nor any of his judges. As they did not wish to wash, Pilate got up. 2 And then Herod the king ordered the Lord to be taken away. He said to them, "What I ordered you to do to him, do it."

3 Joseph, who was a friend of Pilate and of the Lord, stood there and, seeing that they were about to crucify him, came to Pilate and requested the body of the Lord for burial. 4 Pilate sent to Herod and requested his body. 5 Herod said, "Brother Pilate, if someone had not asked for him, we would have buried him, for the Sabbath dawns. It is written in the Law: the sun is not to set on one who has been killed."[1] And he delivered him to the people on the day before Adzumos (Unleavened Bread), their feast.

6 They took the Lord and they ran, roughed him up, and said, "Let us drag the Son of God (to judgment); we have him in our power." 7 They garbed him in purple and seated him upon the judgment seat and said, "Judge justly, king of Israel!" 8 And one of them brought a crown of thorns and put it on the Lord's head. 9 Others standing there spit in his face; others slapped his cheeks; some struck him with a reed, and whipped him, saying, "By this honor, we honor the Son of God!"

10 And they brought two criminals, and they crucified the Lord between them. He was silent as if he had no pain. 11 When they had set up the cross, they inscribed on it, "This is the King of Israel." 12 And when they had taken away his clothes, in front of him they divided them and cast lots for them. 13 But one of the criminals reviled them and said, "We suffer thus because of the evil we did; this man is the Savior of men, what wrong did he do you?" 14 So they were angry with the thief and gave orders that the criminal's legs should not be broken; thus, he died in torment.

15 It was noon, and darkness gripped all Judea. (The Jews) were worried and anguished lest the sun had already set, since he (Jesus) still lived. It is written for them that the sun is not to set on one who has been killed.[2] 16 One of them said, "Give him gall mixed with vinegar to drink." They mixed it and gave it to him to drink. 17 Indeed, they fulfilled everything, and they brought their sins to full fruition on their own heads. 18 Many went around with lamps; they thought it was night. They

fell. 19 And the Lord cried out, "My power, power, you have left me!" He said this and was taken up. 20 That same hour the veil of the Jerusalem Temple was split in two.

21 Then they pulled the spikes out of the Lord's hands, and they placed him on the ground. There was an earthquake which shook the whole earth, and there was great fear. 22 Then the sun shone again and they realized it was the ninth hour. 23 The Jews rejoiced, and they gave his body to Joseph in order that he should bury it, because he had seen what good things he (Jesus) did. 24 He took the Lord, washed him, wrapped him in linen, and placed him in his own tomb, called the Garden of Joseph.

25 Then the Jews, the elders, and the priests, knowing what evil they did to themselves, began to beat their breasts and say, "Woe, on account of our sins; the judgment and the end of Jerusalem are at hand." 26 I with my companions was aggrieved. We trembled and were wounded to the heart; we were hiding, for we were sought by them as criminals, as if we wished to burn down the Temple. 27 Because of all these things, we fasted and sat mourning and crying night and day until the Sabbath.

28 The scribes, Pharisees, and elders gathered together and, hearing that all the people murmured and beat their breasts, said, "If such great miracles have happened at his death, behold how righteous he is!" 29 The elders were afraid, and they came begging to Pilate and said, "Give us soldiers in order that they may guard his tomb for three days, so that his disciples will not come and steal him, for then the people will assume that he is risen from the dead and they will harm us." 31 Pilate gave them Petronius, the centurion, along with soldiers to guard the tomb; and the elders and scribes came with them to the tomb. 32 They with the centurion and the soldiers—since they were all there together—rolled a huge stone and placed it over the door of the tomb. 33 They sealed it with seven seals, erected a tent there, and stood guard.

34 The morning of the Sabbath dawned; a crowd came from Jerusalem and its surroundings in order that they might see the tomb sealed up. 35 In the night before the dawn of the Lord's day,

---

[1]Deut 21:22–23   [2]Deut 21:22–23

while the soldiers guarded two by two, there was a great noise in heaven, 36 and they saw the heavens open and two men, having great splendor, come down from there and draw near the tomb. 37 The stone which had been placed at the door rolled away by itself and moved to the side. The tomb was opened and the two youths went in.

38 When the soldiers saw this, they awakened the centurion and the elders, for they were there on guard. 39 As they recounted what they had seen, again they saw three men coming out of the tomb; two supported one of them and a cross followed them. 40 The heads of the two reached to heaven, but the one whom they bore with their hands reached beyond the heavens. 41 And they heard a voice speaking from the heavens, "Have you preached to those who are sleeping?" 42 And, obediently, (a voice) was heard from the cross, "Yes."

43 Therefore, they decided among themselves to go and reveal these things to Pilate. 44 While they were deciding, again the heavens were seen to open, and a certain man descended and went into the tomb. 45 When they saw these things, those with the centurion went quickly by night to Pilate, abandoning the tomb they guarded. They explained everything which they had seen; they were greatly upset and said, "Truly he was a Son of God." 46 Pilate answered, "I am pure in regard to the blood of the Son of God; this was your decision." 47 Then they all approached and begged him to order the centurion and the soldiers to say nothing of what they had seen. 48 "For it would be better for us," they said, "to bear the guilt of a great sin before God than to fall into the hands of the Jewish people and to be stoned." 49 Pilate, therefore, ordered the centurion and the soldiers to say nothing.

50 At the dawn of the Lord's day, Mary Magdalene, a disciple of the Lord, afraid because of the Jews since they were inflamed by wrath, had not done at the tomb what custom demanded that women should do for those who had died and whom they loved. 51 [Thus she] brought with her some friends and came to the tomb where he was buried. 52 They were afraid lest the Jews should see them, and they said, "Because we were not able to weep and beat our breasts on the day he was crucified, let us now do these things at his tomb. 53 But who will roll away for us the stone placed before the door of the tomb, so that, when we go in, we can sit beside him and do what ought to be done? 54 For the stone is huge, and we are afraid lest someone should see us. Even if we are not able to enter, at least we can place beside the door that which we bring in his memory; let us weep and beat our breasts until we return to our house."

55 They came and found the tomb opened and, approaching, they bent down to look in. There they saw a youth seated in the middle of the tomb; he was handsome and wore a shining robe. He said to them, 56 "Why did you come? Whom do you seek? Not him who was crucified? He is risen and has gone. If you do not believe, bend over and see the place where he was laid, because he is not there. For he is risen and has gone to the place from which he was sent." 57 Then the women were frightened and fled.

58 It was the last day of Adzumos, and many returned to their homes; the feast was over. 59 We, the twelve disciples of the Lord, wept and were grief-stricken. Each, grieving at what had happened, returned to his own house. 60 But I, Simon Peter, and Andrew, my brother, took our nets and went to the sea; and with us was Levi, the son of Alphaeus, whom the Lord . . . [text breaks off at this point].

The Infancy Gospel of Thomas

Many early Christians were naturally curious to learn the details of Jesus' life. As stories circulated about the inspired teachings and miraculous deeds of Jesus' public ministry, some Christians began to speculate on what he said and did before it began. Only a couple of incidents involving Jesus prior to his baptism are found in the New Testament Gospels: the narratives of his birth and infancy in Matthew and Luke and the account, unique to Luke, of his pilgrimage to the Jerusalem Temple as a twelve-year-old (Luke 2:41–52). Other stories of Jesus as a youth, however, were soon in circulation. Behind many of these legends lay a fundamental question: if Jesus was a miracle-working Son of God as an adult, what was he like as a child?

The *Infancy Gospel of Thomas,* not to be confused with the Coptic *Gospel of Thomas* discovered near Nag Hammadi Egypt, is one of the earliest accounts of these legends. The book was allegedly written by "Thomas, the Israelite." It is not clear whether or not the author intended his readers to recognize him as Judas Thomas, thought by some early Christians to have been Jesus' own brother. If he did, then his accounts of Jesus as a youth, needless to say, would have been based on indisputable authority.

The narrative begins with Jesus as a five-year-old boy and relates a number of incidents, most of them miraculous, that betray a streak of the mischievous in Joseph and Mary's precocious son. Here are anecdotes of Jesus at play with his childhood companions (sometimes harming them with his divine power, sometimes healing them), in confrontation with his elders (usually bettering them), at school with his teachers (revealing their ignorance), and in the workshop with his father (miraculously correcting his mistakes). For modern readers it is difficult to decide whether such stories were meant as serious accounts of Jesus' early life or simply as speculative and entertaining stories of the youthful Son of God.

The text provides few clues to help us fix the time of its composition. Most scholars believe that such "infancy Gospels" began to circulate during the first half of the second century; some have dated the *Infancy Gospel of Thomas* itself as early as 125 C.E.

1 I, Thomas the Israelite, announce and make known to all you brethren from the Gentiles the childhood and great deeds of our Lord Jesus Christ, which he did when he was born in our country. This is the beginning.

2 When this child Jesus was five years old, he was playing at the ford of a stream. He made pools of the rushing water and made it immediately pure; he ordered this by word alone. 2 He made soft clay and modeled twelve sparrows from it. It was the Sabbath when he did this. There were many other children playing with him. 3 A certain Jew saw what Jesus did while playing on the Sabbath; he immediately went and announced to his father Joseph, "See, your child is at the stream, and has taken clay and modeled twelve birds; he has

profaned the Sabbath." 4 Joseph came to the place, and seeing what Jesus did he cried out, "Why do you do on the Sabbath what it is not lawful to do?" Jesus clapped his hands and cried to the sparrows, "Be gone." And the sparrows flew off chirping. 5 The Jews saw this and were amazed. They went away and described to their leaders what they had seen Jesus do.

3 The son of Annas the scribe was standing there with Joseph. He took a branch of a willow and scattered the water which Jesus had arranged. 2 Jesus saw what he did and became angry and said to him, "You unrighteous, impious ignoramus, what did the pools and the water do to harm you? Behold, you shall also wither as a tree, and you shall not bear leaves nor roots nor fruit." 3 And immediately that child was all withered. Jesus left and went to the house of Joseph. The parents of the withered one bore him away, bemoaning his lost youth. They led him to Joseph and reproached him, "What kind of child do you have who does such things?"

4 Once again he was going through the village, and a child who was running banged into his shoulder. Jesus was angered and said to him, "You shall go no further on your way." And immediately the child fell down dead. Some people saw this happen and said, "From whence was this child begotten, for his every word is an act accomplished?" 2 The parents of the dead boy went to Joseph and blamed him: "Because you have such a boy, you cannot live with us in the village; your alternative is to teach him to bless and not to curse, for he is killing our children."

5 Joseph took the child aside privately and warned him, saying, "Why do you do such things? These people are suffering and they hate us and are persecuting us!" Jesus said, "I know that these are not your words, but on account of you I will be silent. However, they shall bear their punishment. Immediately, those who accused him were blinded. 2 Those who saw were very frightened and puzzled, and they said about him, "Every word he speaks, whether good or evil, happens and is a miracle." When he saw what Jesus had done, Joseph arose and took hold of Jesus' ear and pulled it hard. 3 The child was angry and said to him, "It is fitting for you to seek and not find. You have act-

ed very stupidly. Do you not know I am yours? Do not vex me."

6 A man named Zaccheus, a teacher, was standing there and he heard, in part, Jesus saying these things to his father. He was greatly astonished that he said such things, since he was just a child. 2 And after a few days he approached Joseph and said to him, "You have a smart child, and he has a mind. Come, hand him over to me so that he may learn writing. I will give him all understanding with the letters, and teach him to greet all the elders and to honor them as grandfathers and fathers and to love his peers." 3 He told him all the letters from the Alpha to the Omega plainly, with much discussion. But Jesus looked at Zaccheus the teacher, and said to him, "You do not know the Alpha according to nature, how do you teach others the Beta? You hypocrite! First, if you know it, teach the Alpha, then we shall believe you about the Beta." Then he began to question the teacher about the first letter and he could not answer him. 4 Many heard as the child said to Zaccheus, "Listen, teacher, to the order of the first element, and pay attention to this, how it has lines, and a central mark which goes through the two lines you see, (they) converge, go up, again come to head, become the same three times, subordinate, and hypostatic, isometric . . . [The text is unreliable.] You now have the lines of Alpha."

7 When the teacher, Zaccheus, heard so many such allegories of the first letter spoken by the child, he was puzzled about such expoundings and his teaching. He said to those present, "Woe is me, I am wretched and puzzled; I have shamed myself trying to handle this child. 2 I beg you, brother Joseph, take him away. I cannot bear the severity of his glance. I cannot understand his speech at all. This child is not earthborn; he is able to tame even fire. Perhaps he was begotten before the world's creation. What belly bore him, what womb nurtured him, I do not know. Woe is me, friend, he completely confuses me. I cannot follow his understanding. I have fooled myself; I am thrice wretched. I worked anxiously to have a disciple, and I found myself with a teacher. 3 I consider my shame, friends; I am an old man and have been conquered by a child; for at this hour I cannot look into his gaze. When they all say that I have been conquered by a little child, what can I say? What can I discuss about the lines of the first element he spoke to me? I do not know, O friends, for I do not know its beginning and end. Therefore, I beg you, brother Joseph, take him into your house. He is something great: a God, an angel, or what I should say I do not know."

8 While the Jews were comforting Zaccheus, the child gave a great laugh, saying, "Now let what is yours bear fruit, and the blind in heart see. I am from above in order that I may curse them and call them into the things which are above, because he who sent me on your account ordered it." 2 And as the child ceased talking, immediately all those who had fallen under his curse were saved (or, healed). And after that no one dared to anger him, lest he should curse him, and he should be crippled.

9 After some days Jesus was playing upstairs in a certain house, and one of the children playing with him fell from the house and died. And when the other children saw this they ran away, and Jesus remained alone. 2 The parents of the dead child came and accused Jesus of throwing him down. Jesus replied, "I did not throw him down." But still they accused him. 3 Then Jesus leaped down from the roof and stood by the body of the child and cried out in a great voice, saying "Zenon!"—that was his name—"rise up and tell me, did I throw you down?" He immediately rose up and said: "No, Lord, you did not throw me down, but you raised me." Those who saw this were astonished. The parents of the child glorified God because of this sign that happened, and they worshiped Jesus.

10 After a few days a young man was splitting wood in the vicinity; the axe fell and split the bottom of his foot, and he was bleeding to death. 2 There was an outcry and people gathered. The child Jesus ran there. He pushed through the crowd, and seized the injured foot of the youth; immediately he was healed. He said to the youth, "Now get up, split your wood, and remember me." The crowd, seeing what had happened, worshiped the child, saying, "Truly, the Spirit of God lives in this child!"

11 When he was six, his mother sent him to draw water and to bring it into the house, giving him a pitcher. But in the crowd, he had a collision; the water jug was broken. 2 Jesus spread out the garment he had on, filled it with water, and bore it to his mother. When his mother saw the miracle she kissed him, and she kept to herself the mysteries which she saw him do.

12 Again, during planting time the child went with his father to sow seed in their field. While they planted, his father sowed, and the child Jesus planted one grain of wheat. 2 When he had reaped and threshed it, it yielded one hundred measures, and he called all the poor of the village to the threshing floor and gave them the grain. Joseph took the remainder of the grain. He was eight when he did this sign.

13 His father was a carpenter and at that time made ploughs and yokes. He received an order from a certain rich man to make a bed for him. One beam came out shorter than the other, and he did not know what to do. The child Jesus said to Joseph his father, "Lay the two pieces of wood alongside each other, and make them even at one end." 2 Joseph did as the child told him. Jesus stood at the other end and grasped the shorter beam; he stretched it and made it equal with the other. His father Joseph saw and was astonished, and embracing the child he kissed him and said, "I am blessed because God has given this child to me."

14 When Joseph saw the mind and age of the child, that he was growing up, he again wished him not to be ignorant of letters. And he took him and gave him to another teacher. But the teacher said to Joseph, "First I will teach him Greek, and then Hebrew." For the teacher knew the child's learning and feared him. Nevertheless he wrote the alphabet and taught him for many hours, but Jesus did not answer him. 2 Then Jesus said to him, "If you really are a teacher, and you know the letters well, tell me the power of Alpha and I will tell you that of Beta." The teacher was angered and hit Jesus on the head. The child was hurt and cursed him. Immediately the teacher fainted, falling to the ground upon his face. 3 The child returned to the house of Joseph. But Joseph was grief-stricken and gave this order to his mother: "Do not let him go outside the door, because anyone who angers him dies."

15 After some time there was another teacher, a good friend of Joseph. He said to him, "Bring the child to me at school, maybe by flattery I can teach him letters." Joseph said, "If you dare, brother, take him with you." He took him with fear and much anxiety, but the child went with pleasure. 2 Jesus went boldly into the school and found a book lying on the lectern, and taking it, did not read the letters in it, but opened his mouth and spoke by the Holy Spirit and taught the Law to those standing nearby. A great crowd gathered and stood listening to him. They were astonished at the beauty of his teaching and the eloquence of his words, that being a babe he could say such things. 3 Joseph heard and was frightened. He ran into the school, wondering whether this teacher was also without skill, but the teacher said to Joseph, "Know, brother, that I took the child as a disciple, but he is full of much grace and wisdom, and I beg you brother, take him into your house." 4 When the child heard this, immediately he smiled at him and said, "Since you spoke correctly and witnessed correctly, on account of you the one who was stricken shall be healed." And immediately the other teacher was healed. Joseph took the child and returned home.

16 Joseph sent his son James to gather wood and to bring it into the house. The child Jesus followed him. While James was gathering the sticks, a snake bit James's hand. 2 As he lay dying, Jesus came near and breathed on the bite. Immediately James ceased suffering, the snake burst, and James was healed.

17 After this, in the neighborhood of Joseph a certain child took sick and died. His mother wept bitterly. Jesus, hearing the great mourning and clamor, ran quickly and found the child dead. He touched his breast and said, "I say to you, child, do not die, but live and be with your mother!" And immediately the child looked up and laughed. Jesus said to the woman, "Pick him up and give him milk, and remember me." 2 The crowd standing around saw and was amazed, and they said, "Truly this child is a God or an angel of God, because his every word becomes a finished deed." And Jesus left there and played with the other children.

18 After some time a house was being built and there was a great clamor. Jesus arose and went there. Seeing a man lying dead he took his hand and said, "I say to you, man, arise, to your work!" And immediately he arose and worshiped him. 2 Seeing this, the crowd was astonished and said, "This is a heavenly child, for he saved many souls from death, and can save them all his life."

19 When he was twelve his parents, according to custom, went to Jerusalem to the Passover with their traveling companions. After the Passover they returned to their house. While they were going home, the child Jesus went back to Jerusalem. His parents thought that he was in the caravan. 2 After a day's travel, they sought him among their kinfolk and when they did not find him they were troubled. They returned again to the city to seek him. After three days they found him in the Temple, seated in the midst of the teachers, listening and questioning them. They all were attentive and amazed at how he, being a child, could argue with the elders and teachers of the people, solving the chief problems of the Law and the parables of the prophets. 3 His mother, Mary, came up and said to him, "How can you have done this to us, child? Behold, we have looked everywhere for you, grieving." And Jesus said to them, "Why did you look for me? Do you not know that I must be in my Father's house?" 4 The scribes and Pharisees said, "Are you the mother of this child?" She said, "I am." They said to her, "You are blessed among women, because God has blessed the fruit of your womb. We have never before seen or heard such glory or such excellence and wisdom." 5 Jesus arose and followed his mother and was obedient to his parents. But his mother kept (in her heart) all that had happened. Jesus grew in wisdom and stature and grace. Glory be to him forever and ever. Amen.

The Secret Gospel of Mark

The *Secret Gospel of Mark* is a longer edition of Mark's Gospel that has been known only since 1958. While cataloguing manuscripts in the library of the Greek Orthodox monastery of Mar Saba, located southeast of Jerusalem, an American scholar, Morton Smith, came upon a seventeenth-century edition of the letters of Ignatius. On the final blank pages of this volume, an eighteenth-century scribe had copied a portion of a letter allegedly from Clement of Alexandria, a church father who lived at the end of the second century and the beginning of the third. In this letter, Clement indicates that Mark had produced two versions of his Gospel, one for church members at large and the other for the spiritual elite who could grasp the full mysteries of the Kingdom. Clement indicates that this second expanded edition, the so-called *Secret Gospel,* had been entrusted to the Christians of Alexandria, his own city, but that it had come to be misused by members of the Carpocratian sect, a group of Gnostic Christians known for their illicit sexual rituals.

Clement then narrates two of the accounts found in the *Secret Gospel.* The contents of the stories, especially the first, show why this version of the Gospel could have seemed so dangerous in the hands of the initiated, and so interesting to the Carpocratians. Jesus raises a youth from the dead, who then loves Jesus and begs to be allowed to stay with him (the story is reminiscent of both the raising of Lazarus in John 11 and of the story of the "rich young man" of Matt 17:16–22 and Mark 10:17–31). After six days, the youth comes to Jesus in the evening, clothed with nothing but a linen garment over his naked body (cf. Mark 14:51). They spend the night together, with Jesus initiating the youth into the mysteries of the kingdom.

The highly unusual character of this story, in particular its homoerotic overtones, has led scholars to debate virtually every aspect of the *Secret Gospel.* Did Clement of Alexandria actually write this letter, preserved only in an eighteenth-century fragment that no one except Morton Smith has actually seen (Smith published photographs of the document, but the original is inaccessible). Is it a modern forgery? An ancient forgery? If the letter is actually by Clement, were the stories that it narrates known before the end of the second century? Do they actually come from a second edition of Mark's Gospel? Could they, instead, have originally been part of the *first* edition of the Gospel, only to be deleted by orthodox Christian scribes concerned with their ethical implications? Were these stories already widely known by Christians of the first century (such as the author of the Fourth Gospel)? Could they, in fact, have actually happened?

These and other questions have made the *Secret Gospel of Mark* one of the most hotly debated Christian texts to have been discovered in modern times.

Citation I (follows Mark 10:32–34)

And they came to Bethany, and there was a woman there whose brother had died. She came and prostrated herself before Jesus and said to him: "Son of David, pity me." The disciples rebuked her, and Jesus in anger set out with her for the garden where the tomb was. Immediately a loud voice was heard from the tomb, and Jesus approached and rolled the stone away from the entrance to the tomb. And going in immediately where the young man was he stretched out his hand and raised him up, taking him by the hand. The young man looked on him and loved him, and began to beseech him that he might be with him. They came out of the tomb and went into the young man's house, for he was rich. After six days Jesus laid a charge upon him, and when evening came the young man comes to him, with a linen robe thrown over his naked body; and he stayed with him that night, for Jesus was teaching him the mystery of the kingdom of God. When he departed thence, he returned to the other side of the Jordan.

Citation II (follows Mark 10:46a)

And there was the sister of the young man whom Jesus loved and his mother and Salome; and Jesus did not receive them.

Papyrus Egerton 2: The Unknown Gospel

The fragmentary manuscript known as *Papyrus Egerton 2* contains a noncanonical Gospel that was completely unknown until its publication in 1935. The fragments had been discovered among a collection of papyri purchased by the British Museum. They had come from Egypt and are usually dated to 150 C.E. or so. The so-called "Unknown Gospel" narrated in these papyri, however, must have been older. While some scholars have argued that it was written before the canonical Gospels, most have concluded that it was produced sometime during the first half of the second century.

Since the *Unknown Gospel* is preserved only in fragments, it is impossible to judge its original length and contents. The surviving remains contain four separate stories: (1) an account of Jesus' controversy with Jewish leaders that is similar to the stories found in John 5:39–47 and 10:31–39; (2) the healing of a leper, reminiscent of Matthew 8:1–4, Mark 1:40–45, Luke 5:12–16, and 17:11–14; (3) a controversy over paying tribute to Caesar, comparable to Matthew 22:15–22, Mark 12:13–17, and Luke 20:20–26; and (4) a fragmentary account of a miracle by Jesus on the bank of the Jordan River, evidently performed to illustrate his parable about the miraculous growth of seeds. This final story has no parallel in the canonical Gospels.

Scholars continue to debate whether the author of this Gospel (a) used the four canonical Gospels as literary sources for his accounts, (b) quoted from memory stories that he knew from the canonical Gospels (changing them in the process), or (c) acquired his stories, not from the canonical Gospels, but from the oral traditions of Jesus in wide circulation in the first and second centuries.

1.

[And Jesus said] to the lawyers, "[Punish] every wrong-doer and transgressor, and not me . . . what he does as he does it." Then, turning to the rulers of the people, he spoke this word, "Search the scriptures, in which you think you have life; it is they which bear witness to me. Do not think that I have come to accuse you to my Father; your accuser is Moses, on whom you have set your hope." When they said, "We know well that God spoke to Moses; but as for you, we do not know where you come from," Jesus said in reply, "Now your unbelief is exposed to the one who was witnessed to by him. If you had believed [in Moses] you would have believed me, because he wrote to your fathers about me . . ."

"Papyrus Egerton 2: The Unknown Gospel," from *The Apocryphal New Testament,* translated by J. K. Elliott. © Oxford University Press 1993. Reprinted by permission of Oxford University Press.

2.

. . . collect stones and stone him. The rulers sought to lay their hands on him in order to arrest him and hand him over to the crowd; but they could not arrest him, because the hour of his betrayal had not yet come. The Lord himself, passing out through their midst, escaped from them.

And behold, a leper approached him and said, "Teacher Jesus, while journeying with lepers and eating with them in the inn, I myself also became a leper. If, therefore, you are willing, I am cleansed." The Lord said to him, "I am willing: be cleansed." And immediately the leprosy departed from him, and the Lord said, "Go, show yourself to the priests and make an offering for your cleansing as Moses commanded, and sin no more . . ."

3.

. . . came to him to tempt him, saying, "Teacher Jesus, we know that you have come from God, for the things which you do bear witness beyond all the prophets. Tell us then: Is it lawful to render to kings what pertains to their rule? Shall we render it to them or not?" But Jesus, knowing their mind, said to them in indignation, "Why do you call me teacher with your mouth, when you do not do what I say? Well did Isaiah prophesy of you when he said: This people honours me with its lips, but their heart is far from me; in vain do they worship me, (teaching as doctrines merely human) commandments."[1]

4.

". . . enclosed in its place, . . . placed below invisibly, . . . its weight immeasurable." . . . And when they were perplexed at his strange question, Jesus, as he walked, stood on the bank of Jordan and, stretching out his right hand, filled it [with seed] and sowed it on the river. Then . . . the water which had been sown [with seed] . . . in their presence and it produced much fruit . . . to their joy . . .

---

[1]Isa 29:13

The Gospel of the Ebionites

The Ebionites were a group of Jewish Christians located in different regions of the Mediterranean from at least the second to the fourth centuries. The distinguishing characteristic of this group, at least in the eyes of their Christian opponents, was their attempt to combine Jewish views and lifestyles with the belief that Jesus was the Messiah. In particular, they were said to have emphasized their monotheistic belief in only one God to such an extreme that they denied, as a consequence, Jesus' own divinity. At the same time, the Ebionites differed from non-Christian Jews in asserting that Jesus was the sacrifice for the sins of the world and that all other sacrifices had therefore become meaningless. Among other things, this belief led them to embrace a vegetarian diet (since most meat was procured, in the ancient world, through the religious act of sacrificing an animal).

The *Gospel of the Ebionites* does not survive intact but only in quotations of an opponent of Jewish Christians, the fourth-century heresy hunter, Epiphanius of Salamis. These quotations, however, give us a good idea of what the entire Gospel must have looked like. It was written in Greek and represented a kind of harmony of the Gospels of Matthew, Mark, and Luke. This can be seen most clearly in the account of the voice at Jesus' baptism. In the three canonical accounts, the voice says slightly different things. These differences are harmonized, however, in the *Gospel of the Ebionites,* where the voice comes from heaven three times, saying something slightly different on each occasion (corresponding to the words found in each of the Synoptics).

Some of the Ebionites' distinctive concerns were embodied in their Gospel. This can be seen, for example, in the reference to the diet of John the Baptist, in which the canonical statement that he ate locusts (i.e., meat) and wild honey is modified by the change of simply one letter, so that now the Baptist, in anticipation of the Ebionites themselves, maintains a vegetarian cuisine: here he is said to have eaten *pancakes* and wild honey.

It is difficult to assign a date to this Gospel, but since it betrays a knowledge of Matthew, Mark, and Luke, and presupposes a thriving community of Jewish Christians, it is perhaps best to locate it sometime early in the second century.

Epiphanius, *adv. Haer.* 30.1–3

1.

And there was a man named Jesus, and he was about thirty years old; he has chosen us and he came into Capernaum and entered into the house of Simon, surnamed Peter, and he opened his mouth and said, "As I walked by the sea of Tiberias, I chose John and James, the sons of Zebedee, and Simon and Andrew and Thaddaeus and Simon Zelotes, and Judas Iscariot; you also, Matthew, when you were sitting at the receipt of

"The Gospel According to the Ebionites," from *The Apocryphal New Testament,* translated by J. K. Elliott. © Oxford University Press 1993. Reprinted by permission of Oxford University Press.

custom, did I call and you followed me. According to my intention you shall be twelve apostles for a testimony to Israel."

2.

And it came to pass when John baptized, that the Pharisees came to him and were baptized, and all Jerusalem also. He had a garment of camels' hair, and a leathern girdle about his loins. And his meat was wild honey, which tasted like manna, formed like cakes of oil.[1]

3.

The beginning of their Gospel reads thus: "It came to pass in the days of Herod, King of Judaea, that John came and baptized with the baptism of repentance in the river Jordan; he is said to be from the tribe of Aaron and a son of Zacharias the priest and of Elizabeth, and all went out to him."

4.

And after many other words it goes on: "After the people had been baptized, Jesus came also, and was baptized by John. And as he came out of the water, the heavens opened, and he saw the Holy Spirit descending in the form of a dove and entering into him. And a voice was heard from heaven, "You are my beloved Son, and in you am I well pleased." And again, "This day have I begotten you." And suddenly a great light shone in that place. And John, seeing him, said, "Who are you, Lord?" Then a voice was heard from heaven, "This is my beloved Son, in whom I am well pleased." Thereat John fell at his feet and said, "I pray you, Lord, baptize me." But he would not, saying, "Suffer it, for thus it is fitting that all should be accomplished."[2]

Epiphanius *adv. Haer.* 30.14:

5.

They also deny that he is a man, basing their assertion on the word which he said when he was told: "Behold your mother and your brethren stand outside." "Who is my mother and who are my brethren?" And he stretched forth his hand toward his disciples and said, "My brethren and my mother and sisters are those who do the will of my Father."[3]

Epiphanius *adv. Haer.* 30.16:

6.

They say that he is not begotten by God the Father but created like one of the archangels, being greater than they. He rules over the angels and the beings created by God and he came and declared, as the gospel used by them records: "I have come to abolish the sacrifices: if you do not cease from sacrificing, the wrath [of God] will not cease from weighing upon you."

Epiphanius *adv. Haer.* 30.22:

7.

Those who reject meat have inconsiderately fallen into error and said, "I have no desire to eat the flesh of this Paschal Lamb with you." They leave the true order of words and distort the word which is clear to all from the connection of the words and make the disciples say: "Where do you want us to prepare for you to eat the Passover?"[4] To which he replied, "I have no desire to eat the flesh of this Paschal Lamb with you."

---

[1]Matt 3:4–5; Mark 1:5–6 [2]Matt 3:13–17; Mark 1:9–11; Luke 3:21–22 [3]Matt 12:46–50; Mark 3:31–35; Luke 8:19–21 [4]Matt 26:17; Mark 14:12

The Gospel of the Nazareans

Written in Aramaic, possibly near the end of the first century or at the beginning of the second, the *Gospel of the Nazareans* was popular among Jewish Christians (sometimes called "Nazareans") living in and around Palestine. Eventually the Gospel fell into disfavor with the Christian community at large, both because few Christians in later centuries could read Aramaic and because the Gospel's Jewish emphases were widely considered suspicious. We know of the work, therefore, only through quotations of its text (in Greek) by church fathers like Jerome, and by references to it in the margins of several Greek manuscripts of the Gospel according to Matthew.

According to some of the church fathers, this Gospel was in fact nothing other than an Aramaic revision of Matthew's Gospel. If these fathers are correct, then part of the revision may have involved the deletion of Matthew's first two chapters, which record the events surrounding Jesus' miraculous birth. According to many Jewish Christians, Jesus was not born of a virgin, but was a normal human being who was specially chosen to be the Messiah simply because God considered him to be more righteous than anyone else. Scholars debate, however, whether the church fathers were right in their assessment of the book: its author may simply have known traditions about Jesus similar to those also available to Matthew. The fragments of the Gospel that do survive, in any event, share with Matthew a concern for the Jewish Law and the question of whether the Jewish people are able to keep it.

Unlike other noncanonical Gospels, the *Gospel of the Nazareans* was similar in form and scope to those that were eventually included among the writings of the New Testament; it included, for example, stories of Jesus' baptism, public ministry, death, and resurrection. The following are among the longer fragments of the Gospel quoted in our surviving sources.

1. Pseudo-Origen *on Matt.* 15:14

It is written in a certain Gospel. . . . Another rich man said to him, "Master, what good thing shall I do to live?" He said to him, "O man, fulfil the law and the prophets." He replied, "I have done that." He said to him, "Go sell all that you possess and distribute it to the poor, and come, follow me." But the rich man began to scratch his head and it did not please him. And the Lord said to him, "How can you say, 'I have fulfilled the law and the prophets,' since it is written in the law: 'You shall love your neighbor as yourself,'[1] and lo! many of your brethren, sons of Abraham, are clothed in filth, dying of hunger, and your house is full of many goods, and nothing at all goes out of it to them?" And returning to Simon, his disciple, who was sitting by him, he said, "Simon, son of Jonas, it is easier for a camel to enter the eye of a needle than for a rich man (to enter) into the kingdom of heaven."[2]

2. Eusebius, *Theophania* 4:12

The cause therefore of the divisions of souls that take place in houses Christ himself taught, as we have found in a place in the Gospel existing among the Jews in the Hebrew language, in which it is said: "I will choose for myself the best which my Father in heaven has given me."

3. Jerome, *de Vir. Ill.* 6:11

In the Gospel . . . for the "supersubstantial bread" I found "Mahar" which signifies "tomorrow's," so that the meaning would be: "give us this day the bread for the morrow."[3]

4. Jerome, *de Vir. Ill.* 12:13

In the Gospel that the Nazarenes and Ebionites use, which I recently translated from the Hebrew into Greek and which most people designate as the authentic text of Matthew, we read that the man with the withered hand was a mason, who asked for help with these words: "I was a mason, working for my bread with my hands. I pray to you, Jesus, restore me to health so that I do not eat my bread in disgrace."

5. Jerome, *de Vir. Ill.* 23:35

In the Gospel which the Nazarenes use we find it written for "son of Barachias,"[4] "Son of Johoiada."

6. Jerome, *de Vir. Ill.* 27:16

In the so-called Gospel of the Hebrews, Barabbas who was condemned for sedition and murder is interpreted by "son of their teacher."[5]

7. Jerome, *de Vir. Ill.* 27:51

In the Gospel often mentioned we read that "the very great lintel of the Temple broke and fell into pieces."

8. Jerome, *on Isa.*, pref. to book 18

For when the apostles thought him to be a spirit or, in the words of the Gospel of the Hebrews which the Nazarenes read, "a bodiless demon" he said to them . . .

9. Jerome, *Dialogi contra Pelagianos* 3:2

In the Gospel of the Hebrews which is written in the Syro-Chaldaic tongue but in Hebrew characters, which the Nazarenes make use of at this day, and which is also called the "Gospel of the Apostles," or as many think, "that of Matthew," and which is in the library of Caesarea, the following narrative is given: "Behold, the mother of the Lord and his brothers said to him, 'John the Baptist baptizes for the remission of sins; let us go and be baptized by him.' But he said, 'What have I committed, that I should be baptized of him, unless it be that in saying this I am in ignorance?' " In the same volume (i.e. in the Gospel of the Hebrews) we read, "If your brother has sinned in word against you and has made satisfaction, forgive him up to seven times a day." Simon, his disciple, said to him, "Seven times?" The Lord answered saying, "Verily I say to you: until seventy times seven![6] For even in the prophets the word of sin is found after they have been anointed with the Holy Spirit."

---

[1]Lev 19:18 [2]Matt 19:24 [3]Matt 6:11; Luke 11:3 [4]Matt 23:35
[5]Matt 27:16 [6]Matt 18:21–22

10.

The following are "corrections" of the Gospel of Matthew made by scribes of several Greek manuscripts (= *MS,* as numbered below), who based their alterations on the text found in the Gospel of the Nazareans.

Matt 4:5. The Jewish copy has not "to the holy city" but "in Jerusalem." *MS* 566

Matt 5:22. The word "without cause" is not inserted in some copies, nor in the Jewish. *MS* 1424

Matt 7:5. The Jewish has here: "If you are in my bosom and do not do the will of my Father which is in heaven, out of my bosom will I cast you away." *MS* 1424

Matt 10:16. The Jewish has: "(wise) more than serpents" instead of "as serpents." *MS* 1424

Matt 11:12. (The kingdom of heaven suffers violence.) The Jewish has: "is ravished (or plundered)." *MS* 1424

Matt 12:40. The Jewish does not have: "three days and three nights (in the heart of the earth)." *MS* 899

Matt 15:5. The Jewish: "Corban, by which you shall be profited by us." *MS* 1424

Matt 16:2, 3. Omitted by the Jewish (as by many extant manuscripts). *MS* 1424

Matt 16:17. The Jewish: "[Simon] son of John." *MSS* 566, 1424.

Matt 18:22. The Jewish has, immediately after the seventy times seven: "For in the prophets, after they were anointed with the Holy Spirit, there was found in them a word (matter) of sin." *MSS* 566, 899

Matt 26:74. The Jewish: "and he denied and swore and cursed." *MSS* 4, 273, 566, 899, 1424

Matt 27:65. The Jewish: "And he delivered to them armed men, that they might sit opposite the cave and keep watch on it day and night." *MS* 1424.

The Gospel According to the Hebrews

The *Gospel according to the Hebrews* was evidently used by Jewish Christians in the city of Alexandria, Egypt, during the first half of the second century. As with the other distinctively Jewish–Christian Gospels of the Nazareans and of the Ebionites, the *Gospel according to the Hebrews* does not survive intact, but only in the quotations of church fathers like Clement of Alexandria and Origen.

The book was evidently given its name to differentiate it from another Gospel used extensively in Alexandria, but among the non-Jewish Christian population, the *Gospel of the Egyptians.* The *Gospel according to the Hebrews* was written in Greek and narrated important events of Jesus' life, including his baptism, temptation, and resurrection. It appears, however, that these stories were not simply taken over and modified from the Gospels that were later included in the New Testament. They were instead alternative forms of these traditions that had been passed along orally until the unknown author of this Gospel heard them and wrote them down.

Some of the quotations of this Gospel show that it embodied a distinctively gnostic slant, in which the goal of salvation is to discover the truth that will allow one to rise above the trappings of the material world to find rest in the realm of the spirit. Christ, then, is understood to be the one who comes down from that realm to bring the message that can lead to salvation.

1. Clement of Alexandria, *Strom.* 2.9.45

As it is also written in the Gospel of the Hebrews, "He who wonders shall reign, and he who reigns shall rest."

2. Origen, *on John* 2:12

If any should lend credence to the Gospel according to the Hebrews, where the Saviour himself says,

"My mother, the Holy Spirit, took me just now by one of my hairs and carried me off to the great Mount Tabor," he will have difficulty in explaining how the Holy Spirit can be the mother of Christ.

3. Jerome, *on Eph.* 5:4

As we read in the Hebrew Gospel where the Lord says to his disciples, "Never be glad unless you are in charity with your brother."

4. Jerome, *de Vir. Ill.* 2

The Gospel also entitled "according to the Hebrews" which I lately translated into Greek and Latin, and which Origen often quotes, contains the following narrative after the Resurrection: "Now the Lord, when he had given the cloth to the servant of the priest, went to James and appeared to him." For James had taken an oath that he would not eat bread from that hour on which he had drunk the cup of the Lord till he saw him risen from the dead. Again a little later the Lord said, "Bring a table and bread," and forthwith it is added: "He took bread and blessed and broke it and gave to James the Just and said to him, 'My brother, eat your bread, for the Son of Man is risen from those who sleep.'"

5. Jerome, *on Ezek.* 18:7

In the Gospel of the Hebrews, which the Nazarenes are in the habit of reading, it belongs to the greatest sins when "one afflicts the spirit of his brother."

6. Jerome, *on Isa.* 11:2

But in the Gospel which is written in Hebrew and which the Nazarenes read, "the whole fountain of the Holy Spirit shall descend upon him." And the Lord is spirit, and where the Spirit of the Lord is, there is liberty. And in the Gospel referred to above I find this written: "And it came to pass, as the Lord came up out of the water, the whole fountain of the Holy Spirit descended upon him and rested upon him and said to him, 'My son, in all the prophets I expected that you might come and that I might rest upon you. You are my rest, you are my firstborn Son, who reigns in eternity.'"

EARLY CHRISTIAN
ACTS

The Acts of the Apostles

The Book of Acts is the only historical account of the spread of Christianity that derives from the early church itself. It is self-consciously a sequel to the Gospel of Luke. Like its predecessor, it too is addressed to a person named "Theophilus," and it purports to continue the story that was started there (1:1–2). The book has been traditionally ascribed to Luke, the traveling companion of Paul, largely on the basis of several passages in which the author uses the first person plural (cf. 16:11–15). Some scholars have maintained, however, that the author is not directly referring to himself in these passages but has incorporated as a source a travelogue written by one of Paul's companions.

The narrative picks up where the Gospel ends, at the postresurrection appearances of Jesus to his disciples. In Acts he is said to have spent forty days with them, prior to commissioning them to spread the good news of his death and resurrection throughout the world (1:8) and then ascending into heaven (1:9–11). The book is principally about the fulfillment of this apostolic commission, as the apostles and their converts proclaim the gospel in Jerusalem, Judea and Samaria, and eventually in such predominantly Gentile regions as Asia Minor, Macedonia, Achaea, and Rome. The principal actors in the first portion of the narrative (chaps. 1–12) are the eleven apostles (joined by Matthias as the replacement for Judas Iscariot) and their converts. Much of this early narrative focuses on the apostle Peter. Just as Jesus received the Spirit in the Gospel of Luke, and so was empowered to preach and heal (see Luke 3:22; 4:18), so too his apostles receive the Spirit here (Acts 2:1–4) and, like Jesus, heal the sick (3:1–10), cast out demons (5:16; 8:6–7), raise the dead (9:36–41), and attract the multitudes by their proclamation. Also, like him, they are rejected and punished by the Jewish leadership in Jerusalem (4:1–3).

A key event occurs in chapter 9 with the conversion of Saul of Tarsus, also known as Paul. Most of the second part of the narrative, chapters 13–28, describes Paul's missionary journeys (chaps. 13–20), his trip to Jerusalem where he is arrested and several times put on trial (chaps. 20–26), and his final voyage to Rome (chaps. 27–28), where the book ends with him under house arrest preaching the gospel.

Far more than being a disinterested historical sketch of the spread of the Christian church, the Book of Acts is intent to show that the Christian mission could not fail because God himself planned it (see 5:33–39). Even the rejection of the gospel by the Jewish leadership in Jerusalem and, subsequently, by most Jewish communities throughout the empire, occurs according to divine initiative. For this rejection moves the apostles to take the gospel to the Gentiles (see chaps. 10–11). When the question arises as to whether Gentiles must first become Jews prior to being admitted into the Christian church, the apostolic band shows remarkable unanimity in concluding that Gentile men do not need to be circumcised to be followers of Jesus (see chap. 15).

Along with its companion volume, then, the Book of Acts shows how the one true God has brought salvation through Christ, not just to the Jews, but to the entire world.

From the New Revised Standard Version Bible, © 1989.

1 In the first book, Theophilus, I wrote about all that Jesus did and taught from the beginning 2 until the day when he was taken up to heaven, after giving instructions through the Holy Spirit to the apostles whom he had chosen. 3 After his suffering he presented himself alive to them by many convincing proofs, appearing to them during forty days and speaking about the kingdom of God. 4 While staying[a] with them, he ordered them not to leave Jerusalem, but to wait there for the promise of the Father. "This," he said, "is what you have heard from me; 5 for John baptized with water, but you will be baptized with[b] the Holy Spirit not many days from now."

6 So when they had come together, they asked him, "Lord, is this the time when you will restore the kingdom to Israel?" 7 He replied, "It is not for you to know the times or periods that the Father has set by his own authority. 8 But you will receive power when the Holy Spirit has come upon you; and you will be my witnesses in Jerusalem, in all Judea and Samaria, and to the ends of the earth." 9 When he had said this, as they were watching, he was lifted up, and a cloud took him out of their sight. 10 While he was going and they were gazing up toward heaven, suddenly two men in white robes stood by them. 11 They said, "Men of Galilee, why do you stand looking up toward heaven? This Jesus, who has been taken up from you into heaven, will come in the same way as you saw him go into heaven."

12 Then they returned to Jerusalem from the mount called Olivet, which is near Jerusalem, a sabbath day's journey away. 13 When they had entered the city, they went to the room upstairs where they were staying, Peter, and John, and James, and Andrew, Philip and Thomas, Bartholomew and Matthew, James son of Alphaeus, and Simon the Zealot, and Judas son of[c] James. 14 All these were constantly devoting themselves to prayer, together with certain women, including Mary the mother of Jesus, as well as his brothers.

15 In those days Peter stood up among the believers[d] (together the crowd numbered about one hundred twenty persons) and said, 16 "Friends,[e] the scripture had to be fulfilled, which the Holy Spirit through David foretold concerning Judas, who became a guide for those who arrested Jesus— 17 for he was numbered among us and was

allotted his share in this ministry." 18 (Now this man acquired a field with the reward of his wickedness; and falling headlong,[f] he burst open in the middle and all his bowels gushed out. 19 This became known to all the residents of Jerusalem, so that the field was called in their language Hakeldama, that is, Field of Blood.) 20 "For it is written in the book of Psalms,

'Let his homestead become
          desolate,
     and let there be no one to live
               in it';[1]

and

     'Let another take his position of
               overseer.'[2]

21 So one of the men who have accompanied us during all the time that the Lord Jesus went in and out among us, 22 beginning from the baptism of John until the day when he was taken up from us— one of these must become a witness with us to his resurrection." 23 So they proposed two, Joseph called Barsabbas, who was also known as Justus, and Matthias. 24 Then they prayed and said, "Lord, you know everyone's heart. Show us which one of these two you have chosen 25 to take the place[g] in this ministry and apostleship from which Judas turned aside to go to his own place." 26 And they cast lots for them, and the lot fell on Matthias; and he was added to the eleven apostles.

2 When the day of Pentecost had come, they were all together in one place. 2 And suddenly from heaven there came a sound like the rush of a violent wind, and it filled the entire house where they were sitting. 3 Divided tongues, as of fire, appeared among them, and a tongue rested on each of them. 4 All of them were filled with the Holy Spirit and began to speak in other languages, as the Spirit gave them ability.

5 Now there were devout Jews from every nation under heaven living in Jerusalem. 6 And at this sound the crowd gathered and was bewildered, because each one heard them speaking in the native language of each. 7 Amazed and astonished, they asked, "Are not all these who are speaking Galileans? 8 And how is it that we hear,

---

[a]Or *eating* [b]Or *by* [c]Or *the brother of* [d]Gk *brothers* [e]Gk *Men, brothers* [f]Or *swelling up* [g]Other ancient authorities read *the share*

[1]Ps 69:25 [2]Ps 109:8

each of us, in our own native language? 9 Parthians, Medes, Elamites, and residents of Mesopotamia, Judea and Cappadocia, Pontus and Asia, 10 Phrygia and Pamphylia, Egypt and the parts of Libya belonging to Cyrene, and visitors from Rome, both Jews and proselytes, 11 Cretans and Arabs—in our own languages we hear them speaking about God's deeds of power." 12 All were amazed and perplexed, saying to one another, "What does this mean?" 13 But others sneered and said, "They are filled with new wine."

14 But Peter, standing with the eleven, raised his voice and addressed them, "Men of Judea and all who live in Jerusalem, let this be known to you, and listen to what I say. 15 Indeed, these are not drunk, as you suppose, for it is only nine o'clock in the morning. 16 No, this is what was spoken through the prophet Joel:

17   'In the last days it will be, God
            declares,
        that I will pour out my Spirit
            upon all flesh,
        and your sons and your
            daughters shall prophesy,
        and your young men shall see
            visions,
        and your old men shall dream
            dreams.
18   Even upon my slaves, both men
            and women,
        in those days I will pour out my
            Spirit;
        and they shall prophesy.
19   And I will show portents in the
            heaven above
        and signs on the earth below,
        blood, and fire, and smoky
            mist.
20   The sun shall be turned to
            darkness
        and the moon to blood,
        before the coming of the
            Lord's great and glorious
            day.
21   Then everyone who calls on the
            name of the Lord shall be
            saved.'[3]

22 "You that are Israelites,[h] listen to what I have to say: Jesus of Nazareth,[i] a man attested to you by God with deeds of power, wonders, and signs that God did through him among you, as you yourselves know— 23 this man, handed over to you according to the definite plan and foreknowledge of God, you crucified and killed by the hands of those outside the law. 24 But God raised him up, having freed him from death,[j] because it was impossible for him to be held in its power. 25 For David says concerning him,

        'I saw the Lord always before me,
            for he is at my right hand so
                that I will not be shaken;
26   therefore my heart was glad, and
                my tongue rejoiced;
            moreover my flesh will live in
                hope.
27   For you will not abandon my soul
                to Hades,
            or let your Holy One experience
                corruption.
28   You have made known to me the
                ways of life;
            you will make me full of
                gladness with your
                presence.'[4]

29 "Fellow Israelites,[k] I may say to you confidently of our ancestor David that he both died and was buried, and his tomb is with us to this day. 30 Since he was a prophet, he knew that God had sworn with an oath to him that he would put one of his descendants on his throne. 31 Foreseeing this, David[l] spoke of the resurrection of the Messiah,[m] saying,

        'He was not abandoned to Hades,
            nor did his flesh experience
                corruption.'[5]

32 This Jesus God raised up, and of that all of us are witnesses. 33 Being therefore exalted at[n] the right hand of God, and having received from the Father the promise of the Holy Spirit, he has poured out this that you both see and hear. 34 For David did not ascend into the heavens, but he himself says,

        'The Lord said to my Lord,
            "Sit at my right hand,

[h]Gk *Men, Israelites*   [i]Gk *the Nazorean*   [j]Gk *the pains of death*   [k]Gk *Men, brothers*   [l]Gk *he*   [m]Or *the Christ*   [n]Or *by*

[3]Joel 2:28–32   [4]Ps 16:8–11   [5]Ps 16:10

35   until I make your enemies your
           footstool.'"[6]

36 Therefore let the entire house of Israel know with certainty that God has made him both Lord and Messiah,[o] this Jesus whom you crucified."

37 Now when they heard this, they were cut to the heart and said to Peter and to the other apostles, "Brothers,[p] what should we do?" 38 Peter said to them, "Repent, and be baptized every one of you in the name of Jesus Christ so that your sins may be forgiven; and you will receive the gift of the Holy Spirit. 39 For the promise is for you, for your children, and for all who are far away, everyone whom the Lord our God calls to him." 40 And he testified with many other arguments and exhorted them, saying, "Save yourselves from this corrupt generation." 41 So those who welcomed his message were baptized, and that day about three thousand persons were added. 42 They devoted themselves to the apostles' teaching and fellowship, to the breaking of bread and the prayers.

43 Awe came upon everyone, because many wonders and signs were being done by the apostles. 44 All who believed were together and had all things in common; 45 they would sell their possessions and goods and distribute the proceeds[q] to all, as any had need. 46 Day by day, as they spent much time together in the temple, they broke bread at home[r] and ate their food with glad and generous[s] hearts, 47 praising God and having the goodwill of all the people. And day by day the Lord added to their number those who were being saved.

3 One day Peter and John were going up to the temple at the hour of prayer, at three o'clock in the afternoon. 2 And a man lame from birth was being carried in. People would lay him daily at the gate of the temple called the Beautiful Gate so that he could ask for alms from those entering the temple. 3 When he saw Peter and John about to go into the temple, he asked them for alms. 4 Peter looked intently at him, as did John, and said, "Look at us." 5 And he fixed his attention on them, expecting to receive something from them. 6 But Peter said, "I have no silver or gold, but what I have I give you; in the name of Jesus Christ of Nazareth,[t] stand up and walk." 7 And he took him by the right hand and raised him up; and immediately his feet and ankles were made strong.

8 Jumping up, he stood and began to walk, and he entered the temple with them, walking and leaping and praising God. 9 All the people saw him walking and praising God, 10 and they recognized him as the one who used to sit and ask for alms at the Beautiful Gate of the temple; and they were filled with wonder and amazement at what had happened to him.

11 While he clung to Peter and John, all the people ran together to them in the portico called Solomon's Portico, utterly astonished. 12 When Peter saw it, he addressed the people, "You Israelites,[u] why do you wonder at this, or why do you stare at us, as though by our own power or piety we had made him walk? 13 The God of Abraham, the God of Isaac, and the God of Jacob, the God of our ancestors has glorified his servant[v] Jesus, whom you handed over and rejected in the presence of Pilate, though he had decided to release him. 14 But you rejected the Holy and Righteous One and asked to have a murderer given to you, 15 and you killed the Author of life, whom God raised from the dead. To this we are witnesses. 16 And by faith in his name, his name itself has made this man strong, whom you see and know; and the faith that is through Jesus[w] has given him this perfect health in the presence of all of you.

17 "And now, friends,[x] I know that you acted in ignorance, as did also your rulers. 18 In this way God fulfilled what he had foretold through all the prophets, that his Messiah[y] would suffer. 19 Repent therefore, and turn to God so that your sins may be wiped out, 20 so that times of refreshing may come from the presence of the Lord, and that he may send the Messiah[z] appointed for you, that is, Jesus, 21 who must remain in heaven until the time of universal restoration that God announced long ago through his holy prophets. 22 Moses said, 'The Lord your God will raise up for you from your own people[x] a prophet like me. You must listen to whatever he tells you. 23 And it will be that everyone who does not listen to that prophet will be utterly rooted out of the people.'[7]

---

[o]Or *Christ*   [p]Gk *Men, brothers*   [q]Gk *them*   [r]Or *from house to house*
[s]Or *sincere*   [t]Gk *the Nazorean*   [u]Gk *Men, Israelites*   [v]Or *child*
[w]Gk *him*   [x]Gk *brothers*   [y]Or *his Christ*   [z]Or *the Christ*

---

[6]Ps 110:1   [7]Deut 18:15–19

24 And all the prophets, as many as have spoken, from Samuel and those after him, also predicted these days. 25 You are the descendants of the prophets and of the covenant that God gave to your ancestors, saying to Abraham, 'And in your descendants all the families of the earth shall be blessed.'[8] 26 When God raised up his servant,[a] he sent him first to you, to bless you by turning each of you from your wicked ways."

4 While Peter and John[b] were speaking to the people, the priests, the captain of the temple, and the Sadducees came to them, 2 much annoyed because they were teaching the people and proclaiming that in Jesus there is the resurrection of the dead. 3 So they arrested them and put them in custody until the next day, for it was already evening. 4 But many of those who heard the word believed; and they numbered about five thousand.

5 The next day their rulers, elders, and scribes assembled in Jerusalem, 6 with Annas the high priest, Caiaphas, John,[c] and Alexander, and all who were of the high-priestly family. 7 When they had made the prisoners[d] stand in their midst, they inquired, "By what power or by what name did you do this?" 8 Then Peter, filled with the Holy Spirit, said to them, "Rulers of the people and elders, 9 if we are questioned today because of a good deed done to someone who was sick and are asked how this man has been healed, 10 let it be known to all of you, and to all the people of Israel, that this man is standing before you in good health by the name of Jesus Christ of Nazareth,[e] whom you crucified, whom God raised from the dead. 11 This Jesus[f] is

'the stone that was rejected by
you, the builders;
it has become the cornerstone.'[g9]

12 There is salvation in no one else, for there is no other name under heaven given among mortals by which we must be saved."

13 Now when they saw the boldness of Peter and John and realized that they were uneducated and ordinary men, they were amazed and recognized them as companions of Jesus. 14 When they saw the man who had been cured standing beside them, they had nothing to say in opposition. 15 So they ordered them to leave the council while they discussed the matter with one another. 16 They said, "What will we do with them? For it is obvious to all who live in Jerusalem that a notable sign has been done through them; we cannot deny it. 17 But to keep it from spreading further among the people, let us warn them to speak no more to anyone in this name." 18 So they called them and ordered them not to speak or teach at all in the name of Jesus. 19 But Peter and John answered them, "Whether it is right in God's sight to listen to you rather than to God, you must judge; 20 for we cannot keep from speaking about what we have seen and heard." 21 After threatening them again, they let them go, finding no way to punish them because of the people, for all of them praised God for what had happened. 22 For the man on whom this sign of healing had been performed was more than forty years old.

23 After they were released, they went to their friends[h] and reported what the chief priests and the elders had said to them. 24 When they heard it, they raised their voices together to God and said, "Sovereign Lord, who made the heaven and the earth, the sea, and everything in them, 25 it is you who said by the Holy Spirit through our ancestor David, your servant:[a]

'Why did the Gentiles rage,
and the peoples imagine vain
things?
26 The kings of the earth took their
stand,
and the rulers have gathered
together
against the Lord and against
his Messiah.'[i10]

27 For in this city, in fact, both Herod and Pontius Pilate, with the Gentiles and the peoples of Israel, gathered together against your holy servant[a] Jesus, whom you anointed, 28 to do whatever your hand and your plan had predestined to take place. 29 And now, Lord, look at their threats, and grant to your servants[j] to speak your word with all boldness, 30 while you stretch out your hand to heal, and signs and wonders are performed through the name of your holy servant[a] Jesus." 31 When they had prayed, the place in which they were gathered

---

[a]Or child   [b]Gk While they   [c]Other ancient authorities read Jonathan   [d]Gk them   [e]Gk the Nazorean   [f]Gk This   [g]Or keystone   [h]Gk their own   [i]Or his Christ   [j]Gk slaves

[8]Gen 22:18; 26:4   [9]Ps 118:22   [10]Ps 2:1–2

together was shaken; and they were all filled with the Holy Spirit and spoke the word of God with boldness.

32 Now the whole group of those who believed were of one heart and soul, and no one claimed private ownership of any possessions, but everything they owned was held in common. 33 With great power the apostles gave their testimony to the resurrection of the Lord Jesus, and great grace was upon them all. 34 There was not a needy person among them, for as many as owned lands or houses sold them and brought the proceeds of what was sold. 35 They laid it at the apostles' feet, and it was distributed to each as any had need. 36 There was a Levite, a native of Cyprus, Joseph, to whom the apostles gave the name Barnabas (which means "son of encouragement"). 37 He sold a field that belonged to him, then brought the money, and laid it at the apostles' feet.

5 But a man named Ananias, with the consent of his wife Sapphira, sold a piece of property; 2 with his wife's knowledge, he kept back some of the proceeds, and brought only a part and laid it at the apostles' feet. 3 "Ananias," Peter asked, "why has Satan filled your heart to lie to the Holy Spirit and to keep back part of the proceeds of the land? 4 While it remained unsold, did it not remain your own? And after it was sold, were not the proceeds at your disposal? How is it that you have contrived this deed in your heart? You did not lie to us[k] but to God!" 5 Now when Ananias heard these words, he fell down and died. And great fear seized all who heard of it. 6 The young men came and wrapped up his body,[l] then carried him out and buried him.

7 After an interval of about three hours his wife came in, not knowing what had happened. 8 Peter said to her, "Tell me whether you and your husband sold the land for such and such a price." And she said, "Yes, that was the price." 9 Then Peter said to her, "How is it that you have agreed together to put the Spirit of the Lord to the test? Look, the feet of those who have buried your husband are at the door, and they will carry you out." 10 Immediately she fell down at his feet and died. When the young men came in they found her dead, so they carried her out and buried her beside her husband. 11 And great fear seized the whole church and all who heard of these things.

12 Now many signs and wonders were done among the people through the apostles. And they were all together in Solomon's Portico. 13 None of the rest dared to join them, but the people held them in high esteem. 14 Yet more than ever believers were added to the Lord, great numbers of both men and women, 15 so that they even carried out the sick into the streets, and laid them on cots and mats, in order that Peter's shadow might fall on some of them as he came by. 16 A great number of people would also gather from the towns around Jerusalem, bringing the sick and those tormented by unclean spirits, and they were all cured.

17 Then the high priest took action; he and all who were with him (that is, the sect of the Sadducees), being filled with jealousy, 18 arrested the apostles and put them in the public prison. 19 But during the night an angel of the Lord opened the prison doors, brought them out, and said, 20 "Go, stand in the temple and tell the people the whole message about this life." 21 When they heard this, they entered the temple at daybreak and went on with their teaching.

When the high priest and those with him arrived, they called together the council and the whole body of the elders of Israel, and sent to the prison to have them brought. 22 But when the temple police went there, they did not find them in the prison; so they returned and reported, 23 "We found the prison securely locked and the guards standing at the doors, but when we opened them, we found no one inside." 24 Now when the captain of the temple and the chief priests heard these words, they were perplexed about them, wondering what might be going on. 25 Then someone arrived and announced, "Look, the men whom you put in prison are standing in the temple and teaching the people!" 26 Then the captain went with the temple police and brought them, but without violence, for they were afraid of being stoned by the people.

27 When they had brought them, they had them stand before the council. The high priest questioned them, 28 saying, "We gave you strict orders not to teach in this name,[m] yet here you have filled Jerusalem with your teaching and you are

---

[k]Gk *to men* [l]Meaning of Gk uncertain [m]Other ancient authorities read *Did we not give you strict orders not to teach in this name?*

determined to bring this man's blood on us."
29 But Peter and the apostles answered, "We must obey God rather than any human authority.[n] 30 The God of our ancestors raised up Jesus, whom you had killed by hanging him on a tree. 31 God exalted him at his right hand as Leader and Savior that he might give repentance to Israel and forgiveness of sins. 32 And we are witnesses to these things, and so is the Holy Spirit whom God has given to those who obey him."

33 When they heard this, they were enraged and wanted to kill them. 34 But a Pharisee in the council named Gamaliel, a teacher of the law, respected by all the people, stood up and ordered the men to be put outside for a short time. 35 Then he said to them, "Fellow Israelites,[o] consider carefully what you propose to do to these men. 36 For some time ago Theudas rose up, claiming to be somebody, and a number of men, about four hundred, joined him; but he was killed, and all who followed him were dispersed and disappeared. 37 After him Judas the Galilean rose up at the time of the census and got people to follow him; he also perished, and all who followed him were scattered. 38 So in the present case, I tell you, keep away from these men and let them alone; because if this plan or this undertaking is of human origin, it will fail; 39 but if it is of God, you will not be able to overthrow them—in that case you may even be found fighting against God!"

They were convinced by him, 40 and when they had called in the apostles, they had them flogged. Then they ordered them not to speak in the name of Jesus, and let them go. 41 As they left the council, they rejoiced that they were considered worthy to suffer dishonor for the sake of the name. 42 And every day in the temple and at home[p] they did not cease to teach and proclaim Jesus as the Messiah.[q]

6 Now during those days, when the disciples were increasing in number, the Hellenists complained against the Hebrews because their widows were being neglected in the daily distribution of food. 2 And the twelve called together the whole community of the disciples and said, "It is not right that we should neglect the word of God in order to wait on tables.[r] 3 Therefore, friends,[s] select from among yourselves seven men

of good standing, full of the Spirit and of wisdom, whom we may appoint to this task, 4 while we, for our part, will devote ourselves to prayer and to serving the word." 5 What they said pleased the whole community, and they chose Stephen, a man full of faith and the Holy Spirit, together with Philip, Prochorus, Nicanor, Timon, Parmenas, and Nicolaus, a proselyte of Antioch. 6 They had these men stand before the apostles, who prayed and laid their hands on them.

7 The word of God continued to spread; the number of the disciples increased greatly in Jerusalem, and a great many of the priests became obedient to the faith.

8 Stephen, full of grace and power, did great wonders and signs among the people. 9 Then some of those who belonged to the synagogue of the Freedmen (as it was called), Cyrenians, Alexandrians, and others of those from Cilicia and Asia, stood up and argued with Stephen. 10 But they could not withstand the wisdom and the Spirit[t] with which he spoke. 11 Then they secretly instigated some men to say, "We have heard him speak blasphemous words against Moses and God." 12 They stirred up the people as well as the elders and the scribes; then they suddenly confronted him, seized him, and brought him before the council. 13 They set up false witnesses who said, "This man never stops saying things against this holy place and the law; 14 for we have heard him say that this Jesus of Nazareth[u] will destroy this place and will change the customs that Moses handed on to us." 15 And all who sat in the council looked intently at him, and they saw that his face was like the face of an angel.

7 Then the high priest asked him, "Are these things so?" 2 And Stephen replied:

"Brothers[v] and fathers, listen to me. The God of glory appeared to our ancestor Abraham when he was in Mesopotamia, before he lived in Haran, 3 and said to him, 'Leave your country and your relatives and go to the land that I will show you.'[11] 4 Then he left the country of the Chaldeans and settled in Haran. After his father died, God had

---

[n]Gk *than men*   [o]Gk *Men, Israelites*   [p]Or *from house to house*
[q]Or *the Christ*   [r]Or *keep accounts*   [s]Gk *brothers*   [t]Or *spirit*
[u]Gk *the Nazorean*   [v]Gk *Men, brothers*

---

[11]Gen 12:1

him move from there to this country in which you are now living. 5 He did not give him any of it as a heritage, not even a foot's length, but promised to give it to him as his possession and to his descendants after him, even though he had no child. 6 And God spoke in these terms, that his descendants would be resident aliens in a country belonging to others, who would enslave them and mistreat them during four hundred years. 7 'But I will judge the nation that they serve,' said God, 'and after that they shall come out and worship me in this place.'[12] 8 Then he gave him the covenant of circumcision. And so Abraham[w] became the father of Isaac and circumcised him on the eighth day; and Isaac became the father of Jacob, and Jacob of the twelve patriarchs.

9 "The patriarchs, jealous of Joseph, sold him into Egypt; but God was with him, 10 and rescued him from all his afflictions, and enabled him to win favor and to show wisdom when he stood before Pharaoh, king of Egypt, who appointed him ruler over Egypt and over all his household. 11 Now there came a famine throughout Egypt and Canaan, and great suffering, and our ancestors could find no food. 12 But when Jacob heard that there was grain in Egypt, he sent our ances-tors there on their first visit. 13 On the second visit Joseph made himself known to his brothers, and Joseph's family became known to Pharaoh. 14 Then Joseph sent and invited his father Jacob and all his relatives to come to him, seventy-five in all; 15 so Jacob went down to Egypt. He himself died there as well as our ancestors, 16 and their bodies[x] were brought back to Shechem and laid in the tomb that Abraham had bought for a sum of silver from the sons of Hamor in Shechem.

17 "But as the time drew near for the fulfillment of the promise that God had made to Abraham, our people in Egypt increased and multiplied 18 until another king who had not known Joseph ruled over Egypt. 19 He dealt craftily with our race and forced our ancestors to abandon their infants so that they would die. 20 At this time Moses was born, and he was beautiful before God. For three months he was brought up in his father's house; 21 and when he was abandoned, Pharaoh's daughter adopted him and brought him up as her own son. 22 So Moses was instructed in all the wisdom

of the Egyptians and was powerful in his words and deeds.

23 "When he was forty years old, it came into his heart to visit his relatives, the Israelites.[y] 24 When he saw one of them being wronged, he defended the oppressed man and avenged him by striking down the Egyptian. 25 He supposed that his kinsfolk would understand that God through him was rescuing them, but they did not understand. 26 The next day he came to some of them as they were quarreling and tried to reconcile them, saying, 'Men, you are brothers; why do you wrong each other?' 27 But the man who was wronging his neighbor pushed Moses[z] aside, saying, 'Who made you a ruler and a judge over us? 28 Do you want to kill me as you killed the Egyptian yesterday?'[13] 29 When he heard this, Moses fled and became a resident alien in the land of Midian. There he became the father of two sons.

30 "Now when forty years had passed, an angel appeared to him in the wilderness of Mount Sinai, in the flame of a burning bush. 31 When Moses saw it, he was amazed at the sight; and as he approached to look, there came the voice of the Lord: 32 'I am the God of your ancestors, the God of Abraham, Isaac, and Jacob.' Moses began to tremble and did not dare to look. 33 Then the Lord said to him, 'Take off the sandals from your feet, for the place where you are standing is holy ground. 34 I have surely seen the mistreatment of my people who are in Egypt and have heard their groaning, and I have come down to rescue them. Come now, I will send you to Egypt.'[14]

35 "It was this Moses whom they rejected when they said, 'Who made you a ruler and a judge?'[15] and whom God now sent as both ruler and liberator through the angel who appeared to him in the bush. 36 He led them out, having performed wonders and signs in Egypt, at the Red Sea, and in the wilderness for forty years. 37 This is the Moses who said to the Israelites, 'God will raise up a prophet for you from your own people[a] as he raised me up.'[16] 38 He is the one who was in the congregation in the wilderness with the angel who

---

[w]Gk *he*   [x]Gk *they*   [y]Gk *his brothers, the sons of Israel*   [z]Gk *him*
[a]Gk *your brothers*

---

[12]Gen 15:13–14; Exod 3:12   [13]Exod 2:14   [14]Exod 3:2–10   [15]Exod 2:14   [16]Deut 18:15

spoke to him at Mount Sinai, and with our ancestors; and he received living oracles to give to us. 39 Our ancestors were unwilling to obey him; instead, they pushed him aside, and in their hearts they turned back to Egypt, 40 saying to Aaron, 'Make gods for us who will lead the way for us; as for this Moses who led us out from the land of Egypt, we do not know what has happened to him.'[17] 41 At that time they made a calf, offered a sacrifice to the idol, and reveled in the works of their hands. 42 But God turned away from them and handed them over to worship the host of heaven, as it is written in the book of the prophets:

'Did you offer to me slain victims
     and sacrifices
   forty years in the wilderness,
       O house of Israel?
43   No; you took along the tent of
             Moloch,
     and the star of your god
             Rephan,
       the images that you made to
             worship;
   so I will remove you beyond
             Babylon.'[18]

44 "Our ancestors had the tent of testimony in the wilderness, as God[b] directed when he spoke to Moses, ordering him to make it according to the pattern he had seen. 45 Our ancestors in turn brought it in with Joshua when they dispossessed the nations that God drove out before our ancestors. And it was there until the time of David, 46 who found favor with God and asked that he might find a dwelling place for the house of Jacob.[c] 47 But it was Solomon who built a house for him. 48 Yet the Most High does not dwell in houses made with human hands;[d] as the prophet says,

49   'Heaven is my throne,
     and the earth is my footstool.
   What kind of house will you build
       for me, says the Lord,
     or what is the place of my rest?
50   Did not my hand make all these
             things?'[19]

51 "You stiff-necked people, uncircumcised in heart and ears, you are forever opposing the Holy Spirit, just as your ancestors used to do. 52 Which of the prophets did your ancestors not persecute? They killed those who foretold the coming of the

Righteous One, and now you have become his betrayers and murderers. 53 You are the ones that received the law as ordained by angels, and yet you have not kept it."

54 When they heard these things, they became enraged and ground their teeth at Stephen.[e] 55 But filled with the Holy Spirit, he gazed into heaven and saw the glory of God and Jesus standing at the right hand of God. 56 "Look," he said, "I see the heavens opened and the Son of Man standing at the right hand of God!" 57 But they covered their ears, and with a loud shout all rushed together against him. 58 Then they dragged him out of the city and began to stone him; and the witnesses laid their coats at the feet of a young man named Saul. 59 While they were stoning Stephen, he prayed, "Lord Jesus, receive my spirit." 60 Then he knelt down and cried out in a loud voice, "Lord, do not hold this sin against them." When he had said this, he died.[f]

8 And Saul approved of their killing him.
    That day a severe persecution began against the church in Jerusalem, and all except the apostles were scattered throughout the countryside of Judea and Samaria. 2 Devout men buried Stephen and made loud lamentation over him. 3 But Saul was ravaging the church by entering house after house; dragging off both men and women, he committed them to prison.

4 Now those who were scattered went from place to place, proclaiming the word. 5 Philip went down to the city[g] of Samaria and proclaimed the Messiah[h] to them. 6 The crowds with one accord listened eagerly to what was said by Philip, hearing and seeing the signs that he did, 7 for unclean spirits, crying with loud shrieks, came out of many who were possessed; and many others who were paralyzed or lame were cured. 8 So there was great joy in that city.

9 Now a certain man named Simon had previously practiced magic in the city and amazed the people of Samaria, saying that he was someone great. 10 All of them, from the least to the greatest, listened to him eagerly, saying, "This man is

---

[b]Gk he   [c]Other ancient authorities read for the God of Jacob   [d]Gk with hands   [e]Gk him   [f]Gk fell asleep   [g]Other ancient authorities read a city   [h]Or the Christ

[17]Exod 32:1, 23   [18]Amos 5:25–27   [19]Isa 66:1–2

the power of God that is called Great." 11 And they listened eagerly to him because for a long time he had amazed them with his magic. 12 But when they believed Philip, who was proclaiming the good news about the kingdom of God and the name of Jesus Christ, they were baptized, both men and women. 13 Even Simon himself believed. After being baptized, he stayed constantly with Philip and was amazed when he saw the signs and great miracles that took place.

14 Now when the apostles at Jerusalem heard that Samaria had accepted the word of God, they sent Peter and John to them. 15 The two went down and prayed for them that they might receive the Holy Spirit 16 (for as yet the Spirit had not come[i] upon any of them; they had only been baptized in the name of the Lord Jesus). 17 Then Peter and John[j] laid their hands on them, and they received the Holy Spirit. 18 Now when Simon saw that the Spirit was given through the laying on of the apostles' hands, he offered them money, 19 saying, "Give me also this power so that anyone on whom I lay my hands may receive the Holy Spirit." 20 But Peter said to him, "May your silver perish with you, because you thought you could obtain God's gift with money! 21 You have no part or share in this, for your heart is not right before God. 22 Repent therefore of this wickedness of yours, and pray to the Lord that, if possible, the intent of your heart may be forgiven you. 23 For I see that you are in the gall of bitterness and the chains of wickedness." 24 Simon answered, "Pray for me to the Lord, that nothing of what you[k] have said may happen to me."

25 Now after Peter and John[l] had testified and spoken the word of the Lord, they returned to Jerusalem, proclaiming the good news to many villages of the Samaritans.

26 Then an angel of the Lord said to Philip, "Get up and go toward the south[m] to the road that goes down from Jerusalem to Gaza." (This is a wilderness road.) 27 So he got up and went. Now there was an Ethiopian eunuch, a court official of the Candace, queen of the Ethiopians, in charge of her entire treasury. He had come to Jerusalem to worship 28 and was returning home; seated in his chariot, he was reading the prophet Isaiah. 29 Then the Spirit said to Philip, "Go over to this chariot and join it." 30 So Philip ran up to it and heard him reading the prophet Isaiah. He asked, "Do you understand what you are reading?" 31 He replied, "How can I, unless someone guides me?" And he invited Philip to get in and sit beside him. 32 Now the passage of the scripture that he was reading was this:

> "Like a sheep he was led to the
>   slaughter,
>   and like a lamb silent before its
>   shearer,
>   so he does not open his
>   mouth.
>
> 33 In his humiliation justice was
>   denied him.
>   Who can describe his
>   generation?
>   For his life is taken away
>   from the earth."[20]

34 The eunuch asked Philip, "About whom, may I ask you, does the prophet say this, about himself or about someone else?" 35 Then Philip began to speak, and starting with this scripture, he proclaimed to him the good news about Jesus. 36 As they were going along the road, they came to some water; and the eunuch said, "Look, here is water! What is to prevent me from being baptized?"[n] 38 He commanded the chariot to stop, and both of them, Philip and the eunuch, went down into the water, and Philip[o] baptized him. 39 When they came up out of the water, the Spirit of the Lord snatched Philip away; the eunuch saw him no more, and went on his way rejoicing. 40 But Philip found himself at Azotus, and as he was passing through the region, he proclaimed the good news to all the towns until he came to Caesarea.

9 Meanwhile Saul, still breathing threats and murder against the disciples of the Lord, went to the high priest 2 and asked him for letters to the synagogues at Damascus, so that if he found any who belonged to the Way, men or women, he

---

[i]Gk *fallen*   [j]Gk *they*   [k]The Greek word for *you* and the verb *pray* are plural   [l]Gk *after they*   [m]Or *go at noon*   [n]Other ancient authorities add all or most of verse 37, *And Philip said, "If you believe with all your heart, you may." And he replied, "I believe that Jesus Christ is the Son of God."*   [o]Gk *he*

---

[20]Isa 53:7–8

might bring them bound to Jerusalem. 3 Now as he was going along and approaching Damascus, suddenly a light from heaven flashed around him. 4 He fell to the ground and heard a voice saying to him, "Saul, Saul, why do you persecute me?" 5 He asked, "Who are you, Lord?" The reply came, "I am Jesus, whom you are persecuting. 6 But get up and enter the city, and you will be told what you are to do." 7 The men who were traveling with him stood speechless because they heard the voice but saw no one. 8 Saul got up from the ground, and though his eyes were open, he could see nothing; so they led him by the hand and brought him into Damascus. 9 For three days he was without sight, and neither ate nor drank.

10 Now there was a disciple in Damascus named Ananias. The Lord said to him in a vision, "Ananias." He answered, "Here I am, Lord." 11 The Lord said to him, "Get up and go to the street called Straight, and at the house of Judas look for a man of Tarsus named Saul. At this moment he is praying, 12 and he has seen in a vision[p] a man named Ananias come in and lay his hands on him so that he might regain his sight." 13 But Ananias answered, "Lord, I have heard from many about this man, how much evil he has done to your saints in Jerusalem; 14 and here he has authority from the chief priests to bind all who invoke your name." 15 But the Lord said to him, "Go, for he is an instrument whom I have chosen to bring my name before Gentiles and kings and before the people of Israel; 16 I myself will show him how much he must suffer for the sake of my name." 17 So Ananias went and entered the house. He laid his hands on Saul[q] and said, "Brother Saul, the Lord Jesus, who appeared to you on your way here, has sent me so that you may regain your sight and be filled with the Holy Spirit." 18 And immediately something like scales fell from his eyes, and his sight was restored. Then he got up and was baptized, 19 and after taking some food, he regained his strength.

For several days he was with the disciples in Damascus, 20 and immediately he began to proclaim Jesus in the synagogues, saying, "He is the Son of God." 21 All who heard him were amazed and said, "Is not this the man who made havoc in Jerusalem among those who invoked this name? And has he not come here for the purpose of bring-

ing them bound before the chief priests?" 22 Saul became increasingly more powerful and confounded the Jews who lived in Damascus by proving that Jesus[r] was the Messiah.[s]

23 After some time had passed, the Jews plotted to kill him, 24 but their plot became known to Saul. They were watching the gates day and night so that they might kill him; 25 but his disciples took him by night and let him down through an opening in the wall,[t] lowering him in a basket.

26 When he had come to Jerusalem, he attempted to join the disciples; and they were all afraid of him, for they did not believe that he was a disciple. 27 But Barnabas took him, brought him to the apostles, and described for them how on the road he had seen the Lord, who had spoken to him, and how in Damascus he had spoken boldly in the name of Jesus. 28 So he went in and out among them in Jerusalem, speaking boldly in the name of the Lord. 29 He spoke and argued with the Hellenists; but they were attempting to kill him. 30 When the believers[u] learned of it, they brought him down to Caesarea and sent him off to Tarsus.

31 Meanwhile the church throughout Judea, Galilee, and Samaria had peace and was built up. Living in the fear of the Lord and in the comfort of the Holy Spirit, it increased in numbers.

32 Now as Peter went here and there among all the believers,[v] he came down also to the saints living in Lydda. 33 There he found a man named Aeneas, who had been bedridden for eight years, for he was paralyzed. 34 Peter said to him, "Aeneas, Jesus Christ heals you; get up and make your bed!" And immediately he got up. 35 And all the residents of Lydda and Sharon saw him and turned to the Lord.

36 Now in Joppa there was a disciple whose name was Tabitha, which in Greek is Dorcas.[w] She was devoted to good works and acts of charity. 37 At that time she became ill and died. When they had washed her, they laid her in a room upstairs. 38 Since Lydda was near Joppa, the disciples, who heard that Peter was there, sent two men to him with the request, "Please come to us without de-

lay." 39 So Peter got up and went with them; and when he arrived, they took him to the room upstairs. All the widows stood beside him, weeping and showing tunics and other clothing that Dorcas had made while she was with them. 40 Peter put all of them outside, and then he knelt down and prayed. He turned to the body and said, "Tabitha, get up." Then she opened her eyes, and seeing Peter, she sat up. 41 He gave her his hand and helped her up. Then calling the saints and widows, he showed her to be alive. 42 This became known throughout Joppa, and many believed in the Lord. 43 Meanwhile he stayed in Joppa for some time with a certain Simon, a tanner.

10 In Caesarea there was a man named Cornelius, a centurion of the Italian Cohort, as it was called. 2 He was a devout man who feared God with all his household; he gave alms generously to the people and prayed constantly to God. 3 One afternoon at about three o'clock he had a vision in which he clearly saw an angel of God coming in and saying to him, "Cornelius." 4 He stared at him in terror and said, "What is it, Lord?" He answered, "Your prayers and your alms have ascended as a memorial before God. 5 Now send men to Joppa for a certain Simon who is called Peter; 6 he is lodging with Simon, a tanner, whose house is by the seaside." 7 When the angel who spoke to him had left, he called two of his slaves and a devout soldier from the ranks of those who served him, 8 and after telling them everything, he sent them to Joppa.

9 About noon the next day, as they were on their journey and approaching the city, Peter went up on the roof to pray. 10 He became hungry and wanted something to eat; and while it was being prepared, he fell into a trance. 11 He saw the heaven opened and something like a large sheet coming down, being lowered to the ground by its four corners. 12 In it were all kinds of four-footed creatures and reptiles and birds of the air. 13 Then he heard a voice saying, "Get up, Peter; kill and eat." 14 But Peter said, "By no means, Lord; for I have never eaten anything that is profane or unclean." 15 The voice said to him again, a second time, "What God has made clean, you must not call profane." 16 This happened three times, and the thing was suddenly taken up to heaven.

17 Now while Peter was greatly puzzled about what to make of the vision that he had seen, suddenly the men sent by Cornelius appeared. They were asking for Simon's house and were standing by the gate. 18 They called out to ask whether Simon, who was called Peter, was staying there. 19 While Peter was still thinking about the vision, the Spirit said to him, "Look, three[x] men are searching for you. 20 Now get up, go down, and go with them without hesitation; for I have sent them." 21 So Peter went down to the men and said, "I am the one you are looking for; what is the reason for your coming?" 22 They answered, "Cornelius, a centurion, an upright and God-fearing man, who is well spoken of by the whole Jewish nation, was directed by a holy angel to send for you to come to his house and to hear what you have to say." 23 So Peter[y] invited them in and gave them lodging.

The next day he got up and went with them, and some of the believers[z] from Joppa accompanied him. 24 The following day they came to Caesarea. Cornelius was expecting them and had called together his relatives and close friends. 25 On Peter's arrival Cornelius met him, and falling at his feet, worshiped him. 26 But Peter made him get up, saying, "Stand up; I am only a mortal." 27 And as he talked with him, he went in and found that many had assembled; 28 and he said to them, "You yourselves know that it is unlawful for a Jew to associate with or to visit a Gentile; but God has shown me that I should not call anyone profane or unclean. 29 So when I was sent for, I came without objection. Now may I ask why you sent for me?"

30 Cornelius replied, "Four days ago at this very hour, at three o'clock, I was praying in my house when suddenly a man in dazzling clothes stood before me. 31 He said, 'Cornelius, your prayer has been heard and your alms have been remembered before God. 32 Send therefore to Joppa and ask for Simon, who is called Peter; he is staying in the home of Simon, a tanner, by the sea.' 33 Therefore I sent for you immediately, and you have been kind enough to come. So now all of us are here in the presence of God to listen to all that the Lord has commanded you to say."

---

[x]One ancient authority reads *two*; others lack the word   [y]Gk *he*
[z]Gk *brothers*

34 Then Peter began to speak to them: "I truly understand that God shows no partiality, 35 but in every nation anyone who fears him and does what is right is acceptable to him. 36 You know the message he sent to the people of Israel, preaching peace by Jesus Christ—he is Lord of all. 37 That message spread throughout Judea, beginning in Galilee after the baptism that John announced: 38 how God anointed Jesus of Nazareth with the Holy Spirit and with power; how he went about doing good and healing all who were oppressed by the devil, for God was with him. 39 We are witnesses to all that he did both in Judea and in Jerusalem. They put him to death by hanging him on a tree; 40 but God raised him on the third day and allowed him to appear, 41 not to all the people but to us who were chosen by God as witnesses, and who ate and drank with him after he rose from the dead. 42 He commanded us to preach to the people and to testify that he is the one ordained by God as judge of the living and the dead. 43 All the prophets testify about him that everyone who believes in him receives forgiveness of sins through his name."

44 While Peter was still speaking, the Holy Spirit fell upon all who heard the word. 45 The circumcised believers who had come with Peter were astounded that the gift of the Holy Spirit had been poured out even on the Gentiles, 46 for they heard them speaking in tongues and extolling God. Then Peter said, 47 "Can anyone withhold the water for baptizing these people who have received the Holy Spirit just as we have?" 48 So he ordered them to be baptized in the name of Jesus Christ. Then they invited him to stay for several days.

11 Now the apostles and the believers[a] who were in Judea heard that the Gentiles had also accepted the word of God. 2 So when Peter went up to Jerusalem, the circumcised believers[b] criticized him, 3 saying, "Why did you go to uncircumcised men and eat with them?" 4 Then Peter began to explain it to them, step by step, saying, 5 "I was in the city of Joppa praying, and in a trance I saw a vision. There was something like a large sheet coming down from heaven, being lowered by its four corners; and it came close to me. 6 As I looked at it closely I saw four-footed animals, beasts of prey, reptiles, and birds of the air. 7 I also heard a voice saying to me, 'Get up, Peter; kill and eat.' 8 But I replied, 'By no means, Lord; for nothing profane or unclean has ever entered my mouth.' 9 But a second time the voice answered from heaven, 'What God has made clean, you must not call profane.' 10 This happened three times; then everything was pulled up again to heaven. 11 At that very moment three men, sent to me from Caesarea, arrived at the house where we were. 12 The Spirit told me to go with them and not to make a distinction between them and us.[c] These six brothers also accompanied me, and we entered the man's house. 13 He told us how he had seen the angel standing in his house and saying, 'Send to Joppa and bring Simon, who is called Peter; 14 he will give you a message by which you and your entire household will be saved.' 15 And as I began to speak, the Holy Spirit fell upon them just as it had upon us at the beginning. 16 And I remembered the word of the Lord, how he had said, 'John baptized with water, but you will be baptized with the Holy Spirit.' 17 If then God gave them the same gift that he gave us when we believed in the Lord Jesus Christ, who was I that I could hinder God?" 18 When they heard this, they were silenced. And they praised God, saying, "Then God has given even to the Gentiles the repentance that leads to life."

19 Now those who were scattered because of the persecution that took place over Stephen traveled as far as Phoenicia, Cyprus, and Antioch, and they spoke the word to no one except Jews. 20 But among them were some men of Cyprus and Cyrene who, on coming to Antioch, spoke to the Hellenists[d] also, proclaiming the Lord Jesus. 21 The hand of the Lord was with them, and a great number became believers and turned to the Lord. 22 News of this came to the ears of the church in Jerusalem, and they sent Barnabas to Antioch. 23 When he came and saw the grace of God, he rejoiced, and he exhorted them all to remain faithful to the Lord with steadfast devotion; 24 for he was a good man, full of the Holy Spirit and of faith. And a great many people were brought to the Lord. 25 Then Barnabas went to Tarsus to look for

[a]Gk brothers [b]Gk lacks believers [c]Or not to hesitate [d]Other ancient authorities read Greeks

Saul, 26 and when he had found him, he brought him to Antioch. So it was that for an entire year they met with[e] the church and taught a great many people, and it was in Antioch that the disciples were first called "Christians."

27 At that time prophets came down from Jerusalem to Antioch. 28 One of them named Agabus stood up and predicted by the Spirit that there would be a severe famine over all the world; and this took place during the reign of Claudius. 29 The disciples determined that according to their ability, each would send relief to the believers[f] living in Judea; 30 this they did, sending it to the elders by Barnabas and Saul.

12 About that time King Herod laid violent hands upon some who belonged to the church. 2 He had James, the brother of John, killed with the sword. 3 After he saw that it pleased the Jews, he proceeded to arrest Peter also. (This was during the festival of Unleavened Bread.) 4 When he had seized him, he put him in prison and handed him over to four squads of soldiers to guard him, intending to bring him out to the people after the Passover. 5 While Peter was kept in prison, the church prayed fervently to God for him.

6 The very night before Herod was going to bring him out, Peter, bound with two chains, was sleeping between two soldiers, while guards in front of the door were keeping watch over the prison. 7 Suddenly an angel of the Lord appeared and a light shone in the cell. He tapped Peter on the side and woke him, saying, "Get up quickly." And the chains fell off his wrists. 8 The angel said to him, "Fasten your belt and put on your sandals." He did so. Then he said to him, "Wrap your cloak around you and follow me." 9 Peter[g] went out and followed him; he did not realize that what was happening with the angel's help was real; he thought he was seeing a vision. 10 After they had passed the first and the second guard, they came before the iron gate leading into the city. It opened for them of its own accord, and they went outside and walked along a lane, when suddenly the angel left him. 11 Then Peter came to himself and said, "Now I am sure that the Lord has sent his angel and rescued me from the hands of Herod and from all that the Jewish people were expecting."

12 As soon as he realized this, he went to the house of Mary, the mother of John whose other name was Mark, where many had gathered and were praying. 13 When he knocked at the outer gate, a maid named Rhoda came to answer. 14 On recognizing Peter's voice, she was so overjoyed that, instead of opening the gate, she ran in and announced that Peter was standing at the gate. 15 They said to her, "You are out of your mind!" But she insisted that it was so. They said, "It is his angel." 16 Meanwhile Peter continued knocking; and when they opened the gate, they saw him and were amazed. 17 He motioned to them with his hand to be silent, and described for them how the Lord had brought him out of the prison. And he added, "Tell this to James and to the believers."[f] Then he left and went to another place.

18 When morning came, there was no small commotion among the soldiers over what had become of Peter. 19 When Herod had searched for him and could not find him, he examined the guards and ordered them to be put to death. Then he went down from Judea to Caesarea and stayed there.

20 Now Herod[h] was angry with the people of Tyre and Sidon. So they came to him in a body; and after winning over Blastus, the king's chamberlain, they asked for a reconciliation, because their country depended on the king's country for food. 21 On an appointed day Herod put on his royal robes, took his seat on the platform, and delivered a public address to them. 22 The people kept shouting, "The voice of a god, and not of a mortal!" 23 And immediately, because he had not given the glory to God, an angel of the Lord struck him down, and he was eaten by worms and died.

24 But the word of God continued to advance and gain adherents. 25 Then after completing their mission Barnabas and Saul returned to[i] Jerusalem and brought with them John, whose other name was Mark.

13 Now in the church at Antioch there were prophets and teachers: Barnabas, Simeon who was called Niger, Lucius of Cyrene, Manaen a member of the court of Herod the ruler,[j] and Saul. 2 While they were worshiping the Lord and

---

[e]Or *were guests of*   [f]Gk *brothers*   [g]Gk *He*   [h]Gk *he*   [i]Other ancient authorities read *from*   [j]Gk *tetrarch*

fasting, the Holy Spirit said, "Set apart for me Barnabas and Saul for the work to which I have called them." 3 Then after fasting and praying they laid their hands on them and sent them off.

4 So, being sent out by the Holy Spirit, they went down to Seleucia; and from there they sailed to Cyprus. 5 When they arrived at Salamis, they proclaimed the word of God in the synagogues of the Jews. And they had John also to assist them. 6 When they had gone through the whole island as far as Paphos, they met a certain magician, a Jewish false prophet, named Bar-Jesus. 7 He was with the proconsul, Sergius Paulus, an intelligent man, who summoned Barnabas and Saul and wanted to hear the word of God. 8 But the magician Elymas (for that is the translation of his name) opposed them and tried to turn the proconsul away from the faith. 9 But Saul, also known as Paul, filled with the Holy Spirit, looked intently at him 10 and said, "You son of the devil, you enemy of all righteousness, full of all deceit and villainy, will you not stop making crooked the straight paths of the Lord? 11 And now listen—the hand of the Lord is against you, and you will be blind for a while, unable to see the sun." Immediately mist and darkness came over him, and he went about groping for someone to lead him by the hand. 12 When the proconsul saw what had happened, he believed, for he was astonished at the teaching about the Lord.

13 Then Paul and his companions set sail from Paphos and came to Perga in Pamphylia. John, however, left them and returned to Jerusalem; 14 but they went on from Perga and came to Antioch in Pisidia. And on the sabbath day they went into the synagogue and sat down. 15 After the reading of the law and the prophets, the officials of the synagogue sent them a message, saying, "Brothers, if you have any word of exhortation for the people, give it." 16 So Paul stood up and with a gesture began to speak:

"You Israelites,[k] and others who fear God, listen. 17 The God of this people Israel chose our ancestors and made the people great during their stay in the land of Egypt, and with uplifted arm he led them out of it. 18 For about forty years he put up with[l] them in the wilderness. 19 After he had destroyed seven nations in the land of Canaan, he gave them their land as an inheritance 20 for about four hundred fifty years. After that he gave them judges until the time of the prophet Samuel. 21 Then they asked for a king; and God gave them Saul son of Kish, a man of the tribe of Benjamin, who reigned for forty years. 22 When he had removed him, he made David their king. In his testimony about him he said, 'I have found David, son of Jesse, to be a man after my heart, who will carry out all my wishes.'[21] 23 Of this man's posterity God has brought to Israel a Savior, Jesus, as he promised; 24 before his coming John had already proclaimed a baptism of repentance to all the people of Israel. 25 And as John was finishing his work, he said, 'What do you suppose that I am? I am not he. No, but one is coming after me; I am not worthy to untie the thong of the sandals[m] on his feet.'

26 "My brothers, you descendants of Abraham's family, and others who fear God, to us[n] the message of this salvation has been sent. 27 Because the residents of Jerusalem and their leaders did not recognize him or understand the words of the prophets that are read every sabbath, they fulfilled those words by condemning him. 28 Even though they found no cause for a sentence of death, they asked Pilate to have him killed. 29 When they had carried out everything that was written about him, they took him down from the tree and laid him in a tomb. 30 But God raised him from the dead; 31 and for many days he appeared to those who came up with him from Galilee to Jerusalem, and they are now his witnesses to the people. 32 And we bring you the good news that what God promised to our ancestors 33 he has fulfilled for us, their children, by raising Jesus; as also it is written in the second psalm,

'You are my Son;
today I have begotten you.'[22]

34 As to his raising him from the dead, no more to return to corruption, he has spoken in this way,

'I will give you the holy promises
made to David.'[23]

35 Therefore he has also said in another psalm,

'You will not let your Holy One
experience corruption.'[24]

[k]Gk *Men, Israelites* [l]Other ancient authorities read *cared for*
[m]Gk *untie the sandals* [n]Other ancient authorities read *you*

[21]Ps 89:20; 1 Sam 13:14 [22]Ps 2:7 [23]Isa 55:3 [24]Ps 16:10

36 For David, after he had served the purpose of God in his own generation, died,[o] was laid beside his ancestors, and experienced corruption; 37 but he whom God raised up experienced no corruption. 38 Let it be known to you therefore, my brothers, that through this man forgiveness of sins is proclaimed to you; 39 by this Jesus[p] everyone who believes is set free from all those sins[q] from which you could not be freed by the law of Moses. 40 Beware, therefore, that what the prophets said does not happen to you:

41   'Look, you scoffers!
            Be amazed and perish,
        for in your days I am doing a
            work,
        a work that you will never
            believe, even if someone
            tells you.'"[25]

42 As Paul and Barnabas[r] were going out, the people urged them to speak about these things again the next sabbath. 43 When the meeting of the synagogue broke up, many Jews and devout converts to Judaism followed Paul and Barnabas, who spoke to them and urged them to continue in the grace of God.

44 The next sabbath almost the whole city gathered to hear the word of the Lord.[s] 45 But when the Jews saw the crowds, they were filled with jealousy; and blaspheming, they contradicted what was spoken by Paul. 46 Then both Paul and Barnabas spoke out boldly, saying, "It was necessary that the word of God should be spoken first to you. Since you reject it and judge yourselves to be unworthy of eternal life, we are now turning to the Gentiles. 47 For so the Lord has commanded us, saying,

        'I have set you to be a light for
            the Gentiles,
        so that you may bring salvation
            to the ends of the earth.'"[26]

48 When the Gentiles heard this, they were glad and praised the word of the Lord; and as many as had been destined for eternal life became believers. 49 Thus the word of the Lord spread throughout the region. 50 But the Jews incited the devout women of high standing and the leading men of the city, and stirred up persecution against Paul and Barnabas, and drove them out of their region. 51 So they shook the dust off their feet in protest against them, and went to Iconium. 52 And the disciples were filled with joy and with the Holy Spirit.

14 The same thing occurred in Iconium, where Paul and Barnabas[r] went into the Jewish synagogue and spoke in such a way that a great number of both Jews and Greeks became believers. 2 But the unbelieving Jews stirred up the Gentiles and poisoned their minds against the brothers. 3 So they remained for a long time, speaking boldly for the Lord, who testified to the word of his grace by granting signs and wonders to be done through them. 4 But the residents of the city were divided; some sided with the Jews, and some with the apostles. 5 And when an attempt was made by both Gentiles and Jews, with their rulers, to mistreat them and to stone them, 6 the apostles[r] learned of it and fled to Lystra and Derbe, cities of Lycaonia, and to the surrounding country; 7 and there they continued proclaiming the good news.

8 In Lystra there was a man sitting who could not use his feet and had never walked, for he had been crippled from birth. 9 He listened to Paul as he was speaking. And Paul, looking at him intently and seeing that he had faith to be healed, 10 said in a loud voice, "Stand upright on your feet." And the man[t] sprang up and began to walk. 11 When the crowds saw what Paul had done, they shouted in the Lycaonian language, "The gods have come down to us in human form!" 12 Barnabas they called Zeus, and Paul they called Hermes, because he was the chief speaker. 13 The priest of Zeus, whose temple was just outside the city,[u] brought oxen and garlands to the gates; he and the crowds wanted to offer sacrifice. 14 When the apostles Barnabas and Paul heard of it, they tore their clothes and rushed out into the crowd, shouting, 15 "Friends,[v] why are you doing this? We are mortals just like you, and we bring you good news, that you should turn from these worthless things to the living God, who made the heaven and the earth and the sea and all that is in them. 16 In past generations he allowed all the nations to

[o]Gk *fell asleep*   [p]Gk *this*   [q]Gk *all*   [r]Gk *they*   [s]Other ancient authorities read *God*   [t]Gk *he*   [u]Or *The priest of Zeus-Outside-the-City*   [v]Gk *Men*

[25]Hab 1:5   [26]Isa 49:6

follow their own ways; 17 yet he has not left himself without a witness in doing good—giving you rains from heaven and fruitful seasons, and filling you with food and your hearts with joy." 18 Even with these words, they scarcely restrained the crowds from offering sacrifice to them.

19 But Jews came there from Antioch and Iconium and won over the crowds. Then they stoned Paul and dragged him out of the city, supposing that he was dead. 20 But when the disciples surrounded him, he got up and went into the city. The next day he went on with Barnabas to Derbe.

21 After they had proclaimed the good news to that city and had made many disciples, they returned to Lystra, then on to Iconium and Antioch. 22 There they strengthened the souls of the disciples and encouraged them to continue in the faith, saying, "It is through many persecutions that we must enter the kingdom of God." 23 And after they had appointed elders for them in each church, with prayer and fasting they entrusted them to the Lord in whom they had come to believe.

24 Then they passed through Pisidia and came to Pamphylia. 25 When they had spoken the word in Perga, they went down to Attalia. 26 From there they sailed back to Antioch, where they had been commended to the grace of God for the work[w] that they had completed. 27 When they arrived, they called the church together and related all that God had done with them, and how he had opened a door of faith for the Gentiles. 28 And they stayed there with the disciples for some time.

15

Then certain individuals came down from Judea and were teaching the brothers, "Unless you are circumcised according to the custom of Moses, you cannot be saved." 2 And after Paul and Barnabas had no small dissension and debate with them, Paul and Barnabas and some of the others were appointed to go up to Jerusalem to discuss this question with the apostles and the elders. 3 So they were sent on their way by the church, and as they passed through both Phoenicia and Samaria, they reported the conversion of the Gentiles, and brought great joy to all the believers.[x] 4 When they came to Jerusalem, they were welcomed by the church and the apostles and the elders, and they reported all that God had done with them. 5 But some believers who belonged to the sect of the Pharisees stood

up and said, "It is necessary for them to be circumcised and ordered to keep the law of Moses."

6 The apostles and the elders met together to consider this matter. 7 After there had been much debate, Peter stood up and said to them, "My brothers,[y] you know that in the early days God made a choice among you, that I should be the one through whom the Gentiles would hear the message of the good news and become believers. 8 And God, who knows the human heart, testified to them by giving them the Holy Spirit, just as he did to us; 9 and in cleansing their hearts by faith he has made no distinction between them and us. 10 Now therefore why are you putting God to the test by placing on the neck of the disciples a yoke that neither our ancestors nor we have been able to bear? 11 On the contrary, we believe that we will be saved through the grace of the Lord Jesus, just as they will."

12 The whole assembly kept silence, and listened to Barnabas and Paul as they told of all the signs and wonders that God had done through them among the Gentiles. 13 After they finished speaking, James replied, "My brothers,[y] listen to me. 14 Simeon has related how God first looked favorably on the Gentiles, to take from among them a people for his name. 15 This agrees with the words of the prophets, as it is written,

16   'After this I will return,
         and I will rebuild the dwelling of
               David, which has fallen;
            from its ruins I will rebuild it,
               and I will set it up,
17   so that all other peoples may seek
               the Lord—
            even all the Gentiles over whom
               my name has been called.
         Thus says the Lord, who has
               been making these things
18   known from long ago.'[z][27]

19 Therefore I have reached the decision that we should not trouble those Gentiles who are turning to God, 20 but we should write to them to abstain only from things polluted by idols and from forni-

---

[w]Or *committed in the grace of God to the work*   [x]Gk *brothers*
[y]Gk *Men, brothers*   [z]Other ancient authorities read *things.* [18]*Known to God from of old are all his works.'*

---

[27]Amos 9:11–12

cation and from whatever has been strangled[a] and from blood. 21 For in every city, for generations past, Moses has had those who proclaim him, for he has been read aloud every sabbath in the synagogues."

22 Then the apostles and the elders, with the consent of the whole church, decided to choose men from among their members[b] and to send them to Antioch with Paul and Barnabas. They sent Judas called Barsabbas, and Silas, leaders among the brothers, 23 with the following letter: "The brothers, both the apostles and the elders, to the believers[c] of Gentile origin in Antioch and Syria and Cilicia, greetings. 24 Since we have heard that certain persons who have gone out from us, though with no instructions from us, have said things to disturb you and have unsettled your minds,[d] 25 we have decided unanimously to choose representatives[e] and send them to you, along with our beloved Barnabas and Paul, 26 who have risked their lives for the sake of our Lord Jesus Christ. 27 We have therefore sent Judas and Silas, who themselves will tell you the same things by word of mouth. 28 For it has seemed good to the Holy Spirit and to us to impose on you no further burden than these essentials: 29 that you abstain from what has been sacrificed to idols and from blood and from what is strangled[a] and from fornication. If you keep yourselves from these, you will do well. Farewell."

30 So they were sent off and went down to Antioch. When they gathered the congregation together, they delivered the letter. 31 When its members[f] read it, they rejoiced at the exhortation. 32 Judas and Silas, who were themselves prophets, said much to encourage and strengthen the believers.[c] 33 After they had been there for some time, they were sent off in peace by the believers[c] to those who had sent them.[g] 35 But Paul and Barnabas remained in Antioch, and there, with many others, they taught and proclaimed the word of the Lord.

36 After some days Paul said to Barnabas, "Come, let us return and visit the believers[c] in every city where we proclaimed the word of the Lord and see how they are doing." 37 Barnabas wanted to take with them John called Mark. 38 But Paul decided not to take with them one who had deserted them in Pamphylia and had not accompanied them in the work. 39 The disagreement became so sharp that they parted company; Barnabas took Mark with him and sailed away to Cyprus. 40 But Paul chose Silas and set out, the believers[c] commending him to the grace of the Lord. 41 He went through Syria and Cilicia, strengthening the churches.

16 Paul[h] went on also to Derbe and to Lystra, where there was a disciple named Timothy, the son of a Jewish woman who was a believer; but his father was a Greek. 2 He was well spoken of by the believers[c] in Lystra and Iconium. 3 Paul wanted Timothy to accompany him; and he took him and had him circumcised because of the Jews who were in those places, for they all knew that his father was a Greek. 4 As they went from town to town, they delivered to them for observance the decisions that had been reached by the apostles and elders who were in Jerusalem. 5 So the churches were strengthened in the faith and increased in numbers daily.

6 They went through the region of Phrygia and Galatia, having been forbidden by the Holy Spirit to speak the word in Asia. 7 When they had come opposite Mysia, they attempted to go into Bithynia, but the Spirit of Jesus did not allow them; 8 so, passing by Mysia, they went down to Troas. 9 During the night Paul had a vision: there stood a man of Macedonia pleading with him and saying, "Come over to Macedonia and help us." 10 When he had seen the vision, we immediately tried to cross over to Macedonia, being convinced that God had called us to proclaim the good news to them.

11 We set sail from Troas and took a straight course to Samothrace, the following day to Neapolis, 12 and from there to Philippi, which is a leading city of the district[i] of Macedonia and a Roman colony. We remained in this city for some days. 13 On the sabbath day we went outside the gate by the river, where we supposed there was a place of prayer; and we sat down and spoke to the women who had gathered there. 14 A certain

[a]Other ancient authorities lack *and from whatever has been strangled*
[b]Gk *from among them*   [c]Gk *brothers*   [d]Other ancient authorities add
saying, 'You must be circumcised and keep the law,'   [e]Gk *men*
[f]Gk *When they*   [g]Other ancient authorities add verse 34, *But it
seemed good to Silas to remain there*   [h]Gk *He*   [i]Other authorities
read *a city of the first district*

woman named Lydia, a worshiper of God, was listening to us; she was from the city of Thyatira and a dealer in purple cloth. The Lord opened her heart to listen eagerly to what was said by Paul. 15 When she and her household were baptized, she urged us, saying, "If you have judged me to be faithful to the Lord, come and stay at my home." And she prevailed upon us.

16 One day, as we were going to the place of prayer, we met a slave-girl who had a spirit of divination and brought her owners a great deal of money by fortune-telling. 17 While she followed Paul and us, she would cry out, "These men are slaves of the Most High God, who proclaim to you[j] a way of salvation." 18 She kept doing this for many days. But Paul, very much annoyed, turned and said to the spirit, "I order you in the name of Jesus Christ to come out of her." And it came out that very hour.

19 But when her owners saw that their hope of making money was gone, they seized Paul and Silas and dragged them into the marketplace before the authorities. 20 When they had brought them before the magistrates, they said, "These men are disturbing our city; they are Jews 21 and are advocating customs that are not lawful for us as Romans to adopt or observe." 22 The crowd joined in attacking them, and the magistrates had them stripped of their clothing and ordered them to be beaten with rods. 23 After they had given them a severe flogging, they threw them into prison and ordered the jailer to keep them securely. 24 Following these instructions, he put them in the innermost cell and fastened their feet in the stocks.

25 About midnight Paul and Silas were praying and singing hymns to God, and the prisoners were listening to them. 26 Suddenly there was an earthquake, so violent that the foundations of the prison were shaken; and immediately all the doors were opened and everyone's chains were unfastened. 27 When the jailer woke up and saw the prison doors wide open, he drew his sword and was about to kill himself, since he supposed that the prisoners had escaped. 28 But Paul shouted in a loud voice, "Do not harm yourself, for we are all here." 29 The jailer[k] called for lights, and rushing in, he fell down trembling before Paul and Silas. 30 Then he brought them outside and said, "Sirs, what must I do to be saved?" 31 They answered, "Believe on the Lord Jesus, and you will be saved, you and your household." 32 They spoke the word of the Lord[l] to him and to all who were in his house. 33 At the same hour of the night he took them and washed their wounds; then he and his entire family were baptized without delay. 34 He brought them up into the house and set food before them; and he and his entire household rejoiced that he had become a believer in God.

35 When morning came, the magistrates sent the police, saying, "Let those men go." 36 And the jailer reported the message to Paul, saying, "The magistrates sent word to let you go; therefore come out now and go in peace." 37 But Paul replied, "They have beaten us in public, uncondemned, men who are Roman citizens, and have thrown us into prison; and now are they going to discharge us in secret? Certainly not! Let them come and take us out themselves." 38 The police reported these words to the magistrates, and they were afraid when they heard that they were Roman citizens; 39 so they came and apologized to them. And they took them out and asked them to leave the city. 40 After leaving the prison they went to Lydia's home; and when they had seen and encouraged the brothers and sisters[m] there, they departed.

17 After Paul and Silas[n] had passed through Amphipolis and Apollonia, they came to Thessalonica, where there was a synagogue of the Jews. 2 And Paul went in, as was his custom, and on three sabbath days argued with them from the scriptures, 3 explaining and proving that it was necessary for the Messiah[o] to suffer and to rise from the dead, and saying, "This is the Messiah,[o] Jesus whom I am proclaiming to you." 4 Some of them were persuaded and joined Paul and Silas, as did a great many of the devout Greeks and not a few of the leading women. 5 But the Jews became jealous, and with the help of some ruffians in the marketplaces they formed a mob and set the city in an uproar. While they were searching for Paul and Silas to bring them out to the assembly, they attacked Jason's house. 6 When they could not find them, they dragged Jason and some be-

---

[j]Other ancient authorities read *to us* [k]Gk *He* [l]Other ancient authorities read *word of God* [m]Gk *brothers* [n]Gk *they* [o]Or *the Christ*

lievers[p] before the city authorities,[q] shouting, "These people who have been turning the world upside down have come here also, 7 and Jason has entertained them as guests. They are all acting contrary to the decrees of the emperor, saying that there is another king named Jesus." 8 The people and the city officials were disturbed when they heard this, 9 and after they had taken bail from Jason and the others, they let them go.

10 That very night the believers[p] sent Paul and Silas off to Beroea; and when they arrived, they went to the Jewish synagogue. 11 These Jews were more receptive than those in Thessalonica, for they welcomed the message very eagerly and examined the scriptures every day to see whether these things were so. 12 Many of them therefore believed, including not a few Greek women and men of high standing. 13 But when the Jews of Thessalonica learned that the word of God had been proclaimed by Paul in Beroea as well, they came there too, to stir up and incite the crowds. 14 Then the believers[p] immediately sent Paul away to the coast, but Silas and Timothy remained behind. 15 Those who conducted Paul brought him as far as Athens; and after receiving instructions to have Silas and Timothy join him as soon as possible, they left him.

16 While Paul was waiting for them in Athens, he was deeply distressed to see that the city was full of idols. 17 So he argued in the synagogue with the Jews and the devout persons, and also in the marketplace[r] every day with those who happened to be there. 18 Also some Epicurean and Stoic philosophers debated with him. Some said, "What does this babbler want to say?" Others said, "He seems to be a proclaimer of foreign divinities." (This was because he was telling the good news about Jesus and the resurrection.) 19 So they took him and brought him to the Areopagus and asked him, "May we know what this new teaching is that you are presenting? 20 It sounds rather strange to us, so we would like to know what it means." 21 Now all the Athenians and the foreigners living there would spend their time in nothing but telling or hearing something new.

22 Then Paul stood in front of the Areopagus and said, "Athenians, I see how extremely religious you are in every way. 23 For as I went through the city and looked carefully at the objects of your worship, I found among them an altar with the inscription, 'To an unknown god.' What therefore you worship as unknown, this I proclaim to you. 24 The God who made the world and everything in it, he who is Lord of heaven and earth, does not live in shrines made by human hands, 25 nor is he served by human hands, as though he needed anything, since he himself gives to all mortals life and breath and all things. 26 From one ancestor[s] he made all nations to inhabit the whole earth, and he allotted the times of their existence and the boundaries of the places where they would live, 27 so that they would search for God[t] and perhaps grope for him and find him—though indeed he is not far from each one of us. 28 For 'In him we live and move and have our being'; as even some of your own poets have said,

'For we too are his offspring.'

29 Since we are God's offspring, we ought not to think that the deity is like gold, or silver, or stone, an image formed by the art and imagination of mortals. 30 While God has overlooked the times of human ignorance, now he commands all people everywhere to repent, 31 because he has fixed a day on which he will have the world judged in righteousness by a man whom he has appointed, and of this he has given assurance to all by raising him from the dead."

32 When they heard of the resurrection of the dead, some scoffed; but others said, "We will hear you again about this." 33 At that point Paul left them. 34 But some of them joined him and became believers, including Dionysius the Areopagite and a woman named Damaris, and others with them.

18 After this Paul[u] left Athens and went to Corinth. 2 There he found a Jew named Aquila, a native of Pontus, who had recently come from Italy with his wife Priscilla, because Claudius had ordered all Jews to leave Rome. Paul[v] went to see them, 3 and, because he was of the same trade, he stayed with them, and they worked together—by trade they were tentmakers. 4 Every sabbath he would argue in the synagogue and would try to convince Jews and Greeks.

5 When Silas and Timothy arrived from Mace-

[p]Gk *brothers*   [q]Gk *politarchs*   [r]Or *civic center*; Gk *agora*
[s]Gk *From one*; other ancient authorities read *From one blood*   [t]Other ancient authorities read *the Lord*   [u]Gk *he*   [v]Gk *He*

donia, Paul was occupied with proclaiming the word,[w] testifying to the Jews that the Messiah[x] was Jesus. 6 When they opposed and reviled him, in protest he shook the dust from his clothes[y] and said to them, "Your blood be on your own heads! I am innocent. From now on I will go to the Gentiles." 7 Then he left the synagogue[z] and went to the house of a man named Titius[a] Justus, a worshiper of God; his house was next door to the synagogue. 8 Crispus, the official of the synagogue, became a believer in the Lord, together with all his household; and many of the Corinthians who heard Paul became believers and were baptized. 9 One night the Lord said to Paul in a vision, "Do not be afraid, but speak and do not be silent; 10 for I am with you, and no one will lay a hand on you to harm you, for there are many in this city who are my people." 11 He stayed there a year and six months, teaching the word of God among them.

12 But when Gallio was proconsul of Achaia, the Jews made a united attack on Paul and brought him before the tribunal. 13 They said, "This man is persuading people to worship God in ways that are contrary to the law." 14 Just as Paul was about to speak, Gallio said to the Jews, "If it were a matter of crime or serious villainy, I would be justified in accepting the complaint of you Jews; 15 but since it is a matter of questions about words and names and your own law, see to it yourselves; I do not wish to be a judge of these matters." 16 And he dismissed them from the tribunal. 17 Then all of them[b] seized Sosthenes, the official of the synagogue, and beat him in front of the tribunal. But Gallio paid no attention to any of these things.

18 After staying there for a considerable time, Paul said farewell to the believers[c] and sailed for Syria, accompanied by Priscilla and Aquila. At Cenchreae he had his hair cut, for he was under a vow. 19 When they reached Ephesus, he left them there, but first he himself went into the synagogue and had a discussion with the Jews. 20 When they asked him to stay longer, he declined; 21 but on taking leave of them, he said, "I[d] will return to you, if God wills." Then he set sail from Ephesus.

22 When he had landed at Caesarea, he went up to Jerusalem[e] and greeted the church, and then went down to Antioch. 23 After spending some time there he departed and went from place to place through the region of Galatia[f] and Phrygia, strengthening all the disciples.

24 Now there came to Ephesus a Jew named Apollos, a native of Alexandria. He was an eloquent man, well-versed in the scriptures. 25 He had been instructed in the Way of the Lord; and he spoke with burning enthusiasm and taught accurately the things concerning Jesus, though he knew only the baptism of John. 26 He began to speak boldly in the synagogue; but when Priscilla and Aquila heard him, they took him aside and explained the Way of God to him more accurately. 27 And when he wished to cross over to Achaia, the believers[c] encouraged him and wrote to the disciples to welcome him. On his arrival he greatly helped those who through grace had become believers, 28 for he powerfully refuted the Jews in public, showing by the scriptures that the Messiah[y] is Jesus.

19 While Apollos was in Corinth, Paul passed through the interior regions and came to Ephesus, where he found some disciples. 2 He said to them, "Did you receive the Holy Spirit when you became believers?" They replied, "No, we have not even heard that there is a Holy Spirit." 3 Then he said, "Into what then were you baptized?" They answered, "Into John's baptism." 4 Paul said, "John baptized with the baptism of repentance, telling the people to believe in the one who was to come after him, that is, in Jesus." 5 On hearing this, they were baptized in the name of the Lord Jesus. 6 When Paul had laid his hands on them, the Holy Spirit came upon them, and they spoke in tongues and prophesied— 7 altogether there were about twelve of them.

8 He entered the synagogue and for three months spoke out boldly, and argued persuasively about the kingdom of God. 9 When some stubbornly refused to believe and spoke evil of the Way before the congregation, he left them, taking the disciples with him, and argued daily in the lecture hall of Tyrannus.[g] 10 This continued for two years, so that all the residents of

---

[w]Gk *with the word*   [x]Or *the Christ*   [y]Gk *reviled him, he shook out his clothes*   [z]Gk *left there*   [a]Other ancient authorities read *Titus*   [b]Other ancient authorities read *all the Greeks*   [c]Gk *brothers*   [d]Other ancient authorities read *I must at all costs keep the approaching festival in Jerusalem, but I*   [e]Gk *went up*   [f]Gk *the Galatian region*   [g]Other ancient authorities read *of a certain Tyrannus, from eleven o'clock in the morning to four in the afternoon*

Asia, both Jews and Greeks, heard the word of the Lord.

11 God did extraordinary miracles through Paul, 12 so that when the handkerchiefs or aprons that had touched his skin were brought to the sick, their diseases left them, and the evil spirits came out of them. 13 Then some itinerant Jewish exorcists tried to use the name of the Lord Jesus over those who had evil spirits, saying, "I adjure you by the Jesus whom Paul proclaims." 14 Seven sons of a Jewish high priest named Sceva were doing this. 15 But the evil spirit said to them in reply, "Jesus I know, and Paul I know; but who are you?" 16 Then the man with the evil spirit leaped on them, mastered them all, and so overpowered them that they fled out of the house naked and wounded. 17 When this became known to all residents of Ephesus, both Jews and Greeks, everyone was awestruck; and the name of the Lord Jesus was praised. 18 Also many of those who became believers confessed and disclosed their practices. 19 A number of those who practiced magic collected their books and burned them publicly; when the value of these books[h] was calculated, it was found to come to fifty thousand silver coins. 20 So the word of the Lord grew mightily and prevailed.

21 Now after these things had been accomplished, Paul resolved in the Spirit to go through Macedonia and Achaia, and then to go on to Jerusalem. He said, "After I have gone there, I must also see Rome." 22 So he sent two of his helpers, Timothy and Erastus, to Macedonia, while he himself stayed for some time longer in Asia.

23 About that time no little disturbance broke out concerning the Way. 24 A man named Demetrius, a silversmith who made silver shrines of Artemis, brought no little business to the artisans. 25 These he gathered together, with the workers of the same trade, and said, "Men, you know that we get our wealth from this business. 26 You also see and hear that not only in Ephesus but in almost the whole of Asia this Paul has persuaded and drawn away a considerable number of people by saying that gods made with hands are not gods. 27 And there is danger not only that this trade of ours may come into disrepute but also that the temple of the great goddess Artemis will be scorned, and she will be deprived of her majesty that brought all Asia and the world to worship her."

28 When they heard this, they were enraged and shouted, "Great is Artemis of the Ephesians!" 29 The city was filled with the confusion; and people[i] rushed together to the theater, dragging with them Gaius and Aristarchus, Macedonians who were Paul's travel companions. 30 Paul wished to go into the crowd, but the disciples would not let him; 31 even some officials of the province of Asia,[j] who were friendly to him, sent him a message urging him not to venture into the theater. 32 Meanwhile, some were shouting one thing, some another; for the assembly was in confusion, and most of them did not know why they had come together. 33 Some of the crowd gave instructions to Alexander, whom the Jews had pushed forward. And Alexander motioned for silence and tried to make a defense before the people. 34 But when they recognized that he was a Jew, for about two hours all of them shouted in unison, "Great is Artemis of the Ephesians!" 35 But when the town clerk had quieted the crowd, he said, "Citizens of Ephesus, who is there that does not know that the city of the Ephesians is the temple keeper of the great Artemis and of the statue that fell from heaven?[k] 36 Since these things cannot be denied, you ought to be quiet and do nothing rash. 37 You have brought these men here who are neither temple robbers nor blasphemers of our[l] goddess. 38 If therefore Demetrius and the artisans with him have a complaint against anyone, the courts are open, and there are proconsuls; let them bring charges there against one another. 39 If there is anything further[m] you want to know, it must be settled in the regular assembly. 40 For we are in danger of being charged with rioting today, since there is no cause that we can give to justify this commotion." 41 When he had said this, he dismissed the assembly.

20 After the uproar had ceased, Paul sent for the disciples; and after encouraging them and saying farewell, he left for Macedonia. 2 When he had gone through those regions and had given the believers[n] much encouragement, he

[h]Gk *them* [i]Gk *they* [j]Gk *some of the Asiarchs* [k]Meaning of Gk uncertain [l]Other ancient authorities read *your* [m]Other ancient authorities read *about other matters* [n]Gk *given them*

came to Greece, 3 where he stayed for three months. He was about to set sail for Syria when a plot was made against him by the Jews, and so he decided to return through Macedonia. 4 He was accompanied by Sopater son of Pyrrhus from Beroea, by Aristarchus and Secundus from Thessalonica, by Gaius from Derbe, and by Timothy, as well as by Tychicus and Trophimus from Asia. 5 They went ahead and were waiting for us in Troas; 6 but we sailed from Philippi after the days of Unleavened Bread, and in five days we joined them in Troas, where we stayed for seven days.

7 On the first day of the week, when we met to break bread, Paul was holding a discussion with them; since he intended to leave the next day, he continued speaking until midnight. 8 There were many lamps in the room upstairs where we were meeting. 9 A young man named Eutychus, who was sitting in the window, began to sink off into a deep sleep while Paul talked still longer. Overcome by sleep, he fell to the ground three floors below and was picked up dead. 10 But Paul went down, and bending over him took him in his arms, and said, "Do not be alarmed, for his life is in him." 11 Then Paul went upstairs, and after he had broken bread and eaten, he continued to converse with them until dawn; then he left. 12 Meanwhile they had taken the boy away alive and were not a little comforted.

13 We went ahead to the ship and set sail for Assos, intending to take Paul on board there; for he had made this arrangement, intending to go by land himself. 14 When he met us in Assos, we took him on board and went to Mitylene. 15 We sailed from there, and on the following day we arrived opposite Chios. The next day we touched at Samos, and[o] the day after that we came to Miletus. 16 For Paul had decided to sail past Ephesus, so that he might not have to spend time in Asia; he was eager to be in Jerusalem, if possible, on the day of Pentecost.

17 From Miletus he sent a message to Ephesus, asking the elders of the church to meet him. 18 When they came to him, he said to them:

"You yourselves know how I lived among you the entire time from the first day that I set foot in Asia, 19 serving the Lord with all humility and with tears, enduring the trials that came to me through the plots of the Jews. 20 I did not shrink from doing anything helpful, proclaiming the message to you and teaching you publicly and from house to house, 21 as I testified to both Jews and Greeks about repentance toward God and faith toward our Lord Jesus. 22 And now, as a captive to the Spirit,[p] I am on my way to Jerusalem, not knowing what will happen to me there, 23 except that the Holy Spirit testifies to me in every city that imprisonment and persecutions are waiting for me. 24 But I do not count my life of any value to myself, if only I may finish my course and the ministry that I received from the Lord Jesus, to testify to the good news of God's grace.

25 "And now I know that none of you, among whom I have gone about proclaiming the kingdom, will ever see my face again. 26 Therefore I declare to you this day that I am not responsible for the blood of any of you, 27 for I did not shrink from declaring to you the whole purpose of God. 28 Keep watch over yourselves and over all the flock, of which the Holy Spirit has made you overseers, to shepherd the church of God[q] that he obtained with the blood of his own Son.[r] 29 I know that after I have gone, savage wolves will come in among you, not sparing the flock. 30 Some even from your own group will come distorting the truth in order to entice the disciples to follow them. 31 Therefore be alert, remembering that for three years I did not cease night or day to warn everyone with tears. 32 And now I commend you to God and to the message of his grace, a message that is able to build you up and to give you the inheritance among all who are sanctified. 33 I coveted no one's silver or gold or clothing. 34 You know for yourselves that I worked with my own hands to support myself and my companions. 35 In all this I have given you an example that by such work we must support the weak, remembering the words of the Lord Jesus, for he himself said, 'It is more blessed to give than to receive.' "

36 When he had finished speaking, he knelt down with them all and prayed. 37 There was much weeping among them all; they embraced Paul and kissed him, 38 grieving especially because of what he had said, that they would not see him again. Then they brought him to the ship.

---

[o]Other ancient authorities add *after remaining at Trogyllium*
[p]Or *And now, bound in the spirit*   [q]Other ancient authorities read *of the Lord*   [r]Or *with his own blood*; Gk *with the blood of his Own*

21 When we had parted from them and set sail, we came by a straight course to Cos, and the next day to Rhodes, and from there to Patara.ˢ 2 When we found a ship bound for Phoenicia, we went on board and set sail. 3 We came in sight of Cyprus; and leaving it on our left, we sailed to Syria and landed at Tyre, because the ship was to unload its cargo there. 4 We looked up the disciples and stayed there for seven days. Through the Spirit they told Paul not to go on to Jerusalem. 5 When our days there were ended, we left and proceeded on our journey; and all of them, with wives and children, escorted us outside the city. There we knelt down on the beach and prayed 6 and said farewell to one another. Then we went on board the ship, and they returned home.

7 When we had finishedᵗ the voyage from Tyre, we arrived at Ptolemais; and we greeted the believersᵘ and stayed with them for one day. 8 The next day we left and came to Caesarea; and we went into the house of Philip the evangelist, one of the seven, and stayed with him. 9 He had four unmarried daughtersᵛ who had the gift of prophecy. 10 While we were staying there for several days, a prophet named Agabus came down from Judea. 11 He came to us and took Paul's belt, bound his own feet and hands with it, and said, "Thus says the Holy Spirit, 'This is the way the Jews in Jerusalem will bind the man who owns this belt and will hand him over to the Gentiles.'" 12 When we heard this, we and the people there urged him not to go up to Jerusalem. 13 Then Paul answered, "What are you doing, weeping and breaking my heart? For I am ready not only to be bound but even to die in Jerusalem for the name of the Lord Jesus." 14 Since he would not be persuaded, we remained silent except to say, "The Lord's will be done."

15 After these days we got ready and started to go up to Jerusalem. 16 Some of the disciples from Caesarea also came along and brought us to the house of Mnason of Cyprus, an early disciple, with whom we were to stay.

17 When we arrived in Jerusalem, the brothers welcomed us warmly. 18 The next day Paul went with us to visit James; and all the elders were present. 19 After greeting them, he related one by one the things that God had done among the Gentiles through his ministry. 20 When they heard it, they praised God. Then they said to him, "You see, brother, how many thousands of believers there are among the Jews, and they are all zealous for the law. 21 They have been told about you that you teach all the Jews living among the Gentiles to forsake Moses, and that you tell them not to circumcise their children or observe the customs. 22 What then is to be done? They will certainly hear that you have come. 23 So do what we tell you. We have four men who are under a vow. 24 Join these men, go through the rite of purification with them, and pay for the shaving of their heads. Thus all will know that there is nothing in what they have been told about you, but that you yourself observe and guard the law. 25 But as for the Gentiles who have become believers, we have sent a letter with our judgment that they should abstain from what has been sacrificed to idols and from blood and from what is strangledʷ and from fornication." 26 Then Paul took the men, and the next day, having purified himself, he entered the temple with them, making public the completion of the days of purification when the sacrifice would be made for each of them.

27 When the seven days were almost completed, the Jews from Asia, who had seen him in the temple, stirred up the whole crowd. They seized him, 28 shouting, "Fellow Israelites, help! This is the man who is teaching everyone everywhere against our people, our law, and this place; more than that, he has actually brought Greeks into the temple and has defiled this holy place." 29 For they had previously seen Trophimus the Ephesian with him in the city, and they supposed that Paul had brought him into the temple. 30 Then all the city was aroused, and the people rushed together. They seized Paul and dragged him out of the temple, and immediately the doors were shut. 31 While they were trying to kill him, word came to the tribune of the cohort that all Jerusalem was in an uproar. 32 Immediately he took soldiers and centurions and ran down to them. When they saw the tribune and the soldiers, they stopped beating Paul. 33 Then the tribune came, arrested him, and ordered him to be bound with two chains; he inquired who he was and what he had done. 34 Some

ˢOther ancient authorities add *and Myra*   ᵗOr *continued*
ᵘGk *brothers*   ᵛGk *four daughters, virgins,*   ʷOther ancient authorities lack *and from what is strangled*

in the crowd shouted one thing, some another; and as he could not learn the facts because of the uproar, he ordered him to be brought into the barracks. 35 When Paul[x] came to the steps, the violence of the mob was so great that he had to be carried by the soldiers. 36 The crowd that followed kept shouting, "Away with him!"

37 Just as Paul was about to be brought into the barracks, he said to the tribune, "May I say something to you?" The tribune[y] replied, "Do you know Greek? 38 Then you are not the Egyptian who recently stirred up a revolt and led the four thousand assassins out into the wilderness?" 39 Paul replied, "I am a Jew, from Tarsus in Cilicia, a citizen of an important city; I beg you, let me speak to the people." 40 When he had given him permission, Paul stood on the steps and motioned to the people for silence; and when there was a great hush, he addressed them in the Hebrew[z] language, saying:

22

"Brothers and fathers, listen to the defense that I now make before you."

2 When they heard him addressing them in Hebrew,[z] they became even more quiet. Then he said:

3 "I am a Jew, born in Tarsus in Cilicia, but brought up in this city at the feet of Gamaliel, educated strictly according to our ancestral law, being zealous for God, just as all of you are today. 4 I persecuted this Way up to the point of death by binding both men and women and putting them in prison, 5 as the high priest and the whole council of elders can testify about me. From them I also received letters to the brothers in Damascus, and I went there in order to bind those who were there and to bring them back to Jerusalem for punishment.

6 "While I was on my way and approaching Damascus, about noon a great light from heaven suddenly shone about me. 7 I fell to the ground and heard a voice saying to me, 'Saul, Saul, why are you persecuting me?' 8 I answered, 'Who are you, Lord?' Then he said to me, 'I am Jesus of Nazareth[a] whom you are persecuting.' 9 Now those who were with me saw the light but did not hear the voice of the one who was speaking to me. 10 I asked, 'What am I to do, Lord?' The Lord said to me, 'Get up and go to Damascus; there you will be told everything that has been assigned to you to do.' 11 Since I could not see because of the brightness of that light, those who were with me took my hand and led me to Damascus.

12 "A certain Ananias, who was a devout man according to the law and well spoken of by all the Jews living there, 13 came to me; and standing beside me, he said, 'Brother Saul, regain your sight!' In that very hour I regained my sight and saw him. 14 Then he said, 'The God of our ancestors has chosen you to know his will, to see the Righteous One and to hear his own voice; 15 for you will be his witness to all the world of what you have seen and heard. 16 And now why do you delay? Get up, be baptized, and have your sins washed away, calling on his name.'

17 "After I had returned to Jerusalem and while I was praying in the temple, I fell into a trance 18 and saw Jesus[b] saying to me, 'Hurry and get out of Jerusalem quickly, because they will not accept your testimony about me.' 19 And I said, 'Lord, they themselves know that in every synagogue I imprisoned and beat those who believed in you. 20 And while the blood of your witness Stephen was shed, I myself was standing by, approving and keeping the coats of those who killed him.' 21 Then he said to me, 'Go, for I will send you far away to the Gentiles.'"

22 Up to this point they listened to him, but then they shouted, "Away with such a fellow from the earth! For he should not be allowed to live." 23 And while they were shouting, throwing off their cloaks, and tossing dust into the air, 24 the tribune directed that he was to be brought into the barracks, and ordered him to be examined by flogging, to find out the reason for this outcry against him. 25 But when they had tied him up with thongs,[c] Paul said to the centurion who was standing by, "Is it legal for you to flog a Roman citizen who is uncondemned?" 26 When the centurion heard that, he went to the tribune and said to him, "What are you about to do? This man is a Roman citizen." 27 The tribune came and asked Paul,[b] "Tell me, are you a Roman citizen?" And he said, "Yes." 28 The tribune answered, "It cost me a large sum of money to get my citizenship." Paul said, "But I was born a citizen." 29 Immediately those who were about to examine him drew back

---

[x] Gk he   [y] Gk He   [z] That is, *Aramaic*   [a] Gk *the Nazorean*   [b] Gk *him*
[c] Or *up for the lashes*

from him; and the tribune also was afraid, for he realized that Paul was a Roman citizen and that he had bound him.

30 Since he wanted to find out what Paul[d] was being accused of by the Jews, the next day he released him and ordered the chief priests and the entire council to meet. He brought Paul down and had him stand before them.

23

While Paul was looking intently at the council he said, "Brothers,[e] up to this day I have lived my life with a clear conscience before God." 2 Then the high priest Ananias ordered those standing near him to strike him on the mouth. 3 At this Paul said to him, "God will strike you, you whitewashed wall! Are you sitting there to judge me according to the law, and yet in violation of the law you order me to be struck?" 4 Those standing nearby said, "Do you dare to insult God's high priest?" 5 And Paul said, "I did not realize, brothers, that he was high priest; for it is written, 'You shall not speak evil of a leader of your people.'"[28]

6 When Paul noticed that some were Sadducees and others were Pharisees, he called out in the council, "Brothers, I am a Pharisee, a son of Pharisees. I am on trial concerning the hope of the resurrection[f] of the dead." 7 When he said this, a dissension began between the Pharisees and the Sadducees, and the assembly was divided. 8 (The Sadducees say that there is no resurrection, or angel, or spirit; but the Pharisees acknowledge all three.) 9 Then a great clamor arose, and certain scribes of the Pharisees' group stood up and contended, "We find nothing wrong with this man. What if a spirit or an angel has spoken to him?" 10 When the dissension became violent, the tribune, fearing that they would tear Paul to pieces, ordered the soldiers to go down, take him by force, and bring him into the barracks.

11 That night the Lord stood near him and said, "Keep up your courage! For just as you have testified for me in Jerusalem, so you must bear witness also in Rome."

12 In the morning the Jews joined in a conspiracy and bound themselves by an oath neither to eat nor drink until they had killed Paul. 13 There were more than forty who joined in this conspiracy. 14 They went to the chief priests and elders and said, "We have strictly bound ourselves by an

oath to taste no food until we have killed Paul. 15 Now then, you and the council must notify the tribune to bring him down to you, on the pretext that you want to make a more thorough examination of his case. And we are ready to do away with him before he arrives."

16 Now the son of Paul's sister heard about the ambush; so he went and gained entrance to the barracks and told Paul. 17 Paul called one of the centurions and said, "Take this young man to the tribune, for he has something to report to him." 18 So he took him, brought him to the tribune, and said, "The prisoner Paul called me and asked me to bring this young man to you; he has something to tell you." 19 The tribune took him by the hand, drew him aside privately, and asked, "What is it that you have to report to me?" 20 He answered, "The Jews have agreed to ask you to bring Paul down to the council tomorrow, as though they were going to inquire more thoroughly into his case. 21 But do not be persuaded by them, for more than forty of their men are lying in ambush for him. They have bound themselves by an oath neither to eat nor drink until they kill him. They are ready now and are waiting for your consent." 22 So the tribune dismissed the young man, ordering him, "Tell no one that you have informed me of this."

23 Then he summoned two of the centurions and said, "Get ready to leave by nine o'clock tonight for Caesarea with two hundred soldiers, seventy horsemen, and two hundred spearmen. 24 Also provide mounts for Paul to ride, and take him safely to Felix the governor." 25 He wrote a letter to this effect:

26 "Claudius Lysias to his Excellency the governor Felix, greetings. 27 This man was seized by the Jews and was about to be killed by them, but when I had learned that he was a Roman citizen, I came with the guard and rescued him. 28 Since I wanted to know the charge for which they accused him, I had him brought to their council. 29 I found that he was accused concerning questions of their law, but was charged with nothing deserving death or imprisonment. 30 When I was informed that

---

[d]Gk *he*   [e]Gk *Men, brothers*   [f]Gk *concerning hope and resurrection*

[28]Exod 22:28

there would be a plot against the man, I sent him to you at once, ordering his accusers also to state before you what they have against him.[g]"

31 So the soldiers, according to their instructions, took Paul and brought him during the night to Antipatris. 32 The next day they let the horsemen go on with him, while they returned to the barracks. 33 When they came to Caesarea and delivered the letter to the governor, they presented Paul also before him. 34 On reading the letter, he asked what province he belonged to, and when he learned that he was from Cilicia, 35 he said, "I will give you a hearing when your accusers arrive." Then he ordered that he be kept under guard in Herod's headquarters.[h]

24 Five days later the high priest Ananias came down with some elders and an attorney, a certain Tertullus, and they reported their case against Paul to the governor. 2 When Paul[i] had been summoned, Tertullus began to accuse him, saying:

"Your Excellency,[j] because of you we have long enjoyed peace, and reforms have been made for this people because of your foresight. 3 We welcome this in every way and everywhere with utmost gratitude. 4 But, to detain you no further, I beg you to hear us briefly with your customary graciousness. 5 We have, in fact, found this man a pestilent fellow, an agitator among all the Jews throughout the world, and a ringleader of the sect of the Nazarenes.[k] 6 He even tried to profane the temple, and so we seized him.[l] 8 By examining him yourself you will be able to learn from him concerning everything of which we accuse him."

9 The Jews also joined in the charge by asserting that all this was true.

10 When the governor motioned to him to speak, Paul replied:

"I cheerfully make my defense, knowing that for many years you have been a judge over this nation. 11 As you can find out, it is not more than twelve days since I went up to worship in Jerusalem. 12 They did not find me disputing with anyone in the temple or stirring up a crowd either in the synagogues or throughout the city. 13 Neither can they prove to you the charge that they now bring against me. 14 But this I admit to you, that according to the Way, which they call a sect, I worship the God of our ancestors, believing everything laid down according to the law or written in the prophets. 15 I have a hope in God—a hope that they themselves also accept—that there will be a resurrection of both[m] the righteous and the unrighteous. 16 Therefore I do my best always to have a clear conscience toward God and all people. 17 Now after some years I came to bring alms to my nation and to offer sacrifices. 18 While I was doing this, they found me in the temple, completing the rite of purification, without any crowd or disturbance. 19 But there were some Jews from Asia—they ought to be here before you to make an accusation, if they have anything against me. 20 Or let these men here tell what crime they had found when I stood before the council, 21 unless it was this one sentence that I called out while standing before them, 'It is about the resurrection of the dead that I am on trial before you today.'"

22 But Felix, who was rather well informed about the Way, adjourned the hearing with the comment, "When Lysias the tribune comes down, I will decide your case." 23 Then he ordered the centurion to keep him in custody, but to let him have some liberty and not to prevent any of his friends from taking care of his needs.

24 Some days later when Felix came with his wife Drusilla, who was Jewish, he sent for Paul and heard him speak concerning faith in Christ Jesus. 25 And as he discussed justice, self-control, and the coming judgment, Felix became frightened and said, "Go away for the present; when I have an opportunity, I will send for you." 26 At the same time he hoped that money would be given him by Paul, and for that reason he used to send for him very often and converse with him.

27 After two years had passed, Felix was succeeded by Porcius Festus; and since he wanted to grant the Jews a favor, Felix left Paul in prison.

25 Three days after Festus had arrived in the province, he went up from Caesarea to Jerusalem 2 where the chief priests and the leaders of the Jews gave him a report against Paul. They appealed to him 3 and requested, as a favor

[g]Other ancient authorities add *Farewell*   [h]Gk *praetorium*   [i]Gk *he*
[j]Gk lacks *Your Excellency*   [k]Gk *Nazoreans*   [l]Other ancient
authorities add *and we would have judged him according to our law.*
*[7]But the chief captain Lysias came and with great violence took him
out of our hands, [8]commanding his accusers to come before you.*
[m]Other ancient authorities read *of the dead, both of*

to them against Paul,[n] to have him transferred to Jerusalem. They were, in fact, planning an ambush to kill him along the way. 4 Festus replied that Paul was being kept at Caesarea, and that he himself intended to go there shortly. 5 "So," he said, "let those of you who have the authority come down with me, and if there is anything wrong about the man, let them accuse him."

6 After he had stayed among them not more than eight or ten days, he went down to Caesarea; the next day he took his seat on the tribunal and ordered Paul to be brought. 7 When he arrived, the Jews who had gone down from Jerusalem surrounded him, bringing many serious charges against him, which they could not prove. 8 Paul said in his defense, "I have in no way committed an offense against the law of the Jews, or against the temple, or against the emperor." 9 But Festus, wishing to do the Jews a favor, asked Paul, "Do you wish to go up to Jerusalem and be tried there before me on these charges?" 10 Paul said, "I am appealing to the emperor's tribunal; this is where I should be tried. I have done no wrong to the Jews, as you very well know. 11 Now if I am in the wrong and have committed something for which I deserve to die, I am not trying to escape death; but if there is nothing to their charges against me, no one can turn me over to them. I appeal to the emperor." 12 Then Festus, after he had conferred with his council, replied, "You have appealed to the emperor; to the emperor you will go."

13 After several days had passed, King Agrippa and Bernice arrived at Caesarea to welcome Festus. 14 Since they were staying there several days, Festus laid Paul's case before the king, saying, "There is a man here who was left in prison by Felix. 15 When I was in Jerusalem, the chief priests and the elders of the Jews informed me about him and asked for a sentence against him. 16 I told them that it was not the custom of the Romans to hand over anyone before the accused had met the accusers face to face and had been given an opportunity to make a defense against the charge. 17 So when they met here, I lost no time, but on the next day took my seat on the tribunal and ordered the man to be brought. 18 When the accusers stood up, they did not charge him with any of the crimes[o] that I was expecting. 19 Instead they had certain points of disagreement with him

about their own religion and about a certain Jesus, who had died, but whom Paul asserted to be alive. 20 Since I was at a loss how to investigate these questions, I asked whether he wished to go to Jerusalem and be tried there on these charges.[p] 21 But when Paul had appealed to be kept in custody for the decision of his Imperial Majesty, I ordered him to be held until I could send him to the emperor." 22 Agrippa said to Festus, "I would like to hear the man myself." "Tomorrow," he said, "you will hear him."

23 So on the next day Agrippa and Bernice came with great pomp, and they entered the audience hall with the military tribunes and the prominent men of the city. Then Festus gave the order and Paul was brought in. 24 And Festus said, "King Agrippa and all here present with us, you see this man about whom the whole Jewish community petitioned me, both in Jerusalem and here, shouting that he ought not to live any longer. 25 But I found that he had done nothing deserving death; and when he appealed to his Imperial Majesty, I decided to send him. 26 But I have nothing definite to write to our sovereign about him. Therefore I have brought him before all of you, and especially before you, King Agrippa, so that, after we have examined him, I may have something to write— 27 for it seems to me unreasonable to send a prisoner without indicating the charges against him."

26 Agrippa said to Paul, "You have permission to speak for yourself." Then Paul stretched out his hand and began to defend himself:

2 "I consider myself fortunate that it is before you, King Agrippa, I am to make my defense today against all the accusations of the Jews, 3 because you are especially familiar with all the customs and controversies of the Jews; therefore I beg of you to listen to me patiently.

4 "All the Jews know my way of life from my youth, a life spent from the beginning among my own people and in Jerusalem. 5 They have known for a long time, if they are willing to testify, that I have belonged to the strictest sect of our religion and lived as a Pharisee. 6 And now I stand here on

[n]Gk *him* [o]Other ancient authorities read *with anything* [p]Gk *on them*

trial on account of my hope in the promise made by God to our ancestors, 7 a promise that our twelve tribes hope to attain, as they earnestly worship day and night. It is for this hope, your Excellency,q that I am accused by Jews! 8 Why is it thought incredible by any of you that God raises the dead?

9 "Indeed, I myself was convinced that I ought to do many things against the name of Jesus of Nazareth.r 10 And that is what I did in Jerusalem; with authority received from the chief priests, I not only locked up many of the saints in prison, but I also cast my vote against them when they were being condemned to death. 11 By punishing them often in all the synagogues I tried to force them to blaspheme; and since I was so furiously enraged at them, I pursued them even to foreign cities.

12 "With this in mind, I was traveling to Damascus with the authority and commission of the chief priests, 13 when at midday along the road, your Excellency,q I saw a light from heaven, brighter than the sun, shining around me and my companions. 14 When we had all fallen to the ground, I heard a voice saying to me in the Hebrews language, 'Saul, Saul, why are you persecuting me? It hurts you to kick against the goads.' 15 I asked, 'Who are you, Lord?' The Lord answered, 'I am Jesus whom you are persecuting. 16 But get up and stand on your feet; for I have appeared to you for this purpose, to appoint you to serve and testify to the things in which you have seen met and to those in which I will appear to you. 17 I will rescue you from your people and from the Gentiles—to whom I am sending you 18 to open their eyes so that they may turn from darkness to light and from the power of Satan to God, so that they may receive forgiveness of sins and a place among those who are sanctified by faith in me.'

19 "After that, King Agrippa, I was not disobedient to the heavenly vision, 20 but declared first to those in Damascus, then in Jerusalem and throughout the countryside of Judea, and also to the Gentiles, that they should repent and turn to God and do deeds consistent with repentance. 21 For this reason the Jews seized me in the temple and tried to kill me. 22 To this day I have had help from God, and so I stand here, testifying to both small and great, saying nothing but what the prophets and Moses said would take place: 23 that the Messiahu must suffer, and that, by being the first to rise from the dead, he would proclaim light both to our people and to the Gentiles."

24 While he was making this defense, Festus exclaimed, "You are out of your mind, Paul! Too much learning is driving you insane!" 25 But Paul said, "I am not out of my mind, most excellent Festus, but I am speaking the sober truth. 26 Indeed the king knows about these things, and to him I speak freely; for I am certain that none of these things has escaped his notice, for this was not done in a corner. 27 King Agrippa, do you believe the prophets? I know that you believe." 28 Agrippa said to Paul, "Are you so quickly persuading me to become a Christian?"v 29 Paul replied, "Whether quickly or not, I pray to God that not only you but also all who are listening to me today might become such as I am—except for these chains."

30 Then the king got up, and with him the governor and Bernice and those who had been seated with them; 31 and as they were leaving, they said to one another, "This man is doing nothing to deserve death or imprisonment." 32 Agrippa said to Festus, "This man could have been set free if he had not appealed to the emperor."

27

When it was decided that we were to sail for Italy, they transferred Paul and some other prisoners to a centurion of the Augustan Cohort, named Julius. 2 Embarking on a ship of Adramyttium that was about to set sail to the ports along the coast of Asia, we put to sea, accompanied by Aristarchus, a Macedonian from Thessalonica. 3 The next day we put in at Sidon; and Julius treated Paul kindly, and allowed him to go to his friends to be cared for. 4 Putting out to sea from there, we sailed under the lee of Cyprus, because the winds were against us. 5 After we had sailed across the sea that is off Cilicia and Pamphylia, we came to Myra in Lycia. 6 There the centurion found an Alexandrian ship bound for Italy and put us on board. 7 We sailed slowly for a number of days and arrived with difficulty off Cnidus, and as the wind was against us, we sailed under the lee of Crete off Salmone. 8 Sailing past

qGk O king   rGk the Nazorean   sThat is, Aramaic   tOther ancient authorities read the things that you have seen   uOr the Christ   vOr Quickly you will persuade me to play the Christian

it with difficulty, we came to a place called Fair Havens, near the city of Lasea.

9 Since much time had been lost and sailing was now dangerous, because even the Fast had already gone by, Paul advised them, 10 saying, "Sirs, I can see that the voyage will be with danger and much heavy loss, not only of the cargo and the ship, but also of our lives." 11 But the centurion paid more attention to the pilot and to the owner of the ship than to what Paul said. 12 Since the harbor was not suitable for spending the winter, the majority was in favor of putting to sea from there, on the chance that somehow they could reach Phoenix, where they could spend the winter. It was a harbor of Crete, facing southwest and northwest.

13 When a moderate south wind began to blow, they thought they could achieve their purpose; so they weighed anchor and began to sail past Crete, close to the shore. 14 But soon a violent wind, called the northeaster, rushed down from Crete.[w] 15 Since the ship was caught and could not be turned head-on into the wind, we gave way to it and were driven. 16 By running under the lee of a small island called Cauda[x] we were scarcely able to get the ship's boat under control. 17 After hoisting it up they took measures[y] to undergird the ship; then, fearing that they would run on the Syrtis, they lowered the sea anchor and so were driven. 18 We were being pounded by the storm so violently that on the next day they began to throw the cargo overboard, 19 and on the third day with their own hands they threw the ship's tackle overboard. 20 When neither sun nor stars appeared for many days, and no small tempest raged, all hope of our being saved was at last abandoned.

21 Since they had been without food for a long time, Paul then stood up among them and said, "Men, you should have listened to me and not have set sail from Crete and thereby avoided this damage and loss. 22 I urge you now to keep up your courage, for there will be no loss of life among you, but only of the ship. 23 For last night there stood by me an angel of the God to whom I belong and whom I worship, 24 and he said, 'Do not be afraid, Paul; you must stand before the emperor; and indeed, God has granted safety to all those who are sailing with you.' 25 So keep up your courage, men, for I have faith in God that it will be exactly as I have been told. 26 But we will have to run aground on some island."

27 When the fourteenth night had come, as we were drifting across the sea of Adria, about midnight the sailors suspected that they were nearing land. 28 So they took soundings and found twenty fathoms; a little farther on they took soundings again and found fifteen fathoms. 29 Fearing that we might run on the rocks, they let down four anchors from the stern and prayed for day to come. 30 But when the sailors tried to escape from the ship and had lowered the boat into the sea, on the pretext of putting out anchors from the bow, 31 Paul said to the centurion and the soldiers, "Unless these men stay in the ship, you cannot be saved." 32 Then the soldiers cut away the ropes of the boat and set it adrift.

33 Just before daybreak, Paul urged all of them to take some food, saying, "Today is the fourteenth day that you have been in suspense and remaining without food, having eaten nothing. 34 Therefore I urge you to take some food, for it will help you survive; for none of you will lose a hair from your heads." 35 After he had said this, he took bread; and giving thanks to God in the presence of all, he broke it and began to eat. 36 Then all of them were encouraged and took food for themselves. 37 (We were in all two hundred seventy-six[z] persons in the ship.) 38 After they had satisfied their hunger, they lightened the ship by throwing the wheat into the sea.

39 In the morning they did not recognize the land, but they noticed a bay with a beach, on which they planned to run the ship ashore, if they could. 40 So they cast off the anchors and left them in the sea. At the same time they loosened the ropes that tied the steering-oars; then hoisting the foresail to the wind, they made for the beach. 41 But striking a reef,[a] they ran the ship aground; the bow stuck and remained immovable, but the stern was being broken up by the force of the waves. 42 The soldiers' plan was to kill the prisoners, so that none might swim away and escape; 43 but the centuri-

---

[w] Gk it   [x] Other ancient authorities read *Clauda*   [y] Gk *helps*   [z] Other ancient authorities read *seventy-six*; others, *about seventy-six*
[a] Gk *place of two seas*

on, wishing to save Paul, kept them from carrying out their plan. He ordered those who could swim to jump overboard first and make for the land, 44 and the rest to follow, some on planks and others on pieces of the ship. And so it was that all were brought safely to land.

28

After we had reached safety, we then learned that the island was called Malta. 2 The natives showed us unusual kindness. Since it had begun to rain and was cold, they kindled a fire and welcomed all of us around it. 3 Paul had gathered a bundle of brushwood and was putting it on the fire, when a viper, driven out by the heat, fastened itself on his hand. 4 When the natives saw the creature hanging from his hand, they said to one another, "This man must be a murderer; though he has escaped from the sea, justice has not allowed him to live." 5 He, however, shook off the creature into the fire and suffered no harm. 6 They were expecting him to swell up or drop dead, but after they had waited a long time and saw that nothing unusual had happened to him, they changed their minds and began to say that he was a god.

7 Now in the neighborhood of that place were lands belonging to the leading man of the island, named Publius, who received us and entertained us hospitably for three days. 8 It so happened that the father of Publius lay sick in bed with fever and dysentery. Paul visited him and cured him by praying and putting his hands on him. 9 After this happened, the rest of the people on the island who had diseases also came and were cured. 10 They bestowed many honors on us, and when we were about to sail, they put on board all the provisions we needed.

11 Three months later we set sail on a ship that had wintered at the island, an Alexandrian ship with the Twin Brothers as its figurehead. 12 We put in at Syracuse and stayed there for three days; 13 then we weighed anchor and came to Rhegium. After one day there a south wind sprang up, and on the second day we came to Puteoli. 14 There we found believers[b] and were invited to stay with them for seven days. And so we came to Rome. 15 The believers[b] from there, when they heard of us, came as far as the Forum of Appius and Three Taverns to meet us. On seeing them, Paul thanked God and took courage.

16 When we came into Rome, Paul was allowed to live by himself, with the soldier who was guarding him.

17 Three days later he called together the local leaders of the Jews. When they had assembled, he said to them, "Brothers, though I had done nothing against our people or the customs of our ancestors, yet I was arrested in Jerusalem and handed over to the Romans. 18 When they had examined me, the Romans[c] wanted to release me, because there was no reason for the death penalty in my case. 19 But when the Jews objected, I was compelled to appeal to the emperor—even though I had no charge to bring against my nation. 20 For this reason therefore I have asked to see you and speak with you,[d] since it is for the sake of the hope of Israel that I am bound with this chain." 21 They replied, "We have received no letters from Judea about you, and none of the brothers coming here has reported or spoken anything evil about you. 22 But we would like to hear from you what you think, for with regard to this sect we know that everywhere it is spoken against."

23 After they had set a day to meet with him, they came to him at his lodgings in great numbers. From morning until evening he explained the matter to them, testifying to the kingdom of God and trying to convince them about Jesus both from the law of Moses and from the prophets. 24 Some were convinced by what he had said, while others refused to believe. 25 So they disagreed with each other; and as they were leaving, Paul made one further statement: "The Holy Spirit was right in saying to your ancestors through the prophet Isaiah,

26   'Go to this people and say,
You will indeed listen, but never
            understand,
    and you will indeed look, but
            never perceive.
27   For this people's heart has grown
            dull,
        and their ears are hard of hearing,
        and they have shut their eyes;
            so that they might not look
                with their eyes,

---

[b]Gk *brothers*   [c]Gk *they*   [d]Or *I have asked you to see me and speak with me*

and listen with their ears,
and understand with their heart
and turn—
and I would heal them.'[29]

28 Let it be known to you then that this salvation of God has been sent to the Gentiles; they will listen."[e]

30 He lived there two whole years at his own expense[f] and welcomed all who came to him,

31 proclaiming the kingdom of God and teaching about the Lord Jesus Christ with all boldness and without hindrance.

[e]Other ancient authorities add verse 29, *And when he had said these words, the Jews departed, arguing vigorously among themselves*
[f]Or *in his own hired dwelling*

[29]Isa 6:9–10

The Acts of Paul and Thecla

The *Acts of Paul and Thecla* is a legendary account of the escapades of Thecla, a woman converted to the Christian faith through the preaching of the apostle Paul. Paul himself appears only on the fringes of the story, as a Christian preacher who converts women to a lifestyle of strict asceticism and sexual renunciation, much to the chagrin of their husbands and fiances. When Thecla herself hears Paul's message, she abandons her fiance and joins the apostle on his journeys, liberated from the concerns of marriage and potential domination by a future husband. Thecla's decision to renounce marriage, however, has serious social implications; seeking revenge, her fiance brings her up before the authorities on the charge of being a Christian. In a miraculous series of episodes, however, God intervenes on her behalf, preserving her from death and reuniting her with her beloved apostle, who authorizes her to share fully in his ministry of teaching the word.

It is difficult to know when the *Acts of Paul and Thecla* was written. It appears to have circulated in the second century along with other narratives of the missionary endeavors of Paul that are collectively entitled the *Acts of Paul.* Most scholars identify this collection with a book known to the church father Tertullian, who, around 200 C.E., claimed that it had been forged by a presbyter of Asia Minor who was caught red-handed. According to Tertullian, the author had concocted his account "out of love of Paul."

There is some evidence to suggest, however, that narratives about Thecla were in circulation at a much earlier stage, possibly at the beginning of the second century. Some scholars have maintained, in fact, that the Pastoral Epistles of the New Testament (1 and 2 Timothy and Titus), which warn against women who spread "old wives' tales" (1 Tim 4:7) and who exercise authority over men and teach (see 1 Tim 2:1–11), represent a reaction to views embodied here in the *Acts of Paul and Thecla.*

Whether or not this particular account of Thecla was composed by the beginning of the second century, it appears to incorporate Christian traditions popular then, as women in Christian communities began to recognize the value of an ascetic lifestyle, especially as it could bring liberation from the constraints of male-dominated marriages.

1 As Paul was going to Iconium after his flight from Antioch, his fellow-travelers were Demas and Hermogenes, the coppersmith, who were full of hypocrisy and flattered Paul as if they loved him. Paul, looking only to the goodness of Christ, did them no harm but loved them exceedingly so that he made sweet to them all the words of the Lord and the interpretation of the gospel concerning the birth and resurrection of the Beloved; and he gave them an account, word for word, of the

"The Acts of Paul and Thecla," from *The Apocryphal New Testament,* translated by J. K. Elliott. © Oxford University Press 1993. Reprinted by permission of Oxford University Press.

great deeds of Christ as they were revealed to him.

2 And a certain man, by name Onesiphorus, hearing that Paul was to come to Iconium, went out to meet him with his children Simmias and Zeno and his wife Lectra, in order that he might entertain him. Titus had informed him what Paul looked like, for he had not seen him in the flesh, but only in the spirit.

3 And he went along the royal road to Lystra and kept looking at the passers-by according to the description of Titus. And he saw Paul coming, a man small in size, bald-headed, bandy-legged, of noble mien, with eyebrows meeting, rather hook-nosed, full of grace. Sometimes he seemed like a man, and sometimes he had the face of an angel.

4 And Paul, seeing Onesiphorus, smiled; and Onesiphorus said, "Hail, O servant of the blessed God." And he said, "Grace be with you and your house." And Demas and Hermogenes were jealous and showed greater hypocrisy, so that Demas said, "Are we not of the blessed God that you have not thus saluted us?" And Onesiphorus said, "I do not see in you the fruit of righteousness, but if such you be, come also into my house and refresh yourselves."

5 And after Paul had gone into the house of Onesiphorus there was great joy and bowing of knees and breaking of bread and the word of God about abstinence and the resurrection. Paul said, "Blessed are the pure in heart, for they shall see God;[1] blessed are those who have kept the flesh chaste, for they shall become a temple of God; blessed are the continent, for God shall speak with them; blessed are those who have kept aloof from this world, for they shall be pleasing to God; blessed are those who have wives as not having them, for they shall experience God; blessed are those who have fear of God, for they shall become angels of God.

6 "Blessed are those who respect the word of God, for they shall be comforted; blessed are those who have received the wisdom of Jesus Christ, for they shall be called the sons of the Most High; blessed are those who have kept the baptism, for they shall be refreshed by the Father and the Son; blessed are those who have come to a knowledge of Jesus Christ, for they shall be in the light; blessed are those who through love of God no longer conform to the world, for they shall judge

angels, and shall be blessed at the right hand of the Father; blessed are the merciful, for they shall obtain mercy[2] and shall not see the bitter day of judgment; blessed are the bodies of the virgins, for they shall be well pleasing to God and shall not lose the reward of their chastity. For the word of the Father shall become to them a work of salvation in the day of the Son, and they shall have rest for ever and ever."

7 And while Paul was speaking in the midst of the church in the house of Onesiphorus a certain virgin named Thecla, the daughter of Theoclia, betrothed to a man named Thamyris, was sitting at the window close by and listened day and night to the discourse of virginity, as proclaimed by Paul. And she did not look away from the window, but was led on by faith, rejoicing exceedingly. And when she saw many women and virgins going in to Paul she also had an eager desire to be deemed worthy to stand in Paul's presence and hear the word of Christ. For she had not yet seen Paul in person, but only heard his word.

8 As she did not move from the window her mother sent to Thamyris. And he came gladly as if already receiving her in marriage. And Thamyris said to Theoclia, "Where, then, is my Thecla [that I may see her]?" And Theoclia answered, "I have a strange story to tell you, Thamyris. For three days and three nights Thecla does not rise from the window either to eat or to drink; but looking earnestly as if upon some pleasant sight she is devoted to a foreigner teaching deceitful and artful discourses, so that I wonder how a virgin of her great modesty exposes herself to such extreme discomfort.

9 "Thamyris, this man will overturn the city of the Iconians and your Thecla too; for all the women and the young men go in to him to be taught by him. He says one must fear only one God and live in chastity. Moreover, my daughter, clinging to the window like a spider, lays hold of what is said by him with a strange eagerness and fearful emotion. For the virgin looks eagerly at what is said by him and has been captivated. But go near and speak to her, for she is betrothed to you."

10 And Thamyris greeted her with a kiss, but at the same time being afraid of her overpowering emotion said, "Thecla, my betrothed, why do you

---

[1]Matt 5:8   [2]Matt 5:7

sit thus? And what sort of feeling holds you distracted? Come back to your Thamyris and be ashamed." Moreover, her mother said the same, "Why do you sit thus looking down, my child, and answering nothing, like a sick woman?" And those who were in the house wept bitterly, Thamyris for the loss of a wife, Theoclia for that of a child, and the maidservants for that of a mistress. And there was a great outpouring of lamentation in the house. And while these things were going on Thecla did not turn away but kept attending to the word of Paul.

11 And Thamyris, jumping up, went into the street, and watched all who went in to Paul and came out. And he saw two men bitterly quarrelling with each other and he said to them, "Men, who are you and tell me who is this man among you, leading astray the souls of young men and deceiving virgins so that they should not marry but remain as they are? I promise you money enough if you tell me about him, for I am the chief man of this city."

12 And Demas and Hermogenes said to him, "Who he is we do not know. But he deprives the husbands of wives and maidens of husbands, saying, 'There is for you no resurrection unless you remain chaste and do not pollute the flesh.'"

13 And Thamyris said to them, "Come into my house and refresh yourselves." And they went to a sumptuous supper and much wine and great wealth and a splendid table. And Thamyris made them drink, for he loved Thecla and wished to take her as wife. And during the supper Thamyris said, "Men, tell me what is his teaching that I also may know it, for I am greatly distressed about Thecla, because she so loves the stranger and I am prevented from marrying."

14 And Demas and Hermogenes said, "Bring him before the Governor Castellius because he persuades the multitude to embrace the new teaching of the Christians, and he will destroy him and you shall have Thecla as your wife. And we shall teach you about the resurrection which he says is to come, that it has already taken place in the children and that we rise again, after having come to the knowledge of the true God."

15 And when Thamyris heard these things he rose up early in the morning and, filled with jealousy and anger, went into the house of Onesipho-

rus with rulers and officers and a great crowd with batons and said to Paul, "You have deceived the city of the Iconians and especially my betrothed bride so that she will not have me! Let us go to the governor Castellius!" And the whole crowd cried, "Away with the sorcerer for he has misled all our wives!", and the multitude was also incited.

16 And Thamyris standing before the tribunal said with a great shout, "O proconsul, this man—we do not know where he comes from—makes virgins averse to marriage. Let him say before you why he teaches thus." But Demas and Hermogenes said to Thamyris, "Say that he is a Christian and he will die at once." But the governor kept his resolve and called Paul, saying, "Who are you and what do you teach? For they bring no small accusation against you."

17 And Paul, lifting up his voice, said, "If I today must tell any of my teachings then listen, O proconsul. The living God, the God of vengeance, the jealous God, the God who has need of nothing, who seeks the salvation of people, has sent me that I may rescue them from corruption and uncleanness and from all pleasure, and from death, that they may sin no more. On this account God sent his Son whose gospel I preach and teach, that in him people have hope, who alone has had compassion upon a world led astray, that people may be no longer under judgment but may have faith and fear of God and knowledge of honesty and love of truth. If then I teach the things revealed to me by God what harm do I do, O proconsul?" When the governor heard this he ordered Paul to be bound and sent to prison until he had time to hear him more attentively.

18 And Thecla, by night, took off her bracelets and gave them to the gatekeeper; and when the door was opened to her she went into the prison. To the jailer she gave a silver mirror and was thus enabled to go in to Paul and, sitting at his feet, she heard the great deeds of God. And Paul was afraid of nothing, but trusted in God. And her faith also increased and she kissed his bonds.

19 And when Thecla was sought for by her family and Thamyris they were hunting through the streets as if she had been lost. One of the gatekeeper's fellow slaves informed them that she had gone out by night. And they examined the gatekeeper who said to them, "She has gone to the for-

eigner in the prison." And they went and found her, so to say, chained to him by affection. And having gone out from there they incited the people and informed the governor what had happened.

20 And he ordered Paul to be brought before the tribunal, but Thecla was riveted to the place where Paul had sat whilst in prison. And the governor ordered her also to be brought to the tribunal, and she came with an exceedingly great joy. And when Paul had been led forth the crowd vehemently cried out, "He is a sorcerer. Away with him!" But the governor gladly heard Paul speak about the holy works of Christ. And having taken counsel, he summoned Thecla and said, "Why do you not marry Thamyris, according to the law of the Iconians?" But she stood looking earnestly at Paul. And when she gave no answer Theoclia, her mother, cried out saying, "Burn the wicked one; burn her who will not marry in the midst of the theatre, that all the women who have been taught by this man may be afraid."

21 And the governor was greatly moved, and after scourging Paul he cast him out of the city. But Thecla he condemned to be burned. And immediately the governor arose and went away to the theatre. And the whole multitude went out to witness the spectacle. But as a lamb in the wilderness looks around for the shepherd, so Thecla kept searching for Paul. And having looked into the crowd she saw the Lord sitting in the likeness of Paul and said, "As if I were unable to endure, Paul has come to look after me." And she gazed upon him with great earnestness, but he went up into heaven.

22 And the boys and girls brought wood and straw in order that Thecla might be burned. And when she came in naked the governor wept and admired the power that was in her. And the executioners arranged the wood and told her to go up on the pile. And having made the sign of the cross she went up on the pile. And they lighted the fire. And though a great fire was blazing it did not touch her. For God, having compassion upon her, made an underground rumbling, and a cloud full of water and hail overshadowed the theatre from above, and all its contents were poured out so that many were in danger of death. And the fire was put out and Thecla saved.

23 And Paul was fasting with Onesiphorus and his wife and his children in a new tomb on the way which led from Iconium to Daphne. And after many days had been spent in fasting the children said to Paul, "We are hungry." And they had nothing with which to buy bread, for Onesiphorus had left the things of this world and followed Paul with all his house. And Paul, having taken off his cloak, said "Go, my child, sell this and buy some loaves and bring them." And when the child was buying them he saw Thecla their neighbor and was astonished and said, "Thecla, where are you going?" And she said, "I have been saved from the fire and am following Paul." And the child said, "Come, I shall take you to him; for he has been mourning for you and praying and fasting six days already."

24 And when she had come to the tomb Paul was kneeling and praying, "Father of Christ, let not the fire touch Thecla but stand by her, for she is yours"; she, standing behind him, cried out, "O Father who made the heaven and the earth, the Father of your beloved Son Jesus Christ, I praise you that you have saved me from the fire that I may see Paul again." And Paul, rising up, saw her and said, "O God, who knows the heart, Father of our Lord Jesus Christ, I praise you because you have speedily heard my prayer."

25 And there was great love in the tomb as Paul and Onesiphorus and the others all rejoiced. And they had five loaves and vegetables and water, and they rejoiced in the holy works of Christ. And Thecla said to Paul, "I will cut my hair off and I shall follow you wherever you go." But he said, "Times are evil and you are beautiful. I am afraid lest another temptation come upon you worse than the first and that you do not withstand it but become mad after men." And Thecla said, "Only give me the seal in Christ, and no temptation shall touch me." And Paul said, "Thecla, be patient; you shall receive the water."

26 And Paul sent away Onesiphorus and all his family to Iconium and went into Antioch, taking Thecla with him. And as soon as they had arrived a certain Syrian, Alexander by name, an influential citizen of Antioch, seeing Thecla, became enamored of her and tried to bribe Paul with gifts and presents. But Paul said, "I know not the woman of whom you speak, nor is she mine." But he, being of great power, embraced her in the street. But she would not endure it and looked about for Paul. And she cried out bitterly, saying,

"Do not force the stranger; do not force the servant of God. I am one of the chief persons of the Iconians and because I would not marry Thamyris I have been cast out of the city." And taking hold of Alexander, she tore his cloak and pulled off his crown and made him a laughing-stock.

27 And he, although loving her, nevertheless felt ashamed of what had happened and led her before the governor; and as she confessed that she had done these things he condemned her to the wild beasts. The women of the city cried out before the tribunal, "Evil judgment! impious judgment!" and Thecla asked the governor that she might remain pure until she was to fight with the wild beasts. And a rich woman named Queen Tryphaena, whose daughter was dead, took her under her protection and had her for a consolation.

28 And when the beasts were exhibited they bound her to a fierce lioness, and Queen Tryphaena followed her. And the lioness, with Thecla sitting upon her, licked her feet; and all the multitude was astonished. And the charge on her inscription was "Sacrilegious." And the women and children cried out again and again, "O God, outrageous things take place in this city." And after the exhibition Tryphaena received her again. For her dead daughter Falconilla had said to her in a dream, "Mother, receive this stranger, the forsaken Thecla, in my place, that she may pray for me and I may come to the place of the just."

29 And when, after the exhibition, Tryphaena had received her she was grieved because Thecla had to fight on the following day with the wild beasts, but on the other hand she loved her dearly like her daughter Falconilla and said, "Thecla, my second child, come, pray for my child that she may live in eternity, for this I saw in my sleep." And without hesitation she lifted up her voice and said, "My God, Son of the Most High, who are in heaven, grant her wish that her daughter Falconilla may live in eternity." And when Thecla had spoken Tryphaena grieved very much, considering that such beauty was to be thrown to the wild beasts.

30 And when it was dawn Alexander came to her, for it was he who arranged the exhibition of wild beasts, and said, "The governor has taken his seat and the crowd is clamoring for us; get ready, I will take her to fight with the wild beasts." And Tryphaena put him to flight with a loud cry, say-

ing, "A second mourning for my Falconilla has come upon my house, and there is no one to help, neither child for she is dead, nor kinsman for I am a widow. God of Thecla, my child, help Thecla."

31 And the governor sent soldiers to bring Thecla. Tryphaena did not leave her but took her by the hand and led her away saying, "My daughter Falconilla I took away to the tomb, but you, Thecla, I take to fight the wild beasts." And Thecla wept bitterly and sighed to the Lord, "O Lord God, in whom I trust, to whom I have fled for refuge, who did deliver me from the fire, reward Tryphaena who has had compassion on your servant and because she kept me pure."

32 And there arose a tumult: the wild beasts roared, the people and the women sitting together were crying, some saying, "Away with the sacrilegious person!", others saying, "O that the city would be destroyed on account of this iniquity! Kill us all, proconsul; miserable spectacle, evil judgment!"

33 And Thecla, having been taken from the hands of Tryphaena, was stripped and received a girdle and was thrown into the arena. And lions and bears were let loose upon her. And a fierce lioness ran up and lay down at her feet. And the multitude of the women cried aloud. And a bear ran upon her, but the lioness went to meet it and tore the bear to pieces. And again a lion that had been trained to fight against men, which belonged to Alexander, ran upon her. And the lioness, encountering the lion, was killed along with it. And the women cried the more since the lioness, her protector, was dead.

34 Then they sent in many beasts as she was standing and stretching forth her hands and praying. And when she had finished her prayer she turned around and saw a large pit full of water and said, "Now it is time to wash myself." And she threw herself in saying, "In the name of Jesus Christ I baptize myself on my last day." When the women and the multitude saw it they wept and said, "Do not throw yourself into the water!"; even the governor shed tears because the seals were to devour such beauty. She then threw herself into the water in the name of Jesus Christ, but the seals, having seen a flash of lightning, floated dead on the surface. And there was round her a cloud of fire so that neither could the beasts touch her nor could she be seen naked.

35 But the women lamented when other and fiercer animals were let loose; some threw petals, others nard, others cassia, others amomum, so that there was an abundance of perfumes. And all the wild beasts were hypnotized and did not touch her. And Alexander said to the governor, "I have some terrible bulls to which we will bind her." And the governor consented grudgingly, "Do what you will." And they bound her by the feet between the bulls and put red-hot irons under their genitals so that they, being rendered more furious, might kill her. They rushed forward but the burning flame around her consumed the ropes, and she was as if she had not been bound.

36 And Tryphaena fainted standing beside the arena, so that the servants said, "Queen Tryphaena is dead." And the governor put a stop to the games and the whole city was in dismay. And Alexander fell down at the feet of the governor and cried, "Have mercy upon me and upon the city and set the woman free, lest the city also be destroyed. For if Caesar hear of these things he will possibly destroy the city along with us because his kinswoman, Queen Tryphaena, has died at the theatre gate."

37 And the governor summoned Thecla out of the midst of the beasts and said to her, "Who are you? And what is there about you that not one of the wild beasts touched you?" She answered, "I am a servant of the living God and, as to what there is about me, I have believed in the Son of God in whom he is well pleased; that is why not one of the beasts touched me. For he alone is the goal of salvation and the basis of immortal life. For he is a refuge to the tempest-tossed, a solace to the afflicted, a shelter to the despairing; in brief, whoever does not believe in him shall not live but be dead forever."

38 When the governor heard these things he ordered garments to be brought and to be put on her. And she said, "He who clothed me when I was naked among the beasts will in the day of judgment clothe me with salvation." And taking the garments she put them on.

And the governor immediately issued an edict saying, "I release to you the pious Thecla, the servant of God." And the women shouted aloud and with one voice praised God, "One is the God, who saved Thecla", so that the whole city was shaken by their voices.

39 And Tryphaena, having received the good news, went with the multitude to meet Thecla. After embracing her she said, "Now I believe that the dead are raised! Now I believe that my child lives. Come inside and all that is mine I shall assign to you." And Thecla went in with her and rested eight days, instructing her in the word of God, so that many of the maidservants believed. And there was great joy in the house.

40 And Thecla longed for Paul and sought him, looking in every direction. And she was told that he was in Myra. And wearing a mantle that she had altered so as to make a man's cloak, she came with a band of young men and maidens to Myra, where she found Paul speaking the word of God and went to him. And he was astonished at seeing her and her companions, thinking that some new temptation was coming upon her. And perceiving this, she said to him, "I have received baptism, O Paul; for he who worked with you for the gospel has worked with me also for baptism."

41 And Paul, taking her, led her to the house of Hermias and heard everything from her, so that he greatly wondered and those who heard were strengthened and prayed for Tryphaena. And Thecla rose up and said to Paul, "I am going to Iconium." Paul answered, "Go, and teach the word of God." And Tryphaena sent her much clothing and gold so that she could leave many things to Paul for the service of the poor.

42 And coming to Iconium she went into the house of Onesiphorus and fell upon the place where Paul had sat and taught the word of God, and she cried and said, "My God and God of this house where the light shone upon me, Jesus Christ, Son of God, my help in prison, my help before the governors, my help in the fire, my help among the wild beasts, you alone are God and to you be glory for every. Amen."

43 And she found Thamyris dead but her mother alive. And calling her mother she said, "Theoclia, my mother, can you believe that the Lord lives in heaven? For if you desire wealth the Lord will give it to you through me; or if you desire your child, behold, I am standing beside you."

And having thus testified, she went to Seleucia and enlightened many by the word of God; then she rested in a glorious sleep.

EARLY CHRISTIAN LETTERS ATTRIBUTED TO PAUL

The Letter to the Romans

The Letter to the Romans is unique among the Pauline epistles. Whereas each of Paul's other letters was written to address doctrinal or practical problems that had arisen in churches that Paul himself had founded, Romans is directed to a community he had never seen. This is not to say that the letter lacks a concrete occasion. On the contrary, Paul's own circumstances appear to have prompted his writing.

Near the end of the letter Paul indicates that he plans to make a missionary journey to Spain and to spend time with the Christians in Rome en route; in particular, he hopes that the Roman Christians will speed him along his journey (15:23–24). Before seeing them, however, he plans to deliver money that he has collected from his churches for the poor saints in Jerusalem (15:25–28). The delivery of this collection from Gentile to Jewish believers was important for Paul because it symbolized the unity of Jew and Gentile in Christ. Indeed, the message of this unity lies at the very heart of Paul's gospel. Paul devotes the bulk of Romans to expounding this message. It appears that Paul's principal reason for the exposition is to win the support of the Roman community, either moral or financial, for his westward mission. It is possible that he is impelled to do so, in part, because the Romans have been misinformed about his message, or at least that he thinks they have been.

Because of this unusual occasion, the letter to the Romans preserves the clearest and most carefully reasoned expression of Paul's gospel. In it he explains how both Jew and Gentile are in need of God's salvation, how the Jewish Law is unable to provide that salvation, and how God has instead provided it through the death and resurrection of Christ (chaps. 1–3). Those who believe in Christ are restored to a right relationship with God (or "justified"; chaps 3–4); being restored to this right relationship brings a release from the dreaded cosmic powers that have been unleashed against this world, including the powers of sin, the flesh, and death (chaps. 5–8).

Paul insists that God's act of justification of Jew and Gentile apart from works prescribed by the Law does not mean that God has gone back on his promises to the Jews to be his chosen people (chaps. 9–11). On the contrary, God's word cannot be revoked; indeed, the Jewish Scriptures themselves demonstrate that God justifies all people, Jew and Gentile, on the basis of faith rather than law (3:31; 4:1–25). Moreover, even though many Jews have rejected the message of God's salvation, in the end, in fulfillment of God's promises, all of Israel too will be saved (11:25–26).

Finally, Paul is adamant that, contrary to what some persons have maintained, his law-free gospel does not lead to lawless behavior. Instead, those who have been restored to a right standing with God will live upright and responsible lives in the Spirit, manifesting love for their neighbors and thereby fulfilling the injunctions of the Law (chaps. 12–15).

From the New Revised Standard Version Bible, © 1989.

1 Paul, a servant[a] of Jesus Christ, called to be an apostle, set apart for the gospel of God, 2 which he promised beforehand through his prophets in the holy scriptures, 3 the gospel concerning his Son, who was descended from David according to the flesh 4 and was declared to be Son of God with power according to the spirit[b] of holiness by resurrection from the dead, Jesus Christ our Lord, 5 through whom we have received grace and apostleship to bring about the obedience of faith among all the Gentiles for the sake of his name, 6 including yourselves who are called to belong to Jesus Christ,

7 To all God's beloved in Rome, who are called to be saints:

Grace to you and peace from God our Father and the Lord Jesus Christ.

8 First, I thank my God through Jesus Christ for all of you, because your faith is proclaimed throughout the world. 9 For God, whom I serve with my spirit by announcing the gospel[c] of his Son, is my witness that without ceasing I remember you always in my prayers, 10 asking that by God's will I may somehow at last succeed in coming to you. 11 For I am longing to see you so that I may share with you some spiritual gift to strengthen you— 12 or rather so that we may be mutually encouraged by each other's faith, both yours and mine. 13 I want you to know, brothers and sisters,[d] that I have often intended to come to you (but thus far have been prevented), in order that I may reap some harvest among you as I have among the rest of the Gentiles. 14 I am a debtor both to Greeks and to barbarians, both to the wise and to the foolish 15 —hence my eagerness to proclaim the gospel to you also who are in Rome.

16 For I am not ashamed of the gospel; it is the power of God for salvation to everyone who has faith, to the Jew first and also to the Greek. 17 For in it the righteousness of God is revealed through faith for faith; as it is written, "The one who is righteous will live by faith."[e][1]

18 For the wrath of God is revealed from heaven against all ungodliness and wickedness of those who by their wickedness suppress the truth. 19 For what can be known about God is plain to them, because God has shown it to them. 20 Ever since the creation of the world his eternal power and divine nature, invisible though they are, have been understood and seen through the things he has made. So they are without excuse; 21 for though they knew God, they did not honor him as God or give thanks to him, but they became futile in their thinking, and their senseless minds were darkened. 22 Claiming to be wise, they became fools; 23 and they exchanged the glory of the immortal God for images resembling a mortal human being or birds or four-footed animals or reptiles.

24 Therefore God gave them up in the lusts of their hearts to impurity, to the degrading of their bodies among themselves, 25 because they exchanged the truth about God for a lie and worshiped and served the creature rather than the Creator, who is blessed forever! Amen.

26 For this reason God gave them up to degrading passions. Their women exchanged natural intercourse for unnatural, 27 and in the same way also the men, giving up natural intercourse with women, were consumed with passion for one another. Men committed shameless acts with men and received in their own persons the due penalty for their error.

28 And since they did not see fit to acknowledge God, God gave them up to a debased mind and to things that should not be done. 29 They were filled with every kind of wickedness, evil, covetousness, malice. Full of envy, murder, strife, deceit, craftiness, they are gossips, 30 slanderers, God-haters,[f] insolent, haughty, boastful, inventors of evil, rebellious toward parents, 31 foolish, faithless, heartless, ruthless. 32 They know God's decree, that those who practice such things deserve to die—yet they not only do them but even applaud others who practice them.

2 Therefore you have no excuse, whoever you are, when you judge others; for in passing judgment on another you condemn yourself, because you, the judge, are doing the very same things. 2 You say,[g] "We know that God's judgment on those who do such things is in accordance with truth." 3 Do you imagine, whoever you are, that when you judge those who do such things and

---

[a]Gk *slave*   [b]Or *Spirit*   [c]Gk *my spirit in the gospel*   [d]Gk *brothers*
[e]Or *The one who is righteous through faith will live*   [f]Or *God-hated*
[g]Gk lacks *You say*

---

[1]Hab 2:4

yet do them yourself, you will escape the judgment of God? 4 Or do you despise the riches of his kindness and forbearance and patience? Do you not realize that God's kindness is meant to lead you to repentance? 5 But by your hard and impenitent heart you are storing up wrath for yourself on the day of wrath, when God's righteous judgment will be revealed. 6 For he will repay according to each one's deeds: 7 to those who by patiently doing good seek for glory and honor and immortality, he will give eternal life; 8 while for those who are self-seeking and who obey not the truth but wickedness, there will be wrath and fury. 9 There will be anguish and distress for everyone who does evil, the Jew first and also the Greek, 10 but glory and honor and peace for everyone who does good, the Jew first and also the Greek. 11 For God shows no partiality.

12 All who have sinned apart from the law will also perish apart from the law, and all who have sinned under the law will be judged by the law. 13 For it is not the hearers of the law who are righteous in God's sight, but the doers of the law who will be justified. 14 When Gentiles, who do not possess the law, do instinctively what the law requires, these, though not having the law, are a law to themselves. 15 They show that what the law requires is written on their hearts, to which their own conscience also bears witness; and their conflicting thoughts will accuse or perhaps excuse them 16 on the day when, according to my gospel, God, through Jesus Christ, will judge the secret thoughts of all.

17 But if you call yourself a Jew and rely on the law and boast of your relation to God 18 and know his will and determine what is best because you are instructed in the law, 19 and if you are sure that you are a guide to the blind, a light to those who are in darkness, 20 a corrector of the foolish, a teacher of children, having in the law the embodiment of knowledge and truth, 21 you, then, that teach others, will you not teach yourself? While you preach against stealing, do you steal? 22 You that forbid adultery, do you commit adultery? You that abhor idols, do you rob temples? 23 You that boast in the law, do you dishonor God by breaking the law? 24 For, as it is written, "The name of God is blasphemed among the Gentiles because of you."[2]

25 Circumcision indeed is of value if you obey the law; but if you break the law, your circumcision has become uncircumcision. 26 So, if those who are uncircumcised keep the requirements of the law, will not their uncircumcision be regarded as circumcision? 27 Then those who are physically uncircumcised but keep the law will condemn you that have the written code and circumcision but break the law. 28 For a person is not a Jew who is one outwardly, nor is true circumcision something external and physical. 29 Rather, a person is a Jew who is one inwardly, and real circumcision is a matter of the heart—it is spiritual and not literal. Such a person receives praise not from others but from God.

3 Then what advantage has the Jew? Or what is the value of circumcision? 2 Much, in every way. For in the first place the Jews[h] were entrusted with the oracles of God. 3 What if some were unfaithful? Will their faithlessness nullify the faithfulness of God? 4 By no means! Although everyone is a liar, let God be proved true, as it is written,

"So that you may be justified in
your words,
and prevail in your judging."[i][3]

5 But if our injustice serves to confirm the justice of God, what should we say? That God is unjust to inflict wrath on us? (I speak in a human way.) 6 By no means! For then how could God judge the world? 7 But if through my falsehood God's truthfulness abounds to his glory, why am I still being condemned as a sinner? 8 And why not say (as some people slander us by saying that we say), "Let us do evil so that good may come"? Their condemnation is deserved!

9 What then? Are we any better off?[j] No, not at all; for we have already charged that all, both Jews and Greeks, are under the power of sin, 10 as it is written:

"There is no one who is righteous,
not even one;[4]
11 there is no one who has
understanding,
there is no one who seeks
God.

---

[h]Gk *they* [i]Gk *when you are being judged* [j]Or *at any disadvantage?*

[2]Isa 52:5; Ezek 36:20 [3]Ps 51:4 [4]Eccl 7:20

12   All have turned aside, together
         they have become
         worthless;
      there is no one who shows
         kindness,
      there is not even one."[5]
13   "Their throats are opened graves;
      they use their tongues to
         deceive."[6]
      "The venom of vipers is under
         their lips."[7]
14   "Their mouths are full of
         cursing and bitterness."[8]
15   "Their feet are swift to shed
         blood;
16   ruin and misery are in their
         paths,
17   and the way of peace they have
         not known."[9]
18   "There is no fear of God before
         their eyes."[10]

19 Now we know that whatever the law says, it speaks to those who are under the law, so that every mouth may be silenced, and the whole world may be held accountable to God. 20 For "no human being will be justified in his sight" by deeds prescribed by the law, for through the law comes the knowledge of sin.

21 But now, apart from law, the righteousness of God has been disclosed, and is attested by the law and the prophets, 22 the righteousness of God through faith in Jesus Christ[k] for all who believe. For there is no distinction, 23 since all have sinned and fall short of the glory of God; 24 they are now justified by his grace as a gift, through the redemption that is in Christ Jesus, 25 whom God put forward as a sacrifice of atonement[l] by his blood, effective through faith. He did this to show his righteousness, because in his divine forbearance he had passed over the sins previously committed; 26 it was to prove at the present time that he himself is righteous and that he justifies the one who has faith in Jesus.[m]

27 Then what becomes of boasting? It is excluded. By what law? By that of works? No, but by the law of faith. 28 For we hold that a person is justified by faith apart from works prescribed by the law. 29 Or is God the God of Jews only? Is he

not the God of Gentiles also? Yes, of Gentiles also, 30 since God is one; and he will justify the circumcised on the ground of faith and the uncircumcised through that same faith. 31 Do we then overthrow the law by this faith? By no means! On the contrary, we uphold the law.

4 What then are we to say was gained by[n] Abraham, our ancestor according to the flesh? 2 For if Abraham was justified by works, he has something to boast about, but not before God. 3 For what does the scripture say? "Abraham believed God, and it was reckoned to him as righteousness."[11] 4 Now to one who works, wages are not reckoned as a gift but as something due. 5 But to one who without works trusts him who justifies the ungodly, such faith is reckoned as righteousness. 6 So also David speaks of the blessedness of those to whom God reckons righteousness apart from works:

7   "Blessed are those whose iniquities
         are forgiven,
      and whose sins are covered;
8   blessed is the one against whom
         the Lord will not reckon
         sin."[12]

9 Is this blessedness, then, pronounced only on the circumcised, or also on the uncircumcised? We say, "Faith was reckoned to Abraham as righteousness."[13] 10 How then was it reckoned to him? Was it before or after he had been circumcised? It was not after, but before he was circumcised. 11 He received the sign of circumcision as a seal of the righteousness that he had by faith while he was still uncircumcised. The purpose was to make him the ancestor of all who believe without being circumcised and who thus have righteousness reckoned to them, 12 and likewise the ancestor of the circumcised who are not only circumcised but who also follow the example of the faith that our ancestor Abraham had before he was circumcised.

13 For the promise that he would inherit the world did not come to Abraham or to his descen-

---

[k]Or *through the faith of Jesus Christ*   [l]Or *a place of atonement*
[m]Or *who has the faith of Jesus*   [n]Other ancient authorities read *say about*

[5]Ps 14:1–3; 53:1–3   [6]Ps 5:9   [7]Ps 140:3   [8]Ps 10:7   [9]Isa 59:7–8
[10]Ps 36:1   [11]Gen 15:6   [12]Ps 32:1–2   [13]Gen 15:6

dants through the law but through the righteous-ness of faith. 14 If it is the adherents of the law who are to be the heirs, faith is null and the promise is void. 15 For the law brings wrath; but where there is no law, neither is there violation.

16 For this reason it depends on faith, in order that the promise may rest on grace and be guaran-teed to all his descendants, not only to the adher-ents of the law but also to those who share the faith of Abraham (for he is the father of all of us, 17 as it is written, "I have made you the father of many nations"[14])—in the presence of the God in whom he believed, who gives life to the dead and calls into existence the things that do not exist. 18 Hop-ing against hope, he believed that he would be-come "the father of many nations,"[15] according to what was said, "So numerous shall your descen-dants be."[16] 19 He did not weaken in faith when he considered his own body, which was already[o] as good as dead (for he was about a hundred years old), or when he considered the barrenness of Sarah's womb. 20 No distrust made him waver concerning the promise of God, but he grew strong in his faith as he gave glory to God, 21 being ful-ly convinced that God was able to do what he had promised. 22 Therefore his faith[p] "was reckoned to him as righteousness."[17] 23 Now the words, "it was reckoned to him," were written not for his sake alone, 24 but for ours also. It will be reck-oned to us who believe in him who raised Jesus our Lord from the dead, 25 who was handed over to death for our trespasses and was raised for our justification.

5 Therefore, since we are justified by faith, we[q] have peace with God through our Lord Jesus Christ, 2 through whom we have obtained access[r] to this grace in which we stand; and we[s] boast in our hope of sharing the glory of God. 3 And not only that, but we[s] also boast in our suf-ferings, knowing that suffering produces en-durance, 4 and endurance produces character, and character produces hope, 5 and hope does not dis-appoint us, because God's love has been poured into our hearts through the Holy Spirit that has been given to us.

6 For while we were still weak, at the right time Christ died for the ungodly. 7 Indeed, rarely will anyone die for a righteous person—though per-haps for a good person someone might actually dare to die. 8 But God proves his love for us in that while we still were sinners Christ died for us. 9 Much more surely then, now that we have been justified by his blood, will we be saved through him from the wrath of God.[t] 10 For if while we were enemies, we were reconciled to God through the death of his Son, much more surely, having been reconciled, will we be saved by his life. 11 But more than that, we even boast in God through our Lord Jesus Christ, through whom we have now received reconciliation.

12 Therefore, just as sin came into the world through one man, and death came through sin, and so death spread to all because all have sinned— 13 sin was indeed in the world before the law, but sin is not reckoned when there is no law. 14 Yet death exercised dominion from Adam to Moses, even over those whose sins were not like the trans-gression of Adam, who is a type of the one who was to come.

15 But the free gift is not like the trespass. For if the many died through the one man's trespass, much more surely have the grace of God and the free gift in the grace of the one man, Jesus Christ, abounded for the many. 16 And the free gift is not like the effect of the one man's sin. For the judg-ment following one trespass brought condemna-tion, but the free gift following many trespasses brings justification. 17 If, because of the one man's trespass, death exercised dominion through that one, much more surely will those who receive the abundance of grace and the free gift of righteous-ness exercise dominion in life through the one man, Jesus Christ.

18 Therefore just as one man's trespass led to condemnation for all, so one man's act of righ-teousness leads to justification and life for all. 19 For just as by the one man's disobedience the many were made sinners, so by the one man's obe-dience the many will be made righteous. 20 But law came in, with the result that the trespass mul-tiplied; but where sin increased, grace abounded all the more, 21 so that, just as sin exercised do-

---

[o]Other ancient authorities lack *already* [p]Gk *Therefore it* [q]Other ancient authorities read *let us* [r]Other ancient authorities add *by faith* [s]Or *let us* [t]Gk *the wrath*

---

[14]Gen 17:5 [15]Gen 17:5 [16]Gen 15:5 [17]Gen 15:6

minion in death, so grace might also exercise dominion through justification[u] leading to eternal life through Jesus Christ our Lord.

6 What then are we to say? Should we continue in sin in order that grace may abound? 2 By no means! How can we who died to sin go on living in it? 3 Do you not know that all of us who have been baptized into Christ Jesus were baptized into his death? 4 Therefore we have been buried with him by baptism into death, so that, just as Christ was raised from the dead by the glory of the Father, so we too might walk in newness of life.

5 For if we have been united with him in a death like his, we will certainly be united with him in a resurrection like his. 6 We know that our old self was crucified with him so that the body of sin might be destroyed, and we might no longer be enslaved to sin. 7 For whoever has died is freed from sin. 8 But if we have died with Christ, we believe that we will also live with him. 9 We know that Christ, being raised from the dead, will never die again; death no longer has dominion over him. 10 The death he died, he died to sin, once for all; but the life he lives, he lives to God. 11 So you also must consider yourselves dead to sin and alive to God in Christ Jesus.

12 Therefore, do not let sin exercise dominion in your mortal bodies, to make you obey their passions. 13 No longer present your members to sin as instruments[v] of wickedness, but present yourselves to God as those who have been brought from death to life, and present your members to God as instruments[v] of righteousness. 14 For sin will have no dominion over you, since you are not under law but under grace.

15 What then? Should we sin because we are not under law but under grace? By no means! 16 Do you not know that if you present yourselves to anyone as obedient slaves, you are slaves of the one whom you obey, either of sin, which leads to death, or of obedience, which leads to righteousness? 17 But thanks be to God that you, having once been slaves of sin, have become obedient from the heart to the form of teaching to which you were entrusted, 18 and that you, having been set free from sin, have become slaves of righteousness. 19 I am speaking in human terms because of your natural limitations.[w] For just as you once presented your members as slaves to impurity and to greater and greater iniquity, so now present your members as slaves to righteousness for sanctification.

20 When you were slaves of sin, you were free in regard to righteousness. 21 So what advantage did you then get from the things of which you now are ashamed? The end of those things is death. 22 But now that you have been freed from sin and enslaved to God, the advantage you get is sanctification. The end is eternal life. 23 For the wages of sin is death, but the free gift of God is eternal life in Christ Jesus our Lord.

7 Do you not know, brothers and sisters[x]—for I am speaking to those who know the law— that the law is binding on a person only during that person's lifetime? 2 Thus a married woman is bound by the law to her husband as long as he lives; but if her husband dies, she is discharged from the law concerning the husband. 3 Accordingly, she will be called an adulteress if she lives with another man while her husband is alive. But if her husband dies, she is free from that law, and if she marries another man, she is not an adulteress.

4 In the same way, my friends,[x] you have died to the law through the body of Christ, so that you may belong to another, to him who has been raised from the dead in order that we may bear fruit for God. 5 While we were living in the flesh, our sinful passions, aroused by the law, were at work in our members to bear fruit for death. 6 But now we are discharged from the law, dead to that which held us captive, so that we are slaves not under the old written code but in the new life of the Spirit.

7 What then should we say? That the law is sin? By no means! Yet, if it had not been for the law, I would not have known sin. I would not have known what it is to covet if the law had not said, "You shall not covet."[18] 8 But sin, seizing an opportunity in the commandment, produced in me all kinds of covetousness. Apart from the law sin lies dead. 9 I was once alive apart from the law, but when the commandment came, sin revived 10 and I died, and the very commandment that promised

[u]Or righteousness [v]Or weapons [w]Gk the weakness of your flesh
[x]Gk brothers

18Exod 20:17; Deut 5:21

life proved to be death to me. 11 For sin, seizing an opportunity in the commandment, deceived me and through it killed me. 12 So the law is holy, and the commandment is holy and just and good.

13 Did what is good, then, bring death to me? By no means! It was sin, working death in me through what is good, in order that sin might be shown to be sin, and through the commandment might become sinful beyond measure.

14 For we know that the law is spiritual; but I am of the flesh, sold into slavery under sin.[y] 15 I do not understand my own actions. For I do not do what I want, but I do the very thing I hate. 16 Now if I do what I do not want, I agree that the law is good. 17 But in fact it is no longer I that do it, but sin that dwells within me. 18 For I know that nothing good dwells within me, that is, in my flesh. I can will what is right, but I cannot do it. 19 For I do not do the good I want, but the evil I do not want is what I do. 20 Now if I do what I do not want, it is no longer I that do it, but sin that dwells within me.

21 So I find it to be a law that when I want to do what is good, evil lies close at hand. 22 For I delight in the law of God in my inmost self, 23 but I see in my members another law at war with the law of my mind, making me captive to the law of sin that dwells in my members. 24 Wretched man that I am! Who will rescue me from this body of death? 25 Thanks be to God through Jesus Christ our Lord!

So then, with my mind I am a slave to the law of God, but with my flesh I am a slave to the law of sin.

8 There is therefore now no condemnation for those who are in Christ Jesus. 2 For the law of the Spirit[z] of life in Christ Jesus has set you[a] free from the law of sin and of death. 3 For God has done what the law, weakened by the flesh, could not do: by sending his own Son in the likeness of sinful flesh, and to deal with sin,[b] he condemned sin in the flesh, 4 so that the just requirement of the law might be fulfilled in us, who walk not according to the flesh but according to the Spirit.[z] 5 For those who live according to the flesh set their minds on the things of the flesh, but those who live according to the Spirit[z] set their minds on the things of the Spirit.[z] 6 To set the mind on the flesh is death, but to set the mind on the Spirit[z] is life and peace. 7 For this reason the mind that is set on the flesh is hostile to God; it does not submit to God's law—indeed it cannot, 8 and those who are in the flesh cannot please God.

9 But you are not in the flesh; you are in the Spirit,[z] since the Spirit of God dwells in you. Anyone who does not have the Spirit of Christ does not belong to him. 10 But if Christ is in you, though the body is dead because of sin, the Spirit[z] is life because of righteousness. 11 If the Spirit of him who raised Jesus from the dead dwells in you, he who raised Christ[c] from the dead will give life to your mortal bodies also through[d] his Spirit that dwells in you.

12 So then, brothers and sisters,[e] we are debtors, not to the flesh, to live according to the flesh— 13 for if you live according to the flesh, you will die; but if by the Spirit you put to death the deeds of the body, you will live. 14 For all who are led by the Spirit of God are children of God. 15 For you did not receive a spirit of slavery to fall back into fear, but you have received a spirit of adoption. When we cry, "Abba![f] Father!" 16 it is that very Spirit bearing witness[g] with our spirit that we are children of God, 17 and if children, then heirs, heirs of God and joint heirs with Christ—if, in fact, we suffer with him so that we may also be glorified with him.

18 I consider that the sufferings of this present time are not worth comparing with the glory about to be revealed to us. 19 For the creation waits with eager longing for the revealing of the children of God; 20 for the creation was subjected to futility, not of its own will but by the will of the one who subjected it, in hope 21 that the creation itself will be set free from its bondage to decay and will obtain the freedom of the glory of the children of God. 22 We know that the whole creation has been groaning in labor pains until now; 23 and not only the creation, but we ourselves, who have the first fruits of the Spirit, groan inwardly while we wait for adoption, the redemption of our bodies.

[y]Gk *sold under sin* [z]Or *spirit* [a]Here the Greek word *you* is singular number; other ancient authorities read *me* or *us* [b]Or *and as a sin offering* [c]Other ancient authorities read *the Christ* or *Christ Jesus* or *Jesus Christ* [d]Other ancient authorities read *on account of* [e]Gk *brothers* [f]Aramaic for *Father* [g]Or [15]*a spirit of adoption, by which we cry, "Abba! Father!"* [16]*The Spirit itself bears witness*

24 For in[h] hope we were saved. Now hope that is seen is not hope. For who hopes[i] for what is seen? 25 But if we hope for what we do not see, we wait for it with patience.

26 Likewise the Spirit helps us in our weakness; for we do not know how to pray as we ought, but that very Spirit intercedes[j] with sighs too deep for words. 27 And God,[k] who searches the heart, knows what is the mind of the Spirit, because the Spirit[l] intercedes for the saints according to the will of God.[m]

28 We know that all things work together for good[n] for those who love God, who are called according to his purpose. 29 For those whom he foreknew he also predestined to be conformed to the image of his Son, in order that he might be the firstborn within a large family.[o] 30 And those whom he predestined he also called; and those whom he called he also justified; and those whom he justified he also glorified.

31 What then are we to say about these things? If God is for us, who is against us? 32 He who did not withhold his own Son, but gave him up for all of us, will he not with him also give us everything else? 33 Who will bring any charge against God's elect? It is God who justifies. 34 Who is to condemn? It is Christ Jesus, who died, yes, who was raised, who is at the right hand of God, who indeed intercedes for us.[p] 35 Who will separate us from the love of Christ? Will hardship, or distress, or persecution, or famine, or nakedness, or peril, or sword? 36 As it is written,

> "For your sake we are being killed
>   all day long;
>   we are accounted as sheep to be
>   slaughtered."[19]

37 No, in all these things we are more than conquerors through him who loved us. 38 For I am convinced that neither death, nor life, nor angels, nor rulers, nor things present, nor things to come, nor powers, 39 nor height, nor depth, nor anything else in all creation, will be able to separate us from the love of God in Christ Jesus our Lord.

9 I am speaking the truth in Christ—I am not lying; my conscience confirms it by the Holy Spirit— 2 I have great sorrow and unceasing anguish in my heart. 3 For I could wish that I myself were accursed and cut off from Christ for the sake of my own people,[q] my kindred according to the flesh. 4 They are Israelites, and to them belong the adoption, the glory, the covenants, the giving of the law, the worship, and the promises; 5 to them belong the patriarchs, and from them, according to the flesh, comes the Messiah,[r] who is over all, God blessed forever.[s] Amen.

6 It is not as though the word of God had failed. For not all Israelites truly belong to Israel, 7 and not all of Abraham's children are his true descendants; but "It is through Isaac that descendants shall be named for you."[20] 8 This means that it is not the children of the flesh who are the children of God, but the children of the promise are counted as descendants. 9 For this is what the promise said, "About this time I will return and Sarah shall have a son."[21] 10 Nor is that all; something similar happened to Rebecca when she had conceived children by one husband, our ancestor Isaac. 11 Even before they had been born or had done anything good or bad (so that God's purpose of election might continue, 12 not by works but by his call) she was told, "The elder shall serve the younger."[22] 13 As it is written,

> "I have loved Jacob,
>   but I have hated Esau."[23]

14 What then are we to say? Is there injustice on God's part? By no means! 15 For he says to Moses,

> "I will have mercy on whom I
>   have mercy,
>   and I will have compassion on
>   whom I have compassion."[24]

16 So it depends not on human will or exertion, but on God who shows mercy. 17 For the scripture says to Pharaoh, "I have raised you up for the very purpose of showing my power in you, so that my name may be proclaimed in all the earth."[25] 18 So then he has mercy on whomever he chooses, and he hardens the heart of whomever he chooses.

---

[h]Or *by* [i]Other ancient authorities read *awaits* [j]Other ancient authorities add *for us* [k]Gk *the one* [l]Gk *he or it* [m]Gk *according to God* [n]Other ancient authorities read *God makes all things work together for good*, or *in all things God works for good* [o]Gk *among many brothers* [p]Or *Is it Christ Jesus . . . for us?* [q]Gk *my brothers* [r]Or *the Christ* [s]Or *Messiah, who is God over all, blessed forever*; or *Messiah. May he who is God over all be blessed forever*

[19]Ps 44:22 [20]Gen 21:12 [21]Gen 18:10, 14 [22]Gen 25:23 [23]Mal 1:2–3 [24]Exod 33:19 [25]Exod 9:16

19 You will say to me then, "Why then does he still find fault? For who can resist his will?" 20 But who indeed are you, a human being, to argue with God? Will what is molded say to the one who molds it, "Why have you made me like this?" 21 Has the potter no right over the clay, to make out of the same lump one object for special use and another for ordinary use? 22 What if God, desiring to show his wrath and to make known his power, has endured with much patience the objects of wrath that are made for destruction; 23 and what if he has done so in order to make known the riches of his glory for the objects of mercy, which he has prepared beforehand for glory— 24 including us whom he has called, not from the Jews only but also from the Gentiles? 25 As indeed he says in Hosea,

> "Those who were not my people I
>   will call 'my people,'
> and her who was not beloved I
>   will call 'beloved.'"[26]
>
26   "And in the very place where it
>   was said to them, 'You are
>   not my people,'
> there they shall be called
>   children of the living God."[27]

27 And Isaiah cries out concerning Israel, "Though the number of the children of Israel were like the sand of the sea, only a remnant of them will be saved; 28 for the Lord will execute his sentence on the earth quickly and decisively."[t][28] 29 And as Isaiah predicted,

> "If the Lord of hosts had not left
>   survivors[u] to us,
> we would have fared like
>   Sodom
> and been made like Gomorrah."[29]

30 What then are we to say? Gentiles, who did not strive for righteousness, have attained it, that is, righteousness through faith; 31 but Israel, who did strive for the righteousness that is based on the law, did not succeed in fulfilling that law. 32 Why not? Because they did not strive for it on the basis of faith, but as if it were based on works. They have stumbled over the stumbling stone, 33 as it is written,

> "See, I am laying in Zion a stone
>   that will make people
>   stumble, a rock that will

> make them fall,
> and whoever believes in him[v]
>   will not be put to shame."[30]

10 Brothers and sisters,[w] my heart's desire and prayer to God for them is that they may be saved. 2 I can testify that they have a zeal for God, but it is not enlightened. 3 For, being ignorant of the righteousness that comes from God, and seeking to establish their own, they have not submitted to God's righteousness. 4 For Christ is the end of the law so that there may be righteousness for everyone who believes.

5 Moses writes concerning the righteousness that comes from the law, that "the person who does these things will live by them."[31] 6 But the righteousness that comes from faith says, "Do not say in your heart, 'Who will ascend into heaven?'" (that is, to bring Christ down) 7 "or 'Who will descend into the abyss?'" (that is, to bring Christ up from the dead). 8 But what does it say?

> "The word is near you,
>   on your lips and in your heart"[32]

(that is, the word of faith that we proclaim); 9 because[x] if you confess with your lips that Jesus is Lord and believe in your heart that God raised him from the dead, you will be saved. 10 For one believes with the heart and so is justified, and one confesses with the mouth and so is saved. 11 The scripture says, "No one who believes in him will be put to shame."[33] 12 For there is no distinction between Jew and Greek; the same Lord is Lord of all and is generous to all who call on him. 13 For, "Everyone who calls on the name of the Lord shall be saved."[34]

14 But how are they to call on one in whom they have not believed? And how are they to believe in one of whom they have never heard? And how are they to hear without someone to proclaim him? 15 And how are they to proclaim him unless they are sent? As it is written, "How beautiful are the feet of those who bring good news!"[35] 16 But not all have obeyed the good news;[y] for Isaiah says,

---

[t]Other ancient authorities read *for he will finish his work and cut it short in righteousness, because the Lord will make the sentence shortened on the earth*   [u]Or *descendants*; Gk *seed*   [v]Or *trusts in it*   [w]Gk *Brothers*   [x]Or *namely, that*   [y]Or *gospel*

---

[26]Hos 2:23   [27]Hos 1:10   [28]Isa 10:22–23   [29]Isa 1:9   [30]Isa 28:16; 8:14   [31]Lev 18:5   [32]Deut 30:12–14   [33]Isa 28:16   [34]Joel 2:32 [35]Isa 52:7

"Lord, who has believed our message?"[36] 17 So faith comes from what is heard, and what is heard comes through the word of Christ.[z]

18 But I ask, have they not heard? Indeed they have; for

"Their voice has gone out to all
the earth,
and their words to the ends of
the world."[37]

19 Again I ask, did Israel not understand? First Moses says,

"I will make you jealous of those
who are not a nation;
with a foolish nation I will
make you angry."[38]

20 Then Isaiah is so bold as to say,

"I have been found by those who
did not seek me;
I have shown myself to those
who did not ask for me."[39]

21 But of Israel he says, "All day long I have held out my hands to a disobedient and contrary people."[40]

11

I ask, then, has God rejected his people? By no means! I myself am an Israelite, a descendant of Abraham, a member of the tribe of Benjamin. 2 God has not rejected his people whom he foreknew. Do you not know what the scripture says of Elijah, how he pleads with God against Israel? 3 "Lord, they have killed your prophets, they have demolished your altars; I alone am left, and they are seeking my life."[41] 4 But what is the divine reply to him? "I have kept for myself seven thousand who have not bowed the knee to Baal."[42] 5 So too at the present time there is a remnant, chosen by grace. 6 But if it is by grace, it is no longer on the basis of works, otherwise grace would no longer be grace.[a]

7 What then? Israel failed to obtain what it was seeking. The elect obtained it, but the rest were hardened, 8 as it is written,

"God gave them a sluggish spirit,
eyes that would not see
and ears that would not hear,
down to this very day."[43]

9 And David says,

"Let their table become a snare
and a trap,

a stumbling block and a
retribution for them;
10   let their eyes be darkened so that
they cannot see,
and keep their backs forever
bent."[44]

11 So I ask, have they stumbled so as to fall? By no means! But through their stumbling[b] salvation has come to the Gentiles, so as to make Israel[c] jealous. 12 Now if their stumbling[b] means riches for the world, and if their defeat means riches for Gentiles, how much more will their full inclusion mean!

13 Now I am speaking to you Gentiles. Inasmuch then as I am an apostle to the Gentiles, I glorify my ministry 14 in order to make my own people[d] jealous, and thus save some of them. 15 For if their rejection is the reconciliation of the world, what will their acceptance be but life from the dead! 16 If the part of the dough offered as first fruits is holy, then the whole batch is holy; and if the root is holy, then the branches also are holy.

17 But if some of the branches were broken off, and you, a wild olive shoot, were grafted in their place to share the rich root[e] of the olive tree, 18 do not boast over the branches. If you do boast, remember that it is not you that support the root, but the root that supports you. 19 You will say, "Branches were broken off so that I might be grafted in." 20 That is true. They were broken off because of their unbelief, but you stand only through faith. So do not become proud, but stand in awe. 21 For if God did not spare the natural branches, perhaps he will not spare you.[f] 22 Note then the kindness and the severity of God: severity toward those who have fallen, but God's kindness toward you, provided you continue in his kindness; otherwise you also will be cut off. 23 And even those of Israel,[g] if they do not persist

---

[z]Or *about Christ*; other ancient authorities read *of God*   [a]Other ancient authorities add *But if it is by works, it is no longer on the basis of grace, otherwise work would no longer be work*
[b]Gk *transgression*   [c]Gk *them*   [d]Gk *my flesh*   [e]Other ancient authorities read *the richness*   [f]Other ancient authorities read *neither will he spare you*   [g]Gk lacks *of Israel*

---

[36]Isa 53:1   [37]Ps 19:4   [38]Deut 32:21   [39]Isa 65:1   [40]Isa 65:2
[41]1 Kgs 19:10, 14   [42]1 Kgs 19:18   [43]Deut 29:4; Isa 29:10   [44]Ps 69:22–23

in unbelief, will be grafted in, for God has the power to graft them in again. 24 For if you have been cut from what is by nature a wild olive tree and grafted, contrary to nature, into a cultivated olive tree, how much more will these natural branches be grafted back into their own olive tree.

25 So that you may not claim to be wiser than you are, brothers and sisters,[h] I want you to understand this mystery: a hardening has come upon part of Israel, until the full number of the Gentiles has come in. 26 And so all Israel will be saved; as it is written,

"Out of Zion will come the
Deliverer;
he will banish ungodliness from
Jacob."
27 "And this is my covenant with
them,
when I take away their sins."[45]
28 As regards the gospel they are enemies of God[i] for your sake; but as regards election they are beloved, for the sake of their ancestors; 29 for the gifts and the calling of God are irrevocable. 30 Just as you were once disobedient to God but have now received mercy because of their disobedience, 31 so they have now been disobedient in order that, by the mercy shown to you, they too may now[j] receive mercy. 32 For God has imprisoned all in disobedience so that he may be merciful to all.

33 O the depth of the riches and wisdom and knowledge of God! How unsearchable are his judgments and how inscrutable his ways!
34 "For who has known the mind of
the Lord?
Or who has been his
counselor?"[46]
35 "Or who has given a gift to him,
to receive a gift in return?"[47]
36 For from him and through him and to him are all things. To him be the glory forever. Amen.

12 I appeal to you therefore, brothers and sisters,[h] by the mercies of God, to present your bodies as a living sacrifice, holy and acceptable to God, which is your spiritual[k] worship. 2 Do not be conformed to this world,[l] but be transformed by the renewing of your minds, so that you may discern what is the will of God—what is good and acceptable and perfect.[m]

3 For by the grace given to me I say to everyone among you not to think of yourself more highly than you ought to think, but to think with sober judgment, each according to the measure of faith that God has assigned. 4 For as in one body we have many members, and not all the members have the same function, 5 so we, who are many, are one body in Christ, and individually we are members one of another. 6 We have gifts that differ according to the grace given to us: prophecy, in proportion to faith; 7 ministry, in ministering; the teacher, in teaching; 8 the exhorter, in exhortation; the giver, in generosity; the leader, in diligence; the compassionate, in cheerfulness.

9 Let love be genuine; hate what is evil, hold fast to what is good; 10 love one another with mutual affection; outdo one another in showing honor. 11 Do not lag in zeal, be ardent in spirit, serve the Lord.[n] 12 Rejoice in hope, be patient in suffering, persevere in prayer. 13 Contribute to the needs of the saints; extend hospitality to strangers.

14 Bless those who persecute you; bless and do not curse them. 15 Rejoice with those who rejoice, weep with those who weep. 16 Live in harmony with one another; do not be haughty, but associate with the lowly;[o] do not claim to be wiser than you are. 17 Do not repay anyone evil for evil, but take thought for what is noble in the sight of all. 18 If it is possible, so far as it depends on you, live peaceably with all. 19 Beloved, never avenge yourselves, but leave room for the wrath of God;[p] for it is written, "Vengeance is mine, I will repay, says the Lord."[48] 20 No, "if your enemies are hungry, feed them; if they are thirsty, give them something to drink; for by doing this you will heap burning coals on their heads."[49] 21 Do not be overcome by evil, but overcome evil with good.

13 Let every person be subject to the governing authorities; for there is no authority except from God, and those authorities that ex-

---

[h]Gk brothers [i]Gk lacks of God [j]Other ancient authorities lack now [k]Or reasonable [l]Gk age [m]Or what is the good and acceptable and perfect will of God [n]Other ancient authorities read serve the opportune time [o]Or give yourselves to humble tasks [p]Gk the wrath

[45]Isa 59:20–21; 27:9 [46]Isa 40:13 [47]Job 41:3, 11 [48]Deut 32:35 [49]Prov 25:21–22

ist have been instituted by God. 2 Therefore whoever resists authority resists what God has appointed, and those who resist will incur judgment. 3 For rulers are not a terror to good conduct, but to bad. Do you wish to have no fear of the authority? Then do what is good, and you will receive its approval; 4 for it is God's servant for your good. But if you do what is wrong, you should be afraid, for the authority[q] does not bear the sword in vain! It is the servant of God to execute wrath on the wrongdoer. 5 Therefore one must be subject, not only because of wrath but also because of conscience. 6 For the same reason you also pay taxes, for the authorities are God's servants, busy with this very thing. 7 Pay to all what is due them—taxes to whom taxes are due, revenue to whom revenue is due, respect to whom respect is due, honor to whom honor is due.

8 Owe no one anything, except to love one another; for the one who loves another has fulfilled the law. 9 The commandments, "You shall not commit adultery; You shall not murder; You shall not steal; You shall not covet";[50] and any other commandment, are summed up in this word, "Love your neighbor as yourself."[51] 10 Love does no wrong to a neighbor; therefore, love is the fulfilling of the law.

11 Besides this, you know what time it is, how it is now the moment for you to wake from sleep. For salvation is nearer to us now than when we became believers; 12 the night is far gone, the day is near. Let us then lay aside the works of darkness and put on the armor of light; 13 let us live honorably as in the day, not in reveling and drunkenness, not in debauchery and licentiousness, not in quarreling and jealousy. 14 Instead, put on the Lord Jesus Christ, and make no provision for the flesh, to gratify its desires.

14 Welcome those who are weak in faith,[r] but not for the purpose of quarreling over opinions. 2 Some believe in eating anything, while the weak eat only vegetables. 3 Those who eat must not despise those who abstain, and those who abstain must not pass judgment on those who eat; for God has welcomed them. 4 Who are you to pass judgment on servants of another? It is before their own lord that they stand or fall. And they will be upheld, for the Lord[s] is able to make them stand.

5 Some judge one day to be better than another, while others judge all days to be alike. Let all be fully convinced in their own minds. 6 Those who observe the day, observe it in honor of the Lord. Also those who eat, eat in honor of the Lord, since they give thanks to God; while those who abstain, abstain in honor of the Lord and give thanks to God.

7 We do not live to ourselves, and we do not die to ourselves. 8 If we live, we live to the Lord, and if we die, we die to the Lord; so then, whether we live or whether we die, we are the Lord's. 9 For to this end Christ died and lived again, so that he might be Lord of both the dead and the living.

10 Why do you pass judgment on your brother or sister?[t] Or you, why do you despise your brother or sister?[t] For we will all stand before the judgment seat of God.[u] 11 For it is written,

"As I live, says the Lord, every
knee shall bow to me,
and every tongue shall give
praise to[v] God."[52]

12 So then, each of us will be accountable to God.[w]

13 Let us therefore no longer pass judgment on one another, but resolve instead never to put a stumbling block or hindrance in the way of another.[x] 14 I know and am persuaded in the Lord Jesus that nothing is unclean in itself; but it is unclean for anyone who thinks it unclean. 15 If your brother or sister[t] is being injured by what you eat, you are no longer walking in love. Do not let what you eat cause the ruin of one for whom Christ died. 16 So do not let your good be spoken of as evil. 17 For the kingdom of God is not food and drink but righteousness and peace and joy in the Holy Spirit. 18 The one who thus serves Christ is acceptable to God and has human approval. 19 Let us then pursue what makes for peace and for mutual upbuilding. 20 Do not, for the sake of food, destroy the work of God. Everything is indeed clean, but it is wrong for you to make others fall by what you eat; 21 it is good not to eat meat or drink wine or do anything that makes your

---

[q]Gk it   [r]Or conviction   [s]Other ancient authorities read for God
[t]Gk brother   [u]Other ancient authorities read of Christ   [v]Or confess
[w]Other ancient authorities lack to God   [x]Gk of a brother

[50]Exod 20:13–15, 17; Deut 5:17–19, 21   [51]Lev 19:18   [52]Isa 45:23

brother or sister[y] stumble.[z] 22 The faith that you have, have as your own conviction before God. Blessed are those who have no reason to condemn themselves because of what they approve. 23 But those who have doubts are condemned if they eat, because they do not act from faith;[a] for whatever does not proceed from faith[a] is sin.[b]

15 We who are strong ought to put up with the failings of the weak, and not to please ourselves. 2 Each of us must please our neighbor for the good purpose of building up the neighbor. 3 For Christ did not please himself; but, as it is written, "The insults of those who insult you have fallen on me."[53] 4 For whatever was written in former days was written for our instruction, so that by steadfastness and by the encouragement of the scriptures we might have hope. 5 May the God of steadfastness and encouragement grant you to live in harmony with one another, in accordance with Christ Jesus, 6 so that together you may with one voice glorify the God and Father of our Lord Jesus Christ.

7 Welcome one another, therefore, just as Christ has welcomed you, for the glory of God. 8 For I tell you that Christ has become a servant of the circumcised on behalf of the truth of God in order that he might confirm the promises given to the patriarchs, 9 and in order that the Gentiles might glorify God for his mercy. As it is written,

"Therefore I will confess[c] you
among the Gentiles,
and sing praises to your name";[54]

10 and again he says,

"Rejoice, O Gentiles, with his
people";[55]

11 and again,

"Praise the Lord, all you Gentiles,
and let all the peoples praise
him";[56]

12 and again Isaiah says,

"The root of Jesse shall come,
the one who rises to rule the
Gentiles;[57]
in him the Gentiles shall hope."

13 May the God of hope fill you with all joy and peace in believing, so that you may abound in hope by the power of the Holy Spirit.

14 I myself feel confident about you, my brothers and sisters,[d] that you yourselves are full of goodness, filled with all knowledge, and able to instruct one another. 15 Nevertheless on some points I have written to you rather boldly by way of reminder, because of the grace given me by God 16 to be a minister of Christ Jesus to the Gentiles in the priestly service of the gospel of God, so that the offering of the Gentiles may be acceptable, sanctified by the Holy Spirit. 17 In Christ Jesus, then, I have reason to boast of my work for God. 18 For I will not venture to speak of anything except what Christ has accomplished[e] through me to win obedience from the Gentiles, by word and deed, 19 by the power of signs and wonders, by the power of the Spirit of God,[f] so that from Jerusalem and as far around as Illyricum I have fully proclaimed the good news[g] of Christ. 20 Thus I make it my ambition to proclaim the good news,[e] not where Christ has already been named, so that I do not build on someone else's foundation, 21 but as it is written,

"Those who have never been told
of him shall see,
and those who have never heard
of him shall understand."[58]

22 This is the reason that I have so often been hindered from coming to you. 23 But now, with no further place for me in these regions, I desire, as I have for many years, to come to you 24 when I go to Spain. For I do hope to see you on my journey and to be sent on by you, once I have enjoyed your company for a little while. 25 At present, however, I am going to Jerusalem in a ministry to the saints; 26 for Macedonia and Achaia have been pleased to share their resources with the poor among the saints at Jerusalem. 27 They were pleased to do this, and indeed they owe it to them; for if the Gentiles have come to share in their spiritual blessings, they ought also to be of service to them in material things. 28 So, when I have completed this, and have delivered to them what has

---

[y]Gk brother [z]Other ancient authorities add or be upset or be weakened [a]Or conviction [b]Other authorities, some ancient, add here 16.25-27 [c]Or thank [d]Gk brothers [e]Gk speak of those things that Christ has not accomplished [f]Other ancient authorities read of the Spirit or of the Holy Spirit [g]Or gospel

[53]Ps 69:9 [54]Ps 18:49; 2 Sam 22:50 [55]Deut 32:43 [56]Ps 117:1 [57]Isa 11:10 [58]Isa 52:15

been collected,[h] I will set out by way of you to Spain; 29 and I know that when I come to you, I will come in the fullness of the blessing[i] of Christ.

30 I appeal to you, brothers and sisters,[j] by our Lord Jesus Christ and by the love of the Spirit, to join me in earnest prayer to God on my behalf, 31 that I may be rescued from the unbelievers in Judea, and that my ministry[k] to Jerusalem may be acceptable to the saints, 32 so that by God's will I may come to you with joy and be refreshed in your company. 33 The God of peace be with all of you.[l] Amen.

16 I commend to you our sister Phoebe, a deacon[m] of the church at Cenchreae, 2 so that you may welcome her in the Lord as is fitting for the saints, and help her in whatever she may require from you, for she has been a benefactor of many and of myself as well.

3 Greet Prisca and Aquila, who work with me in Christ Jesus, 4 and who risked their necks for my life, to whom not only I give thanks, but also all the churches of the Gentiles. 5 Greet also the church in their house. Greet my beloved Epaenetus, who was the first convert[n] in Asia for Christ. 6 Greet Mary, who has worked very hard among you. 7 Greet Andronicus and Junia,[o] my relatives[p] who were in prison with me; they are prominent among the apostles, and they were in Christ before I was. 8 Greet Ampliatus, my beloved in the Lord. 9 Greet Urbanus, our co-worker in Christ, and my beloved Stachys. 10 Greet Apelles, who is approved in Christ. Greet those who belong to the family of Aristobulus. 11 Greet my relative[q] Herodion. Greet those in the Lord who belong to the family of Narcissus. 12 Greet those workers in the Lord, Tryphaena and Tryphosa. Greet the beloved Persis, who has worked hard in the Lord. 13 Greet Rufus, chosen in the Lord; and greet his mother—a mother to me also. 14 Greet Asyncritus, Phlegon, Hermes, Patrobas, Hermas, and the brothers and sisters[j] who are with them. 15 Greet Philologus, Julia, Nereus

and his sister, and Olympas, and all the saints who are with them. 16 Greet one another with a holy kiss. All the churches of Christ greet you.

17 I urge you, brothers and sisters,[j] to keep an eye on those who cause dissensions and offenses, in opposition to the teaching that you have learned; avoid them. 18 For such people do not serve our Lord Christ, but their own appetites,[r] and by smooth talk and flattery they deceive the hearts of the simple-minded. 19 For while your obedience is known to all, so that I rejoice over you, I want you to be wise in what is good and guileless in what is evil. 20 The God of peace will shortly crush Satan under your feet. The grace of our Lord Jesus Christ be with you.[r]

21 Timothy, my co-worker, greets you; so do Lucius and Jason and Sosipater, my relatives.[p]

22 I Tertius, the writer of this letter, greet you in the Lord.[t]

23 Gaius, who is host to me and to the whole church, greets you. Erastus, the city treasurer, and our brother Quartus, greet you.[u]

25 Now to God[v] who is able to strengthen you according to my gospel and the proclamation of Jesus Christ, according to the revelation of the mystery that was kept secret for long ages 26 but is now disclosed, and through the prophetic writings is made known to all the Gentiles, according to the command of the eternal God, to bring about the obedience of faith— 27 to the only wise God, through Jesus Christ, to whom[w] be the glory forever! Amen.[x]

---

[h]Gk *have sealed to them this fruit* [i]Other ancient authorities add *of the gospel* [j]Gk *brothers* [k]Other ancient authorities read *my bringing of a gift* [l]One ancient authority adds 16.25-27 here [m]Or *minister* [n]Gk *first fruits* [o]Or *Junias*; other ancient authorities read *Julia* [p]Or *compatriots* [q]Or *compatriot* [r]Gk *their own belly* [s]Other ancient authorities lack this sentence [t]Or *I Tertius, writing this letter in the Lord, greet you* [u]Other ancient authorities add verse 24, *The grace of our Lord Jesus Christ be with all of you. Amen.* [v]Gk *the one* [w]Other ancient authorities lack *to whom*. The verse then reads, *to the only wise God be the glory through Jesus Christ forever. Amen.* [x]Other ancient authorities lack 16.25-27 or include it after 14.23 or 15.33; others put verse 24 after verse 27

The First Letter to the Corinthians

Paul himself established the church in Corinth, the capital of the Roman province of Achaia (in modern-day Greece), along with his two companions Timothy and Silvanus. The three of them spent considerable time in the city (a year and a half, according to Acts 18:11), preaching the gospel and teaching their converts.

After leaving Corinth, Paul journeyed across the Aegean to the city of Ephesus. While there, he heard word concerning his Corinthian converts from several persons called "Chloe's people" (possibly slaves of a prominent Corinthian woman named Chloe, who were conducting business in Ephesus; 1:11); moreover, he received a letter from members of the congregation who had pressing ethical concerns (cf. 7:1). From Paul's perspective, the news he learned from these sources was not good. He wrote the letter of 1 Corinthians to deal with the problems.

The church had grown fragmented, as different leaders asserted themselves, each claiming special spiritual powers, each acquiring a following (chaps. 1–4). The resultant disunity of the community manifested itself in numerous ways: some members were taking others to court (over what, we are not told; chap. 6); during the communal meals, some were gorging themselves and getting drunk, others had to come late and got nothing to eat (chap. 11); the worship services were chaotic, as different members tried to manifest their spiritual abilities, especially the ability to speak in "tongues" (i.e., unknown languages given by God), more loudly and forcefully than the others (chaps. 12–14). And there were other ethical problems; some men were visiting prostitutes and bragging about it in church (chap. 6); one man was sleeping with his stepmother (chap. 5).

Paul addresses these issues one by one in the letter. But near the end he gets to the heart of the matter. The sundry problems had arisen because the Corinthians did not understand the full meaning of the gospel. Having put their faith in Christ, many Corinthians believed that the salvation they had received was already complete, that they were already living an exalted spiritual life with Christ, ruling with him, not subject to the powers of sin and death that were in the world. Their physical and social lives were therefore of no ultimate consequence to them. Paul, however, thought otherwise. Those who believe in Christ do indeed have a right standing with God, but evil is still present in the world and will continue to be so until the end of the age, when Christ returns to destroy all that is opposed to God and to raise all believers out of their mortal, sinful bodies into bodies that are imperishable and perfect (chap. 15).

Until that time, according the Paul, believers do not yet reign in the heavenly places with Christ; instead, they still partake of this weak and sinful existence. The Corinthians were to realize that they lived in an age of sin and death, and they were to refrain from participating in it. They were to manifest love for one another and to maintain an upright demeanor for those who were outside the church. Above all, they were to await the return of Christ from heaven, when he would dispose of this evil world and bring his followers into his glorious kingdom.

From the New Revised Standard Version Bible, © 1989.

1 Paul, called to be an apostle of Christ Jesus by the will of God, and our brother Sosthenes,

2 To the church of God that is in Corinth, to those who are sanctified in Christ Jesus, called to be saints, together with all those who in every place call on the name of our Lord Jesus Christ, both their Lord[a] and ours:

3 Grace to you and peace from God our Father and the Lord Jesus Christ.

4 I give thanks to my[b] God always for you because of the grace of God that has been given you in Christ Jesus, 5 for in every way you have been enriched in him, in speech and knowledge of every kind— 6 just as the testimony of[c] Christ has been strengthened among you— 7 so that you are not lacking in any spiritual gift as you wait for the revealing of our Lord Jesus Christ. 8 He will also strengthen you to the end, so that you may be blameless on the day of our Lord Jesus Christ. 9 God is faithful; by him you were called into the fellowship of his Son, Jesus Christ our Lord.

10 Now I appeal to you, brothers and sisters,[d] by the name of our Lord Jesus Christ, that all of you be in agreement and that there be no divisions among you, but that you be united in the same mind and the same purpose. 11 For it has been reported to me by Chloe's people that there are quarrels among you, my brothers and sisters.[e] 12 What I mean is that each of you says, "I belong to Paul," or "I belong to Apollos," or "I belong to Cephas," or "I belong to Christ." 13 Has Christ been divided? Was Paul crucified for you? Or were you baptized in the name of Paul? 14 I thank God[f] that I baptized none of you except Crispus and Gaius, 15 so that no one can say that you were baptized in my name. 16 (I did baptize also the household of Stephanas; beyond that, I do not know whether I baptized anyone else.) 17 For Christ did not send me to baptize but to proclaim the gospel, and not with eloquent wisdom, so that the cross of Christ might not be emptied of its power.

18 For the message about the cross is foolishness to those who are perishing, but to us who are being saved it is the power of God. 19 For it is written,

"I will destroy the wisdom of the
        wise,

and the discernment of the
        discerning I will thwart."[1]

20 Where is the one who is wise? Where is the scribe? Where is the debater of this age? Has not God made foolish the wisdom of the world? 21 For since, in the wisdom of God, the world did not know God through wisdom, God decided, through the foolishness of our proclamation, to save those who believe. 22 For Jews demand signs and Greeks desire wisdom, 23 but we proclaim Christ crucified, a stumbling block to Jews and foolishness to Gentiles, 24 but to those who are the called, both Jews and Greeks, Christ the power of God and the wisdom of God. 25 For God's foolishness is wiser than human wisdom, and God's weakness is stronger than human strength.

26 Consider your own call, brothers and sisters:[d] not many of you were wise by human standards,[g] not many were powerful, not many were of noble birth. 27 But God chose what is foolish in the world to shame the wise; God chose what is weak in the world to shame the strong; 28 God chose what is low and despised in the world, things that are not, to reduce to nothing things that are, 29 so that no one[h] might boast in the presence of God. 30 He is the source of your life in Christ Jesus, who became for us wisdom from God, and righteousness and sanctification and redemption, 31 in order that, as it is written, "Let the one who boasts, boast in[i] the Lord."[2]

2 When I came to you, brothers and sisters,[d] I did not come proclaiming the mystery[j] of God to you in lofty words or wisdom. 2 For I decided to know nothing among you except Jesus Christ, and him crucified. 3 And I came to you in weakness and in fear and in much trembling. 4 My speech and my proclamation were not with plausible words of wisdom,[k] but with a demonstration of the Spirit and of power, 5 so that your faith might rest not on human wisdom but on the power of God.

6 Yet among the mature we do speak wisdom,

---

[a]Gk *theirs*   [b]Other ancient authorities lack *my*   [c]Or *to*
[d]Gk *brothers*   [e]Gk *my brothers*   [f]Other ancient authorities read *I am thankful*   [g]Gk *according to the flesh*   [h]Gk *no flesh*   [i]Or *of*   [j]Other ancient authorities read *testimony*   [k]Other ancient authorities read *the persuasiveness of wisdom*

[1]Isa 29:14   [2]Jer 9:24

though it is not a wisdom of this age or of the rulers of this age, who are doomed to perish. 7 But we speak God's wisdom, secret and hidden, which God decreed before the ages for our glory. 8 None of the rulers of this age understood this; for if they had, they would not have crucified the Lord of glory. 9 But, as it is written,

"What no eye has seen, nor ear
    heard,
  nor the human heart conceived,
what God has prepared for those
  who love him"—[3]

10 these things God has revealed to us through the Spirit; for the Spirit searches everything, even the depths of God. 11 For what human being knows what is truly human except the human spirit that is within? So also no one comprehends what is truly God's except the Spirit of God. 12 Now we have received not the spirit of the world, but the Spirit that is from God, so that we may understand the gifts bestowed on us by God. 13 And we speak of these things in words not taught by human wisdom but taught by the Spirit, interpreting spiritual things to those who are spiritual.[1]

14 Those who are unspiritual[m] do not receive the gifts of God's Spirit, for they are foolishness to them, and they are unable to understand them because they are spiritually discerned. 15 Those who are spiritual discern all things, and they are themselves subject to no one else's scrutiny.

16   "For who has known the mind of
       the Lord
    so as to instruct him?"[4]

But we have the mind of Christ.

3 And so, brothers and sisters,[n] I could not speak to you as spiritual people, but rather as people of the flesh, as infants in Christ. 2 I fed you with milk, not solid food, for you were not ready for solid food. Even now you are still not ready, 3 for you are still of the flesh. For as long as there is jealousy and quarreling among you, are you not of the flesh, and behaving according to human inclinations? 4 For when one says, "I belong to Paul," and another, "I belong to Apollos," are you not merely human?

5 What then is Apollos? What is Paul? Servants through whom you came to believe, as the Lord assigned to each. 6 I planted, Apollos watered, but God gave the growth. 7 So neither the one

who plants nor the one who waters is anything, but only God who gives the growth. 8 The one who plants and the one who waters have a common purpose, and each will receive wages according to the labor of each. 9 For we are God's servants, working together; you are God's field, God's building.

10 According to the grace of God given to me, like a skilled master builder I laid a foundation, and someone else is building on it. Each builder must choose with care how to build on it. 11 For no one can lay any foundation other than the one that has been laid; that foundation is Jesus Christ. 12 Now if anyone builds on the foundation with gold, silver, precious stones, wood, hay, straw— 13 the work of each builder will become visible, for the Day will disclose it, because it will be revealed with fire, and the fire will test what sort of work each has done. 14 If what has been built on the foundation survives, the builder will receive a reward. 15 If the work is burned up, the builder will suffer loss; the builder will be saved, but only as through fire.

16 Do you not know that you are God's temple and that God's Spirit dwells in you?[o] 17 If anyone destroys God's temple, God will destroy that person. For God's temple is holy, and you are that temple.

18 Do not deceive yourselves. If you think that you are wise in this age, you should become fools so that you may become wise. 19 For the wisdom of this world is foolishness with God. For it is written,

"He catches the wise in their
    craftiness,"[5]

20 and again,

"The Lord knows the thoughts of
    the wise,
  that they are futile."[6]

21 So let no one boast about human leaders. For all things are yours, 22 whether Paul or Apollos or Cephas or the world or life or death or the present or the future—all belong to you, 23 and you belong to Christ, and Christ belongs to God.

---

[1]Or *interpreting spiritual things in spiritual language*, or *comparing spiritual things with spiritual* [m]Or *natural* [n]Gk *brothers* [o]In verses 16 and 17 the Greek word for *you* is plural

[3]Isa 64:4; 52:15 [4]Isa 40:13 [5]Job 5:13 [6]Ps 94:11

4 Think of us in this way, as servants of Christ and stewards of God's mysteries. 2 Moreover, it is required of stewards that they be found trustworthy. 3 But with me it is a very small thing that I should be judged by you or by any human court. I do not even judge myself. 4 I am not aware of anything against myself, but I am not thereby acquitted. It is the Lord who judges me. 5 Therefore do not pronounce judgment before the time, before the Lord comes, who will bring to light the things now hidden in darkness and will disclose the purposes of the heart. Then each one will receive commendation from God.

6 I have applied all this to Apollos and myself for your benefit, brothers and sisters,[p] so that you may learn through us the meaning of the saying, "Nothing beyond what is written," so that none of you will be puffed up in favor of one against another. 7 For who sees anything different in you?[q] What do you have that you did not receive? And if you received it, why do you boast as if it were not a gift?

8 Already you have all you want! Already you have become rich! Quite apart from us you have become kings! Indeed, I wish that you had become kings, so that we might be kings with you! 9 For I think that God has exhibited us apostles as last of all, as though sentenced to death, because we have become a spectacle to the world, to angels and to mortals. 10 We are fools for the sake of Christ, but you are wise in Christ. We are weak, but you are strong. You are held in honor, but we in disrepute. 11 To the present hour we are hungry and thirsty, we are poorly clothed and beaten and homeless, 12 and we grow weary from the work of our own hands. When reviled, we bless; when persecuted, we endure; 13 when slandered, we speak kindly. We have become like the rubbish of the world, the dregs of all things, to this very day.

14 I am not writing this to make you ashamed, but to admonish you as my beloved children. 15 For though you might have ten thousand guardians in Christ, you do not have many fathers. Indeed, in Christ Jesus I became your father through the gospel. 16 I appeal to you, then, be imitators of me. 17 For this reason I sent[r] you Timothy, who is my beloved and faithful child in the Lord, to remind you of my ways in Christ Jesus, as I teach them everywhere in every church. 18 But some of you, thinking that I am not coming to you, have become arrogant. 19 But I will come to you soon, if the Lord wills, and I will find out not the talk of these arrogant people but their power. 20 For the kingdom of God depends not on talk but on power. 21 What would you prefer? Am I to come to you with a stick, or with love in a spirit of gentleness?

5 It is actually reported that there is sexual immorality among you, and of a kind that is not found even among pagans; for a man is living with his father's wife. 2 And you are arrogant! Should you not rather have mourned, so that he who has done this would have been removed from among you?

3 For though absent in body, I am present in spirit; and as if present I have already pronounced judgment 4 in the name of the Lord Jesus on the man who has done such a thing.[s] When you are assembled, and my spirit is present with the power of our Lord Jesus, 5 you are to hand this man over to Satan for the destruction of the flesh, so that his spirit may be saved in the day of the Lord.[t]

6 Your boasting is not a good thing. Do you not know that a little yeast leavens the whole batch of dough? 7 Clean out the old yeast so that you may be a new batch, as you really are unleavened. For our paschal lamb, Christ, has been sacrificed. 8 Therefore, let us celebrate the festival, not with the old yeast, the yeast of malice and evil, but with the unleavened bread of sincerity and truth.

9 I wrote to you in my letter not to associate with sexually immoral persons— 10 not at all meaning the immoral of this world, or the greedy and robbers, or idolaters, since you would then need to go out of the world. 11 But now I am writing to you not to associate with anyone who bears the name of brother or sister[u] who is sexually immoral or greedy, or is an idolater, reviler, drunkard, or robber. Do not even eat with such a one. 12 For what have I to do with judging those outside? Is it not those who are inside that you are to judge? 13 God will judge those outside. "Drive out the wicked person from among you."[7]

[p]Gk brothers [q]Or Who makes you different from another? [r]Or am sending [s]Or on the man who has done such a thing in the name of the Lord Jesus [t]Other ancient authorities add Jesus [u]Gk brother

[7]Deut 17:7

6 When any of you has a grievance against another, do you dare to take it to court before the unrighteous, instead of taking it before the saints? 2 Do you not know that the saints will judge the world? And if the world is to be judged by you, are you incompetent to try trivial cases? 3 Do you not know that we are to judge angels—to say nothing of ordinary matters? 4 If you have ordinary cases, then, do you appoint as judges those who have no standing in the church? 5 I say this to your shame. Can it be that there is no one among you wise enough to decide between one believer[v] and another, 6 but a believer[v] goes to court against a believer[v]—and before unbelievers at that?

7 In fact, to have lawsuits at all with one another is already a defeat for you. Why not rather be wronged? Why not rather be defrauded? 8 But you yourselves wrong and defraud—and believers[w] at that.

9 Do you not know that wrongdoers will not inherit the kingdom of God? Do not be deceived! Fornicators, idolaters, adulterers, male prostitutes, sodomites, 10 thieves, the greedy, drunkards, revilers, robbers—none of these will inherit the kingdom of God. 11 And this is what some of you used to be. But you were washed, you were sanctified, you were justified in the name of the Lord Jesus Christ and in the Spirit of our God.

12 "All things are lawful for me," but not all things are beneficial. "All things are lawful for me," but I will not be dominated by anything. 13 "Food is meant for the stomach and the stomach for food,"[x] and God will destroy both one and the other. The body is meant not for fornication but for the Lord, and the Lord for the body. 14 And God raised the Lord and will also raise us by his power. 15 Do you not know that your bodies are members of Christ? Should I therefore take the members of Christ and make them members of a prostitute? Never! 16 Do you not know that whoever is united to a prostitute becomes one body with her? For it is said, "The two shall be one flesh."[8] 17 But anyone united to the Lord becomes one spirit with him. 18 Shun fornication! Every sin that a person commits is outside the body; but the fornicator sins against the body itself. 19 Or do you not know that your body is a temple[y] of the Holy Spirit within you, which you have from God, and that you are not your own? 20 For you were bought with a price; therefore glorify God in your body.

7 Now concerning the matters about which you wrote: "It is well for a man not to touch a woman." 2 But because of cases of sexual immorality, each man should have his own wife and each woman her own husband. 3 The husband should give to his wife her conjugal rights, and likewise the wife to her husband. 4 For the wife does not have authority over her own body, but the husband does; likewise the husband does not have authority over his own body, but the wife does. 5 Do not deprive one another except perhaps by agreement for a set time, to devote yourselves to prayer, and then come together again, so that Satan may not tempt you because of your lack of self-control. 6 This I say by way of concession, not of command. 7 I wish that all were as I myself am. But each has a particular gift from God, one having one kind and another a different kind.

8 To the unmarried and the widows I say that it is well for them to remain unmarried as I am. 9 But if they are not practicing self-control, they should marry. For it is better to marry than to be aflame with passion.

10 To the married I give this command—not I but the Lord—that the wife should not separate from her husband 11 (but if she does separate, let her remain unmarried or else be reconciled to her husband), and that the husband should not divorce his wife.

12 To the rest I say—I and not the Lord—that if any believer[z] has a wife who is an unbeliever, and she consents to live with him, he should not divorce her. 13 And if any woman has a husband who is an unbeliever, and he consents to live with her, she should not divorce him. 14 For the unbelieving husband is made holy through his wife, and the unbelieving wife is made holy through her husband. Otherwise, your children would be unclean, but as it is, they are holy. 15 But if the unbelieving partner separates, let it be so; in such a case the brother or sister is not bound. It is to peace

---

[v]Gk *brother*   [w]Gk *brothers*   [x]The quotation may extend to the word *other*   [y]Or *sanctuary*   [z]Gk *brother*

---

[8]Gen 2:24

that God has called you.[a] 16 Wife, for all you know, you might save your husband. Husband, for all you know, you might save your wife.

17 However that may be, let each of you lead the life that the Lord has assigned, to which God called you. This is my rule in all the churches. 18 Was anyone at the time of his call already circumcised? Let him not seek to remove the marks of circumcision. Was anyone at the time of his call uncircumcised? Let him not seek circumcision. 19 Circumcision is nothing, and uncircumcision is nothing; but obeying the commandments of God is everything. 20 Let each of you remain in the condition in which you were called.

21 Were you a slave when called? Do not be concerned about it. Even if you can gain your freedom, make use of your present condition now more than ever.[b] 22 For whoever was called in the Lord as a slave is a freed person belonging to the Lord, just as whoever was free when called is a slave of Christ. 23 You were bought with a price; do not become slaves of human masters. 24 In whatever condition you were called, brothers and sisters,[c] there remain with God.

25 Now concerning virgins, I have no command of the Lord, but I give my opinion as one who by the Lord's mercy is trustworthy. 26 I think that, in view of the impending[d] crisis, it is well for you to remain as you are. 27 Are you bound to a wife? Do not seek to be free. Are you free from a wife? Do not seek a wife. 28 But if you marry, you do not sin, and if a virgin marries, she does not sin. Yet those who marry will experience distress in this life,[e] and I would spare you that. 29 I mean, brothers and sisters,[c] the appointed time has grown short; from now on, let even those who have wives be as though they had none, 30 and those who mourn as though they were not mourning, and those who rejoice as though they were not rejoicing, and those who buy as though they had no possessions, 31 and those who deal with the world as though they had no dealings with it. For the present form of this world is passing away.

32 I want you to be free from anxieties. The unmarried man is anxious about the affairs of the Lord, how to please the Lord; 33 but the married man is anxious about the affairs of the world, how to please his wife, 34 and his interests are divided. And the unmarried woman and the virgin are anxious about the affairs of the Lord, so that they may be holy in body and spirit; but the married woman is anxious about the affairs of the world, how to please her husband. 35 I say this for your own benefit, not to put any restraint upon you, but to promote good order and unhindered devotion to the Lord.

36 If anyone thinks that he is not behaving properly toward his fiancée,[f] if his passions are strong, and so it has to be, let him marry as he wishes; it is no sin. Let them marry. 37 But if someone stands firm in his resolve, being under no necessity but having his own desire under control, and has determined in his own mind to keep her as his fiancée,[f] he will do well. 38 So then, he who marries his fiancée[f] does well; and he who refrains from marriage will do better.

39 A wife is bound as long as her husband lives. But if the husband dies,[g] she is free to marry anyone she wishes, only in the Lord. 40 But in my judgment she is more blessed if she remains as she is. And I think that I too have the Spirit of God.

8 Now concerning food sacrificed to idols: we know that "all of us possess knowledge." Knowledge puffs up, but love builds up. 2 Anyone who claims to know something does not yet have the necessary knowledge; 3 but anyone who loves God is known by him.

4 Hence, as to the eating of food offered to idols, we know that "no idol in the world really exists," and that "there is no God but one." 5 Indeed, even though there may be so-called gods in heaven or on earth—as in fact there are many gods and many lords— 6 yet for us there is one God, the Father, from whom are all things and for whom we exist, and one Lord, Jesus Christ, through whom are all things and through whom we exist.

7 It is not everyone, however, who has this knowledge. Since some have become so accustomed to idols until now, they still think of the food they eat as food offered to an idol; and their conscience, being weak, is defiled. 8 "Food will not bring us close to God."[h] We are no worse off if we do not eat, and no better off if we do. 9 But

---

[a]Other ancient authorities read *us*   [b]Or *avail yourself of the opportunity*   [c]Gk *brothers*   [d]Or *present*   [e]Gk *in the flesh*   [f]Gk *virgin*   [g]Gk *falls asleep*   [h]The quotation may extend to the end of the verse

take care that this liberty of yours does not somehow become a stumbling block to the weak. 10 For if others see you, who possess knowledge, eating in the temple of an idol, might they not, since their conscience is weak, be encouraged to the point of eating food sacrificed to idols? 11 So by your knowledge those weak believers for whom Christ died are destroyed.[i] 12 But when you thus sin against members of your family,[j] and wound their conscience when it is weak, you sin against Christ. 13 Therefore, if food is a cause of their falling,[k] I will never eat meat, so that I may not cause one of them[l] to fall.

9 Am I not free? Am I not an apostle? Have I not seen Jesus our Lord? Are you not my work in the Lord? 2 If I am not an apostle to others, at least I am to you; for you are the seal of my apostleship in the Lord.

3 This is my defense to those who would examine me. 4 Do we not have the right to our food and drink? 5 Do we not have the right to be accompanied by a believing wife,[m] as do the other apostles and the brothers of the Lord and Cephas? 6 Or is it only Barnabas and I who have no right to refrain from working for a living? 7 Who at any time pays the expenses for doing military service? Who plants a vineyard and does not eat any of its fruit? Or who tends a flock and does not get any of its milk?

8 Do I say this on human authority? Does not the law also say the same? 9 For it is written in the law of Moses, "You shall not muzzle an ox while it is treading out the grain."[9] Is it for oxen that God is concerned? 10 Or does he not speak entirely for our sake? It was indeed written for our sake, for whoever plows should plow in hope and whoever threshes should thresh in hope of a share in the crop. 11 If we have sown spiritual good among you, is it too much if we reap your material benefits? 12 If others share this rightful claim on you, do not we still more?

Nevertheless, we have not made use of this right, but we endure anything rather than put an obstacle in the way of the gospel of Christ. 13 Do you not know that those who are employed in the temple service get their food from the temple, and those who serve at the altar share in what is sacrificed on the altar? 14 In the same way, the Lord

commanded that those who proclaim the gospel should get their living by the gospel.

15 But I have made no use of any of these rights, nor am I writing this so that they may be applied in my case. Indeed, I would rather die than that— no one will deprive me of my ground for boasting! 16 If I proclaim the gospel, this gives me no ground for boasting, for an obligation is laid on me, and woe to me if I do not proclaim the gospel! 17 For if I do this of my own will, I have a reward; but if not of my own will, I am entrusted with a commission. 18 What then is my reward? Just this: that in my proclamation I may make the gospel free of charge, so as not to make full use of my rights in the gospel.

19 For though I am free with respect to all, I have made myself a slave to all, so that I might win more of them. 20 To the Jews I became as a Jew, in order to win Jews. To those under the law I became as one under the law (though I myself am not under the law) so that I might win those under the law. 21 To those outside the law I became as one outside the law (though I am not free from God's law but am under Christ's law) so that I might win those outside the law. 22 To the weak I became weak, so that I might win the weak. I have become all things to all people, that I might by all means save some. 23 I do it all for the sake of the gospel, so that I may share in its blessings.

24 Do you not know that in a race the runners all compete, but only one receives the prize? Run in such a way that you may win it. 25 Athletes exercise self-control in all things; they do it to receive a perishable wreath, but we an imperishable one. 26 So I do not run aimlessly, nor do I box as though beating the air; 27 but I punish my body and enslave it, so that after proclaiming to others I myself should not be disqualified.

10 I do not want you to be unaware, brothers and sisters,[n] that our ancestors were all under the cloud, and all passed through the sea, 2 and all were baptized into Moses in the cloud and in the sea, 3 and all ate the same spiritual food,

---

[i] Gk the weak brother . . . is destroyed   [j] Gk against the brothers
[k] Gk my brother's falling   [l] Gk cause my brother   [m] Gk a sister as wife   [n] Gk brothers

[9] Deut 25:4

4 and all drank the same spiritual drink. For they drank from the spiritual rock that followed them, and the rock was Christ. 5 Nevertheless, God was not pleased with most of them, and they were struck down in the wilderness.

6 Now these things occurred as examples for us, so that we might not desire evil as they did. 7 Do not become idolaters as some of them did; as it is written, "The people sat down to eat and drink, and they rose up to play."[10] 8 We must not indulge in sexual immorality as some of them did, and twenty-three thousand fell in a single day. 9 We must not put Christ[o] to the test, as some of them did, and were destroyed by serpents. 10 And do not complain as some of them did, and were destroyed by the destroyer. 11 These things happened to them to serve as an example, and they were written down to instruct us, on whom the ends of the ages have come. 12 So if you think you are standing, watch out that you do not fall. 13 No testing has overtaken you that is not common to everyone. God is faithful, and he will not let you be tested beyond your strength, but with the testing he will also provide the way out so that you may be able to endure it.

14 Therefore, my dear friends,[p] flee from the worship of idols. 15 I speak as to sensible people; judge for yourselves what I say. 16 The cup of blessing that we bless, is it not a sharing in the blood of Christ? The bread that we break, is it not a sharing in the body of Christ? 17 Because there is one bread, we who are many are one body, for we all partake of the one bread. 18 Consider the people of Israel;[q] are not those who eat the sacrifices partners in the altar? 19 What do I imply then? That food sacrificed to idols is anything, or that an idol is anything? 20 No, I imply that what pagans sacrifice, they sacrifice to demons and not to God. I do not want you to be partners with demons. 21 You cannot drink the cup of the Lord and the cup of demons. You cannot partake of the table of the Lord and the table of demons. 22 Or are we provoking the Lord to jealousy? Are we stronger than he?

23 "All things are lawful," but not all things are beneficial. "All things are lawful," but not all things build up. 24 Do not seek your own advantage, but that of the other. 25 Eat whatever is sold in the meat market without raising any question on the ground of conscience, 26 for "the earth and its fullness are the Lord's."[11] 27 If an unbeliever invites you to a meal and you are disposed to go, eat whatever is set before you without raising any question on the ground of conscience. 28 But if someone says to you, "This has been offered in sacrifice," then do not eat it, out of consideration for the one who informed you, and for the sake of conscience— 29 I mean the other's conscience, not your own. For why should my liberty be subject to the judgment of someone else's conscience? 30 If I partake with thankfulness, why should I be denounced because of that for which I give thanks?

31 So, whether you eat or drink, or whatever you do, do everything for the glory of God. 32 Give no offense to Jews or to Greeks or to the church of God, 33 just as I try to please everyone in everything I do, not seeking my own advantage, but that of many, so that they may be saved.

11 Be imitators of me, as I am of Christ.

2 I commend you because you remember me in everything and maintain the traditions just as I handed them on to you. 3 But I want you to understand that Christ is the head of every man, and the husband[r] is the head of his wife,[s] and God is the head of Christ. 4 Any man who prays or prophesies with something on his head disgraces his head, 5 but any woman who prays or prophesies with her head unveiled disgraces her head—it is one and the same thing as having her head shaved. 6 For if a woman will not veil herself, then she should cut off her hair; but if it is disgraceful for a woman to have her hair cut off or to be shaved, she should wear a veil. 7 For a man ought not to have his head veiled, since he is the image and reflection[t] of God; but woman is the reflection[t] of man. 8 Indeed, man was not made from woman, but woman from man. 9 Neither was man created for the sake of woman, but woman for the sake of man. 10 For this reason a woman ought to have a symbol of[u] authority on

---

[o]Other ancient authorities read *the Lord* [p]Gk *my beloved* [q]Gk *Israel according to the flesh* [r]The same Greek word means *man* or *husband* [s]Or *head of the woman* [t]Or *glory* [u]Gk lacks *a symbol of*

[10]Exod 32:6 [11]Ps 24:1

her head,[v] because of the angels. 11 Nevertheless, in the Lord woman is not independent of man or man independent of woman. 12 For just as woman came from man, so man comes through woman; but all things come from God. 13 Judge for yourselves: is it proper for a woman to pray to God with her head unveiled? 14 Does not nature itself teach you that if a man wears long hair, it is degrading to him, 15 but if a woman has long hair, it is her glory? For her hair is given to her for a covering. 16 But if anyone is disposed to be contentious—we have no such custom, nor do the churches of God.

17 Now in the following instructions I do not commend you, because when you come together it is not for the better but for the worse. 18 For, to begin with, when you come together as a church, I hear that there are divisions among you; and to some extent I believe it. 19 Indeed, there have to be factions among you, for only so will it become clear who among you are genuine. 20 When you come together, it is not really to eat the Lord's supper. 21 For when the time comes to eat, each of you goes ahead with your own supper, and one goes hungry and another becomes drunk. 22 What! Do you not have homes to eat and drink in? Or do you show contempt for the church of God and humiliate those who have nothing? What should I say to you? Should I commend you? In this matter I do not commend you!

23 For I received from the Lord what I also handed on to you, that the Lord Jesus on the night when he was betrayed took a loaf of bread, 24 and when he had given thanks, he broke it and said, "This is my body that is for[w] you. Do this in remembrance of me." 25 In the same way he took the cup also, after supper, saying, "This cup is the new covenant in my blood. Do this, as often as you drink it, in remembrance of me." 26 For as often as you eat this bread and drink the cup, you proclaim the Lord's death until he comes.

27 Whoever, therefore, eats the bread or drinks the cup of the Lord in an unworthy manner will be answerable for the body and blood of the Lord. 28 Examine yourselves, and only then eat of the bread and drink of the cup. 29 For all who eat and drink[x] without discerning the body,[y] eat and drink judgment against themselves. 30 For this reason many of you are weak and ill, and some have

died.[z] 31 But if we judged ourselves, we would not be judged. 32 But when we are judged by the Lord, we are disciplined[a] so that we may not be condemned along with the world.

33 So then, my brothers and sisters,[b] when you come together to eat, wait for one another. 34 If you are hungry, eat at home, so that when you come together, it will not be for your condemnation. About the other things I will give instructions when I come.

12 Now concerning spiritual gifts,[c] brothers and sisters,[b] I do not want you to be uninformed. 2 You know that when you were pagans, you were enticed and led astray to idols that could not speak. 3 Therefore I want you to understand that no one speaking by the Spirit of God ever says "Let Jesus be cursed!" and no one can say "Jesus is Lord" except by the Holy Spirit.

4 Now there are varieties of gifts, but the same Spirit; 5 and there are varieties of services, but the same Lord; 6 and there are varieties of activities, but it is the same God who activates all of them in everyone. 7 To each is given the manifestation of the Spirit for the common good. 8 To one is given through the Spirit the utterance of wisdom, and to another the utterance of knowledge according to the same Spirit, 9 to another faith by the same Spirit, to another gifts of healing by the one Spirit, 10 to another the working of miracles, to another prophecy, to another the discernment of spirits, to another various kinds of tongues, to another the interpretation of tongues. 11 All these are activated by one and the same Spirit, who allots to each one individually just as the Spirit chooses.

12 For just as the body is one and has many members, and all the members of the body, though many, are one body, so it is with Christ. 13 For in the one Spirit we were all baptized into one body—Jews or Greeks, slaves or free—and we were all made to drink of one Spirit.

14 Indeed, the body does not consist of one member but of many. 15 If the foot would say, "Because I am not a hand, I do not belong to the

---

[v]Or *have freedom of choice regarding her head*   [w]Other ancient authorities read *is broken for*   [x]Other ancient authorities add *in an unworthy manner*,   [y]Other ancient authorities read *the Lord's body*   [z]Gk *fallen asleep*   [a]Or *When we are judged, we are being disciplined by the Lord*   [b]Gk *brothers*   [c]Or *spiritual persons*

body," that would not make it any less a part of the body. 16 And if the ear would say, "Because I am not an eye, I do not belong to the body," that would not make it any less a part of the body. 17 If the whole body were an eye, where would the hearing be? If the whole body were hearing, where would the sense of smell be? 18 But as it is, God arranged the members in the body, each one of them, as he chose. 19 If all were a single member, where would the body be? 20 As it is, there are many members, yet one body. 21 The eye cannot say to the hand, "I have no need of you," nor again the head to the feet, "I have no need of you." 22 On the contrary, the members of the body that seem to be weaker are indispensable, 23 and those members of the body that we think less honorable we clothe with greater honor, and our less respectable members are treated with greater respect; 24 whereas our more respectable members do not need this. But God has so arranged the body, giving the greater honor to the inferior member, 25 that there may be no dissension within the body, but the members may have the same care for one another. 26 If one member suffers, all suffer together with it; if one member is honored, all rejoice together with it.

27 Now you are the body of Christ and individually members of it. 28 And God has appointed in the church first apostles, second prophets, third teachers; then deeds of power, then gifts of healing, forms of assistance, forms of leadership, various kinds of tongues. 29 Are all apostles? Are all prophets? Are all teachers? Do all work miracles? 30 Do all possess gifts of healing? Do all speak in tongues? Do all interpret? 31 But strive for the greater gifts. And I will show you a still more excellent way.

13 If I speak in the tongues of mortals and of angels, but do not have love, I am a noisy gong or a clanging cymbal. 2 And if I have prophetic powers, and understand all mysteries and all knowledge, and if I have all faith, so as to remove mountains, but do not have love, I am nothing. 3 If I give away all my possessions, and if I hand over my body so that I may boast,[d] but do not have love, I gain nothing.

4 Love is patient; love is kind; love is not envious or boastful or arrogant 5 or rude. It does not insist on its own way; it is not irritable or resent-

ful; 6 it does not rejoice in wrongdoing, but rejoices in the truth. 7 It bears all things, believes all things, hopes all things, endures all things.

8 Love never ends. But as for prophecies, they will come to an end; as for tongues, they will cease; as for knowledge, it will come to an end. 9 For we know only in part, and we prophesy only in part; 10 but when the complete comes, the partial will come to an end. 11 When I was a child, I spoke like a child, I thought like a child, I reasoned like a child; when I became an adult, I put an end to childish ways. 12 For now we see in a mirror, dimly,[e] but then we will see face to face. Now I know only in part; then I will know fully, even as I have been fully known. 13 And now faith, hope, and love abide, these three; and the greatest of these is love.

14 Pursue love and strive for the spiritual gifts, and especially that you may prophesy. 2 For those who speak in a tongue do not speak to other people but to God; for nobody understands them, since they are speaking mysteries in the Spirit. 3 On the other hand, those who prophesy speak to other people for their upbuilding and encouragement and consolation. 4 Those who speak in a tongue build up themselves, but those who prophesy build up the church. 5 Now I would like all of you to speak in tongues, but even more to prophesy. One who prophesies is greater than one who speaks in tongues, unless someone interprets, so that the church may be built up.

6 Now, brothers and sisters,[f] if I come to you speaking in tongues, how will I benefit you unless I speak to you in some revelation or knowledge or prophecy or teaching? 7 It is the same way with lifeless instruments that produce sound, such as the flute or the harp. If they do not give distinct notes, how will anyone know what is being played? 8 And if the bugle gives an indistinct sound, who will get ready for battle? 9 So with yourselves; if in a tongue you utter speech that is not intelligible, how will anyone know what is being said? For you will be speaking into the air. 10 There are doubtless many different kinds of sounds in the world, and nothing is without sound. 11 If then I do not know the meaning of a sound, I

---

[d]Other ancient authorities read *body to be burned*   [e]Gk *in a riddle*
[f]Gk *brothers*

will be a foreigner to the speaker and the speaker a foreigner to me. 12 So with yourselves; since you are eager for spiritual gifts, strive to excel in them for building up the church.

13 Therefore, one who speaks in a tongue should pray for the power to interpret. 14 For if I pray in a tongue, my spirit prays but my mind is unproductive. 15 What should I do then? I will pray with the spirit, but I will pray with the mind also; I will sing praise with the spirit, but I will sing praise with the mind also. 16 Otherwise, if you say a blessing with the spirit, how can anyone in the position of an outsider say the "Amen" to your thanksgiving, since the outsider does not know what you are saying? 17 For you may give thanks well enough, but the other person is not built up. 18 I thank God that I speak in tongues more than all of you; 19 nevertheless, in church I would rather speak five words with my mind, in order to instruct others also, than ten thousand words in a tongue.

20 Brothers and sisters,[g] do not be children in your thinking; rather, be infants in evil, but in thinking be adults. 21 In the law it is written,

"By people of strange tongues
and by the lips of foreigners
I will speak to this people;
yet even then they will not
listen to me,"[12]

says the Lord. 22 Tongues, then, are a sign not for believers but for unbelievers, while prophecy is not for unbelievers but for believers. 23 If, therefore, the whole church comes together and all speak in tongues, and outsiders or unbelievers enter, will they not say that you are out of your mind? 24 But if all prophesy, an unbeliever or outsider who enters is reproved by all and called to account by all. 25 After the secrets of the unbeliever's heart are disclosed, that person will bow down before God and worship him, declaring, "God is really among you."

26 What should be done then, my friends?[g] When you come together, each one has a hymn, a lesson, a revelation, a tongue, or an interpretation. Let all things be done for building up. 27 If anyone speaks in a tongue, let there be only two or at most three, and each in turn; and let one interpret. 28 But if there is no one to interpret, let them be silent in church and speak to themselves and to

God. 29 Let two or three prophets speak, and let the others weigh what is said. 30 If a revelation is made to someone else sitting nearby, let the first person be silent. 31 For you can all prophesy one by one, so that all may learn and all be encouraged. 32 And the spirits of prophets are subject to the prophets, 33 for God is a God not of disorder but of peace.

(As in all the churches of the saints, 34 women should be silent in the churches. For they are not permitted to speak, but should be subordinate, as the law also says. 35 If there is anything they desire to know, let them ask their husbands at home. For it is shameful for a woman to speak in church.[h] 36 Or did the word of God originate with you? Or are you the only ones it has reached?)

37 Anyone who claims to be a prophet, or to have spiritual powers, must acknowledge that what I am writing to you is a command of the Lord. 38 Anyone who does not recognize this is not to be recognized. 39 So, my friends,[i] be eager to prophesy, and do not forbid speaking in tongues; 40 but all things should be done decently and in order.

15 Now I would remind you, brothers and sisters,[g] of the good news[j] that I proclaimed to you, which you in turn received, in which also you stand, 2 through which also you are being saved, if you hold firmly to the message that I proclaimed to you—unless you have come to believe in vain.

3 For I handed on to you as of first importance what I in turn had received: that Christ died for our sins in accordance with the scriptures, 4 and that he was buried, and that he was raised on the third day in accordance with the scriptures, 5 and that he appeared to Cephas, then to the twelve. 6 Then he appeared to more than five hundred brothers and sisters[g] at one time, most of whom are still alive, though some have died.[k] 7 Then he appeared to James, then to all the apostles. 8 Last of all, as to one untimely born, he appeared also to me. 9 For I am the least of the apostles, unfit to be called an apostle, because I persecuted the church

---

[g]Gk *brothers* [h]Other ancient authorities put verses 34-35 after verse 40 [i]Gk *my brothers* [j]Or *gospel* [k]Gk *fallen asleep*

---

[12]Isa 28:11–12

of God. 10 But by the grace of God I am what I am, and his grace toward me has not been in vain. On the contrary, I worked harder than any of them—though it was not I, but the grace of God that is with me. 11 Whether then it was I or they, so we proclaim and so you have come to believe.

12 Now if Christ is proclaimed as raised from the dead, how can some of you say there is no resurrection of the dead? 13 If there is no resurrection of the dead, then Christ has not been raised; 14 and if Christ has not been raised, then our proclamation has been in vain and your faith has been in vain. 15 We are even found to be misrepresenting God, because we testified of God that he raised Christ—whom he did not raise if it is true that the dead are not raised. 16 For if the dead are not raised, then Christ has not been raised. 17 If Christ has not been raised, your faith is futile and you are still in your sins. 18 Then those also who have died[l] in Christ have perished. 19 If for this life only we have hoped in Christ, we are of all people most to be pitied.

20 But in fact Christ has been raised from the dead, the first fruits of those who have died.[l] 21 For since death came through a human being, the resurrection of the dead has also come through a human being; 22 for as all die in Adam, so all will be made alive in Christ. 23 But each in his own order: Christ the first fruits, then at his coming those who belong to Christ. 24 Then comes the end,[m] when he hands over the kingdom to God the Father, after he has destroyed every ruler and every authority and power. 25 For he must reign until he has put all his enemies under his feet. 26 The last enemy to be destroyed is death. 27 For "God[n] has put all things in subjection under his feet."[13] But when it says, "All things are put in subjection," it is plain that this does not include the one who put all things in subjection under him. 28 When all things are subjected to him, then the Son himself will also be subjected to the one who put all things in subjection under him, so that God may be all in all.

29 Otherwise, what will those people do who receive baptism on behalf of the dead? If the dead are not raised at all, why are people baptized on their behalf?

30 And why are we putting ourselves in danger every hour? 31 I die every day! That is as certain, brothers and sisters,[o] as my boasting of you—a boast that I make in Christ Jesus our Lord. 32 If with merely human hopes I fought with wild animals at Ephesus, what would I have gained by it? If the dead are not raised,

> "Let us eat and drink,
>   for tomorrow we die."[14]

33 Do not be deceived:

> "Bad company ruins good
>   morals."

34 Come to a sober and right mind, and sin no more; for some people have no knowledge of God. I say this to your shame.

35 But someone will ask, "How are the dead raised? With what kind of body do they come?" 36 Fool! What you sow does not come to life unless it dies. 37 And as for what you sow, you do not sow the body that is to be, but a bare seed, perhaps of wheat or of some other grain. 38 But God gives it a body as he has chosen, and to each kind of seed its own body. 39 Not all flesh is alike, but there is one flesh for human beings, another for animals, another for birds, and another for fish. 40 There are both heavenly bodies and earthly bodies, but the glory of the heavenly is one thing, and that of the earthly is another. 41 There is one glory of the sun, and another glory of the moon, and another glory of the stars; indeed, star differs from star in glory.

42 So it is with the resurrection of the dead. What is sown is perishable, what is raised is imperishable. 43 It is sown in dishonor, it is raised in glory. It is sown in weakness, it is raised in power. 44 It is sown a physical body, it is raised a spiritual body. If there is a physical body, there is also a spiritual body. 45 Thus it is written, "The first man, Adam, became a living being";[15] the last Adam became a life-giving spirit. 46 But it is not the spiritual that is first, but the physical, and then the spiritual. 47 The first man was from the earth, a man of dust; the second man is[p] from heaven. 48 As was the man of dust, so are those who are of the dust; and as is the man of heaven, so are those

---

[l]Gk *fallen asleep*   [m]Or *Then come the rest*   [n]Gk *he*   [o]Gk *brothers*
[p]Other ancient authorities add *the Lord*

[13]Ps 8:6   [14]Isa 22:13   [15]Gen 2:7

who are of heaven. 49 Just as we have borne the image of the man of dust, we will[q] also bear the image of the man of heaven.

50 What I am saying, brothers and sisters,[r] is this: flesh and blood cannot inherit the kingdom of God, nor does the perishable inherit the imperishable. 51 Listen, I will tell you a mystery! We will not all die,[s] but we will all be changed, 52 in a moment, in the twinkling of an eye, at the last trumpet. For the trumpet will sound, and the dead will be raised imperishable, and we will be changed. 53 For this perishable body must put on imperishability, and this mortal body must put on immortality. 54 When this perishable body puts on imperishability, and this mortal body puts on immortality, then the saying that is written will be fulfilled:

"Death has been swallowed up in
victory."[16]
55   "Where, O death, is your
victory?
Where, O death, is your
sting?"[17]

56 The sting of death is sin, and the power of sin is the law. 57 But thanks be to God, who gives us the victory through our Lord Jesus Christ.

58 Therefore, my beloved,[t] be steadfast, immovable, always excelling in the work of the Lord, because you know that in the Lord your labor is not in vain.

16 Now concerning the collection for the saints: you should follow the directions I gave to the churches of Galatia. 2 On the first day of every week, each of you is to put aside and save whatever extra you earn, so that collections need not be taken when I come. 3 And when I arrive, I will send any whom you approve with letters to take your gift to Jerusalem. 4 If it seems advisable that I should go also, they will accompany me.

5 I will visit you after passing through Macedonia—for I intend to pass through Macedonia— 6 and perhaps I will stay with you or even spend the winter, so that you may send me on my way, wherever I go. 7 I do not want to see you now just in passing, for I hope to spend some time with you,

if the Lord permits. 8 But I will stay in Ephesus until Pentecost, 9 for a wide door for effective work has opened to me, and there are many adversaries.

10 If Timothy comes, see that he has nothing to fear among you, for he is doing the work of the Lord just as I am; 11 therefore let no one despise him. Send him on his way in peace, so that he may come to me; for I am expecting him with the brothers.

12 Now concerning our brother Apollos, I strongly urged him to visit you with the other brothers, but he was not at all willing[u] to come now. He will come when he has the opportunity.

13 Keep alert, stand firm in your faith, be courageous, be strong. 14 Let all that you do be done in love.

15 Now, brothers and sisters,[r] you know that members of the household of Stephanas were the first converts in Achaia, and they have devoted themselves to the service of the saints; 16 I urge you to put yourselves at the service of such people, and of everyone who works and toils with them. 17 I rejoice at the coming of Stephanas and Fortunatus and Achaicus, because they have made up for your absence; 18 for they refreshed my spirit as well as yours. So give recognition to such persons.

19 The churches of Asia send greetings. Aquila and Prisca, together with the church in their house, greet you warmly in the Lord. 20 All the brothers and sisters[r] send greetings. Greet one another with a holy kiss.

21 I, Paul, write this greeting with my own hand. 22 Let anyone be accursed who has no love for the Lord. Our Lord, come![v] 23 The grace of the Lord Jesus be with you. 24 My love be with all of you in Christ Jesus.[w]

---

[q]Other ancient authorities read *let us* [r]Gk *brothers* [s]Gk *fall asleep*
[t]Gk *beloved brothers* [u]Or *it was not at all God's will for him*
[v]Gk *Marana tha*. These Aramaic words can also be read *Maran atha*,
meaning *Our Lord has come* [w]Other ancient authorities add *Amen*

[16]Isa 25:8 [17]Hos 13:14

The Second Letter to the Corinthians

To speak of Paul's "second" letter to the Corinthians may be something of a misnomer, for in the opinion of many scholars, 2 Corinthians represents at least two different Pauline letters (or possibly four or five), which were later cut and pasted together for broader circulation, possibly by someone in the Corinthian community. The principal reason for this scholarly opinion is the drastic shift from the joyful and caring tone of chapters 1–9 to the harsh and condemnatory language of chapters 10–13. If this theory is right, then the final four chapters were taken from a letter that was written earlier than the one embodied in chapters 1–9. Neither letter, on this score, is preserved intact.

Establishing a plausible historical backdrop for each of the letter fragments can facilitate our understanding of their message. In 1 Corinthians 16:5–7 Paul had promised to pay the Corinthians another visit. He evidently fulfilled this promise prior to the writing of 2 Corinthians 1–9, because there he indicates that he does not wish to make "another" painful visit to them (2:1–4). This suggests that the second time he came things did not go well (he was there for the first time when he established the congregation, a visit that was by no means painful). It appears that while he was there, another group of apostles, whom he disparagingly calls the "super-apostles" (11:5), had arrived, claiming for themselves special supernatural gifts and powers that Paul himself could not match. Paul evidently left town in a huff.

He then fired off a letter attacking the super-apostles and all they stood for. In this letter, embodied in part in chapters 10–13, he reasserted some of the main points he had made in 1 Corinthians, but more forcefully and in response to the situation at hand. Contrary to the claims of the super-apostles, Christian existence in the present age is not one of glory and exaltation but of pain and suffering (12:9–10). The true apostle in particular experiences the pain of this world (11:20–31). Anyone who claims to live an exalted existence, therefore, is not a true apostle. Paul threatens now to come a third time in judgment (13:1–4).

He sent this letter through his companion Titus, and it evidently brought remarkable success. The Corinthians had a change of heart, returned to his fold (7:5–12), and punished a person who had publicly humiliated Paul on his second visit (2:5–11). Paul then wrote a friendly and grateful letter in response; most of this letter is now found in chapters 1–9. In it he reaffirms his conviction that, while this is an age dominated by the forces of evil, God's grace is sufficient for those who suffer (1:3–11). He urges his converts to look forward to the time when salvation will be complete, in which present affliction will be rewarded with "an eternal weight of glory beyond all measure" (4:17). This is the final word we hear from Paul concerning his Corinthian congregation; it is impossible for us to know whether the breach was completely mended or whether similar problems arose again later in their relationship with one another.

1 Paul, an apostle of Christ Jesus by the will of God, and Timothy our brother,

To the church of God that is in Corinth, including all the saints throughout Achaia:

2 Grace to you and peace from God our Father and the Lord Jesus Christ.

3 Blessed be the God and Father of our Lord Jesus Christ, the Father of mercies and the God of all consolation, 4 who consoles us in all our affliction, so that we may be able to console those who are in any affliction with the consolation with which we ourselves are consoled by God. 5 For just as the sufferings of Christ are abundant for us, so also our consolation is abundant through Christ. 6 If we are being afflicted, it is for your consolation and salvation; if we are being consoled, it is for your consolation, which you experience when you patiently endure the same sufferings that we are also suffering. 7 Our hope for you is unshaken; for we know that as you share in our sufferings, so also you share in our consolation.

8 We do not want you to be unaware, brothers and sisters,[a] of the affliction we experienced in Asia; for we were so utterly, unbearably crushed that we despaired of life itself. 9 Indeed, we felt that we had received the sentence of death so that we would rely not on ourselves but on God who raises the dead. 10 He who rescued us from so deadly a peril will continue to rescue us; on him we have set our hope that he will rescue us again, 11 as you also join in helping us by your prayers, so that many will give thanks on our[b] behalf for the blessing granted us through the prayers of many.

12 Indeed, this is our boast, the testimony of our conscience: we have behaved in the world with frankness[c] and godly sincerity, not by earthly wisdom but by the grace of God—and all the more toward you. 13 For we write you nothing other than what you can read and also understand; I hope you will understand until the end— 14 as you have already understood us in part—that on the day of the Lord Jesus we are your boast even as you are our boast.

15 Since I was sure of this, I wanted to come to you first, so that you might have a double favor;[d] 16 I wanted to visit you on my way to Macedonia, and to come back to you from Macedonia and have

you send me on to Judea. 17 Was I vacillating when I wanted to do this? Do I make my plans according to ordinary human standards,[e] ready to say "Yes, yes" and "No, no" at the same time? 18 As surely as God is faithful, our word to you has not been "Yes and No." 19 For the Son of God, Jesus Christ, whom we proclaimed among you, Silvanus and Timothy and I, was not "Yes and No"; but in him it is always "Yes." 20 For in him every one of God's promises is a "Yes." For this reason it is through him that we say the "Amen," to the glory of God. 21 But it is God who establishes us with you in Christ and has anointed us, 22 by putting his seal on us and giving us his Spirit in our hearts as a first installment.

23 But I call on God as witness against me: it was to spare you that I did not come again to Corinth. 24 I do not mean to imply that we lord it over your faith; rather, we are workers with you for your joy, because you stand firm in the faith.

2 So I made up my mind not to make you another painful visit. 2 For if I cause you pain, who is there to make me glad but the one whom I have pained? 3 And I wrote as I did, so that when I came, I might not suffer pain from those who should have made me rejoice; for I am confident about all of you, that my joy would be the joy of all of you. 4 For I wrote you out of much distress and anguish of heart and with many tears, not to cause you pain, but to let you know the abundant love that I have for you.

5 But if anyone has caused pain, he has caused it not to me, but to some extent—not to exaggerate it—to all of you. 6 This punishment by the majority is enough for such a person; 7 so now instead you should forgive and console him, so that he may not be overwhelmed by excessive sorrow. 8 So I urge you to reaffirm your love for him. 9 I wrote for this reason: to test you and to know whether you are obedient in everything. 10 Anyone whom you forgive, I also forgive. What I have forgiven, if I have forgiven anything, has been for your sake in the presence of Christ. 11 And we do this so that we may not be outwitted by Satan; for we are not ignorant of his designs.

12 When I came to Troas to proclaim the good

---

[a]Gk brothers [b]Other ancient authorities read your [c]Other ancient authorities read holiness [d]Other ancient authorities read pleasure [e]Gk according to the flesh

news of Christ, a door was opened for me in the Lord; 13 but my mind could not rest because I did not find my brother Titus there. So I said farewell to them and went on to Macedonia.

14 But thanks be to God, who in Christ always leads us in triumphal procession, and through us spreads in every place the fragrance that comes from knowing him. 15 For we are the aroma of Christ to God among those who are being saved and among those who are perishing; 16 to the one a fragrance from death to death, to the other a fragrance from life to life. Who is sufficient for these things? 17 For we are not peddlers of God's word like so many;[f] but in Christ we speak as persons of sincerity, as persons sent from God and standing in his presence.

3 Are we beginning to commend ourselves again? Surely we do not need, as some do, letters of recommendation to you or from you, do we? 2 You yourselves are our letter, written on our[g] hearts, to be known and read by all; 3 and you show that you are a letter of Christ, prepared by us, written not with ink but with the Spirit of the living God, not on tablets of stone but on tablets of human hearts.

4 Such is the confidence that we have through Christ toward God. 5 Not that we are competent of ourselves to claim anything as coming from us; our competence is from God, 6 who has made us competent to be ministers of a new covenant, not of letter but of spirit; for the letter kills, but the Spirit gives life.

7 Now if the ministry of death, chiseled in letters on stone tablets,[h] came in glory so that the people of Israel could not gaze at Moses' face because of the glory of his face, a glory now set aside, 8 how much more will the ministry of the Spirit come in glory? 9 For if there was glory in the ministry of condemnation, much more does the ministry of justification abound in glory! 10 Indeed, what once had glory has lost its glory because of the greater glory; 11 for if what was set aside came through glory, much more has the permanent come in glory!

12 Since, then, we have such a hope, we act with great boldness, 13 not like Moses, who put a veil over his face to keep the people of Israel from gazing at the end of the glory that[i] was being set aside. 14 But their minds were hardened. Indeed, to this very day, when they hear the reading of the old covenant, that same veil is still there, since only in Christ is it set aside. 15 Indeed, to this very day whenever Moses is read, a veil lies over their minds; 16 but when one turns to the Lord, the veil is removed. 17 Now the Lord is the Spirit, and where the Spirit of the Lord is, there is freedom. 18 And all of us, with unveiled faces, seeing the glory of the Lord as though reflected in a mirror, are being transformed into the same image from one degree of glory to another; for this comes from the Lord, the Spirit.

4 Therefore, since it is by God's mercy that we are engaged in this ministry, we do not lose heart. 2 We have renounced the shameful things that one hides; we refuse to practice cunning or to falsify God's word; but by the open statement of the truth we commend ourselves to the conscience of everyone in the sight of God. 3 And even if our gospel is veiled, it is veiled to those who are perishing. 4 In their case the god of this world has blinded the minds of the unbelievers, to keep them from seeing the light of the gospel of the glory of Christ, who is the image of God. 5 For we do not proclaim ourselves; we proclaim Jesus Christ as Lord and ourselves as your slaves for Jesus' sake. 6 For it is the God who said, "Let light shine out of darkness," who has shone in our hearts to give the light of the knowledge of the glory of God in the face of Jesus Christ.

7 But we have this treasure in clay jars, so that it may be made clear that this extraordinary power belongs to God and does not come from us. 8 We are afflicted in every way, but not crushed; perplexed, but not driven to despair; 9 persecuted, but not forsaken; struck down, but not destroyed; 10 always carrying in the body the death of Jesus, so that the life of Jesus may also be made visible in our bodies. 11 For while we live, we are always being given up to death for Jesus' sake, so that the life of Jesus may be made visible in our mortal flesh. 12 So death is at work in us, but life in you.

13 But just as we have the same spirit of faith that is in accordance with scripture—"I believed, and so I spoke"[1]—we also believe, and so we

---

[f]Other ancient authorities read *like the others*   [g]Other ancient authorities read *your*   [h]Gk *on stones*   [i]Gk *of what*

[1]Ps 116:10

speak, 14 because we know that the one who raised the Lord Jesus will raise us also with Jesus, and will bring us with you into his presence. 15 Yes, everything is for your sake, so that grace, as it extends to more and more people, may increase thanksgiving, to the glory of God.

16 So we do not lose heart. Even though our outer nature is wasting away, our inner nature is being renewed day by day. 17 For this slight momentary affliction is preparing us for an eternal weight of glory beyond all measure, 18 because we look not at what can be seen but at what cannot be seen; for what can be seen is temporary, but what cannot be seen is eternal.

5 For we know that if the earthly tent we live in is destroyed, we have a building from God, a house not made with hands, eternal in the heavens. 2 For in this tent we groan, longing to be clothed with our heavenly dwelling— 3 if indeed, when we have taken it off[j] we will not be found naked. 4 For while we are still in this tent, we groan under our burden, because we wish not to be unclothed but to be further clothed, so that what is mortal may be swallowed up by life. 5 He who has prepared us for this very thing is God, who has given us the Spirit as a guarantee.

6 So we are always confident; even though we know that while we are at home in the body we are away from the Lord— 7 for we walk by faith, not by sight. 8 Yes, we do have confidence, and we would rather be away from the body and at home with the Lord. 9 So whether we are at home or away, we make it our aim to please him. 10 For all of us must appear before the judgment seat of Christ, so that each may receive recompense for what has been done in the body, whether good or evil.

11 Therefore, knowing the fear of the Lord, we try to persuade others; but we ourselves are well known to God, and I hope that we are also well known to your consciences. 12 We are not commending ourselves to you again, but giving you an opportunity to boast about us, so that you may be able to answer those who boast in outward appearance and not in the heart. 13 For if we are beside ourselves, it is for God; if we are in our right mind, it is for you. 14 For the love of Christ urges us on, because we are convinced that one has died for all; therefore all have died. 15 And he died for

all, so that those who live might live no longer for themselves, but for him who died and was raised for them.

16 From now on, therefore, we regard no one from a human point of view;[k] even though we once knew Christ from a human point of view,[k] we know him no longer in that way. 17 So if anyone is in Christ, there is a new creation: everything old has passed away; see, everything has become new! 18 All this is from God, who reconciled us to himself through Christ, and has given us the ministry of reconciliation; 19 that is, in Christ God was reconciling the world to himself,[l] not counting their trespasses against them, and entrusting the message of reconciliation to us. 20 So we are ambassadors for Christ, since God is making his appeal through us; we entreat you on behalf of Christ, be reconciled to God. 21 For our sake he made him to be sin who knew no sin, so that in him we might become the righteousness of God.

6 As we work together with him,[m] we urge you also not to accept the grace of God in vain. 2 For he says,

"At an acceptable time I have
   listened to you,
and on a day of salvation I have
   helped you."[2]

See, now is the acceptable time; see, now is the day of salvation! 3 We are putting no obstacle in anyone's way, so that no fault may be found with our ministry, 4 but as servants of God we have commended ourselves in every way: through great endurance, in afflictions, hardships, calamities, 5 beatings, imprisonments, riots, labors, sleepless nights, hunger; 6 by purity, knowledge, patience, kindness, holiness of spirit, genuine love, 7 truthful speech, and the power of God; with the weapons of righteousness for the right hand and for the left; 8 in honor and dishonor, in ill repute and good repute. We are treated as impostors, and yet are true; 9 as unknown, and yet are well known; as dying, and see—we are alive; as punished, and yet not killed; 10 as sorrowful, yet al-

---

[j]Other ancient authorities read *put it on*   [k]*Gk according to the flesh*
[l]Or *God was in Christ reconciling the world to himself*   [m]*Gk As we work together*

[2]Isa 49:8

ways rejoicing; as poor, yet making many rich; as having nothing, and yet possessing everything.

11 We have spoken frankly to you Corinthians; our heart is wide open to you. 12 There is no restriction in our affections, but only in yours. 13 In return—I speak as to children—open wide your hearts also.

14 Do not be mismatched with unbelievers. For what partnership is there between righteousness and lawlessness? Or what fellowship is there between light and darkness? 15 What agreement does Christ have with Beliar? Or what does a believer share with an unbeliever? 16 What agreement has the temple of God with idols? For we[n] are the temple of the living God; as God said,

> "I will live in them and walk
>   among them,
>   and I will be their God,
>   and they shall be my people.[3]
>
> 17   Therefore come out from them,
>   and be separate from them, says
>   the Lord,
>   and touch nothing unclean;
>   then I will welcome you,[4]
> 18   and I will be your father,
>   and you shall be my sons and
>   daughters,
>   says the Lord Almighty."[5]

7 Since we have these promises, beloved, let us cleanse ourselves from every defilement of body and of spirit, making holiness perfect in the fear of God.

2 Make room in your hearts[o] for us; we have wronged no one, we have corrupted no one, we have taken advantage of no one. 3 I do not say this to condemn you, for I said before that you are in our hearts, to die together and to live together. 4 I often boast about you; I have great pride in you; I am filled with consolation; I am overjoyed in all our affliction.

5 For even when we came into Macedonia, our bodies had no rest, but we were afflicted in every way—disputes without and fears within. 6 But God, who consoles the downcast, consoled us by the arrival of Titus, 7 and not only by his coming, but also by the consolation with which he was consoled about you, as he told us of your longing, your

mourning, your zeal for me, so that I rejoiced still more. 8 For even if I made you sorry with my letter, I do not regret it (though I did regret it, for I see that I grieved you with that letter, though only briefly). 9 Now I rejoice, not because you were grieved, but because your grief led to repentance; for you felt a godly grief, so that you were not harmed in any way by us. 10 For godly grief produces a repentance that leads to salvation and brings no regret, but worldly grief produces death. 11 For see what earnestness this godly grief has produced in you, what eagerness to clear yourselves, what indignation, what alarm, what longing, what zeal, what punishment! At every point you have proved yourselves guiltless in the matter. 12 So although I wrote to you, it was not on account of the one who did the wrong, nor on account of the one who was wronged, but in order that your zeal for us might be made known to you before God. 13 In this we find comfort.

In addition to our own consolation, we rejoiced still more at the joy of Titus, because his mind has been set at rest by all of you. 14 For if I have been somewhat boastful about you to him, I was not disgraced; but just as everything we said to you was true, so our boasting to Titus has proved true as well. 15 And his heart goes out all the more to you, as he remembers the obedience of all of you, and how you welcomed him with fear and trembling. 16 I rejoice, because I have complete confidence in you.

8 We want you to know, brothers and sisters,[p] about the grace of God that has been granted to the churches of Macedonia; 2 for during a severe ordeal of affliction, their abundant joy and their extreme poverty have overflowed in a wealth of generosity on their part. 3 For, as I can testify, they voluntarily gave according to their means, and even beyond their means, 4 begging us earnestly for the privilege[q] of sharing in this ministry to the saints— 5 and this, not merely as we expected; they gave themselves first to the Lord and, by the will of God, to us, 6 so that we might

---

[n]Other ancient authorities read *you*   [o]Gk lacks *in your hearts*
[p]Gk *brothers*   [q]Gk *grace*

[3]Lev 26:11–12; Jer 32:38; Ezek 37:27   [4]Isa 52:11; Ezek 20:34, 41
[5]2 Sam 7:8, 14; Isa 43:6; Jer 31:9

urge Titus that, as he had already made a beginning, so he should also complete this generous undertaking[r] among you. 7 Now as you excel in everything—in faith, in speech, in knowledge, in utmost eagerness, and in our love for you[s]—so we want you to excel also in this generous undertaking.[r]

8 I do not say this as a command, but I am testing the genuineness of your love against the earnestness of others. 9 For you know the generous act[t] of our Lord Jesus Christ, that though he was rich, yet for your sakes he became poor, so that by his poverty you might become rich. 10 And in this matter I am giving my advice: it is appropriate for you who began last year not only to do something but even to desire to do something— 11 now finish doing it, so that your eagerness may be matched by completing it according to your means. 12 For if the eagerness is there, the gift is acceptable according to what one has— not according to what one does not have. 13 I do not mean that there should be relief for others and pressure on you, but it is a question of a fair balance between 14 your present abundance and their need, so that their abundance may be for your need, in order that there may be a fair balance. 15 As it is written,

> "The one who had much did not
>   have too much,
> and the one who had little did
>   not have too little."[6]

16 But thanks be to God who put in the heart of Titus the same eagerness for you that I myself have. 17 For he not only accepted our appeal, but since he is more eager than ever, he is going to you of his own accord. 18 With him we are sending the brother who is famous among all the churches for his proclaiming the good news;[u] 19 and not only that, but he has also been appointed by the churches to travel with us while we are administering this generous undertaking[r] for the glory of the Lord himself[v] and to show our goodwill. 20 We intend that no one should blame us about this generous gift that we are administering, 21 for we intend to do what is right not only in the Lord's sight but also in the sight of others. 22 And with them we are sending our brother whom we have often tested and found eager in many matters, but who is now more eager than ever because of

his great confidence in you. 23 As for Titus, he is my partner and co-worker in your service; as for our brothers, they are messengers[w] of the churches, the glory of Christ. 24 Therefore openly before the churches, show them the proof of your love and of our reason for boasting about you.

9 Now it is not necessary for me to write you about the ministry to the saints, 2 for I know your eagerness, which is the subject of my boasting about you to the people of Macedonia, saying that Achaia has been ready since last year; and your zeal has stirred up most of them. 3 But I am sending the brothers in order that our boasting about you may not prove to have been empty in this case, so that you may be ready, as I said you would be; 4 otherwise, if some Macedonians come with me and find that you are not ready, we would be humiliated—to say nothing of you—in this undertaking.[x] 5 So I thought it necessary to urge the brothers to go on ahead to you, and arrange in advance for this bountiful gift that you have promised, so that it may be ready as a voluntary gift and not as an extortion.

6 The point is this: the one who sows sparingly will also reap sparingly, and the one who sows bountifully will also reap bountifully. 7 Each of you must give as you have made up your mind, not reluctantly or under compulsion, for God loves a cheerful giver. 8 And God is able to provide you with every blessing in abundance, so that by always having enough of everything, you may share abundantly in every good work. 9 As it is written,

> "He scatters abroad, he gives to
>   the poor;
> his righteousness[y] endures
>   forever."[7]

10 He who supplies seed to the sower and bread for food will supply and multiply your seed for sowing and increase the harvest of your righteousness.[y] 11 You will be enriched in every way for your great generosity, which will produce thanksgiving to God through us; 12 for the rendering of

---

[r]Gk *this grace*   [s]Other ancient authorities read *your love for us*
[t]Gk *the grace*   [u]Or *the gospel*   [v]Other ancient authorities lack
himself   [w]Gk *apostles*   [x]Other ancient authorities add *of boasting*
[y]Or *benevolence*

[6]Exod 16:18   [7]Ps 112:9

this ministry not only supplies the needs of the saints but also overflows with many thanksgivings to God. 13 Through the testing of this ministry you glorify God by your obedience to the confession of the gospel of Christ and by the generosity of your sharing with them and with all others, 14 while they long for you and pray for you because of the surpassing grace of God that he has given you. 15 Thanks be to God for his indescribable gift!

10 I myself, Paul, appeal to you by the meekness and gentleness of Christ—I who am humble when face to face with you, but bold toward you when I am away!— 2 I ask that when I am present I need not show boldness by daring to oppose those who think we are acting according to human standards.ᶻ 3 Indeed, we live as human beings,ᵃ but we do not wage war according to human standards;ᶻ 4 for the weapons of our warfare are not merely human,ᵇ but they have divine power to destroy strongholds. We destroy arguments 5 and every proud obstacle raised up against the knowledge of God, and we take every thought captive to obey Christ. 6 We are ready to punish every disobedience when your obedience is complete.

7 Look at what is before your eyes. If you are confident that you belong to Christ, remind yourself of this, that just as you belong to Christ, so also do we. 8 Now, even if I boast a little too much of our authority, which the Lord gave for building you up and not for tearing you down, I will not be ashamed of it. 9 I do not want to seem as though I am trying to frighten you with my letters. 10 For they say, "His letters are weighty and strong, but his bodily presence is weak, and his speech contemptible." 11 Let such people understand that what we say by letter when absent, we will also do when present.

12 We do not dare to classify or compare ourselves with some of those who commend themselves. But when they measure themselves by one another, and compare themselves with one another, they do not show good sense. 13 We, however, will not boast beyond limits, but will keep within the field that God has assigned to us, to reach out even as far as you. 14 For we were not overstepping our limits when we reached you; we were the first to come all the way to you with the good newsᶜ of Christ. 15 We do not boast beyond limits, that is, in the labors of others; but our hope is that, as your faith increases, our sphere of action among you may be greatly enlarged, 16 so that we may proclaim the good newsᶜ in lands beyond you, without boasting of work already done in someone else's sphere of action. 17 "Let the one who boasts, boast in the Lord."[8] 18 For it is not those who commend themselves that are approved, but those whom the Lord commends.

11 I wish you would bear with me in a little foolishness. Do bear with me! 2 I feel a divine jealousy for you, for I promised you in marriage to one husband, to present you as a chaste virgin to Christ. 3 But I am afraid that as the serpent deceived Eve by its cunning, your thoughts will be led astray from a sincere and pureᵈ devotion to Christ. 4 For if someone comes and proclaims another Jesus than the one we proclaimed, or if you receive a different spirit from the one you received, or a different gospel from the one you accepted, you submit to it readily enough. 5 I think that I am not in the least inferior to these super-apostles. 6 I may be untrained in speech, but not in knowledge; certainly in every way and in all things we have made this evident to you.

7 Did I commit a sin by humbling myself so that you might be exalted, because I proclaimed God's good newsᵉ to you free of charge? 8 I robbed other churches by accepting support from them in order to serve you. 9 And when I was with you and was in need, I did not burden anyone, for my needs were supplied by the friendsᶠ who came from Macedonia. So I refrained and will continue to refrain from burdening you in any way. 10 As the truth of Christ is in me, this boast of mine will not be silenced in the regions of Achaia. 11 And why? Because I do not love you? God knows I do!

12 And what I do I will also continue to do, in order to deny an opportunity to those who want an opportunity to be recognized as our equals in what they boast about. 13 For such boasters are false apostles, deceitful workers, disguising themselves

---

ᶻGk *according to the flesh*   ᵃGk *in the flesh*   ᵇGk *fleshly*   ᶜOr *the gospel*   ᵈOther ancient authorities lack *and pure*   ᵉGk *the gospel of God*   ᶠGk *brothers*

[8]Jer 9:24

as apostles of Christ. 14 And no wonder! Even Satan disguises himself as an angel of light. 15 So it is not strange if his ministers also disguise themselves as ministers of righteousness. Their end will match their deeds.

16 I repeat, let no one think that I am a fool; but if you do, then accept me as a fool, so that I too may boast a little. 17 What I am saying in regard to this boastful confidence, I am saying not with the Lord's authority, but as a fool; 18 since many boast according to human standards,[g] I will also boast. 19 For you gladly put up with fools, being wise yourselves! 20 For you put up with it when someone makes slaves of you, or preys upon you, or takes advantage of you, or puts on airs, or gives you a slap in the face. 21 To my shame, I must say, we were too weak for that!

But whatever anyone dares to boast of—I am speaking as a fool—I also dare to boast of that. 22 Are they Hebrews? So am I. Are they Israelites? So am I. Are they descendants of Abraham? So am I. 23 Are they ministers of Christ? I am talking like a madman—I am a better one: with far greater labors, far more imprisonments, with countless floggings, and often near death. 24 Five times I have received from the Jews the forty lashes minus one. 25 Three times I was beaten with rods. Once I received a stoning. Three times I was shipwrecked; for a night and a day I was adrift at sea; 26 on frequent journeys, in danger from rivers, danger from bandits, danger from my own people, danger from Gentiles, danger in the city, danger in the wilderness, danger at sea, danger from false brothers and sisters;[h] 27 in toil and hardship, through many a sleepless night, hungry and thirsty, often without food, cold and naked. 28 And, besides other things, I am under daily pressure because of my anxiety for all the churches. 29 Who is weak, and I am not weak? Who is made to stumble, and I am not indignant?

30 If I must boast, I will boast of the things that show my weakness. 31 The God and Father of the Lord Jesus (blessed be he forever!) knows that I do not lie. 32 In Damascus, the governor[i] under King Aretas guarded the city of Damascus in order to[j] seize me, 33 but I was let down in a basket through a window in the wall,[k] and escaped from his hands.

12 It is necessary to boast; nothing is to be gained by it, but I will go on to visions and revelations of the Lord. 2 I know a person in Christ who fourteen years ago was caught up to the third heaven—whether in the body or out of the body I do not know; God knows. 3 And I know that such a person—whether in the body or out of the body I do not know; God knows— 4 was caught up into Paradise and heard things that are not to be told, that no mortal is permitted to repeat. 5 On behalf of such a one I will boast, but on my own behalf I will not boast, except of my weaknesses. 6 But if I wish to boast, I will not be a fool, for I will be speaking the truth. But I refrain from it, so that no one may think better of me than what is seen in me or heard from me, 7 even considering the exceptional character of the revelations. Therefore, to keep[l] me from being too elated, a thorn was given me in the flesh, a messenger of Satan to torment me, to keep me from being too elated.[m] 8 Three times I appealed to the Lord about this, that it would leave me, 9 but he said to me, "My grace is sufficient for you, for power[n] is made perfect in weakness." So, I will boast all the more gladly of my weaknesses, so that the power of Christ may dwell in me. 10 Therefore I am content with weaknesses, insults, hardships, persecutions, and calamities for the sake of Christ; for whenever I am weak, then I am strong.

11 I have been a fool! You forced me to it. Indeed you should have been the ones commending me, for I am not at all inferior to these super-apostles, even though I am nothing. 12 The signs of a true apostle were performed among you with utmost patience, signs and wonders and mighty works. 13 How have you been worse off than the other churches, except that I myself did not burden you? Forgive me this wrong!

14 Here I am, ready to come to you this third time. And I will not be a burden, because I do not want what is yours but you; for children ought not to lay up for their parents, but parents for their children. 15 I will most gladly spend and be spent for you. If I love you more, am I to be loved less?

[g]Gk *according to the flesh* [h]Gk *brothers* [i]Gk *ethnarch* [j]Other ancient authorities read *and wanted to* [k]Gk *through the wall* [l]Other ancient authorities read *To keep* [m]Other ancient authorities lack *to keep me from being too elated* [n]Other ancient authorities read *my power*

16 Let it be assumed that I did not burden you. Nevertheless (you say) since I was crafty, I took you in by deceit. 17 Did I take advantage of you through any of those whom I sent to you? 18 I urged Titus to go, and sent the brother with him. Titus did not take advantage of you, did he? Did we not conduct ourselves with the same spirit? Did we not take the same steps?

19 Have you been thinking all along that we have been defending ourselves before you? We are speaking in Christ before God. Everything we do, beloved, is for the sake of building you up. 20 For I fear that when I come, I may find you not as I wish, and that you may find me not as you wish; I fear that there may perhaps be quarreling, jealousy, anger, selfishness, slander, gossip, conceit, and disorder. 21 I fear that when I come again, my God may humble me before you, and that I may have to mourn over many who previously sinned and have not repented of the impurity, sexual immorality, and licentiousness that they have practiced.

13 This is the third time I am coming to you. "Any charge must be sustained by the evidence of two or three witnesses."[9] 2 I warned those who sinned previously and all the others, and I warn them now while absent, as I did when present on my second visit, that if I come again, I will not be lenient— 3 since you desire proof that Christ is speaking in me. He is not weak in dealing with you, but is powerful in you. 4 For he was

crucified in weakness, but lives by the power of God. For we are weak in him,[o] but in dealing with you we will live with him by the power of God.

5 Examine yourselves to see whether you are living in the faith. Test yourselves. Do you not realize that Jesus Christ is in you?—unless, indeed, you fail to meet the test! 6 I hope you will find out that we have not failed. 7 But we pray to God that you may not do anything wrong—not that we may appear to have met the test, but that you may do what is right, though we may seem to have failed. 8 For we cannot do anything against the truth, but only for the truth. 9 For we rejoice when we are weak and you are strong. This is what we pray for, that you may become perfect. 10 So I write these things while I am away from you, so that when I come, I may not have to be severe in using the authority that the Lord has given me for building up and not for tearing down.

11 Finally, brothers and sisters,[p] farewell.[q] Put things in order, listen to my appeal,[r] agree with one another, live in peace; and the God of love and peace will be with you. 12 Greet one another with a holy kiss. All the saints greet you.

13 The grace of the Lord Jesus Christ, the love of God, and the communion of[s] the Holy Spirit be with all of you.

[o]Other ancient authorities read *with him*   [p]Gk *brothers*   [q]Or *rejoice*
[r]Or *encourage one another*   [s]Or *and the sharing in*

---

[9]Deut 19:15

The Letter to the Galatians

Paul wrote the letter of Galatians to churches in the Roman province of Galatia in central Asia Minor (modern-day Turkey). The letter does not indicate where in the province, exactly, these churches were located, whether among the southern cities evangelized by Paul in Acts (Acts 14) or in the more northern climes, where people were historically more apt to call themselves "Galatians" (3:1). In any event, the occasion for the letter is relatively clear. After Paul had established churches among Gentiles in this region (4:12–20), other Christian missionaries arrived proclaiming a message different from his. According to them, Gentiles who had placed their faith in Christ should also follow the prescriptions of the Jewish Law. Specifically, the males of the congregation were to be circumcised.

We do not know how these missionaries argued their case; they may simply have claimed that since Jesus was the Jewish messiah sent from the Jewish God to the Jewish people in fulfillment of the promises given to the Jewish patriarchs in the Jewish Scriptures, anyone who believes in Christ must obviously accept the Jewish Law. Paul, however, had maintained that people were made right with God through Christ alone, apart from doing the works of the Law. For him, this was not an honest disagreement among well-meaning Christian brothers and sisters. His opponents' views were a frontal attack on the core of his gospel message and on his own authorization to preach it.

Paul's anger is clear at the outset; this is his only letter that does not begin by thanking God for the congregation but, instead, with a rebuke to those who have abandoned Paul's message for "another gospel." Far from having earned God's blessing, such persons stand under God's curse (1:6–9).

Paul devotes the first portion of the letter (most of the first two chapters) to showing that his gospel was "not of human origin," but instead was given to him directly "through a revelation of Jesus Christ" (1:11–12). Contrary to the claims of his opponents, Paul did not modify the original Christian message preached by the apostles before him, because he did not receive his message from them. He got it directly from God (1:13–2:14). Paul then argues at length, in the heart of the letter (2:15–5:12), that a person is made right with God (justified) not by doing works of the Law, but by faith in Christ. Those who insist on doing works of the Law for justification have totally misunderstood and misrepresented the gospel. For if justification could come through the Law, then Christ "died for nothing" (2:21).

This is not to say, however, that those who have been justified apart from the Law can lead lawless lives. Paul concludes the letter by showing that those who now belong to God's people through Christ have received God's Spirit and so are empowered to do God's will, loving their neighbors as themselves, and so fulfilling the Law (5:13–26).

From the New Revised Standard Version Bible, © 1989.

1 Paul an apostle—sent neither by human commission nor from human authorities, but through Jesus Christ and God the Father, who raised him from the dead— 2 and all the members of God's family[a] who are with me,

To the churches of Galatia:

3 Grace to you and peace from God our Father and the Lord Jesus Christ, 4 who gave himself for our sins to set us free from the present evil age, according to the will of our God and Father, 5 to whom be the glory forever and ever. Amen.

6 I am astonished that you are so quickly deserting the one who called you in the grace of Christ and are turning to a different gospel— 7 not that there is another gospel, but there are some who are confusing you and want to pervert the gospel of Christ. 8 But even if we or an angel[b] from heaven should proclaim to you a gospel contrary to what we proclaimed to you, let that one be accursed! 9 As we have said before, so now I repeat, if anyone proclaims to you a gospel contrary to what you received, let that one be accursed!

10 Am I now seeking human approval, or God's approval? Or am I trying to please people? If I were still pleasing people, I would not be a servant[c] of Christ.

11 For I want you to know, brothers and sisters,[d] that the gospel that was proclaimed by me is not of human origin; 12 for I did not receive it from a human source, nor was I taught it, but I received it through a revelation of Jesus Christ.

13 You have heard, no doubt, of my earlier life in Judaism. I was violently persecuting the church of God and was trying to destroy it. 14 I advanced in Judaism beyond many among my people of the same age, for I was far more zealous for the traditions of my ancestors. 15 But when God, who had set me apart before I was born and called me through his grace, was pleased 16 to reveal his Son to me,[e] so that I might proclaim him among the Gentiles, I did not confer with any human being, 17 nor did I go up to Jerusalem to those who were already apostles before me, but I went away at once into Arabia, and afterwards I returned to Damascus.

18 Then after three years I did go up to Jerusalem to visit Cephas and stayed with him fifteen days; 19 but I did not see any other apostle except James the Lord's brother. 20 In what I am writing to you, before God, I do not lie! 21 Then I went into the regions of Syria and Cilicia, 22 and I was still unknown by sight to the churches of Judea that are in Christ; 23 they only heard it said, "The one who formerly was persecuting us is now proclaiming the faith he once tried to destroy." 24 And they glorified God because of me.

2 Then after fourteen years I went up again to Jerusalem with Barnabas, taking Titus along with me. 2 I went up in response to a revelation. Then I laid before them (though only in a private meeting with the acknowledged leaders) the gospel that I proclaim among the Gentiles, in order to make sure that I was not running, or had not run, in vain. 3 But even Titus, who was with me, was not compelled to be circumcised, though he was a Greek. 4 But because of false believers[f] secretly brought in, who slipped in to spy on the freedom we have in Christ Jesus, so that they might enslave us— 5 we did not submit to them even for a moment, so that the truth of the gospel might always remain with you. 6 And from those who were supposed to be acknowledged leaders (what they actually were makes no difference to me; God shows no partiality)—those leaders contributed nothing to me. 7 On the contrary, when they saw that I had been entrusted with the gospel for the uncircumcised, just as Peter had been entrusted with the gospel for the circumcised 8 (for he who worked through Peter making him an apostle to the circumcised also worked through me in sending me to the Gentiles), 9 and when James and Cephas and John, who were acknowledged pillars, recognized the grace that had been given to me, they gave to Barnabas and me the right hand of fellowship, agreeing that we should go to the Gentiles and they to the circumcised. 10 They asked only one thing, that we remember the poor, which was actually what I was[g] eager to do.

11 But when Cephas came to Antioch, I opposed him to his face, because he stood self-condemned; 12 for until certain people came from James, he used to eat with the Gentiles. But after they came, he drew back and kept himself separate for fear of the circumcision faction. 13 And the other Jews

joined him in this hypocrisy, so that even Barnabas was led astray by their hypocrisy. 14 But when I saw that they were not acting consistently with the truth of the gospel, I said to Cephas before them all, "If you, though a Jew, live like a Gentile and not like a Jew, how can you compel the Gentiles to live like Jews?"[h]

15 We ourselves are Jews by birth and not Gentile sinners; 16 yet we know that a person is justified[i] not by the works of the law but through faith in Jesus Christ.[j] And we have come to believe in Christ Jesus, so that we might be justified by faith in Christ,[k] and not by doing the works of the law, because no one will be justified by the works of the law. 17 But if, in our effort to be justified in Christ, we ourselves have been found to be sinners, is Christ then a servant of sin? Certainly not! 18 But if I build up again the very things that I once tore down, then I demonstrate that I am a transgressor. 19 For through the law I died to the law, so that I might live to God. I have been crucified with Christ; 20 and it is no longer I who live, but it is Christ who lives in me. And the life I now live in the flesh I live by faith in the Son of God,[l] who loved me and gave himself for me. 21 I do not nullify the grace of God; for if justification[m] comes through the law, then Christ died for nothing.

3 You foolish Galatians! Who has bewitched you? It was before your eyes that Jesus Christ was publicly exhibited as crucified! 2 The only thing I want to learn from you is this: Did you receive the Spirit by doing the works of the law or by believing what you heard? 3 Are you so foolish? Having started with the Spirit, are you now ending with the flesh? 4 Did you experience so much for nothing?—if it really was for nothing. 5 Well then, does God[n] supply you with the Spirit and work miracles among you by your doing the works of the law, or by your believing what you heard?

6 Just as Abraham "believed God, and it was reckoned to him as righteousness,"[1] 7 so, you see, those who believe are the descendants of Abraham. 8 And the scripture, foreseeing that God would justify the Gentiles by faith, declared the gospel beforehand to Abraham, saying, "All the Gentiles shall be blessed in you."[2] 9 For this reason, those who believe are blessed with Abraham who believed.

10 For all who rely on the works of the law are under a curse; for it is written, "Cursed is everyone who does not observe and obey all the things written in the book of the law."[3] 11 Now it is evident that no one is justified before God by the law; for "The one who is righteous will live by faith."[o][4] 12 But the law does not rest on faith; on the contrary, "Whoever does the works of the law[p] will live by them."[5] 13 Christ redeemed us from the curse of the law by becoming a curse for us—for it is written, "Cursed is everyone who hangs on a tree"[6]— 14 in order that in Christ Jesus the blessing of Abraham might come to the Gentiles, so that we might receive the promise of the Spirit through faith.

15 Brothers and sisters,[q] I give an example from daily life: once a person's will[r] has been ratified, no one adds to it or annuls it. 16 Now the promises were made to Abraham and to his offspring;[s] it does not say, "And to offsprings,"[t] as of many; but it says, "And to your offspring,"[s][7] that is, to one person, who is Christ. 17 My point is this: the law, which came four hundred thirty years later, does not annul a covenant previously ratified by God, so as to nullify the promise. 18 For if the inheritance comes from the law, it no longer comes from the promise; but God granted it to Abraham through the promise.

19 Why then the law? It was added because of transgressions, until the offspring[s] would come to whom the promise had been made; and it was ordained through angels by a mediator. 20 Now a mediator involves more than one party; but God is one.

21 Is the law then opposed to the promises of God? Certainly not! For if a law had been given that could make alive, then righteousness would indeed come through the law. 22 But the scripture has imprisoned all things under the power of sin, so that what was promised through faith in Jesus Christ[u] might be given to those who believe.

---

[h]Some interpreters hold that the quotation extends into the following paragraph   [i]Or *reckoned as righteous;* and so elsewhere   [j]Or *the faith of Jesus Christ*   [k]Or *the faith of Christ*   [l]Or *by the faith of the Son of God*   [m]Or *righteousness*   [n]Gk *he*   [o]Or *The one who is righteous through faith will live*   [p]Gk *does them*   [q]Gk *Brothers*   [r]Or *covenant* (as in verse 17)   [s]Gk *seed*   [t]Gk *seeds*   [u]Or *through the faith of Jesus Christ*

[1]Gen 15:6   [2]Gen 12:3   [3]Deut 27:26; 28:58   [4]Hab 2:4   [5]Lev 18:5   [6]Duet 21:23   [7]Gen 12:7; 13:15; 17:7; 24:7

23 Now before faith came, we were imprisoned and guarded under the law until faith would be revealed. 24 Therefore the law was our disciplinarian until Christ came, so that we might be justified by faith. 25 But now that faith has come, we are no longer subject to a disciplinarian, 26 for in Christ Jesus you are all children of God through faith. 27 As many of you as were baptized into Christ have clothed yourselves with Christ. 28 There is no longer Jew or Greek, there is no longer slave or free, there is no longer male and female; for all of you are one in Christ Jesus. 29 And if you belong to Christ, then you are Abraham's offspring,[v] heirs according to the promise.

4 My point is this: heirs, as long as they are minors, are no better than slaves, though they are the owners of all the property; 2 but they remain under guardians and trustees until the date set by the father. 3 So with us; while we were minors, we were enslaved to the elemental spirits[w] of the world. 4 But when the fullness of time had come, God sent his Son, born of a woman, born under the law, 5 in order to redeem those who were under the law, so that we might receive adoption as children. 6 And because you are children, God has sent the Spirit of his Son into our[x] hearts, crying, "Abba![y] Father!" 7 So you are no longer a slave but a child, and if a child then also an heir, through God.[z]

8 Formerly, when you did not know God, you were enslaved to beings that by nature are not gods. 9 Now, however, that you have come to know God, or rather to be known by God, how can you turn back again to the weak and beggarly elemental spirits?[a] How can you want to be enslaved to them again? 10 You are observing special days, and months, and seasons, and years. 11 I am afraid that my work for you may have been wasted.

12 Friends,[b] I beg you, become as I am, for I also have become as you are. You have done me no wrong. 13 You know that it was because of a physical infirmity that I first announced the gospel to you; 14 though my condition put you to the test, you did not scorn or despise me, but welcomed me as an angel of God, as Christ Jesus. 15 What has become of the goodwill you felt? For I testify that, had it been possible, you would have torn out your eyes and given them to me. 16 Have I now become your enemy by telling you the truth? 17 They make much of you, but for no good purpose; they want to exclude you, so that you may make much of them. 18 It is good to be made much of for a good purpose at all times, and not only when I am present with you. 19 My little children, for whom I am again in the pain of childbirth until Christ is formed in you, 20 I wish I were present with you now and could change my tone, for I am perplexed about you.

21 Tell me, you who desire to be subject to the law, will you not listen to the law? 22 For it is written that Abraham had two sons, one by a slave woman and the other by a free woman. 23 One, the child of the slave, was born according to the flesh; the other, the child of the free woman, was born through the promise. 24 Now this is an allegory: these women are two covenants. One woman, in fact, is Hagar, from Mount Sinai, bearing children for slavery. 25 Now Hagar is Mount Sinai in Arabia[c] and corresponds to the present Jerusalem, for she is in slavery with her children. 26 But the other woman corresponds to the Jerusalem above; she is free, and she is our mother. 27 For it is written,

"Rejoice, you childless one, you
who bear no children,
burst into song and shout, you
who endure no birth pangs;
for the children of the desolate
woman are more numerous
than the children of the one
who is married."[8]

28 Now you,[d] my friends,[e] are children of the promise, like Isaac. 29 But just as at that time the child who was born according to the flesh persecuted the child who was born according to the Spirit, so it is now also. 30 But what does the scripture say? "Drive out the slave and her child; for the child of the slave will not share the inheritance with the child of the free woman."[9] 31 So then, friends,[e] we are children, not of the slave but of the free woman.

[v] Gk *seed* [w] Or *the rudiments* [x] Other ancient authorities read *your* [y] Aramaic for *Father* [z] Other ancient authorities read *an heir of God through Christ* [a] Or *beggarly rudiments* [b] Gk *Brothers* [c] Other ancient authorities read *For Sinai is a mountain in Arabia* [d] Other ancient authorities read *we* [e] Gk *brothers*

[8] Isa 54:1 [9] Gen 21:10

5 For freedom Christ has set us free. Stand firm, therefore, and do not submit again to a yoke of slavery.

2 Listen! I, Paul, am telling you that if you let yourselves be circumcised, Christ will be of no benefit to you. 3 Once again I testify to every man who lets himself be circumcised that he is obliged to obey the entire law. 4 You who want to be justified by the law have cut yourselves off from Christ; you have fallen away from grace. 5 For through the Spirit, by faith, we eagerly wait for the hope of righteousness. 6 For in Christ Jesus neither circumcision nor uncircumcision counts for anything; the only thing that counts is faith working[f] through love.

7 You were running well; who prevented you from obeying the truth? 8 Such persuasion does not come from the one who calls you. 9 A little yeast leavens the whole batch of dough. 10 I am confident about you in the Lord that you will not think otherwise. But whoever it is that is confusing you will pay the penalty. 11 But my friends,[g] why am I still being persecuted if I am still preaching circumcision? In that case the offense of the cross has been removed. 12 I wish those who unsettle you would castrate themselves!

13 For you were called to freedom, brothers and sisters;[g] only do not use your freedom as an opportunity for self-indulgence,[h] but through love become slaves to one another. 14 For the whole law is summed up in a single commandment, "You shall love your neighbor as yourself."[10] 15 If, however, you bite and devour one another, take care that you are not consumed by one another.

16 Live by the Spirit, I say, and do not gratify the desires of the flesh. 17 For what the flesh desires is opposed to the Spirit, and what the Spirit desires is opposed to the flesh; for these are opposed to each other, to prevent you from doing what you want. 18 But if you are led by the Spirit, you are not subject to the law. 19 Now the works of the flesh are obvious: fornication, impurity, licentiousness, 20 idolatry, sorcery, enmities, strife, jealousy, anger, quarrels, dissensions, factions, 21 envy,[i] drunkenness, carousing, and things like these. I am warning you, as I warned you before: those who do such things will not inherit the kingdom of God.

22 By contrast, the fruit of the Spirit is love, joy, peace, patience, kindness, generosity, faithfulness, 23 gentleness, and self-control. There is no law against such things. 24 And those who belong to Christ Jesus have crucified the flesh with its passions and desires. 25 If we live by the Spirit, let us also be guided by the Spirit. 26 Let us not become conceited, competing against one another, envying one another.

6 My friends,[j] if anyone is detected in a transgression, you who have received the Spirit should restore such a one in a spirit of gentleness. Take care that you yourselves are not tempted. 2 Bear one another's burdens, and in this way you will fulfill[k] the law of Christ. 3 For if those who are nothing think they are something, they deceive themselves. 4 All must test their own work; then that work, rather than their neighbor's work, will become a cause for pride. 5 For all must carry their own loads.

6 Those who are taught the word must share in all good things with their teacher.

7 Do not be deceived; God is not mocked, for you reap whatever you sow. 8 If you sow to your own flesh, you will reap corruption from the flesh; but if you sow to the Spirit, you will reap eternal life from the Spirit. 9 So let us not grow weary in doing what is right, for we will reap at harvest time, if we do not give up. 10 So then, whenever we have an opportunity, let us work for the good of all, and especially for those of the family of faith.

11 See what large letters I make when I am writing in my own hand! 12 It is those who want to make a good showing in the flesh that try to compel you to be circumcised—only that they may not be persecuted for the cross of Christ. 13 Even the circumcised do not themselves obey the law, but they want you to be circumcised so that they may boast about your flesh. 14 May I never boast of anything except the cross of our Lord Jesus Christ, by which[l] the world has been crucified to me, and I to the world. 15 For[m] neither circumcision nor uncircumcision is anything; but a new creation is

---

[f]Or *made effective*   [g]Gk *brothers*   [h]Gk *the flesh*   [i]Other ancient authorities add *murder*   [j]Gk *Brothers*   [k]Other ancient authorities read *in this way fulfill*   [l]Or *through whom*   [m]Other ancient authorities add *in Christ Jesus*

[10]Lev 19:18

everything! 16 As for those who will follow this rule—peace be upon them, and mercy, and upon the Israel of God.

17 From now on, let no one make trouble for me; for I carry the marks of Jesus branded on my body.

18 May the grace of our Lord Jesus Christ be with your spirit, brothers and sisters.[n] Amen.

[n]Gk *brothers*

The Letter to the Ephesians

Ephesians is unique among the letters that go under Paul's name in that it appears to have originally been a circular letter. In the earliest and best manuscripts, the words "in Ephesus" are lacking from 1:1, so that rather than being addressed to the saints of Ephesus, it was addressed to saints everywhere (including, no doubt, Ephesus, where a copyist then supplied the words "in Ephesus" in order to personalize the letter). Indeed, the problems that are addressed in this letter are not specific to a particular locale; they are problems that had emerged in numerous Christian communities, possibly throughout Asia Minor, at the time of its writing.

The overriding purpose of the letter is to remind its Gentile readers that, whereas they had formerly been alienated from both God and his people, the Jews, they have now been reconciled through the work of Christ (2:1–22). Jesus' death tore down the barrier that had previously separated Jew and Gentile—that is the Jewish Law—so that both groups were now equal and able to live in harmony with one another (2:11–18). Moreover, through Christ's death all people, Jew and Gentile, have become united with God (2:18–22) and raised up to enjoy a glorified existence in the heavenly places (2:1–10). This was the "mystery" that God had concealed from earlier generations but had now revealed through Paul to the world (3:1–13).

While still living in the world, believers are to manifest the unity that they have in Christ in their various relationships: among themselves in the church (4:1–16), with respect to the rest of society (4:17–5:20), and in the social roles in which they find themselves (5:21–6:9). The letter closes with exhortation to continue the fight against the Satanic forces trying to disrupt the life of the congregation (6:10–20).

Even though Ephesians has a number of similarities with some of the undisputedly Pauline letters (e.g., Romans), the majority of critical scholars today are persuaded that Paul himself did not write this letter. Even more than Colossians (see that introduction), the vocabulary and especially the style of writing are strikingly different from Paul's; the exalted view of the believers as already reigning with Christ is even more pronounced here than in Colossians (contrast 2:5–6 with Rom 6:1–6 and 1 Corinthians 15); and several Pauline ideas have taken on new shades of meaning (e.g., Paul's opposition to "works" of the Jewish Law as a means of salvation has here become an opposition to reliance on "good deeds"; 2:1–10). It appears, then, that an author living near the end of the first century has developed some of Paul's views in directions not taken by the apostle himself. Possibly using some of the letters circulating under Paul's name (especially Colossians, with which Ephesians has a good deal in common), the author writes a circular letter to reaffirm what he saw to be the core of Paul's message, that Christ brought a unification of Jew and Gentile with one another and of both with God, and that those who are in Christ should manifest this unity in their lives together.

1 Paul, an apostle of Christ Jesus by the will of God,

To the saints who are in Ephesus and are faithful[a] in Christ Jesus:

2 Grace to you and peace from God our Father and the Lord Jesus Christ.

3 Blessed be the God and Father of our Lord Jesus Christ, who has blessed us in Christ with every spiritual blessing in the heavenly places, 4 just as he chose us in Christ[b] before the foundation of the world to be holy and blameless before him in love. 5 He destined us for adoption as his children through Jesus Christ, according to the good pleasure of his will, 6 to the praise of his glorious grace that he freely bestowed on us in the Beloved. 7 In him we have redemption through his blood, the forgiveness of our trespasses, according to the riches of his grace 8 that he lavished on us. With all wisdom and insight 9 he has made known to us the mystery of his will, according to his good pleasure that he set forth in Christ, 10 as a plan for the fullness of time, to gather up all things in him, things in heaven and things on earth. 11 In Christ we have also obtained an inheritance,[c] having been destined according to the purpose of him who accomplishes all things according to his counsel and will, 12 so that we, who were the first to set our hope on Christ, might live for the praise of his glory. 13 In him you also, when you had heard the word of truth, the gospel of your salvation, and had believed in him, were marked with the seal of the promised Holy Spirit; 14 this[d] is the pledge of our inheritance toward redemption as God's own people, to the praise of his glory.

15 I have heard of your faith in the Lord Jesus and your love[e] toward all the saints, and for this reason 16 I do not cease to give thanks for you as I remember you in my prayers. 17 I pray that the God of our Lord Jesus Christ, the Father of glory, may give you a spirit of wisdom and revelation as you come to know him, 18 so that, with the eyes of your heart enlightened, you may know what is the hope to which he has called you, what are the riches of his glorious inheritance among the saints, 19 and what is the immeasurable greatness of his power for us who believe, according to the working of his great power. 20 God[f] put this power to work in Christ when he raised him from the dead

and seated him at his right hand in the heavenly places, 21 far above all rule and authority and power and dominion, and above every name that is named, not only in this age but also in the age to come. 22 And he has put all things under his feet and has made him the head over all things for the church, 23 which is his body, the fullness of him who fills all in all.

2 You were dead through the trespasses and sins 2 in which you once lived, following the course of this world, following the ruler of the power of the air, the spirit that is now at work among those who are disobedient. 3 All of us once lived among them in the passions of our flesh, following the desires of flesh and senses, and we were by nature children of wrath, like everyone else. 4 But God, who is rich in mercy, out of the great love with which he loved us 5 even when we were dead through our trespasses, made us alive together with Christ[g]—by grace you have been saved— 6 and raised us up with him and seated us with him in the heavenly places in Christ Jesus, 7 so that in the ages to come he might show the immeasurable riches of his grace in kindness toward us in Christ Jesus. 8 For by grace you have been saved through faith, and this is not your own doing; it is the gift of God— 9 not the result of works, so that no one may boast. 10 For we are what he has made us, created in Christ Jesus for good works, which God prepared beforehand to be our way of life.

11 So then, remember that at one time you Gentiles by birth,[h] called "the uncircumcision" by those who are called "the circumcision"—a physical circumcision made in the flesh by human hands— 12 remember that you were at that time without Christ, being aliens from the commonwealth of Israel, and strangers to the covenants of promise, having no hope and without God in the world. 13 But now in Christ Jesus you who once were far off have been brought near by the blood of Christ. 14 For he is our peace; in his flesh he has made both groups into one and has broken down the dividing wall, that is, the hostility between us. 15 He has abolished the law with its

[a]Other ancient authorities lack *in Ephesus*, reading *saints who are also faithful* [b]Gk *in him* [c]Or *been made a heritage* [d]Other ancient authorities read *who* [e]Other ancient authorities lack *and your love* [f]Gk *He* [g]Other ancient authorities read *in Christ* [h]Gk *in the flesh*

commandments and ordinances, that he might create in himself one new humanity in place of the two, thus making peace, 16 and might reconcile both groups to God in one body[i] through the cross, thus putting to death that hostility through it.[j] 17 So he came and proclaimed peace to you who were far off and peace to those who were near; 18 for through him both of us have access in one Spirit to the Father. 19 So then you are no longer strangers and aliens, but you are citizens with the saints and also members of the household of God, 20 built upon the foundation of the apostles and prophets, with Christ Jesus himself as the cornerstone.[k] 21 In him the whole structure is joined together and grows into a holy temple in the Lord; 22 in whom you also are built together spiritually[l] into a dwelling place for God.

3 This is the reason that I Paul am a prisoner for[m] Christ Jesus for the sake of you Gentiles— 2 for surely you have already heard of the commission of God's grace that was given me for you, 3 and how the mystery was made known to me by revelation, as I wrote above in a few words, 4 a reading of which will enable you to perceive my understanding of the mystery of Christ. 5 In former generations this mystery[n] was not made known to humankind, as it has now been revealed to his holy apostles and prophets by the Spirit: 6 that is, the Gentiles have become fellow heirs, members of the same body, and sharers in the promise in Christ Jesus through the gospel.

7 Of this gospel I have become a servant according to the gift of God's grace that was given me by the working of his power. 8 Although I am the very least of all the saints, this grace was given to me to bring to the Gentiles the news of the boundless riches of Christ, 9 and to make everyone see[o] what is the plan of the mystery hidden for ages in[p] God who created all things; 10 so that through the church the wisdom of God in its rich variety might now be made known to the rulers and authorities in the heavenly places. 11 This was in accordance with the eternal purpose that he has carried out in Christ Jesus our Lord, 12 in whom we have access to God in boldness and confidence through faith in him.[q] 13 I pray therefore that you[r] may not lose heart over my sufferings for you; they are your glory.

14 For this reason I bow my knees before the Fa-ther,[s] 15 from whom every family[t] in heaven and on earth takes its name. 16 I pray that, according to the riches of his glory, he may grant that you may be strengthened in your inner being with power through his Spirit, 17 and that Christ may dwell in your hearts through faith, as you are being rooted and grounded in love. 18 I pray that you may have the power to comprehend, with all the saints, what is the breadth and length and height and depth, 19 and to know the love of Christ that surpasses knowledge, so that you may be filled with all the fullness of God.

20 Now to him who by the power at work within us is able to accomplish abundantly far more than all we can ask or imagine, 21 to him be glory in the church and in Christ Jesus to all generations, forever and ever. Amen.

4 I therefore, the prisoner in the Lord, beg you to lead a life worthy of the calling to which you have been called, 2 with all humility and gentleness, with patience, bearing with one another in love, 3 making every effort to maintain the unity of the Spirit in the bond of peace. 4 There is one body and one Spirit, just as you were called to the one hope of your calling, 5 one Lord, one faith, one baptism, 6 one God and Father of all, who is above all and through all and in all.

7 But each of us was given grace according to the measure of Christ's gift. 8 Therefore it is said,
"When he ascended on high he
made captivity itself a
captive;
he gave gifts to his people."[1]
9 (When it says, "He ascended," what does it mean but that he had also descended[u] into the lower parts of the earth? 10 He who descended is the same one who ascended far above all the heavens, so that he might fill all things.) 11 The gifts he gave were that some would be apostles, some prophets, some evangelists, some pastors and teachers, 12 to equip the saints for the work of ministry, for building up the body of Christ,

---

[i] Or *reconcile both of us in one body for God*   [j] Or *in him*, or *in himself*   [k] Or *keystone*   [l] Gk *in the Spirit*   [m] Or *of*   [n] Gk *it*   [o] Other ancient authorities read *to bring to light*   [p] Or *by*   [q] Or *the faith of him*   [r] Or *I*   [s] Other ancient authorities add *of our Lord Jesus Christ*   [t] Gk *fatherhood*   [u] Other ancient authorities add *first*

[1] Ps 68:18

13 until all of us come to the unity of the faith and of the knowledge of the Son of God, to maturity, to the measure of the full stature of Christ. 14 We must no longer be children, tossed to and fro and blown about by every wind of doctrine, by people's trickery, by their craftiness in deceitful scheming. 15 But speaking the truth in love, we must grow up in every way into him who is the head, into Christ, 16 from whom the whole body, joined and knit together by every ligament with which it is equipped, as each part is working properly, promotes the body's growth in building itself up in love.

17 Now this I affirm and insist on in the Lord: you must no longer live as the Gentiles live, in the futility of their minds. 18 They are darkened in their understanding, alienated from the life of God because of their ignorance and hardness of heart. 19 They have lost all sensitivity and have abandoned themselves to licentiousness, greedy to practice every kind of impurity. 20 That is not the way you learned Christ! 21 For surely you have heard about him and were taught in him, as truth is in Jesus. 22 You were taught to put away your former way of life, your old self, corrupt and deluded by its lusts, 23 and to be renewed in the spirit of your minds, 24 and to clothe yourselves with the new self, created according to the likeness of God in true righteousness and holiness.

25 So then, putting away falsehood, let all of us speak the truth to our neighbors, for we are members of one another. 26 Be angry but do not sin; do not let the sun go down on your anger, 27 and do not make room for the devil. 28 Thieves must give up stealing; rather let them labor and work honestly with their own hands, so as to have something to share with the needy. 29 Let no evil talk come out of your mouths, but only what is useful for building up,[v] as there is need, so that your words may give grace to those who hear. 30 And do not grieve the Holy Spirit of God, with which you were marked with a seal for the day of redemption. 31 Put away from you all bitterness and wrath and anger and wrangling and slander, together with all malice, 32 and be kind to one another, tenderhearted, forgiving one another, as God in Christ has forgiven you.[w]

5 Therefore be imitators of God, as beloved children, 2 and live in love, as Christ loved us[x] and gave himself up for us, a fragrant offering and sacrifice to God.

3 But fornication and impurity of any kind, or greed, must not even be mentioned among you, as is proper among saints. 4 Entirely out of place is obscene, silly, and vulgar talk; but instead, let there be thanksgiving. 5 Be sure of this, that no fornicator or impure person, or one who is greedy (that is, an idolater), has any inheritance in the kingdom of Christ and of God.

6 Let no one deceive you with empty words, for because of these things the wrath of God comes on those who are disobedient. 7 Therefore do not be associated with them. 8 For once you were darkness, but now in the Lord you are light. Live as children of light— 9 for the fruit of the light is found in all that is good and right and true. 10 Try to find out what is pleasing to the Lord. 11 Take no part in the unfruitful works of darkness, but instead expose them. 12 For it is shameful even to mention what such people do secretly; 13 but everything exposed by the light becomes visible, 14 for everything that becomes visible is light. Therefore it says,

> "Sleeper, awake!
> 　Rise from the dead,
> 　and Christ will shine on you."

15 Be careful then how you live, not as unwise people but as wise, 16 making the most of the time, because the days are evil. 17 So do not be foolish, but understand what the will of the Lord is. 18 Do not get drunk with wine, for that is debauchery; but be filled with the Spirit, 19 as you sing psalms and hymns and spiritual songs among yourselves, singing and making melody to the Lord in your hearts, 20 giving thanks to God the Father at all times and for everything in the name of our Lord Jesus Christ.

21 Be subject to one another out of reverence for Christ.

22 Wives, be subject to your husbands as you are to the Lord. 23 For the husband is the head of the wife just as Christ is the head of the church, the body of which he is the Savior. 24 Just as the church is subject to Christ, so also wives ought to be, in everything, to their husbands.

---

[v]Other ancient authorities read *building up faith*　[w]Other ancient authorities read *us*　[x]Other ancient authorities read *you*

25 Husbands, love your wives, just as Christ loved the church and gave himself up for her, 26 in order to make her holy by cleansing her with the washing of water by the word, 27 so as to present the church to himself in splendor, without a spot or wrinkle or anything of the kind—yes, so that she may be holy and without blemish. 28 In the same way, husbands should love their wives as they do their own bodies. He who loves his wife loves himself. 29 For no one ever hates his own body, but he nourishes and tenderly cares for it, just as Christ does for the church, 30 because we are members of his body.[y] 31 "For this reason a man will leave his father and mother and be joined to his wife, and the two will become one flesh."[2] 32 This is a great mystery, and I am applying it to Christ and the church. 33 Each of you, however, should love his wife as himself, and a wife should respect her husband.

6 Children, obey your parents in the Lord,[z] for this is right. 2 "Honor your father and mother"—this is the first commandment with a promise: 3 "so that it may be well with you and you may live long on the earth."[3]

4 And, fathers, do not provoke your children to anger, but bring them up in the discipline and instruction of the Lord.

5 Slaves, obey your earthly masters with fear and trembling, in singleness of heart, as you obey Christ; 6 not only while being watched, and in order to please them, but as slaves of Christ, doing the will of God from the heart. 7 Render service with enthusiasm, as to the Lord and not to men and women, 8 knowing that whatever good we do, we will receive the same again from the Lord, whether we are slaves or free.

9 And, masters, do the same to them. Stop threatening them, for you know that both of you have the same Master in heaven, and with him there is no partiality.

10 Finally, be strong in the Lord and in the strength of his power. 11 Put on the whole armor of God, so that you may be able to stand against the wiles of the devil. 12 For our[a] struggle is not against enemies of blood and flesh, but against the rulers, against the authorities, against the cosmic powers of this present darkness, against the spiritual forces of evil in the heavenly places. 13 Therefore take up the whole armor of God, so that you may be able to withstand on that evil day, and having done everything, to stand firm. 14 Stand therefore, and fasten the belt of truth around your waist, and put on the breastplate of righteousness. 15 As shoes for your feet put on whatever will make you ready to proclaim the gospel of peace. 16 With all of these,[b] take the shield of faith, with which you will be able to quench all the flaming arrows of the evil one. 17 Take the helmet of salvation, and the sword of the Spirit, which is the word of God.

18 Pray in the Spirit at all times in every prayer and supplication. To that end keep alert and always persevere in supplication for all the saints. 19 Pray also for me, so that when I speak, a message may be given to me to make known with boldness the mystery of the gospel,[c] 20 for which I am an ambassador in chains. Pray that I may declare it boldly, as I must speak.

21 So that you also may know how I am and what I am doing, Tychicus will tell you everything. He is a dear brother and a faithful minister in the Lord. 22 I am sending him to you for this very purpose, to let you know how we are, and to encourage your hearts.

23 Peace be to the whole community,[d] and love with faith, from God the Father and the Lord Jesus Christ. 24 Grace be with all who have an undying love for our Lord Jesus Christ.[e]

---

[y]Other ancient authorities add *of his flesh and of his bones* [z]Other ancient authorities lack *in the Lord* [a]Other ancient authorities read *your* [b]Or *In all circumstances* [c]Other ancient authorities lack *of the gospel* [d]Gk *to the brothers* [e]Other ancient authorities add *Amen*

---

[2]Gen 2:24 [3]Exod 20:12; Deut 5:16

The Letter to the Philippians

Scholars debate whether Paul's letter to the Philippians represents a solitary letter or a collection of two or more letters, later spliced together for broader distribution (cf. 2 Corinthians). In any event, it is clear that prior to the writing of the letter(s) a considerable amount of correspondence had been going on between Paul and the church that he founded in Philippi, in the province of Macedonia.

At the time of his writing, Paul was in prison awaiting trial and anticipating his own death (1:7, 12–26). We do not know where he was, exactly, whether in Rome, Ephesus, or somewhere else. His Philippian converts had learned of his situation and sent one of their members, a man named Epaphroditus, with a monetary gift to assist him in his time of suffering (4:10–20). After arriving, however, Epaphroditus himself fell gravely ill, nearly to the point of death. The Philippians heard of the situation and grew deeply concerned. When Epaphroditus's health returned he himself became distraught over the anxiety he had caused.

All of these issues, and several others, are addressed in the short and joyful letter (or letters) that Paul wrote from the midst of his own sufferings to those who had made a tangible expression of their love and concern for him. In part, the letter serves as a thank-you note for the gift Paul had received (4:10–20); in part it provides reassurance to the Philippians concerning the recovery of Epaphroditus (2:25–30); and in part it expresses Paul's joy in the midst of suffering and his urgent request that others follow him in rejoicing that God's work goes forward despite the harsh realities of life in this evil world (1:3–30).

Perhaps most important, Paul uses the occasion of the letter to urge the Philippians not only to rejoice in what God was doing but also to model themselves after what he had already done through his servants. They are to give themselves to one another, following the examples provided by Epaphroditus and ultimately by Christ himself, who for the sake of others humbled himself by "taking the form of a slave," being "born in human likeness," and ultimately becoming "obedient to the point of death" (2:6–8). It was because of Christ's self-condescension that God then exalted him (2:9–11), and the Philippians should follow his lead. There should be no strife or contention in the congregation; they should treat one another as more important than themselves (2:1–4); and they should stay true to the teachings they have received, avoiding teachers in their midst who might possibly lead them astray (3:2–11).

1

Paul and Timothy, servants[a] of Christ Jesus,
To all the saints in Christ Jesus who are in
Philippi, with the bishops[b] and deacons:[c]

2 Grace to you and peace from God our Father
and the Lord Jesus Christ.

3 I thank my God every time I remember you,
4 constantly praying with joy in every one of my
prayers for all of you, 5 because of your sharing
in the gospel from the first day until now. 6 I am
confident of this, that the one who began a good
work among you will bring it to completion by the
day of Jesus Christ. 7 It is right for me to think this
way about all of you, because you hold me in your
heart,[d] for all of you share in God's grace[e] with me,
both in my imprisonment and in the defense and
confirmation of the gospel. 8 For God is my witness, how I long for all of you with the compassion of Christ Jesus. 9 And this is my prayer, that
your love may overflow more and more with
knowledge and full insight 10 to help you to determine what is best, so that in the day of Christ you
may be pure and blameless, 11 having produced
the harvest of righteousness that comes through
Jesus Christ for the glory and praise of God.

12 I want you to know, beloved,[f] that what has
happened to me has actually helped to spread the
gospel, 13 so that it has become known throughout
the whole imperial guard[g] and to everyone else that
my imprisonment is for Christ; 14 and most of the
brothers and sisters,[f] having been made confident
in the Lord by my imprisonment, dare to speak the
word[h] with greater boldness and without fear.

15 Some proclaim Christ from envy and rivalry,
but others from goodwill. 16 These proclaim
Christ out of love, knowing that I have been put
here for the defense of the gospel; 17 the others
proclaim Christ out of selfish ambition, not sincerely but intending to increase my suffering in
my imprisonment. 18 What does it matter? Just
this, that Christ is proclaimed in every way,
whether out of false motives or true; and in that I
rejoice.

Yes, and I will continue to rejoice, 19 for I
know that through your prayers and the help of the
Spirit of Jesus Christ this will turn out for my de-
liverance. 20 It is my eager expectation and hope
that I will not be put to shame in any way, but that
by my speaking with all boldness, Christ will be-
exalted now as always in my body, whether by life
or by death. 21 For to me, living is Christ and dying is gain. 22 If I am to live in the flesh, that
means fruitful labor for me; and I do not know
which I prefer. 23 I am hard pressed between the
two: my desire is to depart and be with Christ, for
that is far better; 24 but to remain in the flesh is
more necessary for you. 25 Since I am convinced
of this, I know that I will remain and continue with
all of you for your progress and joy in faith, 26 so
that I may share abundantly in your boasting in
Christ Jesus when I come to you again.

27 Only, live your life in a manner worthy of the
gospel of Christ, so that, whether I come and see
you or am absent and hear about you, I will know
that you are standing firm in one spirit, striving
side by side with one mind for the faith of the
gospel, 28 and are in no way intimidated by your
opponents. For them this is evidence of their destruction, but of your salvation. And this is God's
doing. 29 For he has graciously granted you the
privilege not only of believing in Christ, but of
suffering for him as well— 30 since you are having the same struggle that you saw I had and now
hear that I still have.

2

If then there is any encouragement in Christ,
any consolation from love, any sharing in
the Spirit, any compassion and sympathy, 2 make
my joy complete: be of the same mind, having the
same love, being in full accord and of one mind.
3 Do nothing from selfish ambition or conceit, but
in humility regard others as better than yourselves.
4 Let each of you look not to your own interests,
but to the interests of others. 5 Let the same mind
be in you that was[i] in Christ Jesus,

6   who, though he was in the form
            of God,
           did not regard equality with
            God
           as something to be exploited,

7   but emptied himself,
           taking the form of a slave,
           being born in human
            likeness.

[a]Gk slaves [b]Or overseers [c]Or overseers and helpers [d]Or because
I hold you in my heart [e]Gk in grace [f]Gk brothers [g]Gk whole
praetorium [h]Other ancient authorities read word of God [i]Or that
you have

And being found in human
form,
8   he humbled himself
and became obedient to the
point of death—
even death on a cross.

9   Therefore God also highly exalted
him
and gave him the name
that is above every name,
10   so that at the name of Jesus
every knee should bend,
in heaven and on earth and
under the earth,
11   and every tongue should confess
that Jesus Christ is Lord,
to the glory of God the Father.

12 Therefore, my beloved, just as you have always obeyed me, not only in my presence, but
much more now in my absence, work out your
own salvation with fear and trembling; 13 for it is
God who is at work in you, enabling you both to
will and to work for his good pleasure.

14 Do all things without murmuring and arguing, 15 so that you may be blameless and innocent, children of God without blemish in the midst
of a crooked and perverse generation, in which
you shine like stars in the world. 16 It is by your
holding fast to the word of life that I can boast on
the day of Christ that I did not run in vain or labor
in vain. 17 But even if I am being poured out as a
libation over the sacrifice and the offering of your
faith, I am glad and rejoice with all of you—
18 and in the same way you also must be glad and
rejoice with me.

19 I hope in the Lord Jesus to send Timothy to
you soon, so that I may be cheered by news of you.
20 I have no one like him who will be genuinely
concerned for your welfare. 21 All of them are
seeking their own interests, not those of Jesus
Christ. 22 But Timothy's[j] worth you know, how
like a son with a father he has served with me in
the work of the gospel. 23 I hope therefore to send
him as soon as I see how things go with me;
24 and I trust in the Lord that I will also come soon.

25 Still, I think it necessary to send to you
Epaphroditus—my brother and co-worker and fellow soldier, your messenger[k] and minister to my
need; 26 for he has been longing for[l] all of you,
and has been distressed because you heard that he
was ill. 27 He was indeed so ill that he nearly died.
But God had mercy on him, and not only on him
but on me also, so that I would not have one sorrow after another. 28 I am the more eager to send
him, therefore, in order that you may rejoice at
seeing him again, and that I may be less anxious.
29 Welcome him then in the Lord with all joy, and
honor such people, 30 because he came close to
death for the work of Christ,[m] risking his life to
make up for those services that you could not
give me.

3 Finally, my brothers and sisters,[n] rejoice[o] in
the Lord.

To write the same things to you is not trouble-
some to me, and for you it is a safeguard.

2 Beware of the dogs, beware of the evil workers, beware of those who mutilate the flesh![p]
3 For it is we who are the circumcision, who worship in the Spirit of God[q] and boast in Christ Jesus
and have no confidence in the flesh— 4 even
though I, too, have reason for confidence in the
flesh.

If anyone else has reason to be confident in the
flesh, I have more: 5 circumcised on the eighth
day, a member of the people of Israel, of the tribe
of Benjamin, a Hebrew born of Hebrews; as to
the law, a Pharisee; 6 as to zeal, a persecutor of
the church; as to righteousness under the law,
blameless.

7 Yet whatever gains I had, these I have come to
regard as loss because of Christ. 8 More than that,
I regard everything as loss because of the surpassing value of knowing Christ Jesus my Lord. For
his sake I have suffered the loss of all things, and
I regard them as rubbish, in order that I may gain
Christ 9 and be found in him, not having a righteousness of my own that comes from the law, but
one that comes through faith in Christ,[r] the righteousness from God based on faith. 10 I want to
know Christ[s] and the power of his resurrection and
the sharing of his sufferings by becoming like him

[j]Gk his   [k]Gk apostle   [l]Other ancient authorities read longing to see
[m]Other ancient authorities read of the Lord   [n]Gk my brothers
[o]Or farewell   [p]Gk the mutilation   [q]Other ancient authorities read
worship God in spirit   [r]Or through the faith of Christ   [s]Gk him

in his death, 11 if somehow I may attain the resurrection from the dead.

12 Not that I have already obtained this or have already reached the goal;[t] but I press on to make it my own, because Christ Jesus has made me his own. 13 Beloved,[u] I do not consider that I have made it my own;[v] but this one thing I do: forgetting what lies behind and straining forward to what lies ahead, 14 I press on toward the goal for the prize of the heavenly[w] call of God in Christ Jesus. 15 Let those of us then who are mature be of the same mind; and if you think differently about anything, this too God will reveal to you. 16 Only let us hold fast to what we have attained.

17 Brothers and sisters,[u] join in imitating me, and observe those who live according to the example you have in us. 18 For many live as enemies of the cross of Christ; I have often told you of them, and now I tell you even with tears. 19 Their end is destruction; their god is the belly; and their glory is in their shame; their minds are set on earthly things. 20 But our citizenship[x] is in heaven, and it is from there that we are expecting a Savior, the Lord Jesus Christ. 21 He will transform the body of our humiliation[y] that it may be conformed to the body of his glory,[z] by the power that also enables him to make all things subject to himself.

4 Therefore, my brothers and sisters,[a] whom I love and long for, my joy and crown, stand firm in the Lord in this way, my beloved.

2 I urge Euodia and I urge Syntyche to be of the same mind in the Lord. 3 Yes, and I ask you also, my loyal companion,[b] help these women, for they have struggled beside me in the work of the gospel, together with Clement and the rest of my co-workers, whose names are in the book of life.

4 Rejoice[c] in the Lord always; again I will say, Rejoice.[c] 5 Let your gentleness be known to everyone. The Lord is near. 6 Do not worry about anything, but in everything by prayer and supplication with thanksgiving let your requests be made known to God. 7 And the peace of God, which surpasses all understanding, will guard your hearts and your minds in Christ Jesus.

8 Finally, beloved,[d] whatever is true, whatever is honorable, whatever is just, whatever is pure, whatever is pleasing, whatever is commendable, if there is any excellence and if there is anything worthy of praise, think about[e] these things. 9 Keep on doing the things that you have learned and received and heard and seen in me, and the God of peace will be with you.

10 I rejoice[f] in the Lord greatly that now at last you have revived your concern for me; indeed, you were concerned for me, but had no opportunity to show it.[g] 11 Not that I am referring to being in need; for I have learned to be content with whatever I have. 12 I know what it is to have little, and I know what it is to have plenty. In any and all circumstances I have learned the secret of being well-fed and of going hungry, of having plenty and of being in need. 13 I can do all things through him who strengthens me. 14 In any case, it was kind of you to share my distress.

15 You Philippians indeed know that in the early days of the gospel, when I left Macedonia, no church shared with me in the matter of giving and receiving, except you alone. 16 For even when I was in Thessalonica, you sent me help for my needs more than once. 17 Not that I seek the gift, but I seek the profit that accumulates to your account. 18 I have been paid in full and have more than enough; I am fully satisfied, now that I have received from Epaphroditus the gifts you sent, a fragrant offering, a sacrifice acceptable and pleasing to God. 19 And my God will fully satisfy every need of yours according to his riches in glory in Christ Jesus. 20 To our God and Father be glory forever and ever. Amen.

21 Greet every saint in Christ Jesus. The friends[d] who are with me greet you. 22 All the saints greet you, especially those of the emperor's household.

23 The grace of the Lord Jesus Christ be with your spirit.[h]

[t]Or *have already been made perfect* [u]Gk *Brothers* [v]Other ancient authorities read *my own yet* [w]Gk *upward* [x]Or *commonwealth* [y]Or *our humble bodies* [z]Or *his glorious body* [a]Gk *my brothers* [b]Or *loyal Syzygus* [c]Or *Farewell* [d]Gk *brothers* [e]Gk *take account of* [f]Gk *I rejoiced* [g]Gk lacks *to show it* [h]Other ancient authorities add *Amen*

The Letter to the Colossians

The letter to the Colossians is directed against a group of "false teachers" who had infiltrated the Christian community (2:4). The author does not indicate the precise nature of the teaching, which he labels a "philosophy and empty deceit" (2:8). It appears to have involved some kind of Jewish mysticism, in which aspects of the Jewish Law were to be rigorously followed (2:11–17), an ascetic lifestyle was to be maintained (2:18), and angelic beings were to be worshipped (2:19). These mystical practices were evidently intended to unite believers with the divine.

In response, the author insists that Christ himself is "the image of the invisible God," and that "the fullness of God" dwells in him (1:15, 19). There is no need, therefore, to worship other beings; indeed, Christ himself created these beings and is lord over them (1:16). It is Christ who bestows all blessings on believers (1:21–22; 2:13–15), including the true "spiritual circumcision" (2:9–10). Through his death he destroyed everything that brings alienation from God, including the "legal demands" (2:14) so cherished by the author's opponents.

According to this author, believers in Christ have already been raised with him and are dwelling with him in the heavenly places (3:1); they do not therefore need "visions" of the divine realm. Nor do they need purity regulations that bring only the appearance of piety; in Christ, believers have the full experience of the divine itself (2:20–23). This does not mean, however, that they are free to neglect social and moral obligations in this world. Until Christ himself returns they must continue to avoid vice (3:5–11), embrace virtue (3:12–17), and live appropriately according to their social roles (3:18–4:1).

Scholars continue to debate whether Paul himself wrote this letter. On the one hand, the prescript, the basic layout of the letter, and the closing all sound like Paul, and a number of Pauline themes are sounded throughout. On the other hand, the writing style (as seen in the Greek) is quite different from Paul's, especially in the use of long complex sentences. Even more important, the central claim of the letter, that believers have already been raised with Christ and are presently enjoying the full blessings of heaven (e.g., 3:1), seems to stand at direct odds with what Paul himself says elsewhere. For Paul, believers have already "died" with Christ, but they have *not* yet been raised with him; nor will they be until he returns (cf. Rom 6:1–6, where he is emphatic about just this point). In fact, 1 Corinthians appears to oppose precisely the perspective advanced here, that believers are already residing in the heavenly places and ruling with Christ.

For these reasons many scholars believe this letter to be pseudonymous, written perhaps a generation after Paul by a member of one of his churches who chose to address a new problem that had arisen in his community by appealing to the authority of the apostle in support of his views.

1

Paul, an apostle of Christ Jesus by the will of God, and Timothy our brother,

2 To the saints and faithful brothers and sisters[a] in Christ in Colossae:

Grace to you and peace from God our Father.

3 In our prayers for you we always thank God, the Father of our Lord Jesus Christ, 4 for we have heard of your faith in Christ Jesus and of the love that you have for all the saints, 5 because of the hope laid up for you in heaven. You have heard of this hope before in the word of the truth, the gospel 6 that has come to you. Just as it is bearing fruit and growing in the whole world, so it has been bearing fruit among yourselves from the day you heard it and truly comprehended the grace of God. 7 This you learned from Epaphras, our beloved fellow servant.[b] He is a faithful minister of Christ on your[c] behalf, 8 and he has made known to us your love in the Spirit.

9 For this reason, since the day we heard it, we have not ceased praying for you and asking that you may be filled with the knowledge of God's[d] will in all spiritual wisdom and understanding, 10 so that you may lead lives worthy of the Lord, fully pleasing to him, as you bear fruit in every good work and as you grow in the knowledge of God. 11 May you be made strong with all the strength that comes from his glorious power, and may you be prepared to endure everything with patience, while joyfully 12 giving thanks to the Father, who has enabled[e] you[f] to share in the inheritance of the saints in the light. 13 He has rescued us from the power of darkness and transferred us into the kingdom of his beloved Son, 14 in whom we have redemption, the forgiveness of sins.[g]

15 He is the image of the invisible God, the first-born of all creation; 16 for in[h] him all things in heaven and on earth were created, things visible and invisible, whether thrones or dominions or rulers or powers—all things have been created through him and for him. 17 He himself is before all things, and in[h] him all things hold together. 18 He is the head of the body, the church; he is the beginning, the firstborn from the dead, so that he might come to have first place in everything. 19 For in him all the fullness of God was pleased to dwell, 20 and through him God was pleased to reconcile to himself all things, whether on earth or in heaven, by making peace through the blood of his cross.

21 And you who were once estranged and hostile in mind, doing evil deeds, 22 he has now reconciled[i] in his fleshly body[j] through death, so as to present you holy and blameless and irreproachable before him— 23 provided that you continue securely established and steadfast in the faith, without shifting from the hope promised by the gospel that you heard, which has been proclaimed to every creature under heaven. I, Paul, became a servant of this gospel.

24 I am now rejoicing in my sufferings for your sake, and in my flesh I am completing what is lacking in Christ's afflictions for the sake of his body, that is, the church. 25 I became its servant according to God's commission that was given to me for you, to make the word of God fully known, 26 the mystery that has been hidden throughout the ages and generations but has now been revealed to his saints. 27 To them God chose to make known how great among the Gentiles are the riches of the glory of this mystery, which is Christ in you, the hope of glory. 28 It is he whom we proclaim, warning everyone and teaching everyone in all wisdom, so that we may present everyone mature in Christ. 29 For this I toil and struggle with all the energy that he powerfully inspires within me.

2

For I want you to know how much I am struggling for you, and for those in Laodicea, and for all who have not seen me face to face. 2 I want their hearts to be encouraged and united in love, so that they may have all the riches of assured understanding and have the knowledge of God's mystery, that is, Christ himself,[k] 3 in whom are hidden all the treasures of wisdom and knowledge. 4 I am saying this so that no one may deceive you with plausible arguments. 5 For though I am absent in body, yet I am with you in spirit, and I rejoice to see your morale and the firmness of your faith in Christ.

6 As you therefore have received Christ Jesus

---

[a]Gk brothers [b]Gk slave [c]Other ancient authorities read our
[d]Gk his [e]Other ancient authorities read called [f]Other ancient authorities read us [g]Other ancient authorities add through his blood
[h]Or by [i]Other ancient authorities read you have now been reconciled
[j]Gk in the body of his flesh [k]Other ancient authorities read of the mystery of God, both of the Father and of Christ

the Lord, continue to live your lives[l] in him, 7 rooted and built up in him and established in the faith, just as you were taught, abounding in thanksgiving.

8 See to it that no one takes you captive through philosophy and empty deceit, according to human tradition, according to the elemental spirits of the universe,[m] and not according to Christ. 9 For in him the whole fullness of deity dwells bodily, 10 and you have come to fullness in him, who is the head of every ruler and authority. 11 In him also you were circumcised with a spiritual circumcision,[n] by putting off the body of the flesh in the circumcision of Christ; 12 when you were buried with him in baptism, you were also raised with him through faith in the power of God, who raised him from the dead. 13 And when you were dead in trespasses and the uncircumcision of your flesh, God[o] made you[p] alive together with him, when he forgave us all our trespasses, 14 erasing the record that stood against us with its legal demands. He set this aside, nailing it to the cross. 15 He disarmed[q] the rulers and authorities and made a public example of them, triumphing over them in it.

16 Therefore do not let anyone condemn you in matters of food and drink or of observing festivals, new moons, or sabbaths. 17 These are only a shadow of what is to come, but the substance belongs to Christ. 18 Do not let anyone disqualify you, insisting on self-abasement and worship of angels, dwelling[r] on visions,[s] puffed up without cause by a human way of thinking,[t] 19 and not holding fast to the head, from whom the whole body, nourished and held together by its ligaments and sinews, grows with a growth that is from God.

20 If with Christ you died to the elemental spirits of the universe,[m] why do you live as if you still belonged to the world? Why do you submit to regulations, 21 "Do not handle, Do not taste, Do not touch"? 22 All these regulations refer to things that perish with use; they are simply human commands and teachings. 23 These have indeed an appearance of wisdom in promoting self-imposed piety, humility, and severe treatment of the body, but they are of no value in checking self-indulgence.[u]

3 So if you have been raised with Christ, seek the things that are above, where Christ is, seated at the right hand of God. 2 Set your minds on things that are above, not on things that are on earth, 3 for you have died, and your life is hidden with Christ in God. 4 When Christ who is your[v] life is revealed, then you also will be revealed with him in glory.

5 Put to death, therefore, whatever in you is earthly: fornication, impurity, passion, evil desire, and greed (which is idolatry). 6 On account of these the wrath of God is coming on those who are disobedient.[w] 7 These are the ways you also once followed, when you were living that life.[x] 8 But now you must get rid of all such things—anger, wrath, malice, slander, and abusive[y] language from your mouth. 9 Do not lie to one another, seeing that you have stripped off the old self with its practices 10 and have clothed yourselves with the new self, which is being renewed in knowledge according to the image of its creator. 11 In that renewal[z] there is no longer Greek and Jew, circumcised and uncircumcised, barbarian, Scythian, slave and free; but Christ is all and in all!

12 As God's chosen ones, holy and beloved, clothe yourselves with compassion, kindness, humility, meekness, and patience. 13 Bear with one another and, if anyone has a complaint against another, forgive each other; just as the Lord[a] has forgiven you, so you also must forgive. 14 Above all, clothe yourselves with love, which binds everything together in perfect harmony. 15 And let the peace of Christ rule in your hearts, to which indeed you were called in the one body. And be thankful. 16 Let the word of Christ[b] dwell in you richly; teach and admonish one another in all wisdom; and with gratitude in your hearts sing psalms, hymns, and spiritual songs to God.[c] 17 And whatever you do, in word or deed, do everything in the name of the Lord Jesus, giving thanks to God the Father through him.

---

[l]Gk to walk   [m]Or the rudiments of the world   [n]Gk a circumcision made without hands   [o]Gk he   [p]Other ancient authorities read made us; others, made   [q]Or divested himself of   [r]Other ancient authorities read not dwelling   [s]Meaning of Gk uncertain   [t]Gk by the mind of his flesh   [u]Or are of no value, serving only to indulge the flesh   [v]Other authorities read our   [w]Other ancient authorities lack on those who are disobedient (Gk the children of disobedience)   [x]Or living among such people   [y]Or filthy   [z]Gk its creator,   [11]where   [a]Other ancient authorities read just as Christ   [b]Other ancient authorities read of God, or of the Lord   [c]Other ancient authorities read to the Lord

18 Wives, be subject to your husbands, as is fitting in the Lord. 19 Husbands, love your wives and never treat them harshly.

20 Children, obey your parents in everything, for this is your acceptable duty in the Lord. 21 Fathers, do not provoke your children, or they may lose heart. 22 Slaves, obey your earthly masters[d] in everything, not only while being watched and in order to please them, but wholeheartedly, fearing the Lord.[d] 23 Whatever your task, put yourselves into it, as done for the Lord and not for your masters,[e] 24 since you know that from the Lord you will receive the inheritance as your reward; you serve[f] the Lord Christ. 25 For the wrongdoer will be paid back for whatever wrong has been done, and there is no partiality.

4 Masters, treat your slaves justly and fairly, for you know that you also have a Master in heaven.

2 Devote yourselves to prayer, keeping alert in it with thanksgiving. 3 At the same time pray for us as well that God will open to us a door for the word, that we may declare the mystery of Christ, for which I am in prison, 4 so that I may reveal it clearly, as I should.

5 Conduct yourselves wisely toward outsiders, making the most of the time.[g] 6 Let your speech always be gracious, seasoned with salt, so that you may know how you ought to answer everyone.

7 Tychicus will tell you all the news about me; he is a beloved brother, a faithful minister, and a fellow servant[h] in the Lord. 8 I have sent him to you for this very purpose, so that you may know how we are[i] and that he may encourage your hearts; 9 he is coming with Onesimus, the faithful and beloved brother, who is one of you. They will tell you about everything here.

10 Aristarchus my fellow prisoner greets you, as does Mark the cousin of Barnabas, concerning whom you have received instructions—if he comes to you, welcome him. 11 And Jesus who is called Justus greets you. These are the only ones of the circumcision among my co-workers for the kingdom of God, and they have been a comfort to me. 12 Epaphras, who is one of you, a servant[h] of Christ Jesus, greets you. He is always wrestling in his prayers on your behalf, so that you may stand mature and fully assured in everything that God wills. 13 For I testify for him that he has worked hard for you and for those in Laodicea and in Hierapolis. 14 Luke, the beloved physician, and Demas greet you. 15 Give my greetings to the brothers and sisters[j] in Laodicea, and to Nym-pha and the church in her house. 16 And when this letter has been read among you, have it read also in the church of the Laodiceans; and see that you read also the letter from Laodicea. 17 And say to Archippus, "See that you complete the task that you have received in the Lord."

18 I, Paul, write this greeting with my own hand. Remember my chains. Grace be with you.[k]

---

[d]In Greek the same word is used for *master* and *Lord*   [e]Gk *not for men*   [f]Or *you are slaves of,* or *be slaves of*   [g]Or *opportunity*   [h]Gk *slave*   [i]Other authorities read *that I may know how you are*   [j]Gk *brothers*   [k]Other ancient authorities add *Amen*

The First Letter to the Thessalonians

First Thessalonians was the first book of the New Testament to be written (ca. 50 C.E.). This makes it the oldest surviving piece of literature from early Christianity. It is addressed by Paul and his two companions, Timothy and Silvanus, to the church that they jointed founded in Thessalonica, capital of the province of Macedonia. It is a particularly personal and joyful letter, full of fond recollections of the relationship these three missionaries shared with their converts when they first were with them.

The community was comprised of Gentiles who had been converted from their polytheistic worship of idols "to serve a living and true God, and to wait for his Son from heaven whom he raised from the dead" (1:9–10). Possibly because Paul had not spent much time among the Thessalonian Christians before moving on, questions had arisen in his absence. Having sent Timothy back to check up on the congregation and having learned of the problems that had emerged, Paul, along with his two fellow-missionaries, now writes this letter in response (3:1–6).

The principal problem appears to have involved Paul's message of the imminent return of Christ in judgment. Paul had persuaded his converts that Jesus, who was now exalted to heaven, was soon to appear again to remove those who believe in him from this sinful world and to allow them to enter into the glorious kingdom that he would bring. But Christ had not yet returned, and in the meantime some of the members of the Thessalonian congregation had died. This caused some consternation among those left behind (4:13). Have those who died missed out on their heavenly reward? Will they not enjoy the blessings of the kingdom when Christ returns?

Paul writes not only to reestablish friendly contact with his Thessalonian converts and to encourage them in their faith, but also to console them in the face of their loss and to affirm that in fact the dead in Christ have not lost out on the glories to be brought at his return. For when Jesus appears from heaven, "the dead in Christ will rise first"; and then "we who are alive, who are left will be caught up in the clouds together with them, to meet the Lord in the air" (4:16–17). The Thessalonians can continue to be assured that this cataclysmic event will come soon. And they should be alert and ready, lest they be caught unawares; for it will come unexpectedly, "like a thief in the night" (5:1–11).

In the meantime, the Thessalonians are to keep the faith, even in the midst of opposition by their non-Christian opponents (4:13–16). They are to live moral and upright lives, avoiding sexual impurity among themselves (4:1–8). And they are to project an acceptable and attractive image to those outside the church by the way they live and relate to one another (4:9–12).

1 Paul, Silvanus, and Timothy,
To the church of the Thessalonians in God the Father and the Lord Jesus Christ:
Grace to you and peace.

2 We always give thanks to God for all of you and mention you in our prayers, constantly 3 remembering before our God and Father your work of faith and labor of love and steadfastness of hope in our Lord Jesus Christ. 4 For we know, brothers and sisters[a] beloved by God, that he has chosen you, 5 because our message of the gospel came to you not in word only, but also in power and in the Holy Spirit and with full conviction; just as you know what kind of persons we proved to be among you for your sake. 6 And you became imitators of us and of the Lord, for in spite of persecution you received the word with joy inspired by the Holy Spirit, 7 so that you became an example to all the believers in Macedonia and in Achaia. 8 For the word of the Lord has sounded forth from you not only in Macedonia and Achaia, but in every place your faith in God has become known, so that we have no need to speak about it. 9 For the people of those regions[b] report about us what kind of welcome we had among you, and how you turned to God from idols, to serve a living and true God, 10 and to wait for his Son from heaven, whom he raised from the dead—Jesus, who rescues us from the wrath that is coming.

2 You yourselves know, brothers and sisters,[a] that our coming to you was not in vain, 2 but though we had already suffered and been shamefully mistreated at Philippi, as you know, we had courage in our God to declare to you the gospel of God in spite of great opposition. 3 For our appeal does not spring from deceit or impure motives or trickery, 4 but just as we have been approved by God to be entrusted with the message of the gospel, even so we speak, not to please mortals, but to please God who tests our hearts. 5 As you know and as God is our witness, we never came with words of flattery or with a pretext for greed; 6 nor did we seek praise from mortals, whether from you or from others, 7 though we might have made demands as apostles of Christ. But we were gentle[c] among you, like a nurse tenderly caring for her own children. 8 So deeply do we care for you that we are determined to share with you not only

the gospel of God but also our own selves, because you have become very dear to us.

9 You remember our labor and toil, brothers and sisters;[a] we worked night and day, so that we might not burden any of you while we proclaimed to you the gospel of God. 10 You are witnesses, and God also, how pure, upright, and blameless our conduct was toward you believers. 11 As you know, we dealt with each one of you like a father with his children, 12 urging and encouraging you and pleading that you lead a life worthy of God, who calls you into his own kingdom and glory.

13 We also constantly give thanks to God for this, that when you received the word of God that you heard from us, you accepted it not as a human word but as what it really is, God's word, which is also at work in you believers. 14 For you, brothers and sisters,[a] became imitators of the churches of God in Christ Jesus that are in Judea, for you suffered the same things from your own compatriots as they did from the Jews, 15 who killed both the Lord Jesus and the prophets,[d] and drove us out; they displease God and oppose everyone 16 by hindering us from speaking to the Gentiles so that they may be saved. Thus they have constantly been filling up the measure of their sins; but God's wrath has overtaken them at last.[e]

17 As for us, brothers and sisters,[a] when, for a short time, we were made orphans by being separated from you—in person, not in heart—we longed with great eagerness to see you face to face. 18 For we wanted to come to you—certainly I, Paul, wanted to again and again—but Satan blocked our way. 19 For what is our hope or joy or crown of boasting before our Lord Jesus at his coming? Is it not you? 20 Yes, you are our glory and joy!

3 Therefore when we could bear it no longer, we decided to be left alone in Athens; 2 and we sent Timothy, our brother and co-worker for God in proclaiming[f] the gospel of Christ, to strengthen and encourage you for the sake of your faith, 3 so that no one would be shaken by these persecutions. Indeed, you yourselves know that this is what we are destined for. 4 In fact, when we were with you, we told you beforehand that we

[a]Gk *brothers*   [b]Gk *For they*   [c]Other ancient authorities read *infants*
[d]Other ancient authorities read *their own prophets*   [e]Or *completely* or *forever*   [f]Gk lacks *proclaiming*

were to suffer persecution; so it turned out, as you know. 5 For this reason, when I could bear it no longer, I sent to find out about your faith; I was afraid that somehow the tempter had tempted you and that our labor had been in vain.

6 But Timothy has just now come to us from you, and has brought us the good news of your faith and love. He has told us also that you always remember us kindly and long to see us—just as we long to see you. 7 For this reason, brothers and sisters,[g] during all our distress and persecution we have been encouraged about you through your faith. 8 For we now live, if you continue to stand firm in the Lord. 9 How can we thank God enough for you in return for all the joy that we feel before our God because of you? 10 Night and day we pray most earnestly that we may see you face to face and restore whatever is lacking in your faith.

11 Now may our God and Father himself and our Lord Jesus direct our way to you. 12 And may the Lord make you increase and abound in love for one another and for all, just as we abound in love for you. 13 And may he so strengthen your hearts in holiness that you may be blameless before our God and Father at the coming of our Lord Jesus with all his saints.

4 Finally, brothers and sisters,[g] we ask and urge you in the Lord Jesus that, as you learned from us how you ought to live and to please God (as, in fact, you are doing), you should do so more and more. 2 For you know what instructions we gave you through the Lord Jesus. 3 For this is the will of God, your sanctification: that you abstain from fornication; 4 that each one of you know how to control your own body[h] in holiness and honor, 5 not with lustful passion, like the Gentiles who do not know God; 6 that no one wrong or exploit a brother or sister[i] in this matter, because the Lord is an avenger in all these things, just as we have already told you beforehand and solemnly warned you. 7 For God did not call us to impurity but in holiness. 8 Therefore whoever rejects this rejects not human authority but God, who also gives his Holy Spirit to you.

9 Now concerning love of the brothers and sisters,[g] you do not need to have anyone write to you, for you yourselves have been taught by God to love one another; 10 and indeed you do love all the brothers and sisters[g] throughout Macedonia. But we urge you, beloved,[g] to do so more and more, 11 to aspire to live quietly, to mind your own affairs, and to work with your hands, as we directed you, 12 so that you may behave properly toward outsiders and be dependent on no one.

13 But we do not want you to be uninformed, brothers and sisters,[g] about those who have died,[j] so that you may not grieve as others do who have no hope. 14 For since we believe that Jesus died and rose again, even so, through Jesus, God will bring with him those who have died.[j] 15 For this we declare to you by the word of the Lord, that we who are alive, who are left until the coming of the Lord, will by no means precede those who have died.[j] 16 For the Lord himself, with a cry of command, with the archangel's call and with the sound of God's trumpet, will descend from heaven, and the dead in Christ will rise first. 17 Then we who are alive, who are left, will be caught up in the clouds together with them to meet the Lord in the air; and so we will be with the Lord forever. 18 Therefore encourage one another with these words.

5 Now concerning the times and the seasons, brothers and sisters,[g] you do not need to have anything written to you. 2 For you yourselves know very well that the day of the Lord will come like a thief in the night. 3 When they say, "There is peace and security," then sudden destruction will come upon them, as labor pains come upon a pregnant woman, and there will be no escape! 4 But you, beloved,[g] are not in darkness, for that day to surprise you like a thief; 5 for you are all children of light and children of the day; we are not of the night or of darkness. 6 So then let us not fall asleep as others do, but let us keep awake and be sober; 7 for those who sleep sleep at night, and those who are drunk get drunk at night. 8 But since we belong to the day, let us be sober, and put on the breastplate of faith and love, and for a helmet the hope of salvation. 9 For God has destined us not for wrath but for obtaining salvation through our Lord Jesus Christ,

[g]Gk brothers   [h]Or how to take a wife for himself   [i]Gk brother
[j]Gk fallen asleep

10 who died for us, so that whether we are awake or asleep we may live with him. 11 Therefore encourage one another and build up each other, as indeed you are doing.

12 But we appeal to you, brothers and sisters,[k] to respect those who labor among you, and have charge of you in the Lord and admonish you; 13 esteem them very highly in love because of their work. Be at peace among yourselves. 14 And we urge you, beloved,[k] to admonish the idlers, encourage the fainthearted, help the weak, be patient with all of them. 15 See that none of you repays evil for evil, but always seek to do good to one another and to all. 16 Rejoice always, 17 pray without ceasing, 18 give thanks in all circumstances; for this is the will of God in Christ Jesus for you. 19 Do not quench the Spirit. 20 Do not despise the words of prophets,[l] 21 but test everything; hold fast to what is good; 22 abstain from every form of evil.

23 May the God of peace himself sanctify you entirely; and may your spirit and soul and body be kept sound[m] and blameless at the coming of our Lord Jesus Christ. 24 The one who calls you is faithful, and he will do this.

25 Beloved,[n] pray for us.

26 Greet all the brothers and sisters[o] with a holy kiss. 27 I solemnly command you by the Lord that this letter be read to all of them.[p]

28 The grace of our Lord Jesus Christ be with you.[q]

---

[k]Gk *brothers*   [l]Gk *despise prophecies*   [m]Or *complete*
[n]Gk *Brothers*   [o]Gk *brothers*   [p]Gk *to all the brothers*   [q]Other ancient authorities add *Amen*

The Second Letter to the Thessalonians

One of the Deutero-Pauline epistles, 2 Thessalonians is a letter assigned by many scholars, not to Paul himself, but to a member of one of his churches—a "second" Paul—some years after his death (see also the introductions to Ephesians and Colossians). Whoever actually wrote the letter, its occasion and purpose are relatively clear. The people to whom it is addressed are experiencing persecution for their faith (1:4–6); moreover, their suffering has led some of their number to believe that the end of the age is absolutely imminent (2:1–2). Some of them have taken this belief to an extreme, having quit their jobs in anticipation of Christ's immediate return. Problems within the community have erupted as a result; those who continue to earn a living are having to support those who do not (3:6–15).

The letter was written in part to comfort those who were being persecuted for their faith. Their enemies would be punished with "eternal destruction" at Christ's return, whereas they themselves would enter into their glorious reward (1:7–12). This cataclysmic event, however, was not to take place in the immediate future. Notwithstanding prophecies made in the church and a letter allegedly from the apostle, the end had not yet arrived (2:1–3). According to this author, an entire sequence of events was to transpire before Christ would return: an anti-Christ figure was to arise who would establish himself in the Jerusalem temple and declare himself to be God (2:3–5). Only then would Christ come for a final confrontation with the forces of evil (2:6–12). The Thessalonians, therefore, were not to think that the end was absolutely imminent. They were to return to work and patiently wait for the end that was destined, eventually, to come (3:6–12).

Parts of this letter bear a close resemblance to writings that are undisputably from Paul, including the prescript (2 Thess 1:1; cf. 1 Thess 2:1) and certain echoes of 1 Thessalonians (3:7–9; cf. 1 Thess 2:9). The difficulty with ascribing it to Paul himself, however, is the apocalyptic scenario that lies at its core. For if in fact a series of earthly events was to transpire before the end could come (such as the public appearance of the anti-Christ), how could Paul have earlier warned the Thessalonians to be prepared at all times for the imminent return of Christ, which would happen "suddenly," "like a thief in the night" (1 Thess 5:1–10)? In the view of most scholars, either Paul seriously changed his mind about a major component of his teaching, or the second letter to the Thessalonians came from a different hand, possibly a member of one of Paul's churches living a generation later, when some Christians *continued* to believe that the end was to come in the immediate future and had begun to act upon this conviction.

1 Paul, Silvanus, and Timothy,
To the church of the Thessalonians in God our Father and the Lord Jesus Christ:

2 Grace to you and peace from God our[a] Father and the Lord Jesus Christ.

3 We must always give thanks to God for you, brothers and sisters,[b] as is right, because your faith is growing abundantly, and the love of everyone of you for one another is increasing. 4 Therefore we ourselves boast of you among the churches of God for your steadfastness and faith during all your persecutions and the afflictions that you are enduring.

5 This is evidence of the righteous judgment of God, and is intended to make you worthy of the kingdom of God, for which you are also suffering. 6 For it is indeed just of God to repay with affliction those who afflict you, 7 and to give relief to the afflicted as well as to us, when the Lord Jesus is revealed from heaven with his mighty angels 8 in flaming fire, inflicting vengeance on those who do not know God and on those who do not obey the gospel of our Lord Jesus. 9 These will suffer the punishment of eternal destruction, separated from the presence of the Lord and from the glory of his might, 10 when he comes to be glorified by his saints and to be marveled at on that day among all who have believed, because our testimony to you was believed. 11 To this end we always pray for you, asking that our God will make you worthy of his call and will fulfill by his power every good resolve and work of faith, 12 so that the name of our Lord Jesus may be glorified in you, and you in him, according to the grace of our God and the Lord Jesus Christ.

2 As to the coming of our Lord Jesus Christ and our being gathered together to him, we beg you, brothers and sisters,[b] 2 not to be quickly shaken in mind or alarmed, either by spirit or by word or by letter, as though from us, to the effect that the day of the Lord is already here. 3 Let no one deceive you in any way; for that day will not come unless the rebellion comes first and the lawless one[c] is revealed, the one destined for destruction.[d] 4 He opposes and exalts himself above every so-called god or object of worship, so that he takes his seat in the temple of God, declaring himself to be God. 5 Do you not remember that I told you these things when I was still with you? 6 And you know what is now restraining him, so that he may be revealed when his time comes. 7 For the mystery of lawlessness is already at work, but only until the one who now restrains it is removed. 8 And then the lawless one will be revealed, whom the Lord Jesus[e] will destroy[f] with the breath of his mouth, annihilating him by the manifestation of his coming. 9 The coming of the lawless one is apparent in the working of Satan, who uses all power, signs, lying wonders, 10 and every kind of wicked deception for those who are perishing, because they refused to love the truth and so be saved. 11 For this reason God sends them a powerful delusion, leading them to believe what is false, 12 so that all who have not believed the truth but took pleasure in unrighteousness will be condemned.

13 But we must always give thanks to God for you, brothers and sisters[b] beloved by the Lord, because God chose you as the first fruits[g] for salvation through sanctification by the Spirit and through belief in the truth. 14 For this purpose he called you through our proclamation of the good news,[h] so that you may obtain the glory of our Lord Jesus Christ. 15 So then, brothers and sisters,[b] stand firm and hold fast to the traditions that you were taught by us, either by word of mouth or by our letter.

16 Now may our Lord Jesus Christ himself and God our Father, who loved us and through grace gave us eternal comfort and good hope, 17 comfort your hearts and strengthen them in every good work and word.

3 Finally, brothers and sisters,[b] pray for us, so that the word of the Lord may spread rapidly and be glorified everywhere, just as it is among you, 2 and that we may be rescued from wicked and evil people; for not all have faith. 3 But the Lord is faithful; he will strengthen you and guard you from the evil one.[i] 4 And we have confidence in the Lord concerning you, that you are doing and will go on doing the things that we command. 5 May the Lord direct your hearts to the love of God and to the steadfastness of Christ.

---

[a]Other ancient authorities read *the*   [b]Gk *brothers*   [c]Gk *the man of lawlessness*; other ancient authorities read *the man of sin*   [d]Gk *the son of destruction*   [e]Other ancient authorities lack *Jesus*   [f]Other ancient authorities read *consume*   [g]Other ancient authorities read *from the beginning*   [h]Or *through our gospel*   [i]Or *from evil*

6 Now we command you, beloved,[j] in the name of our Lord Jesus Christ, to keep away from believers who are[k] living in idleness and not according to the tradition that they[l] received from us. 7 For you yourselves know how you ought to imitate us; we were not idle when we were with you, 8 and we did not eat anyone's bread without paying for it; but with toil and labor we worked night and day, so that we might not burden any of you. 9 This was not because we do not have that right, but in order to give you an example to imitate. 10 For even when we were with you, we gave you this command: Anyone unwilling to work should not eat. 11 For we hear that some of you are living in idleness, mere busybodies, not doing any work. 12 Now such persons we command and exhort in the Lord Jesus Christ to do their work qui-etly and to earn their own living. 13 Brothers and sisters,[m] do not be weary in doing what is right.

14 Take note of those who do not obey what we say in this letter; have nothing to do with them, so that they may be ashamed. 15 Do not regard them as enemies, but warn them as believers.[n]

16 Now may the Lord of peace himself give you peace at all times in all ways. The Lord be with all of you.

17 I, Paul, write this greeting with my own hand. This is the mark in every letter of mine; it is the way I write. 18 The grace of our Lord Jesus Christ be with all of you.[o]

[j]Gk brothers [k]Ck from every brother who is [l]Other ancient authorities read you [m]Gk Brothers [n]Gk a brother [o]Other ancient authorities add Amen

The First Letter to Timothy

1 and 2 Timothy and Titus are commonly designated the Pastoral Epistles. Each of these letters purports to be written by the apostle Paul to a person he has chosen to lead one of his churches; the letters contain pastoral advice concerning how these appointed representatives ("pastors") should tend their Christian flocks. Although each epistle presupposes a slightly different situation, the overarching issues are the same: (a) false teachers creating problems for the congregations and (b) the internal organization of the Christian communities.

Because the vocabulary, theological ideas, and presupposed historical contexts of these letters differ so markedly from those of the undisputedly Pauline letters, the majority of scholars today maintain that the Pastoral Epistles did not actually come from Paul's hand, but from a later author of one of his churches, who wrote in the apostle's name to authorize his own opposition to "false" teachers and to sanction his vision of how the church should be organized. Both the rigorous church structure promoted here and the gnostic character of the author's opponents point to a time of composition several decades after Paul's death, possibly near the end of the first century or the beginning of the second.

In order to advance his views, this pseudonymous and otherwise unknown author embedded a plausible historical context within each of his letters. The letter of 1 Timothy presupposes that Paul has left Timothy behind in the city of Ephesus in order to bring the false teachers within the Christian congregation under control (1:3–11), to establish order in the church (2:1–15), and to appoint moral and upright leaders to administer the community's affairs (3:1–13). Most of the letter consists of instructions concerning Christian living and social interaction, with respect, for example, to Christians' treatment of the elderly, widows, and their own leaders, and Christians' disposition toward needless asceticism, material wealth, and heretics who corrupt the truth.

Since these heretics are said to have been enthralled with "myths and endless genealogies" (1:4), to have used the Jewish Scriptures to support their views (1:6), to have demanded strict ascetic practices (4:3), and to have promoted the "contradictions of what is falsely called knowledge" (*gnosis*) (6:20), they may have represented an early form of Jewish-Christian Gnosticism. It may be that some of the prominent women in the congregation were particularly attracted to this perspective; this would explain the author's insistence that women be silenced and brought under control (see 2:11–15 and 5:4–16). In any event, the author of this letter urges his readers to spurn these gnostic teachers and to organize the leadership of the church in such a way as to present a unified front against them.

From the New Revised Standard Version Bible, © 1989.

1 Paul, an apostle of Christ Jesus by the command of God our Savior and of Christ Jesus our hope,

2 To Timothy, my loyal child in the faith:

Grace, mercy, and peace from God the Father and Christ Jesus our Lord.

3 I urge you, as I did when I was on my way to Macedonia, to remain in Ephesus so that you may instruct certain people not to teach any different doctrine, 4 and not to occupy themselves with myths and endless genealogies that promote speculations rather than the divine training[a] that is known by faith. 5 But the aim of such instruction is love that comes from a pure heart, a good conscience, and sincere faith. 6 Some people have deviated from these and turned to meaningless talk, 7 desiring to be teachers of the law, without understanding either what they are saying or the things about which they make assertions.

8 Now we know that the law is good, if one uses it legitimately. 9 This means understanding that the law is laid down not for the innocent but for the lawless and disobedient, for the godless and sinful, for the unholy and profane, for those who kill their father or mother, for murderers, 10 fornicators, sodomites, slave traders, liars, perjurers, and whatever else is contrary to the sound teaching 11 that conforms to the glorious gospel of the blessed God, which he entrusted to me.

12 I am grateful to Christ Jesus our Lord, who has strengthened me, because he judged me faithful and appointed me to his service, 13 even though I was formerly a blasphemer, a persecutor, and a man of violence. But I received mercy because I had acted ignorantly in unbelief, 14 and the grace of our Lord overflowed for me with the faith and love that are in Christ Jesus. 15 The saying is sure and worthy of full acceptance, that Christ Jesus came into the world to save sinners— of whom I am the foremost. 16 But for that very reason I received mercy, so that in me, as the foremost, Jesus Christ might display the utmost patience, making me an example to those who would come to believe in him for eternal life. 17 To the King of the ages, immortal, invisible, the only God, be honor and glory forever and ever.[b] Amen.

18 I am giving you these instructions, Timothy, my child, in accordance with the prophecies made earlier about you, so that by following them you may fight the good fight, 19 having faith and a good conscience. By rejecting conscience, certain persons have suffered shipwreck in the faith; 20 among them are Hymenaeus and Alexander, whom I have turned over to Satan, so that they may learn not to blaspheme.

2 First of all, then, I urge that supplications, prayers, intercessions, and thanksgivings be made for everyone, 2 for kings and all who are in high positions, so that we may lead a quiet and peaceable life in all godliness and dignity. 3 This is right and is acceptable in the sight of God our Savior, 4 who desires everyone to be saved and to come to the knowledge of the truth. 5 For

> there is one God;
> there is also one mediator
>   between God and
>   humankind,
> Christ Jesus, himself human,
> 6   who gave himself a ransom for
>   all

—this was attested at the right time. 7 For this I was appointed a herald and an apostle (I am telling the truth,[c] I am not lying), a teacher of the Gentiles in faith and truth.

8 I desire, then, that in every place the men should pray, lifting up holy hands without anger or argument; 9 also that the women should dress themselves modestly and decently in suitable clothing, not with their hair braided, or with gold, pearls, or expensive clothes, 10 but with good works, as is proper for women who profess reverence for God. 11 Let a woman[d] learn in silence with full submission. 12 I permit no woman[d] to teach or to have authority over a man;[e] she is to keep silent. 13 For Adam was formed first, then Eve; 14 and Adam was not deceived, but the woman was deceived and became a transgressor. 15 Yet she will be saved through childbearing, provided they continue in faith and love and holiness, with modesty.

3 The saying is sure:[f] whoever aspires to the office of bishop[g] desires a noble task.

---

[a]Or *plan* [b]Gk *to the ages of the ages* [c]Other ancient authorities add *in Christ* [d]Or *wife* [e]Or *her husband* [f]Some interpreters place these words at the end of the previous paragraph. Other ancient authorities read *The saying is commonly accepted* [g]Or *overseer*

2 Now a bishop[h] must be above reproach, married only once,[i] temperate, sensible, respectable, hospitable, an apt teacher, 3 not a drunkard, not violent but gentle, not quarrelsome, and not a lover of money. 4 He must manage his own household well, keeping his children submissive and respectful in every way— 5 for if someone does not know how to manage his own household, how can he take care of God's church? 6 He must not be a recent convert, or he may be puffed up with conceit and fall into the condemnation of the devil. 7 Moreover, he must be well thought of by outsiders, so that he may not fall into disgrace and the snare of the devil.

8 Deacons likewise must be serious, not double-tongued, not indulging in much wine, not greedy for money; 9 they must hold fast to the mystery of the faith with a clear conscience. 10 And let them first be tested; then, if they prove themselves blameless, let them serve as deacons. 11 Women[j] likewise must be serious, not slanderers, but temperate, faithful in all things. 12 Let deacons be married only once,[k] and let them manage their children and their households well; 13 for those who serve well as deacons gain a good standing for themselves and great boldness in the faith that is in Christ Jesus.

14 I hope to come to you soon, but I am writing these instructions to you so that, 15 if I am delayed, you may know how one ought to behave in the household of God, which is the church of the living God, the pillar and bulwark of the truth. 16 Without any doubt, the mystery of our religion is great:

> He[l] was revealed in flesh,
> vindicated[m] in spirit,[n]
> seen by angels,
> proclaimed among Gentiles,
> believed in throughout the
> world,
> taken up in glory.

4 Now the Spirit expressly says that in later[o] times some will renounce the faith by paying attention to deceitful spirits and teachings of demons, 2 through the hypocrisy of liars whose consciences are seared with a hot iron. 3 They forbid marriage and demand abstinence from foods, which God created to be received with thanksgiving by those who believe and know the truth. 4 For everything created by God is good, and nothing is to be rejected, provided it is received with thanksgiving; 5 for it is sanctified by God's word and by prayer.

6 If you put these instructions before the brothers and sisters,[p] you will be a good servant[q] of Christ Jesus, nourished on the words of the faith and of the sound teaching that you have followed. 7 Have nothing to do with profane myths and old wives' tales. Train yourself in godliness, 8 for, while physical training is of some value, godliness is valuable in every way, holding promise for both the present life and the life to come. 9 The saying is sure and worthy of full acceptance. 10 For to this end we toil and struggle,[r] because we have our hope set on the living God, who is the Savior of all people, especially of those who believe.

11 These are the things you must insist on and teach. 12 Let no one despise your youth, but set the believers an example in speech and conduct, in love, in faith, in purity. 13 Until I arrive, give attention to the public reading of scripture,[s] to exhorting, to teaching. 14 Do not neglect the gift that is in you, which was given to you through prophecy with the laying on of hands by the council of elders.[t] 15 Put these things into practice, devote yourself to them, so that all may see your progress. 16 Pay close attention to yourself and to your teaching; continue in these things, for in doing this you will save both yourself and your hearers.

5 Do not speak harshly to an older man,[u] but speak to him as to a father, to younger men as brothers, 2 to older women as mothers, to younger women as sisters—with absolute purity.

3 Honor widows who are really widows. 4 If a widow has children or grandchildren, they should first learn their religious duty to their own family and make some repayment to their parents; for this is pleasing in God's sight. 5 The real widow, left alone, has set her hope on God and continues in

---

[h]Or *an overseer* [i]Gk *the husband of one wife* [j]Or *Their wives*, or *Women deacons* [k]Gk *be husbands of one wife* [l]Gk *Who*; other ancient authorities read *God*; others, *Which* [m]Or *justified* [n]Or *by the Spirit* [o]Or *the last* [p]Gk *brothers* [q]Or *deacon* [r]Other ancient authorities read *suffer reproach* [s]Gk *to the reading* [t]Gk *by the presbytery* [u]Or *an elder*, or *a presbyter*

supplications and prayers night and day; 6 but the widow[v] who lives for pleasure is dead even while she lives. 7 Give these commands as well, so that they may be above reproach. 8 And whoever does not provide for relatives, and especially for family members, has denied the faith and is worse than an unbeliever.

9 Let a widow be put on the list if she is not less than sixty years old and has been married only once;[w] 10 she must be well attested for her good works, as one who has brought up children, shown hospitality, washed the saints' feet, helped the afflicted, and devoted herself to doing good in every way. 11 But refuse to put younger widows on the list; for when their sensual desires alienate them from Christ, they want to marry, 12 and so they incur condemnation for having violated their first pledge. 13 Besides that, they learn to be idle, gadding about from house to house; and they are not merely idle, but also gossips and busybodies, saying what they should not say. 14 So I would have younger widows marry, bear children, and manage their households, so as to give the adversary no occasion to revile us. 15 For some have already turned away to follow Satan. 16 If any believing woman[x] has relatives who are really widows, let her assist them; let the church not be burdened, so that it can assist those who are real widows.

17 Let the elders who rule well be considered worthy of double honor,[y] especially those who labor in preaching and teaching; 18 for the scripture says, "You shall not muzzle an ox while it is treading out the grain,"[1] and, "The laborer deserves to be paid."[2] 19 Never accept any accusation against an elder except on the evidence of two or three witnesses. 20 As for those who persist in sin, rebuke them in the presence of all, so that the rest also may stand in fear. 21 In the presence of God and of Christ Jesus and of the elect angels, I warn you to keep these instructions without prejudice, doing nothing on the basis of partiality. 22 Do not ordain[z] anyone hastily, and do not participate in the sins of others; keep yourself pure.

23 No longer drink only water, but take a little wine for the sake of your stomach and your frequent ailments.

24 The sins of some people are conspicuous and precede them to judgment, while the sins of others follow them there. 25 So also good works are conspicuous; and even when they are not, they cannot remain hidden.

6 Let all who are under the yoke of slavery regard their masters as worthy of all honor, so that the name of God and the teaching may not be blasphemed. 2 Those who have believing masters must not be disrespectful to them on the ground that they are members of the church;[a] rather they must serve them all the more, since those who benefit by their service are believers and beloved.[b]

Teach and urge these duties. 3 Whoever teaches otherwise and does not agree with the sound words of our Lord Jesus Christ and the teaching that is in accordance with godliness, 4 is conceited, understanding nothing, and has a morbid craving for controversy and for disputes about words. From these come envy, dissension, slander, base suspicions, 5 and wrangling among those who are depraved in mind and bereft of the truth, imagining that godliness is a means of gain.[c] 6 Of course, there is great gain in godliness combined with contentment; 7 for we brought nothing into the world, so that[d] we can take nothing out of it; 8 but if we have food and clothing, we will be content with these. 9 But those who want to be rich fall into temptation and are trapped by many senseless and harmful desires that plunge people into ruin and destruction. 10 For the love of money is a root of all kinds of evil, and in their eagerness to be rich some have wandered away from the faith and pierced themselves with many pains.

11 But as for you, man of God, shun all this; pursue righteousness, godliness, faith, love, endurance, gentleness. 12 Fight the good fight of the faith; take hold of the eternal life, to which you were called and for which you made[e] the good confession in the presence of many witnesses. 13 In the presence of God, who gives life to all things, and of Christ Jesus, who in his testimony

---

[v]Gk *she* [w]Gk *the wife of one husband* [x]Other ancient authorities read *believing man or woman*; others, *believing man*
[y]Or *compensation* [z]Gk *Do not lay hands on* [a]Gk *are brothers*
[b]Or *since they are believers and beloved, who devote themselves to good deeds* [c]Other ancient authorities add *Withdraw yourself from such people* [d]Other ancient authorities read *world—it is certain that*
[e]Gk *confessed*

[1]Deut 25:4 [2]Matt 10:10; Luke 10:7

before Pontius Pilate made the good confession, I charge you 14 to keep the commandment without spot or blame until the manifestation of our Lord Jesus Christ, 15 which he will bring about at the right time—he who is the blessed and only Sovereign, the King of kings and Lord of lords. 16 It is he alone who has immortality and dwells in unapproachable light, whom no one has ever seen or can see; to him be honor and eternal dominion. Amen.

17 As for those who in the present age are rich, command them not to be haughty, or to set their hopes on the uncertainty of riches, but rather on God who richly provides us with everything for our enjoyment. 18 They are to do good, to be rich in good works, generous, and ready to share, 19 thus storing up for themselves the treasure of a good foundation for the future, so that they may take hold of the life that really is life.

20 Timothy, guard what has been entrusted to you. Avoid the profane chatter and contradictions of what is falsely called knowledge; 21 by professing it some have missed the mark as regards the faith.

Grace be with you.[f]

---

[f]The Greek word for *you* here is plural; in other ancient authorities it is singular. Other ancient authorities add *Amen*

The Second Letter to Timothy

Even though 2 Timothy differs from the other Pastoral Epistles in content and tone, it appears to have been written by the same pseudonymous author (see the introduction to 1 Timothy). The vocabulary and writing style are similar to those of 1 Timothy (cf. 1 Tim 1:2 and 2 Tim 1:2), and the concerns for the administration of the church and the weeding out of false teachers are still to the fore.

Unlike in the other Pastoral Epistles, "Paul" in this letter is in prison in Rome (1:8, 16–17), expecting soon to be put to death after a second judicial proceeding (4:6–8, 17; the first one evidently did not go well). He writes Timothy not only to encourage him in his pastoral duties and to urge him, yet again, to contend with the false teachers in his church (2:14–19), but also to ask him to come to Rome as soon as possible with some of the apostle's personal belongings (4:13, 21).

Timothy appears to be portrayed here as a third-generation Christian who was preceded in his faith by his mother Eunice and grandmother Lois (1:5). He is said to have been trained in the Scriptures from his childhood (3:15); as an adult, he became a companion of "Paul" and collaborated with him in his mission to Asia Minor (3:10–11). He was ordained to the ministry through a ceremony of laying on of hands (1:6; 4:1–5). As one of Paul's few trusted companions (see 1:16–17; 4:10–18), he was put in charge of the major church of Ephesus and especially commissioned with overcoming those who were leading the saints astray with their idle talk and corrupt lives (2:16–18, 23–26; 3:1–9; 4:3–5).

Because this letter has a far more personal tone to it than the other Pastoral Epistles, some scholars have maintained that it has been interspersed with fragments of Paul's genuine correspondence. Recently, though, scholars have come to think that its personal character relates more closely to its unique genre; unlike 1 Timothy and Titus, 2 Timothy represents the "last will and testament" of the apostle Paul, a kind of letter that we know about from other pseudonymous writings, especially Jewish, of the period. Here the apostle bids his farewell to a person dear to him, extending his final blessings, warnings, and exhortations, and urging his reader(s) to endure suffering with the same fortitude and faithfulness that he himself has displayed.

1 Paul, an apostle of Christ Jesus by the will of God, for the sake of the promise of life that is in Christ Jesus,

2 To Timothy, my beloved child:

Grace, mercy, and peace from God the Father and Christ Jesus our Lord.

3 I am grateful to God—whom I worship with a clear conscience, as my ancestors did—when I remember you constantly in my prayers night and day. 4 Recalling your tears, I long to see you so that I may be filled with joy. 5 I am reminded of your sincere faith, a faith that lived first in your

grandmother Lois and your mother Eunice and now, I am sure, lives in you. 6 For this reason I remind you to rekindle the gift of God that is within you through the laying on of my hands; 7 for God did not give us a spirit of cowardice, but rather a spirit of power and of love and of self-discipline.

8 Do not be ashamed, then, of the testimony about our Lord or of me his prisoner, but join with me in suffering for the gospel, relying on the power of God, 9 who saved us and called us with a holy calling, not according to our works but according to his own purpose and grace. This grace was given to us in Christ Jesus before the ages began, 10 but it has now been revealed through the appearing of our Savior Christ Jesus, who abolished death and brought life and immortality to light through the gospel. 11 For this gospel I was appointed a herald and an apostle and a teacher,[a] 12 and for this reason I suffer as I do. But I am not ashamed, for I know the one in whom I have put my trust, and I am sure that he is able to guard until that day what I have entrusted to him.[b] 13 Hold to the standard of sound teaching that you have heard from me, in the faith and love that are in Christ Jesus. 14 Guard the good treasure entrusted to you, with the help of the Holy Spirit living in us.

15 You are aware that all who are in Asia have turned away from me, including Phygelus and Hermogenes. 16 May the Lord grant mercy to the household of Onesiphorus, because he often refreshed me and was not ashamed of my chain; 17 when he arrived in Rome, he eagerly[c] searched for me and found me 18 —may the Lord grant that he will find mercy from the Lord on that day! And you know very well how much service he rendered in Ephesus.

2 You then, my child, be strong in the grace that is in Christ Jesus; 2 and what you have heard from me through many witnesses entrust to faithful people who will be able to teach others as well. 3 Share in suffering like a good soldier of Christ Jesus. 4 No one serving in the army gets entangled in everyday affairs; the soldier's aim is to please the enlisting officer. 5 And in the case of an athlete, no one is crowned without competing according to the rules. 6 It is the farmer who does the work who ought to have the first share of the crops. 7 Think over what I say, for the Lord will give you understanding in all things.

8 Remember Jesus Christ, raised from the dead, a descendant of David—that is my gospel, 9 for which I suffer hardship, even to the point of being chained like a criminal. But the word of God is not chained. 10 Therefore I endure everything for the sake of the elect, so that they may also obtain the salvation that is in Christ Jesus, with eternal glory. 11 The saying is sure:

If we have died with him, we will
    also live with him;
12   if we endure, we will also reign
      with him;
    if we deny him, he will also deny
      us;
13   if we are faithless, he remains
      faithful—
    for he cannot deny himself.

14 Remind them of this, and warn them before God[d] that they are to avoid wrangling over words, which does no good but only ruins those who are listening. 15 Do your best to present yourself to God as one approved by him, a worker who has no need to be ashamed, rightly explaining the word of truth. 16 Avoid profane chatter, for it will lead people into more and more impiety, 17 and their talk will spread like gangrene. Among them are Hymenaeus and Philetus, 18 who have swerved from the truth by claiming that the resurrection has already taken place. They are upsetting the faith of some. 19 But God's firm foundation stands, bearing this inscription: "The Lord knows those who are his,"[1] and, "Let everyone who calls on the name of the Lord turn away from wickedness."[2]

20 In a large house there are utensils not only of gold and silver but also of wood and clay, some for special use, some for ordinary. 21 All who cleanse themselves of the things I have mentioned[e] will become special utensils, dedicated and useful to the owner of the house, ready for every good work. 22 Shun youthful passions and pursue righteousness, faith, love, and peace, along with those who

---

[a]Other ancient authorities add *of the Gentiles* [b]Or *what has been entrusted to me* [c]Or *promptly* [d]Other ancient authorities read *the Lord* [e]Gk *of these things*

[1]Num 16:5 [2]Num 16:26; Job 36:10; Isa 26:13

call on the Lord from a pure heart. 23 Have nothing to do with stupid and senseless controversies; you know that they breed quarrels. 24 And the Lord's servant[f] must not be quarrelsome but kindly to everyone, an apt teacher, patient, 25 correcting opponents with gentleness. God may perhaps grant that they will repent and come to know the truth, 26 and that they may escape from the snare of the devil, having been held captive by him to do his will.[g]

3 You must understand this, that in the last days distressing times will come. 2 For people will be lovers of themselves, lovers of money, boasters, arrogant, abusive, disobedient to their parents, ungrateful, unholy, 3 inhuman, implacable, slanderers, profligates, brutes, haters of good, 4 treacherous, reckless, swollen with conceit, lovers of pleasure rather than lovers of God, 5 holding to the outward form of godliness but denying its power. Avoid them! 6 For among them are those who make their way into households and captivate silly women, overwhelmed by their sins and swayed by all kinds of desires, 7 who are always being instructed and can never arrive at a knowledge of the truth. 8 As Jannes and Jambres opposed Moses, so these people, of corrupt mind and counterfeit faith, also oppose the truth. 9 But they will not make much progress, because, as in the case of those two men,[h] their folly will become plain to everyone.

10 Now you have observed my teaching, my conduct, my aim in life, my faith, my patience, my love, my steadfastness, 11 my persecutions, and my suffering the things that happened to me in Antioch, Iconium, and Lystra. What persecutions I endured! Yet the Lord rescued me from all of them. 12 Indeed, all who want to live a godly life in Christ Jesus will be persecuted. 13 But wicked people and impostors will go from bad to worse, deceiving others and being deceived. 14 But as for you, continue in what you have learned and firmly believed, knowing from whom you learned it, 15 and how from childhood you have known the sacred writings that are able to instruct you for salvation through faith in Christ Jesus. 16 All scripture is inspired by God and is[i] useful for teaching, for reproof, for correction, and for training in righteousness, 17 so that everyone who be-longs to God may be proficient, equipped for every good work.

4 In the presence of God and of Christ Jesus, who is to judge the living and the dead, and in view of his appearing and his kingdom, I solemnly urge you: 2 proclaim the message; be persistent whether the time is favorable or unfavorable; convince, rebuke, and encourage, with the utmost patience in teaching. 3 For the time is coming when people will not put up with sound doctrine, but having itching ears, they will accumulate for themselves teachers to suit their own desires, 4 and will turn away from listening to the truth and wander away to myths. 5 As for you, always be sober, endure suffering, do the work of an evangelist, carry out your ministry fully.

6 As for me, I am already being poured out as a libation, and the time of my departure has come. 7 I have fought the good fight, I have finished the race, I have kept the faith. 8 From now on there is reserved for me the crown of righteousness, which the Lord, the righteous judge, will give me on that day, and not only to me but also to all who have longed for his appearing.

9 Do your best to come to me soon, 10 for Demas, in love with this present world, has deserted me and gone to Thessalonica; Crescens has gone to Galatia,[j] Titus to Dalmatia. 11 Only Luke is with me. Get Mark and bring him with you, for he is useful in my ministry. 12 I have sent Tychicus to Ephesus. 13 When you come, bring the cloak that I left with Carpus at Troas, also the books, and above all the parchments. 14 Alexander the coppersmith did me great harm; the Lord will pay him back for his deeds. 15 You also must beware of him, for he strongly opposed our message.

16 At my first defense no one came to my support, but all deserted me. May it not be counted against them! 17 But the Lord stood by me and gave me strength, so that through me the message might be fully proclaimed and all the Gentiles might hear it. So I was rescued from the lion's mouth. 18 The Lord will rescue me from every

---

[f]Gk *slave*   [g]Or *by him, to do his* (that is, God's) *will*   [h]Gk lacks *two men*   [i]Or *Every scripture inspired by God is also*   [j]Other ancient authorities read *Gaul*

evil attack and save me for his heavenly kingdom. To him be the glory forever and ever. Amen.

19 Greet Prisca and Aquila, and the household of Onesiphorus. 20 Erastus remained in Corinth; Trophimus I left ill in Miletus. 21 Do your best to come before winter. Eubulus sends greetings to you, as do Pudens and Linus and Claudia and all the brothers and sisters.[k]

22 The Lord be with your spirit. Grace be with you.[l]

[k] Gk *all the brothers* [l] The Greek word for *you* here is plural. Other ancient authorities add *Amen*

The Letter to Titus

There can be little doubt that the Letter to Titus was produced by the same pseudonymous author who wrote the two other Pastoral Epistles (see the introduction to 1 Timothy). In many ways Titus seems like a condensed version of 1 Timothy: its overarching concern with church organization, its lists of qualifications for church leaders, and the nature of its moral instructions are very much the same.

The situation presupposed in this letter is that "Paul" has left his entrusted colleague Titus behind on the island of Crete to appoint Christian elders in the churches there (1:4–9). He is now writing to urge Titus to correct the erroneous ideas promoted by false teachers; as in 1 Timothy, these teachings involve complicated "mythologies" that confuse the faithful (1:10–16), "genealogies," and "quarrels about the law" (3:9). Here again, then, the opponents may have represented an early form of Jewish-Christian Gnosticism. Titus is not to argue with such people, but to warn them twice to change their views and afterwards simply to ignore them (3:9–11). It appears that, as with 1 Timothy, the tight church organization promoted by the letter is designed to provide a unified front against those who advance such dangerous opinions.

A good portion of the epistle provides advice to various social groups within the Christian congregation, "older men" (2:2), "older women" (2:3), "younger women" (2:4–5), "younger men" (2:6–8), and "slaves" (2:9–10). Near the conclusion of the letter, the advice becomes more general in nature, involving basic admonitions to Christians to engage in the kind of moral behavior that is appropriate for those who have been saved (3:1–7).

1 Paul, a servant[a] of God and an apostle of Jesus Christ, for the sake of the faith of God's elect and the knowledge of the truth that is in accordance with godliness, 2 in the hope of eternal life that God, who never lies, promised before the ages began— 3 in due time he revealed his word through the proclamation with which I have been entrusted by the command of God our Savior,

4 To Titus, my loyal child in the faith we share:

Grace[b] and peace from God the Father and Christ Jesus our Savior.

5 I left you behind in Crete for this reason, so that you should put in order what remained to be done, and should appoint elders in every town, as I directed you: 6 someone who is blameless, married only once,[c] whose children are believers, not accused of debauchery and not rebellious. 7 For a bishop,[d] as God's steward, must be blameless; he must not be arrogant or quick-tempered or addicted to wine or violent or greedy for gain; 8 but he must be hospitable, a lover of goodness, prudent, upright, devout, and self-controlled. 9 He must have a firm grasp of the word that is trustworthy in accordance with the teaching, so that he may be able both to preach with sound doctrine and to refute those who contradict it.

10 There are also many rebellious people, idle talkers and deceivers, especially those of the circumcision; 11 they must be silenced, since they are upsetting whole families by teaching for sor-

[a]Gk slave   [b]Other ancient authorities read Grace, mercy,
[c]Gk husband of one wife   [d]Or an overseer

did gain what it is not right to teach. 12 It was one of them, their very own prophet, who said,

> "Cretans are always liars, vicious
> brutes, lazy gluttons."

13 That testimony is true. For this reason rebuke them sharply, so that they may become sound in the faith, 14 not paying attention to Jewish myths or to commandments of those who reject the truth. 15 To the pure all things are pure, but to the corrupt and unbelieving nothing is pure. Their very minds and consciences are corrupted. 16 They profess to know God, but they deny him by their actions. They are detestable, disobedient, unfit for any good work.

2 But as for you, teach what is consistent with sound doctrine. 2 Tell the older men to be temperate, serious, prudent, and sound in faith, in love, and in endurance.

3 Likewise, tell the older women to be reverent in behavior, not to be slanderers or slaves to drink; they are to teach what is good, 4 so that they may encourage the young women to love their husbands, to love their children, 5 to be self-controlled, chaste, good managers of the household, kind, being submissive to their husbands, so that the word of God may not be discredited.

6 Likewise, urge the younger men to be self-controlled. 7 Show yourself in all respects a model of good works, and in your teaching show integrity, gravity, 8 and sound speech that cannot be censured; then any opponent will be put to shame, having nothing evil to say of us.

9 Tell slaves to be submissive to their masters and to give satisfaction in every respect; they are not to talk back, 10 not to pilfer, but to show complete and perfect fidelity, so that in everything they may be an ornament to the doctrine of God our Savior.

11 For the grace of God has appeared, bringing salvation to all,[e] 12 training us to renounce impiety and worldly passions, and in the present age to live lives that are self-controlled, upright, and godly, 13 while we wait for the blessed hope and the manifestation of the glory of our great God and Savior,[f] Jesus Christ. 14 He it is who gave himself for us that he might redeem us from all iniquity and purify for himself a people of his own who are zealous for good deeds.

15 Declare these things; exhort and reprove with all authority.[g] Let no one look down on you.

3 Remind them to be subject to rulers and authorities, to be obedient, to be ready for every good work, 2 to speak evil of no one, to avoid quarreling, to be gentle, and to show every courtesy to everyone. 3 For we ourselves were once foolish, disobedient, led astray, slaves to various passions and pleasures, passing our days in malice and envy, despicable, hating one another. 4 But when the goodness and loving kindness of God our Savior appeared, 5 he saved us, not because of any works of righteousness that we had done, but according to his mercy, through the water[h] of rebirth and renewal by the Holy Spirit. 6 This Spirit he poured out on us richly through Jesus Christ our Savior, 7 so that, having been justified by his grace, we might become heirs according to the hope of eternal life. 8 The saying is sure.

I desire that you insist on these things, so that those who have come to believe in God may be careful to devote themselves to good works; these things are excellent and profitable to everyone. 9 But avoid stupid controversies, genealogies, dissensions, and quarrels about the law, for they are unprofitable and worthless. 10 After a first and second admonition, have nothing more to do with anyone who causes divisions, 11 since you know that such a person is perverted and sinful, being self-condemned.

12 When I send Artemas to you, or Tychicus, do your best to come to me at Nicopolis, for I have decided to spend the winter there. 13 Make every effort to send Zenas the lawyer and Apollos on their way, and see that they lack nothing. 14 And let people learn to devote themselves to good works in order to meet urgent needs, so that they may not be unproductive.

15 All who are with me send greetings to you. Greet those who love us in the faith.

Grace be with all of you.[i]

---

[e]Or *has appeared to all, bringing salvation* [f]Or *of the great God and our Savior* [g]Gk *commandment* [h]Gk *washing* [i]Other ancient authorities add *Amen*

The Letter to Philemon

No more than a page in length, Philemon is the only undisputed Pauline letter written to an individual. Rather than addressing practical and doctrinal problems that had arisen in the church, the letter concerns a single man, the runaway slave Onesimus, and his fate at the hands of his master, a Christian named Philemon.

At the time of his writing, Paul is in prison (v. 1), although it is impossible to determine whether he is in Ephesus, Rome, or elsewhere. While in prison, he has seen and converted Onesimus, who has become his servant (v. 10). He is now sending him back to his legal owner, Philemon, whom Paul knows well, evidently as one of his own converts (v. 19).

Tradition says that Philemon lived in the small town of Colossae in Asia Minor. Paul wants him to receive Onesimus back without punishing him or charging him for the financial loss that he incurred (he may have run off with some of his master's property; v. 18). He appeals to Philemon's personal indebtedness to him, and informs him that he himself will make up any loss he has suffered, possibly in anticipation that this will not be necessary (v. 19). Onesimus, Paul informs Philemon, has proved "useful" to him and can still be "useful" to Philemon (v. 11). Here Paul is playing on words. The name Onesimus means "useful" in Greek.

Scholars have sometimes had difficulty explaining how Onesimus and Paul happened to meet. Given the enormity of the empire, it seems unlikely that Paul and the slave of a former convert would end up in the same jail cell by chance. The problem has been resolved by recent studies of ancient slavery, which have shown that it was an accepted practice for mistreated or runaway slaves to appeal to a respected friend of their master for help in pleading their cause. Evidently, Onesimus took advantage of this practice. When he met Paul, however, he heard the same gospel that had converted his master and, like him, came then to believe in Christ.

Onesimus's conversion made it easier for him to return home without penalty, for Paul could now encourage Philemon to receive him "no longer as a slave but more than a slave, a beloved brother" (v. 16). It may be that Paul hopes for even something more, that Philemon will set Onesimus free or, possibly, give him over to the apostle for his own ongoing work (vv. 20–21).

1 Paul, a prisoner of Christ Jesus, and Timothy our brother,[a]

To Philemon our dear friend and co-worker, 2 to Apphia our sister,[b] to Archippus our fellow soldier, and to the church in your house:

3 Grace to you and peace from God our Father and the Lord Jesus Christ.

4 When I remember you[c] in my prayers, I always thank my God 5 because I hear of your love for all the saints and your faith toward the Lord Jesus. 6 I pray that the sharing of your faith may become effective when you perceive all the good that we[d] may do for Christ. 7 I have indeed received much joy and encouragement from your love, because the hearts of the saints have been refreshed through you, my brother.

8 For this reason, though I am bold enough in Christ to command you to do your duty, 9 yet I would rather appeal to you on the basis of love— and I, Paul, do this as an old man, and now also as a prisoner of Christ Jesus.[e] 10 I am appealing to you for my child, Onesimus, whose father I have become during my imprisonment. 11 Formerly he was useless to you, but now he is indeed useful[f] both to you and to me. 12 I am sending him, that is, my own heart, back to you. 13 I wanted to keep him with me, so that he might be of service to me in your place during my imprisonment for the gospel; 14 but I preferred to do nothing without your consent, in order that your good deed might be voluntary and not something forced. 15 Perhaps this is the reason he was separated from you for a while, so that you might have him back forever, 16 no longer as a slave but more than a slave, a beloved brother—especially to me but how much more to you, both in the flesh and in the Lord.

17 So if you consider me your partner, welcome him as you would welcome me. 18 If he has wronged you in any way, or owes you anything, charge that to my account. 19 I, Paul, am writing this with my own hand: I will repay it. I say nothing about your owing me even your own self. 20 Yes, brother, let me have this benefit from you in the Lord! Refresh my heart in Christ. 21 Confident of your obedience, I am writing to you, knowing that you will do even more than I say.

22 One thing more—prepare a guest room for me, for I am hoping through your prayers to be restored to you.

23 Epaphras, my fellow prisoner in Christ Jesus, sends greetings to you,[g] 24 and so do Mark, Aristarchus, Demas, and Luke, my fellow workers.

25 The grace of the Lord Jesus Christ be with your spirit.[h]

[a]Gk the brother [b]Gk the sister [c]From verse 4 through verse 21, you is singular [d]Other ancient authorities read you (plural) [e]Or as an ambassador of Christ Jesus, and now also his prisoner [f]The name Onesimus means useful or (compare verse 20) beneficial [g]Here you is singular [h]Other ancient authorities add Amen

The Third Letter to the Corinthians

As its name suggests, *3 Corinthians* is a letter pseudonymously penned in Paul's name, ostensibly to the Christian community that he founded in Corinth. Near the end of the second century, the letter came to be included in the narrative of Paul's missionary travels known as the *Acts of Paul.* The letter itself, however, may have been in circulation at an earlier date. It addressed theological issues known already to have been debated during the first half of the second century, and many of its views are reminiscent of those advanced by the Pastoral Epistles at the end of the first century and by Ignatius of Antioch at the beginning of the second. The letter may have been composed, then, sometime in the early part of the second century.

Within the *Acts of Paul, 3 Corinthians* represents Paul's response to a letter sent to him by the Corinthian congregation, in which they express their concern over the views of two false teachers in their midst, Simon and Cleobius. These heretics have led members of the church astray into a form of gnostic teaching that maintains that the true God did not create the world or inspire the Jewish prophets, that there is to be no future fleshly resurrection, and that Jesus himself was not a fleshly human being, born of a human mother.

In opposition to these teachings, *3 Corinthians* emphasizes the fleshly nature both of Jesus and of the salvation that he brings; the flesh is not destined for annihilation but for redemption. Thus Jesus really was "born to Mary," after the Holy Spirit came into her from heaven (v. 5; cf. vv. 12–14); Jesus came into this world "to redeem all flesh through his own flesh" (v. 6; cf. vv. 14–15); and there is to be a resurrection of all flesh from the dead (vv. 6, 24, 17, 33).

All these things had been taught, according to the author, through the Jewish prophets (vv. 9–10), the earliest apostles (v. 4), and Paul himself. Those who accept this teaching will "receive a reward" by being raised bodily from the dead for eternal life (v. 36); but those who turn away from it are destined for the destruction of fire (vv. 37–38).

1 Paul, the prisoner of Jesus Christ, to the brethren at Corinth—greeting! 2 Being in many afflictions, I marvel not that the teachings of the evil one had such rapid success. 3 For my Lord Jesus Christ will quickly come, since he is rejected by those who falsify his teaching. 4 For I delivered to you first of all what I received from the apostles before me who were always with Jesus Christ, 5 that our Lord Jesus Christ was born of Mary of the seed of David, the Father having sent the spir-

"The Third Letter to the Corinthians," from *The Apocryphal New Testament,* translated by J. K. Elliott. © Oxford University Press 1993. Reprinted by permission of Oxford University Press.

it from heaven into her 6 that he might come into this world and save all flesh by his own flesh and that he might raise us in the flesh from the dead as he has presented himself to us as our example. 7 And since man is created by his Father, 8 for this reason was he sought by him when he was lost, to become alive by adoption. 9 For the almighty God, maker of heaven and earth, sent the prophets first to the Jews to deliver them from their sins, 10 for he wished to save the house of Israel; therefore he took from the spirit of Christ and poured it out upon the prophets who proclaimed the true worship of God for a long period of time. 11 For the wicked prince who wished to be God himself laid his hands on them and killed them and bound all flesh of man to his pleasure. 12 But the almighty God, being just, and not wishing to repudiate his creation had mercy 13 and sent his Spirit into Mary the Galilean, 15 that the evil one might be conquered by the same flesh by which he held sway, and be convinced that he is not God. 16 For by his own body Jesus Christ saved all flesh, 17 presenting in his own body a temple of righteousness 18 through which we are saved. 19 They who follow them are not children of righteousness but of wrath, who despise the wisdom of God and in their disbelief assert that heaven and earth and all that is in them are not a work of God. 20 They have the accursed belief of the serpent. 21 Turn away from them and keep aloof from their teaching. 24 And those who say that there is no resurrection of the flesh shall have no resurrection,

25 for they do not believe him who had thus risen. 26 For they do not know, O Corinthians, about the sowing of wheat or some other grain that it is cast naked into the ground and having perished rises up again by the will of God in a body and clothed. 27 And he not only raises the body which is sown, but blesses it manifold. 28 And if one will not take the parable of the seeds 29 let him look at Jonah, the son of Amathios who, being unwilling to preach to the Ninevites, was swallowed up by the whale. 30 And after three days and three nights God heard the prayer of Jonah out of deepest hell, and nothing was corrupted, not even a hair nor an eyelid. 31 How much more will he raise you up, who have believed in Christ Jesus, as he himself was raised up. 32 When a corpse was thrown on the bones of the prophet Elisha by one of the children of Israel the corpse rose from death; how much more shall you rise up on that day with a whole body, after you have been thrown upon the body and bones and Spirit of the Lord. 34 If, however, you receive anything else let no one trouble me, 35 for I have these bonds on me that I may win Christ, and I bear his marks that I may attain to the resurrection of the dead. 36 And whoever accepts this rule which we have received by the blessed prophets and the holy gospel, shall receive a reward, 37 but for whomsoever deviates from this rule fire shall be for him and for those who preceded him therein 38 since they are Godless people, a generation of vipers. 39 Resist them in the power of the Lord. 40 Peace be with you.

GENERAL EPISTLES
AND OTHER EARLY
CHRISTIAN WRITINGS

The Letter to the Hebrews

The book traditionally called "Paul's Letter to the Hebrews" is probably misnamed. It was not written by Paul, it is not a letter, and it was evidently not addressed to Jews.

The book was eventually accepted as canonical only when enough fourth-century Christian leaders became convinced that Paul had written it; the book itself, however, makes no such claim. Already in antiquity there were scholars who knew that Paul did not write it. The writing style and vocabulary differ from his, some of its important terms (e.g., "faith," 11:1) mean something other than in Paul's letters, and its major concerns are issues Paul never discusses, let alone emphasizes (e.g., Jesus' superiority to the Jewish priests and the Jewish sacrificial system).

Although the book has an epistolary conclusion, it does not begin as a letter. There is, for example, no prescript that names its author or addressees. Instead the book appears to be a sermon addressed by a Christian preacher to his congregation (13:22). The congregation may have been comprised largely of Gentile converts to Christianity: in the course of his exhortation, when the preacher recalls the instructions they had received upon first coming into the fold, he mentions faith in God, the resurrection of the dead, and eternal judgment (6:1–2). It seems unlikely that converts from Judaism would have needed instruction about such matters.

The sermon is principally concerned with the superiority of Christ to the Jewish religion. According to this author, the Jewish Law is partial and imperfect, unable to bring people into a right standing before God. The inadequacy of Judaism, he maintains, is recognized by the Jewish Scriptures themselves, which state that God had planned all along to provide a "new covenant" to do what the "old" one could not (8:7–13). This old covenant was foreshadowed in the legislation given by Moses (8:5, 10:1), but has been fulfilled only in the work of Christ. Christ, in fact, is superior to the religion of Judaism: he surpasses the Jewish prophets (1:1–3), the Jewish lawgiver Moses (3:1–6), the Jewish priests (chaps. 4–7), and the Jewish sacrifices (chap. 10).

The point of this exposition is a practical one. Some members of the preacher's community had forsaken the Christian church for the synagogue, or at least were being tempted to do so, perhaps in an effort to avoid persecution (see 10:32–34). The author wants to stop them. For him, Christians would be foolish to turn to the "imperfect" religion of Judaism after they have already experienced the full reality of Christ. Indeed, to do so would be to call the wrath of God down upon themselves (6:1–6; 10:26–29).

We do not know when this book was written. Given the fact that the references to Judaism are drawn exclusively from the Jewish Scriptures rather than from cultic practices of the first century, many scholars prefer a date after the Jerusalem Temple was destroyed (70 C.E.), possibly sometime nearer the end of the first century.

From the New Revised Standard Version Bible, © 1989.

1 Long ago God spoke to our ancestors in many and various ways by the prophets, 2 but in these last days he has spoken to us by a Son,[a] whom he appointed heir of all things, through whom he also created the worlds. 3 He is the reflection of God's glory and the exact imprint of God's very being, and he sustains[b] all things by his powerful word. When he had made purification for sins, he sat down at the right hand of the Majesty on high, 4 having become as much superior to angels as the name he has inherited is more excellent than theirs.

5 For to which of the angels did God ever say,
"You are my Son;
today I have begotten you"?[1]
Or again,
"I will be his Father,
and he will be my Son"?[2]
6 And again, when he brings the firstborn into the world, he says,
"Let all God's angels worship
him."[3]
7 Of the angels he says,
"He makes his angels winds,
and his servants flames of fire."[4]
8 But of the Son he says,
"Your throne, O God, is[c] forever
and ever,
and the righteous scepter is the
scepter of your[d] kingdom.[5]
9   You have loved righteousness and
hated wickedness;
therefore God, your God, has
anointed you
with the oil of gladness beyond
your companions."[5]
10 And,
"In the beginning, Lord, you
founded the earth,
and the heavens are the work of
your hands;
11   they will perish, but you remain;
they will all wear out like
clothing;
12   like a cloak you will roll them up,
and like clothing[e] they will be
changed.
But you are the same,
and your years will never end."[6]

13 But to which of the angels has he ever said,
"Sit at my right hand
until I make your enemies a
footstool for your feet"?[7]
14 Are not all angels[f] spirits in the divine service, sent to serve for the sake of those who are to inherit salvation?

2 Therefore we must pay greater attention to what we have heard, so that we do not drift away from it. 2 For if the message declared through angels was valid, and every transgression or disobedience received a just penalty, 3 how can we escape if we neglect so great a salvation? It was declared at first through the Lord, and it was attested to us by those who heard him, 4 while God added his testimony by signs and wonders and various miracles, and by gifts of the Holy Spirit, distributed according to his will.

5 Now God[g] did not subject the coming world, about which we are speaking, to angels. 6 But someone has testified somewhere,
"What are human beings that you
are mindful of them,[h]
or mortals, that you care for
them?[i]
7   You have made them for a little
while lower[j] than the
angels;
you have crowned them with
glory and honor,[k]
8   subjecting all things under their
feet."[8]
Now in subjecting all things to them, God[g] left nothing outside their control. As it is, we do not yet see everything in subjection to them, 9 but we do see Jesus, who for a little while was made lower[l] than the angels, now crowned with glory and honor because of the suffering of death, so that by the grace of God[m] he might taste death for everyone. 10 It was fitting that God,[g] for whom and

---

[a]Or *the Son* [b]Or *bears along* [c]Or *God is your throne* [d]Other ancient authorities read *his* [e]Other ancient authorities lack *like clothing* [f]Gk *all of them* [g]Gk *he* [h]Gk *What is man that you are mindful of him?* [i]Gk *or the son of man that you care for him?* In the Hebrew of Psalm 8.4-6 both *man* and *son of man* refer to all humankind [j]Or *them only a little lower* [k]Other ancient authorities add *and set them over the works of your hands* [l]Or *who was made a little lower* [m]Other ancient authorities read *apart from God*

---

[1]Ps 2:7 [2]2 Sam 7:14; 1 Chron 17:13 [3]Deut 32:43 [4]Ps 104:4 [5]Ps 45:6–7 [6]Ps 102:25–27 [7]Ps 110:1 [8]Ps 8:4–6

through whom all things exist, in bringing many children to glory, should make the pioneer of their salvation perfect through sufferings. 11 For the one who sanctifies and those who are sanctified all have one Father.[n] For this reason Jesus[o] is not ashamed to call them brothers and sisters,[p] 12 saying,

> "I will proclaim your name to my
> brothers and sisters,[p]
> in the midst of the congregation
> I will praise you."[9]

13 And again,

> "I will put my trust in him."

And again,

> "Here am I and the children
> whom God has given me."[10]

14 Since, therefore, the children share flesh and blood, he himself likewise shared the same things, so that through death he might destroy the one who has the power of death, that is, the devil, 15 and free those who all their lives were held in slavery by the fear of death. 16 For it is clear that he did not come to help angels, but the descendants of Abraham. 17 Therefore he had to become like his brothers and sisters[p] in every respect, so that he might be a merciful and faithful high priest in the service of God, to make a sacrifice of atonement for the sins of the people. 18 Because he himself was tested by what he suffered, he is able to help those who are being tested.

3 Therefore, brothers and sisters,[p] holy partners in a heavenly calling, consider that Jesus, the apostle and high priest of our confession, 2 was faithful to the one who appointed him, just as Moses also "was faithful in all[q] God's[r] house."[11] 3 Yet Jesus[s] is worthy of more glory than Moses, just as the builder of a house has more honor than the house itself. 4 (For every house is built by someone, but the builder of all things is God.) 5 Now Moses was faithful in all God's[r] house as a servant, to testify to the things that would be spoken later. 6 Christ, however, was faithful over God's[r] house as a son, and we are his house if we hold firm[t] the confidence and the pride that belong to hope.

7 Therefore, as the Holy Spirit says,

> "Today, if you hear his voice,
> 8   do not harden your hearts as in
>   the rebellion,
>   as on the day of testing in the
>   wilderness,
> 9   where your ancestors put me to
>   the test,
>   though they had seen my works
> 10   for forty years.
>   Therefore I was angry with that
>   generation,
>   and I said, 'They always go astray
>   in their hearts,
>   and they have not known my
>   ways.'
> 11   As in my anger I swore,
>   'They will not enter my rest.'"[12]

12 Take care, brothers and sisters,[p] that none of you may have an evil, unbelieving heart that turns away from the living God. 13 But exhort one another every day, as long as it is called "today," so that none of you may be hardened by the deceitfulness of sin. 14 For we have become partners of Christ, if only we hold our first confidence firm to the end. 15 As it is said,

> "Today, if you hear his voice,
>   do not harden your hearts as in
>   the rebellion."[13]

16 Now who were they who heard and yet were rebellious? Was it not all those who left Egypt under the leadership of Moses? 17 But with whom was he angry forty years? Was it not those who sinned, whose bodies fell in the wilderness? 18 And to whom did he swear that they would not enter his rest, if not to those who were disobedient? 19 So we see that they were unable to enter because of unbelief.

4 Therefore, while the promise of entering his rest is still open, let us take care that none of you should seem to have failed to reach it. 2 For indeed the good news came to us just as to them; but the message they heard did not benefit them, because they were not united by faith with those who listened.[u] 3 For we who have believed enter that rest, just as God[v] has said,

---

[n]Gk *are all of one*   [o]Gk *he*   [p]Gk *brothers*   [q]Other ancient authorities lack *all*   [r]Gk *his*   [s]Gk *this one*   [t]Other ancient authorities add *to the end*   [u]Other ancient authorities read *it did not meet with faith in those who listened*   [v]Gk *he*

[9]Ps 22:22   [10]Isa 8:17–18   [11]Num 12:7   [12]Ps 95:7–11   [13]Ps 95:7–8

"As in my anger I swore,
'They shall not enter my rest,'"[14]
though his works were finished at the foundation of the world. 4 For in one place it speaks about the seventh day as follows, "And God rested on the seventh day from all his works."[15] 5 And again in this place it says, "They shall not enter my rest."[16] 6 Since therefore it remains open for some to enter it, and those who formerly received the good news failed to enter because of disobedience, 7 again he sets a certain day—"today"—saying through David much later, in the words already quoted,

"Today, if you hear his voice,
do not harden your hearts."[17]

8 For if Joshua had given them rest, God[w] would not speak later about another day. 9 So then, a sabbath rest still remains for the people of God; 10 for those who enter God's rest also cease from their labors as God did from his. 11 Let us therefore make every effort to enter that rest, so that no one may fall through such disobedience as theirs.

12 Indeed, the word of God is living and active, sharper than any two-edged sword, piercing until it divides soul from spirit, joints from marrow; it is able to judge the thoughts and intentions of the heart. 13 And before him no creature is hidden, but all are naked and laid bare to the eyes of the one to whom we must render an account.

14 Since, then, we have a great high priest who has passed through the heavens, Jesus, the Son of God, let us hold fast to our confession. 15 For we do not have a high priest who is unable to sympathize with our weaknesses, but we have one who in every respect has been tested[x] as we are, yet without sin. 16 Let us therefore approach the throne of grace with boldness, so that we may receive mercy and find grace to help in time of need.

5 Every high priest chosen from among mortals is put in charge of things pertaining to God on their behalf, to offer gifts and sacrifices for sins. 2 He is able to deal gently with the ignorant and wayward, since he himself is subject to weakness; 3 and because of this he must offer sacrifice for his own sins as well as for those of the people. 4 And one does not presume to take this honor, but takes it only when called by God, just as Aaron was.

5 So also Christ did not glorify himself in becoming a high priest, but was appointed by the one who said to him,

"You are my Son,
today I have begotten you";[18]

6 as he says also in another place,

"You are a priest forever,
according to the order of
Melchizedek."[19]

7 In the days of his flesh, Jesus[w] offered up prayers and supplications, with loud cries and tears, to the one who was able to save him from death, and he was heard because of his reverent submission. 8 Although he was a Son, he learned obedience through what he suffered; 9 and having been made perfect, he became the source of eternal salvation for all who obey him, 10 having been designated by God a high priest according to the order of Melchizedek.

11 About this[y] we have much to say that is hard to explain, since you have become dull in understanding. 12 For though by this time you ought to be teachers, you need someone to teach you again the basic elements of the oracles of God. You need milk, not solid food; 13 for everyone who lives on milk, being still an infant, is unskilled in the word of righteousness. 14 But solid food is for the mature, for those whose faculties have been trained by practice to distinguish good from evil.

6 Therefore let us go on toward perfection,[z] leaving behind the basic teaching about Christ, and not laying again the foundation: repentance from dead works and faith toward God, 2 instruction about baptisms, laying on of hands, resurrection of the dead, and eternal judgment. 3 And we will do[a] this, if God permits. 4 For it is impossible to restore again to repentance those who have once been enlightened, and have tasted the heavenly gift, and have shared in the Holy Spirit, 5 and have tasted the goodness of the word of God and the powers of the age to come, 6 and then have fallen away, since on their own they are crucifying again the Son of God and are holding him up to contempt. 7 Ground that drinks up the

---

[w]Gk *he* [x]Or *tempted* [y]Or *him* [z]Or *toward maturity* [a]Other ancient authorities read *let us do*

[14]Ps 95:11 [15]Gen 2:2 [16]Ps 95:11 [17]Ps 95:7–8 [18]Ps 2:7 [19]Ps 110:4

rain falling on it repeatedly, and that produces a crop useful to those for whom it is cultivated, receives a blessing from God. 8 But if it produces thorns and thistles, it is worthless and on the verge of being cursed; its end is to be burned over.

9 Even though we speak in this way, beloved, we are confident of better things in your case, things that belong to salvation. 10 For God is not unjust; he will not overlook your work and the love that you showed for his sake[b] in serving the saints, as you still do. 11 And we want each one of you to show the same diligence so as to realize the full assurance of hope to the very end, 12 so that you may not become sluggish, but imitators of those who through faith and patience inherit the promises.

13 When God made a promise to Abraham, because he had no one greater by whom to swear, he swore by himself, 14 saying, "I will surely bless you and multiply you."[20] 15 And thus Abraham,[c] having patiently endured, obtained the promise. 16 Human beings, of course, swear by someone greater than themselves, and an oath given as confirmation puts an end to all dispute. 17 In the same way, when God desired to show even more clearly to the heirs of the promise the unchangeable character of his purpose, he guaranteed it by an oath, 18 so that through two unchangeable things, in which it is impossible that God would prove false, we who have taken refuge might be strongly encouraged to seize the hope set before us. 19 We have this hope, a sure and steadfast anchor of the soul, a hope that enters the inner shrine behind the curtain, 20 where Jesus, a forerunner on our behalf, has entered, having become a high priest forever according to the order of Melchizedek.

7 This "King Melchizedek of Salem, priest of the Most High God, met Abraham as he was returning from defeating the kings and blessed him"; 2 and to him Abraham apportioned "one-tenth of everything." His name, in the first place, means "king of righteousness"; next he is also king of Salem, that is, "king of peace."[21] 3 Without father, without mother, without genealogy, having neither beginning of days nor end of life, but resembling the Son of God, he remains a priest forever.

4 See how great he is! Even[d] Abraham the pa-triarch gave him a tenth of the spoils. 5 And those descendants of Levi who receive the priestly office have a commandment in the law to collect tithes[e] from the people, that is, from their kindred,[f] though these also are descended from Abraham. 6 But this man, who does not belong to their ancestry, collected tithes[e] from Abraham and blessed him who had received the promises. 7 It is beyond dispute that the inferior is blessed by the superior. 8 In the one case, tithes are received by those who are mortal; in the other, by one of whom it is testified that he lives. 9 One might even say that Levi himself, who receives tithes, paid tithes through Abraham, 10 for he was still in the loins of his ancestor when Melchizedek met him.

11 Now if perfection had been attainable through the levitical priesthood—for the people received the law under this priesthood—what further need would there have been to speak of another priest arising according to the order of Melchizedek, rather than one according to the order of Aaron? 12 For when there is a change in the priesthood, there is necessarily a change in the law as well. 13 Now the one of whom these things are spoken belonged to another tribe, from which no one has ever served at the altar. 14 For it is evident that our Lord was descended from Judah, and in connection with that tribe Moses said nothing about priests.

15 It is even more obvious when another priest arises, resembling Melchizedek, 16 one who has become a priest, not through a legal requirement concerning physical descent, but through the power of an indestructible life. 17 For it is attested of him,

"You are a priest forever,
according to the order of
Melchizedek."[22]

18 There is, on the one hand, the abrogation of an earlier commandment because it was weak and ineffectual 19 (for the law made nothing perfect); there is, on the other hand, the introduction of a better hope, through which we approach God.

20 This was confirmed with an oath; for others who became priests took their office without an

---

[b]Gk *for his name*   [c]Gk *he*   [d]Other ancient authorities lack *Even*
[e]Or *a tenth*   [f]Gk *brothers*

[20]Gen 22:16–17   [21]Gen 14:17–20   [22]Ps 110:4

oath, 21 but this one became a priest with an oath, because of the one who said to him,

> "The Lord has sworn
>   and will not change his mind,
>   'You are a priest forever'"—[23]

22 accordingly Jesus has also become the guarantee of a better covenant.

23 Furthermore, the former priests were many in number, because they were prevented by death from continuing in office; 24 but he holds his priesthood permanently, because he continues forever. 25 Consequently he is able for all time to save[g] those who approach God through him, since he always lives to make intercession for them.

26 For it was fitting that we should have such a high priest, holy, blameless, undefiled, separated from sinners, and exalted above the heavens. 27 Unlike the other[h] high priests, he has no need to offer sacrifices day after day, first for his own sins, and then for those of the people; this he did once for all when he offered himself. 28 For the law appoints as high priests those who are subject to weakness, but the word of the oath, which came later than the law, appoints a Son who has been made perfect forever.

8 Now the main point in what we are saying is this: we have such a high priest, one who is seated at the right hand of the throne of the Majesty in the heavens, 2 a minister in the sanctuary and the true tent[i] that the Lord, and not any mortal, has set up. 3 For every high priest is appointed to offer gifts and sacrifices; hence it is necessary for this priest also to have something to offer. 4 Now if he were on earth, he would not be a priest at all, since there are priests who offer gifts according to the law. 5 They offer worship in a sanctuary that is a sketch and shadow of the heavenly one; for Moses, when he was about to erect the tent,[i] was warned, "See that you make everything according to the pattern that was shown you on the mountain."[24] 6 But Jesus[j] has now obtained a more excellent ministry, and to that degree he is the mediator of a better covenant, which has been enacted through better promises. 7 For if that first covenant had been faultless, there would have been no need to look for a second one.

8 God[k] finds fault with them when he says:

> "The days are surely coming, says
>   the Lord,
>   when I will establish a new
>   covenant with the house of
>   Israel
>   and with the house of Judah;
> 9 not like the covenant that I made
>   with their ancestors,
>   on the day when I took them
>   by the hand to lead them
>   out of the land of Egypt;
>   for they did not continue in my
>   covenant,
>   and so I had no concern for
>   them, says the Lord.
> 10 This is the covenant that I will
>   make with the house of
>   srael
>   after those days, says the Lord:
>   I will put my laws in their minds,
>   and write them on their hearts,
>   and I will be their God,
>   and they shall be my people.
> 11 And they shall not teach one
>   another
>   or say to each other, 'Know the
>   Lord,'
>   for they shall all know me,
>   from the least of them to the
>   greatest.
> 12 For I will be merciful toward their
>   iniquities,
>   and I will remember their sins
>   no more."[25]

13 In speaking of "a new covenant," he has made the first one obsolete. And what is obsolete and growing old will soon disappear.

9 Now even the first covenant had regulations for worship and an earthly sanctuary. 2 For a tent[i] was constructed, the first one, in which were the lampstand, the table, and the bread of the Presence;[l] this is called the Holy Place. 3 Behind the second curtain was a tent[i] called the Holy of

---

[g]Or *able to save completely*   [h]Gk lacks *other*   [i]Or *tabernacle*
[j]Gk *he*   [k]Gk *He*   [l]Gk *the presentation of the loaves*

[23]Ps 110:4   [24]Exod 25:40   [25]Jer 31:31–34

Holies. 4 In it stood the golden altar of incense and the ark of the covenant overlaid on all sides with gold, in which there were a golden urn holding the manna, and Aaron's rod that budded, and the tablets of the covenant; 5 above it were the cherubim of glory overshadowing the mercy seat.[m] Of these things we cannot speak now in detail.

6 Such preparations having been made, the priests go continually into the first tent[n] to carry out their ritual duties; 7 but only the high priest goes into the second, and he but once a year, and not without taking the blood that he offers for himself and for the sins committed unintentionally by the people. 8 By this the Holy Spirit indicates that the way into the sanctuary has not yet been disclosed as long as the first tent[n] is still standing. 9 This is a symbol[o] of the present time, during which gifts and sacrifices are offered that cannot perfect the conscience of the worshiper, 10 but deal only with food and drink and various baptisms, regulations for the body imposed until the time comes to set things right.

11 But when Christ came as a high priest of the good things that have come,[p] then through the greater and perfect[q] tent[n] (not made with hands, that is, not of this creation), 12 he entered once for all into the Holy Place, not with the blood of goats and calves, but with his own blood, thus obtaining eternal redemption. 13 For if the blood of goats and bulls, with the sprinkling of the ashes of a heifer, sanctifies those who have been defiled so that their flesh is purified, 14 how much more will the blood of Christ, who through the eternal Spirit[r] offered himself without blemish to God, purify our[s] conscience from dead works to worship the living God!

15 For this reason he is the mediator of a new covenant, so that those who are called may receive the promised eternal inheritance, because a death has occurred that redeems them from the transgressions under the first covenant.[t] 16 Where a will[t] is involved, the death of the one who made it must be established. 17 For a will[t] takes effect only at death, since it is not in force as long as the one who made it is alive. 18 Hence not even the first covenant was inaugurated without blood. 19 For when every commandment had been told to

all the people by Moses in accordance with the law, he took the blood of calves and goats,[u] with water and scarlet wool and hyssop, and sprinkled both the scroll itself and all the people, 20 saying, "This is the blood of the covenant that God has ordained for you."[26] 21 And in the same way he sprinkled with the blood both the tent[n] and all the vessels used in worship. 22 Indeed, under the law almost everything is purified with blood, and without the shedding of blood there is no forgiveness of sins.

23 Thus it was necessary for the sketches of the heavenly things to be purified with these rites, but the heavenly things themselves need better sacrifices than these. 24 For Christ did not enter a sanctuary made by human hands, a mere copy of the true one, but he entered into heaven itself, now to appear in the presence of God on our behalf. 25 Nor was it to offer himself again and again, as the high priest enters the Holy Place year after year with blood that is not his own; 26 for then he would have had to suffer again and again since the foundation of the world. But as it is, he has appeared once for all at the end of the age to remove sin by the sacrifice of himself. 27 And just as it is appointed for mortals to die once, and after that the judgment, 28 so Christ, having been offered once to bear the sins of many, will appear a second time, not to deal with sin, but to save those who are eagerly waiting for him.

10 Since the law has only a shadow of the good things to come and not the true form of these realities, it[v] can never, by the same sacrifices that are continually offered year after year, make perfect those who approach. 2 Otherwise, would they not have ceased being offered, since the worshipers, cleansed once for all, would no longer have any consciousness of sin? 3 But in these sacrifices there is a reminder of sin year after year. 4 For it is impossible for the blood of bulls and goats to take away sins. 5 Conse-

[m]Or *the place of atonement* [n]Or *tabernacle* [o]Gk *parable* [p]Other ancient authorities read *good things to come* [q]Gk *more perfect* [r]Other ancient authorities read *Holy Spirit* [s]Other ancient authorities read *your* [t]The Greek word used here means both *covenant* and *will* [u]Other ancient authorities lack *and goats* [v]Other ancient authorities read *they*

26Exod 24:8

quently, when Christ[w] came into the world, he said,

> "Sacrifices and offerings you have
> not desired,
> but a body you have prepared
> for me;
> 6 in burnt offerings and sin
> offerings
> you have taken no pleasure.
> 7 Then I said, 'See, God, I have
> come to do your will,
> O God'
> (in the scroll of the book[x] it is
> written of me)."[27]

8 When he said above, "You have neither desired nor taken pleasure in sacrifices and offerings and burnt offerings and sin offerings"[28] (these are offered according to the law), 9 then he added, "See, I have come to do your will."[29] He abolishes the first in order to establish the second. 10 And it is by God's will[y] that we have been sanctified through the offering of the body of Jesus Christ once for all.

11 And every priest stands day after day at his service, offering again and again the same sacrifices that can never take away sins. 12 But when Christ[z] had offered for all time a single sacrifice for sins, "he sat down at the right hand of God," 13 and since then has been waiting "until his enemies would be made a footstool for his feet."[30] 14 For by a single offering he has perfected for all time those who are sanctified. 15 And the Holy Spirit also testifies to us, for after saying,

> 16 "This is the covenant that I will
> make with them
> after those days, says the Lord:
> I will put my laws in their hearts,
> and I will write them on their
> minds,"[31]

17 he also adds,

> "I will remember[a] their sins and
> their lawless deeds no
> more."[32]

18 Where there is forgiveness of these, there is no longer any offering for sin.

19 Therefore, my friends,[b] since we have confidence to enter the sanctuary by the blood of Jesus, 20 by the new and living way that he opened for us through the curtain (that is, through his flesh),

21 and since we have a great priest over the house of God, 22 let us approach with a true heart in full assurance of faith, with our hearts sprinkled clean from an evil conscience and our bodies washed with pure water. 23 Let us hold fast to the confession of our hope without wavering, for he who has promised is faithful. 24 And let us consider how to provoke one another to love and good deeds, 25 not neglecting to meet together, as is the habit of some, but encouraging one another, and all the more as you see the Day approaching.

26 For if we willfully persist in sin after having received the knowledge of the truth, there no longer remains a sacrifice for sins, 27 but a fearful prospect of judgment, and a fury of fire that will consume the adversaries. 28 Anyone who has violated the law of Moses dies without mercy "on the testimony of two or three witnesses."[33] 29 How much worse punishment do you think will be deserved by those who have spurned the Son of God, profaned the blood of the covenant by which they were sanctified, and outraged the Spirit of grace? 30 For we know the one who said, "Vengeance is mine, I will repay."[34] And again, "The Lord will judge his people."[35] 31 It is a fearful thing to fall into the hands of the living God.

32 But recall those earlier days when, after you had been enlightened, you endured a hard struggle with sufferings, 33 sometimes being publicly exposed to abuse and persecution, and sometimes being partners with those so treated. 34 For you had compassion for those who were in prison, and you cheerfully accepted the plundering of your possessions, knowing that you yourselves possessed something better and more lasting. 35 Do not, therefore, abandon that confidence of yours; it brings a great reward. 36 For you need endurance, so that when you have done the will of God, you may receive what was promised. 37 For yet

> "in a very little while,
> the one who is coming will
> come and will not delay;
> 38 but my righteous one will live by
> faith.

---

[w]Gk he　[x]Meaning of Gk uncertain　[y]Gk by that will　[z]Gk this one
[a]Gk on their minds and I will remember　[b]Gk Therefore, brothers

---

[27]Ps 40:6–8　[28]Ps 40:6　[29]Ps 40:7　[30]Ps 110:1　[31]Jer 31:33　[32]Jer 31:34　[33]Deut 19:15　[34]Deut 32:35　[35]Deut 32:36; Ps 135:14

My soul takes no pleasure in
anyone who shrinks back."[36]

39 But we are not among those who shrink back and so are lost, but among those who have faith and so are saved.

11 Now faith is the assurance of things hoped for, the conviction of things not seen. 2 Indeed, by faith[c] our ancestors received approval. 3 By faith we understand that the worlds were prepared by the word of God, so that what is seen was made from things that are not visible.[d]

4 By faith Abel offered to God a more acceptable[e] sacrifice than Cain's. Through this he received approval as righteous, God himself giving approval to his gifts; he died, but through his faith[f] he still speaks. 5 By faith Enoch was taken so that he did not experience death; and "he was not found, because God had taken him."[37] For it was attested before he was taken away that "he had pleased God."[38] 6 And without faith it is impossible to please God, for whoever would approach him must believe that he exists and that he rewards those who seek him. 7 By faith Noah, warned by God about events as yet unseen, respected the warning and built an ark to save his household; by this he condemned the world and became an heir to the righteousness that is in accordance with faith.

8 By faith Abraham obeyed when he was called to set out for a place that he was to receive as an inheritance; and he set out, not knowing where he was going. 9 By faith he stayed for a time in the land he had been promised, as in a foreign land, living in tents, as did Isaac and Jacob, who were heirs with him of the same promise. 10 For he looked forward to the city that has foundations, whose architect and builder is God. 11 By faith he received power of procreation, even though he was too old—and Sarah herself was barren—because he considered him faithful who had promised.[g] 12 Therefore from one person, and this one as good as dead, descendants were born, "as many as the stars of heaven and as the innumerable grains of sand by the seashore."[39]

13 All of these died in faith without having received the promises, but from a distance they saw and greeted them. They confessed that they were strangers and foreigners on the earth, 14 for people who speak in this way make it clear that they are seeking a homeland. 15 If they had been thinking of the land that they had left behind, they would have had opportunity to return. 16 But as it is, they desire a better country, that is, a heavenly one. Therefore God is not ashamed to be called their God; indeed, he has prepared a city for them.

17 By faith Abraham, when put to the test, offered up Isaac. He who had received the promises was ready to offer up his only son, 18 of whom he had been told, "It is through Isaac that descendants shall be named for you."[40] 19 He considered the fact that God is able even to raise someone from the dead—and figuratively speaking, he did receive him back. 20 By faith Isaac invoked blessings for the future on Jacob and Esau. 21 By faith Jacob, when dying, blessed each of the sons of Joseph, "bowing in worship over the top of his staff."[41] 22 By faith Joseph, at the end of his life, made mention of the exodus of the Israelites and gave instructions about his burial.[h]

23 By faith Moses was hidden by his parents for three months after his birth, because they saw that the child was beautiful; and they were not afraid of the king's edict.[i] 24 By faith Moses, when he was grown up, refused to be called a son of Pharaoh's daughter, 25 choosing rather to share ill-treatment with the people of God than to enjoy the fleeting pleasures of sin. 26 He considered abuse suffered for the Christ[j] to be greater wealth than the treasures of Egypt, for he was looking ahead to the reward. 27 By faith he left Egypt, unafraid of the king's anger; for he persevered as though[k] he saw him who is invisible. 28 By faith he kept the Passover and the sprinkling of blood, so that the destroyer of the firstborn would not touch the firstborn of Israel.[l]

29 By faith the people passed through the Red Sea as if it were dry land, but when the Egyptians attempted to do so they were drowned. 30 By faith

---

[c]Gk by this [d]Or was not made out of visible things [e]Gk greater [f]Gk through it [g]Or By faith Sarah herself, though barren, received power to conceive, even when she was too old, because she considered him faithful who had promised. [h]Gk his bones [i]Other ancient authorities add By faith Moses, when he was grown up, killed the Egyptian, because he observed the humiliation of his people (Gk brothers) [j]Or the Messiah [k]Or because [l]Gk would not touch them

[36]Hab 2:3–4 [37]Gen 5:24; Sir 44:16 [38]Gen 5:22 [39]Gen 22:17 [40]Gen 21:12 [41]Gen 47:31

the walls of Jericho fell after they had been encircled for seven days. 31 By faith Rahab the prostitute did not perish with those who were disobedient,[m] because she had received the spies in peace.

32 And what more should I say? For time would fail me to tell of Gideon, Barak, Samson, Jephthah, of David and Samuel and the prophets— 33 who through faith conquered kingdoms, administered justice, obtained promises, shut the mouths of lions, 34 quenched raging fire, escaped the edge of the sword, won strength out of weakness, became mighty in war, put foreign armies to flight. 35 Women received their dead by resurrection. Others were tortured, refusing to accept release, in order to obtain a better resurrection. 36 Others suffered mocking and flogging, and even chains and imprisonment. 37 They were stoned to death, they were sawn in two,[n] they were killed by the sword; they went about in skins of sheep and goats, destitute, persecuted, tormented— 38 of whom the world was not worthy. They wandered in deserts and mountains, and in caves and holes in the ground.

39 Yet all these, though they were commended for their faith, did not receive what was promised, 40 since God had provided something better so that they would not, apart from us, be made perfect.

12

Therefore, since we are surrounded by so great a cloud of witnesses, let us also lay aside every weight and the sin that clings so closely,[o] and let us run with perseverance the race that is set before us, 2 looking to Jesus the pioneer and perfecter of our faith, who for the sake of[p] the joy that was set before him endured the cross, disregarding its shame, and has taken his seat at the right hand of the throne of God.

3 Consider him who endured such hostility against himself from sinners,[q] so that you may not grow weary or lose heart. 4 In your struggle against sin you have not yet resisted to the point of shedding your blood. 5 And you have forgotten the exhortation that addresses you as children—

> "My child, do not regard lightly
>   the discipline of the Lord,
>   or lose heart when you are
>   punished by him;
6 for the Lord disciplines those
>   whom he loves,

and chastises every child whom
      he accepts."[42]

7 Endure trials for the sake of discipline. God is treating you as children; for what child is there whom a parent does not discipline? 8 If you do not have that discipline in which all children share, then you are illegitimate and not his children. 9 Moreover, we had human parents to discipline us, and we respected them. Should we not be even more willing to be subject to the Father of spirits and live? 10 For they disciplined us for a short time as seemed best to them, but he disciplines us for our good, in order that we may share his holiness. 11 Now, discipline always seems painful rather than pleasant at the time, but later it yields the peaceful fruit of righteousness to those who have been trained by it.

12 Therefore lift your drooping hands and strengthen your weak knees, 13 and make straight paths for your feet, so that what is lame may not be put out of joint, but rather be healed.

14 Pursue peace with everyone, and the holiness without which no one will see the Lord. 15 See to it that no one fails to obtain the grace of God; that no root of bitterness springs up and causes trouble, and through it many become defiled. 16 See to it that no one becomes like Esau, an immoral and godless person, who sold his birthright for a single meal. 17 You know that later, when he wanted to inherit the blessing, he was rejected, for he found no chance to repent,[r] even though he sought the blessing[s] with tears.

18 You have not come to something[t] that can be touched, a blazing fire, and darkness, and gloom, and a tempest, 19 and the sound of a trumpet, and a voice whose words made the hearers beg that not another word be spoken to them. 20 (For they could not endure the order that was given, "If even an animal touches the mountain, it shall be stoned to death."[43] 21 Indeed, so terrifying was the sight that Moses said, "I tremble with fear."[44]) 22 But you have come to Mount Zion and to the city of the living God, the heavenly Jerusalem, and to in-

---

[m]Or *unbelieving*   [n]Other ancient authorities add *they were tempted*
[o]Other ancient authorities read *sin that easily distracts*   [p]Or *who instead of*   [q]Other ancient authorities read *such hostility from sinners against themselves*   [r]Or *no chance to change his father's mind*
[s]Gk *it*   [t]Other ancient authorities read *a mountain*

---

[42]Prov 3:11–12   [43]Exod 19:12–13   [44]Deut 9:19

numerable angels in festal gathering, 23 and to the assembly[u] of the firstborn who are enrolled in heaven, and to God the judge of all, and to the spirits of the righteous made perfect, 24 and to Jesus, the mediator of a new covenant, and to the sprinkled blood that speaks a better word than the blood of Abel.

25 See that you do not refuse the one who is speaking; for if they did not escape when they refused the one who warned them on earth, how much less will we escape if we reject the one who warns from heaven! 26 At that time his voice shook the earth; but now he has promised, "Yet once more I will shake not only the earth but also the heaven."[45] 27 This phrase, "Yet once more," indicates the removal of what is shaken—that is, created things—so that what cannot be shaken may remain. 28 Therefore, since we are receiving a kingdom that cannot be shaken, let us give thanks, by which we offer to God an acceptable worship with reverence and awe; 29 for indeed our God is a consuming fire.

13 Let mutual love continue. 2 Do not neglect to show hospitality to strangers, for by doing that some have entertained angels without knowing it. 3 Remember those who are in prison, as though you were in prison with them; those who are being tortured, as though you yourselves were being tortured.[v] 4 Let marriage be held in honor by all, and let the marriage bed be kept undefiled; for God will judge fornicators and adulterers. 5 Keep your lives free from the love of money, and be content with what you have; for he has said, "I will never leave you or forsake you."[46] 6 So we can say with confidence,

> "The Lord is my helper;
>   I will not be afraid.
> What can anyone do to me?"[47]

7 Remember your leaders, those who spoke the word of God to you; consider the outcome of their way of life, and imitate their faith. 8 Jesus Christ is the same yesterday and today and forever. 9 Do not be carried away by all kinds of strange teachings; for it is well for the heart to be strengthened by grace, not by regulations about food,[w] which

have not benefited those who observe them. 10 We have an altar from which those who officiate in the tent[x] have no right to eat. 11 For the bodies of those animals whose blood is brought into the sanctuary by the high priest as a sacrifice for sin are burned outside the camp. 12 Therefore Jesus also suffered outside the city gate in order to sanctify the people by his own blood. 13 Let us then go to him outside the camp and bear the abuse he endured. 14 For here we have no lasting city, but we are looking for the city that is to come. 15 Through him, then, let us continually offer a sacrifice of praise to God, that is, the fruit of lips that confess his name. 16 Do not neglect to do good and to share what you have, for such sacrifices are pleasing to God.

17 Obey your leaders and submit to them, for they are keeping watch over your souls and will give an account. Let them do this with joy and not with sighing—for that would be harmful to you.

18 Pray for us; we are sure that we have a clear conscience, desiring to act honorably in all things. 19 I urge you all the more to do this, so that I may be restored to you very soon.

20 Now may the God of peace, who brought back from the dead our Lord Jesus, the great shepherd of the sheep, by the blood of the eternal covenant, 21 make you complete in everything good so that you may do his will, working among us[y] that which is pleasing in his sight, through Jesus Christ, to whom be the glory forever and ever. Amen.

22 I appeal to you, brothers and sisters,[z] bear with my word of exhortation, for I have written to you briefly. 23 I want you to know that our brother Timothy has been set free; and if he comes in time, he will be with me when I see you. 24 Greet all your leaders and all the saints. Those from Italy send you greetings. 25 Grace be with all of you.[a]

---

[u]Or *angels, and to the festal gathering* [23]*and assembly*   [v]Gk *were in the body*   [w]Gk *not by foods*   [x]Or *tabernacle*   [y]Other ancient authorities read *you*   [z]Gk *brothers*   [a]Other ancient authorities add *Amen*

---

[45]Hag 2:6   [46]Deut 31:6, 8; Josh 1:5   [47]Ps 118:6

The Letter of James

The Letter of James consists of a series of ethical admonitions to those who "believe in our glorious Lord Jesus Christ" (2:1). The author, who calls himself "James, a servant of God" (1:1), has been traditionally identified as James the brother of Jesus (see Gal 1:19). It is not clear, however, that the author intends this identification. For one thing, "James" was a common name in the first century; even within the New Testament several other persons have it (see, e.g., Matt 4:21; 10:3; 27:56). Moreover, nowhere in the letter does the author claim to be a member of Jesus' family or to have any firsthand knowledge of his teachings.

Scholars occasionally have been struck by the unique character of this book, especially by how little of it seems distinctively Christian: the figure of Jesus himself appears only on the periphery (he is named only in 1:1 and 2:1), nearly all of the moral injunctions are paralleled in non-Christian Jewish writings, and the examples of ethical behavior are consistently drawn, not from the lives of Jesus and his apostles, but from stories of the Jewish Scriptures (Abraham, 2:21; Rahab, 2:25; Job, 5:11; Elijah, 5:17). Even the communities of believers who are addressed are portrayed in Jewish guise: they are "the twelve tribes in the Dispersion" (1:1), and their assembly place is literally called a "synagogue" (2:2).

Both the author and his audience, however, are clearly Christian (1:1; 2:1). Moreover, as a number of scholars have observed, many of the ethical injunctions here are similar to Jesus' own teachings as preserved in the Gospels (cf. 2:8 with Matt 19:23–24; 5:1–6 with Matt 19:23–24; and 5:12 with Matt 5:33–37). It appears, then, that the author has culled a number of important ethical admonitions from a variety of sources, such as Jewish books of wisdom (comparable to the book of Proverbs) and traditions of Jesus' own teaching. In doing so he has been particularly keen to admonish his readers to control their speech (1:26; 3:1–12), to beware of the dangers of wealth (1:9–11; 4:13–17; 5:1–6), and to be patient in the midst of suffering (1:2–8, 12–16; 5:7–11).

Above all else, James is concerned to show that no one can be made right with God by faith alone, without doing good deeds (1:22–27; 2:14–26). Since the Reformation, some interpreters have thought that James is directly opposing Paul's teaching that a person is "justified by faith, not by works of the law" (Rom 3:28). It may be more accurate to say, however, that James is opposed to an extreme interpretation of Paul, which states that people can live any way they want, so long as they have "faith." For James, faith must be manifest in one's life, for "faith without works is dead" (2:26).

From the New Revised Standard Version Bible, © 1989.

1

James, a servant[a] of God and of the Lord Jesus Christ,

To the twelve tribes in the Dispersion: Greetings.

2 My brothers and sisters,[b] whenever you face trials of any kind, consider it nothing but joy, 3 because you know that the testing of your faith produces endurance; 4 and let endurance have its full effect, so that you may be mature and complete, lacking in nothing.

5 If any of you is lacking in wisdom, ask God, who gives to all generously and ungrudgingly, and it will be given you. 6 But ask in faith, never doubting, for the one who doubts is like a wave of the sea, driven and tossed by the wind; 7, 8 for the doubter, being double-minded and unstable in every way, must not expect to receive anything from the Lord.

9 Let the believer[c] who is lowly boast in being raised up, 10 and the rich in being brought low, because the rich will disappear like a flower in the field. 11 For the sun rises with its scorching heat and withers the field; its flower falls, and its beauty perishes. It is the same way with the rich; in the midst of a busy life, they will wither away.

12 Blessed is anyone who endures temptation. Such a one has stood the test and will receive the crown of life that the Lord[d] has promised to those who love him. 13 No one, when tempted, should say, "I am being tempted by God"; for God cannot be tempted by evil and he himself tempts no one. 14 But one is tempted by one's own desire, being lured and enticed by it; 15 then, when that desire has conceived, it gives birth to sin, and that sin, when it is fully grown, gives birth to death. 16 Do not be deceived, my beloved.[e]

17 Every generous act of giving, with every perfect gift, is from above, coming down from the Father of lights, with whom there is no variation or shadow due to change.[f] 18 In fulfillment of his own purpose he gave us birth by the word of truth, so that we would become a kind of first fruits of his creatures.

19 You must understand this, my beloved:[e] let everyone be quick to listen, slow to speak, slow to anger; 20 for your anger does not produce God's righteousness. 21 Therefore rid yourselves of all sordidness and rank growth of wickedness, and welcome with meekness the implanted word that has the power to save your souls.

22 But be doers of the word, and not merely hearers who deceive themselves. 23 For if any are hearers of the word and not doers, they are like those who look at themselves[g] in a mirror; 24 for they look at themselves and, on going away, immediately forget what they were like. 25 But those who look into the perfect law, the law of liberty, and persevere, being not hearers who forget but doers who act—they will be blessed in their doing.

26 If any think they are religious, and do not bridle their tongues but deceive their hearts, their religion is worthless. 27 Religion that is pure and undefiled before God, the Father, is this: to care for orphans and widows in their distress, and to keep oneself unstained by the world.

2

My brothers and sisters,[h] do you with your acts of favoritism really believe in our glorious Lord Jesus Christ?[i] 2 For if a person with gold rings and in fine clothes comes into your assembly, and if a poor person in dirty clothes also comes in, 3 and if you take notice of the one wearing the fine clothes and say, "Have a seat here, please," while to the one who is poor you say, "Stand there," or, "Sit at my feet,"[j] 4 have you not made distinctions among yourselves, and become judges with evil thoughts? 5 Listen, my beloved brothers and sisters.[b] Has not God chosen the poor in the world to be rich in faith and to be heirs of the kingdom that he has promised to those who love him? 6 But you have dishonored the poor. Is it not the rich who oppress you? Is it not they who drag you into court? 7 Is it not they who blaspheme the excellent name that was invoked over you?

8 You do well if you really fulfill the royal law according to the scripture, "You shall love your neighbor as yourself."[1] 9 But if you show partiality, you commit sin and are convicted by the law

---

[a]Gk slave [b]Gk brothers [c]Gk brother [d]Gk he; other ancient authorities read God [e]Gk my beloved brothers [f]Other ancient authorities read variation due to a shadow of turning [g]Gk at the face of his birth [h]Gk My brothers [i]Or hold the faith of our glorious Lord Jesus Christ without acts of favoritism [j]Gk Sit under my footstool

[1]Lev 19:18

as transgressors. 10 For whoever keeps the whole law but fails in one point has become accountable for all of it. 11 For the one who said, "You shall not commit adultery,"[2] also said, "You shall not murder."[3] Now if you do not commit adultery but if you murder, you have become a transgressor of the law. 12 So speak and so act as those who are to be judged by the law of liberty. 13 For judgment will be without mercy to anyone who has shown no mercy; mercy triumphs over judgment.

14 What good is it, my brothers and sisters,[k] if you say you have faith but do not have works? Can faith save you? 15 If a brother or sister is naked and lacks daily food, 16 and one of you says to them, "Go in peace; keep warm and eat your fill," and yet you do not supply their bodily needs, what is the good of that? 17 So faith by itself, if it has no works, is dead.

18 But someone will say, "You have faith and I have works." Show me your faith apart from your works, and I by my works will show you my faith. 19 You believe that God is one; you do well. Even the demons believe—and shudder. 20 Do you want to be shown, you senseless person, that faith apart from works is barren? 21 Was not our ancestor Abraham justified by works when he offered his son Isaac on the altar? 22 You see that faith was active along with his works, and faith was brought to completion by the works. 23 Thus the scripture was fulfilled that says, "Abraham believed God, and it was reckoned to him as righteousness,"[4] and he was called the friend of God. 24 You see that a person is justified by works and not by faith alone. 25 Likewise, was not Rahab the prostitute also justified by works when she welcomed the messengers and sent them out by another road? 26 For just as the body without the spirit is dead, so faith without works is also dead.

3 Not many of you should become teachers, my brothers and sisters,[k] for you know that we who teach will be judged with greater strictness. 2 For all of us make many mistakes. Anyone who makes no mistakes in speaking is perfect, able to keep the whole body in check with a bridle. 3 If we put bits into the mouths of horses to make them obey us, we guide their whole bodies. 4 Or look at ships: though they are so large that it takes strong winds to drive them, yet they are guided by a very small rudder wherever the will of the pilot directs. 5 So also the tongue is a small member, yet it boasts of great exploits.

How great a forest is set ablaze by a small fire! 6 And the tongue is a fire. The tongue is placed among our members as a world of iniquity; it stains the whole body, sets on fire the cycle of nature,[l] and is itself set on fire by hell.[m] 7 For every species of beast and bird, of reptile and sea creature, can be tamed and has been tamed by the human species, 8 but no one can tame the tongue—a restless evil, full of deadly poison. 9 With it we bless the Lord and Father, and with it we curse those who are made in the likeness of God. 10 From the same mouth come blessing and cursing. My brothers and sisters,[n] this ought not to be so. 11 Does a spring pour forth from the same opening both fresh and brackish water? 12 Can a fig tree, my brothers and sisters,[o] yield olives, or a grapevine figs? No more can salt water yield fresh.

13 Who is wise and understanding among you? Show by your good life that your works are done with gentleness born of wisdom. 14 But if you have bitter envy and selfish ambition in your hearts, do not be boastful and false to the truth. 15 Such wisdom does not come down from above, but is earthly, unspiritual, devilish. 16 For where there is envy and selfish ambition, there will also be disorder and wickedness of every kind. 17 But the wisdom from above is first pure, then peaceable, gentle, willing to yield, full of mercy and good fruits, without a trace of partiality or hypocrisy. 18 And a harvest of righteousness is sown in peace for[p] those who make peace.

4 Those conflicts and disputes among you, where do they come from? Do they not come from your cravings that are at war within you? 2 You want something and do not have it; so you commit murder. And you covet[q] something and cannot obtain it; so you engage in disputes and conflicts. You do not have, because you do not ask. 3 You ask and do not receive, because you ask wrongly, in order to spend what you get on your pleasures. 4 Adulterers! Do you not know that friendship with the world is enmity with God?

[k]Gk *brothers*   [l]Or *wheel of birth*   [m]Gk *Gehenna*   [n]Gk *My brothers*
[o]Gk *my brothers*   [p]Or *by*   [q]Or *you murder and you covet*

[2]Exod 20:14; Deut 5:18   [3]Exod 20:13; Deut 5:17   [4]Gen 15:6

Therefore whoever wishes to be a friend of the world becomes an enemy of God. 5 Or do you suppose that it is for nothing that the scripture says, "God[r] yearns jealously for the spirit that he has made to dwell in us"? 6 But he gives all the more grace; therefore it says,

"God opposes the proud,
    but gives grace to the humble."[5]

7 Submit yourselves therefore to God. Resist the devil, and he will flee from you. 8 Draw near to God, and he will draw near to you. Cleanse your hands, you sinners, and purify your hearts, you double-minded. 9 Lament and mourn and weep. Let your laughter be turned into mourning and your joy into dejection. 10 Humble yourselves before the Lord, and he will exalt you.

11 Do not speak evil against one another, brothers and sisters.[s] Whoever speaks evil against another or judges another, speaks evil against the law and judges the law; but if you judge the law, you are not a doer of the law but a judge. 12 There is one lawgiver and judge who is able to save and to destroy. So who, then, are you to judge your neighbor?

13 Come now, you who say, "Today or tomorrow we will go to such and such a town and spend a year there, doing business and making money." 14 Yet you do not even know what tomorrow will bring. What is your life? For you are a mist that appears for a little while and then vanishes. 15 Instead you ought to say, "If the Lord wishes, we will live and do this or that." 16 As it is, you boast in your arrogance; all such boasting is evil. 17 Anyone, then, who knows the right thing to do and fails to do it, commits sin.

5 Come now, you rich people, weep and wail for the miseries that are coming to you. 2 Your riches have rotted, and your clothes are moth-eaten. 3 Your gold and silver have rusted, and their rust will be evidence against you, and it will eat your flesh like fire. You have laid up treasure[t] for the last days. 4 Listen! The wages of the laborers who mowed your fields, which you kept back by fraud, cry out, and the cries of the harvesters have reached the ears of the Lord of hosts. 5 You have lived on the earth in luxury and in plea-sure; you have fattened your hearts in a day of slaughter. 6 You have condemned and murdered the righteous one, who does not resist you.

7 Be patient, therefore, beloved,[s] until the coming of the Lord. The farmer waits for the precious crop from the earth, being patient with it until it receives the early and the late rains. 8 You also must be patient. Strengthen your hearts, for the coming of the Lord is near.[u] 9 Beloved,[v] do not grumble against one another, so that you may not be judged. See, the Judge is standing at the doors! 10 As an example of suffering and patience, beloved,[s] take the prophets who spoke in the name of the Lord. 11 Indeed we call blessed those who showed endurance. You have heard of the endurance of Job, and you have seen the purpose of the Lord, how the Lord is compassionate and merciful.

12 Above all, my beloved,[s] do not swear, either by heaven or by earth or by any other oath, but let your "Yes" be yes and your "No" be no, so that you may not fall under condemnation.

13 Are any among you suffering? They should pray. Are any cheerful? They should sing songs of praise. 14 Are any among you sick? They should call for the elders of the church and have them pray over them, anointing them with oil in the name of the Lord. 15 The prayer of faith will save the sick, and the Lord will raise them up; and anyone who has committed sins will be forgiven. 16 Therefore confess your sins to one another, and pray for one another, so that you may be healed. The prayer of the righteous is powerful and effective. 17 Elijah was a human being like us, and he prayed fervently that it might not rain, and for three years and six months it did not rain on the earth. 18 Then he prayed again, and the heaven gave rain and the earth yielded its harvest.

19 My brothers and sisters,[w] if anyone among you wanders from the truth and is brought back by another, 20 you should know that whoever brings back a sinner from wandering will save the sinner's[x] soul from death and will cover a multitude of sins.

---

[r]Gk *He*   [s]Gk *brothers*   [t]Or *will eat your flesh, since you have stored up fire*   [u]Or *is at hand*   [v]Gk *Brothers*   [w]Gk *My brothers*   [x]Gk *his*

[5]Prov 3:34

The Letter of 1 Peter

The Letter of 1 Peter is addressed to Christian "exiles" scattered throughout several provinces of Asia Minor: "Pontus, Galatia, Cappadocia, Asia, and Bythinia" (1:1). Scholars have debated whether the recipients were literally "exiles" and "aliens" (2:1)—that is, people who were socially marginalized as foreigners in their places of residence—or whether these terms are figurative designations for Christians whose real allegiance is heaven and who are, therefore, simply "in exile" here on earth for a short while (cf. 1:13, 17). In either case, the immediate social context of the letter is clear. The people addressed are experiencing persecution and it has grown serious (2:12; 3:14; 4:12). The word for suffering occurs more frequently in this short letter than in any other book of the New Testament.

The antagonism toward the Christians has evidently come from the grass roots; they are being opposed by former colleagues and friends who do not understand or appreciate their new allegiances to the church (4:4). Some Christians may have been placed on trial before civil authorities (3:15), possibly simply for being Christian.

The author of the letter is concerned that his readers not abandon the Christian faith because of their suffering. And so he repeatedly reminds them that they are special before God as the chosen people set apart from the rest of the world (1:4, 17, 19, 23; 2:4–9). He is even more emphatic that Christians should suffer for doing what is right, in imitation of Christ, rather than for what is wrong (3:15–17). They are, therefore, to continue to lead moral, upright lives and to be good family members and model citizens, showing that they have done nothing to deserve their punishment and putting to shame those who wrongly harm them (3:16; 4:16–16).

The letter claims to have been written by Simon Peter, Jesus' disciple, evidently from Rome (assuming that "Babylon" in 5:13 is a codeword for the capital of the empire; see Rev 17:5; 18:2). Scholars, however, have long questioned this claim. Virtually the only things known about Peter are that he was a Jewish fisherman from Galilee, a peasant known to be illiterate, whose native language was probably Aramaic (Mark 1:6; Acts 4:13). This letter, on the other hand, was written by a highly literate Greek-speaking Christian familiar with the Greek Old Testament and Greek rhetorical strategies.

Some scholars have resolved this dilemma by suggesting that Silvanus, mentioned in 5:12, was the actual author of the letter (or that, as Peter's scribe, Silvanus put the letter into more rhetorically effective language). Others have noted the large number of other early Christian writings pseudonymously produced in Peter's name, including three apocalypses, several Acts, and other letters. 1 Peter may itself belong to this group of Petrine pseudepigrapha, a letter written in the apostle's name to deal with problems that had arisen some decades after his death.

From the New Revised Standard Version Bible, © 1989.

1 Peter, an apostle of Jesus Christ,

To the exiles of the Dispersion in Pontus, Galatia, Cappadocia, Asia, and Bithynia, 2 who have been chosen and destined by God the Father and sanctified by the Spirit to be obedient to Jesus Christ and to be sprinkled with his blood:

May grace and peace be yours in abundance.

3 Blessed be the God and Father of our Lord Jesus Christ! By his great mercy he has given us a new birth into a living hope through the resurrection of Jesus Christ from the dead, 4 and into an inheritance that is imperishable, undefiled, and unfading, kept in heaven for you, 5 who are being protected by the power of God through faith for a salvation ready to be revealed in the last time. 6 In this you rejoice,[a] even if now for a little while you have had to suffer various trials, 7 so that the genuineness of your faith—being more precious than gold that, though perishable, is tested by fire—may be found to result in praise and glory and honor when Jesus Christ is revealed. 8 Although you have not seen[b] him, you love him; and even though you do not see him now, you believe in him and rejoice with an indescribable and glorious joy, 9 for you are receiving the outcome of your faith, the salvation of your souls.

10 Concerning this salvation, the prophets who prophesied of the grace that was to be yours made careful search and inquiry, 11 inquiring about the person or time that the Spirit of Christ within them indicated when it testified in advance to the sufferings destined for Christ and the subsequent glory. 12 It was revealed to them that they were serving not themselves but you, in regard to the things that have now been announced to you through those who brought you good news by the Holy Spirit sent from heaven—things into which angels long to look!

13 Therefore prepare your minds for action;[c] discipline yourselves; set all your hope on the grace that Jesus Christ will bring you when he is revealed. 14 Like obedient children, do not be conformed to the desires that you formerly had in ignorance. 15 Instead, as he who called you is holy, be holy yourselves in all your conduct; 16 for it is written, "You shall be holy, for I am holy."[1]

17 If you invoke as Father the one who judges all people impartially according to their deeds, live in reverent fear during the time of your exile.

18 You know that you were ransomed from the futile ways inherited from your ancestors, not with perishable things like silver or gold, 19 but with the precious blood of Christ, like that of a lamb without defect or blemish. 20 He was destined before the foundation of the world, but was revealed at the end of the ages for your sake. 21 Through him you have come to trust in God, who raised him from the dead and gave him glory, so that your faith and hope are set on God.

22 Now that you have purified your souls by your obedience to the truth[d] so that you have genuine mutual love, love one another deeply[e] from the heart.[f] 23 You have been born anew, not of perishable but of imperishable seed, through the living and enduring word of God.[g] 24 For

"All flesh is like grass
    and all its glory like the flower
        of grass.
The grass withers,
    and the flower falls,
25   but the word of the Lord endures
        forever."[2]

That word is the good news that was announced to you.

2 Rid yourselves, therefore, of all malice, and all guile, insincerity, envy, and all slander. 2 Like newborn infants, long for the pure, spiritual milk, so that by it you may grow into salvation— 3 if indeed you have tasted that the Lord is good.

4 Come to him, a living stone, though rejected by mortals yet chosen and precious in God's sight, and 5 like living stones, let yourselves be built[h] into a spiritual house, to be a holy priesthood, to offer spiritual sacrifices acceptable to God through Jesus Christ. 6 For it stands in scripture:

"See, I am laying in Zion a stone,
    a cornerstone chosen and
        precious;
and whoever believes in him[i] will
    not be put to shame."[3]

---

[a]Or *Rejoice in this* [b]Other ancient authorities read *known* [c]Gk *gird up the loins of your mind* [d]Other ancient authorities add *through the Spirit* [e]Or *constantly* [f]Other ancient authorities read *a pure heart* [g]Or *through the word of the living and enduring God* [h]Or *you yourselves are being built* [i]Or *it*

---

[1]Lev 11:45; 19:2 [2]Isa 40:6–8 [3]Isa 28:16

7 To you then who believe, he is precious; but for those who do not believe,

> "The stone that the builders
>   rejected
>   has become the very head of the
>   corner,"[4]

8 and

> "A stone that makes them
>   stumble,
>   and a rock that makes them
>   fall."[5]

They stumble because they disobey the word, as they were destined to do.

9 But you are a chosen race, a royal priesthood, a holy nation, God's own people,[j] in order that you may proclaim the mighty acts of him who called you out of darkness into his marvelous light.

10
> Once you were not a people,
>   but now you are God's people;
> once you had not received mercy,
>   but now you have received
>   mercy.

11 Beloved, I urge you as aliens and exiles to abstain from the desires of the flesh that wage war against the soul. 12 Conduct yourselves honorably among the Gentiles, so that, though they malign you as evildoers, they may see your honorable deeds and glorify God when he comes to judge.[k]

13 For the Lord's sake accept the authority of every human institution,[l] whether of the emperor as supreme, 14 or of governors, as sent by him to punish those who do wrong and to praise those who do right. 15 For it is God's will that by doing right you should silence the ignorance of the foolish. 16 As servants[m] of God, live as free people, yet do not use your freedom as a pretext for evil. 17 Honor everyone. Love the family of believers.[n] Fear God. Honor the emperor.

18 Slaves, accept the authority of your masters with all deference, not only those who are kind and gentle but also those who are harsh. 19 For it is a credit to you if, being aware of God, you endure pain while suffering unjustly. 20 If you endure when you are beaten for doing wrong, what credit is that? But if you endure when you do right and suffer for it, you have God's approval. 21 For to this you have been called, because Christ also suffered for you, leaving you an example, so that you should follow in his steps.

22
> "He committed no sin,
>   and no deceit was found in his
>   mouth."[6]

23 When he was abused, he did not return abuse; when he suffered, he did not threaten; but he entrusted himself to the one who judges justly. 24 He himself bore our sins in his body on the cross,[o] so that, free from sins, we might live for righteousness; by his wounds[p] you have been healed. 25 For you were going astray like sheep, but now you have returned to the shepherd and guardian of your souls.

3 Wives, in the same way, accept the authority of your husbands, so that, even if some of them do not obey the word, they may be won over without a word by their wives' conduct, 2 when they see the purity and reverence of your lives. 3 Do not adorn yourselves outwardly by braiding your hair, and by wearing gold ornaments or fine clothing; 4 rather, let your adornment be the inner self with the lasting beauty of a gentle and quiet spirit, which is very precious in God's sight. 5 It was in this way long ago that the holy women who hoped in God used to adorn themselves by accepting the authority of their husbands. 6 Thus Sarah obeyed Abraham and called him lord. You have become her daughters as long as you do what is good and never let fears alarm you.

7 Husbands, in the same way, show consideration for your wives in your life together, paying honor to the woman as the weaker sex,[q] since they too are also heirs of the gracious gift of life—so that nothing may hinder your prayers.

8 Finally, all of you, have unity of spirit, sympathy, love for one another, a tender heart, and a humble mind. 9 Do not repay evil for evil or abuse for abuse; but, on the contrary, repay with a blessing. It is for this that you were called—that you might inherit a blessing. 10 For

> "Those who desire life
>   and desire to see good days,
>   let them keep their tongues from
>   evil

---

[j]Gk *a people for his possession*   [k]Gk *God on the day of visitation*
[l]Or *every institution ordained for human beings*   [m]Gk *slaves*
[n]Gk *Love the brotherhood*   [o]Or *carried up our sins in his body to the tree*   [p]Gk *bruise*   [q]Gk *vessel*

---

[4]Ps 118:22   [5]Isa 8:14   [6]Isa 53:9

and their lips from speaking
deceit;

11   let them turn away from evil and
do good;
let them seek peace and pursue
it.

12   For the eyes of the Lord are on
the righteous,
and his ears are open to their
prayer.
But the face of the Lord is against
those who do evil."[7]

13 Now who will harm you if you are eager to do what is good? 14 But even if you do suffer for doing what is right, you are blessed. Do not fear what they fear,[r] and do not be intimidated, 15 but in your hearts sanctify Christ as Lord. Always be ready to make your defense to anyone who demands from you an accounting for the hope that is in you; 16 yet do it with gentleness and reverence.[s] Keep your conscience clear, so that, when you are maligned, those who abuse you for your good conduct in Christ may be put to shame. 17 For it is better to suffer for doing good, if suffering should be God's will, than to suffer for doing evil. 18 For Christ also suffered[t] for sins once for all, the righteous for the unrighteous, in order to bring you[u] to God. He was put to death in the flesh, but made alive in the spirit, 19 in which also he went and made a proclamation to the spirits in prison, 20 who in former times did not obey, when God waited patiently in the days of Noah, during the building of the ark, in which a few, that is, eight persons, were saved through water. 21 And baptism, which this prefigured, now saves you—not as a removal of dirt from the body, but as an appeal to God for[v] a good conscience, through the resurrection of Jesus Christ, 22 who has gone into heaven and is at the right hand of God, with angels, authorities, and powers made subject to him.

4 Since therefore Christ suffered in the flesh,[w] arm yourselves also with the same intention (for whoever has suffered in the flesh has finished with sin), 2 so as to live for the rest of your earthly life[x] no longer by human desires but by the will of God. 3 You have already spent enough time in doing what the Gentiles like to do, living in licentiousness, passions, drunkenness, revels, carous-

ing, and lawless idolatry. 4 They are surprised that you no longer join them in the same excesses of dissipation, and so they blaspheme.[y] 5 But they will have to give an accounting to him who stands ready to judge the living and the dead. 6 For this is the reason the gospel was proclaimed even to the dead, so that, though they had been judged in the flesh as everyone is judged, they might live in the spirit as God does.

7 The end of all things is near;[z] therefore be serious and discipline yourselves for the sake of your prayers. 8 Above all, maintain constant love for one another, for love covers a multitude of sins. 9 Be hospitable to one another without complaining. 10 Like good stewards of the manifold grace of God, serve one another with whatever gift each of you has received. 11 Whoever speaks must do so as one speaking the very words of God; whoever serves must do so with the strength that God supplies, so that God may be glorified in all things through Jesus Christ. To him belong the glory and the power forever and ever. Amen.

12 Beloved, do not be surprised at the fiery ordeal that is taking place among you to test you, as though something strange were happening to you. 13 But rejoice insofar as you are sharing Christ's sufferings, so that you may also be glad and shout for joy when his glory is revealed. 14 If you are reviled for the name of Christ, you are blessed, because the spirit of glory,[a] which is the Spirit of God, is resting on you.[b] 15 But let none of you suffer as a murderer, a thief, a criminal, or even as a mischief maker. 16 Yet if any of you suffers as a Christian, do not consider it a disgrace, but glorify God because you bear this name. 17 For the time has come for judgment to begin with the household of God; if it begins with us, what will be the end for those who do not obey the gospel of God? 18 And

"If it is hard for the righteous to
be saved,

---

[r]Gk *their fear*   [s]Or *respect*   [t]Other ancient authorities read *died*
[u]Other ancient authorities read *us*   [v]Or *a pledge to God from*
[w]Other ancient authorities add *for us*; others, *for you*   [x]Gk *rest of the time in the flesh*   [y]Or *they malign you*   [z]Or *is at hand*   [a]Other ancient authorities add *and of power*   [b]Other ancient authorities add *On their part he is blasphemed, but on your part he is glorified*

---

[7]Ps 34:12–16

what will become of the

ungodly and the sinners?"[8]

19 Therefore, let those suffering in accordance with God's will entrust themselves to a faithful Creator, while continuing to do good.

5 Now as an elder myself and a witness of the sufferings of Christ, as well as one who shares in the glory to be revealed, I exhort the elders among you 2 to tend the flock of God that is in your charge, exercising the oversight,[c] not under compulsion but willingly, as God would have you do it[d]—not for sordid gain but eagerly. 3 Do not lord it over those in your charge, but be examples to the flock. 4 And when the chief shepherd appears, you will win the crown of glory that never fades away. 5 In the same way, you who are younger must accept the authority of the elders.[e] And all of you must clothe yourselves with humility in your dealings with one another, for

"God opposes the proud,

but gives grace to the humble."[9]

6 Humble yourselves therefore under the mighty hand of God, so that he may exalt you in due time. 7 Cast all your anxiety on him, because he cares for you. 8 Discipline yourselves, keep alert.[f] Like a roaring lion your adversary the devil prowls around, looking for someone to devour. 9 Resist him, steadfast in your faith, for you know that your brothers and sisters[g] in all the world are undergoing the same kinds of suffering. 10 And after you have suffered for a little while, the God of all grace, who has called you to his eternal glory in Christ, will himself restore, support, strengthen, and establish you. 11 To him be the power forever and ever. Amen.

12 Through Silvanus, whom I consider a faithful brother, I have written this short letter to encourage you and to testify that this is the true grace of God. Stand fast in it. 13 Your sister church[h] in Babylon, chosen together with you, sends you greetings; and so does my son Mark. 14 Greet one another with a kiss of love.

Peace to all of you who are in Christ.[i]

---

[c]Other ancient authorities lack *exercising the oversight*   [d]Other ancient authorities lack *as God would have you do it*   [e]Or *of those who are older*   [f]Or *be vigilant*   [g]Gk *your brotherhood*   [h]Gk *She who is*   [i]Other ancient authorities add *Amen*

[8]Prov 11:31   [9]Prov 3:34

The Letter of 2 Peter

The author of 2 Peter claims to be the apostle "Simeon Peter," who beheld Jesus' glory and heard the voice from heaven on the Mount of Transfiguration (1:1, 17–18). On the basis of internal evidence in the letter itself, however, the majority of critical scholars have concluded that it is pseudonymous, written some decades after Peter's death by an author intent on providing apostolic support for his own views. For one thing, the book was written at a time when the imminent end of the world, so widely anticipated among the earliest Christians, had become a source of ridicule against them (3:3–10). Moreover, as is sometimes pointed out, it was written by a relatively sophisticated Greek-speaking Christian, rather than an Aramaic-speaking Jewish peasant. It is striking that no church writer evidences any knowledge of this book at all until the beginning of the third century; this would be peculiar if it were known to be an actual letter by Jesus' apostle.

The author claims to be Peter precisely in order to show that, unlike his opponents, he has no need of "cleverly devised myths" to understand Jesus (1:16); he knows about him firsthand. His opponents appear to be early Christian Gnostics who propound idiosyncratic interpretations of Scripture (1:20) and who appeal to the writings of Paul for support (3:16). The author never explains what, exactly, these views were, but instead launches an attack on the immoral lives of those who advance them (chap. 2). They are said to be "insatiable for sin," they speak "bombastic nonsense," and they are full of "licentious desires" (2:14, 18). Much of this vituperative attack appears to have been borrowed from the book of Jude.

In particular, the author opposes those who scoff at Christians for thinking, against all appearances, that the end of the world is imminent (3:3–4). For him, the end is indeed soon to come, and those who mock have erred in measuring time in human terms. For with God "one day is like a thousand years and a thousand years are like one day" (3:8). The end, the author maintains, has been delayed for good reason: to allow people a chance to repent. This they must do without delay, for when the "day of God" comes, "the heavens will be set ablaze and dissolved, and the elements will melt with fire," but those who are prepared will be rewarded with "new heavens and a new earth, where righteousness is at home" (3:12–13).

1 Simeon[a] Peter, a servant[b] and apostle of Jesus Christ,

To those who have received a faith as precious as ours through the righteousness of our God and Savior Jesus Christ:[c]

2 May grace and peace be yours in abundance in the knowledge of God and of Jesus our Lord.

3 His divine power has given us everything needed for life and godliness, through the knowledge of him who called us by[d] his own glory and goodness. 4 Thus he has given us, through these things, his precious and very great promises, so that through them you may escape from the cor-

---

[a]Other ancient authorities read *Simon*   [b]Gk *slave*   [c]Or *of our God and the Savior Jesus Christ*   [d]Other ancient authorities read *through*

ruption that is in the world because of lust, and may become participants of the divine nature. 5 For this very reason, you must make every effort to support your faith with goodness, and goodness with knowledge, 6 and knowledge with self-control, and self-control with endurance, and endurance with godliness, 7 and godliness with mutual[e] affection, and mutual[e] affection with love. 8 For if these things are yours and are increasing among you, they keep you from being ineffective and unfruitful in the knowledge of our Lord Jesus Christ. 9 For anyone who lacks these things is nearsighted and blind, and is forgetful of the cleansing of past sins. 10 Therefore, brothers and sisters,[f] be all the more eager to confirm your call and election, for if you do this, you will never stumble. 11 For in this way, entry into the eternal kingdom of our Lord and Savior Jesus Christ will be richly provided for you.

12 Therefore I intend to keep on reminding you of these things, though you know them already and are established in the truth that has come to you. 13 I think it right, as long as I am in this body,[g] to refresh your memory, 14 since I know that my death[h] will come soon, as indeed our Lord Jesus Christ has made clear to me. 15 And I will make every effort so that after my departure you may be able at any time to recall these things.

16 For we did not follow cleverly devised myths when we made known to you the power and coming of our Lord Jesus Christ, but we had been eyewitnesses of his majesty. 17 For he received honor and glory from God the Father when that voice was conveyed to him by the Majestic Glory, saying, "This is my Son, my Beloved,[i] with whom I am well pleased."[1] 18 We ourselves heard this voice come from heaven, while we were with him on the holy mountain.

19 So we have the prophetic message more fully confirmed. You will do well to be attentive to this as to a lamp shining in a dark place, until the day dawns and the morning star rises in your hearts. 20 First of all you must understand this, that no prophecy of scripture is a matter of one's own interpretation, 21 because no prophecy ever came by human will, but men and women moved by the Holy Spirit spoke from God.[j]

2 But false prophets also arose among the people, just as there will be false teachers among you, who will secretly bring in destructive opinions. They will even deny the Master who bought them—bringing swift destruction on themselves. 2 Even so, many will follow their licentious ways, and because of these teachers[k] the way of truth will be maligned. 3 And in their greed they will exploit you with deceptive words. Their condemnation, pronounced against them long ago, has not been idle, and their destruction is not asleep.

4 For if God did not spare the angels when they sinned, but cast them into hell[l] and committed them to chains[m] of deepest darkness to be kept until the judgment; 5 and if he did not spare the ancient world, even though he saved Noah, a herald of righteousness, with seven others, when he brought a flood on a world of the ungodly; 6 and if by turning the cities of Sodom and Gomorrah to ashes he condemned them to extinction[n] and made them an example of what is coming to the ungodly;[o] 7 and if he rescued Lot, a righteous man greatly distressed by the licentiousness of the lawless 8 (for that righteous man, living among them day after day, was tormented in his righteous soul by their lawless deeds that he saw and heard), 9 then the Lord knows how to rescue the godly from trial, and to keep the unrighteous under punishment until the day of judgment 10 —especially those who indulge their flesh in depraved lust, and who despise authority.

Bold and willful, they are not afraid to slander the glorious ones,[p] 11 whereas angels, though greater in might and power, do not bring against them a slanderous judgment from the Lord.[q] 12 These people, however, are like irrational animals, mere creatures of instinct, born to be caught and killed. They slander what they do not understand, and when those creatures are destroyed,[r] they also will be destroyed, 13 suffering[s] the penalty for doing wrong. They count it a pleasure to revel in the daytime. They are blots and blem-

---

[e]Gk *brotherly*   [f]Gk *brothers*   [g]Gk *tent*   [h]Gk *the putting off of my tent*   [i]Other ancient authorities read *my beloved Son*   [j]Other ancient authorities read *but moved by the Holy Spirit saints of God spoke*   [k]Gk *because of them*   [l]Gk *Tartaros*   [m]Other ancient authorities read *pits*   [n]Other ancient authorities lack *to extinction*   [o]Other ancient authorities read *an example to those who were to be ungodly*   [p]Or *angels*; Gk *glories*   [q]Other ancient authorities read *before the Lord*; others lack the phrase   [r]Gk *in their destruction*   [s]Other ancient authorities read *receiving*

[1]Matt 17:5; Mk 9:7

ishes, reveling in their dissipation[t] while they feast with you. 14 They have eyes full of adultery, insatiable for sin. They entice unsteady souls. They have hearts trained in greed. Accursed children! 15 They have left the straight road and have gone astray, following the road of Balaam son of Bosor,[u] who loved the wages of doing wrong, 16 but was rebuked for his own transgression; a speechless donkey spoke with a human voice and restrained the prophet's madness.

17 These are waterless springs and mists driven by a storm; for them the deepest darkness has been reserved. 18 For they speak bombastic nonsense, and with licentious desires of the flesh they entice people who have just[v] escaped from those who live in error. 19 They promise them freedom, but they themselves are slaves of corruption; for people are slaves to whatever masters them. 20 For if, after they have escaped the defilements of the world through the knowledge of our Lord and Savior Jesus Christ, they are again entangled in them and overpowered, the last state has become worse for them than the first. 21 For it would have been better for them never to have known the way of righteousness than, after knowing it, to turn back from the holy commandment that was passed on to them. 22 It has happened to them according to the true proverb,

> "The dog turns back to its own
> vomit,"[2]

and,

> "The sow is washed only to
> wallow in the mud."

3 This is now, beloved, the second letter I am writing to you; in them I am trying to arouse your sincere intention by reminding you 2 that you should remember the words spoken in the past by the holy prophets, and the commandment of the Lord and Savior spoken through your apostles. 3 First of all you must understand this, that in the last days scoffers will come, scoffing and indulging their own lusts 4 and saying, "Where is the promise of his coming? For ever since our ancestors died,[w] all things continue as they were from the beginning of creation!" 5 They deliberately ignore this fact, that by the word of God heavens existed long ago and an earth was formed out of water and by means of water, 6 through

which the world of that time was deluged with water and perished. 7 But by the same word the present heavens and earth have been reserved for fire, being kept until the day of judgment and destruction of the godless.

8 But do not ignore this one fact, beloved, that with the Lord one day is like a thousand years, and a thousand years are like one day. 9 The Lord is not slow about his promise, as some think of slowness, but is patient with you,[x] not wanting any to perish, but all to come to repentance. 10 But the day of the Lord will come like a thief, and then the heavens will pass away with a loud noise, and the elements will be dissolved with fire, and the earth and everything that is done on it will be disclosed.[y]

11 Since all these things are to be dissolved in this way, what sort of persons ought you to be in leading lives of holiness and godliness, 12 waiting for and hastening[z] the coming of the day of God, because of which the heavens will be set ablaze and dissolved, and the elements will melt with fire? 13 But, in accordance with his promise, we wait for new heavens and a new earth, where righteousness is at home.

14 Therefore, beloved, while you are waiting for these things, strive to be found by him at peace, without spot or blemish; 15 and regard the patience of our Lord as salvation. So also our beloved brother Paul wrote to you according to the wisdom given him, 16 speaking of this as he does in all his letters. There are some things in them hard to understand, which the ignorant and unstable twist to their own destruction, as they do the other scriptures. 17 You therefore, beloved, since you are forewarned, beware that you are not carried away with the error of the lawless and lose your own stability. 18 But grow in the grace and knowledge of our Lord and Savior Jesus Christ. To him be the glory both now and to the day of eternity. Amen.[a]

---

[t]Other ancient authorities read *love-feasts* [u]Other ancient authorities read *Beor* [v]Other ancient authorities read *actually* [w]Gk *our fathers fell asleep* [x]Other ancient authorities read *on your account* [y]Other ancient authorities read *will be burned up* [z]Or *earnestly desiring* [a]Other ancient authorities lack *Amen*

[2]Prov 26:11

The Letter of 1 John

Although traditionally called an "epistle," the book of 1 John lacks the standard conventions of ancient letters: the author does not introduce himself, name his addressees, or offer an opening greeting or prayer on their behalf; nor does he conclude with well-wishings, final prayers, or even a farewell. The book appears to be a persuasive essay written by a Christian leader to a Christian community; it was possibly accompanied by a cover letter that has since been lost.

The occasion for the essay is relatively clear. The author refers to a group of persons who had formerly belonged to the community but have since left: "They went out from us, but they did not belong to us; for if they had belonged to us, they would have remained with us" (2:19). In other places he calls these persons "liars" and "antichrists" (i.e., those who are opposed to Christ; 2:4, 18, 22). Some evidence in the letter suggests that these persons were Christians who believed so strongly in the divinity of Jesus that they had come to deny his humanity. That is to say, they did not think that, as a divine being, Jesus fully participated in human existence; he did not have have a real flesh-and-blood body. Not finding acceptance in the community, these people withdrew, possibly in order to start a new community of their own.

The author counteracts his opponents' views by stressing that Christ actually did "come in the flesh" (4:2), that the "Word of Life" could be "heard . . . seen with our eyes . . . and touched with our hands" (1:1–2), and that it was his real blood that brought forgiveness of sins (1:7; 2:2; 4:10). Moreover, he maintains that the real fleshly existence of Christ has moral implications for the believer. He charges that his opponents, more concerned with the spirit than the flesh, are lax in keeping God's commandments and in loving their brothers and sisters (2:4, 9–11); they practice sin while claiming to be spiritual beings who have no contact with it (1:6–10). In contrast, the author stresses that his readers are to manifest real, active love among one another as the children of God (e.g., 3:18; 4:7).

We do not know who actually wrote this book, as the writer kept his identity anonymous. Readers have long noted the similarity in vocabulary and theology to the Fourth Gospel, and so have traditionally ascribed the book to the same author. Since, however, the issues raised here differ markedly from those addressed by the Gospel—the conflict with the Jewish synagogue, for example, is entirely lacking—most scholars today prefer to see the book as stemming from a later author living in the same community, one who possibly knew the gospel traditions and understood himself (as opposed to those who withdrew from the community) to stand in continuity with them.

1 We declare to you what was from the beginning, what we have heard, what we have seen with our eyes, what we have looked at and touched with our hands, concerning the word of life— 2 this life was revealed, and we have seen it and testify to it, and declare to you the eternal life that was with the Father and was revealed to us— 3 we declare to you what we have seen and heard

so that you also may have fellowship with us; and truly our fellowship is with the Father and with his Son Jesus Christ. 4 We are writing these things so that our[a] joy may be complete.

5 This is the message we have heard from him and proclaim to you, that God is light and in him there is no darkness at all. 6 If we say that we have fellowship with him while we are walking in darkness, we lie and do not do what is true; 7 but if we walk in the light as he himself is in the light, we have fellowship with one another, and the blood of Jesus his Son cleanses us from all sin. 8 If we say that we have no sin, we deceive ourselves, and the truth is not in us. 9 If we confess our sins, he who is faithful and just will forgive us our sins and cleanse us from all unrighteousness. 10 If we say that we have not sinned, we make him a liar, and his word is not in us.

2 My little children, I am writing these things to you so that you may not sin. But if anyone does sin, we have an advocate with the Father, Jesus Christ the righteous; 2 and he is the atoning sacrifice for our sins, and not for ours only but also for the sins of the whole world.

3 Now by this we may be sure that we know him, if we obey his commandments. 4 Whoever says, "I have come to know him," but does not obey his commandments, is a liar, and in such a person the truth does not exist; 5 but whoever obeys his word, truly in this person the love of God has reached perfection. By this we may be sure that we are in him: 6 whoever says, "I abide in him," ought to walk just as he walked.

7 Beloved, I am writing you no new commandment, but an old commandment that you have had from the beginning; the old commandment is the word that you have heard. 8 Yet I am writing you a new commandment that is true in him and in you, because[b] the darkness is passing away and the true light is already shining. 9 Whoever says, "I am in the light," while hating a brother or sister,[c] is still in the darkness. 10 Whoever loves a brother or sister[d] lives in the light, and in such a person[e] there is no cause for stumbling. 11 But whoever hates another believer[f] is in the darkness, walks in the darkness, and does not know the way to go, because the darkness has brought on blindness.

12   I am writing to you, little
               children,

because your sins are forgiven
on account of his name.
13   I am writing to you, fathers,
              because you know him who is
                   from the beginning.
        I am writing to you, young
              people,
              because you have conquered the
                   evil one.
14   I write to you, children,
              because you know the Father.
        I write to you, fathers,
              because you know him who is
                   from the beginning.
        I write to you, young people,
              because you are strong
              and the word of God abides in
                   you,
                   and you have overcome the
                        evil one.

15 Do not love the world or the things in the world. The love of the Father is not in those who love the world; 16 for all that is in the world—the desire of the flesh, the desire of the eyes, the pride in riches—comes not from the Father but from the world. 17 And the world and its desire[g] are passing away, but those who do the will of God live forever.

18 Children, it is the last hour! As you have heard that antichrist is coming, so now many antichrists have come. From this we know that it is the last hour. 19 They went out from us, but they did not belong to us; for if they had belonged to us, they would have remained with us. But by going out they made it plain that none of them belongs to us. 20 But you have been anointed by the Holy One, and all of you have knowledge.[h] 21 I write to you, not because you do not know the truth, but because you know it, and you know that no lie comes from the truth. 22 Who is the liar but the one who denies that Jesus is the Christ?[i] This is the antichrist, the one who denies the Father and the Son. 23 No one who denies the Son has the Father; everyone who confesses the Son has the Father also. 24 Let what you heard from the begin-

[a]Other ancient authorities read *your*   [b]Or *that*   [c]Gk *hating a brother* [d]Gk *loves a brother*   [e]Or *in it*   [f]Gk *hates a brother*   [g]Or *the desire for it*   [h]Other ancient authorities read *you know all things*   [i]Or *the Messiah*

ning abide in you. If what you heard from the beginning abides in you, then you will abide in the Son and in the Father. 25 And this is what he has promised us,[j] eternal life.

26 I write these things to you concerning those who would deceive you. 27 As for you, the anointing that you received from him abides in you, and so you do not need anyone to teach you. But as his anointing teaches you about all things, and is true and is not a lie, and just as it has taught you, abide in him.[k]

28 And now, little children, abide in him, so that when he is revealed we may have confidence and not be put to shame before him at his coming.

29 If you know that he is righteous, you may be sure that everyone who does right has been born of him.

3 See what love the Father has given us, that we should be called children of God; and that is what we are. The reason the world does not know us is that it did not know him. 2 Beloved, we are God's children now; what we will be has not yet been revealed. What we do know is this: when he[k] is revealed, we will be like him, for we will see him as he is. 3 And all who have this hope in him purify themselves, just as he is pure.

4 Everyone who commits sin is guilty of lawlessness; sin is lawlessness. 5 You know that he was revealed to take away sins, and in him there is no sin. 6 No one who abides in him sins; no one who sins has either seen him or known him. 7 Little children, let no one deceive you. Everyone who does what is right is righteous, just as he is righteous. 8 Everyone who commits sin is a child of the devil; for the devil has been sinning from the beginning. The Son of God was revealed for this purpose, to destroy the works of the devil. 9 Those who have been born of God do not sin, because God's seed abides in them;[l] they cannot sin, because they have been born of God. 10 The children of God and the children of the devil are revealed in this way: all who do not do what is right are not from God, nor are those who do not love their brothers and sisters.[m]

11 For this is the message you have heard from the beginning, that we should love one another. 12 We must not be like Cain who was from the evil one and murdered his brother. And why did he murder him? Because his own deeds were evil and

his brother's righteous. 13 Do not be astonished, brothers and sisters,[n] that the world hates you. 14 We know that we have passed from death to life because we love one another. Whoever does not love abides in death. 15 All who hate a brother or sister[m] are murderers, and you know that murderers do not have eternal life abiding in them. 16 We know love by this, that he laid down his life for us—and we ought to lay down our lives for one another. 17 How does God's love abide in anyone who has the world's goods and sees a brother or sister[o] in need and yet refuses help?

18 Little children, let us love, not in word or speech, but in truth and action. 19 And by this we will know that we are from the truth and will reassure our hearts before him 20 whenever our hearts condemn us; for God is greater than our hearts, and he knows everything. 21 Beloved, if our hearts do not condemn us, we have boldness before God; 22 and we receive from him whatever we ask, because we obey his commandments and do what pleases him.

23 And this is his commandment, that we should believe in the name of his Son Jesus Christ and love one another, just as he has commanded us. 24 All who obey his commandments abide in him, and he abides in them. And by this we know that he abides in us, by the Spirit that he has given us.

4 Beloved, do not believe every spirit, but test the spirits to see whether they are from God; for many false prophets have gone out into the world. 2 By this you know the Spirit of God: every spirit that confesses that Jesus Christ has come in the flesh is from God, 3 and every spirit that does not confess Jesus[p] is not from God. And this is the spirit of the antichrist, of which you have heard that it is coming; and now it is already in the world. 4 Little children, you are from God, and have conquered them; for the one who is in you is greater than the one who is in the world. 5 They are from the world; therefore what they say is from the world, and the world listens to them. 6 We are from God. Whoever knows God listens to us, and whoever is not from God does not listen to us.

[j]Other ancient authorities read *you* [k]Or *it* [l]Or *because the children of God abide in him* [m]Gk *his brother* [n]Gk *brothers* [o]Gk *brother* [p]Other ancient authorities read *does away with Jesus* (Gk *dissolves Jesus*)

From this we know the spirit of truth and the spirit of error.

7 Beloved, let us love one another, because love is from God; everyone who loves is born of God and knows God. 8 Whoever does not love does not know God, for God is love. 9 God's love was revealed among us in this way: God sent his only Son into the world so that we might live through him. 10 In this is love, not that we loved God but that he loved us and sent his Son to be the atoning sacrifice for our sins. 11 Beloved, since God loved us so much, we also ought to love one another. 12 No one has ever seen God; if we love one another, God lives in us, and his love is perfected in us.

13 By this we know that we abide in him and he in us, because he has given us of his Spirit. 14 And we have seen and do testify that the Father has sent his Son as the Savior of the world. 15 God abides in those who confess that Jesus is the Son of God, and they abide in God. 16 So we have known and believe the love that God has for us.

God is love, and those who abide in love abide in God, and God abides in them. 17 Love has been perfected among us in this: that we may have boldness on the day of judgment, because as he is, so are we in this world. 18 There is no fear in love, but perfect love casts out fear; for fear has to do with punishment, and whoever fears has not reached perfection in love. 19 We love[q] because he first loved us. 20 Those who say, "I love God," and hate their brothers or sisters,[r] are liars; for those who do not love a brother or sister[s] whom they have seen, cannot love God whom they have not seen. 21 The commandment we have from him is this: those who love God must love their brothers and sisters[r] also.

5 Everyone who believes that Jesus is the Christ[t] has been born of God, and everyone who loves the parent loves the child. 2 By this we know that we love the children of God, when we love God and obey his commandments. 3 For the love of God is this, that we obey his commandments. And his commandments are not burdensome, 4 for whatever is born of God conquers the world. And this is the victory that conquers the world, our faith. 5 Who is it that conquers the world but the one who believes that Jesus is the Son of God?

6 This is the one who came by water and blood, Jesus Christ, not with the water only but with the water and the blood. And the Spirit is the one that testifies, for the Spirit is the truth. 7 There are three that testify:[u] 8 the Spirit and the water and the blood, and these three agree. 9 If we receive human testimony, the testimony of God is greater; for this is the testimony of God that he has testified to his Son. 10 Those who believe in the Son of God have the testimony in their hearts. Those who do not believe in God[v] have made him a liar by not believing in the testimony that God has given concerning his Son. 11 And this is the testimony: God gave us eternal life, and this life is in his Son. 12 Whoever has the Son has life; whoever does not have the Son of God does not have life.

13 I write these things to you who believe in the name of the Son of God, so that you may know that you have eternal life.

14 And this is the boldness we have in him, that if we ask anything according to his will, he hears us. 15 And if we know that he hears us in whatever we ask, we know that we have obtained the requests made of him. 16 If you see your brother or sister[w] committing what is not a mortal sin, you will ask, and God[x] will give life to such a one—to those whose sin is not mortal. There is sin that is mortal; I do not say that you should pray about that. 17 All wrongdoing is sin, but there is sin that is not mortal.

18 We know that those who are born of God do not sin, but the one who was born of God protects them, and the evil one does not touch them. 19 We know that we are God's children, and that the whole world lies under the power of the evil one. 20 And we know that the Son of God has come and has given us understanding so that we may know him who is true;[y] and we are in him who is true, in his Son Jesus Christ. He is the true God and eternal life.

21 Little children, keep yourselves from idols.[z]

---

[q]Other ancient authorities add *him*; others add *God*   [r]Gk *brothers*   [s]Gk *brother*   [t]Or *the Messiah*   [u]A few other authorities read (with variations) [7]*There are three that testify in heaven, the Father, the Word, and the Holy Spirit, and these three are one.* [8]*And there are three that testify on earth:*   [v]Other ancient authorities read *in the Son*   [w]Gk *your brother*   [x]Gk *he*   [y]Other ancient authorities read *know the true God*   [z]Other ancient authorities add *Amen*

The Letter of 2 John

Unlike 1 John (see that introduction), the book of 2 John is an actual epistle, sent by someone who calls himself "the elder" to an unnamed person called "the elect lady" (v. 1). Because in the course of his letter the author stops speaking to this "lady" and begins addressing a group of people ("you," plural, in v. 6), many scholars assume that the term *elect lady* refers to a Christian community that understands itself to be the chosen of God.

The issues and concerns of this letter are closely aligned with those of 1 John, as are the vocabulary and writing style, leading most scholars to conclude that they were written by the same author, probably to the same community. Here too there is a concern over "deceivers" and "antichrists" who deny that "Jesus has come in the flesh" (v. 7); here too there is an emphasis on the need for those within the community to love one another by keeping God's commandments (vv. 5–6).

The author strongly opposes those who do not share his views in such matters, insisting that the community show no hospitality to anyone who takes a contrary position (vv. 9–11). He concludes by indicating his eagerness to join the congregation soon and by sending greetings from its "elect sister," that is, presumably, his own Christian community (v. 13). Like 1 John, the book was probably produced after the Fourth Gospel, sometime near the end of the first century.

1 The elder to the elect lady and her children, whom I love in the truth, and not only I but also all who know the truth, 2 because of the truth that abides in us and will be with us forever:

3 Grace, mercy, and peace will be with us from God the Father and from[a] Jesus Christ, the Father's Son, in truth and love.

4 I was overjoyed to find some of your children walking in the truth, just as we have been commanded by the Father. 5 But now, dear lady, I ask you, not as though I were writing you a new commandment, but one we have had from the beginning, let us love one another. 6 And this is love, that we walk according to his commandments; this is the commandment just as you have heard it from the beginning—you must walk in it.

7 Many deceivers have gone out into the world, those who do not confess that Jesus Christ has come in the flesh; any such person is the deceiver and the antichrist! 8 Be on your guard, so that you do not lose what we[b] have worked for, but may receive a full reward. 9 Everyone who does not abide in the teaching of Christ, but goes beyond it, does not have God; whoever abides in the teaching has both the Father and the Son. 10 Do not receive into the house or welcome anyone who comes to you and does not bring this teaching; 11 for to welcome is to participate in the evil deeds of such a person.

12 Although I have much to write to you, I would rather not use paper and ink; instead I hope to come to you and talk with you face to face, so that our joy may be complete.

13 The children of your elect sister send you their greetings.[c]

[a]Other ancient authorities add *the Lord* [b]Other ancient authorities read *you* [c]Other ancient authorities add *Amen*

The Letter of 3 John

Like 2 John, the book of 3 John is a real letter; it was evidently written by the same author. Rather than addressing the entire Christian community, however, here the author addresses an individual within it, a man named Gaius. It appears that Gaius had shown some hospitality to a group of traveling Christians (missionaries?), possibly sent by the author himself, and the author is writing to express his gratitude (vv. 5–8).

At the same time, the letter reveals a serious bit of tension in Gaius's Christian community, for another leader named Diotrephes has refused to receive these visitors and has defamed the author of the letter himself (vv. 9–10). It remains unclear whether Gaius and Diotrephes were heads of different house churches within the same community or were, instead, leading spokespersons within the same church.

In any event, the author commends to Gaius another of his envoys, Demetrius, possibly as the one bearing the letter (v. 12). As in 2 John, he concludes by expressing his desire to visit soon and by sending greetings from members of his own church (vv. 13–15).

1 The elder to the beloved Gaius, whom I love in truth.

2 Beloved, I pray that all may go well with you and that you may be in good health, just as it is well with your soul. 3 I was overjoyed when some of the friends[a] arrived and testified to your faithfulness to the truth, namely how you walk in the truth. 4 I have no greater joy than this, to hear that my children are walking in the truth.

5 Beloved, you do faithfully whatever you do for the friends,[a] even though they are strangers to you; 6 they have testified to your love before the church. You will do well to send them on in a manner worthy of God; 7 for they began their journey for the sake of Christ,[b] accepting no support from non-believers.[c] 8 Therefore we ought to support such people, so that we may become co-workers with the truth.

9 I have written something to the church; but Diotrephes, who likes to put himself first, does not acknowledge our authority. 10 So if I come, I will call attention to what he is doing in spreading false charges against us. And not content with those charges, he refuses to welcome the friends,[a] and even prevents those who want to do so and expels them from the church.

11 Beloved, do not imitate what is evil but imitate what is good. Whoever does good is from God; whoever does evil has not seen God. 12 Everyone has testified favorably about Demetrius, and so has the truth itself. We also testify for him,[d] and you know that our testimony is true.

13 I have much to write to you, but I would rather not write with pen and ink; 14 instead I hope to see you soon, and we will talk together face to face.

15 Peace to you. The friends send you their greetings. Greet the friends there, each by name.

[a]Gk brothers   [b]Gk for the sake of the name   [c]Gk the Gentiles
[d]Gk lacks for him

The Letter of Jude

The brief Letter of Jude is principally concerned with false teachers who have infiltrated the Christian community and led many of its members astray (v. 4). The author does not indicate what, exactly, these "intruders" taught, but he considers their teachings extremely dangerous: he maintains that they actually "deny our Master and Lord Jesus Christ" (v. 4). In particular he is concerned with the moral views these teachers embody. He claims that they behave like "irrational animals" (v. 10), engage in ungodly activities (v. 15), and indulge in their own lusts (v. 16). He likens them to the children of Israel who reveled in their wanton acts of adultery and idolatry after escaping Egypt, and to the inhabitants of Sodom and Gomorrah who "indulged in sexual immorality and pursued unnatural lust" (vv. 5–7).

Much of the epistle is filled with invective and name-calling against these opponents (see vv. 12–13). The author warns them to take heed and repent, or, like the inhabitants of Sodom and Gomorrah, they would be made "an example by undergoing a punishment of eternal fire" (v. 7).

The letter claims to be written by "Jude . . . the brother of James" (v. 1). Since Jesus was known to have two brothers named Jude and James (Mark 6:3), the latter of whom became the leader of the Jerusalem church (e.g., Gal 1:19; 2:9), the author appears to be claiming to be Jesus' own brother. Many scholars, however, suspect that the letter is pseudonymous. We know from historical sources that Jude's family was comprised of uneducated peasants, whereas this book is written by someone well-trained in Greek and conversant with a wide range of apocryphal Jewish literature (he quotes, for example from a lost apocryphal account in v. 9 and the book of 1 Enoch in v. 14). The book may have been written near the end of the first century, when Christian communities were coming under the influence of a wide array of teachers and leaders, many of whom stood at odds with one another and engaged in vitriolic attacks on one another's moral character.

1 Jude,[a] a servant[b] of Jesus Christ and brother of James,

To those who are called, who are beloved[c] in[d] God the Father and kept safe for[d] Jesus Christ:

2 May mercy, peace, and love be yours in abundance.

3 Beloved, while eagerly preparing to write to you about the salvation we share, I find it necessary to write and appeal to you to contend for the faith that was once for all entrusted to the saints. 4 For certain intruders have stolen in among you, people who long ago were designated for this condemnation as ungodly, who pervert the grace of our God into licentiousness and deny our only Master and Lord, Jesus Christ.[e]

[a]Gk *Judas* [b]Gk *slave* [c]Other ancient authorities read *sanctified*
[d]Or *by* [e]Or *the only Master and our Lord Jesus Christ*

5 Now I desire to remind you, though you are fully informed, that the Lord, who once for all saved[f] a people out of the land of Egypt, afterward destroyed those who did not believe. 6 And the angels who did not keep their own position, but left their proper dwelling, he has kept in eternal chains in deepest darkness for the judgment of the great day. 7 Likewise, Sodom and Gomorrah and the surrounding cities, which, in the same manner as they, indulged in sexual immorality and pursued unnatural lust,[g] serve as an example by undergoing a punishment of eternal fire.

8 Yet in the same way these dreamers also defile the flesh, reject authority, and slander the glorious ones.[h] 9 But when the archangel Michael contended with the devil and disputed about the body of Moses, he did not dare to bring a condemnation of slander[i] against him, but said, "The Lord rebuke you!" 10 But these people slander whatever they do not understand, and they are destroyed by those things that, like irrational animals, they know by instinct. 11 Woe to them! For they go the way of Cain, and abandon themselves to Balaam's error for the sake of gain, and perish in Korah's rebellion. 12 These are blemishes[j] on your love-feasts, while they feast with you without fear, feeding themselves.[k] They are waterless clouds carried along by the winds; autumn trees without fruit, twice dead, uprooted; 13 wild waves of the sea, casting up the foam of their own shame; wandering stars, for whom the deepest darkness has been reserved forever.

14 It was also about these that Enoch, in the seventh generation from Adam, prophesied, saying, "See, the Lord is coming[l] with ten thousands of his holy ones, 15 to execute judgment on all, and to convict everyone of all the deeds of ungodliness that they have committed in such an ungodly way, and of all the harsh things that ungodly sinners have spoken against him."[1] 16 These are grumblers and malcontents; they indulge their own lusts; they are bombastic in speech, flattering people to their own advantage.

17 But you, beloved, must remember the predictions of the apostles of our Lord Jesus Christ; 18 for they said to you, "In the last time there will be scoffers, indulging their own ungodly lusts." 19 It is these worldly people, devoid of the Spirit, who are causing divisions. 20 But you, beloved, build yourselves up on your most holy faith; pray in the Holy Spirit; 21 keep yourselves in the love of God; look forward to the mercy of our Lord Jesus Christ that leads to[m] eternal life. 22 And have mercy on some who are wavering; 23 save others by snatching them out of the fire; and have mercy on still others with fear, hating even the tunic defiled by their bodies.[n]

24 Now to him who is able to keep you from falling, and to make you stand without blemish in the presence of his glory with rejoicing, 25 to the only God our Savior, through Jesus Christ our Lord, be glory, majesty, power, and authority, before all time and now and forever. Amen.

[f]Other ancient authorities read *though you were once for all fully informed, that Jesus* (or *Joshua*) *who saved* [g]Gk *went after other flesh* [h]Or *angels*; Gk *glories* [i]Or *condemnation for blasphemy* [j]Or *reefs* [k]Or *without fear. They are shepherds who care only for themselves* [l]Gk *came* [m]Gk *Christ to* [n]Gk *by the flesh*. The Greek text of verses 22-23 is uncertain at several points

[1]1 Enoc 1:9

The Letter of 1 Clement

The letter of 1 Clement was sent from "the church of God in Rome" to "the church of God in Corinth" (1:1). Although traditionally ascribed to Clement, thought to have been the third bishop of Rome, the letter itself never names its actual author or mentions Clement. The purpose of the writing, in any event, is perfectly clear. There has been a division in the church in Corinth, an "odious and unholy breach of unity" (1:1) in which the elders of the church were forcibly deposed from their office and others took their place (3:2–4). For the Roman Christians, this is an altogether unacceptable arrangement: "it is disgraceful, exceedingly disgraceful, and unworthy of your Christian upbringing, to have it reported that because of one or two individuals the solid and ancient Corinthian church is in revolt against its presbyters" (47:6). This letter urges the congregation to do something about the situation: they are to remove the new leaders and reinstate the old.

At the core of the letter's argument against the Corinthian usurpers lies one of the earliest expressions of the notion of "apostolic succession," which came to play such a significant role in theological controversies of the second century. According to this view, the original leaders of the Christian churches had been appointed by the apostles, who were themselves chosen by Christ, who was sent from God. Anyone who deposes these leaders, therefore, is in direct rebellion against God himself (chaps. 42–44).

Much of the argument revolves around the history of the people of God as known from the Jewish Scriptures. According to 1 Clement, from the time of Cain and Abel onward, envy and strife have always been promoted by sinners opposed to the righteous. The new leaders of the Corinthian congregation stand within this nefarious line: they have swindled their way into power out of jealousy and rivalry. But for this author, God opposes those who exalt themselves over the ones he has himself chosen. This is shown not only from writings of the Jewish prophets, but also from the teachings of Jesus and the writings of the apostles (e.g., chaps. 12 and 46).

The letter provides several hints as to the time of its composition. It indicates that there were still church leaders throughout the Christian world who had been handpicked by the apostles (chap. 44); and yet the Corinthian church is called "ancient" (chap. 47). Moreover, Peter and Paul are said here to have been martyred in Rome in "our own generation" (chap. 5; they are generally thought to have been executed under Nero ca. 64 C.E.), and hostilities against the Christians have recently been renewed. These various hints suggest that the book was written near the end of the first century, possibly around 95 C.E. during the reign of Domitian.

"The Letter of 1 Clement," from *Early Christian Fathers*, edited by Cyril D. Richardson (Library of Christian Classics). © 1953 by Westminster Press. Reprinted by permission of Westminster John Knox Press.

The church of God, living in exile in Rome, to the church of God, exiled in Corinth—to you who are called and sanctified by God's will through our Lord Jesus Christ. Abundant grace and peace be yours from God Almighty through Jesus Christ.

1 Due, dear friends, to the sudden and successive misfortunes and accidents we have encountered, we have, we admit, been rather long in turning our attention to your quarrels. We refer to the abominable and unholy schism, so alien and foreign to those whom God has chosen, which a few impetuous and headstrong fellows have fanned to such a pitch of insanity that your good name, once so famous and dear to us all, has fallen into the gravest ill repute. 2 Has anyone, indeed, stayed with you without attesting the excellence and firmness of your faith? without admiring your sensible and considerate Christian piety? without broadcasting your spirit of unbounded hospitality? without praising your perfect and trustworthy knowledge? 3 For you always acted without partiality and walked in God's laws. You obeyed your rulers and gave your elders the proper respect. You disciplined the minds of your young people in moderation and dignity. You instructed your women to do everything with a blameless and pure conscience, and to give their husbands the affection they should. You taught them, too, to abide by the rule of obedience and to run their homes with dignity and thorough discretion.

2 You were all humble and without any pretensions, obeying orders rather than issuing them, more gladly giving than receiving. Content with Christ's rations and mindful of them, you stored his words carefully up in your hears and held his sufferings before your eyes.

2 In consequence, you were all granted a profound and rich peace and an insatiable longing to do good, while the Holy Spirit was abundantly poured out on you all. 3 You were full of holy counsels, and, with zeal for the good and devout confidence, you stretched out your hands to almighty God, beseeching him to have mercy should you involuntarily have fallen into any sin. 4 Day and night you labored for the whole brotherhood, that by your pity and sympathy the sum of his elect might be saved. 5 You were sincere and guileless and bore no grudges. 6 All sedition and

schism were an abomination to you. You wept for the faults of your neighbors, while you reckoned their shortcomings as your own. 7 You never regretted all the good you did, being ready for any good deed. 8 Possessed of an excellent and devout character, you did everything in his fear. The commands and decrees of the Lord were engraven on the tablets of your heart.

3 You were granted great popularity and growing numbers, so that the word of Scripture was fulfilled: "My beloved ate and drank and filled out and grew fat and started to kick."[1]

2 From this there arose rivalry and envy, strife and sedition, persecution and anarchy, war and captivity. 3 And so the dishonored rose up against those who were held in honor, those of no reputation against the notable, the stupid against the wise, the young against their elders. 4 For this reason righteousness and peace are far from you, since each has abandoned the fear of God and grown purblind in his faith, and ceased to walk by the rules of his precepts or to behave in a way worthy of Christ. Rather does each follow the lusts of his evil heart, by reviving that wicked and unholy rivalry, by which, indeed, death came into the world.

4 For Scripture runs thus: "And it happened after some days that Cain brought God a sacrifice from the fruits of the earth, while Abel made his offering from the first-born of the sheep and of their fat. 2 And God looked with favor on Abel and on his gifts; but he did not heed Cain and his sacrifices. 3 And Cain was greatly upset and his face fell. 4 And God said to Cain, 'Why are you so upset, and why has your face fallen? If you have made a correct offering but not divided it correctly, have you not sinned? 5 Keep quiet. Your brother will turn to you and you shall rule over him.' 6 And Cain said to his brother Abel, 'Let us go into the field.' And it happened that while they were in the field Cain attacked his brother Abel and killed him."[2]

7 You see, brothers, rivalry and envy are responsible for fratricide. 8 Because of rivalry our forefather Jacob fled from the presence of his brother Esau. 9 It was rivalry that caused Joseph to be murderously persecuted and reduced to slav-

---

[1]Deut 32:15   [2]Gen 4:3–8

ery. 10 Rivalry forced Moses to flee from the presence of Pharaoh, the king of Egypt, when he heard his fellow clansman say: "Who made you a ruler or judge over us? Do you want to slay me as you did the Egyptian yesterday?"[3] 11 By reason of rivalry Aaron and Miriam were excluded from the camp. 12 Rivalry cast Dathan and Abiram alive into Hades because they revolted against Moses, God's servant. 13 Because of rivalry David not only incurred the envy of foreigners but was even persecuted by Saul, the king of Israel.

5 But, passing from examples in antiquity, let us come to the heroes nearest our own times. Let us take the noble examples of our own generation. 2 By reason of rivalry and envy the greatest and most righteous pillars [of the Church] 3 were persecuted, and battled to the death. Let us set before our eyes the noble apostles: 4 Peter, who by reason of wicked jealousy, not only once or twice but frequently endured suffering and thus, bearing his witness, went to the glorious place which he merited. 5 By reason of rivalry and contention Paul showed how to win the prize for patient endurance. 6 Seven times he was in chains; he was exiled, stoned, became a herald [of the gospel] in East and West, and won the noble renown which his faith merited. 7 To the whole world he taught righteousness, and reaching the limits of the West he bore his witness before rulers. And so, released from this world, he was taken up into the holy place and became the greatest example of patient endurance.

6 To these men who lived such holy lives there was joined a great multitude of the elect who by reason of rivalry were the victims of many outrages and tortures and who became outstanding examples among us. 2 By reason of rivalry women were persecuted in the roles of Danaïds and Dircae. Victims of dreadful and blasphemous outrages, they ran with sureness the course of faith to the finish, and despite their physical weakness won a notable prize. 3 It was rivalry that estranged wives from their husbands and annulled the saying of our father, Adam, "This is now bone of my bone and flesh of my flesh."[4] 4 Rivalry and contention have overthrown great cities and uprooted mighty nations.

7 We are writing in this vein, dear friends, not only to admonish you but also to remind our-

selves. For we are in the same arena and involved in the same struggle. 2 Hence we should give up empty and futile concerns, and turn to the glorious and holy rule of our tradition. 3 Let us note what is good, what is pleasing and acceptable to him who made us. 4 Let us fix our eyes on the blood of Christ and let us realize how precious it is to his Father, since it was poured out for our salvation and brought the grace of repentance to the whole world. 5 Let us go through all the generations and observe that from one generation to another the Master has afforded an opportunity of repentance to those who are willing to turn to him. 6 Noah preached repentance and those who heeded him were saved. 7 Jonah preached destruction to the Ninevites; and when they had repented of their sins, they propitiated God with their prayers and gained salvation despite the fact they were not God's people.

8 The ministers of God's grace spoke about repentance through the Holy Spirit, 2 and the Master of the universe himself spoke of repentance with an oath: "For as I live, says the Lord, I do not desire the death of the sinner, but his repentance." 3 He added, too, this generous consideration: "Repent, O house of Israel, of your iniquity. Say to the sons of my people, Should your sins reach from earth to heaven, and be redder than scarlet and blacker than sackcloth, and should you turn to me with your whole heart and say 'Father!' I will heed you as though you were a holy people."[5] 4 And in another place this is what he says: "Wash and become clean: rid your souls of wickedness before my eyes. Cease from your wickedness, learn to behave well, devote yourselves to justice, rescue the wronged, uphold the rights of the orphan and grant the widow justice. And come, let us reason together, says the Lord; and if your sins are like purple, I will make them white as snow, and if they are like scarlet, I will make them white as wool. And if you are willing and heed me, you shall eat the good things of the earth. But if you are unwilling and do not heed me, the sword shall devour you. For it is the mouth of the Lord that has spoken thus."[6] Since, therefore, he wanted all those he loved to have an opportunity to repent, he confirmed this by his almighty will.

---

[3] Exod 2:14   [4] Gen 2:23   [5] Ezek 33:11–27   [6] Isa 1:16–20

9 So, then, let us fall in with his magnificent and glorious intention, and let us prostrate ourselves before him as suppliants of his mercy and kindness. Let us turn to his compassion and give up useless ventures and strife, and rivalry that leads to death. 2 Let us fasten our eyes on those who have served his magnificent glory to perfection. 3 Let us take Enoch, for instance, who, because he proved upright by his obedience, was translated and never died. 4 Noah proved faithful in his ministry and preached a new birth to the world. Through him, therefore, the Master saved those living creates that entered peacefully into the ark.

10 Abraham, who was called "The Friend," proved faithful in obeying God's words. 2 It was obedience which led him to quit his country, his kindred, and his father's house, so that, by leaving a paltry country, a mean kindred, and an insignificant house, he might inherit God's promises. 3 For he told him: "Depart from your country and from your kindred and from the house of your father, and go to a land which I will show you. And I will make you great among the nations and I will bless you and I will make your name great and you will be blessed. And I will bless those who bless you and curse those who curse you, and all the tribes of the earth will be blessed through you."[7] 4 And again, when he separated from Lot, God told him: "Lift up your eyes and from where you now are look to the North, the South, the East, and the West, for all the land that you see I will give you and your seed forever. 5 And I will make your seed like the dust of the earth. If anybody can count the dust of the earth, then your seed will be counted."[8] 6 And again he says: "God led Abraham out and told him: Look up to heaven and count the stars, if you can. That is how numerous your seed will be! And Abraham believed God and this was put down to his credit as an upright deed."[9] 7 Because of his faith and hospitality a son was granted to him in his old age, and he obediently offered him as a sacrifice to God on one of the hills which he indicated.

11 Because of his hospitality and religious devotion, Lot was saved from Sodom, when the whole countryside was condemned to fire and brimstone. In that way the Master made it clear that he does not forsake those who put their hope on him, but delivers to punishment and torment those who turn away from him. 2 Of this latter, to be sure, his wife became an example. After quitting the city with him, she changed her mind and fell out with him, with the result that she became a pillar of salt that exists to this day. In this way it was made evident to all that the double-minded and those who question God's power are condemned and become a warning to all generations.

12 Because of her faith and hospitality Rahab the harlot was saved. 2 For when the spies were sent to Jericho by Joshua the son of Nun, the king of the land got to know that they had come to spy on his country. Consequently he sent out men to capture them, intending to arrest them and put them to death. 3 The hospitable Rahab, however, took them in and hid them in a room upstairs under stalks of flax. 4 When the king's men learned of it, they said to her: "The men who are spying on our country went into your house. Bring them out, for this is the king's command." But she at once answered, "The men you seek came into my house, but they immediately departed and are on their way," and she pointed in the opposite direction. 5 And she said to the men: "I am absolutely certain that the Lord God is handing this country over to you; for fear and terror of you have fallen on all its people. When, therefore, you come to take it, rescue me and my father's house." 6 And they said to her: "It shall be exactly as you say. When you learn of our approach, you shall gather together all your family under your roof and they shall be saved. But whoever is found outside the house will perish." 7 And in addition they gave her a sign that she should hang a piece of scarlet from her house. By this they made it clear that it was by the blood of the Lord that redemption was going to come to all who believe in God and hope on him. 8 You see, dear friends, that not only faith but prophecy as well is exemplified in this woman.

13 Let us then, brothers, be humble and be rid of all pretensions and arrogance and silliness and anger. Let us act as Scripture bids us, for the Holy Spirit says: "Let not the wise man boast of his wisdom or the strong man of his might

---

[7]Gen 12:1–3   [8]Gen 13:14–16   [9]Gen 15:5–6

or the rich man of his wealth. But let him that boasts boast of the Lord; and so he will seek Him out and act justly and uprightly."[10] Especially let us recall the words of the Lord Jesus, which he uttered to teach considerateness and patience. 2 For this is what he said: "Show mercy, that you may be shown mercy. Forgive, that you may be forgiven. As you behave to others, so they will behave to you. As you give, so will you get. As you judge, so you will be judged. As you show kindness, so will you receive kindness. The measure you give will be the measure you get."[11] 3 Let us firmly hold on to this commandment and these injunctions so that in our conduct we may obey his holy words and be humble. 4 For Holy Scripture says, "On whom shall I look except on him who is humble and gentle and who trembles at my words?"[12]

14 It is right, then, and holy, brothers, that we should obey God rather than follow those arrogant and disorderly fellows who take the lead in stirring up loathsome rivalry. 2 For we shall incur no ordinary harm, but rather great danger, if we recklessly give ourselves over to the designs of those who launch out into strife and sedition to alienate us from what is right. 3 Let us be kind to one another in line with the compassion and tenderness of him who created us. 4 For it is written: "The kind shall inhabit the land, and the innocent shall be left upon it. But those who transgress shall be destroyed from off it."[13] 5 And again he says: "I saw an ungodly man exalted and elevated like the cedars of Lebanon. But I passed by and, look, he had vanished! And I searched for his place and could not find it. Maintain innocence and have an eye for uprightness, for a man of peace will have descendants."[14]

15 Let us, then, attach ourselves to those who are religiously devoted to peace, and not to those who wish for it hypocritically. 2 For somewhere it is said, "This people honors me with its lips, but its heart is far removed from me."[15] 3 And again, "They blessed with their mouth, but they cursed with their heart."[16] 4 And again it says: "They loved him with their mouth, but they lied to him with their tongue. Their heart was not straightforward with him, and they were not faithful to his covenant. 5 Therefore let the deceitful lips that speak evil against the righteous be struck dumb."[17] And again: "May the Lord destroy all deceitful lips and the tongue that boasts unduly and those who say, 'We will boast of our tongues; our lips are our own; who is Lord over us?' 6 Because of the wretchedness of the poor and the groans of the needy I will now arise, says the Lord. I will place him in safety: I will act boldly in his cause."[18]

16 It is to the humble that Christ belongs, not to those who exalt themselves above his flock. 2 The scepter of God's majesty, the Lord Jesus Christ, did not come with the pomp of pride or arrogance, though he could have done so. But he came in humility just as the Holy Spirit said of him. 3 For Scripture reads: "Lord, who has believed what we heard? And to whom has the arm of the Lord been revealed? Before him we announced that he was like a child, like a root in thirsty ground. He has no comeliness or glory. We saw him, and he had neither comeliness nor beauty. But his appearance was ignominious, deficient when compared to a person's stature. He was a man marred by stripes and toil, and experienced in enduring weakness. Because his face was turned away, he was dishonored and disregarded. 4 He it is who bears our sins and suffers pain for us. And we regarded him as subject to toil and stripes and affliction. 5 But it was for our sins that he was wounded and for our transgressions that he suffered. To bring us peace he was punished: by his stripes we were healed. 6 Like sheep we have all gone astray: each one went astray in his own way. 7 And the Lord delivered him up for our sins; and he does not open his mouth because he is abused. Like a sheep he is led off to be slaughtered; and just as a lamb before its shearers is dumb, so he does not open his mouth. In his humiliation his condemnation ended. Who shall tell about his posterity? 8 For his life was taken away from the earth. 9 Because of the transgressions of my people he came to his death. 10 And I will give the wicked as an offering for his burial and the rich for his death. For he did no iniquity and no deceit was found in his mouth. And the Lord's will is to cleanse him of his stripes. 11 If you make an offering for sin, your soul will see a long-lived pos-

---

[10]Jer 9:23–24   [11]Matt 5:7; 6:14–15; 7:1, 2, 12; Luke 6:31, 36–38
[12]Isa 66:2   [13]Prov 2:21–22; Ps 37:9, 38   [14]Ps 37:35–37   [15]Isa
29:13; Mark 7:6   [16]Ps 78:36–37; 62:4   [17]Ps 31:18   [18]Ps 12:3–5

terity. 12 And the Lord's will is to do away with the toil of his soul, to show him light and to form him with understanding, to justify an upright man who serves many well. And he himself will bear their sins. 13 For this reason he shall have many heirs and he shall share the spoils of the strong, because his life was delivered up to death and he was reckoned among transgressors. And he it was who bore the sins of many and was delivered up because of their sins."[19]

15 And again he himself says: "I am a worm and not a man, a disgrace to mankind and despised by the people. 16 All those who saw me mocked me, they made mouths at me and shook their heads, saying: 'He hoped on the Lord. Let him rescue him, let him save him, since he is pleased with him!'"[20]

17 You see, dear friends, the kind of example we have been given. And so, if the Lord humbled himself in this way, what should we do who through him have come under the yoke of his grace?

17 Let us be imitators even of those who wandered around in the skins of goats and sheep, and preached the coming of the Christ. We refer to the prophets Elijah and Elisha—yes, and Ezekiel, too—and to the heroes of old as well. 2 Abraham was widely renowned and called the Friend of God. When he gazed on God's glory, he declared in his humility, "I am only dust and ashes."[21] 3 This is what is written about Job: "Job was an upright and innocent man, sincere, devout, and one who avoided all evil."[22] 4 But he was his own accuser when he said, "There is none who is free from stain, not even if his life lasts but a single day."[23] 5 Moses was called "faithful in all God's house"[24] and God used him to bring his judgment on Egypt with scourges and torments. Yet even he, despite the great glory he was given, did not boast; but when he was granted an oracle from the bush, said: "Who am I that you send me? 6 I have a feeble voice and a slow tongue."[25] And again he says, "I am but steam from a pot."

18 And what shall we say of the famous David? God said of him, "I have discovered a man after my own heart, David the son of Jesse: I have anointed him with eternal mercy."[26] 2 But he too says to God: "Have mercy upon me, O God, according to your great mercy; and according to the wealth of your compassion wipe out my transgression. 3 Wash me thoroughly from my iniquity and cleanse me from my sin, for I acknowledge my transgression and my sin is ever before me. 4 Against you only have I sinned; and I have done evil in your sight. The result is that you are right when you speak and are acquitted when you are judged. 5 For, see, I was conceived in iniquity, and in sin did my mother bear me. 6 For, see, you have loved the truth: you have revealed to me the mysteries and secrets of your wisdom. 7 You shall sprinkle me with hyssop and I shall be cleansed. You shall wash me and I shall be whiter than snow. 8 You will make me hear joy and gladness: the bones which have been humbled shall rejoice. 9 Turn your face from my sins and wipe away all my iniquities. 10 Create in me a pure heart, O God, and renew a right spirit in my very core. 11 Cast me not away from your presence, and do not take your Holy Spirit away from me. 12 Give me back the gladness of your salvation, and strengthen me with your guiding spirit. 13 I will teach your ways to the wicked, and the godless shall turn back to you. 14 Save me from bloodguiltiness, O God, the God of my salvation. My tongue will rejoice in your righteousness. 15 You will open my mouth, O Lord, and my lips will proclaim your praise. 16 For if you had wanted sacrifice, I would have given it. You will not find pleasure in burnt offerings. 17 The sacrifice for God is a broken spirit: a broken and a humbled heart, O God, you will not despise."[27]

19 The humility and obedient submissiveness of so many and so famous heroes have improved not only us but our fathers before us, and all who have received his oracles in fear and sincerity. 2 Since, then, we have benefited by many great and glorious deeds, let us run on to the goal of peace, which was handed down to us from the beginning. Let us fix our eyes on the Father and Creator of the universe and cling to his magnificent and excellent gifts of peace and kindness to us. 3 Let us see him in our minds and look with the eyes of our souls on his patient purpose. Let us consider how free he is from anger toward his whole creation.

---

[19]Isa 53:1–12 [20]Ps 22:6–8 [21]Gen 18:27 [22]Job 1:1 [23]Job 14:4–5 [24]Num 12:7; Heb 3:2 [25]Exod 3:11; 4:10 [26]Ps 89:20; Acts 13:22 [27]Ps 51:1–17

20

The heavens move at his direction and peacefully obey him. 2 Day and night observe the course he has appointed them, without getting in each other's way. 3 The sun and the moon and the choirs of stars roll on harmoniously in their appointed courses at his command, and with never a deviation. 4 By his will and without dissension or altering anything he has decreed the earth becomes fruitful at the proper seasons and brings forth abundant food for people and beasts and every living thing upon it. 5 The unsearchable, abysmal depths and the indescribable regions of the underworld are subject to the same decrees. 6 The basin of the boundless sea is by his arrangement constructed to hold the heaped up waters, so that the sea does not flow beyond the barriers surrounding it, but does just as he bids it. 7 For he said, "Thus far you shall come, and your waves shall break within you."[28] 8 The ocean which people cannot pass, and the worlds beyond it, are governed by the same decrees of the Master. 9 The seasons, spring, summer, autumn, and winter, peacefully give way to each other. 10 The winds from their different points perform their service at the proper time and without hindrance. Perennial springs, created for enjoyment and health, never fail to offer their life-giving breasts to people. The tiniest creatures come together in harmony and peace. 11 All these things the great Creator and Master of the universe ordained to exist in peace and harmony. Thus, he showered his benefits on them all, but most abundantly on us who have taken refuge in his compassion through our Lord Jesus Christ, 12 to whom be glory and majesty forever and ever. Amen.

21

Take care, dear friends, that his many blessings do not turn out to be our condemnation, which will be the case if we fail to live worthily of him, to act in concert, and to do what is good and pleasing to him. 2 For he says somewhere, "The Spirit of the Lord is a lamp which searches the hidden depths of the heart."[29] 3 Let us realize how near he is, and that none of our thoughts or of the ideas we have escapes his notice. 4 It is right, therefore, that we should not be deserters, disobeying his will. 5 Rather than offend God, let us offend foolish and stupid people who exalt themselves and boast with their pretensions to fine speech. 6 Let us reverence the Lord Jesus Christ whose blood was given for us. Let us respect those who rule over us. Let us honor our elders. Let us rear the young in the fear of God. Let us direct our women to what is good. 7 Let them show a purity of character we can admire. Let them reveal a genuine sense of modesty. By their reticence let them show that their tongues are considerate. Let them not play favorites in showing affection, but in holiness let them love all equally, who fear God. 8 Let our children have a Christian training. Let them learn the value God sets on humility, what power pure love has with him, how good and excellent it is to fear him, and how this means salvation to everybody who lives in his fear with holiness and a pure conscience. 9 For he is the searcher of thoughts and of desires. It is his breath which is in us; and when he wants to, he will take it away.

22

Now Christian faith confirms all this. For this is how Christ addresses us through his Holy Spirit: "Come, my children, listen to me. 2 I will teach you the fear of the Lord. What person is there that desires life, and loves to see good days? 3 Keep your tongue from evil and your lips from uttering deceit. 4 Refrain from evil and do good. 5 Seek peace and follow after it. 6 The eyes of the Lord are over the upright and his ears are open to their petitions. But the face of the Lord is turned against those who do evil, to eradicate their memory from the earth. 7 The upright person cried out and the Lord heeded him and delivered him out of all his troubles. 8 Manifold are the plagues of the sinner, but his mercy will enfold those who hope on the Lord."[30]

23

The all-merciful and beneficent Father has compassion on those who fear him, and with kindness and love he grants his favors to those who approach him with a sincere heart. 2 For this reason we must not be double-minded, and our souls must not harbor wrong notions about his excellent and glorious gifts. 3 Let that verse of Scripture be remote from us, which says: "Wretched are the double-minded, those who doubt in their soul and say, 'We have heard these things even in our fathers' times, and, see, we have grown old and none of them has happened to us.' You fools! 4 Compare yourselves to a tree. Take a

---

[28]Job 38:11 [29]Prov 20:27 [30]Ps 34:11–17; Ps 32:10

vine: first it sheds its leaves, then comes a bud, then a leaf, then a flower, and after this a sour grape, and finally a ripe bunch." You note that the fruit of the tree reaches its maturity in a short time. 5 So, to be sure, swiftly and suddenly his purpose will be accomplished, just as Scripture, too, testifies: "Quickly he will come and not delay, and the Lord will come suddenly into his temple, even the Holy One whom you expect."[31]

24 Let us consider, dear friends, how the Master continually points out to us that there will be a future resurrection. Of this he made the Lord Jesus Christ the first fruits by raising him from the dead. 2 Let us take note, dear friends, of the resurrection at the natural seasons. 3 Day and night demonstrate resurrection. Night passes and day comes. Day departs and night returns. 4 Take the crops as examples. How and in what way is the seeding done? 5 The sower goes out and casts each of his seeds in the ground. When they fall on the ground they are dry and bare, and they decay. But then the marvelous providence of the Master resurrects them from their decay, and from a single seed many grow and bear fruit.

25 Let us note the remarkable token which comes from the East, from the neighborhood, that is, of Arabia. 2 There is a bird which is called a phoenix. It is the only one of its kind and lives five hundred years. When the time for its departure and death draws near, it makes a burial nest for itself from frankincense, myrrh, and other spices; and when the time is up, it gets into it and dies. 3 From its decaying flesh a worm is produced, which is nourished by the secretions of the dead creature and grows wings. When it is full-fledged, it takes up the burial nest containing the bones of its predecessor, and manages to carry them all the way from Arabia to the Egyptian city called Heliopolis. 4 And in broad daylight, so that everyone can see, it lights at the altar of the sun and puts them down there, and so starts home again. 5 The priests then look up their dated records and discover it has come after a lapse of five hundred years.

26 Shall we, then, imagine that it is something great and surprising if the Creator of the universe raises up those who have served him in holiness and in the assurance born of a good faith, when he uses a mere bird to illustrate the greatness of his promise? 2 For he says somewhere: "And you shall raise me up and I shall give you thanks"[32]; And, "I lay down and slept: I rose up because you are with me."[33] 3 And again Job says, "And you will make this flesh of mine, which has endured all this, to rise up."[34]

27 With this hope, then, let us attach ourselves to him who is faithful to his promises and just in his judgments. 2 He who bids us to refrain from lying is all the less likely to lie himself. 3 For nothing is impossible to God save lying. Let us, then, rekindle our faith in him, and bear in mind that nothing is beyond his reach. 4 By his majestic word he established the universe, and by his word he can bring it to an end. "Who shall say to him, What have you done? Or who shall resist his mighty strength?"[35] He will do everything when he wants to and as he wants to. And not one of the things he has decreed will fail. 6 Everything is open to his sight and nothing escapes his will. 7 For "the heavens declare God's glory and the sky proclaims the work of his hands. Day pours forth words to day; and night imparts knowledge to night. And there are neither words nor speech, and their voices are not heard."[36]

28 Since, then, he sees and hears everything, we should fear him and rid ourselves of wicked desires that issue in base deeds. By so doing we shall be sheltered by his mercy from the judgments to come. 2 For where can any of us flee to escape his might hand? What world is there to receive anyone who deserts him? 3 For Scripture says somewhere: "Where shall I go and where shall I hide from your presence? If I go up to heaven, you are there. If I go off to the ends of the earth, there is your right hand. If I make my bed in the depths, there is your spirit."[37] 4 Where, then, can anyone go or where can he flee to escape from him who embraces everything?

29 We must, then, approach him with our souls holy, lifting up pure and undefiled hands to him, loving our kind and compassionate Father, who has made us his chosen portion. 2 For thus it is written: "When the Most High divided the nations, when he dispersed the sons of Adam, he fixed the boundaries of the nations to suit the

---

[31]Mal 3:1   [32]Ps 28:7 (?)   [33]Ps 3:5   [34]Job 19:26   [35]Wisd 12:12   [36]Ps 19:1–3   [37]Ps 139:7–8

number of God's angels. The Lord's portion became his people, Jacob: Israel was the lot that fell to him."[38] 3 And in another place it says: "Behold, the Lord takes for himself a people from among the nations, just as a man takes the first fruits of his threshing floor; and the Holy of Holies shall come forth from that nation."[39]

30 Since, then, we are a holy portion, we should do everything that makes for holiness. We should flee from slandering, vile and impure embraces, drunkenness, rioting, filthy lusts, detestable adultery, and disgusting arrogance. 2 "For God," says Scripture, "resists the arrogant, but gives grace to the humble."[40] 3 We should attach ourselves to those to whom God's grace has been given. We should clothe ourselves with concord, being humble, self-controlled, far removed from all gossiping and slandering, and justified by our deeds, not by words. 4 For it says: "He who talks a lot will hear much in reply. 5 Or does the prattler imagine he is right? Blessed is the one his mother bore to be short-lived. Do not indulge in talking overmuch."[41] 6 We should leave God to praise us and not praise ourselves. 7 For God detests self-praisers. Let others applaud our good deeds, as it was with our righteous forefathers. 8 Presumption, audacity, and recklessness are traits of those accursed by God. But considerateness, humility, and modesty are the traits of those whom God has blessed.

31 Let us, then, cling to his blessing and note what leads to it. 2 Let us unfold the tale of the ancient past. Why was our father Abraham blessed? Was it not because he acted in righteousness and truth, prompted by faith? 3 Isaac, fully realizing what was going to happen, gladly let himself be led to sacrifice. 4 In humility Jacob quit his homeland because of his brother. He went to Laban and became his slave, and to him there were given the twelve scepters of the tribes of Israel.

32 And if anyone will candidly look into each example, he will realize the magnificence of the gifts God gives.

2 For from Jacob there came all the priests and the Levites who serve at God's altar. From him comes the Lord Jesus so far as his human nature goes. From him there come the kings and rulers and governors of Judah. Nor is the glory of the other tribes derived from him insignificant. For God promised that "your seed shall be as the stars of heaven."[42] 3 So all of them received honor and greatness, not through themselves or their own deeds or the right things they did, but through his will. 4 And we, therefore, who by his will have been called in Jesus Christ, are not justified of ourselves or by our wisdom or insight or religious devotion or the holy deeds we have done from the heart, but by that faith by which almighty God has justified all people from the very beginning. To him be glory forever and ever. Amen.

33 What, then, brothers, ought we to do? Should we grow slack in doing good and give up love? May the Lord never permit this to happen at any rate to us! Rather should we be energetic in doing every good deed with earnestness and eagerness. 2 For the Creator and Master of the universe himself rejoices in his works. 3 Thus by his almighty power he established the heavens and by his inscrutable wisdom he arranged them. He separated the land from the water surrounding it and fixed it upon the sure foundation of his own will. By his decree he brought into existence the living creatures which roam on it; and after creating the sea and the creatures which inhabit it, he fixed its boundaries by his power. 4 Above all, with his holy and pure hands he formed man, his outstanding and greatest achievement, stamped with his own image. 5 For this is what God said: "Let us make man in our own image and likeness. 6 And God made man: male and female he created."[43] And so, when he had finished all this, he praised it and blessed it and said, "Increase and multiply."[44] 7 We should observe that all the righteous have been adorned with good deeds and the very Lord adorns himself with good deeds and rejoices. 8 Since, then, we have this example, we should unhesitatingly give ourselves to his will, and put all our effort into acting uprightly.

34 The good laborer accepts the bread he has earned with his head held high; the lazy and negligent worker cannot look his employer in the face. 2 We must, then, be eager to do good; for everything comes from him. 3 For he

---

[38]Deut 32:8–9   [39]Deut 4:34; 14:2; Num 18:27; 2 Chron 31:14; Ezek 48:12   [40]Prov 3:34; James 4:6; 1 Pet 5:5   [41]Job 11:2–3   [42]Gen 15:5; 22:17; 26:4   [43]Gen 1:26–27   [44]Gen 1:28

warns us: "See, the Lord is coming. He is bringing his reward with him, to pay each one according to his work."[45] 4 He bids us, therefore, to believe on him with all our heart, and not to be slack or negligent in every good deed. 5 He should be the basis of our boasting and assurance. We should be subject to his will. We should note how the whole throng of his angels stand ready to serve his will. 6 For Scripture says: "Ten thousand times ten thousand stood by him, and thousands of thousands ministered to him and cried out: Holy, holy, holy is the Lord of Hosts: all creation is full of his glory."[46] 7 We too, then, should gather together for worship in concord and mutual trust, and earnestly beseech him as it were with one mouth, that we may share in his great and glorious promises. 8 For he says, "Eye has not seen and ear has not heard and man's heart has not conceived what he has prepared for those who patiently wait for him."[47]

35 How blessed and amazing are God's gifts, dear friends! 2 Life with immortality, splendor with righteousness, truth with confidence, faith with assurance, self-control with holiness! 3 And all these things are within our comprehension. What, then, is being prepared for those who wait for him? The Creator and Father of eternity, the all-holy, himself knows how great and wonderful it is. 4 We, then, should make every effort to be found in the number of those who are patiently looking for him, so that we may share in the gifts he has promised. 5 And how shall this be, dear friends? If our mind is faithfully fixed on God; if we seek out what pleases and delights him; if we do what is in accord with his pure will, and follow in the way of truth. If we rid ourselves of all wickedness, evil, avarice, contentiousness, malice, fraud, gossip, slander, hatred of God, arrogance, pretension, conceit, and inhospitality. 6 God hates those who act in this way; and not only those who do these things but those who applaud them. 7 For Scripture says: "But God told the sinner: Why do you speak of my statutes and have my covenant on your lips? You hated discipline and turned your back on my words. If you saw a thief you went along with him, and you threw in your lot with adulterers. Your mouth overflowed with iniquity, and your tongue wove deceit. You sat there slandering your brother and putting a stumbling block in the way of your mother's son.

9 This you did, and I kept silent. You suspected, you wicked one, that I would be like you. 10 I will reproach you and show you your very self. 11 Ponder, then, these things, you who forget God, lest he seize you like a lion and there be no one to save you. 12 A sacrifice of praise will glorify me, and that is the way by which I will show him God's salvation."[48]

36 This is the way, dear friends, in which we found our salvation, Jesus Christ, the high priest of our offerings, the protector and helper of our weakness. 2 Through him we fix our gaze on the heights of heaven. In him we see mirrored God's pure and transcendent face. Through him the eyes of our hearts have been opened. Through him our foolish and darkened understanding springs up to the light. Through him the Master has willed that we should taste immortal knowledge. For, "since he reflects God's splendor, he is as superior to the angels as his title is more distinguished than theirs."[49] 3 For thus it is written: "He who makes his angels winds, and his ministers flames of fire."[50] 4 But of his son this is what the Master said: "You are my son: today I have begotten you. Ask me and I will give you the nations for you to inherit, and the ends of the earth for you to keep."[51] 5 And again he says to him: "Sit at my right hand until I make your enemies your footstool."[52] 6 Who are meant by "enemies"? Those who are wicked and resist his will.

37 Really in earnest, then, brothers, we must march under his irreproachable orders. 2 Let us note with what discipline, readiness, and obedience those who serve under our generals carry out orders. 3 Not everybody is a general, colonel, captain, sergeant, and so on. But each in his own rank carries out the orders of the emperor and of the generals. 4 The great cannot exist without the small; neither can the small exist without the great. 5 All are linked together; and this has an advantage. Take our body, for instance. The head cannot get along without the feet. Nor, similarly, can the feet get along without the head. The tiniest parts of our body are essential to it, and are valuable to the total body. Yes, they all act in con-

---

[45]Isa 40:10; 62:11; Prov 24:12; Rev 22:12   [46]Dan 7:3; Isa 6:3
[47]1 Cor 2:9   [48]Ps 50:16–23   [49]Heb 1:3–4   [50]Heb 1:7; Ps 104:4
[51]Heb 1:5; Ps 2:7–8   [52]Heb 1:13; Ps 110:1

cord, and are united in a single obedience to preserve the whole body.

38 Following this out, we must preserve our Christian body too in its entirety. Each must be subject to his neighbor, according to his special gifts. 2 The strong must take care of the weak; the weak must look up to the strong. The rich must provide for the poor; the poor must thank God for giving him someone to meet his needs. The wise person must show his wisdom not in words but in good deeds. The humble must not brag about his humility; but should give others occasion to mention it. He who is continent must not put on airs. He must recognize that his self-control is a gift from another. 3 We must take to heart, brothers, from what stuff we were created, what kind of creatures we were when we entered the world, from what a dark grave he who fashioned and created us brought us into his world. And we must realize the preparations he so generously made before we were born. 4 Since, then, we owe all this to him, we ought to give him unbounded thanks. To him be glory forever and ever. Amen.

39 Thoughtless, silly, senseless, and ignorant folk mock and jeer at us, in an effort, so they imagine, to exalt themselves. 2 But what can a mere mortal do? What power has a creature of earth? 3 For it is written: "There was no shape before my eyes, but I heard a breath and a voice. What! 4 Can a mortal be pure before the Lord? Or can a person be blameless for his actions, if he does not believe in his servants and finds something wrong with his angels? 5 Not even heaven is pure in his sight: let alone those who live in houses of clay—of the very same clay of which we ourselves are made. He smites them like a moth; and they do not last from dawn to dusk. They perish, for they cannot help themselves. 6 He breathes on them, and they die for lack of wisdom. 7 Call out and see if anyone will heed you, or if you will see any of the holy angels. For wrath destroys a stupid person, and rivalry is the death of one in error. 8 I have seen the foolish taking root, but suddenly their home is swept away. 9 May their sons be far from safety! May they be mocked at the doors of lesser men, and there will be none to deliver them. For what has been prepared by them, the righteous will eat; and they shall not be delivered from troubles."[53]

40 Now that this is clear to us and we have peered into the depths of the divine knowledge, we are bound to do in an orderly fashion all that the Master has bidden us to do at the proper times he set. 2 He ordered sacrifices and services to be performed; and required this to be done, not in a careless and disorderly way, but at the times and seasons he fixed. 3 Where he wants them performed, and by whom, he himself fixed by his supreme will, so that everything should be done in a holy way and with his approval, and should be acceptable to his will. 4 Those, therefore, who make their offerings at the time set, win his approval and blessing. For they follow the Master's orders and do no wrong. 5 The high priest is given his particular duties: the priests are assigned their special place, while on the Levites particular tasks are imposed. The layman is bound by the layman's code.

41 Each of us, brothers, in his own rank must win God's approval and have a clear conscience. We must not transgress the rules laid down for our ministry, but must perform it reverently. 2 Not everywhere, brothers, are the different sacrifices—the daily ones, the freewill offerings, and those for sins and trespasses—offered, but only in Jerusalem. And even there sacrifices are not made at any point, but only in front of the sanctuary, at the altar, after the high priest and the ministers mentioned have inspected the offering for blemishes. 3 Those, therefore, who act in any way at variance with his will, suffer the penalty of death. 4 You see, brothers, the more knowledge we are given, the greater risks we run.

42 The apostles received the gospel for us from the Lord Jesus Christ; Jesus, the Christ, was sent from God. 2 Thus Christ is from God and the apostles from Christ. In both instances the orderly procedure depends on God's will. 3 And so the apostles, after receiving their orders and being fully convinced by the resurrection of our Lord Jesus Christ and assured by God's word, went out in the confidence of the Holy Spirit to preach the good news that God's Kingdom was about to come. 4 They preached in country and city, and appointed their first converts, after testing them by the Spirit, to be the bishops and

---

[53]Job 4:16–18; 15:15; 4:19–5:5

deacons of future believers. 5 Nor was this any novelty, for Scripture had mentioned bishops and deacons long before. For this is what Scripture says somewhere: "I will appoint their bishops in righteousness and their deacons in faith."[54]

43 And is it any wonder that those Christians whom God had entrusted with such a duty should have appointed the officers mentioned? For the blessed Moses too, who was a faithful servant in all God's house, recorded in the sacred books all the orders given to him, and the rest of the prophets followed in his train by testifying with him to his legislation. 2 Now, when rivalry for the priesthood arose and the tribes started quarreling as to which of them should be honored with this glorious privilege, Moses bid the twelve tribal chiefs bring him rods, on each of which was written the name of one of the tribes. These he took and bound, sealing them with the rings of the tribal leaders; and he put them in the tent of testimony on God's table. 3 Then he shut the tent and put seals on the keys just as he had on the rods. 4 And he told them: "Brothers, the tribe whose rod puts forth buds is the one God has chosen for the priesthood and for his ministry." 5 Early the next morning he called all Israel together, six hundred thousand strong, and showed the seals to the tribal chiefs and opened the tent of testimony and brought out the rods. And it was discovered that Aaron's rod had not only budded, but was actually bearing fruit. What do you think, dear friends? 6 Did not Moses know in advance that this was going to happen? Why certainly. But he acted the way he did in order to forestall anarchy in Israel, and so that the name of the true and only God might be glorified. To Him be the glory forever and ever. Amen.

44 Now our apostles, thanks to our Lord Jesus Christ, knew that there was going to be strife over the title of bishop. 2 It was for this reason and because they had been given an accurate knowledge of the future, that they appointed the officers we have mentioned. Furthermore, they later added a codicil to the effect that, should these die, other approved men should succeed to their ministry. 3 In the light of this, we view it as a breach of justice to remove from their ministry those who were appointed either by them [i.e., the apostles] or later on and with the whole church's consent, by others of the proper standing, and who, long enjoying everybody's approval, have ministered to Christ's flock faultlessly, humbly, quietly, and unassumingly. 4 For we shall be guilty of no slight sin if we eject from the episcopate men who have offered the sacrifices with innocence and holiness. 5 Happy, indeed, are those presbyters who have already passed on, and who ended a life of fruitfulness with their task complete. For they need not fear that anyone will remove them from their secure positions. 6 But you, we observe, have removed a number of people, despite their good conduct, from a ministry they have fulfilled with honor and integrity.

45 Your contention and rivalry, brothers, thus touches matters that bear on our salvation.

2 You have studied Holy Scripture, which contains the truth and is inspired by the Holy Spirit. 3 You realize that there is nothing wrong or misleading written in it. You will not find that upright people have ever been disowned by holy people. 4 The righteous, to be sure, have been persecuted, but by wicked people. They have been imprisoned, but by the godless. They have been stoned by transgressors, slain by people prompted by abominable and wicked rivalry. 5 Yet in such sufferings they bore up nobly. 6 What shall we say, brothers? Was Daniel cast into a den of lions by those who revered God? 7 Or was Ananias, Azarias, or Mishael shut up in the fiery furnace by people devoted to the magnificent and glorious worship of the Most High? Not for a moment! Who, then, was it that did such things? Detestable people, thoroughly and completely wicked, whose factiousness drove them to such a pitch of fury that they tormented those who resolutely served God in holiness and innocence. They failed to realize that the Most High is the champion and defender of those who worship his excellent name with a pure conscience. To him be the glory forever and ever. Amen. 8 But those who held out with confidence inherited glory and honor. They were exalted, and God inscribed them on his memory forever and ever. Amen.

46 Brothers, we must follow such examples. For it is written: "Follow the saints, be-

---

[54]Isa 60:17

cause those who follow them will become saints." 3 Again, it says in another place: "In the company of the innocent, you will be innocent; in the company of the elect, you will be elect; and in a crooked person's company you will go wrong."[55] 4 Let us, then, follow the innocent and the upright. 5 They, it is, who are God's elect. Why is it that you harbor strife, bad temper, dissension, schism, and quarreling? 6 Do we not have one God, one Christ, one Spirit of grace which was poured out on us? And is there not one calling in Christ? 7 Why do we rend and tear asunder Christ's members and raise a revolt against our own body? Why do we reach such a pitch of insanity that we are oblivious of the fact we are members of each other? 8 Recall the words of our Lord Jesus. For he said: "Woe to that man! It were better for him not to have been born than to be the occasion of one of my chosen ones stumbling. It were better for him to have a millstone around his neck and to be drowned in the sea, than to pervert one of my chosen."[56] 9 Your schism has led many astray; it has made many despair; it has made many doubt; and it has distressed us all. Yet it goes on!

47 Pick up the letter of the blessed apostle Paul. What was the primary thing he wrote to you, when he started preaching the gospel? 3 To be sure, under the Spirit's guidance, he wrote to you about himself and Cephas and Apollos, because even then you had formed cliques. 4 Factiousness, however, at that time was a less serious sin, since you were partisans of notable apostles and of a man they endorsed. 5 But think now who they are who have led you astray and degraded your honorable and celebrated love of the brethren. 6 It is disgraceful, exceedingly disgraceful, and unworthy of your Christian upbringing, to have it reported that because of one or two individuals the solid and ancient Corinthian Church is in revolt against its presbyters. 7 This report, moreover, has reached not only us, but those who dissent from us as well. The result is that the Lord's name is being blasphemed because of your stupidity, and you are exposing yourselves to danger.

48 We must, then, put a speedy end to this. We must prostrate ourselves before the Master, and beseech him with tears to have mercy on us and be reconciled to us and bring us back to our honorable and holy practice of brotherly love. 2 For it is this which is the gate of righteousness, which opens the way to life, as it is written: "Open the gates of righteousness for me, so that I may enter by them and praise the Lord. 3 This is the Lord's gate: the righteous shall enter by it."[57] While there are many gates open, the gate of righteousness is the Christian gate. Blessed are all those who enter by it and direct their way in holiness and righteousness, by doing everything without disorder.

5 Let a person be faithful, let him be capable of uttering knowledge, let him be wise in judging arguments, let him be pure in conduct. 6 But the greater he appears to be, the more humble he ought to be, and the more ready to seek the common good in preference to his own.

49 Whoever has Christian love must keep Christ's commandments. 2 Who can describe the bond of God's love? 3 Who is capable of expressing its great beauty? 4 The heights to which love leads are beyond description. 5 Love unites us to God. Love hides a multitude of sins. Love puts up with everything and is always patient. There is nothing vulgar about love, nothing arrogant. Love knows nothing of schism or revolt. Love does everything in harmony. By love all God's elect were made perfect. Without love nothing can please God. 6 By love the Master accepted us. Because of the love he had for us, and in accordance with God's will, Jesus Christ our Lord gave his blood for us, his flesh for our flesh, and his life for ours.

50 You see, brothers, how great and amazing love is, and how its perfection is beyond description. 2 Who is able to possess it save those to whom God has given the privilege? Let us, then, beg and implore him mercifully to grant us love without human bias and to make us irreproachable. 3 All the generations from Adam to our day have passed away, but those who, by the grace of God, have been made perfect in love have a place among the saints, who will appear when Christ's Kingdom comes. 4 For it is written: "Go into your closets for a very little while, until my wrath and anger pass, and I will remember a good

---

[55]Ps 18:25–26   [56]Matt 26:24; Mark 14:21; Matt 18:6; Mark 9:42; Luke 17:2   [57]Ps 118:19–20

day and I will raise you up from your graves."[58] 5 Happy are we, dear friends, if we keep God's commandments in the harmony of love, so that by love our sins may be forgiven us. 6 For it is written: "Happy are those whose iniquities are forgiven and whose sins are covered. Happy is the one whose sin the Lord will not reckon, and on whose lips there is no deceit."[59] 7 This is the blessing which was given to those whom God chose through Jesus Christ our Lord. To him be the glory forever and ever. Amen.

51 Let us, then, ask pardon for our failings and for whatever we have done through the prompting of the adversary. And those who are the ringleaders of the revolt and dissension ought to reflect upon the common nature of our hope. 2 Those, certainly, who live in fear and love would rather suffer outrages themselves than have their neighbors do so. They prefer to endure condemnation themselves rather than bring in reproach our tradition of noble and righteous harmony. 3 It is better for a person to confess his sins than to harden his heart in the way those rebels against God's servant Moses hardened theirs. The verdict against them was made very plain. 4 For they went down to Hades alive, and death will be their shepherd. 5 Pharaoh and his host and all the princes of Egypt and the chariots and their riders were engulfed in the Red Sea and perished, for no other reason than that they hardened their foolish hearts after Moses, God's servant, had done signs and wonders in Egypt.

52 The Master, brothers, has no need of anything. He wants nothing of anybody save that he should praise him. 2 For his favorite, David, says: "I will praise the Lord; and this will please him more than a young calf with horns and hoofs. Let the poor observe this and rejoice."[60] 3 And again he says: "Offer to God the sacrifice of praise, and pay your vows to the Most High. Call on me in the day of your affliction and I will rescue you, and you will glorify me. 4 For the sacrifice God wants is a broken spirit."[61]

53 You know the Holy Scriptures, dear friends—you know them well—and you have studied God's oracles. It is to remind you of them that we write the way we do. 2 When Moses ascended the mountain and spent forty days and forty nights in fasting and humiliation, God said to him: "Get quickly down from here, for your people, whom you led out the land of Egypt, have broken the law. They have quickly turned from the way you bid them take. They have cast idols for themselves."[62] 3 And the Lord told him: "I have spoken to you once, yes, twice, saying, I have looked at this people and, see, it is obstinate. Let me exterminate them, and I will wipe out their name from under heaven, and I will make you into a great and wonderful nation, much larger than this one."[63] 4 And Moses answered: "No, no, Lord. Pardon my people's sin, or else eliminate me too from the roll of the living."[64]

5 O great love! O unsurpassed perfection! The servant speaks openly to his Lord. He begs pardon for his people or requests that he too will be wiped out along with them.

54 Well, then, who of your number is noble, large-hearted, and full of love? 2 Let him say: "If it is my fault that revolt, strife, and schism have arisen, I will leave, I will go away wherever you wish, and do what the congregation orders. Only let Christ's flock live in peace with their appointed presbyters." 3 The one who does this will win for himself great glory in Christ, and will be welcome everywhere. For the earth and its fullness belong to the Lord. This has been the conduct and will always be the conduct of those who have no regrets that they belong to the city of God.

55 Let us take some heathen examples: In times of plague many kings and rulers, prompted by oracles, have given themselves up to death in order to rescue their subjects by their own blood. Many have quit their own cities to put an end to sedition. 2 We know many of our own number who have had themselves imprisoned in order to ransom others. Many have sold themselves into slavery and given the price to feed others. 3 Many women, empowered by God's grace, have performed deeds worthy of men. 4 The blessed Judith, when her city was under siege, begged of the elders to be permitted to leave it for the enemy's camp. 5 So she exposed herself to danger and for love of her country and of her be-

---

[58]Isa 26:20; Ezek 37:12   [59]Ps 32:1–2; Rom 4:7–9   [60]Ps 69:30–32
[61]Ps 50:14–15; 51:17   [62]Deut 9:12 (Exod 32:7–8)   [63]Deut 9:13–14
(Exod 32:9–10)   [64]Exod 32:31–32

sieged people, she departed. And the Lord delivered Holofernes into the hands of a woman. 6 To no less danger did Esther, that woman of perfect faith, expose herself in order to rescue the twelve tribes of Israel when they were on the point of being destroyed. For by her fasting and humiliation she implored the all-seeing Master, the eternal God; and he beheld the humility of her soul and rescued her people for whose sake she had faced danger.

56 So we too must intercede for any who have fallen into sin, that considerateness and humility may be granted to them and that they may submit, not to us, but to God's will. For in that way they will prove fruitful and perfect when God and the saints remember them with mercy. 2 We must accept correction, dear friends. No one should resent it. Warnings we give each other are good and thoroughly beneficial. For they bind us to God's will. 3 This is what the Holy Word says about it: "The Lord has disciplined me severely and has not given me up to death. 4 For the Lord disciplines the one he loves, and punishes every son he accepts."[65] 5 For, it says, "the upright person will discipline me with mercy and reprove me. But let not the oil of sinners anoint my head."[66] And again it says: "Happy is the one the Lord reproves. Do not refuse the Almighty's warning. For he inflicts pain, and then makes all well again. 7 He smites, but his hands heal. 8 Six times will he rescue you from trouble; and on the seventh evil will not touch you. 9 In famine he will rescue you from death; in war he will deliver you from the edge of the sword. 10 From the scourge of the tongue he will hide you, and you will not be afraid of evils when they come. 11 You will ridicule the wicked and lawless, and not be afraid of wild beasts; 12 for wild beasts will leave you in peace. 13 Then you will discover that your house will be peaceful, and the tent in which you dwell will be safe. 14 You will find, too, that your seed will be numerous, and your children like the grass of the fields. 15 You will come to your tomb like ripe wheat harvested at the appropriate season, or like a heap on the threshing floor gathered together at the right time."[67]

16 You see, dear friends, how well protected they are whom the Master disciplines. Yes, he is like a good Father, and disciplines us so that the outcome of his holy discipline may mean mercy for us.

57 And that is why you who are responsible for the revolt must submit to the presbyters. You must humble your hearts and be disciplined so that you repent. 2 You must learn obedience, and be done with your proud boasting and curb your arrogant tongues. For it is better for you to have an insignificant yet creditable place in Christ's flock than to appear eminent and be excluded from Christ's hope. 3 For this is what the excellent Wisdom says: "See, I will declare to you the utterance of my Spirit: I will teach you my word. 4 Since I called and you did not listen, since I poured out words and you did not heed, but disregarded my plans and disobeyed my reproofs, therefore I will laugh at your destruction. And I will rejoice when ruin befalls you and when confusion suddenly overtakes you, and catastrophe descends like a hurricane, or when persecution and siege come upon you. 5 Yes, it will be like this: when you call upon me, I will not heed you. The wicked shall look for me and shall not find me. For they detested wisdom, and did not choose the fear of the Lord. They had no desire to heed my counsels, and mocked at my reproofs. 6 For this reason they shall eat the fruit of their ways and fill themselves with impiety. 7 Because they wronged babes, they will be slain; and by being searched out the impious shall be destroyed. But he that listens to me will dwell in confident hope and live quietly, free from the fear of any misfortune."[68]

58 So, then, let us obey his most holy and glorious name and escape the threats which Wisdom has predicted against the disobedient. In that way we shall live in peace, having our confidence in his most holy and majestic name. 2 Accept our advice, and you will never regret it. For as God lives, and as the Lord Jesus Christ lives and the Holy Spirit (on whom the elect believe and hope), the person who with humility and eager considerateness and with no regrets does what God has decreed and ordered will be enlisted and enrolled in the ranks of those who are saved

---

[65]Ps 118:18; Prov 3:12 (Heb 12:6)   [66]Ps 141:5   [67]Job 5:17–26
[68]Prov 1:23–33

through Jesus Christ. Through him be the glory to God forever and ever. Amen.

59 If, on the other hand, there be some who fail to obey what God has told them through us, they must realize that they will enmesh themselves in sin and in no insignificant danger. 2 We, for our part, will not be responsible for such a sin. But we will beg with earnest prayer and supplication that the Creator of the universe will keep intact the precise number of his elect in the whole world, through his beloved Child Jesus Christ. It was through him that he called us from darkness to light, from ignorance to the recognition of his glorious name, 3 to hope on Your name, which is the origin of all creation. You have opened the eyes of our hearts so that we realize you alone are highest among the highest, and ever remain holy among the holy. You humble the pride of the arrogant, overrule the plans of the nations, raise up the humble and humble the haughty. You make rich and make poor; you slay and bring to life; you alone are the guardian of spirits and the God of all flesh. You see into the depths: you look upon people's deeds; you aid those in danger and save those in despair. You are the creator of every spirit and watch over them. You multiply the nations on the earth, and from out of them all you have chosen those who love you through Jesus Christ, your beloved Son. Through him you have trained us, made us saints, and honored us.

4 We ask you, Master, be our helper and defender. Rescue those of our number in distress; raise up the fallen; assist the needy; heal the sick; turn back those of your people who stray; feed the hungry; release our captives; revive the weak; encourage those who lose heart. Let all the nations realize that you are the only God, that Jesus Christ is your Child, and that we are your people and the sheep of your pasture.

60 You brought into being the everlasting structure of the world by what you did. You, Lord, made the earth. You who are faithful in all generations, righteous in judgment, marvelous in strength and majesty, wise in creating, prudent in making creation endure, visibly good, kind to those who trust in you, merciful and compassionate—forgive us our sins, wickedness, trespasses, and failings. 2 Do not take account of every sin of

your slaves, men and women, but cleanse us with the cleansing of your truth, and guide our steps so that we walk with holy hearts and do what is good and pleasing to you and to our rulers.

3 Yes, Master, turn your radiant face toward us in peace, for our good, that we may be shielded by your powerful hand and rescued from every sin by your uplifted arm. 4 Deliver us, too, from all who hate us without good reason. Give us and all who live on the earth harmony and peace, just as you did to our fathers when they reverently called upon you in faith and truth. And grant that we may be obedient to your almighty and glorious name, and to our rulers and governors on earth.

61 You, Master, gave them imperial power through your majestic and indescribable might, so that we, recognizing it was you who gave them the glory and honor, might submit to them, and in no way oppose your will. Grant them, Lord, health, peace, harmony, and stability, so that they may give no offense in administering the government you have given them. 2 For it is you, Master, the heavenly King of eternity, who give the sons of men glory and honor and authority over the earth's people. Direct their plans, O Lord, in accord with what is good and pleasing to you, so that they may administer the authority you have given them, with peace, considerateness, and reverence, and so win your mercy. 3 We praise you, who alone are able to do this and still better things for us, through the high priest and guardian of our souls, Jesus Christ. Through him be the glory and the majesty to you now and for all generations and forevermore. Amen.

62 We have written enough to you, brothers, about what befits our religion and is most helpful to those who want reverently and uprightly to lead a virtuous life. 2 We have, indeed, touched on every topic—faith, repentance, genuine love, self-control, sobriety, and patience. We have reminded you that you must reverently please almighty God by your uprightness, truthfulness, and long-suffering. You must live in harmony, bearing no grudges, in love, peace, and true considerateness, just as our forefathers, whom we mentioned, won approval by their humble attitude to the Father, God the Creator, and to all people. 3 We were, moreover, all the more delighted to remind you of these things, since we well realized we were writing to people who were real believers and of the highest standing, and who had made a study of the oracles of God's teaching.

63 Hence it is only right that, confronted with such examples and so many of them, we should bow the neck and adopt the attitude of obedience. Thus, by giving up this futile revolt, we may be free from all reproach and gain the true goal ahead of us. 2 Yes, you will make us exceedingly happy if you prove obedient to what we, prompted by the Holy Spirit, have written, and if, following the plea of our letter for peace and harmony, you rid yourselves of your wicked and passionate rivalry.

3 We are sending you, moreover, trustworthy and discreet persons who from youth to old age have lived irreproachable lives among us. They will be witnesses to mediate between us. 4 We have done this to let you know that our whole concern has been, and is, to have peace speedily restored among you.

64 And now may the all-seeing God and Master of spirits and Lord of all flesh, who chose the Lord Jesus Christ and us through him to be his own people, grant to every soul over whom his magnificent and holy name has been invoked, faith, fear, peace, patience, long suffering, self-control, purity, and sobriety. So may we win his approval through our high priest and defender, Jesus Christ. Through him be glory, majesty, might, and honor to God, now and forevermore. Amen.

65 Be quick to return our delegates in peace and joy, Claudius Ephebus and Valerius Bito, along with Fortunatus. In that way they will the sooner bring us news of that peace and harmony we have prayed for and so much desire, and we in turn will the more speedily rejoice over your healthy state.

The grace of our Lord Jesus Christ be with you and with all everywhere whom God has called through him. Through him be glory, honor, might, majesty, and eternal dominion to God, from everlasting to everlasting. Amen.

The Letter of the Romans to the Corinthians

The Didache

Discovered in 1873 in a monastary library in Constantinople, the "Didache (literally, *The Teaching*) of the Twelve Apostles" has made a significant impact on the way in which scholars understand the social life and ritual practices of the early church. It is, in fact, the first "church manual" to have survived from early Christianity.

The book was probably written around 100 C.E., since it appears to be familiar with earlier Christian traditions such as those embodied in Matthew's Gospel in the latter half of the first century, yet does not evidence the rigid form of church hierarchy that had developed later in the second century (even though it speaks of bishops and deacons).

The first part of the book describes the "Two Ways of Life and Death" (see the introduction to the *Letter of Barnabas*). The Way of Life (chaps. 1–4) is paved with upright behavior: the author's readers are to love one another, avoid evil desires, jealousy, and anger, give alms to the poor, obey God's commandments, and generally lead morally respectable lives. Many of these instructions reflect the teachings of Jesus from Matthew's Sermon on the Mount (e.g., praying for one's enemies, turning the other cheek, and going the extra mile). As might be expected, the Way of Death (chap. 5) involves the opposite sorts of behavior: "murders, adulteries, lusts, fornications, thefts," and sundry other transgressive activities.

The bulk of the rest of the book gives instructions for the ritual practices and social interactions of the Christian community (chaps. 7–15), including directions for how to perform baptisms (preferably in cold, running water), when to fast (every Wednesday and Friday), what to pray (the Lord's Prayer, three times a day), and how to celebrate the Eucharist (first giving thanks for the cup, then the bread). Near the end of these instructions the author addresses the problem of wandering "apostles," "teachers," and "prophets" of dubious moral character; evidently, some scoundrels had become itinerant Christian preachers simply for financial gain. The communities are to test the sincerity of these wandering ministers and to limit the length of their stay at the community's expense; moreover, the communities are to appoint leaders of their own to direct their affairs.

The book concludes with a kind of apocalyptic discourse, an exhortation to be prepared for the imminent end of the world, to be brought by "the Lord coming on the clouds of heaven" (16:7).

1 There are two ways, one of life and one of death; and between the two ways there is a great difference.

2 Now, this is the way of life: First, you must love God who made you, and second, your neighbor as yourself. And whatever you want people to refrain from doing to you, you must not do to them.

3 What these maxims teach is this: Bless those who curse you, and pray for your enemies. Moreover, fast for those who persecute you. For what credit is it to you if you love those who love you? Is that not the way the heathen act? But you must love those who hate you, and then you will make no enemies. Abstain from carnal passions. 4 If someone strikes you on the right cheek, turn to him the other too, and you will be perfect. If someone forces you to go one mile with him, go along with him for two; if someone robs you of your overcoat, give him your suit as well. If someone deprives you of your property, do not ask for it back. (You could not get it back anyway!) 5 Give to everybody who begs from you, and ask for no return. For the Father wants his own gifts to be universally shared. Happy is the one who gives as the commandment bids him, for he is guiltless! But alas for the one who receives! If he receives because he is in need, he will be guiltless. But if he is not in need he will have to stand trial why he received and for what purpose. He will be thrown into prison and have his action investigated; and he will not get out until he has paid back the last cent. 6 Indeed, there is a further saying that relates to this: "Let your donation sweat in your hands until you know to whom to give it."

2 The second commandment of the Teaching: 2 Do not murder; do not commit adultery; do not corrupt boys; do not fornicate; do not steal; do not practice magic; do not go in for sorcery; do not murder a child by abortion or kill a newborn infant. 3 Do not covet your neighbor's property; do not commit perjury; do not bear false witness; do not slander; do not bear grudges. 4 Do not be double-minded or double-tongued, for a double tongue is a deadly snare. 5 Your words shall not be dishonest or hollow, but substantiated by action. 6 Do not be greedy or extortionate or hypocritical or malicious or arrogant. Do not plot against your neighbor. 7 Do not hate anybody; but reprove some, pray for others, and still others love more than your own life.

3 My child, flee from all wickedness and from everything of that sort. 2 Do not be irritable, for anger leads to murder. Do not be jealous or contentious or impetuous, for all this breeds murder.

3 My child, do not be lustful, for lust leads to fornication. Do not use foul language or leer, for all this breeds adultery.

4 My child, do not be a diviner, for that leads to idolatry. Do not be an enchanter or an astrologer or a magician. Moreover, have no wish to observe or heed such practices, for all this breeds idolatry.

5 My child, do not be a liar, for lying leads to theft. Do not be avaricious or vain, for all this breeds thievery.

6 My child, do not be a grumbler, for grumbling leads to blasphemy. Do not be stubborn or evil-minded, for all this breeds blasphemy.

7 But be humble since the humble will inherit the earth. 8 Be patient, merciful, harmless, quiet, and good; and always have respect for the teaching you have been given. Do not put on airs or give yourself up to presumptuousness. Do not associate with the high and mighty; but be with the upright and humble. Accept whatever happens to you as good, in the realization that nothing occurs apart from God.

4 My child, day and night you should remember him who preaches God's word to you, and honor him as you would the Lord. For where the Lord's nature is discussed, there the Lord is. 2 Every day you should seek the company of saints to enjoy their refreshing conversation. 3 You must not start a schism, but reconcile those at strife. Your judgments must be fair. You must not play favorites when reproving transgressions. 4 You must not be of two minds about your decision.

5 Do not be one who holds his hand out to take, but shuts it when it comes to giving. 6 If your labor has brought you earnings, pay a ransom for your sins. 7 Do not hesitate to give and do not give with a bad grace; for you will discover who he is that pays you back a reward with a good grace. 8 Do not turn your back on the needy, but share everything with your brother and call nothing your own. For if you have what is eternal in

common, how much more should you have what is transient!

9 Do not neglect your responsibility to your son or your daughter, but from their youth you shall teach them to revere God. 10 Do not be harsh in giving orders to your slaves, men and women. They hope in the same God as you, and the result may be that they cease to revere the God over you both. For when he comes to call us, he will not respect our station, but will call those whom the Spirit has made ready. 11 You slaves, for your part, must obey your masters with reverence and fear, as if they represented God.

12 You must hate all hypocrisy and everything which fails to please the Lord. 13 You must not forsake the Lord's commandments, but observe the ones you have been given, neither adding nor subtracting anything. 14 At the church meeting you must confess your sins, and not approach prayer with a bad conscience. That is the way of life.

5 But the way of death is this: First of all, it is wicked and thoroughly blasphemous: murders, adulteries, lusts, fornications, thefts, idolatries, magic arts, sorceries, robberies, false witness, hypocrisies, duplicity, deceit, arrogance, malice, stubbornness, greediness, filthy talk, jealousy, audacity, haughtiness, boastfulness.

2 Those who persecute good people, who hate truth, who love lies, who are ignorant of the reward of uprightness, who do not abide by goodness or justice, and are on the alert not for goodness but for evil: gentleness and patience are remote from them. They love vanity, look for profit, have no pity for the poor, do not exert themselves for the oppressed, ignore their Maker, murder children, corrupt God's image, turn their backs on the needy, oppress the afflicted, defend the rich, unjustly condemn the poor, and are thoroughly wicked. My children, may you be saved from all this!

6 See that no one leads you astray from this way of the teaching, since such a one's teaching is godless.

2 If you can bear the Lord's full yoke, you will be perfect. But if you cannot, then do what you can.

3 Now about food: undertake what you can. But keep strictly away from what is offered to idols, for that implies worshiping dead gods.

7 Now about baptism: this is how to baptize. Give public instruction on all these points, and then baptize in running water, in the name of the Father and of the Son and of the Holy Spirit. 2 If you do not have running water, baptize in some other. 3 If you cannot in cold, then in warm. If you have neither, then pour water on the head three times in the name of the Father, Son, and Holy Spirit. 4 Before the baptism, moreover, the one who baptizes and the one being baptized must fast, and any others who can. And you must tell the one being baptized to fast for one or two days beforehand.

8 Your fasts must not be identical with those of the hypocrites. They fast on Mondays and Thursdays; but you should fast on Wednesdays and Fridays.

2 You must not pray like the hypocrites, but pray as follows as the Lord bid us in his gospel:

"Our Father in heaven, hallowed be your name; your Kingdom come; your will be done on earth as it is in heaven; give us today our bread for the morrow; and forgive us our debts as we forgive our debtors. And do not lead us into temptation, but save us from the evil one, for yours is the power and the glory forever."[1]

3 You should pray in this way three times a day.

9 Now about the Eucharist: This is how to give thanks: 2 First in connection with the cup:

"We thank you, our Father, for the holy vine of David, your child, which you have revealed through Jesus, your child. To you be glory forever."

3 Then in connection with the piece [broken off the loaf]:

"We thank you, our Father, for the life and knowledge which you have revealed through Jesus, your child. To you be glory forever.

4 "As this piece [of bread] was scattered over the hills and then was brought together and made one, so let your Church be brought together from the ends of the earth into your Kingdom. For yours is the glory and the power through Jesus Christ forever."

5 You must not let anyone eat or drink of your

[1]Matt 6:9–13

Eucharist except those baptized in the Lord's name. For in reference to this the Lord said, "Do not give what is sacred to dogs."[2]

10 After you have finished your meal, say grace in this way:

2 "We thank you, holy Father, for your sacred name which you have lodged in our hearts, and for the knowledge and faith and immortality which you have revealed through Jesus, your child. To you be glory forever.

3 "Almighty Master, you have created everything for the sake of your name, and have given people food and drink to enjoy that they may thank you. But to us you have given spiritual food and drink and eternal life through Jesus, your child.

4 "Above all, we thank you that you are mighty. To you be glory forever.

5 "Remember, Lord, your Church, to save it from all evil and to make it perfect by your love. Make it holy, and gather it together from the four winds into your Kingdom which you have made ready for it. For yours is the power and the glory forever."

6 "Let Grace come and let this world pass away."

"Hosanna to the God of David!"

"If anyone is holy, let him come. If not, let him repent."

"Our Lord, come!"

"Amen."

7 In the case of prophets, however, you should let them give thanks in their own way.

11 Now, you should welcome anyone who comes your way and teaches you all we have been saying. 2 But if the teacher proves himself a renegade and by teaching otherwise contradicts all this, pay no attention to him. But if his teaching furthers the Lord's righteousness and knowledge, welcome him as the Lord.

3 Now about the apostles and prophets: Act in line with the gospel precept. 4 Welcome every apostle on arriving, as if he were the Lord. 5 But he must not stay beyond one day. In case of necessity, however, the next day too. If he stays three days, he is a false prophet. 6 On departing, an apostle must not accept anything save sufficient food to carry him till his next lodging. If he asks for money, he is a false prophet.

7 While a prophet is making ecstatic utterances, you must not test or examine him. For "every sin will be forgiven," but this sin "will not be forgiven."[3] 8 However, not everybody making ecstatic utterances is a prophet, but only if he behaves like the Lord. It is by their conduct that the false prophet and the [true] prophet can be distinguished. 9 For instance, if a prophet marks out a table in the Spirit, he must not eat from it. If he does, he is a false prophet. 10 Again, every prophet who teaches the truth but fails to practice what he preaches is a false prophet. 11 But every attested and genuine prophet who acts with a view to symbolizing the mystery of the Church, and does not teach you to do all he does, must not be judged by you. His judgment rests with God. For the ancient prophets too acted in this way. 12 But if someone says in the Spirit, "Give me money, or something else," you must not heed him. However, if he tells you to give for others in need, no one must condemn him.

12 Everyone who comes to you in the name of the Lord must be welcomed. Afterward, when you have tested him, you will find out about him, for you have insight into right and wrong. 2 If it is a traveler who arrives, help him all you can. But he must not stay with you more than two days, or, if necessary, three. 3 If he wants to settle with you and is an artisan, he must work for his living. 4 If, however, he has no trade, use your judgment in taking steps for him to live with you as a Christian without being idle. 5 If he refuses to do this, he is trading on Christ. You must be on your guard against such people.

13 Every genuine prophet who wants to settle with you has a right to his support. 2 Similarly, a genuine teacher himself, just like a workman, has a right to his support. 3 Hence take all the first fruits of vintage and harvest, and of cattle and sheep, and give these first fruits to the prophets. For they are your high priests. 4 If, however, you have no prophet, give them to the poor. 5 If you make bread, take the first fruits and give in accordance with the precept. 6 Similarly, when you open a jar of wine or oil, take the first fruits and give them to the prophets. 7 Indeed, of

---

[2]Matt 7:6   [3]Matt 12:31

money, clothes, and of all your possessions, take such first fruits as you think right, and give in accordance with the precept.

14 On every Lord's Day—his special day—come together and break bread and give thanks, first confessing your sins so that your sacrifice may be pure. 2 Anyone at variance with his neighbor must not join you, until they are reconciled, lest your sacrifice be defiled. 3 For it was of this sacrifice that the Lord said, "Always and everywhere offer me a pure sacrifice; for I am a great King, says the Lord, and my name is marveled at by the nations."[4]

15 You must, then, elect for yourselves bishops and deacons who are a credit to the Lord, men who are gentle, generous, faithful, and well tried. For their ministry to you is identical with that of the prophets and teachers. 2 You must not, therefore, despise them, for along with the prophets and teachers they enjoy a place of honor among you.

3 Furthermore, do not reprove each other angrily, but quietly, as you find it in the gospel. Moreover, if anyone has wronged his neighbor, nobody must speak to him, and he must not hear a word from you, until he repents. 4 Say your prayers, give your charity, and do everything just as you find it in the gospel of our Lord.

16 Watch over your life: do not let your lamps go out, and do not keep your loins ungirded; but be ready, for you do not know the hour when our Lord is coming. 2 Meet together frequently in your search for what is good for your souls, since a lifetime of faith will be of no advantage to you unless you prove perfect at the very last. 3 For in the final days multitudes of false prophets and seducers will appear. 4 Sheep will turn into wolves, and love into hatred. For with the increase of iniquity people will hate, persecute, and betray each other. And then the world deceiver will appear in the guise of God's Son. He will work signs and wonders and the earth will fall into his hands and he will commit outrages such as have never occurred before. 5 Then mankind will come to the fiery trial and many will fall away and perish, but those who persevere in their faith will be saved by the Curse himself. 6 Then there will appear the signs of the Truth: first the sign of stretched-out [hands] in heaven, then the sign of a trumpet's blast, and thirdly the resurrection of the dead, though not of all the dead, but as it has been said: 7 "The Lord will come and all his saints with him. Then the world will see the Lord coming on the clouds of the sky."[5]

---

[4]Mal 1:11, 14   [5]Zech 14:5

The Letter of Ignatius to the Ephesians

Ignatius is one of the first Christians known to have been executed on order of the Roman authorities. Arrested in Antioch of Syria, where he served as bishop of the church, Ignatius was sent in chains to face the wild beasts in the Roman amphitheater (1:2; 21:2). While traveling by land through Asia Minor, he was met at various stopping points by representatives of local Christian communities who had heard of his plight. Ignatius in turn penned letters to several of these churches. Altogether, seven letters survive from his hand. They appear to date from around 110 C.E.

The letter to the church in Ephesus was written from the city of Smyrna (21:1). The Ephesian Christians had sent a five-person delegation to meet with Ignatius, headed by the bishop of the church, Onesimus, and one of its deacons, Burrhus (1:3–2:1). Having learned about their congregation, Ignatius writes to express his gratitude and to encourage them in their faith.

Several themes recur throughout this short letter. Most noticeably, Ignatius is concerned that the Ephesian Christians live in harmony with one another and, especially, with their bishop. They are "to act in accord with the bishop's mind" (4:1) and to "avoid resisting the bishop so [as to] be subject to God" (5:2). Indeed, the Ephesians are told to regard Onesimus, their bishop, "as the Lord himself" (6:1).

Much of the letter provides basic instruction on Christian living; the Ephesians are encouraged, for example, to live in love toward one another (14:1), to avoid sin (14:2), not to be overly garrulous (15:1), and to practice what they preach (15:1). In particular, Ignatius had learned that outsiders had come into the congregation proclaiming "wicked teaching" (9:1). He does not indicate the precise nature of the problem, but he does warn the Ephesians to give these interlopers no heed and to remain true to their basic beliefs about Christ. His own summary of these beliefs is strikingly paradoxical: "There is only one physician— of flesh yet spiritual, born yet unbegotten, God incarnate, genuine life in the midst of death, sprung from Mary as well as God, first subject to suffering then beyond it—Jesus Christ our Lord" (7:2).

Ignatius appears to be familiar with a number of traditions about Jesus from the Gospels, and he interprets them in somewhat unusual ways: the star of Bethlehem astonished all the other stars of heaven, which gathered about it in adoration (19:2–3); Jesus' baptism in water purified the waters used in (Christian) baptism (18:2); and his being anointed with oil allowed him to "pass on the aroma of incorruption to the Church" (17:1). It is debated among scholars whether Ignatius had actually read any of our written Gospels (e.g., Matthew) or had instead simply heard some of the oral traditions about Jesus' life.

"The Letter of Ignatius to the Ephesians," from *Early Christian Fathers,* edited by Cyril D. Richardson (Library of Christian Classics). © 1953 by Westminster Press. Reprinted by permission of Westminster John Knox Press.

Heartiest greetings of pure joy in Jesus Christ from Ignatius, the "God-inspired," to the church at Ephesus in Asia. Out of the fullness of God the Father you have been blessed with large numbers and are predestined from eternity to enjoy forever continual and unfading glory. The source of your unity and election is genuine suffering which you undergo by the will of the Father and of Jesus Christ, our God. Hence you deserve to be considered happy.

1 I gave a godly welcome to your church which has so endeared itself to us by reason of your upright nature, marked as it is by faith in Jesus Christ, our Saviour, and by love of him. You are imitators of God; and it was God's blood that stirred you up once more to do the sort of thing you do naturally and have now done to perfection. 2 For you were all zeal to visit me when you heard that I was being shipped as a prisoner from Syria for the sake of our common Name and hope. I hope, indeed, by your prayers to have the good fortune to fight with wild beasts in Rome, so that by doing this I can be a real disciple. 3 In God's name, therefore, I received your large congregation in the person of Onesimus, your bishop in this world, a man whose love is beyond words. My prayer is that you should love him in the spirit of Jesus Christ and all be like him. Blessed is he who let you have such a bishop. You deserved it.

2 Now about my fellow slave Burrhus, your godly deacon, who has been richly blessed. I very much want him to stay with me. He will thus bring honor on you and the bishop. Crocus too, who is a credit both to God and to you, and whom I received as a model of your love, altogether raised my spirits (May the Father of Jesus Christ grant him a similar comfort!), as did Onesimus, Burrhus, Euplus, and Fronto. In them I saw and loved you all. 2 May I always be glad about you, that is, if I deserve to be! It is right, then, for you to render all glory to Jesus Christ, seeing he has glorified you. Thus, united in your submission, and subject to the bishop and the presbytery, you will be real saints.

3 I do not give you orders as if I were somebody important. For even if I am a prisoner for the Name, I have not yet reached Christian perfection. I am only beginning to be a disciple, so I address you as my fellow students. I needed your coaching in faith, encouragement, endurance, and patience. 2 But since love forbids me to keep silent about you, I hasten to urge you to harmonize your actions with God's mind. For Jesus Christ—that life from which we can't be torn—is the Father's mind, as the bishops too, appointed the world over, reflect the mind of Jesus Christ.

4 Hence you should act in accord with the bishop's mind, as you surely do. Your presbytery, indeed, which deserves its name and is a credit to God, is as closely tied to the bishop as the strings to a harp. Wherefore your accord and harmonious love is a hymn to Jesus Christ. 2 Yes, one and all, you should form yourselves into a choir, so that, in perfect harmony and taking your pitch from God, you may sing in unison and with one voice to the Father through Jesus Christ. Thus he will heed you, and by your good deeds he will recognize you are members of his Son. Therefore you need to abide in irreproachable unity if you really want to be God's members forever.

5 If in so short a time I could get so close to your bishop—I do not mean in a natural way, but in a spiritual—how much more do I congratulate you on having such intimacy with him as the Church enjoys with Jesus Christ, and Jesus Christ with the Father. That is how unity and harmony come to prevail everywhere. Make no mistake about it. 2 If anyone is not inside the sanctuary, he lacks God's bread. And if the prayer of one or two has great avail, how much more that of the bishop and the total Church. 3 He who fails to join in your worship shows his arrogance by the very fact of becoming a schismatic. It is written, moreover, "God resists the proud."[1] Let us, then, heartily avoid resisting the bishop so that we may be subject to God.

6 The more anyone sees the bishop modestly silent, the more he should revere him. For everyone the Master of the house sends on his business, we ought to receive as the One who sent him. It is clear, then, that we should regard the bishop as the Lord himself. 2 Indeed, Onesimus spoke very highly of your godly conduct, that you were all living by the truth and harboring no sectarianism. Nay, you heed nobody beyond what he has to say truthfully about Jesus Christ.

---

[1]Prov 3:34

7 Some, indeed, have a wicked and deceitful habit of flaunting the Name about, while acting in a way unworthy of God. You must avoid them like wild beasts. For they are mad dogs which bite on the sly. You must be on your guard against them, for it is hard to heal their bite. 2 There is only one physician—of flesh yet spiritual, born yet unbegotten, God incarnate, genuine life in the midst of death, sprung from Mary as well as God, first subject to suffering then beyond it—Jesus Christ our Lord.

8 Let no one mislead you, as, indeed, you are not misled, being wholly God's. For when you harbor no dissension that can harass you, then you are indeed living in God's way. A cheap sacrifice I am, but I dedicate myself to you Ephesians—a church forever famous. 2 Carnal people cannot act spiritually, or spiritual people carnally, just as faith cannot act like unbelief, or unbelief like faith. But even what you do in the flesh you do spiritually. For you do everything under Christ's control.

9 I have heard that some strangers came your way with a wicked teaching. But you did not let them sow it among you. You stopped up your ears to prevent admitting what they disseminated. Like stones of God's Temple, ready for a building of God the Father, you are being hoisted up by Jesus Christ, as with a crane (that's the cross!), while the rope you use is the Holy Spirit. Your faith is what lifts you up, while love is the way you ascend to God.

2 You are all taking part in a religious procession, carrying along with you your God, shrine, Christ, and your holy objects, and decked out from tip to toe in the commandments of Jesus Christ. I too am enjoying it all, because I can talk with you in a letter, and congratulate you on changing your old way of life and setting your love on God alone.

10 Keep on praying for others too, for there is a chance of their being converted and getting to God. Let them, then, learn from you at least by your actions. 2 Return their bad temper with gentleness; their boasts with humility; their abuse with prayer. In the face of their error, be steadfast in the faith. Return their violence with mildness and do not be intent on getting your own back. 3 By our patience let us show we are their brothers, intent on imitating the Lord, seeing which

of us can be the more wronged, robbed, and despised. Thus no devil's weed will be found among you; but thoroughly pure and self-controlled, you will remain body and soul united to Jesus Christ.

11 The last days are here. So let us abase ourselves and stand in awe of God's patience, lest it turn out to be our condemnation. Either let us fear the wrath to come or let us value the grace we have: one or the other. Only let our lot be genuine life in Jesus Christ. 2 Do not let anything catch your eye besides him, for whom I carry around these chains—my spiritual pearls! Through them I want to rise from the dead by your prayers. May I ever share in these, so that I may be numbered among the Ephesian Christians who, by the might of Jesus Christ, have always been of one mind with the very apostles.

12 I realize who I am and to whom I am writing. I am a convict; you have been freed. I am in danger; you are safe. 2 You are the route for God's victims. You have been initiated into the [Christian] mysteries with Paul, a real saint and martyr, who deserves to be congratulated. When I come to meet God may I follow in his footsteps, who in all his letters mentions your union with Christ Jesus.

13 Try to gather together more frequently to celebrate God's Eucharist and to praise him. For when you meet with frequency, Satan's powers are overthrown and his destructiveness is undone by the unanimity of your faith. 2 There is nothing better than peace, by which all strife in heaven and earth is done away.

14 You will not overlook any of this if you have a thorough belief in Jesus Christ and love him. That is the beginning and end of life: faith the beginning and love the end. And when the two are united you have God, and everything else that has to do with real goodness is dependent on them. 2 No one who professes faith falls into sin, nor does one who has learned to love, hate. "The tree is known by its fruit."[2] Similarly, those who profess to be Christ's will be recognized by their actions. For what matters is not a momentary act of professing, but being persistently motivated by faith.

15 It is better to keep quiet and be real, than to chatter and be unreal. It is a good thing

---

[2]Matt 12:33

to teach if, that is, the teacher practices what he preaches. There was one such Teacher, who spoke and it was done; and what he did in silence is worthy of the Father. 2 He who has really grasped what Jesus said can appreciate his silence. Thus he will be perfect: his words will mean action, and his very silence will reveal his character.

3 The Lord overlooks nothing. Even secrets are open to him. Let us, then, do everything as if he were dwelling in us. Thus we shall be his temples and he will be within us as our God—as he actually is. This will be clear to us just to the extent that we love him rightly.

16 Make no mistake, my brothers: adulterers will not inherit God's Kingdom. 2 If, then, those who act carnally suffer death, how much more shall those who by wicked teaching corrupt God's faith for which Jesus Christ was crucified. Such a vile creature will go to the unquenchable fire along with anyone who listens to him.

17 The reason the Lord let the ointment be poured on his head was that he might pass on the aroma of incorruption to the Church. Do not be anointed with the foul smell of the teaching of the prince of this world, lest he capture you and rob you of the life ahead of you. 2 Why do we not all come to our senses by accepting God's knowledge, which is Jesus Christ? Why do we stupidly perish, ignoring the gift which the Lord has really sent?

18 I am giving my life (not that it's worth much!) for the cross, which unbelievers find a stumbling block, but which means to us salvation and eternal life. Where is the wise man? Where is the debater? Where are the boasts of those supposedly intelligent? 2 For our God, Jesus the Christ, was conceived by Mary, in God's plan being sprung both from the seed of David and from the Holy Spirit. He was born and baptized that by his Passion he might hallow water.

19 Now, Mary's virginity and her giving birth escaped the notice of the prince of this world, as did the Lord's death—those three

secrets crying to be told, but wrought in God's silence. How, then, were they revealed to the ages? 2 A star shone in heaven brighter than all the stars. Its light was indescribable and its novelty caused amazement. The rest of the stars, along with the sun and the moon, formed a ring around it; yet it outshone them all, and there was bewilderment whence this unique novelty had arisen. 3 As a result all magic lost its power and all witchcraft ceased. Ignorance was done away with, and the ancient kingdom [of evil] was utterly destroyed, for God was revealing himself as a man, to bring newness of eternal life. What God had prepared was now beginning. Hence everything was in confusion as the destruction of death was being taken in hand.

20 If Jesus Christ allows me, in answer to your prayers, and it is his will, I will explain to you more about [God's] plan in a second letter I intend to write. I have only touched on this plan in reference to the New Man Jesus Christ, and how it involves believing in him and loving him, and entails his Passion and resurrection. 2 I will do this especially if the Lord shows me that you are all, every one of you, meeting together under the influence of the grace that we owe to the Name, in one faith and in union with Christ, who was descended from David according to the flesh and is Son of man and Son of God. At these meetings you should heed the bishop and presbytery attentively, and break one loaf, which is the medicine of immortality, and the antidote which wards off death but yields continuous life in union with Jesus Christ.

21 I am giving my life for you and for those whom you, to God's honor, sent to Smyrna. I am writing to you from there, giving the Lord thanks and embracing Polycarp and you too in my love. Bear me in mind, as Jesus Christ does you. 2 Pray for the church in Syria, whence I am being sent off to Rome as a prisoner. I am the least of the faithful there—yet I have been privileged to serve God's honor. Farewell in God the Father and in Jesus Christ, our common hope.

The Letter of Ignatius to the Magnesians

Ignatius's letter to the Magnesians is similar in many ways to his letter to the Ephesians (see that introduction). It too was written from Smyrna (15:1), a stopping point along Ignatius's journey to martyrdom in Rome. It too is a response to the support shown Ignatius by the church: the Magnesians had sent a four-person delegation to meet with him, headed by their bishop Damas.

Here too Ignatius stresses the need for church members to live in harmony with one another and the bishop. In particular, he is concerned that the Magnesian Christians not look down upon their bishop for his youthfulness (3:1). They are to "respect him as fully as . . . the authority of God the Father" (3:1), they are to "defer" to him (13:2), they are to allow him "to preside in God's place" (6:1). Under the bishop are the "elders" or "presbyters," whom Ignatius insists are to be respected as the apostles themselves (6:1).

The Magnesian delegation had evidently informed Ignatius of "false teaching" in their midst, and he writes the congregation to be wary of it. In this instance, unlike in the letter to the Ephesians, we learn something about the nature of the problem. There were some members of the congregation who were urging Christians to adopt Jewish customs (8:1; 9:1; 10:3). For Ignatius, this idea is "monstrous" (10:3); for Christianity, he claims, is not based on Judaism, but Judaism on Christianity (10:3). Indeed, for Ignatius, "if we go on observing Judaism, we admit we never received grace" (8:1). For even the prophets of the Jewish Scriptures were persecuted for proclaiming that the one true God "has revealed himself in his son Jesus Christ" (8:2). This letter thus shows that already by the early second century Christians had begun to claim that the Hebrew Bible was a Christian, not a Jewish, book.

Every good wish in God the Father and in Jesus Christ from Ignatius, the "God-inspired," to the church at Magnesia on the Maeander. In Christ Jesus, our Saviour, I greet your church which, by reason of its union with him, is blessed with the favor of God the Father.

1 I was delighted to hear of your well-disciplined and godly love; and hence, impelled by faith in Jesus Christ, I decided to write to you. 2 Privileged as I am to have this distinguished and godly name, I sing the praises of the churches, even while I am a prisoner. I want them to confess that Jesus Christ, our perpetual Life, united flesh with spirit. I want them, too, to unite their faith with love—there is nothing better than that. Above all, I want them to confess the union of Jesus with the Father. If, with him to support us, we put up with all the spite of the prince of this world and manage to escape, we shall get to God.

2 Yes, I had the good fortune to see you, in the persons of Damas your bishop (he's a credit to God!), and of your worthy presbyters, Bassus and Apollonius, and of my fellow slave, the deacon Zotion. I am delighted with him, because he submits to the bishop as to God's grace, and to the presbytery as to the law of Jesus Christ.

3 Now, it is not right to presume on the youthfulness of your bishop. You ought to respect him as fully as you respect the authority of God the Father. Your holy presbyters, I know, have not taken unfair advantage of his apparent youthfulness, but in their godly wisdom have deferred to him—nay, rather, not so much to him as to the Father of Jesus Christ, who is everybody's bishop. 2 For the honor, then, of him who loved us, we ought to obey without any dissembling, since the real issue is not that a person misleads a bishop whom he can see, but that he defrauds the One who is invisible. In such a case he must reckon, not with a human being, but with God who knows his secrets.

4 We have not only to be called Christians, but to *be* Christians. It is the same thing as calling a man a bishop and then doing everything in disregard of him. Such people seem to me to be acting against their conscience, since they do not come to the valid and authorized services.

5 Yes, everything is coming to an end, and we stand before this choice—death or life—and everyone will go to his own place. One might say similarly, there are two coinages, one God's, the other the world's. Each bears its own stamp—unbelievers that of this world; believers, who are spurred by love, the stamp of God the Father through Jesus Christ. And if we do not willingly die in union with his Passion, we do not have his life in us.

6 I believed, then, that I saw your whole congregation in these people I have mentioned, and I loved you all. Hence I urge you to aim to do everything in godly agreement. Let the bishop preside in God's place, and the presbyters take the place of the apostolic council, and let the deacons (my special favorites) be entrusted with the ministry of Jesus Christ who was with the Father from eternity and appeared at the end [of the world].

2 Taking, then, the same attitude as God, you should all respect one another. Let no one think of his neighbor in a carnal way; but always love one another in the spirit of Jesus Christ. Do not let there be anything to divide you, but be in accord with the bishop and your leaders. Thus you will be an example and a lesson of incorruptibility.

7 As, then, the Lord did nothing without the Father (either on his own or by the apostles) because he was at one with him, so you must not do anything without the bishop and presbyters. Do not, moreover, try to convince yourselves that anything done on your own is commendable. Only what you do together is right. Hence you must have one prayer, one petition, one mind, one hope, dominated by love and unsullied joy—that means you must have Jesus Christ. You cannot have anything better than that.

2 Run off—all of you—to one temple of God, as it were, to one altar, to one Jesus Christ, who came forth from one Father, while still remaining one with him, and returned to him.

8 Do not be led astray by wrong views or by outmoded tales that count for nothing. For if we still go on observing Judaism, we admit we never received grace. 2 The divine prophets themselves lived Christ Jesus' way. That is why they were persecuted, for they were inspired by his grace to convince unbelievers that God is one, and that he has revealed himself in his Son Jesus Christ, who is his Word issuing from the silence and who won the complete approval of him who sent him.

9 Those, then, who lived by ancient practices arrived at a new hope. They ceased to keep the Sabbath and lived by the Lord's Day, on which our life as well as theirs shone forth, thanks to Him and his death, though some deny this. Through this mystery we got our faith, and because of it we stand our ground so as to become disciples of Jesus Christ, our sole teacher. 2 How, then, can we live without him when even the prophets, who were his disciples by the Spirit, awaited him as their teacher? He, then, whom they were rightly expecting, raised them from the dead, when he came.

10 We must not, then, be impervious to his kindness. Indeed, were he to act as we do, we should at once be done for. Hence, now we are his disciples, we must learn to live like Christians—to be sure, whoever bears any other name does not belong to God. 2 Get rid, then, of the bad yeast—it has grown stale and sour—and be changed into new yeast, that is, into Jesus Christ. Be salted in him, so that none of you go bad, for your smell will give you away. 3 It is monstrous to talk Jesus Christ and to live like a Jew. For Christianity did not believe in Judaism, but Judaism in Christianity. People of every tongue have come to believe in it, and so been united together in God.

11 I do not write in this way, my dear friends, because I have heard that any of you are like that. Rather do I, well aware of my humble position, want to caution you ahead, lest you fall a prey to stupid ideas, and to urge you to be thoroughly convinced of the birth, Passion, and resurrection, which occurred while Pontius Pilate was governor. Yes, all that was actually and assuredly done by Jesus Christ, our Hope. God forbid that any of you should lose it!

12 I want to be glad about you ever so much, if, that is, I deserve to be. For though I am a prisoner, I cannot compare with one of you who are free. I realize that you are not conceited, for you have Jesus Christ within you. And more, I know you are self-conscious when I praise you, just as Scripture says, "The upright man is his own accuser."[1]

13 Make a real effort, then, to stand firmly by the orders of the Lord and the apostles, so that whatever you do, you may succeed in body and soul, in faith and love, in Son, Father, and Spirit, from first to last, along with your most distinguished bishop, your presbytery (that neatly plaited spiritual wreath!), and your godly deacons. 2 Defer to the bishop and to one another as Jesus Christ did to the Father in the days of his flesh, and as the apostles did to Christ, to the Father, and to the Spirit. In that way we shall achieve complete unity.

14 I realize you are full of God. Hence I have counseled you but briefly. Remember me in your prayers, that I may get to God. Remember too the church in Syria—I do not deserve to be called a member of it. To be sure, I need your united and holy prayers and your love, so that the church in Syria may have the privilege of being refreshed by means of your church.

15 The Ephesians greet you from Smyrna. I am writing to you from there. Like you, they came here for God's glory and have revived me considerably, as has Polycarp, the bishop of Smyrna. The other churches also send their greetings to you in honor of Jesus Christ. Farewell—be at one with God, for you possess an unbreakable spirit, which is what Jesus Christ had.

---

[1]Prov 18:17

The Letter of Ignatius to the Trallians

Like his letters to the Ephesians and the Magnesians, Ignatius's letter to the Trallians was sent from Smyrna (12:1) in response to the support he had received. The church in Tralles had sent its bishop, Polybius, to meet with Ignatius on his road to martyrdom (1:1). Having learned about the congregation, Ignatius writes to urge them to stay united and to stand against heresy.

Thus Ignatius urges the Trallians "to act in no way without the bishop" (2:2) who has the "role of [God] the Father" (3:1) and to "submit even to the presbytery as to the apostles of Jesus Christ," (2:2). He suggests that "whoever does anything without bishop, presbytery, and deacons does not have a clear conscience" (7:2).

He is also concerned with false teaching in the congregation; but rather than opposing Judaism, as he does in the letter to the Magnesians, here Ignatius warns against those who claim that Jesus' sufferings were "a sham" (10:1). These Christians, whom Ignatius labels "atheists" and "unbelievers" (10:1), evidently maintained that, since Jesus was God, he could not have been a real flesh-and-blood human being, capable of being born, suffering, and dying. In response, Ignatius insists that Jesus "was really born, ate, and drank; was really persecuted under Pontius Pilate, was really crucified and died . . . and was really raised from the dead" (9:1–2).

Ignatius concludes his letter by urging the Trallians to flee false teachings (11:1–2), to continue in their harmony with one another (12:1), to pray for his own situation (12:3) and for the church in Syria that he left behind (13:1), and to be submissive to their bishop and presbytery (13:2).

Full hearty greetings in apostolic style, and every good wish from Ignatius, the "God-inspired," to the holy church at Tralles in Asia. You are dear to God, the Father of Jesus Christ, elect and a real credit to him, being completely at peace by reason of the Passion of Jesus Christ, who is our Hope, since we shall rise in union with him.

1 Well do I realize what a character you have—above reproach and steady under strain. It is not just affected, but it comes naturally to you, as I gathered from Polybius, your bishop. By God's will and that of Jesus Christ, he came to me in Smyrna, and so heartily congratulated me on being a prisoner for Jesus Christ that in him I saw your whole congregation. 2 I welcomed, then, your godly good will, which reached me by him, and I gave thanks that I found you, as I heard, to be following God.

2 For when you obey the bishop as if he were Jesus Christ, you are (as I see it) living not in a merely human fashion but in Jesus Christ's way, who for our sakes suffered death that you might believe in his death and so escape dying yourselves. 2 It is essential, therefore, to act in no

way without the bishop, just as you are doing. Rather submit even to the presbytery as to the apostles of Jesus Christ. He is our Hope, and if we live in union with him now, we shall gain eternal life. 3 Those too who are deacons of Jesus Christ's "mysteries" must give complete satisfaction to everyone. For they do not serve mere food and drink, but minister to God's Church. They must therefore avoid leaving themselves open to criticism, as they would shun fire.

3 Correspondingly, everyone must show the deacons respect. They represent Jesus Christ, just as the bishop has the role of the Father, and the presbyters are like God's council and an apostolic band. You cannot have a church without these. 2 I am sure that you agree with me in this.

In your bishop I received the very model of your love, and I have him with me. His very bearing is a great lesson, while his gentleness is most forceful. I imagine even the godless respect him.

3 While I could write about this matter more sharply, I spare you out of love. Since, too, I am a convict, I have not thought it my place to give you orders like an apostle.

4 God has granted me many an inspiration, but I keep my limits, lest boasting should be my undoing. For what I need most at this point is to be on my guard and not to heed flatterers. Those who tell me . . . they are my scourge. 2 To be sure, I am ever so eager to be a martyr, but I do not know if I deserve to be. Many people have no notion of my impetuous ambition. Yet it is all the more a struggle for me. What I need is gentleness by which the prince of this world is overthrown.

5 Am I incapable of writing to you of heavenly things? No, indeed; but I am afraid to harm you, seeing you are mere babes. You must forgive me, but the chances are you could not accept what I have to say and would choke yourselves. 2 Even in my own case, it is not because I am a prisoner and can grasp heavenly mysteries, the ranks of the angels, the array of principalities, things visible and invisible—it is not because of all that that I am a genuine disciple as yet. There is plenty missing, if we are not going to be forsaken by God.

6 I urge you, therefore—not I, but Jesus Christ's love—use only Christian food. Keep off foreign fare, by which I mean heresy. 2 For those

people mingle Jesus Christ with their teachings just to gain your confidence under false pretenses. It is as if they were giving a deadly poison mixed with honey and wine, with the result that the unsuspecting victim gladly accepts it and drinks down death with fatal pleasure.

7 Be on your guard, then, against such people. This you will do by not being puffed up and by keeping very close to [our] God, Jesus Christ, and the bishop and the apostles' precepts. 2 Inside the sanctuary a person is pure; outside he is impure. That means: whoever does anything without bishop, presbytery, and deacons does not have a clear conscience.

8 It is not because I have heard of any such thing in your case that I write thus. No, in my love for you I am warning you ahead, since I foresee the devil's wiles. Recapture, then, your gentleness, and by faith (that's the Lord's flesh) and by love (that's Jesus Christ's blood) make yourselves new creatures. 2 Let none of you hold anything against his neighbor. Do not give the heathen opportunities whereby God's people should be scoffed at through the stupidity of a few. For, "Woe to him by whose folly my name is scoffed at before any."[1]

9 Be deaf, then, to any talk that ignores Jesus Christ, of David's lineage, of Mary; who was really born, ate, and drank; was really persecuted under Pontius Pilate; was really crucified and died, in the sight of heaven and earth and the underworld. 2 He was really raised from the dead, for his Father raised him, just as his Father will raise us, who believe on him, through Christ Jesus, apart from whom we have no genuine life.

10 And if, as some atheists (I mean unbelievers) say, his suffering was a sham (it's really *they* who are a sham!), why, then, am I a prisoner? Why do I want to fight with wild beasts? In that case I shall die to no purpose. Yes, and I am maligning the Lord too!

11 Flee, then, these wicked offshoots which produce deadly fruit. If a person taste of it, he dies outright. They are none of the Father's planting. 2 For had they been, they would have shown themselves as branches of the cross, and borne immortal fruit. It is through the cross, by his

---

[1]Isa 52:5

suffering, that he summons you who are his members. A head cannot be born without limbs, since God stands for unity. It is his nature.

12 From Smyrna I send you my greetings in which the churches of God that are here with me join. They have altogether raised my spirits—yes, completely. 2 My very chains which I carry around for Jesus Christ's sake, in my desire to get to God, exhort you, "Stay united and pray for one another!"

It is right that each one of you and especially the presbyters should encourage the bishop, in honor of the Father, Jesus Christ, and the apostles.

3 Out of love I want you to heed me, so that my letter will not tell against you. Moreover, pray for me. By God's mercy I need your love if I am going to deserve the fate I long for, and not prove a "castaway."

13 The Smyrnaeans and Ephesians send their greetings with love. Remember the church of Syria in your prayers. I am not worthy to be a member of it: I am the least of their number. Farewell in Jesus Christ. 2 Submit to the bishop as to [God's] law, and to the presbytery too. All of you, love one another with an undivided heart. 3 My life is given for you, not only now but especially when I shall get to God. I am still in danger. But the Father is faithful: he will answer my prayer and yours because of Jesus Christ. Under his influence may you prove to be spotless.

The Letter of Ignatius to the Romans

Ignatius's letter to the Romans is unique among the seven writings that survive from his hand. It is not addressed to a church that had sent delegates to support him en route to his martyrdom nor to a church with which he had stayed. It is sent instead to the Christians of Rome, his destination. The letter has one overarching purpose: to persuade these Christians not to interfere with Ignatius's approaching martyrdom. Ignatius is bound for the amphitheater, where he will be thrown to the wild beasts; he pleads with the Roman Christians not to hinder the proceedings.

In Ignatius's own words: "I am voluntarily dying for God—if, that is, you do not interfere. I plead with you, do not do me an unseasonable kindness. Let me be fodder for wild beasts—that is how I can get to God. I am God's wheat and I am being ground by the teeth of wild beasts to make a pure loaf for Christ" (4:1–2). Some of Ignatius's rhetoric has struck modern readers as almost pathological: "What a thrill I shall have from the wild beasts that are ready for me! . . . I shall coax them on to eat me up at once and not to hold off. . . . And if they are reluctant, I shall force them to it. . . . Come fire, cross, battling with wild beasts, wrenching of bones, mangling of limbs, crushing of my whole body, cruel tortures of the devil—only let me get to Jesus Christ" (5:2–3).

In any event, the reason for Ignatius's passionate longing for death is reasonably clear. Ignatius claims to have no desire to live in this world (7:3); he wants to leave it so that he can "get to God" (4:2). Moreover, just as Christ suffered a violent death, so must he, if he wants to be "a real disciple of Jesus Christ" (4:2). Only then will he "imitate the Passion of my God" (6:3). In particular, Ignatius appears concerned that his nerves may fail him when he actually arrives in Rome. And so he beseeches the Christian community there in advance not to intervene on his behalf (1:2), "even if, when I arrive, I make a different plea" (7:2).

As with the letters to the Ephesians, the Magnesians, and the Trallians, this letter was written from Smyrna; unlike them, it is dated, August 24 (10:2). We are not told the year, but most scholars put it around 110 C.E.

Greetings in Jesus Christ, the Son of the Father, from Ignatius, the "God-inspired," to the church that is in charge of affairs in Roman quarters and that the Most High Father and Jesus Christ, his only Son, have magnificently embraced in mercy and love. You have been granted light both by the will of Him who willed all that is, and by virtue of your believing in Jesus Christ, our God, and of loving him. You are a credit to God: you deserve your renown and are to be congratulated. You deserve praise and success and are privileged to be without blemish. Yes, you rank first in love, being true to Christ's law and stamped with the Father's name. To you, then, sincerest greetings in Jesus Christ, our God, for you cleave to his every commandment—observing not only their letter but their spirit—being permanently filled with God's grace and purged of every stain alien to it.

1 Since God has answered my prayer to see you godly people, I have gone on to ask for more. I mean, it is as a prisoner for Christ Jesus that I hope to greet you, if indeed it be [God's] will that I should deserve to meet my end. 2 Things are off to a good start. May I have the good fortune to meet my fate without interference! What I fear is your generosity which may prove detrimental to me. For you can easily do what you want to, whereas it is hard for me to get to God unless you let me alone.

2 I do not want you to please people, but to please God, just as you are doing. For I shall never again have such a chance to get to God, nor can you, if you keep quiet, get credit for a finer deed. For if you quietly let me alone, people will see in me God's Word. But if you are enamored of my mere body, I shall, on the contrary, be a meaningless noise. 2 Grant me no more than to be a sacrifice for God while there is an altar at hand. Then you can form yourselves into a choir and sing praises to the Father in Jesus Christ that God gave the bishop of Syria the privilege of reaching the sun's setting when he summoned him from its rising. It is a grand thing for my life to set on the world, and for me to be on my way to God, so that I may rise in his presence.

3 You never grudged anyone. You taught others. So I want you to substantiate the lessons that you bid them heed. 2 Just pray that I may have strength of soul and body so that I may not only talk [about martyrdom], but really want it. It is not that I want merely to be called a Christian, but actually to *be* one. Yes, if I prove to be one, then I can have the name. Then, too, I shall be a convincing Christian only when the world sees me no more. 3 Nothing you can see has real value. Our God Jesus Christ, indeed, has revealed himself more clearly by returning to the Father. The greatness of Christianity lies in its being hated by the world, not in its being convincing to it.

4 I am corresponding with all the churches and bidding them all realize that I am voluntarily dying for God—if, that is, you do not interfere. I plead with you, do not do me an unseasonable kindness. Let me be fodder for wild beasts—that is how I can get to God. I am God's wheat and I am being ground by the teeth of wild beasts to make a pure loaf for Christ. 2 I would rather that you fawn on the beasts so that they may be my tomb and no scrap of my body be left. Thus, when I have fallen asleep, I shall be a burden to no one. Then I shall be a real disciple of Jesus Christ when the world sees my body no more. Pray Christ for me that by these means I may become God's sacrifice. 3 I do not give you orders like Peter and Paul. They were apostles: I am a convict. They were at liberty: I am still a slave. But if I suffer, I shall be emancipated by Jesus Christ; and united to him, I shall rise to freedom.

Even now as a prisoner, I am learning to forgo my own wishes.

5 All the way from Syria to Rome I am fighting with wild beasts, by land and sea, night and day, chained as I am to ten leopards (I mean to a detachment of soldiers), who only get worse the better you treat them. But by their injustices I am becoming a better disciple, though not for that reason am I acquitted. 2 What a thrill I shall have from the wild beasts that are ready for me! I hope they will make short work of me. I shall coax them on to eat me up at once and not to hold off, as sometimes happens, through fear. And if they are reluctant, I shall force them to it. 3 Forgive me— I know what is good for me. Now is the moment I am beginning to be a disciple. May nothing seen or unseen begrudge me making my way to Jesus Christ. Come fire, cross, battling with wild beasts, wrenching of bones, mangling of limbs, crushing of my whole body, cruel tortures of the devil— only let me get to Jesus Christ!

6 Not the wide bounds of earth nor the kingdoms of this world will avail me anything. I would rather die and get to Jesus Christ, than reign over the ends of the earth. That is whom I am looking for—the One who died for us. That is whom I want—the One who rose for us. 2 I am going through the pangs of being born. Sympathize with me, my brothers! Do not stand in the way of my coming to life—do not wish death on me. Do not give back to the world one who wants to be God's; do not trick him with material things. Let me get into the clear light and manhood will be mine. 3 Let me imitate the Passion of my God. If anyone has Him in him, let him appreciate what I am longing for, and sympathize with me, realizing what I am going through.

7 The prince of this world wants to kidnap me and pervert my godly purpose. None of you, then, who will be there, must abet him. Rather be on my side—that is, on God's. Do not talk Jesus Christ and set your heart on the world. Harbor no envy. 2 If, when I arrive, I make a different plea, pay no attention to me. Rather heed what I am now writing to you. For though alive, it is with a passion for death that I am writing to you. My Desire has been crucified and there burns in me no passion for material things. There is living water in me, which speaks and says inside me, "Come to the Father." 3 I take no delight in corruptible food or in the dainties of this life. What I want is God's bread, which is the flesh of Christ, who came from David's line; and for drink I want his blood: an immortal love feast indeed!

8 I do not want to live any more on a human plane. And so it shall be, if you want it to. Want it to, so that you will be wanted! Despite the brevity of my letter, trust my request. 2 Jesus Christ will clarify it for you and make you see I am really in earnest. He is the guileless mouth by which the Father has spoken truthfully. 3 Pray for me that I reach my goal. I have written prompted, not by human passion, but by God's will. If I suf-

fer, it will be because you favored me. If I am rejected, it will be because you hated me.

9 Remember the church of Syria in your prayers. In my place they have God for their shepherd. Jesus Christ alone will look after them—he, and your love. 2 I blush to be reckoned among them, for I do not deserve it, being the least of them and an afterthought. Yet by his mercy I shall be something, if, that is, I get to God.

3 With my heart I greet you; and the churches which have welcomed me, not as a chance passerby, but in the name of Jesus Christ, send their love. Indeed, even those that did not naturally lie on my route went ahead to prepare my welcome in the different towns.

10 I am sending this letter to you from Smyrna by those praiseworthy Ephesians. With me, along with many others is Crocus—a person very dear to me. 2 I trust you have had word about those who went ahead of me from Syria to Rome for God's glory. Tell them I am nearly there. They are all a credit to God and to you; so you should give them every assistance. 3 I am writing this to you on the twenty-fourth of August. Farewell, and hold out to the end with the patience of Jesus Christ.

The Letter of Ignatius to the Philadelphians

After Ignatius left Smyrna, he passed through the Asia Minor city of Philadelphia, spending time with the church there before journeying on to Troas, still en route to his martyrdom in Rome (6:3–7:1). It was from Troas that he wrote a letter back to the Philadelphians through his traveling companion, Burrhus, a Christian from Ephesus (11:2).

Most of the themes sounded in Ignatius's earlier letters are present here as well. He speaks highly of the bishop of Philadelphia (whom he does not name), being particularly impressed with his quiet strength (1:1) and upright life (1:2). He writes to the church that it needs to be united behind the bishop. It appears that while among them, Ignatius had seen divisions; at the time, he claims, he tried to resolve the problems, doing "all I could as a man utterly devoted to unity" (8:1). The divisions, he believed, had a simple solution: "When I was with you I cried out, raising my voice—it was God's voice—'Pay heed to the bishop, the presbytery, and the deacons.'" He urged the community to "do nothing apart from the bishop; keep your bodies as if they were God's temple; value unity; flee schism" (7:2).

The divisions were evidently rooted in different theological and practical perspectives advanced by some members of the congregation. Among the Philadelphians were Gentile believers who had come to think that Christians needed to follow the practices of Judaism. This was a position with which Ignatius showed little sympathy: "if anyone preaches Judaism to you, pay no attention to him. For it is better to hear about Christianity from one of the circumcision than Judaism from a Gentile" (6:1). While his opponents claimed not to accept anything as true that was not supported in their "original documents," the Hebrew Bible, Ignatius claimed that "it is Jesus Christ who is the original documents" (8:2). For him, the Old Testament patriarchs and prophets were looking forward to Christ and themselves had salvation only through Christ (9:1–2).

The letter concludes with an expression of gratitude that his own church, in Antioch of Syria, had begun to enjoy peace, as the divisions earlier evidenced there had been resolved. Ignatius hopes that the Philadelphian church can send an ambassador to convey its congratulations.

Greetings in the blood of Jesus Christ from Ignatius, the "God-inspired," to the church of God the Father and the Lord Jesus Christ, which is at Philadelphia in Asia—an object of the divine mercy and firmly knit in godly unity. Yours is a deep, abiding joy in the Passion of our Lord; and by his overflowing mercy you are thoroughly convinced of his resurrection. You are the very personification of eternal and perpetual joy. This is especially true if you are at one with the bishop, and with the presbyters and deacons, who are on his side and who have been appointed by the will of Jesus Christ. By his Holy Spirit and in accordance with his own will he validated their appointment.

1 I well realize that this bishop of yours does not owe his ministry to his own efforts or to people. Nor is it to flatter his vanity that he holds this office which serves the common good. Rather does he owe it to the love of God the Father and the Lord Jesus Christ. I have been struck by his charming manner. 2 By being silent he can do more than those who chatter. For he is in tune with the commandments as a harp is with its strings. For this reason I bless his godly mind, recognizing its virtue and perfection, and the way he lives in altogether godly composure, free from fitfulness and anger.

2 Since you are children of the light of truth, flee from schism and false doctrine. Where the Shepherd is, there follow like sheep. 2 For there are many specious wolves who, by means of wicked pleasures, capture those who run God's race. In the face of your unity, however, they will not have a chance.

3 Keep away from bad pasturage. Jesus Christ does not cultivate it since the Father did not plant it. Not that I found schism among you—rather had you been sifted. 2 As many as are God's and Jesus Christ's, they are on the bishop's side; and as many as respect and enter the unity of the church, they shall be God's, and thus they shall live in Jesus Christ's way. 3 Make no mistake, my brothers, if anyone joins a schismatic he will not inherit God's Kingdom. If anyone walks in the way of heresy, he is out of sympathy with the Passion.

4 Be careful, then, to observe a single Eucharist. For there is one flesh of our Lord, Je-

sus Christ, and one cup of his blood that makes us one, and one altar, just as there is one bishop along with the presbytery and the deacons, my fellow slaves. In that way whatever you do is in line with God's will.

5 My brothers, in my abounding love for you I am overjoyed to put you on your guard—though it is not I, but Jesus Christ. Being a prisoner for his cause makes me the more fearful that I am still far from being perfect. Yet your prayers to God will make me perfect so that I may gain that fate which I have mercifully been allotted, by taking refuge in the "Gospel," as in Jesus' flesh, and in the "Apostles," as in the presbytery of the Church. 2 And the "Prophets," let us love them too, because they anticipated the gospel in their preaching and hoped for and awaited him, and were saved by believing on him. Thus they were in Jesus Christ's unity. Saints they were, and we should love and admire them, seeing that Jesus Christ vouched for them and they form a real part of the gospel of our common hope.

6 Now, if anyone preaches Judaism to you, pay no attention to him. For it is better to hear about Christianity from one of the circumcision than Judaism from a Gentile. If both, moreover, fail to talk about Jesus Christ, they are to me tombstones and graves of the dead, on which only human names are inscribed. 2 Flee, then, the wicked tricks and snares of the prince of this world, lest his suggestions wear you down, and you waver in your love. Rather, meet together, all of you, with a single heart. 3 I thank my God that in my relations with you I have nothing to be ashamed of. No one can brag secretly or openly that I was the slightest burden to anyone. I trust, too, that none of those I talked to will need to take what I say as a criticism of them.

7 Some there may be who wanted in a human way to mislead me, but the Spirit is not misled, seeing it comes from God. For it knows whence it comes and whither it goes, and exposes what is secret. When I was with you I cried out, raising my voice—it was God's voice—"Pay heed to the bishop, the presbytery, and the deacons." 2 Some, it is true, suspected that I spoke thus because I had been told in advance that some of you were schismatics. But I swear by him for whose

cause I am a prisoner, that from no human channels did I learn this. It was the Spirit that kept on preaching in these words: "Do nothing apart from the bishop; keep your bodies as if they were God's temple; value unity; flee schism; imitate Jesus Christ as he imitated his Father."

8 I, then, was doing all I could, as a man utterly devoted to unity. Where there is schism and bad feeling, God has no place. The Lord forgives all who repent—if, that is, their repentance brings them into God's unity and to the bishop's council. I put my confidence in the grace of Jesus Christ. He will release you from all your chains.

2 I urge you, do not do things in cliques, but act as Christ's disciples. When I heard some people saying, "If I don't find it in the original documents, I don't believe it in the gospel," I answered them, "But it *is* written there." They retorted, "That's just the question." To my mind it is Jesus Christ who is the original documents. The inviolable archives are his cross and death and his resurrection and the faith that came by him. It is by these things and through your prayers that I want to be justified.

9 Priests are a fine thing, but better still is the High Priest who was entrusted with the Holy of Holies. He alone was entrusted with God's secrets. He is the door to the Father. Through it there enter Abraham, Isaac, and Jacob, the prophets and apostles and the Church. All these find their place in God's unity. 2 But there is something special about the gospel—I mean the coming of the Saviour, our Lord Jesus Christ, his Passion and resurrection. The beloved prophets announced his coming; but the gospel is the crowning achievement forever. All these things, taken together, have their value, provided you hold the faith in love.

10 Thanks to your prayers and to the love that you have for me in Christ Jesus, news has reached me that the church at Antioch in Syria is at peace. Consequently, it would be a nice thing for you, as a church of God, to elect a deacon to go there on a mission, as God's representative, and at a formal service to congratulate them and glorify the Name. 2 He who is privileged to perform such a ministry will enjoy the blessing of Jesus Christ, and you too will win glory. If you really want to do this for God's honor, it is not impossible, just as some of the churches in the vicinity have already sent bishops; others presbyters and deacons.

11 Now about Philo, the deacon from Cilicia. He is well spoken of and right now he is helping me in God's cause, along with Rheus Agathopus—a choice person—who followed me from Syria and so has said good-by to this present life. They speak well of you, and I thank God on your account that you welcomed them, as the Lord does you. I hope that those who slighted them will be redeemed by Jesus Christ's grace. 2 The brothers in Troas send their love and greetings. It is from there that I am sending this letter to you by Burrhus. The Ephesians and Smyrnaeans have done me the honor of sending him to be with me. They in turn will be honored by Jesus Christ, on whom they have set their hope with body, soul, spirit, faith, love, and a single mind. Farewell in Christ Jesus, our common Hope.

The Letter of Ignatius to the Smyrneans

Ignatius had evidently gotten to know the church at Smyrna rather well during his stay there. After leaving town, he traveled to Troas, where he wrote a letter (12:1) greeting a number of the Smyrnean Christians (13:1–2) and urging them to avoid heresy and to remain united behind their bishop.

Ignatius is particularly concerned over those who claimed that Jesus' passion was only a sham, that is, that he was not an actual flesh-and-blood human being who really suffered (2:1). Ignatius denies that such persons are "believers" (2:1) and warns his readers not even to meet and talk with them (4:1). In opposition to their views, Ignatius insists that Jesus was "actually born" (1:1) and was "actually crucified . . . in the flesh" (1:2), he "genuinely suffered" and "genuinely raised himself" (2:1). Even after his resurrection he was "in the flesh" (3:1), as evidenced by the fact that his disciples touched him and saw him eat and drink (3:2–3).

Ignatius is deeply troubled by this christological issue, in part because it relates to his own situation. He himself is on the road to martyrdom; if Christ did not actually suffer in the flesh, there would be little reason for Ignatius himself to do so: "If what our Lord did is a sham, so is my being in chains. Why, then, have I given myself up completely to death, fire, sword, and wild beasts?" (4:2).

The community can best withstand these pernicious teachers, in Ignatius's view, by uniting behind their bishop, the representative of God among the congregation. Whoever "pays the bishop honor has been honored by God," whereas anyone "who acts without the bishop's knowledge is in the devil's service" (9:1). No one, therefore, should be allowed to conduct baptisms or eucharistic meals without the bishop present (8:1).

Near the end of the letter Ignatius enjoins the church to send a delegate to his own church in Antioch, with a letter "extolling the calm which God has granted them" (11:3); he concludes by sending final greetings to members of the congregation he had come to know during his time among them (13:1–2).

Heartiest greetings in all sincerity and in God's Word from Ignatius, the "God-inspired," to the church of God the Father and the beloved Jesus Christ, which is at Smyrna in Asia. By God's mercy you have received every gift; you abound in faith and love, and are lacking in no gift. You are a wonderful credit to God and real saints.

1 I extol Jesus Christ, the God who has granted you such wisdom. For I detected that you were fitted out with an unshakable faith, being

"The Letter of Ignatius to the Smyrneans," from *Early Christian Fathers,* edited by Cyril D. Richardson (Library of Christian Classics). © 1953 by Westminster Press. Reprinted by permission of Westminster John Knox Press.

nailed, as it were, body and soul to the cross of the Lord Jesus Christ, and being rooted in love by the blood of Christ. Regarding our Lord, you are absolutely convinced that on the human side he was actually sprung from David's line, Son of God according to God's will and power, actually born of a virgin, baptized by John, that all righteousness might be fulfilled by him, 2 and actually crucified for us in the flesh, under Pontius Pilate and Herod the Tetrarch. (We are part of his fruit which grew out of his most blessed Passion.) And thus, by his resurrection, he raised a standard to rally his saints and faithful forever—whether Jews or Gentiles—in one body of his Church.

2 For it was for our sakes that he suffered all this, to save us. And he genuinely suffered, as even he genuinely raised himself. It is not as some unbelievers say, that his Passion was a sham. It's they who are a sham! Yes, and their fate will fit their fancies—they will be ghosts and apparitions.

3 For myself, I am convinced and believe that even after the resurrection he was in the flesh. 2 Indeed, when he came to Peter and his friends, he said to them, Take hold of me, touch me and see that I am not a bodiless ghost. And they at once touched him and were convinced, clutching his body and his very breath. For this reason they despised death itself, and proved its victors. Moreover, after the resurrection he ate and drank with them as a real human being, although in spirit he was united with the Father.

4 I urge these things on you, my friends, although I am well aware that you agree with me. But I warn you in advance against wild beasts in human shapes. You must not only refuse to receive them, but if possible, you must avoid meeting them. Just pray for them that they may somehow repent, hard as that is. Yet Jesus Christ, our genuine life, has the power to bring it about. 2 If what our Lord did is a sham, so is my being in chains. Why, then, have I given myself up completely to death, fire, sword, and wild beasts? For the simple reason that near the sword means near God. To be with wild beasts means to be with God. But it must all be in the name of Jesus Christ. To share in his Passion I go through everything, for he who became the perfect man gives me the strength.

5 Yet in their ignorance some deny him—or rather have been denied by him, since they advocate death rather than the truth. The prophets and the law of Moses have failed to convince them—nay, to this very day the gospel and the sufferings of each one of us have also failed, for they class our sufferings with Christ's. 2 What good does anyone do me by praising me and then reviling my Lord by refusing to acknowledge that he carried around live flesh? He who denies this has completely disavowed him and carries a corpse around. 3 The names of these people, seeing they are unbelievers, I am not going to write down. No, far be it from me even to recall them until they repent and acknowledge the Passion, which means our resurrection.

6 Let no one be misled: heavenly beings, the splendor of angels, and principalities, visible and invisible, if they fail to believe in Christ's blood, they too are doomed. Let him accept it who can. Let no one's position swell his head, for faith and love are everything—there is nothing preferable to them.

2 Pay close attention to those who have wrong notions about the grace of Jesus Christ, which has come to us, and note how at variance they are with God's mind. They care nothing about love: they have no concern for widows or orphans, for the oppressed, for those in prison or released, for the hungry or the thirsty.

7 They hold aloof from the Eucharist and from services of prayer, because they refuse to admit that the Eucharist is the flesh of our Saviour Jesus Christ, which suffered for our sins and which, in his goodness, the Father raised [from the dead]. Consequently those who wrangle and dispute God's gift face death. They would have done better to love and so share in the resurrection. 2 The right thing to do, then, is to avoid such people and to talk about them neither in private nor in public. Rather pay attention to the prophets and above all to the gospel. There we get a clear picture of the Passion and see that the resurrection has really happened.

8 Flee from schism as the source of mischief. You should all follow the bishop as Jesus Christ did the Father. Follow, too, the presbytery as you would the apostles; and respect the deacons as you would God's law. Nobody must do anything that has to do with the Church without the bishop's approval. You should regard that Eucharist as valid which is celebrated either by the bishop or by someone he authorizes. 2 Where the bishop is present, there let the congregation gather, just as where Jesus Christ is, there is the Catholic Church. Without the bishop's supervision, no baptisms or love feasts are permitted. On the other hand, whatever he approves pleases God as well. In that way everything you do will be on the safe side and valid.

9 It is well for us to come to our senses at last, while we still have a chance to repent and turn to God. It is a fine thing to acknowledge God and the bishop. He who pays the bishop honor has been honored by God. But he who acts without the bishop's knowledge is in the devil's service.

2 By God's grace may you have an abundance of everything! You deserve it. You have brought me no end of comfort; may Jesus Christ do the same for you! Whether I was absent or present, you gave me your love. May God requite you! If for his sake you endure everything, you will get to him.

10 It was good of you to welcome Philo and Rheus Agathopus as deacons of the Christ God. They accompanied me in God's cause, and they thank the Lord on your behalf that you provided them every comfort. I can assure you you will lose nothing by it. 2 Prisoner as I am, I am giving my life for you—not that it's worth much! You did not scorn my chains and were not ashamed of them. Neither will Jesus Christ be ashamed of you. You can trust him implicitly!

11 Your prayers have reached out as far as the church at Antioch in Syria. From there I have come, chained with these magnificent chains, and I send you all greetings. I do not, of course, deserve to be a member of that church, seeing I am the least among them. Yet it was [God's] will to give me the privilege—not, indeed, for anything I had done of my own accord, but by his grace. Oh, I want that grace to be given me in full measure,

that by your prayers I may get to God! 2 Well, then, so that your own conduct may be perfect on earth and in heaven, it is right that your church should honor God by sending a delegate in his name to go to Syria and to congratulate them on being at peace, on recovering their original numbers, and on having their own corporate life restored to them. 3 To my mind that is what God would want you to do: to send one of your number with a letter, and thus join with them in extolling the calm which God has granted them, and the fact that they have already reached a haven, thanks to your prayers. Seeing you are perfect, your intentions must be perfect as well. Indeed, if you want to do what is right God stands ready to give you his help.

12 The brothers in Troas send their love to you. From there I am sending this letter to you by Burrhus. You joined with your Ephesian brothers in sending him to be with me, and he has altogether raised my spirits. I wish everyone would be like him, since he is a model of what God's ministry should be. God's grace will repay him for all he has done for me. 2 Greetings to your bishop (he is such a credit to God!), and to your splendid presbytery and to my fellow slaves the deacons, and to you all, every one of you, in Jesus Christ's name, in his flesh and blood, in his Passion and resurrection, both bodily and spiritual, and in unity—both God's and yours. Grace be yours, and mercy, peace, and endurance, forever.

13 Greetings to the families of my brothers, along with their wives and children, and to the virgins enrolled with the widows. I bid you farewell in the Father's power. Philo, who is with me, sends you greetings. 2 Greetings to Tavia's family. I want her to be firmly and thoroughly grounded in faith and love. Greetings to Alce, who means a great deal to me, and to the inimitable Daphnus and to Eutecnus and to each one of you. Farewell in God's grace.

The Letter of Ignatius to Polycarp

All of Ignatius's other surviving letters are addressed to Christian communities; the letter to Polycarp is the only sent to an individual. Polycarp was the bishop of Smyrna, one of the churches that Ignatius had visited en route to Rome and to which he addressed one of his other letters. The letter to Polycarp consists principally of advice to the bishop concerning how to shepherd his flock; it is particularly noteworthy for its rich imagery, as Ignatius repeatedly likens the labor of the bishop to the discipline of an athlete and to the work of a sailor. He urges his friend to be diligent, to bring unruly members of his congregation under subjection, to overcome false teachers, and to promote the social well-being of his community (chaps. 1–5).

It is interesting to note that, after the first five chapters, the letter suddenly shifts to address the community at large; it was evidently meant to be read, therefore, to the entire church. Members of the community are urged to heed the bishop, to be united with one another, and to continue the good fight of the faith (chap. 6). The letter includes another request for the church to send a delegate to Ignatius's home church in Antioch, which had just overcome its own internal struggles.

In his conclusion, Ignatius indicates that he is to sail immediately for Neapolis (chap. 8). He asks Polycarp to write churches on his route to inform them of his coming. His final greetings are the last words we have from his hand.

Heartiest greetings from Ignatius, the "God-inspired," to Polycarp, who is bishop of the church at Smyrna—or rather who has God the Father and the Lord Jesus Christ for *his* bishop.

1 While I was impressed with your godly mind, which is fixed, as it were, on an immovable rock, I am more than grateful that I was granted the sight of your holy face. 2 God grant I may never forget it! By the grace which you have put on, I urge you to press forward in your race and to urge everybody to be saved. Vindicate your position by giving your whole attention to its material and spiritual sides. Make unity your concern—there is nothing better than that. Lend everybody a hand, as the Lord does you. Out of love be patient with everyone, as indeed you are. 3 Devote yourself to continual prayer. Ask for increasing insight. Be ever on the watch by keeping your spirit alert. Take a personal interest in those you talk to, just as God does. Bear the diseases of everyone, like an athlete in perfect form. The greater the toil, the greater the gain.

2 It is no credit to you if you are fond of good pupils. Rather by your gentleness subdue those who are annoying. Not every wound is healed by the same plaster. Relieve spasms of pain with poultices. 2 In all circumstances be "wise as a serpent," and perpetually "harmless as a dove."[1] The reason you have a body as well as a soul is that you may win the favor of the visible world. But ask that you may have revelations of what is unseen. In that way you will lack nothing and have an abundance of every gift.

3 Just as pilots demand winds and a storm-tossed sailor a harbor, so times like these demand a person like you. With your help we will get to God. As God's athlete, be sober. The prize, as you very well know, is immortality and eternal life. Bound as I am with chains that you kissed, I give my whole self for you—cheap sacrifice though it is!

3 You must not be panic-stricken by those who have an air of credibility but who teach heresy. Stand your ground like an anvil under the hammer. A great athlete must suffer blows to conquer. And especially for God's sake must we put up with everything, so that he will put up with us. 2 Show more enthusiasm than you do. Mark the times. Be on the alert for him who is above time, the Timeless, the Unseen, the One who became visible for our sakes, who was beyond touch and passion, yet who for our sakes became subject to suffering, and endured everything for us.

4 Widows must not be neglected. After the Lord you must be their protector. Do not let anything be done without your consent; and do not do anything without God's, as indeed you do not. Stand firm. Hold services more often. 2 Seek out everybody by name. 3 Do not treat slaves, men and women, contemptuously. Neither must they grow insolent. But for God's glory they must give more devoted service, so that they may obtain from God a better freedom. Moreover, they must not be overanxious to gain their freedom at the community's expense, lest they prove to be slaves of selfish passion. Flee from such wicked practices—nay, rather, preach against them.

5 Tell my sisters to love the Lord and to be altogether contented with their husbands. Similarly urge my brothers in the name of Jesus Christ to love their wives as the Lord loves the

Church. 2 If anyone can live in chastity for the honor of the Lord's flesh, let him do so without ever boasting. If he boasts of it, he is lost; and if he is more highly honored than the bishop, his chastity is as good as forfeited. It is right for men and women who marry to be united with the bishop's approval. In that way their marriage will follow God's will and not the promptings of lust. Let everything be done so as to advance God's honor.

6 Pay attention to the bishop so that God will pay attention to you. I give my life as a sacrifice (poor as it is) for those who are obedient to the bishop, the presbyters, and the deacons. Along with them may I get my share of God's reward! Share your hard training together—wrestle together, run together, suffer together, go to bed together, get up together, as God's stewards, assessors, and assistants. 2 Give satisfaction to him in whose ranks you serve and from whom you get your pay. Let none of you prove a deserter. Let your baptism be your arms; your faith, your helmet; your love, your spear; your endurance, your armor. Let your deeds be your deposits, so that you will eventually get back considerable savings. Be patient, then, and gentle with each other, as God is with you. May I always be happy about you!

7 News has reached me that, thanks to your prayers, the church at Antioch in Syria is now at peace. At this I have taken new courage and, relying on God, I have set my mind at rest—assuming, that is, I may get to God through suffering, and at the resurrection prove to be your disciple. 2 So, my dear Polycarp (and how richly God has blessed you!), you ought to call a most religious council and appoint somebody whom you regard as especially dear and diligent, and who can act as God's messenger. You should give him the privilege of going to Syria and of advancing God's glory by extolling your untiring generosity. 3 A Christian does not control his own life, but gives his whole time to God. This is God's work, and when you have completed it, it will be yours as well. For God's grace gives me confidence that you are ready to act generously when it comes to his business. It is because I am well aware of your earnest sincerity that I limit my appeal to so few words.

---

[1]Matt 10:16

8 I have been unable to write to all the churches because I am sailing at once (so God has willed it) from Troas to Neapolis. I want you, therefore, as one who has the mind of God, to write to the churches ahead and to bid them to do the same. Those who can should send representatives, while the others should send letters by your own delegates. In that way you will win renown, such as you deserve, by an act that will be remembered forever.

2 Greetings to every one of you personally, and to the widow of Epitropus with her children and her whole family. Greetings to my dear Attalus. Greetings to the one who is to be chosen to go to Syria. Grace will ever be with him and with Polycarp who sends him. 3 I bid you farewell as always in our God, Jesus Christ. May you abide in him and so share in the divine unity and be under God's care. Greetings to Alce, who means a great deal to me. Farewell in the Lord.

The Letter of Polycarp to the Philippians

Sometime after Ignatius visited and wrote to Polycarp, the bishop of Smyrna in Asia Minor, Polycarp himself addressed a letter to the Christian community of Philippi. Scholars have debated the date of this letter: in one passage, Polycarp intimates that Ignatius had just left town, putting its date around 110 C.E. (13:1, where Polycarp indicates that he plans to visit the church in Antioch at Ignatius's request). Another passage implies that Ignatius had already experienced martyrdom (9:1). This has sometimes been taken to suggest that the letter was penned many years later, possibly as late as 135 C.E. Other scholars, though, have maintained that our present book represents two different letters written at different times, later cut and pasted together to form one larger letter for circulation.

Whether representing one writing or two, the occasion of the bulk of the letter as we have it is relatively clear. Polycarp is writing the Philippian church because they have asked his advice on a problem that had arisen in their community: man named Valens, a leader of the church, along with his wife, had been caught embezzling church funds, and the community was not certain how to handle the situation (chap. 11). Polycarp uses the opportunity to denounce those who crave worldly goods and to issue other moral exhortations to his readers; in terms of the specific situation, he advises the Philippians to allow the offending couple to repent and return to the church's good graces.

Polycarp does not recommend a similarly kind treatment to the false teachers that he has learned were plaguing the Philippian church with their denials of the future resurrection of believers and of the fleshly existence of Christ (7:1). Polycarp denounces these teachings and urges the congregation to give such persons no heed.

Much of the rest of the letter consists of general ethical exhortations for the Philippians to love one another, pray for one another, give alms insofar as possible, and live moral, upright lives. Many of these exhortations are drawn from other Christian writings, including the Synoptic Gospels and the letters of Paul. Indeed, in places the letter reads almost like a pastiche of earlier Christian traditions known to the author and, presumably, to many of his Philippian readers.

Polycarp and the presbyters with him, to the church of God that sojourns at Philippi; may mercy and peace be multiplied to you from God Almighty and Jesus Christ, our Saviour.

1 I rejoice with you greatly in our Lord Jesus Christ, in that you have welcomed the models of true Love, and have helped on their way, as opportunity was given you, those men who are

bound in fetters which become the saints, which are indeed the diadems of the true elect of God and of our Lord. 2 And I also rejoice because the firm root of your faith, famous from the earliest times, still abides and bears fruit for our Lord Jesus Christ, who endured for our sins even to face death, "whom God raised up, having loosed the pangs of Hades."[1] 3 In him, "though you have not seen him, you believe with inexpressible and exalted joy"[2]—joy that many have longed to experience—knowing that "you are saved by grace, not because of works,"[3] namely, by the will of God through Jesus Christ.

2 Therefore, girding your loins, serve God in fear and in truth, forsaking empty talkativeness and the erroneous teaching of the crowd, believing on him who raised our Lord Jesus Christ from the dead and gave him glory and a throne on his right hand; to whom he subjected all things, whether in heaven or on earth, whom everything that breathes serves, who will come as judge of the living and the dead, whose blood God will require from those who disobey him. 2 For he who raised him from the dead will raise us also, if we do his will and follow his commandments, and love what he loved, refraining from all wrongdoing, avarice, love of money, slander, and false witness; not returning evil for evil or abuse for abuse, or blow for blow, or curse for curse; but rather remembering what the Lord said when he taught: 3 "Judge not, that you be not judged; forgive, and you will be forgiven; be merciful, that you may be shown mercy; the measure you give will be the measure you get"[4]; and "blessed are the poor and those persecuted for righteousness' sake, for theirs is the Kingdom of God."[5]

3 I write these things about righteousness, brethren, not at my own instance, but because you first invited me to do so. 2 Certainly, neither I nor anyone like me can follow the wisdom of the blessed and glorious Paul, who, when he was present among you face to face with the generation of his time, taught you accurately and firmly the word of truth. Also when absent he wrote you letters that will enable you, if you study them carefully, to grow in the faith delivered to you—which is a mother of us all, accompanied by hope, and led by love to God and Christ and our neighbor. 3 For if anyone is occupied in these, he

has fulfilled the commandment of righteousness; for he who possesses love is far from all sin.

4 But the love of money is the beginning of all evils. Knowing, therefore, that we brought nothing into the world, and we cannot take anything out, let us arm ourselves with the weapons of righteousness, and let us first of all teach ourselves to live by the commandment of the Lord.

2 Then you must teach your wives in the faith delivered to them and in love and purity—to cherish their own husbands in all fidelity, and to love all others equally in all chastity, and to educate their children in the fear of God. 3 And the widows should be discreet in their faith pledged to the Lord, praying unceasingly on behalf of all, refraining from all slander, gossip, false witness, love of money—in fact, from evil of any kind—knowing that they are God's altar, that everything is examined for blemishes, and nothing escapes him whether of thoughts or sentiments, or any of the secrets of the heart.

5 Knowing, then, that "God is not mocked,"[6] we ought to live worthily of his commandment and glory.

2 Likewise the deacons should be blameless before his righteousness, as servants of God and Christ and not of people; not slanderers, or double-tongued, not lovers of money, temperate in all matters, compassionate, careful, living according to the truth of the Lord, who became a servant of all; to whom, if we are pleasing in the present age, we shall also obtain the age to come, inasmuch as he promised to raise us from the dead. And if we bear our citizenship worthy of him, we shall also reign with him—provided, of course, that we have faith.

3 Similarly also the younger ones must be blameless in all things, especially taking thought of purity and bridling themselves from all evil. It is a fine thing to cut oneself off from the lusts that are in the world, for every passion of the flesh wages war against the Spirit, and neither fornicators nor the effeminate nor homosexuals will inherit the Kingdom of God, nor those who do perverse things. Wherefore it is necessary to refrain from all these things, and be obedient to the presbyters and

---

[1]Acts 2:24 [2]1 Pet 1:8 [3]Eph 2:5, 8–9 [4]Matt 7:1–2; Luke 6:36–38 [5]Luke 6:20; Matt 5:3, 10 [6]Gal 6:7

deacons as unto God and Christ. And the young women must live with blameless and pure conscience.

6 Also the presbyters must be compassionate, merciful to all, turning back those who have gone astray, looking after the sick, not neglecting widow or orphan or one that is poor; but always taking thought for what is honorable in the sight of God and of others, refraining from all anger, partiality, unjust judgment, keeping far from all love of money, not hastily believing evil of anyone, nor being severe in judgment, knowing that we all owe the debt of sin. 2 If, then, we pray the Lord to forgive us, we ourselves ought also to forgive, for we are before the eyes of the Lord and God, and "everyone shall stand before the judgment seat of Christ and each of us shall give an account of himself."[7] 3 So then let us "serve him with fear and all reverence,"[8] as he himself has commanded, and also the apostles who preached the gospel to us and the prophets who foretold the coming of the Lord.

7 Let us be zealous for that which is good, refraining from occasions of scandal and from false brethren, and those who bear in hypocrisy the name of the Lord, who deceive empty-headed people. For "whosoever does not confess that Jesus Christ has come in the flesh is antichrist"[9]; and whosoever does not confess the testimony of the cross is of the devil; and whosoever perverts the sayings of the Lord to suit his own lusts and says there is neither resurrection nor judgment—such a one is the first-born of Satan. 2 Let us, therefore, forsake the vanity of the crowd and their false teachings and turn back to the word delivered to us from the beginning, watching unto prayer and continuing steadfast in fasting, beseeching fervently the all-seeing God to lead us not into temptation,[10] even as the Lord said, "The spirit indeed is willing, but the flesh is weak."[11]

8 Let us, then, hold steadfastly and unceasingly to our Hope and to the Pledge of our righteousness, that is, Christ Jesus, "who bore our sins in his own body on the tree, who committed no sin, neither was guile found on his lips"[12]; but for our sakes he endured everything that we might live in him. 2 Therefore let us be imitators of his patient endurance, and if we suffer for the sake of his name, let us glorify him. For he set us this example in his own person, and this is what we believed.

9 Now I exhort all of you to be obedient to the word of righteousness and to exercise all patient endurance, such as you have seen with your very eyes, not only in the blessed Ignatius and Zosimus and Rufus, but also in others who were of your membership, and in Paul himself and the rest of the apostles; being persuaded that all these did not run in vain, but in faith and righteousness, and that they are now in their deserved place with the Lord, in whose suffering they also shared. 2 For they loved not this present world, but him who died on our behalf and was raised by God for our sakes.

10 Stand firm, therefore, in these things and follow the example of the Lord, steadfast and immovable in the faith, loving the brotherhood, cherishing one another, fellow companions in the truth, in the gentleness of the Lord preferring one another and despising no one. 2 Whenever you are able to do a kindness, do not put it off, because almsgiving frees from death. All of you submit yourselves to one another, having your manner of life above reproach from the heathen, so that you may receive praise for your good works and the Lord may not be blasphemed on your account. 3 Woe to them, however, through whom the name of the Lord is blasphemed. Therefore, all of you teach the sobriety in which you are yourselves living.

11 I have been exceedingly grieved on account of Valens, who was sometime a presbyter among you, because he so forgot the office that was given him. I warn you, therefore, to refrain from the love of money and be pure and truthful. 2 Shun evil of every kind. For how shall he who cannot govern himself in these things teach another? If anyone does not refrain from the love of money he will be defiled by idolatry and so be judged as if he were one of the heathen, who are ignorant of the judgment of the Lord. Or "do we not know that the saints will judge the world,"[13] as Paul teaches? However, I have neither observed nor heard of any such thing among you, with whom blessed Paul labored and who

---

[7]Rom 14:10, 12   [8]Ps 2:11   [9]1 Jn 4:2–3; 2 Jn 7   [10]Matt 6:13
[11]Matt 26:41; Mark 14:38   [12]1 Pet 2:24, 22   [13]1 Cor 6:2

were his epistles in the beginning. Of you he was wont to boast in all the churches which at that time alone knew God; for we did not as yet know him. 4 I am, therefore, very grieved indeed for that man and his wife. May the Lord grant them true repentance. But you, too, must be moderate in this matter; and do not consider such persons as enemies, but reclaim them as suffering and straying members, in order that you may save the whole body of you. For in doing this you will edify yourselves.

12 I am confident, indeed, that you are well versed in the sacred Scriptures and that nothing escapes you—something not granted to me—only, as it is said in these Scriptures, "be angry but sin not" and "let not the sun go down on your anger."[14] Blessed is he who remembers this. I believe it is so with you. 2 May God and the Father of our Lord Jesus Christ, and the eternal High Priest himself, the Son of God, Jesus Christ, build you up in faith and truth and in all gentleness, without anger and in patient endurance, in long-suffering, forbearance, and purity; and give you a portion and share among his saints, and to us also along with you, and to all under heaven who are destined to believe in our Lord Jesus Christ and in his Father who raised him from the dead. 3 Pray for all the saints. Pray also for emperors and magistrates and rulers, and for those who persecute and hate you, and for the enemies of the cross, that your fruit may be manifest in all, so that you may be perfected in him.

13 Both you and Ignatius have written me that if anyone is leaving for Syria he should take your letter along too. I shall attend to this if I have a favorable opportunity—either myself or one whom I shall send to represent you as well as me. 2 We are sending you the letters of Ignatius, those he addressed to us and any others we had by us, just as you requested. They are herewith appended to this letter. From them you can derive great benefit, for they are concerned with faith and patient endurance and all the edification pertaining to the Lord. Of Ignatius himself and those who are with him, let us have any reliable information that you know.

14 I am sending you this letter by Crescens, whom I recently commended to you and now commend him again. He has lived with us blamelessly, and I believe he will do so among you. I also commend to you his sister, when she arrives among you. Farewell in the Lord Jesus Christ in grace, both you and all who are yours. Amen.

---

[14]Ps 4:4; Eph 4:26

The Letter of Barnabas

The book of Barnabas has traditionally been called an epistle, even though its opening contains only a greeting, with neither its author nor its recipients named. The second- and third-century Christians who refer to the book attribute it to Barnabas, the companion of the apostle Paul. But this may have involved little more than guesswork on the part of Christians who were eager to have the book read and accepted as "apostolic." It was considered part of the New Testament Scriptures in some Christian communities down to the fourth century.

The book in fact appears to have been written long after Barnabas himself had died: it mentions, for example, the destruction of the Temple (70 C.E.) and refers to the possibility of its soon being rebuilt (16:3–4). This possibility was very much alive in the early decades of the second century, but evaporated when the Emperor Hadrian (132–134 C.E.) had a Roman shrine constructed over the Temple's ruins. Most scholars have concluded, on these grounds, that the book was written sometime during the first half of the second century, possibly around 130 C.E.

The book is concerned with the relationship of Judaism and Christianity. Its basic thrust is that Judaism is, and always has been, a false religion. According to this author, Jews violated God's covenant from the very beginning (4:6–8); they have, as a result, never been God's people or understood their own Scriptures. For this author, the Jewish Scriptures can be understood only in light of Christ; indeed, for him, the Old Testament is a Christian, not a Jewish, book.

As a corollary, Jews who claim that their religion was given by God have been misled by an evil angel who persuaded them to take the laws of Moses literally (9:5). In fact, claims the author, the laws of sabbath observance, kosher food, and circumcision were meant not as literal descriptions of how the Jewish people were to live, but as figurative pointers to Christ and the religion that he was to establish (chaps. 9–10, 15). A good deal of this book, therefore, tries to show how Christ and the Christian religion were foreshadowed in the Old Testament Scriptures.

The book ends on a different note, by describing the Christian doctrine of the "Two Ways": there is the morally upright way of "light" and the morally perverse way of "darkness" (chaps. 18–20; see the introduction to the *Didache*). All people must choose between these two paths, following the righteous practices of the one or the moral improprieties of the other.

1 Greetings, sons and daughters, in the name of the Lord who loved us, in peace.

2 Seeing that God's righteous acts toward you are so extraordinary and abundant, my joy over your favored and illustrious spirits is unbounded—you have received such grace, such an implantation of the pneumatic gift! 3 Wherefore I, who also hope to be saved, inwardly rejoice all the more because I can actually see that the spirit which is on you has been poured out in your midst from the abundance of the fountain of the Lord. My eagerly anticipated visit to you has so wonderfully exceeded all expectations concerning you!

4 Therefore, I am convinced of this—indeed, I am all the more conscious of it because I know that he who spoke many things in your midst was my traveling companion in the Way of Righteousness, the Lord; and for this reason I myself am constrained at all times to love you more than my own soul—for great faith and love dwell in you, with hope of obtaining the life he gives! 5 Therefore, since it has occurred to me that if I am diligent in imparting to you a measure of what I have received it will be to my credit for having ministered to such spirits, I have hastened to send you this brief communication so that along with your faith you might also have perfect *gnosis*[a] [knowledge].

6 There are, then, three basic doctrines of the Lord of life: Hope, the beginning and end of our faith, and Righteousness, the beginning and end of judgment, (and) Love, a witness of the joy and gladness of works done in righteousness.

7 For the Master has made known to us through the prophets what already has come to pass and what is now occurring, and he has given us a foretaste of what is about to happen. Thus as we observe each of these things being worked out as he said, we ought all the more abundantly and enthusiastically draw near in fear of him. 8 And now, not as a Teacher but as one from your very midst, I will point out a few things which will enable you to rejoice in the present circumstances.

2 Since, then, the present days are evil and he who is now at work possesses the power, we ought to walk circumspectly and seek out the Lord's righteous requirements. 2 The auxiliaries of our faith, then, are Fear and Endurance, while Patience and Self-control also fight along at our side. 3 Thus while these allies remain in a pure state in relation to the Lord, there rejoice with them Wisdom, Understanding, Knowledge [Insight], and *Gnosis* [Knowledge].

4 For he made it clear to us through all the prophets that he needs neither sacrifices nor whole burnt offerings nor offerings in general—as he says in one place:

5 "What good is the multitude of your
     sacrifices to me? says the Lord.
I am satiated with burnt offerings of rams
     and the fat of lambs,
     and I do not want the blood of bulls and
        goats—
     not even if you come and appear
      before me!
For who has required these things from
     your hands?
Do not continue to tread my (Temple)
     court.
If you bring finely ground flour, it is vain;
     offering of incense is an abomination to
     me,
      I cannot bear your new moon festivals
      and sabbaths."[1]

6 Therefore he set these things aside, so that the new law of our Lord Jesus Christ, which is not tied to a yoke of necessity, might have its own offering which is not man-made.

7 And again he says to them: "Did I command your fathers, when they were coming out of the land of Egypt, to offer burnt offerings and sacrifices to me? 8 But, rather, this is what I commanded them—

Let none of you hold a grudge in his heart
     against his neighbor,
And love not a false oath."[2]

9 Therefore, since we are not without understanding, we ought to perceive the gracious intention of our Father. For he is speaking to us, desiring that

---

[a]Editor's note: The translator of the *Letter of Barnabas* has chosen not to translate the Greek word *gnosis* and its related forms in several places. He feels that a one-word translation could not convey the complex of meanings. He believes Barnabas uses it as a technical term to convey the concept of an obedient hearer of the Lord's voice. Thus, knowledge of the Lord's requirements is required, as well as a grasp of what salvation is all about. Since most translators render gnosis as "knowledge," we will insert that word in brackets.

---

[1]Isa 1:11–13   [2]Jer 7:22; Zech 8:17

we who are not misled as they were should seek how we might approach him with our offering.

10a To us, then, he speaks thus:
"A sacrifice to God is a broken heart;
An odor well pleasing to the Lord is a
heart which glorifies its creator."[3]

10b Therefore, brethren, we ought to pay strict attention to the matters which concern our salvation, lest the Wicked One causes error to slip in among us and hurls us away from our life!

3 Therefore he speaks again concerning these things to them:
"Why do you make a fast to me, says the
Lord,
so that today your voice is heard
wailing?
This is not the sort of fast I have chosen,
says the Lord, not a person
humiliating his soul.

2   Not even if you bend your neck in the
shape of a circle,
and deck yourselves out in sackcloth and
ashes—
you cannot even call such conduct an
acceptable fast!"[4]

3 But to us he says:
"Behold, this is the fast which I have
chosen, says the Lord.
Loose every bond of injustice,
untie the knots of forcibly extracted
agreements.
Release the downtrodden with forgiveness,
and tear up every unjust contract.
Distribute your food to the hungry,
and if you see someone naked, clothe
him.
Bring the homeless into your home,
and if you see someone of lowly estate,
do not despise him,
nor (despise) anyone of your own
household.

4   Then your light will break forth early,
and your healing will arise quickly.
And your righteousness will go before you,
and the glory of God will surround you.

5   Then you will cry out, and God will listen
to you;
While you are still speaking, he will say
'Here I am'—

if you put away from you bonds and
scornful gestures and words of
complaint
and give your food to the hungry
without hypocrisy,
and have mercy on the person of
lowly estate."[5]

6 For this reason, therefore, brethren, when he foresaw how the people whom he prepared in his Beloved One would believe in childlike innocence, the Patient One gave us a preview concerning everything lest we be shattered to pieces as "proselytes" to their law.

4 We must, then, carefully investigate the present situation and seek out the things which are able to save us.

1b Therefore let us completely flee from all
the works of lawlessness,
lest the works of lawlessness ensnare us;
And let us hate the error of the present age,
so that we might be loved in the age to
come.

2 Let us give no leisure to our own soul so that it has opportunity to associate with the wicked and sinful—lest we become like them!

3 The great final scandal is at hand, concerning which it has been written—as Enoch says. 3b For the Master cut short the times and the days for this reason, that his Beloved One might hasten and come into his inheritance. 4 And the prophet speaks thus:
"Ten kingdoms will reign on the earth.
And afterward there will arise a little
king,
Who will humiliate three of the
kingdoms simultaneously."[6]

5 Similarly, Daniel says concerning the same one:
"And I saw the fourth beast, wicked and
powerful
and more dangerous than all the beasts
of the sea;
And how that ten horns sprouted from him,
and from them budded a little offshoot
of a horn;
And how that it humiliated three of the
great horns simultaneously."[7]

6 Therefore you ought to understand!

---

[3]Ps 51:17, 19   [4]Isa 58:3–5   [5]Isa 58:6–10   [6]Dan 7:24   [7]Dan 7:7–8

6b Furthermore, I also urge you as one of your own, and especially as one who loves you all more than I love my own self, walk circumspectly and do not be like certain people, compounding your sins by claiming that your covenant is irrevocably yours. 6c But they lost it completely in the following manner, after Moses already had received it— 7 for the Scripture says:

"And Moses was on the mountain fasting for forty days and forty nights, and he received the covenant from the Lord, stone tablets inscribed by the finger of the Lord's hand."[8]

But when they turned to idols, they lost it. 8 For the Lord speaks thus:

"Moses, Moses, descend immediately for your people whom you led out from the land of Egypt have sinned."[9]

And Moses understood, and he hurled the two tablets from his hands. 8b And the covenant (of the tablets) was smashed to bits so that the covenant of Jesus, the Beloved One might be sealed in our heart, in hope of his faith.

9 But since I wish to write many things—not as a Teacher would, but as is fitting for a friend to do—and to omit nothing of what we have received, I hurry along. I am your devoted slave.

9b Wherefore let us walk circumspectly in these last days. For the entire period of our life and faith will be wasted unless now, in the lawless time and in the impeding scandals, we resist as befits God's sons. 10 Therefore, lest the Black One make deceitful entrance, let us flee from all that is irrelevant, let us hate completely the works of the wicked way. 10b Do not live monastic lives by retiring to yourselves as though you have already attained the righteous state, but by assembling together, seek out together what is to your mutual advantage. 11 For the Scripture says:

"Woe to those who are wise in their own eyes,
and understanding in their own sight."[10]

11b Let us be pneumatics; let us be a perfect Temple to God. To the best of our ability let us meditate on the fear of God and strive to keep his commandments, so that we might rejoice in his ordinances. 12 The Lord will judge the world impartially. Each one will receive payment in accord with his deeds—if he was good, his righteousness precedes him; if he was wicked, the reward of

wickedness goes before him! 13 Thus on no account should we slumber in ours sins by relaxing as "those who have been called"—and the wicked Archon will take advantage of his power over us and push us away from the kingdom of the Lord. 14 And finally, my brethren, understand this: When you notice what great signs and wonders were performed in Israel and still they have been abandoned, let us take heed lest we be found to be, as it is written, "many called but few chosen."[11]

5 For it was for this reason that the Lord submitted to deliver his flesh to destruction, that by the forgiveness of sins we might be purified—that is, by the sprinkling (for purification) of his blood. 2 For it is written concerning him—partly with reference to Israel and partly to us—and it says thus:

"He was wounded because of our lawless actions,
and he was rendered helpless because of our sins;
by his wounds we were healed.
As a sheep to the slaughter was he led,
and as a lamb he was silent before his shearer."[12]

3 We ought, therefore, to give heartfelt thanks to the Lord because he has both given us *gnosis* [knowledge] of the things which have come to pass, and has given us wisdom in the present events—nor are we without understanding concerning what is about to happen. 4 But the Scripture says:

"It is not unjust to spread out nets for capturing birds."[13]

4b This is what it is saying: It is just that a man should perish if, although he has *gnosis* [knowledge] of the Way of Righteousness, he becomes ensnared in the Way of Darkness.

5 And furthermore, my brethren, consider this: if the Lord submitted to suffer for our souls—he who is Lord of the whole world, to whom God said at the foundation of the world:

"Let us make man in accord with our image and likeness"[14]

—then how is it that he submitted to suffer at the hand of men? Learn! 6 The prophets, after they

[8]Exod 34:28   [9]Exod 32:7   [10]Isa 5:21   [11]Matt 22:14   [12]Isa 53:5, 7   [13]Prov 1:17   [14]Gen 1:26

had received special insight from him, prophesied concerning him. And he submitted so that he might break the power of Death and demonstrate the resurrection from the dead—thus it was necessary for him to be manifested in flesh. 7 Also (he submitted) so that he might fulfill the promise to the fathers and, while he was preparing the new people for himself and while he was still on earth, to prove that after he has brought about the resurrection he will judge.

8 Furthermore, although he was teaching Israel and doing such great wonders and signs, the result was not that they loved him dearly for his preaching! 9 But when he chose his own apostles who were destined to preach his gospel—men who were sinful beyond measure so that he might prove that he came not to call righteous but sinners—it was then that he revealed himself as God's Son. 10 For if he had not come in flesh, how could people be saved by looking at him? They cannot even gaze directly into the rays of the sun, even though it is a work of his hands and is destined to cease existing!

11 Thus the Son of God came in flesh for this reason, that he might bring to summation the total of sins of those who persecuted his prophets to death. 12 So also he submitted for this reason. 12b For God says that the afflicting of his flesh came from them:

"When they smite their own Shepherd,
    then the sheep of the flock will be lost."[15]

13 And he desired to suffer in such a manner, for it was necessary so that he might suffer on the wood. 13b For one who prophesies concerning him says:

"Spare my soul from the sword
and affix my flesh with nails,
    for a synagogue of wicked men have come
        upon me."[16]

14 And again he says:

"Behold, I have bared my back for stripes,
    and my cheeks for smiting.
But I have set my face as a solid rock."[17]

6 When, therefore, he made the commandment, what does he say?

"Who disputes my judgment? Let him
        oppose me.
Or who vindicates himself in my presence?
Let him draw near to the Lord's Servant.

2 Woe to you, for you all will grow old like a
        garment,
    and a moth will devour you!"[18]

2b And again, since he was established as a mighty Stone which crushes, the prophet says of him:

"Behold, I will insert into the foundations of Zion a stone which is precious, chosen, a cornerstone, prized."

3 Then what does he say?

"And whoever trusts in him will live forever."[19]

3b Is our hope, then, on a stone? Not in the least! But he speaks in such a way since the Lord has established his flesh in strength.

3c For he says:

"And he established me as a solid Rock."[20]

4 And again the prophet says:

"The very stone which the builders rejected has become the cornerstone!"

4b And again he says:

"This is the great and awesome Day which the Lord made."[21]

5 I write to you more clearly so that you might understand. I am a slave devoted to your love.

6 What, then, does the prophet say again?

"A synagogue of wicked men encompasses me, they surround me as bees around honey; and for my garments they cast lots."[22]

7 Thus, since he was about to be manifested in flesh and to suffer, his passion was revealed beforehand. 7b For the prophet says concerning Israel:

"Woe to them, for they devised a wicked plot against themselves when they said, 'Let us bind the Righteous One, for he is displeasing to us.'"[23]

8 What does the other prophet, Moses, say to them?

"Behold, thus says the Lord God: Enter into the good land, which the Lord promised to Abraham and Isaac and Jacob, and make it your inheritance—a land flowing milk and honey."[24]

9 And what does *"gnosis"* [knowledge] say? Learn!

"Hope, it says, on that Jesus who is about to appear to you in flesh. For man is land suffering, for Adam was formed from the face of the land."

---

[15]Zech 13:7 [16]Ps 22:20, 16 [17]Isa 50:6–7 [18]Isa 50:8–9 [19]Isa 28:16 [20]Isa 50:7 [21]Ps 118:22, 24 [22]Ps 22:16, 18; 118:12 [23]Isa 3:9–10 [24]Exod 33:1, 3

10 What, then, does he say? "Into the good land—a land flowing milk and honey."

10b Blessed be our Lord, brethren, who has placed in us wisdom and understanding of his secrets. For the prophet says:

"Who can understand a parable of the Lord, except he who is wise and understanding, and who loves his Lord?"

11 Since, then, he renovated us by the forgiveness of sins he made us to be an other sort (of creation), as though we had a child's soul—he fashioned us again, as it were. 12 For the Scripture is speaking about us when he says to the Son:

"Let us make man in accord with our image and likeness, and let them rule over the beasts of the earth and the birds of heaven and the fish of the sea."[25]

12b And when he saw how well we were formed, the Lord said:

"Increase and multiply and fill the earth."[26]
These things (he said) to the Son.

13 Again, I will show you how he says to us that he made a second fashioning in the last times. 13b And the Lord says:

"Behold, I make the last things like the first."[27]

13c It is for this reason, therefore, that the prophet proclaimed: "Enter into the land flowing milk and honey, and exercise lordship over it"[28] 14 See, then, we have been fashioned anew! 14b As he says again in another prophet:

"Behold, says the Lord, I will remove from them—that is, from those on whom he foresaw the Lord's spirit—their stony hearts, and I will insert fleshly hearts."[29]

14c Because he was about to be manifested in flesh and to dwell in us. 15 For, my brethren, our heart being thus inhabited constitutes a holy Temple to the Lord! 16 For the Lord says again:

"And in what manner shall I appear before the Lord my God and be glorified?"[30]

16b He says:

"I will confess you in the assembly of my
        brethren,
and I will praise you in the midst of the
        assembly of saints."[31]

16c Therefore we are those whom he conducts into the good land!

17 What, then, is the "milk and honey"? Because the infant is initiated into life first by honey, then by milk. 17b Thus also, in a similar way, when we have been initiated into life by faith in the promise and by the word, we will live exercising lordship over the land. 18 But as it was already said above: "And they shall increase, and multiply, and rule over the fish. . . ."[32] 18b Who, then, is presently able to rule over beasts or fish or birds of heaven? For we ought to understand that "to rule" implies that one is in control, so that he who gives the orders exercises dominion. 19 If, then, this is not the present situation, he has told us when it will be—when we ourselves have been perfected as heirs of the Lord's covenant.

7 Understand, therefore, children of joy, that the good Lord revealed everything to us beforehand so that we might know whom we ought to praise continually with thanksgiving.

2 If, then, the Son of God, who is Lord and is about to judge the living and dead, suffered so that his being afflicted might bring us life, let us believe that it was not possible for the Son of God to suffer except on our behalf.

3 But he also drank vinegar and gall when he was crucified. 3b Hear how the priests of the Temple made even this clear, when the commandment was written:

"Whoever does not fast during the (Atonement) Fast must surely die."[33]

3c The Lord gave such a commandment since he was destined to offer the vessel of the spirit as a sacrifice for our sins, so that the "type" which is based on Isaac's having been offered up on the altar also might be fulfilled.

4 What, then, does he say in the prophet?

"And they shall eat from the goat which is offered up during the Fast for all sins"—
pay attention more diligently—
"and the priests alone shall all eat the entrails unwashed, with vinegar."

5 For what reason?

"Since I am destined to offer my flesh for the sins of my new people, you (priests) are about to drink gall mixed with vinegar—you alone will eat while the people fast and smite themselves on sackcloth and ashes."

---

[25]Gen 1:26   [26]Gen 1:28   [27]Matt 19:30; 20:16 (?)   [28]Exod 33:3
[29]Ezek 11:19   [30]Ps 42:2   [31]Ps 22:22, 25   [32]Gen 1:28   [33]Lev 23:29

This is to demonstrate that he must suffer at their hands.

6 Pay attention to what he commanded:

"Take two goats which are handsome and alike, and present them; and let the priest take one for a burnt offering for sins."[34]

7 But what do they do with the other?

"Accursed, he says, is the other."

7b Pay attention to how the type of Jesus is made clear!

8 "And you shall all spit on and prick (that goat), and encircle its head with scarlet wool, and thus let it be cast out into the desert."[35]

8b And when this has been done, the one who bears the goat brings (it) into the desert and takes the wool and places it upon a bush which is called *rache,* the buds of which we are accustomed to eat when we find them in the countryside. Thus of the *rache* alone are the fruits sweet.

9 What, then, does it mean—pay attention—that the one is placed on the altar and the other is accursed, and that the accursed one is crowned? 9b Because they will see him then, on that day, wearing the scarlet robe around his flesh, and they will say:

Is not this he whom we once crucified, despising and piercing and spitting on him? Surely this was the one who then said he was God's Son!

10 Now how is this like that situation? For this reason the goats were alike and handsome, equal, so that when they see it coming then, they will be amazed at the similarity of the goat. 10b Therefore notice here the type of Jesus who was destined to suffer.

11 And what does it mean that they place the wool in the midst of the thorns? It is a type of Jesus placed in the church, so that whoever desires to snatch away the scarlet wool must suffer many things because the thornbush is treacherous, and he must obtain it through affliction.

11b In such a way, he says, those who desire to see me and to take hold of my kingdom ought to take me through affliction and suffering.

8 And what do you suppose is the type involved here, in that he commanded to Israel that those men in whom sins are complete should offer a heifer; and when they had slaughtered it, to burn it; and then the children should take the ash-es and put them into a container; and the scarlet wool should be wrapped around a piece of wood—again, note the type, of the cross, and the scarlet wool and the hyssop; and thus the children sprinkle the people individually in order to purify them from sins? 2 Understand how it is told to you in such simplicity: the calf is Jesus; the sinful men who offer it are those who offered him to be slaughtered. Then men (appear) no longer, (it is) no longer (concerned with) the "glory" of sinners! 3 Those who sprinkle are children, they are those who preach to us forgiveness of sins and purification of the heart, to whom he entrusted the authority to proclaim the gospel. 3b There are twelve (of the latter), for a witness to the tribes, since there are twelve tribes of Israel. 4 But why are there (only) three children who sprinkle? This is for a witness to Abraham, Isaac, and Jacob, because they are great before God.

5 And the fact that the wool is on the wood signifies that the kingdom of Jesus is on the wood, and that those who hope on him will live forever. 6 But why are the wool and hyssop together? Because in his kingdom there shall be wicked and vile days, in which we shall be saved. For the one whose flesh is distressed is cured by means of the hyssop's vileness!

7 Wherefore, the things which have come to pass are clear to us, but hidden to them, because they did not hearken to the Lord's voice.

9 For again, he speaks concerning the ears, how he circumcised the ears of our heart. 1b The Lord says in the prophet:

"By listening with the ear, they hearkened to me."[36]

1c And again he says:

"By hearing, those who are far off shall hearken;

The things I have done will become known.

"And circumcise, says the Lord, your hearts."[37]

2 And again he says:

"Hear, Israel, for thus says the Lord your God;

Who is he who desires to live forever?

By hearing, let him hearken to the voice of my servant."[38]

---

[34]Lev 16:7, 9   [35]Lev 16:10, 20–22   [36]Ps 18:44   [37]Isa 33:13; Jer 4:4   [38]Jer 7:2; Ps 34:12–13

3 And again he says:

"Hear, heaven, and give ear, earth; for the Lord has spoken"[39]—

these are mentioned as a witness.

3b And again he says:

"Hear the Lord's word, rulers of this people."[40]

3c And again he says:

"Hear, children, a voice crying in the desert."[41]

4 Therefore he circumcised our ears, so that when we hear the word, we might believe.

4b But he also set aside the circumcision on which they relied. For he said that circumcision was not a matter of the flesh, but they became transgressors because a wicked angel "enlightened" them.

5 And he says to them:

"Thus says the Lord your God"—

here I find a commandment—

"Woe to those who sow among thorns;
Be circumcised to your Lord."[42]

5b And what is he saying?

"Circumcise the wickedness from your heart"[43]

5c And again he says:

"Behold, the Lord says, all the nations
have uncircumcised foreskins,
but this people is uncircumcised in
heart!"[44]

6 But you will say: And yet the people received circumcision as a special sign. But every Syrian and Arab, and all the priests of the idols also (are circumcised). Are they also, then, from their covenant? But even the Egyptians are in circumcision!

7 Learn, then, abundantly concerning everything, children of love; for when Abraham first gave circumcision, he circumcised while looking forward in the spirit to Jesus, and he received the teachings of the three letters. 8 For it says:

"And Abraham circumcised the men of his household, 18 and 300 (in number)."[45]

8b What, then, is the *gnosis* [knowledge] which was given him? Learn! For a distinction is made in that the 18 comes first, then it says 300. Now the (number) 18 (is represented by two letters), J = 10 and E = 18—thus you have "JE," (the abbreviation for) "JEsus."[b] And because the cross, represented by the letter T (= 300), was destined to convey special significance, it also says 300. He makes clear, then, that JEsus is symbolized by the

two letters (JE = 18), while in the one letter (T = 300) is symbolized the cross.

9 He who placed the implanted gift of his teaching in us knows! No one has learned from me a more trustworthy lesson! But I know that you are worthy.

10 Now when Moses said:

"Eat neither pig, nor eagle nor hawk nor crow, nor any fish which is without scales,"[46] he received in his understanding three doctrines. 2 Further, he says to them in Deuteronomy:

"And I will ordain as a covenant for this people my righteous ordinances."[47]

2b Therefore it is not God's commandment that they (literally) should not eat, but Moses spoke in the spirit.

3 For this reason, then, he mentions the "pig": Do not associate, he is saying, with such people—people who are like pigs. That is, people who forget their Lord when they are well off, but when they are in need, they acknowledge the Lord; 3b just as when the pig is feeding it ignores its keeper, but when it is hungry it makes a din, and after it partakes it is quiet again.

4 "Neither eat the eagle nor the hawk nor the kite nor the crow."[48] Do not, he is saying, associate with nor be like such people—people who do not know how to procure their own food by honest labor and sweat, but in their lawlessness they plunder the possessions of others, and they keep sharp watch as they walk around in apparent innocence, and spy out whom they might despoil by plundering; 4b just as those birds are unique in not procuring their own food, but as they perch idly by, they seek how they might devour the flesh of others—pestilent creatures in their wickedness!

5 "And do not eat," he says, "sea eel nor octopus nor cuttlefish."[49] Do not, he is saying, be like such people—people who are completely impious and have already been condemned to death;

---

[b]Because of the repeated numbers (symbolized by letters in Greek) and abbreviations, there is a great deal of confusion among the witnesses to 9:8b. Thus the above translation sometimes takes minor liberties with the text for the sake of the English reader (e.g., the Greek IH [= 18] is transliterated to JE).

---

[39]Isa 1:2 [40]Isa 1:10; 28:14 [41]Isa 40:3 [42]Jer 4:3–4 [43]Deut 10:16
[44]Jer 9:26 [45]Gen 14:14; 17:23 [46]Lev 11:7–15; Deut 14:8–14
[47]Deut 4:1, 10, 13 [48]Lev 11:13–16 [49]Lev 11:10

5b just as those fish are uniquely cursed and loiter in the depths, not swimming about as do the rest but inhabiting the murky region beneath the deep water.

6 But "neither shall you eat the hairy-footed animal."[50] Why not? Do not be, he is saying, one who corrupts children, nor be like such people; 6b because the hare increases unduly its discharge each year, and thus has as many holes as it is years old.

7 But neither shall you eat the hyena. Do not, he is saying, be an adulterer nor a corrupter, nor be like such people. 7b Why? Because this animal changes its nature each year, and at one time it is male while at another it is female.

8 But also he hated the weasel, fittingly. Do not, he is saying, be such a person. We hear of such people, who perform a lawless deed uncleanly with the mouth. Neither associate with those unclean women who perform the lawless deed with the mouth. 8b For this animal conceives through its mouth.

9 Concerning foods, then, when Moses received the three doctrines he spoke out thus, in the spirit. But because of fleshly desires they accepted his words as though they concerned actual food.

10 And David also received *gnosis* [Knowledge] of the same three doctrines—and he says:
10b "Blessed is the one who has not walked
　　　according to the
　　counsel of impious people"—
just as the fish which grope in darkness in the depths—
10c　"nor stood in the way of sinners"—
just as those who appear to fear the Lord sin like the pig—
10d　"nor sat in the seat of pestilent
　　　fellows"[51]—
just like the birds perched for plundering.

10e Now receive complete (understanding) concerning food.
11 Moses says again:
　　"Eat every split-hooved and cud-chewing animal."[52]
11b What is he saying (about the latter)? That (the animal) which receives fodder knows who feeds it, and while it relies on him, it seems content. He spoke fittingly in view of the commandment. 11c What, then, is he saying? Associate with those who fear the Lord, with those who meditate in their heart on the subtleties of the matter, with those who proclaim the Lord's righteous ordinances and keep them, with those who realize that study is a joyful occupation, and who "ruminate" on the Lord's word. 11d And what does the "split-hooved" mean? That the righteous person both walks in this world and anticipates the holy aeon.

11e See how appropriately Moses legislated! 12 But how could they perceive or understand these things? But since we rightly understand the commandments, we are speaking as the Lord desired. 12b This is why he circumcised our ears and hearts, so that we might understand these things.

11 But let us investigate whether the Lord was concerned to reveal beforehand concerning the water and concerning the cross.

1b First, concerning the water, it is written with reference to Israel how they never will accept the baptism which conveys forgiveness of sins, but they will build (cisterns) for themselves. 2 For the prophet says:
　"Be astounded, Heaven, and shudder
　　　greatly at this, Earth,
　For this people has committed two wicked
　　　acts—
　They have forsaken me, the living fount of
　　　water,
　And they have dug out for themselves a pit
　　　of death.
3　Has my holy mount Sinai become an arid
　　　rock?
　For you shall be as fledglings of a bird,
　　　fluttering about when they are taken
　　　from the nest."[53]
4 And again the prophet says:
　"I will go before you, and I will level
　　　mountains
　　　and shatter gates of brass and break iron
　　　bars,
　And I will give you treasures—dark,
　　　hidden, unseen—
　that they might know that I am the Lord
　　　God.
5　And you will dwell in an elevated cave

---

[50]Lev 11:6　[51]Ps 1:1　[52]Lev 11:3; Deut 14:6　[53]Jer 2:12–13; Isa 16:1–2

made from solid rock,
and its water supply is dependable.
You will see a king in his glory,
and your soul will meditate on the fear of
the Lord."[54]

6 And again he says in another prophet:
"And he who does these things will be like
the tree planted by
springs of waters,
which produces its fruit at the proper
time,
and which has leaves that will no
wither;
And everything he does will prosper.

7 The impious are not like this—not in the
least.
But rather, they are like the dust which the
wind drives from the face of the
earth.
For this reason, the impious will not appear
for judgment
nor sinners in the council of the
righteous.
For the Lord knows the Way of the
Righteous,
and the Way of the Impious will
perish."[55]

8 Perceive how he referred to the water and the
cross together.

8b For this is what he is saying: "Blessed" are
those who, having placed their hope in the cross,
descend into the water. 8c For the reward, he says,
comes "at the proper time"—then, he says, I will
repay. 8d But as for the present, what does he say?
"The leaves will not wither." He is saying this, that
every word which flows forth from you—through
your mouth—in faith and love, will be a means of
conversion and hope to many.

9 And again, another prophet says:
"And the Land of Jacob was praised more than
any land"—he is saying this, he glorifies the vessel of his spirit.

10 Then what does he say?
"And there was a river flowing from the
right side,
and beautiful trees came up out of it.
And whoever eats of them will live
forever."[56]

11 He is saying this, that we go down into the water full of sins and vileness, and we come up bearing fruit in our heart, having in the spirit fear and
hope in Jesus.

11b "And whoever eats from these will live forever." He is saying this: Whoever, he says, hears
these things which are spoken and believes will
live forever.

12 Similarly, he explains again concerning
the cross in another prophet who says:
"And when will these things come to pass,
says the Lord?
When a tree falls down and rises up, and
when blood drips from a tree."[57]

1b Again, you have (information) concerning the
cross and the one destined to be crucified.

2 And again he says in the (book of) Moses,
when Israel was under attack from foreigners—
and so that he might remind those who were being
attacked that they had been given over to death because of their sins—the spirit says to Moses, in his
heart, that he should make a type of the cross and
of him who was destined to suffer. 2b If they do
not, he is saying, place their hope on him, they will
be under attack forever. 2c Thus Moses piled one
shield upon another in the midst of the battle, and
as he stood elevated above them all he stretched
out his hands. And as long as he did so, Israel again
prevailed; but whenever he let (his hands) drop,
they were again being killed. 3 Why? So that they
might know that they could not be saved unless
they hoped on him.

4 And again, in another prophet he says:
"The whole day I have stretched out my
hands to a people
who are disobedient and who oppose my
Righteous Way."[58]

5 Again, Moses makes a type of Jesus—(signi-
fying) that it was necessary for him to suffer and
that he whom they supposed had perished would
bestow life—in the standard (set up) when Israel
was smitten (by a plague). 5b For the Lord made
every serpent to bite them, and they were dying,
so that he might demonstrate to them that it was
because of their transgression—since transgression took root in Eve because of the serpent—that
they will be given over to mortal affliction.

---

[54]Isa 45:2–3; 33:16–18 [55]Ps 1:3–6 [56]Ezek 47:1–12 [57]4 Ezra 4:33; 5:5 [58]Isa 65:2

6 Furthermore, it is this same Moses who commanded,

"You shall have neither a cast-metal nor a carved image to your God"[59]—

he it is who makes (such an image) in order to provide a type of Jesus.

6b Moses, then, makes a bronze serpent and sets it up in a prominent place and calls the people together by means of a proclamation. 7 Therefore, when they came together they begged Moses to offer a prayer on their behalf, that they might be healed.

7b But Moses said to them:

"Whenever, he says, anyone is bitten, let him come to the serpent which is erected on the wooden pole. And let him hope, believing that this dead object is able to bestow life, and he will be healed immediately."

7c And they did so.

7d Again, you have also in these things the glory of Jesus—for all things take place in him and for his sake.

8 Again, what does Moses say to "Jesus" son of Naue, when he had given this name to him who was a prophet so that all the people might hearken to him alone? 8b For the Father is making all things clear concerning his Son "Jesus." 9 Thus Moses says to "Jesus" son of Naue, to whom he had given this name when he sent him to spy out the land:

"Take a book in your hands and write what the Lord says, that 'Jesus' the Son of God will cut off the entire house of Amalek by its roots at the end of days."[60]

10 Again, notice "Jesus"—not the son of a man but the Son of God, and manifested in flesh by a type.

10b Since, then, they were going to say that Messiah is David's Son, David himself—fearing and perceiving the error of the sinners—prophesies:

"The Lord said to my Lord, 'Sit at my right hand until I make your enemies a footstool for your feet.'"[61]

11 And again, Isaiah says as follows:

"The Lord said to my Messiah, the Lord, whose right hand I held, that nations would become obedient to him, and 'I will demolish the strength of kings.'"[62]

11b Notice how David says he is "Lord," and does not say "Son."

13

But let us see if this people is the heir; or the former people, and if the covenant is for us or for them.

2 Therefore, hear what the Scripture says concerning "the people":

"And Isaac was making entreaty for Rebecca his wife, because she was barren. And she became pregnant. Then Rebecca also went to inquire of the Lord, and the Lord said to her:

'Two nations are in your womb, and two peoples in your belly. And one of the people will dominate the other, and the greater will be subject to the lesser.'"[63]

3 You ought to perceive who Isaac (represents) and who Rebecca, and with reference to whom he had pointed out that "this people" is "greater" than "that."

4 And in another prophecy Jacob says it even more clearly to his son Joseph, when he says:

"Behold, the Lord has not (yet) deprived me of your presence.

Bring your sons to me, so that I might bless them."[64]

5 And he brought Ephraim and Manasse near, intending that Manasse should receive the blessing since he was older—thus Joseph brought (the latter) to his father Jacob's right hand. 5b But Jacob saw, in the spirit, a type of "the people" which was to come afterward. 5c And what does it say?

"And Jacob crossed his hands and placed his right hand on the head of Ephraim, the second and younger (son) and blessed him. And Joseph said to Jacob: 'You should transpose your right hand to Manasse's head, for he is my firstborn son.' And Jacob said to Joseph: 'I know, child, I know, but the greater will be subject to the lesser.'"[65]

And thus (Ephraim) received the blessing. 6 Take note on which of them he placed (his right hand)—this "people" is to be first, and heir of the covenant!

7 Was, then, this situation also in view in the case of Abraham? We are receiving the perfection of our *gnosis* [knowledge]! 7b What, then, does he say to Abraham when for his belief alone he was established in righteousness?

"Behold, I have established you, Abraham, as

---

[59]Deut 27:15   [60]Exod 17:14   [61]Ps 110:1   [62]Isa 45:1   [63]Gen 25:21–23   [64]Gen 48:11   [65]Gen 48:14–19

the father of nations which believe in God while uncircumcised."[66]

14 Indeed, it was!

1b But let us see if he has given the covenant which he promised the fathers he would give to "the people." 1c He has given it, but they were not worthy to receive it because of their sins. 2 For the prophet says:

"And Moses was fasting on Mount Sinai, when he was to receive the Lord's covenant with the people, for forty days and forty nights. And Moses received from the Lord the two tablets inscribed by the finger of the Lord's hand, in the spirit.[67] And when Moses received (them), he brought (them) down to give to the people. 3 And the Lord said to Moses:

'Moses, Moses, descend immediately, because your people which you led out from the land of Egypt has sinned.'

And Moses understood, for they had again made molten images for themselves, and he hurled the tablets from (his) hands, and the tablets of the Lord's covenant were shattered."[68]

4 Moses, then, received (it), but they did not prove worthy.

4b And how did we receive it? Learn! Moses received it in the capacity of servant, but the Lord himself gave it to us, to a "people" of inheritance, by submitting for us. 5 And he was made manifest so that they might fill up the measure of their sins, and we might receive it through Jesus, who inherits the Lord's covenant. 5b He was prepared for this reason, that by appearing himself liberating from darkness our hearts which had already been paid over to death and given over to the lawlessness of error, he might establish a covenant in us by a word. 6 For it is written how the Father commanded him to prepare a holy people for himself when he had liberated us from the darkness. 7 Therefore the prophet says:

"I, the Lord your God, have called you in righteousness,

and I will grasp your hand and empower you;

And I have given you as a covenant to people, as a light for the nations,

to open the eyes of the blind,

and to release from their bonds those who have been shackled,

and to lead out from their prison house those sitting in darkness."[69]

7b Know, then, whence we were liberated!

8 Again the prophet says:

"Behold, I have placed you as a light for the nations,

that you might beam salvation to the end of the earth.

Thus says the Lord God who liberated you."[70]

9 Again the prophet says:

"The Lord's spirit is on me,

wherefore he anointed me to announce benefaction to the oppressed,

he sent me to heal those who are broken hearted,

to proclaim pardon to the captives and restoration of

sight to the blind,

to announce the acceptable year of the Lord, and the day

of recompense,

to comfort all those who are in mourning."[71]

15 And furthermore, concerning the sabbath. It is written in the "Ten Words" by which (the Lord) spoke to Moses face to face on Mount Sinai:

"And you shall keep the Lord's sabbath holy with clean hands and a clean heart."[72]

2 And elsewhere he says:

"If my sons guard the sabbath, then I will bestow my mercy on them."[73]

3 He mentions "the sabbath" at the beginning of creation:

"And God made the works of his hands in six days,

and he finished on the seventh day.

And he rested on it, and kept it holy."[74]

4 Pay attention, children, to what he says: "He finished in six days." He is saying this, that in six thousand years the Lord will finish everything. For with him the "day" signifies a thousand years. 4b And he bears me witness (on this point) saying:

[66]Gen 17:4 [67]Exod 24:18; 31:18 [68]Exod 32:7–19 [69]Isa 42:6–7 [70]Isa 49:6–7 [71]Isa 61:1–2 [72]Exod 20:8; Deut 5:12 [73]Jer 17:24–25 (?) [74]Gen 2:2

"Behold, a day of the Lord shall be as a thousand years."[75]

4c Therefore, children, "in six days"—in six thousand years—"everything" will be "finished."

5 "And he rested on the seventh day." He is saying this: When his Son comes he will put an end to the time of the Lawless One, and judge the impious, and change the sun and moon and stars—then he will truly rest "on the seventh day."

6 Furthermore he says: "Keep it holy with clean hands and a clean heart." 6b If, then, anyone at present is able, by being clean in heart, to keep holy the day which God hallowed, we have been deceived in everything! 7 But if he keeps it holy at that time by truly resting, when we ourselves are able (to do so) since we have been made righteous and have received the promise—when lawlessness is no more and all things have been made new by the Lord—at that time we will be able to keep it holy, when we ourselves first have been made holy!

8 Further, he says to them:
"I cannot bear your new moon celebrations and sabbaths."[76]

8b See how he is saying that it is not your present sabbaths that are acceptable to me, but that (sabbath) which I have made, in which, when I have rested everything, I will make the beginning of an eighth day—that is, the beginning of another world. 9 Wherefore also we observe the eighth day as a time of rejoicing, for on it Jesus both arose from the dead and, when he had appeared, ascended into the heavens.

16 And finally, concerning the Temple. I will show you how those wretched people, when they went astray, placed their hope on the building and not on their God who created them—as though God has a house! 2 For, roughly speaking, they consecrated him by means of the Temple, as the pagans do! 2b But how does the Lord speak when he sets it aside? Learn!

"Who measured the heaven with a span, or
the earth with a hand?
Was it not I, says the Lord?
The heaven is my throne, and the earth is
the stool for my feet.
What sort of house will you erect for me,
or what place for me to rest?"[77]

2c You knew that their hope was in vain!

3 Furthermore, he says again:
"Behold, those who tore down this Temple
will themselves build it."[78]

4 It is happening. For because of their fighting it was torn down by the enemies. And now the very servants of the enemies will themselves rebuild it.

5 Again, it was made clear that the city and the Temple and the people of Israel were destined to be abandoned. 5b For the Scripture says:
"And it shall be at the end of days that the Lord will abandon the sheep of the pasture, and the sheepfold, and their watchtower to destruction!"[79]

5c And it happened just as the Lord announced!

6 But let us inquire whether there is a Temple of God? There is, where he himself says he makes and prepares (it)! 6b For it is written:
"And it shall come to pass when the "hebdomad"[c] is finished, God's Temple will be built gloriously in the Lord's Name."[80]

7 Thus I find that there is a Temple.

7b How, then, will it "be built in the Lord's Name"? Learn! Before we believed in God the dwelling place of our heart was corrupt and infirm—truly a Temple built by human hands. For it was full of idolatry, and was a house of demons, through doing whatever things were contrary to God. 8 But "it will be built in the Lord's Name"—pay attention—so that the Temple of the Lord may be "built gloriously." 8b How? Learn! When we receive the forgiveness of sins and place our hope on the Name, we become new, created again from the beginning. Wherefore God truly dwells in our "dwelling place"—in us. 9 In what way? The word of his faith, the invitation of his promise, the wisdom of his righteous ordinances, the commandments of his teaching; himself prophesying in us, himself dwelling in us—by opening for us the door of the Temple, which is the mouth, and giving us repentance, he leads those who had been in bondage to death into the incorruptible Temple. 10 For he who longs to be saved looks not to the (external) person, but to him who dwells in him and speaks in him, and he is amazed at the fact that he never either had heard him speak such words from his mouth nor had himself ever desired to

[c]Symbolic week

[75]Ps 90:4 [76]Isa 1:13 [77]Isa 40:12; 66:1 [78]Isa 49:17 [79]1 Enoch 89:56 [80]Dan 9:24–27; 1 Enoch 91:13; Tobit 14:15; 2 Sam 7:13 (?)

hear (them)! 10b This is a pneumatic Temple built for the Lord!

17 To the best of my ability, and in simplicity, (I have tried) to make (these things) clear to you—I hope that I have not neglected anything (vital). 2 For if I keep writing to you concerning things present or to come, you would never comprehend because they are contained in parables. 2b So much, on the one hand, for these matters.

18 But let us move on to another *gnosis* [kind of knowledge] and teaching.

There are two ways of teaching and authority: that of light and that of darkness. And there is a great difference between the two ways.

For over one are appointed lightbearing angels of God,

but over the other, angels of Satan.

2 And the former is Lord from everlasting to everlasting, but the latter is ruler of the present time of lawlessness.

19 Therefore, the way of Light is this— if anyone who desires to traverse the way to the appointed place is diligent in his works.

Therefore, the *gnosis* [knowledge] which is granted to us to walk in it is of this sort:

2 You shall love him who made you; fear him who formed you; glorify him who redeemed you from death.

Be upright in heart and rich in spirit.

Do not associate with those who are proceeding in the way of death.

Hate everything that is not pleasing to God.
Hate all hypocrisy.

Do not forsake the Lord's commandments.

3 Do not exalt yourself, but always be humble-minded.

Do not allow yourself to become arrogant.

Do not take glory on yourself.

Do not plot wickedly against your neighbor.

4 Do not be sexually promiscuous.

Do not commit adultery.

Do not be sexually perverted.

Let not the word of God depart from you with any sort of impurity.

Do not show partiality in reproving anyone for transgressions.

Be meek, be quiet, be one who fears the words which you have heard.

Do not take the Lord's name in vain.

Do not bear a grudge against your brother.

5 Do not be undecided as to whether or not a thing shall come to pass.

Love your neighbor more than yourself.

Do not murder a child by abortion, nor, again, destroy that which is born.

Do not remove your control from your son or your daughter, but from youth up, teach the fear of the Lord.

6 Be not desirous of the things of your neighbor.

Be not greedy, neither be yoked from your soul with the haughty; but associate with the righteous and lowly.

Whatever befalls you, receive these experiences as good, knowing that nothing happens without God.

7 Be not double-minded nor double-tongued for the double tongue is a snare of death.

Be subject to those over you as though to God, in reverence and fear.

Do not give an angry command to your slave or maidservant, who trust in the same God, lest they fear not the God who is over you both; because he came not to call according to status, but to call those in whom he prepared the spirit.

8 Share all things with your neighbor and do not claim that anything is exclusively yours; for if you are sharers in that which is imperishable, how much more so in what is perishable.

Be not overtalkative, for the mouth is death's snare.

To the extent of your ability, be pure for your soul's sake.

9 Do not be one who stretches out his hands to receive but who holds them back when it comes to giving.

Love as the apple of your eye all who proclaim the Lord's word to you.

10 Remember the day of judgment night and day and pursue (the quest) each day either by the word, by toiling and traveling in order to admonish and by taking pains to save a soul by the word or by your hands, by working to provide a ransom for your sins.

11 Do not hesitate to give nor grumble when you give, for you know who is the good paymaster of the reward.

Guard what you received, neither adding nor substracting anything.

Hate evil completely.

Judge justly.

12 Do not cause divisions, but make peace with disputants by bringing them together.

Make confession for your sins.

Do not go to prayer with an evil conscience.

This is the Way of Light.

20 But the Way of the Black One is crooked and full of cursing.

For it is entirely a way of eternal death with punishment, in which lie the things which destroy people's souls—

idolatry, arrogance, pride in power, hypocrisy, duplicity, adultery, murder, robbery, conceit, transgression, guile, malice, stubbornness, sorcery, magic, greediness, without fear of God, persecutors of the good; hating truth, loving a lie; not knowing the reward of righteousness, not associating with what is good;

Not judging justly, not guarding the rights of the widow and orphan;

Being alert not with respect to the fear of God but to that which is wicked—from whom courtesy and patience are far off and distant;

Loving what is worthless, pursuing reward;

Not showing mercy toward the poor, not laboring on behalf of the downtrodden;

Reckless with slanderous speech, not knowing him who made them;

Murderers of children, corrupters of God's creation;

Turning away from the needy, afflicting the oppressed;

Advocates of the rich, lawless judges of the poor—sinful through and through!

21 Therefore it is fitting that when one has learned the ordinances of the Lord—

as many as have been written—he walks in them.

1b For he who does these things will be glorified in God's kingdom;

he who chooses those will perish with his works.

1c For this reason there is resurrection, for this reason there is recompense.

2 I urge those who are in a high position—if you accept any of my well-intentioned advice—to make sure that there are among you those to whom you may do that which is good. Do not fail in this. 3 The day is near in which all things will perish together with the Wicked One. The Lord is near, and his reward.

4 Once more and again I urge you; be good lawgivers among yourselves, persevere as faithful advisers to each other, remove all hypocrisy from among you. 5 And the God who has dominion over the whole universe will give you Wisdom, Insight, Understanding, *Gnosis* [Knowledge] of his ordinances, Endurance.

6 Be taught by God, seeking out what the Lord seeks from you; and so act that you may find (what you seek) in the day of judgment. 7 And if there is any remembrance of what is good, remember me as you meditate on these things, so that my earnest longing and my sleeplessness might lead to some good result.

8 I urge you, begging your favor, while the "good vessel" is still with you do not fail in any respect, but continually seek out these things and fulfill every commandment—for they are worthy. 9 Wherefore, I hastened all the more to write whatever I could. 9b May you be saved, children of love and peace. 9c The Lord of glory and of all grace be with your spirit.

The Preaching of Peter

A popular document in the early church, the *Preaching of Peter* was widely assumed by early church fathers to have been composed by the apostle Peter himself. Most scholars today, however, think that it was written sometime during the first part of the second century.

The book no longer survives intact but is known only through the quotations of later authors, especially Clement of Alexandria, who lived at the end of the second century and the beginning of the third. On the basis of these fragmentary remains it is impossible to judge the original length or contents of the document. Some of its major emphases, however, are reasonably clear: according to its author, Christianity is superior both to the cults of pagans, who naively worship idols and living creatures, and to the religion of the Jews, who in their ignorance worship angels and celestial bodies rather than the true God. In particular, the book emphasizes that Christ fulfilled the predictions of the Jewish Scriptures and brought salvation to all people. Everyone who learns the truth of Christ is to repent for the forgiveness of their sins.

It is possible, given its themes, that the book was one of the first "apologies" for early Christianity, that is, a reasoned defense of the views of Christians against the attacks of their cultured despisers, both pagans and Jews.

1. Clement of Alexandria *Strom.* 1.29.182

And in the Preaching of Peter you may find the Lord called "Law and Word."

2. Clement of Alexandria, *Strom.* 6.5.39–41

But that the most notable of the Greeks do not know God by direct knowledge but indirectly, Peter says in his Preaching, "Know then that there is one God who made the beginning of all things and has power over their end," and "The invisible who sees all things, uncontainable, who contains all, who needs nothing, of whom all things stand in need and for whose sake they exist, incomprehensible, perpetual, incorruptible, uncreated, who made all things by the word of his power . . . that is, the Son." Then he goes on, "This God you must worship, not after the manner of the Greeks . . . showing that we and the notable Greeks worship the same God, though not according to perfect knowledge for they had not learned the tradition of the Son." "Do not," he says, "worship"—he does not say "the God whom the Greeks worship," but "not in the manner of the Greeks": he would

"The Preaching of Peter," from *The Apocryphal New Testament,* translated by J. K. Elliott. © Oxford University Press 1993. Reprinted by permission of Oxford University Press.

change the method of worship of God, not proclaim another God. What, then, is meant by "not in the manner of the Greeks"? Peter himself will explain, for he continues, "Carried away by ignorance and not knowing God as we do, according to the perfect knowledge, but shaping those things over which he gave them power for their use, wood and stones, brass and iron, gold and silver, forgetting their material and proper use, they set up things subservient to their existence and worship them; and what things God has given them for food, the fowls of the air and the creatures that swim in the sea and creep on the earth, wild beasts and four-footed cattle of the field, weasels too and mice, cats and dogs and apes; even their own foodstuffs do they sacrifice to animals that can be consumed and, offering dead things to the dead as if they were gods, they show ingratitude to God since by these practices they deny that he exists. . ." He continues again in this fashion, "Neither worship him as the Jews do for they, who suppose that they alone know God, do not know him, serving angels and archangels, the month and the moon: and if no moon be seen, they do not celebrate what is called the first sabbath, nor keep the new moon, nor the days of unleavened bread, nor the feast of tabernacles, nor the great day (of atonement)."

Then he adds the finale of what is required: "So then learn in a holy and righteous manner that which we deliver to you, observe, worshipping God through Christ in a new way. For we have found in the Scriptures, how the Lord said, 'Behold, I make with you a new covenant, not as the covenant with your fathers in mount Horeb.'[1] He has made a new one with us: for the ways of the Greeks and Jews are old, but we are Christians who worship him in a new way as a third generation."

3. Clement of Alexandria *Strom.* 6.5.43

Therefore Peter says that the Lord said to the apostles, "If then any of Israel will repent and believe in God through my name, his sins shall be forgiven him: and after twelve years go out into the world, lest any say, 'We did not hear'."

4. Clement of Alexandria *Strom.* 6.6.48

For example, in the Preaching of Peter the Lord says, "I chose you twelve, judging you to be disciples worthy of me, whom the Lord willed, and thinking you faithful apostles I sent you into the world to preach the gospel to people throughout the world, that they should know that there is one God; to declare by faith in me [the Christ] what shall be, so that those who have heard and believed may be saved, and that those who have not believed may hear and bear witness, not having any defence so as to say, 'We did not hear.' . . ."

And to all reasonable souls it has been said above: Whatever things any of you did in ignorance, not knowing God clearly, all his sins shall be forgiven him, if he comes to God and repents.

5. Clement of Alexandria *Strom.* 6.15.128

Peter in the Preaching, speaking of the apostles, says, "But, having opened the books of the prophets which we had, we found, sometimes expressed by parables, sometimes by riddles, and sometimes directly and in so many words the name Jesus Christ, both his coming and his death and the cross and all the other torments which the Jews inflicted on him, and his resurrection and assumption into the heavens before Jerusalem was founded, all these things that had been written, what he must suffer and what shall be after him. When, therefore, we gained knowledge of these things, we believed in God through that which had been written of him."

And a little after he adds that the prophecies came by divine providence, in these terms, "For we know that God commanded them, and without the Scripture we say nothing."

6. John of Damascus, *Parall.* A 12

(Of Peter): Wretched that I am, I remembered not that God sees the mind and observes the voice of the soul. Allying myself with sin, I said to myself,

---

[1]Jer 31:31–32

"God is merciful, and will bear with me; and because I was not immediately smitten, I ceased not, but rather despised pardon, and exhausted the long-suffering of God."

(From the Teaching of Peter): Rich is the man who has mercy on many, and, imitating God, gives what he has. For God has given all things to all his creation. Understand then, you rich, that you ought to minister, for you have received more than you yourselves need. Learn that others lack the things you have in superfluity. Be ashamed to keep things that belong to others. Imitate the fairness of God, and no one will be poor.

7. Origen, *de Principiis* i, prol. 8

But if any would produce to us from that book which is called The Doctrine of Peter, the passage where the Saviour is represented as saying to the disciples, "I am not a bodiless demon," . . .

8. Gregory of Nazianaus, *epp.* 16 and 20

"A soul in trouble is near to God," as Peter says somewhere—a marvellous utterance.

The Fragments of Papias

According to the church father Irenaeus, Papias was a companion of Polycarp. The fourth-century church historian Eusebius claims that Papias had been the bishop of Hieropolis in Asia Minor. Otherwise we know very little about the man.

Sometime around 110 or 120 C.E. Papias wrote a five-volume work entitled *Expositions of the Sayings of the Lord.* The work no longer survives intact, but several fragments from it are quoted and discussed by such church fathers as Irenaeus and Eusebius. Papias claims to have acquired his information about Jesus from followers of the disciples; in particular, he names Aristion and "the presbyter John." Eusebius points out that the latter could not have been John the son of Zebedee, whom Papias mentions elsewhere.

Among the most interesting features of the surviving fragments of Papias are the following:

(1) He is forthright in stating his preference for *oral* traditions about Jesus (the "living and abiding voice") over written accounts about him (i.e., the Gospels; it is uncertain if he knew of any besides Matthew and Mark).

(2) He asserts that Mark recorded stories about Jesus as they were told by Peter, but acknowledges that Peter often changed the stories as occasion demanded, that he did not tell them sequentially, and that Mark did not record them "in order." (Many scholars believe that Papias is referring to our canonical Mark, but that is not at all certain; in any event, it should be recalled that he is writing nearly six decades after Mark had been placed in circulation.)

(3) He maintains that Matthew collected Jesus' sayings in Hebrew, and that these sayings were translated (into Greek?) in different ways by different people. (Again, it is not clear that Papias has in mind the New Testament Gospel of Matthew, since this book, unlike the collection of sayings that Papias mentions, was originally composed in Greek rather than Hebrew.)

Eusebius discusses several other features of Papias's writings without quoting them directly. Papias had evidently related the story of a dead person raised to life in his own congregation, an account of a Christian man who drank deadly poison to no ill effect, and an episode similar to the story of the woman taken in adultery that later found its way into manuscripts of the Gospel of John (7:53–8:12).

In particular, Papias emphasized a materialistic understanding of the end time, asserting that there was to be a literal thousand-year millenium on earth after the resurrection of

"The Fragments of Papias," translated by J. B. Lightfoot & J. R. Harmer, *The Apostolic Fathers,* 2nd ed., edited by Michael W. Holmes, by Baker Book House.

the dead. This teaching did not ingratiate Papias with later church writers. Eusebius, for instance, calls him "a man of exceedingly small intelligence" (*Ecclesiastical History* 3.39.13). Perhaps as a result of such views, Papias's writings were not copied and preserved for posterity.

1. Irenaeus of Lyons, *Against Heresies* 5.33.3–4

The blessing thus foretold undoubtedly belongs to the times of the kingdom, when the righteous will rise from the dead and reign, when creation, too, renewed and freed from bondage, will produce an abundance of food of all kinds "from the dew of heaven and from the fertility of the earth," just as the elders, who saw John the disciple of the Lord, recalled having heard from him how the Lord used to teach about those times and say:

"The days will come when vines will grow, each having ten thousand shoots, and on each shoot ten thousand branches, and on each branch ten thousand twigs, and on each twig ten thousand clusters, and in each cluster ten thousand grapes, and each grape when crushed will yield twenty-five measures of wine. And when one of the saints takes hold of a cluster, another cluster will cry out, "I am better, take me, bless the Lord through me." Similarly a grain of wheat will produce ten thousand heads, and every head will have ten thousand grains, and every grain ten pounds of fine flour, white and clean. And the other fruits, seeds, and grass will produce in similar proportions, and all the animals feeding on these fruits produced by the soil will in turn become peaceful and harmonious toward one another, and fully subject to humans."

Papias, a man of the early period, who was a hearer of John and a companion of Polycarp, bears witness to these things in writing in the fourth of his books, for there are five books composed by him. And he goes on to say: "These things are believable to those who believe." "And," he says, "when Judas the traitor did not believe and asked, 'How, then, will such growth be accomplished by the Lord?" the Lord said, 'Those who live until those times will see.'"

2. Eusebius, *Church History* 3.39

Papias himself, in the preface to his discourses, indicates that he was by no means a hearer or eyewitness of the holy apostles, but shows by the language he uses that he received the matters of the faith from those who had known them:

"I will not hesitate to set down for you, along with my interpretations, everything I carefully learned then from the elders and carefully remembered, guaranteeing their truth. For unlike most people I did not enjoy those who have a great deal to say, but those who teach the truth. Nor did I enjoy those who recall someone else's commandments, but those who remember the commandments given by the Lord to the faith and proceeding from the truth itself. And if by chance someone who had been a follower of the elders should come my way, I inquired about the words of the elders—what Andrew or Peter said, or Philip, or Thomas or James, or John or Matthew or any other of the Lord's disciples, and whatever Aristion and the elder John, the Lord's disciples, were saying. For I did not think that information from books would profit me as much as information from a living and abiding voice."

In his writing he also hands on other accounts of the sayings of the Lord belonging to Aristion, who has been mentioned above, and the traditions of John the Elder, to which we refer those interested. For our present purpose we must add to his statements already quoted above a tradition concerning Mark, who wrote the Gospel, which has been set forth in these words:

"And the Elder used to say this: 'Mark, having become Peter's interpreter, wrote down accurately everything he remembered, though not in order, of the things either said or done by Christ. For he neither heard the Lord nor followed him, but afterward, as I said, followed Peter, who adapted his teachings as needed but had no intention of giving an ordered account of the Lord's sayings. Consequently Mark did nothing wrong in writing down some things as he remembered them, for he made it his one concern not to omit anything which he heard or to make any false statement in them.'"

Such, then, is the account given by Papias with respect to Mark. But with respect to Matthew the following was said:

"So Matthew composed the oracles in the Hebrew language and each person interpreted them as best he could."

3. Apollinaris of Laodicaea (Reconstructed from Fragments Compiled by Various Editors)

From Apollinarius: Judas did not die by hanging but lived on, having been cut down before he choked to death. Indeed, the Acts of the Apostles makes this clear: "Falling headlong, he burst open in the middle and his intestines spilled out."[1] Papias, the disciple of John, recounts this more clearly in the fourth book of the *Exposition of the Sayings of the Lord,* as follows:

"Judas was a terrible, walking example of ungodliness in this world, his flesh so bloated that he was not able to pass through a place where a wagon passes easily, not even his bloated head by itself. For his eyelids, they say, were so swollen that he could not see the light at all, and his eyes could not be seen, even by a doctor using an optical instrument, so far had they sunk below the outer surface. His genitals appeared more loathsome and larger than anyone else's, and when he relieved himself there passed through it pus and worms from every part of his body, much to his shame. After much agony and punishment, they say, he finally died in his own place, and because of the stench the area is deserted and uninhabitable even now; in fact, to this day no one can pass that place unless they hold their nose, so great was the discharge from his body and so far did it spread over the ground."

4. Andrew of Caesarea, *On the Apocalypse,* Chap. 34, Serm. 12

But Papias says, word for word:
"Some of them"—obviously meaning those which once were holy—"he assigned to rule over the orderly arrangement of the earth, and commissioned them to rule well." And next he says: "But as it turned out, their administration came to nothing. And the great dragon, the ancient serpent, who is called the Devil and Satan, was cast out; the deceiver of the whole world was cast down to the earth along with his angels."

5. Andrew of Caesarea, *On the Apocalypse,* on Rev. 12:7–9

And Papias spoke in the following manner in his treatises:

"Never does heaven receive his terrestrial thanks, because it is impossible for light to participate in darkness. He fell to earth, here to live; and when mankind came here, where he was, he did not permit them to live in natural passions; on the contrary, he enticed them into much evil. But Michael and his legions, who are guardians of the world, help mankind, as Daniel learned; they gave laws and made the prophets wise. And all this was war against the dragon, who sets stumbling blocks for people. Then the war extended into heaven, even to Christ himself. Therefore Christ came; and the law, which was impossible for anyone else, he fulfilled in his body, according to the apostle. He rejected sin and condemned Satan, and spread abroad

---

[1]Acts 1:18

his righteousness through his death for all. As this occurred, the victory of Michael and his legions, the guardians of mankind, became complete, and the dragon could resist no more. Because the death of Christ destroyed him and threw him to the earth, accordingly Christ said: 'I saw Satan fall from heaven like a lightning bolt.'"[2]

In this sense the teacher understood not his first fall, but the second, which was through the cross; and this did not consist of a spatial fall, as at first, but rather judgment and expectation of a mighty punishment. . . .

---

[2]Luke 10:18

EARLY CHRISTIAN
APOCALYPSES

The Revelation to John

No book of the Christian Bible has so mystified and intrigued readers over the centuries as the Revelation (or Apocalypse) to John. Nor has any other been subject to such wild and divergent interpretations, as readers have tried to demonstrate that its visions of the end time relate directly to events transpiring in their own day.

The book records a series of visions given by God to his prophet John on the Island of Patmos (1:9). The author does not claim to be Jesus' disciple, John the son of Zebedee, although tradition has so identified him. In any event, modern scholars have recognized on linguistic grounds that, whoever wrote this book (John was a common name), it was not the author of the Fourth Gospel.

The first vision is of Christ himself, who appears to the author as "one like the Son of Man" (chap. 1; cf. Dan 7:13) and dictates letters to the seven churches of Asia Minor to comfort and/or admonish them in their Christian lives (chaps. 2–3). The rest of the book narrates a series of heavenly visions concerning the future course of events on earth; the events are catastrophic and take place in three series of sevens: the breaking of seven seals of a scroll that records earth's destiny (chaps. 5–6); the blowing of seven trumpets (chaps. 8–9), which also leads to the appearance of the anti-Christ and his prophet (chaps. 12–13); and the pouring out of seven bowls of God's wrath (chaps. 15–16).

The earthly disasters reach their climax with the destruction of the Great Whore of Babylon, representing Rome, the city "built on seven hills" (17:9, 18), followed by a cosmic battle in which Christ destroys the forces of evil aligned against him (chaps. 17–19). In the end, God sends to earth his kingdom, in which his saints will live a blessed existence forever (chaps. 20–22).

Whereas this description of future events may seem bizarre and unique to modern readers, it is a kind of book that would have been familiar to Jewish and Christian readers in the ancient world. Most of the other ancient "apocalypses" are pseudonymous, written in the names of famous persons from the past like Abraham, Enoch, or Adam. These books record highly symbolic visions given to the prophet by God and interpreted through an angelic mediator; the visions typically reveal the future course of worldly events or indicate the real but hidden meaning of earthly realities. In every instance, the visions are meant to provide hope for their readers: despite appearances to the contrary, God is ultimately in control of the world and its destiny, and those who remain faithful to him will be rewarded in the end. For the Book of Revelation, the enemy of believers is the city of Rome and its emperors (chaps. 17–19); the author's visions show that God will soon intervene on behalf of his persecuted saints, overthrow the evil empire aligned against them, and bestow eternal rewards on those who remain faithful.

While it is difficult to assign a date to the Book of Revelation, most scholars think that some of its visions date to the reign of Nero (ca. 64 C.E.) but that the book as a whole was not completed until near the end of the first century, possibly around 95 C.E. during the reign of Domitian.

1 The revelation of Jesus Christ, which God gave him to show his servants[a] what must soon take place; he made[b] it known by sending his angel to his servant[c] John, 2 who testified to the word of God and to the testimony of Jesus Christ, even to all that he saw.

3 Blessed is the one who reads aloud the words of the prophecy, and blessed are those who hear and who keep what is written in it; for the time is near.

4 John to the seven churches that are in Asia:

Grace to you and peace from him who is and who was and who is to come, and from the seven spirits who are before his throne, 5 and from Jesus Christ, the faithful witness, the firstborn of the dead, and the ruler of the kings of the earth.

To him who loves us and freed[d] us from our sins by his blood, 6 and made[b] us to be a kingdom, priests serving[e] his God and Father, to him be glory and dominion forever and ever. Amen.

7   Look! He is coming with the
            clouds;
        every eye will see him,
      even those who pierced him;
        and on his account all the tribes
            of the earth will wail.

So it is to be. Amen.

8 "I am the Alpha and the Omega," says the Lord God, who is and who was and who is to come, the Almighty.

9 I, John, your brother who share with you in Jesus the persecution and the kingdom and the patient endurance, was on the island called Patmos because of the word of God and the testimony of Jesus.[f] 10 I was in the spirit[g] on the Lord's day, and I heard behind me a loud voice like a trumpet 11 saying, "Write in a book what you see and send it to the seven churches, to Ephesus, to Smyrna, to Pergamum, to Thyatira, to Sardis, to Philadelphia, and to Laodicea."

12 Then I turned to see whose voice it was that spoke to me, and on turning I saw seven golden lampstands, 13 and in the midst of the lampstands I saw one like the Son of Man, clothed with a long robe and with a golden sash across his chest. 14 His head and his hair were white as white wool, white as snow; his eyes were like a flame of fire, 15 his feet were like burnished bronze, refined as

in a furnace, and his voice was like the sound of many waters. 16 In his right hand he held seven stars, and from his mouth came a sharp, two-edged sword, and his face was like the sun shining with full force.

17 When I saw him, I fell at his feet as though dead. But he placed his right hand on me, saying, "Do not be afraid; I am the first and the last, 18 and the living one. I was dead, and see, I am alive forever and ever; and I have the keys of Death and of Hades. 19 Now write what you have seen, what is, and what is to take place after this. 20 As for the mystery of the seven stars that you saw in my right hand, and the seven golden lampstands: the seven stars are the angels of the seven churches, and the seven lampstands are the seven churches.

2 "To the angel of the church in Ephesus write: These are the words of him who holds the seven stars in his right hand, who walks among the seven golden lampstands:

2 "I know your works, your toil and your patient endurance. I know that you cannot tolerate evildoers; you have tested those who claim to be apostles but are not, and have found them to be false. 3 I also know that you are enduring patiently and bearing up for the sake of my name, and that you have not grown weary. 4 But I have this against you, that you have abandoned the love you had at first. 5 Remember then from what you have fallen; repent, and do the works you did at first. If not, I will come to you and remove your lampstand from its place, unless you repent. 6 Yet this is to your credit: you hate the works of the Nicolaitans, which I also hate. 7 Let anyone who has an ear listen to what the Spirit is saying to the churches. To everyone who conquers, I will give permission to eat from the tree of life that is in the paradise of God.

8 "And to the angel of the church in Smyrna write: These are the words of the first and the last, who was dead and came to life:

9 "I know your affliction and your poverty, even though you are rich. I know the slander on the part of those who say that they are Jews and are not, but are a synagogue of Satan. 10 Do not fear what

[a]Gk *slaves*   [b]Gk *and he made*   [c]Gk *slave*   [d]Other ancient authorities read *washed*   [e]Gk *priests to*   [f]Or *testimony to Jesus*   [g]Or *in the Spirit*

you are about to suffer. Beware, the devil is about to throw some of you into prison so that you may be tested, and for ten days you will have affliction. Be faithful until death, and I will give you the crown of life. 11 Let anyone who has an ear listen to what the Spirit is saying to the churches. Whoever conquers will not be harmed by the second death.

12 "And to the angel of the church in Pergamum write: These are the words of him who has the sharp two-edged sword:

13 "I know where you are living, where Satan's throne is. Yet you are holding fast to my name, and you did not deny your faith in me[h] even in the days of Antipas my witness, my faithful one, who was killed among you, where Satan lives. 14 But I have a few things against you: you have some there who hold to the teaching of Balaam, who taught Balak to put a stumbling block before the people of Israel, so that they would eat food sacrificed to idols and practice fornication. 15 So you also have some who hold to the teaching of the Nicolaitans. 16 Repent then. If not, I will come to you soon and make war against them with the sword of my mouth. 17 Let anyone who has an ear listen to what the Spirit is saying to the churches. To everyone who conquers I will give some of the hidden manna, and I will give a white stone, and on the white stone is written a new name that no one knows except the one who receives it.

18 "And to the angel of the church in Thyatira write: These are the words of the Son of God, who has eyes like a flame of fire, and whose feet are like burnished bronze:

19 "I know your works—your love, faith, service, and patient endurance. I know that your last works are greater than the first. 20 But I have this against you: you tolerate that woman Jezebel, who calls herself a prophet and is teaching and beguiling my servants[i] to practice fornication and to eat food sacrificed to idols. 21 I gave her time to repent, but she refuses to repent of her fornication. 22 Beware, I am throwing her on a bed, and those who commit adultery with her I am throwing into great distress, unless they repent of her doings; 23 and I will strike her children dead. And all the churches will know that I am the one who searches minds and hearts, and I will give to each of you

as your works deserve. 24 But to the rest of you in Thyatira, who do not hold this teaching, who have not learned what some call 'the deep things of Satan,' to you I say, I do not lay on you any other burden; 25 only hold fast to what you have until I come. 26 To everyone who conquers and continues to do my works to the end,

I will give authority over the
        nations;
27   to rule[j] them with an iron rod,
          as when clay pots are
            shattered—

28 even as I also received authority from my Father. To the one who conquers I will also give the morning star. 29 Let anyone who has an ear listen to what the Spirit is saying to the churches.

3 "And to the angel of the church in Sardis write: These are the words of him who has the seven spirits of God and the seven stars:

"I know your works; you have a name of being alive, but you are dead. 2 Wake up, and strengthen what remains and is on the point of death, for I have not found your works perfect in the sight of my God. 3 Remember then what you received and heard; obey it, and repent. If you do not wake up, I will come like a thief, and you will not know at what hour I will come to you. 4 Yet you have still a few persons in Sardis who have not soiled their clothes; they will walk with me, dressed in white, for they are worthy. 5 If you conquer, you will be clothed like them in white robes, and I will not blot your name out of the book of life; I will confess your name before my Father and before his angels. 6 Let anyone who has an ear listen to what the Spirit is saying to the churches.

7 "And to the angel of the church in Philadelphia write:
      These are the words of the holy
          one, the true one,
        who has the key of David,
        who opens and no one will
            shut,
        who shuts and no one opens:
8 "I know your works. Look, I have set before you an open door, which no one is able to shut. I

[h]Or *deny my faith*   [i]Gk *slaves*   [j]Or *to shepherd*

know that you have but little power, and yet you have kept my word and have not denied my name. 9 I will make those of the synagogue of Satan who say that they are Jews and are not, but are lying—I will make them come and bow down before your feet, and they will learn that I have loved you. 10 Because you have kept my word of patient endurance, I will keep you from the hour of trial that is coming on the whole world to test the inhabitants of the earth. 11 I am coming soon; hold fast to what you have, so that no one may seize your crown. 12 If you conquer, I will make you a pillar in the temple of my God; you will never go out of it. I will write on you the name of my God, and the name of the city of my God, the new Jerusalem that comes down from my God out of heaven, and my own new name. 13 Let anyone who has an ear listen to what the Spirit is saying to the churches.

14 "And to the angel of the church in Laodicea write: The words of the Amen, the faithful and true witness, the origin[k] of God's creation:

15 "I know your works; you are neither cold nor hot. I wish that you were either cold or hot. 16 So, because you are lukewarm, and neither cold nor hot, I am about to spit you out of my mouth. 17 For you say, 'I am rich, I have prospered, and I need nothing.' You do not realize that you are wretched, pitiable, poor, blind, and naked. 18 Therefore I counsel you to buy from me gold refined by fire so that you may be rich; and white robes to clothe you and to keep the shame of your nakedness from being seen; and salve to anoint your eyes so that you may see. 19 I reprove and discipline those whom I love. Be earnest, therefore, and repent. 20 Listen! I am standing at the door, knocking; if you hear my voice and open the door, I will come in to you and eat with you, and you with me. 21 To the one who conquers I will give a place with me on my throne, just as I myself conquered and sat down with my Father on his throne. 22 Let anyone who has an ear listen to what the Spirit is saying to the churches."

4 After this I looked, and there in heaven a door stood open! And the first voice, which I had heard speaking to me like a trumpet, said, "Come up here, and I will show you what must take place after this." 2 At once I was in the spir-

it,[l] and there in heaven stood a throne, with one seated on the throne! 3 And the one seated there looks like jasper and carnelian, and around the throne is a rainbow that looks like an emerald. 4 Around the throne are twenty-four thrones, and seated on the thrones are twenty-four elders, dressed in white robes, with golden crowns on their heads. 5 Coming from the throne are flashes of lightning, and rumblings and peals of thunder, and in front of the throne burn seven flaming torches, which are the seven spirits of God; 6 and in front of the throne there is something like a sea of glass, like crystal.

Around the throne, and on each side of the throne, are four living creatures, full of eyes in front and behind: 7 the first living creature like a lion, the second living creature like an ox, the third living creature with a face like a human face, and the fourth living creature like a flying eagle. 8 And the four living creatures, each of them with six wings, are full of eyes all around and inside. Day and night without ceasing they sing,

> "Holy, holy, holy,
> the Lord God the Almighty,
> who was and is and is to
> come."

9 And whenever the living creatures give glory and honor and thanks to the one who is seated on the throne, who lives forever and ever, 10 the twenty-four elders fall before the one who is seated on the throne and worship the one who lives forever and ever; they cast their crowns before the throne, singing,

11   "You are worthy, our Lord and
> God,
> to receive glory and honor and
> power,
> for you created all things,
> and by your will they existed
> and were created."

5 Then I saw in the right hand of the one seated on the throne a scroll written on the inside and on the back, sealed[m] with seven seals; 2 and I saw a mighty angel proclaiming with a loud voice, "Who is worthy to open the scroll and break its seals?" 3 And no one in heaven or on earth or under the earth was able to open the scroll or to

[k]Or *beginning*   [l]Or *in the Spirit*   [m]Or *written on the inside, and sealed on the back*

look into it. 4 And I began to weep bitterly because no one was found worthy to open the scroll or to look into it. 5 Then one of the elders said to me, "Do not weep. See, the Lion of the tribe of Judah, the Root of David, has conquered, so that he can open the scroll and its seven seals."

6 Then I saw between the throne and the four living creatures and among the elders a Lamb standing as if it had been slaughtered, having seven horns and seven eyes, which are the seven spirits of God sent out into all the earth. 7 He went and took the scroll from the right hand of the one who was seated on the throne. 8 When he had taken the scroll, the four living creatures and the twenty-four elders fell before the Lamb, each holding a harp and golden bowls full of incense, which are the prayers of the saints. 9 They sing a new song:

> "You are worthy to take the scroll
>   and to open its seals,
> for you were slaughtered and by
>   your blood you ransomed
>   for God
>   saints from[n] every tribe and
>   language and people and
>   nation;
> 10   you have made them to be a
>   kingdom and priests
>   serving[o] our God,
>   and they will reign on earth."

11 Then I looked, and I heard the voice of many angels surrounding the throne and the living creatures and the elders; they numbered myriads of myriads and thousands of thousands, 12 singing with full voice,

> "Worthy is the Lamb that was
>   slaughtered
> to receive power and wealth and
>   wisdom and might
> and honor and glory and
>   blessing!"

13 Then I heard every creature in heaven and on earth and under the earth and in the sea, and all that is in them, singing,

> "To the one seated on the throne
>   and to the Lamb
> be blessing and honor and glory
>   and might
> forever and ever!"

14 And the four living creatures said, "Amen!" And the elders fell down and worshiped.

6 Then I saw the Lamb open one of the seven seals, and I heard one of the four living creatures call out, as with a voice of thunder, "Come!"[p] 2 I looked, and there was a white horse! Its rider had a bow; a crown was given to him, and he came out conquering and to conquer.

3 When he opened the second seal, I heard the second living creature call out, "Come!"[p] 4 And out came[q] another horse, bright red; its rider was permitted to take peace from the earth, so that people would slaughter one another; and he was given a great sword.

5 When he opened the third seal, I heard the third living creature call out, "Come!"[p] I looked, and there was a black horse! Its rider held a pair of scales in his hand, 6 and I heard what seemed to be a voice in the midst of the four living creatures saying, "A quart of wheat for a day's pay,[r] and three quarts of barley for a day's pay,[r] but do not damage the olive oil and the wine!"

7 When he opened the fourth seal, I heard the voice of the fourth living creature call out, "Come!"[p] 8 I looked and there was a pale green horse! Its rider's name was Death, and Hades followed with him; they were given authority over a fourth of the earth, to kill with sword, famine, and pestilence, and by the wild animals of the earth.

9 When he opened the fifth seal, I saw under the altar the souls of those who had been slaughtered for the word of God and for the testimony they had given; 10 they cried out with a loud voice, "Sovereign Lord, holy and true, how long will it be before you judge and avenge our blood on the inhabitants of the earth?" 11 They were each given a white robe and told to rest a little longer, until the number would be complete both of their fellow servants[s] and of their brothers and sisters,[t] who were soon to be killed as they themselves had been killed.

12 When he opened the sixth seal, I looked, and there came a great earthquake; the sun became black as sackcloth, the full moon became like blood, 13 and the stars of the sky fell to the earth as the fig tree drops its winter fruit when shaken

[n]Gk *ransomed for God from* [o]Gk *priests to* [p]Or *"Go!"* [q]Or *went*
[r]Gk *a denarius* [s]Gk *slaves* [t]Gk *brothers*

by a gale. 14 The sky vanished like a scroll rolling itself up, and every mountain and island was removed from its place. 15 Then the kings of the earth and the magnates and the generals and the rich and the powerful, and everyone, slave and free, hid in the caves and among the rocks of the mountains, 16 calling to the mountains and rocks, "Fall on us and hide us from the face of the one seated on the throne and from the wrath of the Lamb; 17 for the great day of their wrath has come, and who is able to stand?"

7 After this I saw four angels standing at the four corners of the earth, holding back the four winds of the earth so that no wind could blow on earth or sea or against any tree. 2 I saw another angel ascending from the rising of the sun, having the seal of the living God, and he called with a loud voice to the four angels who had been given power to damage earth and sea, 3 saying, "Do not damage the earth or the sea or the trees, until we have marked the servants[u] of our God with a seal on their foreheads."

4 And I heard the number of those who were sealed, one hundred forty-four thousand, sealed out of every tribe of the people of Israel:

5 From the tribe of Judah twelve thousand sealed,

from the tribe of Reuben twelve thousand,
from the tribe of Gad twelve thousand,

6 from the tribe of Asher twelve thousand,
from the tribe of Naphtali twelve thousand,
from the tribe of Manasseh twelve thousand,

7 from the tribe of Simeon twelve thousand,
from the tribe of Levi twelve thousand,
from the tribe of Issachar twelve thousand,

8 from the tribe of Zebulun twelve thousand,
from the tribe of Joseph twelve thousand,
from the tribe of Benjamin twelve thousand sealed.

9 After this I looked, and there was a great multitude that no one could count, from every nation, from all tribes and peoples and languages, standing before the throne and before the Lamb, robed in white, with palm branches in their hands. 10 They cried out in a loud voice, saying,

"Salvation belongs to our God
who is seated on the
throne, and to the Lamb!"

11 And all the angels stood around the throne and around the elders and the four living creatures, and they fell on their faces before the throne and worshiped God, 12 singing,

"Amen! Blessing and glory and wisdom
and thanksgiving and honor
and power and might
be to our God forever and ever! Amen."

13 Then one of the elders addressed me, saying, "Who are these, robed in white, and where have they come from?" 14 I said to him, "Sir, you are the one that knows." Then he said to me, "These are they who have come out of the great ordeal; they have washed their robes and made them white in the blood of the Lamb.

15	For this reason they are before the
throne of God,
and worship him day and night
within his temple,
and the one who is seated on
the throne will shelter
them.

16	They will hunger no more, and
thirst no more;
the sun will not strike them,
nor any scorching heat;

17	for the Lamb at the center of the
throne will be their
shepherd,
and he will guide them to
springs of the water of life,
and God will wipe away every
tear from their eyes."

8 When the Lamb opened the seventh seal, there was silence in heaven for about half an hour. 2 And I saw the seven angels who stand before God, and seven trumpets were given to them.

3 Another angel with a golden censer came and stood at the altar; he was given a great quantity of incense to offer with the prayers of all the saints on the golden altar that is before the throne. 4 And the smoke of the incense, with the prayers of the saints, rose before God from the hand of the angel. 5 Then the angel took the censer and filled it with fire from the altar and threw it on the earth; and there were peals of thunder, rumblings, flashes of lightning, and an earthquake.

[u] Gk *slaves*

6 Now the seven angels who had the seven trumpets made ready to blow them.

7 The first angel blew his trumpet, and there came hail and fire, mixed with blood, and they were hurled to the earth; and a third of the earth was burned up, and a third of the trees were burned up, and all green grass was burned up.

8 The second angel blew his trumpet, and something like a great mountain, burning with fire, was thrown into the sea. 9 A third of the sea became blood, a third of the living creatures in the sea died, and a third of the ships were destroyed.

10 The third angel blew his trumpet, and a great star fell from heaven, blazing like a torch, and it fell on a third of the rivers and on the springs of water. 11 The name of the star is Wormwood. A third of the waters became wormwood, and many died from the water, because it was made bitter.

12 The fourth angel blew his trumpet, and a third of the sun was struck, and a third of the moon, and a third of the stars, so that a third of their light was darkened; a third of the day was kept from shining, and likewise the night.

13 Then I looked, and I heard an eagle crying with a loud voice as it flew in midheaven, "Woe, woe, woe to the inhabitants of the earth, at the blasts of the other trumpets that the three angels are about to blow!"

9 And the fifth angel blew his trumpet, and I saw a star that had fallen from heaven to earth, and he was given the key to the shaft of the bottomless pit; 2 he opened the shaft of the bottomless pit, and from the shaft rose smoke like the smoke of a great furnace, and the sun and the air were darkened with the smoke from the shaft. 3 Then from the smoke came locusts on the earth, and they were given authority like the authority of scorpions of the earth. 4 They were told not to damage the grass of the earth or any green growth or any tree, but only those people who do not have the seal of God on their foreheads. 5 They were allowed to torture them for five months, but not to kill them, and their torture was like the torture of a scorpion when it stings someone. 6 And in those days people will seek death but will not find it; they will long to die, but death will flee from them.

7 In appearance the locusts were like horses equipped for battle. On their heads were what looked like crowns of gold; their faces were like human faces, 8 their hair like women's hair, and their teeth like lions' teeth; 9 they had scales like iron breastplates, and the noise of their wings was like the noise of many chariots with horses rushing into battle. 10 They have tails like scorpions, with stingers, and in their tails is their power to harm people for five months. 11 They have as king over them the angel of the bottomless pit; his name in Hebrew is Abaddon,[v] and in Greek he is called Apollyon.[w]

12 The first woe has passed. There are still two woes to come.

13 Then the sixth angel blew his trumpet, and I heard a voice from the four[x] horns of the golden altar before God, 14 saying to the sixth angel who had the trumpet, "Release the four angels who are bound at the great river Euphrates." 15 So the four angels were released, who had been held ready for the hour, the day, the month, and the year, to kill a third of humankind. 16 The number of the troops of cavalry was two hundred million; I heard their number. 17 And this was how I saw the horses in my vision: the riders wore breastplates the color of fire and of sapphire[y] and of sulfur; the heads of the horses were like lions' heads, and fire and smoke and sulfur came out of their mouths. 18 By these three plagues a third of humankind was killed, by the fire and smoke and sulfur coming out of their mouths. 19 For the power of the horses is in their mouths and in their tails; their tails are like serpents, having heads; and with them they inflict harm.

20 The rest of humankind, who were not killed by these plagues, did not repent of the works of their hands or give up worshiping demons and idols of gold and silver and bronze and stone and wood, which cannot see or hear or walk. 21 And they did not repent of their murders or their sorceries or their fornication or their thefts.

10 And I saw another mighty angel coming down from heaven, wrapped in a cloud, with a rainbow over his head; his face was like the sun, and his legs like pillars of fire. 2 He held a little scroll open in his hand. Setting his right foot on the sea and his left foot on the land, 3 he gave a great shout, like a lion roaring. And when he

---

[v]That is, *Destruction*   [w]That is, *Destroyer*   [x]Other ancient authorities lack *four*   [y]Gk *hyacinth*

shouted, the seven thunders sounded. 4 And when the seven thunders had sounded, I was about to write, but I heard a voice from heaven saying, "Seal up what the seven thunders have said, and do not write it down." 5 Then the angel whom I saw standing on the sea and the land

> raised his right hand to heaven
6 and swore by him who lives
> forever and ever,

who created heaven and what is in it, the earth and what is in it, and the sea and what is in it: "There will be no more delay, 7 but in the days when the seventh angel is to blow his trumpet, the mystery of God will be fulfilled, as he announced to his servants[z] the prophets."

8 Then the voice that I had heard from heaven spoke to me again, saying, "Go, take the scroll that is open in the hand of the angel who is standing on the sea and on the land." 9 So I went to the angel and told him to give me the little scroll; and he said to me, "Take it, and eat; it will be bitter to your stomach, but sweet as honey in your mouth." 10 So I took the little scroll from the hand of the angel and ate it; it was sweet as honey in my mouth, but when I had eaten it, my stomach was made bitter.

11 Then they said to me, "You must prophesy again about many peoples and nations and languages and kings."

11 Then I was given a measuring rod like a staff, and I was told, "Come and measure the temple of God and the altar and those who worship there, 2 but do not measure the court outside the temple; leave that out, for it is given over to the nations, and they will trample over the holy city for forty-two months. 3 And I will grant my two witnesses authority to prophesy for one thousand two hundred sixty days, wearing sackcloth."

4 These are the two olive trees and the two lampstands that stand before the Lord of the earth. 5 And if anyone wants to harm them, fire pours from their mouth and consumes their foes; anyone who wants to harm them must be killed in this manner. 6 They have authority to shut the sky, so that no rain may fall during the days of their prophesying, and they have authority over the waters to turn them into blood, and to strike the earth with every kind of plague, as often as they desire.

7 When they have finished their testimony, the beast that comes up from the bottomless pit will make war on them and conquer them and kill them, 8 and their dead bodies will lie in the street of the great city that is prophetically[a] called Sodom and Egypt, where also their Lord was crucified. 9 For three and a half days members of the peoples and tribes and languages and nations will gaze at their dead bodies and refuse to let them be placed in a tomb; 10 and the inhabitants of the earth will gloat over them and celebrate and exchange presents, because these two prophets had been a torment to the inhabitants of the earth.

11 But after the three and a half days, the breath[b] of life from God entered them, and they stood on their feet, and those who saw them were terrified. 12 Then they[c] heard a loud voice from heaven saying to them, "Come up here!" And they went up to heaven in a cloud while their enemies watched them. 13 At that moment there was a great earthquake, and a tenth of the city fell; seven thousand people were killed in the earthquake, and the rest were terrified and gave glory to the God of heaven.

14 The second woe has passed. The third woe is coming very soon.

15 Then the seventh angel blew his trumpet, and there were loud voices in heaven, saying,

> "The kingdom of the world has
> > become the kingdom of our
> Lord
> > and of his Messiah,[d]
> and he will reign forever and
> > ever."

16 Then the twenty-four elders who sit on their thrones before God fell on their faces and worshiped God, 17 singing,

> "We give you thanks, Lord God
> > Almighty,
> who are and who were,
> for you have taken your great
> > power
> and begun to reign.
18 The nations raged,
> > but your wrath has come,
> > and the time for judging the
> > > dead,

---

[z]Gk *slaves*   [a]Or *allegorically*; Gk *spiritually*   [b]Or *the spirit*   [c]Other ancient authorities read *I*   [d]Gk *Christ*

for rewarding your servants,[e] the
prophets
and saints and all who fear your
name,
both small and great,
and for destroying those who
destroy the earth."

19 Then God's temple in heaven was opened, and the ark of his covenant was seen within his temple; and there were flashes of lightning, rumblings, peals of thunder, an earthquake, and heavy hail.

12 A great portent appeared in heaven: a woman clothed with the sun, with the moon under her feet, and on her head a crown of twelve stars. 2 She was pregnant and was crying out in birth pangs, in the agony of giving birth. 3 Then another portent appeared in heaven: a great red dragon, with seven heads and ten horns, and seven diadems on his heads. 4 His tail swept down a third of the stars of heaven and threw them to the earth. Then the dragon stood before the woman who was about to bear a child, so that he might devour her child as soon as it was born. 5 And she gave birth to a son, a male child, who is to rule[f] all the nations with a rod of iron. But her child was snatched away and taken to God and to his throne; 6 and the woman fled into the wilderness, where she has a place prepared by God, so that there she can be nourished for one thousand two hundred sixty days.

7 And war broke out in heaven; Michael and his angels fought against the dragon. The dragon and his angels fought back, 8 but they were defeated, and there was no longer any place for them in heaven. 9 The great dragon was thrown down, that ancient serpent, who is called the Devil and Satan, the deceiver of the whole world—he was thrown down to the earth, and his angels were thrown down with him.

10 Then I heard a loud voice in heaven, proclaiming,

"Now have come the salvation
and the power
and the kingdom of our God
and the authority of his
Messiah,[g]
for the accuser of our comrades[h]

has been thrown down,
who accuses them day and night
before our God.
11 But they have conquered him by
the blood of the Lamb
and by the word of their
testimony,
for they did not cling to life even
in the face of death.
12 Rejoice then, you heavens
and those who dwell in them!
But woe to the earth and the sea,
for the devil has come down to
you
with great wrath,
because he knows that his time
is short!"

13 So when the dragon saw that he had been thrown down to the earth, he pursued[i] the woman who had given birth to the male child. 14 But the woman was given the two wings of the great eagle, so that she could fly from the serpent into the wilderness, to her place where she is nourished for a time, and times, and half a time. 15 Then from his mouth the serpent poured water like a river after the woman, to sweep her away with the flood. 16 But the earth came to the help of the woman; it opened its mouth and swallowed the river that the dragon had poured from his mouth. 17 Then the dragon was angry with the woman, and went off to make war on the rest of her children, those who keep the commandments of God and hold the testimony of Jesus.

18 Then the dragon[j] took his stand on the sand of the seashore.

13 And I saw a beast rising out of the sea, having ten horns and seven heads; and on its horns were ten diadems, and on its heads were blasphemous names. 2 And the beast that I saw was like a leopard, its feet were like a bear's, and its mouth was like a lion's mouth. And the dragon gave it his power and his throne and great authority. 3 One of its heads seemed to have received a death-blow, but its mortal wound[k] had been healed. In amazement the whole earth followed the beast. 4 They worshiped the dragon, for he

[e]Gk *slaves* [f]Or *to shepherd* [g]Gk *Christ* [h]Gk *brothers*
[i]Or *persecuted* [j]Gk *Then he*; other ancient authorities read *Then I stood* [k]Gk *the plague of its death*

had given his authority to the beast, and they worshiped the beast, saying, "Who is like the beast, and who can fight against it?"

5 The beast was given a mouth uttering haughty and blasphemous words, and it was allowed to exercise authority for forty-two months. 6 It opened its mouth to utter blasphemies against God, blaspheming his name and his dwelling, that is, those who dwell in heaven. 7 Also it was allowed to make war on the saints and to conquer them.[l] It was given authority over every tribe and people and language and nation, 8 and all the inhabitants of the earth will worship it, everyone whose name has not been written from the foundation of the world in the book of life of the Lamb that was slaughtered.[m]

9 Let anyone who has an ear listen:
10   If you are to be taken captive,
              into captivity you go;
         if you kill with the sword,
              with the sword you must be
                   killed.
Here is a call for the endurance and faith of the saints.

11 Then I saw another beast that rose out of the earth; it had two horns like a lamb and it spoke like a dragon. 12 It exercises all the authority of the first beast on its behalf, and it makes the earth and its inhabitants worship the first beast, whose mortal wound[n] had been healed. 13 It performs great signs, even making fire come down from heaven to earth in the sight of all; 14 and by the signs that it is allowed to perform on behalf of the beast, it deceives the inhabitants of earth, telling them to make an image for the beast that had been wounded by the sword[o] and yet lived; 15 and it was allowed to give breath[p] to the image of the beast so that the image of the beast could even speak and cause those who would not worship the image of the beast to be killed. 16 Also it causes all, both small and great, both rich and poor, both free and slave, to be marked on the right hand or the forehead, 17 so that no one can buy or sell who does not have the mark, that is, the name of the beast or the number of its name. 18 This calls for wisdom: let anyone with understanding calculate the number of the beast, for it is the number of a person. Its number is six hundred sixty-six.[q]

14 Then I looked, and there was the Lamb, standing on Mount Zion! And with him were one hundred forty-four thousand who had his name and his Father's name written on their foreheads. 2 And I heard a voice from heaven like the sound of many waters and like the sound of loud thunder; the voice I heard was like the sound of harpists playing on their harps, 3 and they sing a new song before the throne and before the four living creatures and before the elders. No one could learn that song except the one hundred forty-four thousand who have been redeemed from the earth. 4 It is these who have not defiled themselves with women, for they are virgins; these follow the Lamb wherever he goes. They have been redeemed from humankind as first fruits for God and the Lamb, 5 and in their mouth no lie was found; they are blameless.

6 Then I saw another angel flying in midheaven, with an eternal gospel to proclaim to those who live[r] on the earth—to every nation and tribe and language and people. 7 He said in a loud voice, "Fear God and give him glory, for the hour of his judgment has come; and worship him who made heaven and earth, the sea and the springs of water."

8 Then another angel, a second, followed, saying, "Fallen, fallen is Babylon the great! She has made all nations drink of the wine of the wrath of her fornication."

9 Then another angel, a third, followed them, crying with a loud voice, "Those who worship the beast and its image, and receive a mark on their foreheads or on their hands, 10 they will also drink the wine of God's wrath, poured unmixed into the cup of his anger, and they will be tormented with fire and sulfur in the presence of the holy angels and in the presence of the Lamb. 11 And the smoke of their torment goes up forever and ever. There is no rest day or night for those who worship the beast and its image and for anyone who receives the mark of its name."

12 Here is a call for the endurance of the saints, those who keep the commandments of God and hold fast to the faith of[s] Jesus.

[l]Other ancient authorities lack this sentence   [m]Or *written in the book of life of the Lamb that was slaughtered from the foundation of the world*   [n]Gk *whose plague of its death*   [o]Or *that had received the plague of the sword*   [p]Or *spirit*   [q]Other ancient authorities read *six hundred sixteen*   [r]Gk *sit*   [s]Or *to their faith in*

13 And I heard a voice from heaven saying, "Write this: Blessed are the dead who from now on die in the Lord." "Yes," says the Spirit, "they will rest from their labors, for their deeds follow them."

14 Then I looked, and there was a white cloud, and seated on the cloud was one like the Son of Man, with a golden crown on his head, and a sharp sickle in his hand! 15 Another angel came out of the temple, calling with a loud voice to the one who sat on the cloud, "Use your sickle and reap, for the hour to reap has come, because the harvest of the earth is fully ripe." 16 So the one who sat on the cloud swung his sickle over the earth, and the earth was reaped.

17 Then another angel came out of the temple in heaven, and he too had a sharp sickle. 18 Then another angel came out from the altar, the angel who has authority over fire, and he called with a loud voice to him who had the sharp sickle, "Use your sharp sickle and gather the clusters of the vine of the earth, for its grapes are ripe." 19 So the angel swung his sickle over the earth and gathered the vintage of the earth, and he threw it into the great wine press of the wrath of God. 20 And the wine press was trodden outside the city, and blood flowed from the wine press, as high as a horse's bridle, for a distance of about two hundred miles.[t]

15 Then I saw another portent in heaven, great and amazing: seven angels with seven plagues, which are the last, for with them the wrath of God is ended.

2 And I saw what appeared to be a sea of glass mixed with fire, and those who had conquered the beast and its image and the number of its name, standing beside the sea of glass with harps of God in their hands. 3 And they sing the song of Moses, the servant[u] of God, and the song of the Lamb:

"Great and amazing are your
deeds,
Lord God the Almighty!
Just and true are your ways,
King of the nations![v]
4 Lord, who will not fear
and glorify your name?
For you alone are holy.
All nations will come
and worship before you,
for your judgments have been
revealed."

5 After this I looked, and the temple of the tent[w] of witness in heaven was opened, 6 and out of the temple came the seven angels with the seven plagues, robed in pure bright linen,[x] with golden sashes across their chests. 7 Then one of the four living creatures gave the seven angels seven golden bowls full of the wrath of God, who lives forever and ever; 8 and the temple was filled with smoke from the glory of God and from his power, and no one could enter the temple until the seven plagues of the seven angels were ended.

16 Then I heard a loud voice from the temple telling the seven angels, "Go and pour out on the earth the seven bowls of the wrath of God."

2 So the first angel went and poured his bowl on the earth, and a foul and painful sore came on those who had the mark of the beast and who worshiped its image.

3 The second angel poured his bowl into the sea, and it became like the blood of a corpse, and every living thing in the sea died.

4 The third angel poured his bowl into the rivers and the springs of water, and they became blood. 5 And I heard the angel of the waters say,

"You are just, O Holy One, who
are and were,
for you have judged these
things;
6 because they shed the blood of
saints and prophets,
you have given them blood to
drink.
It is what they deserve!"
7 And I heard the altar respond,
"Yes, O Lord God, the Almighty,
your judgments are true and
just!"

8 The fourth angel poured his bowl on the sun, and it was allowed to scorch people with fire; 9 they were scorched by the fierce heat, but they cursed the name of God, who had authority over these plagues, and they did not repent and give him glory.

10 The fifth angel poured his bowl on the throne of the beast, and its kingdom was plunged into dark-

[t]Gk *one thousand six hundred stadia*   [u]Gk *slave*   [v]Other ancient authorities read *the ages*   [w]Or *tabernacle*   [x]Other ancient authorities read *stone*

ness; people gnawed their tongues in agony, 11 and cursed the God of heaven because of their pains and sores, and they did not repent of their deeds.

12 The sixth angel poured his bowl on the great river Euphrates, and its water was dried up in order to prepare the way for the kings from the east. 13 And I saw three foul spirits like frogs coming from the mouth of the dragon, from the mouth of the beast, and from the mouth of the false prophet. 14 These are demonic spirits, performing signs, who go abroad to the kings of the whole world, to assemble them for battle on the great day of God the Almighty. 15 ("See, I am coming like a thief! Blessed is the one who stays awake and is clothed,[y] not going about naked and exposed to shame.") 16 And they assembled them at the place that in Hebrew is called Harmagedon.

17 The seventh angel poured his bowl into the air, and a loud voice came out of the temple, from the throne, saying, "It is done!" 18 And there came flashes of lightning, rumblings, peals of thunder, and a violent earthquake, such as had not occurred since people were upon the earth, so violent was that earthquake. 19 The great city was split into three parts, and the cities of the nations fell. God remembered great Babylon and gave her the wine-cup of the fury of his wrath. 20 And every island fled away, and no mountains were to be found; 21 and huge hailstones, each weighing about a hundred pounds,[z] dropped from heaven on people, until they cursed God for the plague of the hail, so fearful was that plague.

17 Then one of the seven angels who had the seven bowls came and said to me, "Come, I will show you the judgment of the great whore who is seated on many waters, 2 with whom the kings of the earth have committed fornication, and with the wine of whose fornication the inhabitants of the earth have become drunk." 3 So he carried me away in the spirit[a] into a wilderness, and I saw a woman sitting on a scarlet beast that was full of blasphemous names, and it had seven heads and ten horns. 4 The woman was clothed in purple and scarlet, and adorned with gold and jewels and pearls, holding in her hand a golden cup full of abominations and the impurities of her fornication; 5 and on her forehead was writ-

ten a name, a mystery: "Babylon the great, mother of whores and of earth's abominations." 6 And I saw that the woman was drunk with the blood of the saints and the blood of the witnesses to Jesus.

When I saw her, I was greatly amazed. 7 But the angel said to me, "Why are you so amazed? I will tell you the mystery of the woman, and of the beast with seven heads and ten horns that carries her. 8 The beast that you saw was, and is not, and is about to ascend from the bottomless pit and go to destruction. And the inhabitants of the earth, whose names have not been written in the book of life from the foundation of the world, will be amazed when they see the beast, because it was and is not and is to come.

9 "This calls for a mind that has wisdom: the seven heads are seven mountains on which the woman is seated; also, they are seven kings, 10 of whom five have fallen, one is living, and the other has not yet come; and when he comes, he must remain only a little while. 11 As for the beast that was and is not, it is an eighth but it belongs to the seven, and it goes to destruction. 12 And the ten horns that you saw are ten kings who have not yet received a kingdom, but they are to receive authority as kings for one hour, together with the beast. 13 These are united in yielding their power and authority to the beast; 14 they will make war on the Lamb, and the Lamb will conquer them, for he is Lord of lords and King of kings, and those with him are called and chosen and faithful."

15 And he said to me, "The waters that you saw, where the whore is seated, are peoples and multitudes and nations and languages. 16 And the ten horns that you saw, they and the beast will hate the whore; they will make her desolate and naked; they will devour her flesh and burn her up with fire. 17 For God has put it into their hearts to carry out his purpose by agreeing to give their kingdom to the beast, until the words of God will be fulfilled. 18 The woman you saw is the great city that rules over the kings of the earth."

18 After this I saw another angel coming down from heaven, having great authority; and the earth was made bright with his splendor. 2 He called out with a mighty voice,

---

[y]Gk *and keeps his robes*   [z]Gk *weighing about a talent*   [a]Or *in the Spirit*

"Fallen, fallen is Babylon the great!
   It has become a dwelling place
     of demons,
a haunt of every foul spirit,
   a haunt of every foul bird,
   a haunt of every foul and hateful
     beast.[b]

3 For all the nations have drunk[c]
   of the wine of the wrath of her
     fornication,
  and the kings of the earth have
     committed fornication with
     her,
  and the merchants of the earth
     have grown rich from the
     power[d] of her luxury."

4 Then I heard another voice from heaven
saying,

"Come out of her, my people,
   so that you do not take part in
     her sins,
and so that you do not share
   in her plagues;
5 for her sins are heaped high as
     heaven,
   and God has remembered her
     iniquities.
6 Render to her as she herself has
     rendered,
   and repay her double for her
     deeds;
   mix a double draught for her in
     the cup she mixed.
7 As she glorified herself and lived
     luxuriously,
   so give her a like measure of
     torment and grief.
Since in her heart she says,
   'I rule as a queen;
I am no widow,
   and I will never see grief,'
8 therefore her plagues will come in
     a single day—
   pestilence and mourning and
     famine—
and she will be burned with fire;
   for mighty is the Lord God who
     judges her."

9 And the kings of the earth, who committed fornication and lived in luxury with her, will weep and wail over her when they see the smoke of her burning; 10 they will stand far off, in fear of her torment, and say,

"Alas, alas, the great city,
   Babylon, the mighty city!
For in one hour your judgment
     has come."

11 And the merchants of the earth weep and mourn for her, since no one buys their cargo anymore, 12 cargo of gold, silver, jewels and pearls, fine linen, purple, silk and scarlet, all kinds of scented wood, all articles of ivory, all articles of costly wood, bronze, iron, and marble, 13 cinnamon, spice, incense, myrrh, frankincense, wine, olive oil, choice flour and wheat, cattle and sheep, horses and chariots, slaves—and human lives.[e]

14   "The fruit for which your soul
       longed
       has gone from you,
and all your dainties and your
       splendor
   are lost to you,
     never to be found again!"

15 The merchants of these wares, who gained wealth from her, will stand far off, in fear of her torment, weeping and mourning aloud,

16   "Alas, alas, the great city,
   clothed in fine linen,
     in purple and scarlet,
   adorned with gold,
     with jewels, and with pearls!
17   For in one hour all this wealth has
     been laid waste!"

And all shipmasters and seafarers, sailors and all whose trade is on the sea, stood far off 18 and cried out as they saw the smoke of her burning,

"What city was like the great
     city?"

19 And they threw dust on their heads, as they wept and mourned, crying out,

"Alas, alas, the great city,
   where all who had ships at sea
   grew rich by her wealth!

[b]Other ancient authorities lack the words *a haunt of every foul beast* and attach the words *and hateful* to the previous line so as to read *a haunt of every foul and hateful bird* [c]Other ancient authorities read *She has made all nations drink* [d]Or *resources* [e]Or *chariots, and human bodies and souls*

For in one hour she has been laid
          waste."

20   Rejoice over her, O heaven,
          you saints and apostles and
              prophets!
      For God has given judgment for
          you against her.

21 Then a mighty angel took up a stone like a
great millstone and threw it into the sea, saying,
      "With such violence Babylon the
          great city
      will be thrown down,
      and will be found no more;

22   and the sound of harpists and
              minstrels and of flutists and
              trumpeters
      will be heard in you no more;
      and an artisan of any trade
          will be found in you no more;
      and the sound of the millstone
          will be heard in you no more;

23   and the light of a lamp
          will shine in you no more;
      and the voice of bridegroom and
              bride
          will be heard in you no more;
      for your merchants were the
              magnates of the earth,
          and all nations were deceived by
              your sorcery.

24   And in you[f] was found the blood
              of prophets and of saints,
          and of all who have been
              slaughtered on earth."

19 After this I heard what seemed to be the
    loud voice of a great multitude in heav-
en, saying,
      "Hallelujah!
      Salvation and glory and power to
          our God,

2   for his judgments are true and
              just;
      he has judged the great whore
          who corrupted the earth with
              her fornication,
      and he has avenged on her the
          blood of his servants."[g]

3 Once more they said,
      "Hallelujah!

The smoke goes up from her
          forever and ever."

4 And the twenty-four elders and the four living
creatures fell down and worshiped God who is
seated on the throne, saying,
      "Amen. Hallelujah!"

5 And from the throne came a voice saying,
      "Praise our God,
          all you his servants,[g]
      and all who fear him,
          small and great."

6 Then I heard what seemed to be the voice of a
great multitude, like the sound of many waters and
like the sound of mighty thunderpeals, crying out,
      "Hallelujah!
      For the Lord our God
          the Almighty reigns.

7   Let us rejoice and exult
          and give him the glory,
      for the marriage of the Lamb has
              come,
          and his bride has made herself
              ready;

8   to her it has been granted to be
              clothed
          with fine linen, bright and
              pure"—

for the fine linen is the righteous deeds of the
saints.

9 And the angel said[h] to me, "Write this:
Blessed are those who are invited to the marriage
supper of the Lamb." And he said to me, "These
are true words of God." 10 Then I fell down at
his feet to worship him, but he said to me, "You
must not do that! I am a fellow servant[i] with you
and your comrades[j] who hold the testimony of Jesus.[k] Worship God! For the testimony of
Jesus[k] is the spirit of prophecy."

11 Then I saw heaven opened, and there was a
white horse! Its rider is called Faithful and True,
and in righteousness he judges and makes war.
12 His eyes are like a flame of fire, and on his head
are many diadems; and he has a name inscribed
that no one knows but himself. 13 He is clothed in
a robe dipped in[l] blood, and his name is called The

[f]Gk her   [g]Gk slaves   [h]Gk he said   [i]Gk slave   [j]Gk brothers
[k]Or to Jesus   [l]Other ancient authorities read sprinkled with

Word of God. 14 And the armies of heaven, wearing fine linen, white and pure, were following him on white horses. 15 From his mouth comes a sharp sword with which to strike down the nations, and he will rule[m] them with a rod of iron; he will tread the wine press of the fury of the wrath of God the Almighty. 16 On his robe and on his thigh he has a name inscribed, "King of kings and Lord of lords."

17 Then I saw an angel standing in the sun, and with a loud voice he called to all the birds that fly in midheaven, "Come, gather for the great supper of God, 18 to eat the flesh of kings, the flesh of captains, the flesh of the mighty, the flesh of horses and their riders—flesh of all, both free and slave, both small and great." 19 Then I saw the beast and the kings of the earth with their armies gathered to make war against the rider on the horse and against his army. 20 And the beast was captured, and with it the false prophet who had performed in its presence the signs by which he deceived those who had received the mark of the beast and those who worshiped its image. These two were thrown alive into the lake of fire that burns with sulfur. 21 And the rest were killed by the sword of the rider on the horse, the sword that came from his mouth; and all the birds were gorged with their flesh.

20 Then I saw an angel coming down from heaven, holding in his hand the key to the bottomless pit and a great chain. 2 He seized the dragon, that ancient serpent, who is the Devil and Satan, and bound him for a thousand years, 3 and threw him into the pit, and locked and sealed it over him, so that he would deceive the nations no more, until the thousand years were ended. After that he must be let out for a little while.

4 Then I saw thrones, and those seated on them were given authority to judge. I also saw the souls of those who had been beheaded for their testimony to Jesus[n] and for the word of God. They had not worshiped the beast or its image and had not received its mark on their foreheads or their hands. They came to life and reigned with Christ a thousand years. 5 (The rest of the dead did not come to life until the thousand years were ended.) This is the first resurrection. 6 Blessed and holy are those who share in the first resurrection. Over these the second death has no power, but they will

be priests of God and of Christ, and they will reign with him a thousand years.

7 When the thousand years are ended, Satan will be released from his prison 8 and will come out to deceive the nations at the four corners of the earth, Gog and Magog, in order to gather them for battle; they are as numerous as the sands of the sea. 9 They marched up over the breadth of the earth and surrounded the camp of the saints and the beloved city. And fire came down from heaven[o] and consumed them. 10 And the devil who had deceived them was thrown into the lake of fire and sulfur, where the beast and the false prophet were, and they will be tormented day and night forever and ever.

11 Then I saw a great white throne and the one who sat on it; the earth and the heaven fled from his presence, and no place was found for them. 12 And I saw the dead, great and small, standing before the throne, and books were opened. Also another book was opened, the book of life. And the dead were judged according to their works, as recorded in the books. 13 And the sea gave up the dead that were in it, Death and Hades gave up the dead that were in them, and all were judged according to what they had done. 14 Then Death and Hades were thrown into the lake of fire. This is the second death, the lake of fire; 15 and anyone whose name was not found written in the book of life was thrown into the lake of fire.

21 Then I saw a new heaven and a new earth; for the first heaven and the first earth had passed away, and the sea was no more. 2 And I saw the holy city, the new Jerusalem, coming down out of heaven from God, prepared as a bride adorned for her husband. 3 And I heard a loud voice from the throne saying,

"See, the home[p] of God is among
          mortals.
He will dwell[p] with them as their
          God;[q]
they will be his peoples,[r]
and God himself will be with
          them;[s]

---

[m]Or *will shepherd*   [n]Or *for the testimony of Jesus*   [o]Other ancient authorities read *from God, out of heaven,* or *out of heaven from God*   [p]Gk *the tabernacle*   [q]Other ancient authorities lack *as their God*   [r]Other ancient authorities read *people*   [s]Other ancient authorities add *and be their God*

4 he will wipe every tear from their
    eyes.
  Death will be no more;
  mourning and crying and pain will
    be no more,
  for the first things have passed
    away."

5 And the one who was seated on the throne said, "See, I am making all things new." Also he said, "Write this, for these words are trustworthy and true." 6 Then he said to me, "It is done! I am the Alpha and the Omega, the beginning and the end. To the thirsty I will give water as a gift from the spring of the water of life. 7 Those who conquer will inherit these things, and I will be their God and they will be my children. 8 But as for the cowardly, the faithless,[t] the polluted, the murderers, the fornicators, the sorcerers, the idolaters, and all liars, their place will be in the lake that burns with fire and sulfur, which is the second death."

9 Then one of the seven angels who had the seven bowls full of the seven last plagues came and said to me, "Come, I will show you the bride, the wife of the Lamb." 10 And in the spirit[u] he carried me away to a great, high mountain and showed me the holy city Jerusalem coming down out of heaven from God. 11 It has the glory of God and a radiance like a very rare jewel, like jasper, clear as crystal. 12 It has a great, high wall with twelve gates, and at the gates twelve angels, and on the gates are inscribed the names of the twelve tribes of the Israelites; 13 on the east three gates, on the north three gates, on the south three gates, and on the west three gates. 14 And the wall of the city has twelve foundations, and on them are the twelve names of the twelve apostles of the Lamb.

15 The angel[v] who talked to me had a measuring rod of gold to measure the city and its gates and walls. 16 The city lies foursquare, its length the same as its width; and he measured the city with his rod, fifteen hundred miles;[w] its length and width and height are equal. 17 He also measured its wall, one hundred forty-four cubits[x] by human measurement, which the angel was using. 18 The wall is built of jasper, while the city is pure gold, clear as glass. 19 The foundations of the wall of the city are adorned with every jewel; the first was jasper, the second sapphire, the third agate, the fourth emerald, 20 the fifth onyx, the sixth car-

nelian, the seventh chrysolite, the eighth beryl, the ninth topaz, the tenth chrysoprase, the eleventh jacinth, the twelfth amethyst. 21 And the twelve gates are twelve pearls, each of the gates is a single pearl, and the street of the city is pure gold, transparent as glass.

22 I saw no temple in the city, for its temple is the Lord God the Almighty and the Lamb. 23 And the city has no need of sun or moon to shine on it, for the glory of God is its light, and its lamp is the Lamb. 24 The nations will walk by its light, and the kings of the earth will bring their glory into it. 25 Its gates will never be shut by day—and there will be no night there. 26 People will bring into it the glory and the honor of the nations. 27 But nothing unclean will enter it, nor anyone who practices abomination or falsehood, but only those who are written in the Lamb's book of life.

22 Then the angel[y] showed me the river of the water of life, bright as crystal, flowing from the throne of God and of the Lamb 2 through the middle of the street of the city. On either side of the river is the tree of life[z] with its twelve kinds of fruit, producing its fruit each month; and the leaves of the tree are for the healing of the nations. 3 Nothing accursed will be found there any more. But the throne of God and of the Lamb will be in it, and his servants[a] will worship him; 4 they will see his face, and his name will be on their foreheads. 5 And there will be no more night; they need no light of lamp or sun, for the Lord God will be their light, and they will reign forever and ever.

6 And he said to me, "These words are trustworthy and true, for the Lord, the God of the spirits of the prophets, has sent his angel to show his servants[a] what must soon take place."

7 "See, I am coming soon! Blessed is the one who keeps the words of the prophecy of this book."

8 I, John, am the one who heard and saw these things. And when I heard and saw them, I fell down to worship at the feet of the angel who showed them to me; 9 but he said to me, "You

---

[t]Or *the unbelieving* [u]Or *in the Spirit* [v]Gk *He* [w]Gk *twelve thousand stadia* [x]That is, almost seventy-five yards [y]Gk *he* [z]Or *the Lamb.* [2]*In the middle of the street of the city, and on either side of the river, is the tree of life* [a]Gk *slaves*

must not do that! I am a fellow servant[b] with you and your comrades[c] the prophets, and with those who keep the words of this book. Worship God!"

10 And he said to me, "Do not seal up the words of the prophecy of this book, for the time is near. 11 Let the evildoer still do evil, and the filthy still be filthy, and the righteous still do right, and the holy still be holy."

12 "See, I am coming soon; my reward is with me, to repay according to everyone's work. 13 I am the Alpha and the Omega, the first and the last, the beginning and the end."

14 Blessed are those who wash their robes,[d] so that they will have the right to the tree of life and may enter the city by the gates. 15 Outside are the dogs and sorcerers and fornicators and murderers and idolaters, and everyone who loves and practices falsehood.

16 "It is I, Jesus, who sent my angel to you with this testimony for the churches. I am the root and the descendant of David, the bright morning star."

17   The Spirit and the bride say,

> "Come."
> And let everyone who hears say,
>   "Come."
> And let everyone who is thirsty
>   come.
> Let anyone who wishes take the
>   water of life as a gift.

18 I warn everyone who hears the words of the prophecy of this book: if anyone adds to them, God will add to that person the plagues described in this book; 19 if anyone takes away from the words of the book of this prophecy, God will take away that person's share in the tree of life and in the holy city, which are described in this book.

20 The one who testifies to these things says, "Surely I am coming soon."

Amen. Come, Lord Jesus!

21 The grace of the Lord Jesus be with all the saints. Amen.[e]

[b]Gk *slave* [c]Gk *brothers* [d]Other ancient authorities read *do his commandments* [e]Other ancient authorities lack *all*; others lack *the saints*; others lack *Amen*

The Shepherd of Hermas

The Shepherd was a popular book among Christians of the first four centuries. Written by Hermas, brother of Pius, bishop of Rome during the first half of the second century, the book was regarded by some churches as canonical Scripture, although it was eventually excluded from the New Testament, in part because it was known not to have been written by an apostle.

The book takes its name from an angelic mediator who appears to Hermas in the form of a shepherd. Other angelic beings appear here as well, in particular an old woman who identifies herself as the personification of the Christian church. These various figures communicate divine revelations to Hermas and, upon request (sometimes grudgingly), interpret their meaning to him.

The book is divided into a series of five visions, twelve sets of commandments (or "mandates"), and ten parables (or "similitudes"). The visions and similitudes are enigmatic and symbolic; they are usually explained to Hermas as having a spiritual significance for the Christian here on earth. The mandates are somewhat easier to interpret, consisting of direct exhortations to speak the truth, give alms, do good, and avoid sexual immorality, drunkenness, gluttony, and other vices.

Indeed, the entire book is driven by an ethical concern: what can Christians do if they have fallen into sin after being baptized? A number of early Christians had insisted that those who returned to lives of sin after joining the church had lost any hope of salvation. An alternative view is advanced by Hermas. This book maintains, on the basis of its divine revelations, that Christians who had fallen again into sin after their baptism had a second chance (but only *one* second chance) to repent and return to God's good graces. Those who refused to avail themselves of this opportunity, however, or who reverted to sin again thereafter, would be forced to face the judgment of God on the day of reckoning that was soon to come.

The book is the longest work to survive from the first hundred years of the Christian church. The following extracts are representative of the whole.

The Visions

Vision I

1 The one who brought me up sold me to a certain Rhoda in Rome. Many years later I met her again, and I began to love her as a sister. 2 Sometime later I saw her bathing in the river Tiber, and I gave her my hand and led her out of the river. When I saw her beauty I thought to myself and said, "I would be happy if I had a wife of such beauty and manner." That was the only thing I thought, nothing more. 3 Sometime later, as I was going to Cumae and praising the creatures of God, as they are so great and remarkable and powerful, while I was walking along I fell asleep and

"The Shepherd of Hermas," translated by Graydon F. Snyder, from *The Apostolic Fathers,* edited by Jack N. Sparks. © 1978 by Thomas Nelson. Reprinted by permission.

a spirit took me and carried me through a certain pathless region, through which a person could not walk. The place was precipitous and broken up by the waters. When I had crossed the river, I came into level ground and I knelt down and began to pray to God and to confess my sins. 4 While I was praying heaven opened, and I saw that woman, whom I had desired, greeting me from heaven, saying, "How do you do, Hermas?" 5 And I looked at her and said to her, "Madam, what are you doing here?" And she answered me, "I have been taken up in order that I might make known your sins before the Lord." 6 I said to her, "Are you now accusing me?" "No," she said, "but listen to the words which I am about to tell you. God who dwells in heaven and created the things that are from that which is not, and has increased and multiplied them for the sake of his holy church, is angry with you because you sinned against me." 7 I answered her and said, "Have I sinned against you? Where or when have I spoken an indecent word to you? Have I not always regarded you as a goddess? Have I not always respected you as a sister? Why do you charge me falsely, O Madam, with these evil and unclean things?" 8 She laughed and said to me, "The desire for evil rose up in your heart. Or do you suppose that it is not an evil thing for a righteous man if an evil desire arises in his heart? It is indeed a sin, and a great one," she said, "for the righteous man wishes righteous things. So when he desires righteous things, his reputation in heaven is set safe, and he finds the Lord favorable in everything he does. But those who in their hearts desire evil things bring death and captivity upon themselves, especially those who gain this world for themselves and pride themselves on their wealth and do not hold fast to the good things that are to come. 9 Their souls will repent: they who have no hope, but have despaired of themselves and their life. But you pray to God and he will heal your sins, your entire house, and all the saints."

2 After she said these words the heavens were closed, and I was shuddering all over and was distressed. I said to myself, "If this sin is recorded against me, how can I be saved? Or how can I propitiate God for the full measure of my sin? Or with what words shall I ask the Lord to be merciful to me?" 2 While I was considering and de-

liberating on these things in my heart, I saw before me a great white chair made of snow-white wool; and an elderly woman in a brightly shining garment came up with a book in her hand, and sat down alone and greeted me, "How do you do, Hermas?" And distressed and weeping I said, "How do you do, Madam?" 3 And she said to me, "Why are you sad, Hermas? You who are so patient, so good-natured, always laughing, why so downcast in appearance and so unhappy?" And I said to her, "Because of a very good woman who says that I have sinned against her." 4 Then she said, "By no means should this thing happen to the servant of God. But certainly a thought arose in your heart concerning her. For the servant of God, it is such a wish as this which brings sin. For it is an evil and shocking wish for a revered and already approved spirit if it desires an evil deed, and especially Hermas, the self-disciplined, who refrains from every evil desire and is full of all sincerity and great innocence."

3 "But it is not because of this that God is angry with you, but so that you might convert your children who have sinned against the Lord and against you, their parents. But being fond of children you have not admonished your family, but you have allowed it to become terribly corrupt. It is for this reason the Lord is angry with you. But he will heal all of your evil deeds which originated in your family, for becomes of their sins and iniquities you have been corrupted by the concerns of this life. 2 But the great compassion of the Lord has been merciful to you and to your family and will make you strong and will establish you in his glory. Only do not be remiss, but have courage and strengthen your family. For just as a smith, beating his work with a hammer, becomes master of the skill which he wishes, so also the righteous word daily repeated becomes master of all evil. So do not cease instructing your children. For I know that if they repent with all their heart, they will be inscribed in the books of life with the saints." 3 After these words of hers had ceased she said to me, "Do you wish to hear me read aloud?" And I said, "Yes I do, Madam." She said to me, "Pay attention and hear the glories of God." I heard of great and wonderful things, which I was not able to remember, for all the words were frightening, such as a person is unable to bear. So I remembered the last words, for they were beneficial to us and mild: 4 "Behold, the God of hosts, who has by his invisible and mighty power and by his great understanding created the world, and by his glorious will clothed his creation with beauty, and by his mighty word fixed the heaven and established the earth upon the waters, and by his own wisdom and providence created his holy church which also he blessed; behold, he is removing all the heavens and the mountains and the hills and the seas, and everything is becoming level for his elect in order that he might keep for them the promise which he made with great glory and joy, if they keep the commandments of God which they received in great faith."

4 So when she had finished reading and had risen from the chair, four young men came and took the chair and went away toward the east. 2 And she called to me and she touched my breast and said to me, "Did my reading please you?" And I said to her, "These latter words are pleasing to me, but the former were hard and difficult." Then she answered me, "These latter words are for the righteous, and the former for the heathen and the apostate." 3 As she was speaking with me, two men appeared and took her by the arms and departed toward the east, where the chair was. And she departed cheerfully, and as she was going away she said to me, "Be a man, Hermas."

Vision II

5 While I was going to Cumae, about the same time as the year before, as I was walking along I recalled the vision of the year before, and again a spirit took me and bore me to the same place as last year. 2 So when I reached the place I knelt down and began to pray to the Lord and to glorify his name, because he had considered me worthy and had made known to me my previous sins. 3 And after I had risen from the prayer I saw before me the elderly lady whom I had seen the year before, walking about and reading a little book aloud. And she said to me, "Are you able to disclose these things to the elect of God?" I said to her, "Madam, I cannot remember so much, but give me the document so that I can copy it." "Take it," she said, "and give it back to me." 4 I took it,

and having gone to another part of the field I copied it all, letter by letter, for I could not distinguish the syllables. After I had finished the letters of the document, the document was suddenly snatched from my hand, but by whom I did not see.

6 Fifteen days later, after I fasted and earnestly asked the Lord, the meaning of the writing was revealed to me. And this is what was written: 2 "Your offspring, Hermas, have rejected God and blasphemed the Lord, and by their great evil have betrayed their parents, and are called betrayers of parents, and their betrayal has not profited them, but still they add to their sin debaucheries and orgies of evil, and so their iniquities have reached the limit. 3 But make these words known to all your children and to your wife, who is about to be your sister. For she does not control her tongue, with which she sins. But when she hears these words she will control herself and will obtain mercy. 4 After you have made known to them these words which the Master commanded me should be revealed to you, then all sins which they have previously committed will be forgiven both them and all the saints who have sinned up to this day if they repent with all their heart and put away double-mindedness from their hearts. 5 For the Master swore by his glory concerning his elect, that if, after this day has been fixed, there is yet sin they will not obtain salvation. For repentance for the just has an end; for the saints the days of repentance are finished, but for the heathen there is repentance until the last day. 6 So speak to the officials of the church so that they will straighten their ways in righteousness, that they may receive the promises in full with great glory. 7 So you who do righteousness be steadfast and be not double-minded, so that your way will be with the holy angels. Blessed are you who endure the great tribulation which is coming and who will not deny their life. 8 For the Lord has sworn by his Son that they who deny their Lord have been rejected from their life, who now are about to deny him in the coming days; but for those who denied him before, he has been merciful because of his great compassion."

7 "But you, Hermas, do not any longer bear a grudge against your children nor leave your sister to herself, so that they may be cleansed of their former sins. For they will be disciplined with a just discipline if you do not bear a grudge against them. Bearing a grudge produces death. But you, Hermas, have undergone great trials of your own because of the transgressions of your family, because you did not care for them; but you neglected them and became entangled in your own evil affairs. 2 But the thing that saves you is that you have not fallen away from the living God, as well as your sincerity and great self-control. These things have saved you, if you stand fast, and save all who do such things and walk in innocence and sincerity. These will be victorious over all and will endure to everlasting life. 3 Blessed are all those who do righteousness. They will never be destroyed. 4 But say to Maximus, 'Behold, persecution is coming; if it seems good to you, deny again.' 'The Lord is near to those who turn to him,' as it is written in the book of Eldad and Modat, who prophesied to the people in the desert."

8 As I was sleeping, brethren, a revelation was given to me by a handsome young man who said to me, "That elderly lady, from whom you received the document, who do you think she is?" I said, "The Sibyl." "You are mistaken," said he, "she is not." "Who then is she?" I said. "The Church," he said. I said to him, "Why then is she elderly?" "Because," said he, "she was created first of all; that is why she is elderly; and for her the world was made." 2 Afterward I saw a vision in my house. The elderly lady came and asked me if I had already given the book to the elders. I admitted I had not. "You have done well," she said, "for I have words to add. So when I finish all the words they will be made known through you to all the elect. 3 So you shall write two little books and you shall send one to Clement and one to Grapte. Then Clement will send one to the other cities, for that has been entrusted to him. And Grapte will instruct the widows and the orphans. But in this city you yourself shall read it aloud with the elders who stand at the head of the church."

Vision III

9 Brethren, what I saw was this. 2 I had fasted many times and I prayed to the Lord that he make known to me the revelation which he promised to show me through that elderly lady;

and on that very night the elderly lady appeared to me and said to me, "Since you are so needy and eager to know everything, go to the field where you raise grain, and about the fifth hour I will appear to you and I will show you that which you ought to see." 3 I asked her saying, "Madam, to what part of the field?" "Wherever you please," said she. I chose a lovely secluded place. But before I could speak to her and tell her which place, she said to me, "I will go wherever you wish." 4 So, brethren, I went to the field and I noted the hour and I went to the place where I had arranged for her to come, and I saw an ivory couch placed there, and on the couch there was a linen cushion and spread out over it a fine linen cloth. 5 When I saw these things standing there, and no one at the place, I was utterly astonished, and a sort of trembling seized me and my hair stood on end; and a sort of shuddering came over me, because I was alone. Then when I came to myself and remembered the glory of God and took courage, kneeling down I confessed to the Lord again my sins, as previously. 6 And she came with six young men, whom I had seen before, and she stood beside me and listened attentively while I prayed and confessed to the Lord my sins. And she touched me and said, "Hermas, stop asking all of these things concerning your sins; ask also concerning righteousness, so that you may take some part of it to your family." 7 And she raised me up by the hand and led me to the couch and said to the young men, "Go and build." 8 And after the young men departed and we were alone, she said to me, "Sit here." I said to her, "Madam, let the elders sit first." "Do as I say," she said, "sit down." 9 Then when I wished to sit on the right side she would not let me, but indicated to me with her hand that I should sit on the left side. Then as I was musing and grieving because she did not allow me to sit on the right side, she said to me, "Are you distressed, Hermas? The place of the right side belongs to others, who have already pleased God and suffered for the name. But you lack much to be able to sit with them. But if you stand fast in your simplicity, as you are doing, you also shall sit with them, and whoever does what they have done and bears what they have borne."

10 "What," said I, "have they borne?" "Listen," she said. "Whips, prisons, great per-

secutions, crosses, wild beasts, for the sake of the name. That is why the right side of the holy place is for them and whoever suffers for the name. But for the remainder there is the left side. But to both, those who sit on the right and those who sit on the left, are the same gifts and the same promises; except the former sit on the right and have a certain glory. 2 And you are very eager to sit on the right with them, but your shortcomings are many. But you will be cleansed of your shortcomings; and all those who are not double-minded will be cleansed of all their sins to this day." 3 When she had said these things she intended to depart, but I fell at her feet and beseeched her by the Lord to show me the vision which she had promised. 4 And again she took me by the hand and raised me up and had me sit on the couch at the left. And she sat down at the right. And lifting a shining staff she said to me, "Do you see something great?" I said to her, "Madam, I see nothing." She said to me, "Look! Do you not see right before you a great tower being built of lustrous square stones upon the water?" 5 And the tower was being built in a square by the six young men who had come with her; but myriads of other men were bringing stones, some from the deep, and some from the land, and were handing them to the six young men. They were taking them and building. 6 All the stones that were dragged from the deep were set in the building just as they were, for they were prepared and fit with the other stones at the joints. And they were joined so closely to each other that their joints did not show. And the structure of the tower looked as if it were built of one stone. 7 And of the other stones which were brought from the dry land, some they rejected, and some they placed in the building; others they broke up and threw far from the tower. 8 And many other stones were lying in a circle around the tower, and they did not use them for the tower. For some of them were rough, others had cracks, some were damaged by cutting, and some were white and round, so that they would not fit into the building. 9 And I saw other stones thrown far from the tower and going to the road and not staying on the road, but rolling off the road into the rough ground; and others were falling into fire and being burned; and others were falling near the water and were not able to roll into

the water, although they wished to roll and go into the water.

11 After showing me these things she wished to hurry away. I said to her, "Madam, what good is it for me to see these things and not know what is happening?" She answered and said to me, "You are a sly one, wishing to know about the tower," "Yes, Madam," I said, "so that I may report to my brethren, and that they may be cheered, and having heard these things may know God in much glory." 2 And she said, "Many will hear, but having heard, some of them will rejoice and others will weep; but even these, if they hear and repent, also shall rejoice. Hear, then, the parable of the tower, for I will reveal everything to you. And do not trouble me any more about a revelation, for these revelations have come to an end, for they have been completed. But you will not stop asking for revelations, for you are so bold. 3 The tower which you see being built is I, the church which appeared to you now and previously. So ask whatever you wish about the tower and I will reveal it to you, so that you may rejoice with the saints." 4 I said to her, "Madam, since once you considered me worthy enough to reveal everything to me, reveal it." And she said to me, "Whatever is possible to be revealed to you will be revealed. Only let your heart return to God and do not be double-minded concerning whatever you see." 5 I asked her, "Why is the tower build on water, Madam?" "As I said to you before," she said, "you are a sly one concerning the Scriptures and you seek diligently. Well, if you seek, you will find the truth. Hear then why the tower is built on water: because your life has been and will be saved through water. And the tower has been established by the word of the almighty and glorious name, and is supported by the unseen power of the Master."

12 I answered her and said, "Madam, this thing is great and wonderful. But the six young men who are building, who are they, Madam?" "These are the holy angels of God who were created first, to whom the Lord committed all his creation to develop and to build up and to govern the entire creation. So through them the building of the tower will be completed." 2 "But who are the others who are bringing the stones?" "They are also angels of God, but the first six are superior to them. So the building of the tower will be completed, and they will all rejoice together around the tower and glorify God because the building of the tower has been completed." 3 I asked her saying, "Madam, I wish to know the destination of the stones and what sort of meaning they have." She answered me and said, "It is not because you are more worthy than all the others that a revelation is given to you, for others were before you and better than you, to whom these visions ought to have been revealed. But in order that the name of God may be glorified, a revelation has been and will be given to you because of the double-minded ones who debate in their hearts whether these things are so or not. Tell them that all these things are true and nothing is apart from the truth, but everything is secure and reliable and well founded.

13 "Hear now about the stones that go into the building. The stones that are square and white and fit their joints are the apostles and bishops and teachers and deacons who have walked according to the holiness of God, and who have sincerely and reverently served the elect of God as bishops and teachers and deacons. Some have fallen asleep while others are still living. And they always agreed with one another and had peace with one another and listened to each other. That is why their joints fit together in the building of the tower." 2 "And the ones that were dragged from the deep and placed in the building and whose joints fit with the other stones that were already laid, who are they?" "They are the ones who have suffered for the name of God." 3 "And I wish to know who are the other stones which were brought from the dry land, Madam." She said, "Those that go into the building and are not hewn out are they whom the Lord approved because they walked in the uprightness of the Lord and carried out his commands." 4 "Who are the ones that are brought and placed in the building?" "They are the new in the faith and are faithful. They have been admonished by the angels to do good, therefore evil has not been found in them." 5 "Who are the ones they were rejecting and throwing away?" "They are the ones who have sinned and wish to repent. For this reason they were not thrown far from the tower, because they

will be useful in the building if they repent. So the ones who are about to repent, if they do repent, shall be secure in the faith, if they repent now while the tower is being built. But if the building is completed they will no longer have a place, but will be excluded. And they have only this—that they lie close to the tower."

14 "Would you like to know who they are that are broken up and thrown far from the tower? They are the sons of iniquity; their faith was in hypocrisy, and no evil escaped them. For this reason they do not have salvation, because they are of no use in the building on account of their evil. That is why they were broken to pieces and thrown far away, because of the wrath of the Lord, for they provoked him to wrath. 2 And the others which did not go into the building, many of which you have seen lying around, the rough ones are those who have known the truth but do not abide in it and do not fit with the saints, therefore are worthless." 3 "Who are the ones that have cracks?" "They are those who oppose each other in their hearts and do not have peace among themselves, but have only the appearance of peace, so whenever they depart from each other, their evil thoughts remain in their hearts. These are the cracks which the stones have. 4 The ones that are damaged by cutting are those who have believed and live for the most part in righteousness and have a certain measure of iniquity. That is why they are damaged and mutilated." 5 "Who are those that are white and round and do not fit into the building, Madam?" She answered and said to me, "How long will you be foolish and senseless, and ask about everything and understand nothing? They are the ones that have faith, but have also the riches of this world. Whenever tribulation comes, because of the riches and their business affairs they deny their Lord." 6 And I answered her and said, "Madam, when then will they be useful for the building?" "Whenever," said she, "their riches which beguile them are hewn off, then they will be useful to God. For just as the round stone, if nothing is hewn off and cast from it, is unable to become square, so also the wealthy in this world, unless their wealth is hewn off, are unable to be used by the Lord. 7 Learn first from your own situation. When you were rich, you were not useful.

Now you are useful and beneficial in life. Be useful to God, for you yourself have been used as one of the same stones."

15 "And the other stones which you saw thrown far from the tower and which reached the road and rolled from the road into the wasteland, they are the ones who have believed, but because of their double-mindedness left their true road. So thinking they can find a better way, they go astray and walk in misery through the wasteland. 2 The ones that fell into the fire and were burned, they are the ones who oppose the living God to the end, and it no longer enters their heart to repent because of their licentious desires and the evil things which they have done. 3 Do you wish to know who are the others who have fallen near the water and are unable to fall into the water? They are the ones who have heard the word and wish to be baptized in the name of the Lord. Then when the purity of the truth comes to their remembrance, they change their minds and again follow after their evil desires." 4 So she ended the explanation of the tower. 5 Still unabashed, I asked her if all the stones that were rejected and did not fit into the structure of the tower could repent and have a place in this tower. "They can repent," she said, "but they cannot fit in this tower. 6 But they will fit in another much inferior place, and that only when they are tormented and fill out the days of their sins. And for this reason they will be changed, because they receive the righteous word. And then it will happen that they are changed from their torments, if the evil deeds which they have done come to their hearts. But if they do not come to their hearts, they will not be saved because of their hardness of heart."

16 When I had stopped asking her concerning these things, she said to me, "Would you like to see something else?" Being very eager to see more, I was very glad to look. 2 She looked at me with a slight smile and said to me, "Do you see seven women around the tower?" "Yes, Madam," I said. "This tower is borne by them by command of the Lord. 3 Now hear about their functions. The first of them, who governs [the others] by gestures, is called Faith. Through her the elect of God are saved. 4 The second, who is girded and appears manly, is called Self-control. She

is the daughter of Faith. So whoever will follow her will be blessed in his life, because he will refrain from all evil works, believing that if he will refrain from every evil desire he will inherit eternal life." 5 "Who are the others, Madam?" "They are daughters of one another, and they are called Sincerity, Knowledge, Innocence, Reverence, and Love. So whenever you do all the works of their mother, you can live." 6 "I wish to know, Madam," I said, "what sort of power they have." "Listen," she said, "to what powers they have. 7 Their powers are governed by one another, and they follow one another in the order in which each is born. From Faith is born Self-control, from Self-control, Sincerity, from Sincerity, Innocence, from Innocence, Reverence, from Reverence, Knowledge, from Knowledge, Love. So their works are pure and reverent and divine. 8 So whoever serves these and has the strength to hold fast to their works will have a dwelling in the tower with the saints of God." 9 I asked her concerning the times, if it were already ended. And she cried out with a loud voice and said, "Oh, foolish man! Do you not see the tower is still being built? So whenever the building of the tower is finished, that is the end. But it will be built up quickly. Do not ask me anything more. Let this reminder and the renewal of your spirits be sufficient for you and the saints. 10 But these things have been revealed not to you alone, but in order that you might show them to everyone—after three days, 11 for you need to understand first of all. I command you first, Hermas, to speak all these things which I am about to say into the ears of the saints in order that they may hear these things and do them and be cleansed of their evil, and you with them."

17 "Listen to me, children, by the mercy of the Lord, who fed you righteousness drop by drop, I nourished you in great sincerity and innocence and reverence in order that you might be righteous and purified from all evil and perversity. But you do not wish to cease from your evil. 2 Now then listen to me and be at peace among yourselves, and be concerned for one another and help one another, and do not take the creation of God for yourselves alone, but share the gravy of life with those also who are in need. 3 For by eating too much some are bringing on themselves illness in the flesh and are injuring their flesh; and the flesh of those who do not have food to eat is injured because there is not sufficient food and their body is wasting away. 4 So this lack of community spirit is harmful to you who have and do not share with the needy. 5 Consider the judgment which is to come. So let those who have more seek out those who are hungry until such a time as the tower is finished. For after the tower is finished you will wish to do good, but you will not have the opportunity. 6 So you who rejoice in your riches see to it that the needy never groan and their groaning go up to the Lord, and you be shut outside the door of the tower with your goods. 7 Now, then, I say to you officials of the church and those who have the seats of honor: do not become like the poisoners. For while the poisoners carry their drugs in bottles, you carry your drug and poison in your heart. 8 You have become callous and do not wish to cleanse your heart and mix your wisdom together in a clean heart in order that you may have mercy from the great king. 9 See to it then, children, that these dissensions of yours do not turn you away from your life. 10 How do you expect to teach the elect of the Lord if you yourselves do not have training? So teach one another and have peace among yourselves so that I too may stand joyfully before the father and give account for all of you to your Lord."

18 So when she finished speaking with me, the six young men who were building came and took her to the tower, and four others picked up the couch and carried it also to the tower. I did not see their faces because they were turned away. 2 But as she was going away I asked her to give me a revelation about the three forms in which she had appeared to me. She answered me and said, "Concerning these things, it is necessary for you to ask someone else to reveal it to you." 3 Now, brethren, last year in the first vision she appeared to me as quite elderly and she was sitting in a chair. 4 But in the second vision she had a younger face, though her body and hair were elderly, and she stood as she talked to me. And she was more cheerful than before. 5 In the third vision she was completely young and remarkable for her beauty, except that her hair was that of an elderly woman. She was cheerful in every respect

and sat on a couch. 6 Concerning these things I was deeply grieved, for I wanted to know this revelation, and in a vision of the night I saw the elderly lady who said to me, "Every request requires humility. So fast, and you will receive what you ask from the Lord." 7 So I fasted one day, and that night a young man appeared to me and said to me, "Why do you continually ask for revelations in your prayer? Be careful, lest by your many requests you injure your body. 8 These revelations are enough for you. Are you able to look at revelations mightier than what you have already seen?" 9 I answered and said to him, "Sir, this is the only thing I ask, that the revelation about the three forms of the elderly lady be completed." He answered me and said, "How long will you people be without understanding? Your double-mindedness makes you unable to understand and you do not turn your heart to the Lord." 10 And again I answered him and said, "But from you, sir, we will know these things more accurately."

19 "Hear," he said, "about the forms concerning which you inquired. 2 Why did she appear to you in the first vision as elderly and sitting on a chair?" Because your spirit is old and already faded and you lack power because of your softness and double-mindedness. 3 For just as old men, who no longer have any hope of becoming young again, look forward to nothing but their falling asleep, so also you who are softened by the cares of life, have given yourselves over to indifference and do not cast your burdens on the Lord. But your disposition was broken and you became old with your griefs." 4 "Why, then, I would like to know, did she sit in a chair, sir?" "Because everyone who is weak sits on a chair on account of his weakness, in order that the weakness of his body might find support. You have the meaning of the first vision."

20 "In the second vision you saw her standing and she had a younger face and was more cheerful than before, but the body and hair were those of an elderly lady. Listen," he said, "to this parable also. 2 Whenever someone is old and has already given up hope for himself because of his weakness and poverty, and waits for nothing but the last day of his life, then unexpectedly an inheritance is left to him, and when he hears of it he arises, and being very glad he is clothed with strength. And he does not recline, but stands up, and his spirit, which previously was broken by his former concerns, is renewed and he no longer sits down, but acts like a man. So also are you who have heard the revelation which the Lord revealed to you. 3 For he had compassion on you and renewed your spirits, and you put aside your weakness, and strength came to you and you were made powerful in the faith; when the Lord saw you were being made strong he rejoiced. And for this reason he showed you the building of the tower, and he will show you other things if with all your heart you remain at peace with one another."

21 "And in the third vision you saw her younger and beautiful and cheerful and her form was lovely. 2 So just as, if some good news comes to someone who is grieving, immediately he forgets the former grief and thinks of nothing but the news which he has heard, and from then on is strengthened to do good and his spirit is renewed because of the joy which he received, so also you have received renewal of your spirits because you have seen these good things. 3 And since you saw her sitting on a couch, the position is secure because the couch has four legs and stands secure, for even the world is supported by four elements. 4 So the ones who fully repent will be young and made secure—the ones who repent with all their heart. You have received the revelation in full, so do not ask anything else concerning the revelation. But if anything is needed, it will be revealed to you."

Vision IV

22 That which I saw, brethren, twenty days after the previous vision had occurred, was as a foreshadowing of the tribulation to come. 2 I was going into the country by the Via Campana. The place is about 6,000 feet from the public thoroughfare, and is easily reached. 3 So as I was walking along by myself I asked the Lord that the revelation and vision which he had shown me through his holy church might be completed, so that he might strengthen me and give repentance to his servants who had been led astray, in order

that his great and glorious name might be glorified, because he regarded me worthy to show me his wonders. 4 And as I was glorifying him and giving him thanks, something like the sound of a voice answered me, "Be not double-minded, Hermas." And I began to reason with myself and to say, "How can I be double-minded, when I have been made so secure by the Lord and have seen such glorious things?" 5 And I walked on a little, brethren, and behold, I saw a cloud of dust reaching as it were up to heaven, and I began to say to myself, "Are there not cattle coming and raising a cloud of dust?" And it was about 600 feet away from me. 6 When the dust cloud became greater and greater, I suspected it was something divine. The sun shone more brightly for a moment and behold, I saw a huge beast, something like a sea monster, and out of its mouth were coming fiery locusts. And the beast was about one hundred feet in length, and it had a head like a jar. 7 And I began to cry and to beseech the Lord to save me from it, and I remembered the word which I had heard, "Do not be double-minded, Hermas." 8 So, brethren, being clothed in the faith of God and remembering the great things he had taught me, taking courage, I entrusted myself to the beast. And the beast came on with a rush as if it could destroy a city. 9 I drew near to it and the sea monster, great as it was, stretched itself out on the ground and did nothing but thrust out its tongue and did not move at all until I had gone by it. 10 And the beast had four colors on its head: black, then the color of fire and blood, then gold, then white.

23 After I had passed by the beast and had gone on about thirty feet, behold, a young lady met me, adorned as if coming from a bridal chamber, all in white and with white sandals, veiled up to the forehead, and her head covering was a snood, but she had white hair. 2 I knew from my previous visions that she was the church, and I became more cheerful. She greeted me saying, "How do you do, friend?" And I greeted her in return, "How do you do, Madam?" 3 She answered me and said, "Did nothing meet you?" I said to her, "Madam, a beast so great as could destroy entire peoples, but by the power of the Lord and by his great compassion I escaped it." 4 "It is only right that you escape," she said, "because you cast your burden upon God and you opened your heart to the Lord, believing that you could not be saved by anything but the great and glorious name. Therefore the Lord sent his angel who has authority over the beasts, whose name is Thegri, and he shut its mouth so that it might not hurt you. You escaped a great tribulation because of your faith and because when you saw so great a beast you did not become double-minded. 5 Go then and tell the elect of the Lord about his great deeds, and say to them that this beast is a foreshadowing of the great tribulation about to come. If then you prepare yourselves in advance and repent with all your heart before the Lord, you will be able to escape it, if your heart becomes pure and blameless and you serve the Lord blamelessly the rest of the days of your life. Cast your burdens upon the Lord and he will set them straight. 6 Have faith in the Lord, you who are double-minded, because he can do all things and turn his wrath from you and send out plagues to you who are double-minded. Woe to those who hear these words and disobey; it would have been better for them not to have been born."

24 I asked her about the four colors that the beast had on its head. She answered me and said, "Again you are inquisitive about such things." "Yes Madam," I said, "make known to me what they are." 2 "Listen," said she, "the black is this world in which you live. 3 The color of fire and blood means it is necessary for this world to be destroyed by blood and fire. 4 And the gold part is you who have fled this world. For just as gold is tested by fire and becomes useful, so also you who live among those people are being tested. Those then who endure and are made red hot by them will be purified. For just as gold casts off its dross, so also you will cast off all grief and distress, and you will be purified and be useful in the construction of the tower. 5 And the white part is the age which is to come, in which the elect of God will live, because those who have been chosen by God for eternal life will be spotless and pure. 6 So speak constantly in the hearing of the saints. You have also the foreshadowing of the great tribulation which is to come. And if you so wish, it will be nothing. Remember those things which have already been written." 7 After she had said these things she departed, and I did not see where she went, for there came a cloud and I turned back in fear, supposing that the beast was coming.

Revelation V

25 After I had prayed in my house and had sat down on the bed, there came in a man glorious in appearance, in the manner of a shepherd, wearing a white goatskin and with a bag on his shoulders and a staff in his hand. And he greeted me, and I returned his greeting. 2 And he sat down beside me at once and said to me, "I have been sent by the most reverend angel to dwell with you the rest of the days of your life." 3 I thought that he came to test me and I said to him, "But who are you? For I know," I said, "to whom I have been entrusted." He said to me, "Do you not recognize me?" "No," said I, "I," he said, "am the shepherd to whom you have been entrusted." 4 While he still spoke his appearance was changed and I recognized him as that one to whom I had been entrusted, and at once I was confused and fear seized me, and I was completely overcome by grief because I had answered him so wickedly and foolishly. 5 And he answered and said to me, "Do not be confused, but be strengthened in my commandments which I am about to give you. For I was sent," he said, "so that I might show you again everything which you saw before, the main points, those which are beneficial to you. So then, first of all, you write down my commandments and parables; but the other things you shall write just as I show them to you. Therefore," he said, "I am commanding you to write first the commandments and the parables, so that you may read them immediately and be able to keep them." 6 So then I wrote down the commandments and parables just as he had commanded me. 7 If when you hear these things you keep them and live by them and do them with a clean heart, you will receive from the Lord whatever he has promised you. But if you hear and do not repent, but still add to your sins, you will receive from the Lord the opposite. The shepherd, the angel of repentance, has commanded me to write all these things in this way.

The Mandates

Mandate I

26 "First of all, believe that God is one, who created and completed all things and made all that is from that which is not and contains all things, and who alone is uncontained. 2 So have faith in him and fear him, and fearing him be self-controlled. Keep these things and you will cast away all evil from yourself, and you will put on every virtue of righteousness and you will live to God, if you keep this commandment."

Mandate II

27 He said to me, "Have simplicity and become innocent, and you will be as little children who do not know the evil that destroys the life of people. 2 First, do not defame anyone nor listen gladly to one who does defame. Otherwise you who listen will also be guilty of the sin of the one who defames, if you believe the defamation which you have heard; for by believing it, you yourself will have something against your brother. So in that way you will be guilty of the sin of the one who defames. 3 Defamation is evil; it is a restless demon, never at peace, but always dwells in dissension. So refrain from it and you will always be at peace with everyone. 4 And put on reverence, in which there is no evil reason for offense, but all is smooth and cheerful. Do good, and from your labors which God has given you give generously to all who are in need, not considering to whom you should give or to whom you should not give. Give to all, for God wishes that from his own gifts there be a giving to all. 5 So those who receive will give account to God as to why they took it and for what purpose; for those who are in distress when they receive something will not be condemned, while those who receive something in hypocrisy will be punished. 6 So the one who gives is guiltless, for as he received from the Lord a service to fulfill, he fulfilled it sincerely, not trying to distinguish to whom he should give or not give. So this service, sincerely fulfilled, becomes glorious before God. So the one who serves sin-cerely will live to God. 7 So keep this commandment, as I have told you, so that the repentance of you and your family may be found sincere and pure and innocent and undefiled.

Mandate III

28 Again he said to me, "Love truth, and let nothing but truth proceed from your mouth, so that the spirit which God caused to dwell in this flesh will be found truthful by all people, and in that way the Lord who dwells in you will be glorified because the Lord is truthful in every word and there is nothing false in him. 2 So those who falsify reject the Lord and become defrauders of the Lord, not returning to him the deposit which they received. For they received from him a spirit free of falseness. If they give this back as a false one, they have defiled the commandment of the Lord and have become defrauders." 3 So when I heard these things I cried a great deal. And when he saw me crying, he said, "Why are you crying?" "Sir," I said, "because I do not know whether I can be saved." "Why?" said he, "Because, sir," I said, "I have never yet in my life spoken a true word, but I have always lived deceitfully with everyone and I have represented my falseness as truth to all people, and no one ever contradicted me, but believed my word. Sir," said I, "having done these things, how then can I live?" 4 "Your judgment," he said, "is right and true, for you ought as God's servant to live in truth, and an evil conscience ought not to dwell with the spirit of truth, nor bring grief to a spirit which is reverent and true." "Never before, sir," I said, "have I heard such words so precisely." 5 "Well now," he said, "you do hear. Keep them so that even the former falsifications which you told in your business, when they are found truthful, will become trustworthy. For they also can become trustworthy. If you keep these things and from now on speak only the truth, you will be able to gain for yourself life, and whoever hears this commandment and refrains from the evilness of lying, will live to God."

Mandate IV

29 "I command you," he said, "to guard chastity, and do not let anything occur in your heart about another man's wife or about some immorality or about any such evil things even similar to these. For if you do this, you commit a great sin. But if you always keep your mind on your own wife, you will never go wrong. 2 For if this desire arises up in your heart, you will sin, and if other things just as evil rise up, you commit sin. For to a servant of God this desire is a great sin, and if anyone commits this evil act, he brings death upon himself. 3 So watch out; refrain from this desire; for where reverence dwells, there iniquity ought not to rise up in the heart of a righteous man." 4 I said to him, "Sir, let me ask you a few questions." "Speak up," he said. "Sir," I said, "if a man has a wife who is faithful in the Lord and he discovers her in some adultery, does the man then sin if he continues to live with her?" 5 "As long as he knows nothing of it," said he, "he does not sin, but if the husband knows of her sin and the wife does not repent, but persists in her evil, and the husband continues to live with her, he becomes guilty of her sin and a partner in her adultery." 6 "What then, sir," I said, "should the husband do if the wife persists in this passion?" "Let him divorce her," he said, "and let the husband live by himself; but if when he has divorced her he marries another woman, he also commits adultery." "So, sir," said I, "after the woman has been divorced, if she repents and wishes to be returned to her own husband, will she not be taken back?" 8 "Yes indeed," he said, "if the husband does not take her back, he sins and brings upon himself a great sin. At least it is necessary to take back the one who has sinned and repented, but not often, for there is one repentance for the servants of God. So in case of repentance, the husband ought not to marry. This course of action is valid for both wife and husband. 9 Not only," said he, "is it adultery if anyone defiles his flesh, but also whoever does anything similar to what the heathen do commits adultery. So if anyone persists in such deeds and does not repent, avoid him and do not live with him, lest you also share in his sin. 10 That is why I order you to live by yourself, whether husband or wife. For in such cases repentance is possible. 11 So I," said he, "am not giving a pretext for this matter to end in this way, but in order that the one who has sinned will sin no longer. Concerning his former sin there is one who is able to heal, for it is he who has power over all things."

30 I asked him again saying, "Since the Lord considers me worthy enough for you to live with me always, endure yet a few more words from me, since I do not understand anything and my heart has been hardened by my former deeds. Make me understand, because I am very foolish and I understand absolutely nothing." 2 He answered me and said, "I," he said, "am in charge of repentance and I give understanding to everyone who repents. Or does it not seem to you," he said, "that this repentance is itself understanding? To repent," he said, "is great understanding. For the one who sins understands that he has done evil before the Lord, and the deed which he has done rises up in his heart, and he repents and no longer commits the evil deed, but does good deeds all the more and humbles and torments his own soul because he sinned. So you see repentance is great understanding." 3 "So that is why, sir," I said, "I inquire so precisely from you into everything; first, because I am a sinner, that I might know what things to do in order to live, for my sins are many and diverse." 4 "You will live," he said, "if you keep my commandments and walk in them. And whoever hears these commandments and keeps them will live to God."

31 "Sir," I said, "I would like to question you still further." "Speak," he said. "Sir," I said, "I have heard from certain teachers that there is no other repentance except that one when we went down into water and received forgiveness of our former sins." 2 He said to me, "You have heard correctly, for that is so. For the one who has received forgiveness of sins ought never to sin again, but live in purity. 3 But since you inquire so precisely into everything, I will show this to you also, but not for giving a pretext for those who are about to believe or to those who just now believe in the Lord. For those who just now believe, or are about to believe, do not have repentance of sins, but they have forgiveness of their former sins. 4 So for those who were called before these days the Lord established repentance; for since the Lord knows the heart and knows everything beforehand, he knew the weakness of people and the cunning of the devil, that he would do something evil to the servants of God and act wickedly toward them. 5 So being full of compassion, the Lord had mercy on what he had made and established this repentance, and authority over this repentance was given to me. 6 But I tell you," he said, "after that great and holy calling, if anyone sins who has been tempted by the devil, he has one repentance. But if he continually sins and repents, it is of no advantage to such a person, for he will hardly live." I said to him, "I was given new life when I heard these things so precisely from you; for I know that if I no longer continue in my sin, I will be saved." "You will be saved," he said, "and everyone else who does these things."

32 I asked him again saying, "Sir, since you endured me once before, make this clear to me also." "Speak," he said, "Sir, if a wife," I said, "or, on the other hand, a husband falls asleep, and one of them marries, the one who marries does not sin, does he?" 2 "He does not sin," he said, "but if he lives by himself, he gains greater honor for himself and great glory with the Lord; but even if he marries he does not sin. 3 So preserve chastity and reverence and you will live to God. From now on, from the day you were entrusted to me, keep these things which I tell you and I am going to tell you, and I will dwell in your house. 4 And there will be forgiveness for your former trespasses if you keep my commandments; and there will also be forgiveness for everyone who keeps these commandments of mine and lives in this purity."

Mandate V

33 "Be patient," he said, "and understanding, and you will overcome all evil deeds and do great righteousness. 2 For if you are patient, the holy Spirit that dwells in you will be pure, not hindered by another spirit which is evil, but dwelling in a spacious room will rejoice and be glad with the vessel in which it dwells and will serve God with great cheerfulness, having peace with itself. 3 But if any ill temper enters, the holy Spirit, which is delicate, is discomforted immedi-

ately, and since it does not have a clean place, it seeks to leave the place. For it is choked by the evil spirit and it does not have room, since it was defiled by ill temper, to serve the Lord as it wishes. For the Lord dwells in patience, but the devil in ill temper. 4 So when both spirits dwell in the same place, it is of no advantage and bad for that person in whom they dwell. 5 For if you take a very little bit of wormwood and pour it into a jar of honey, is not all of the honey spoiled, and is not so much honey ruined by the very least amount of wormwood, and does it not destroy the sweetness of the honey, and it no longer has the same favor with its owner because it has been made bitter and it has lost its usefulness? But if wormwood is not put into the honey, the honey is found sweet and becomes useful to its owner. 6 You see that patience is very sweet, even more than the honey, and is useful to the Lord, and he dwells in it. But ill temper is bitter and useless. If then ill temper is mixed with patience, patience is defiled, and its prayer is no longer useful to God." 7 "Sir," I said, "I wish to know the power of ill temper so that I may guard against it." "Indeed," he said, "if you and your family do not guard against it, you have destroyed all hope. But guard against it, for I am with you and all who repent with all their heart will refrain from it; for I will be with them and I will protect them, for they have all been made righteous by the most revered angel."

34 "Now hear," said he, "about the power of ill temper, how evil it is, and how it misleads the servants of God by its power, and how it makes them stray from righteousness. But it does not lead astray those who are filled with faith nor is it able to do anything to them, for my power is with them; but it does lead the empty headed and double-minded astray. 2 For whenever it sees such people leading a quiet life, it maneuvers itself into the heart of that one, and for no reason at all the man or the woman becomes bitter, because of business matters, or concerning food or some trifle, or concerning a certain friend, or concerning giving or receiving, or some such foolish matters, for all these things are foolish and empty and senseless and harmful to the servants of God. 3 But patience is great and firm and possesses power that is strong and sturdy and thrives in a great expanse, is cheerful, glad, free from care, glorifying the Lord at all times, having no bitterness in itself, remaining always meek and quiet. So this patience dwells with those who have a faith that is whole. 4 But ill temper is first of all foolish, impetuous and senseless. Then from foolishness comes bitterness, from bitterness anger, from anger wrath, and from wrath implacable fury; so this fury, consisting as it does of such evil things, becomes a great and incurable sin. 5 For whenever all these spirits dwell in one vessel, where also dwells the holy Spirit, that vessel does not hold them, but overflows. 6 So the delicate spirit, which does not customarily dwell with an evil spirit, nor with harshness, leaves such a person and seeks to dwell with gentleness and quiet. 7 Thus whenever it departed from that person, where it was dwelling, that person became devoid of the spirit of righteousness and from then on, since he has been filled with evil spirits, he vacillates in everything he does, being pulled here and there by the evil spirits, and totally blinded to a good disposition. So it goes then with all those who are ill tempered. 8 So refrain then from ill temper, the most evil spirit; but put on patience and resist ill temper and bitterness, and you will be found with a reverence that is beloved by the Lord. See to it then that you never neglect this commandment; for if you master this commandment, you will be able also to keep the remaining commandments which I am going to give you. Be strong and made powerful by these, and all who wish to live by them will be made powerful."

The Similitudes

Similitude I

50 He said to me, "You know," said he, "that you servants of God live in a foreign country, for your city is far from this city. If, then, you know," he said, "your city in which you are going to live, why do you prepare lands and expensive possessions and buildings and useless rooms here? 2 So the one who prepares these things for this city does not expect to return to his own city. 3 Foolish and double-minded and miserable man, do you not understand that all these things are another's and are under the authority of someone else? For the lord of this city will say, 'I do not want you to live in my city, but depart from this city for you do not live in accordance with my laws.' 4 So you who have fields and dwellings and many other possessions, what will you do with the field and the dwelling and the other things which you have prepared for yourself, when you are cast out by him? For the lord of this country has the right to say to you, 'Either live according to my rules or get out of my county.' 5 What are you going to do if there is a law in your own city? For the sake of your fields and other possessions will you renounce your law altogether and live according to the law of this city? Beware lest it be disadvantageous for you to deny your law, for if you wish to return to your city, you will not be received because you have denied the law of your city, and you will be excluded from it. 6 So beware. As one living in a foreign country, do not prepare for yourself more than is necessary to be self-sufficient, and be prepared so that whenever the ruler of this city wishes to cast you out for disobeying his law, you can leave his city and go to your city and joyfully live according to your law with decorum. 7 So beware, you who serve the Lord and have him in your hearts. Do the deeds of God, remembering his commandments and the promises which he promised, and trust him, for he will do them if his commandments are observed. 8 So instead of fields, purchase souls that are in distress, as each is able, and care for the widows and orphans, and do not overlook them, and spend your wealth and all your possessions on such fields and houses which you receive from God. 9 For this is the reason the master made you rich, so that you might fulfill these ministries for him. It is much better for you to purchase such fields and possessions and houses as you will find in your city when you go home to it. 10 This wealth is beautiful and cheerful, for it brings neither grief nor fear, but brings joy. Do not strive for the wealth of the heathen, for it has no advantage to you who are servants of God. 11 But strive for your own wealth, in which you are able to rejoice, and do not counterfeit or touch that of another, nor desire it.

For it is wicked to desire that which belongs to someone else. Do your own work and you will be saved."

Similitude II

51 While I was walking in the country, and was observing an elm and a vine, and contrasting them and their fruits, the shepherd appeared to me and said, "What are your thoughts concerning the elm and the vine?" "I think sir," I said, "that they are very well suited to each other." 2 "These two trees," he said, "appear as a type for the servants of God." "I would like to know," I said, "the type of these trees of which you speak." "Do you see," he said, "the elm and the vine?" "I see them, sir," I said. 3 "This vine," he said, "bears fruit, but the elm is a fruitless tree. But if it does not climb up on the elm, this vine is not able to bear much fruit, since it is spread on the ground, and what fruit it does bear is rotten, because it is not hanging on the elm. So whenever the vine is attached to the elm, it bears fruit both from itself and from the elm. 4 So you see, then, that the elm gives much fruit, not less than the vine, but, instead, even more." "How, sir," I said, "does it bear more?" "Because," he said, "the vine which is attached to the elm gives fruit which is plentiful and good, while that which is lying on the ground bears little fruit, which is rotten at that. So this parable applies to the servants of God, to poor and rich." 5 "How, sir?" I said. "Make it known to me." "Listen," he said, "the rich man has wealth, but he is poor in things concerning the Lord, being overburdened concerning his wealth, and his prayer and confession to the Lord are insignificant, and what he has is feeble and small and without authority. So whenever the rich man rests upon the poor man and supplies him his needs, he believes that what he does for the poor man will be able to find a reward with God, because the poor man is rich in his prayer and in confession, and his prayer has much power with God. Therefore the rich man provides everything for the poor man without hesitating. 6 Since he is supported by the rich man, the poor man, when he gives thanks to God, pleads with him on behalf of the one who shared with him, and that one is all the more zealous on behalf of the poor man, in order that he

might not lack anything in his life, for he knows that the prayer of the poor man is acceptable and rich before the Lord. 7 So both complete their work. The poor man works with prayer, in which he is rich, which he received from the Lord; this he gives back to the Lord who supplies it to him. And the rich man likewise without hesitating shares with the poor man the wealth which he received from the Lord. And this work is great and acceptable with God, because he understands about his wealth and works for the poor man out of the gifts of the Lord, and rightly fulfills his ministry. 8 So to humans the elm appears not to bear fruit, and they do not know or understand that whenever there is a drought, the elm, which has water, nourishes the vine, and the vine, which has a constant supply of water, gives double the amount of fruit, both for itself and for the elm. So also those who are poor, by appealing to the Lord on behalf of the rich, complement their wealth, and again those who are rich, by supplying the necessities of life to the poor, complement their prayers. 9 So they both become partners in righteous work. So the one who does these things will not be deserted by God, but will be inscribed in the books of the living. 10 Blessed are those who have and understand that their wealth comes from the Lord, for the one who understands this will also be able to do some good service.

Similitude III

52 He showed me many trees which had no leaves, but appeared to me to be as if dried up; for they were all alike. And he said to me, "Do you see," he said, "these trees?" "I see, sir," I said, "that they are alike and dried up." He answered me and said, "These trees which you see are the ones who dwell in this world." 2 "Why, then, sir," I said, "are they as if dry and all alike?" "Because," said he, "neither the righteous nor the sinners are apparent in this world, but are all alike. For this world is winter for the righteous, and they are not apparent even though they are living with sinners. 3 For just as in the winter, the trees, having shed their leaves, are alike, and it is not apparent which are the dried up or which are the living, so also in this world neither the righteous nor the sinners are apparent, but all are alike."

Similitude IV

53 Again he showed me many trees, some of which were budding, and some dried up, and he said to me, "Do you see," he said, "these trees." "I see, sir," I said, "some budding and some dried up." 2 "These trees which are budding," he said, "are the righteous who are about to dwell in the world to come, for the world to come is summer for the righteous, but winter for the sinners. So when the mercy of the Lord shines forth, then those who serve God will be made known to all. 3 For just as the fruit of every single tree appears by summer and it is known what kind they are, so also the fruit of the righteous will be apparent and, since they are flourishing, they will all be known in that world. 4 But the heathen and the sinners, the dried-up trees which you saw, such will be found dried up and fruitless in that age and will be burned as dry wood and will be distinguishable because their conduct was evil in their life. For the sinners will be burned because they sinned and did not repent, the heathen will be burned because they did not know the one who created them. 5 So bear fruit in yourself, so that in that summer your fruit will be known. Refrain from many affairs and you will in no wise sin. For those who engage in many affairs also sin much since they are overburdened by their affairs and do not serve their Lord. 6 How, then," he said, "can such a person ask anything of the Lord and receive it, when he does not serve the Lord? The ones who serve him, those will receive their requests. But the ones who do not serve the Lord will receive nothing. 7 If anyone is occupied with one concern, he is also able to serve the Lord, for his mind is not corrupted away from the Lord, but he will serve him with a pure mind. 8 So if you do these things, you will be able to bear fruit for the world to come; and whoever does these things will bear fruit."

Similitude V

54 While I was fasting, and sitting on a certain mountain, and thanking the Lord for all he had done for me, I saw the shepherd sitting beside me and saying these things to me, "Why have you come here so early?" "Because, sir," I said, "I am on guard duty." 2 "What," said he, "is the guard?" "I am fasting, sir," I said. "But what," said he, "is this fast that you are keeping?" "Sir," I said, "I am fasting just as I have been accustomed to do." 3 "You do not know how to fast to God," he said, "and this useless fast you are keeping for him is not a fast." "Why, sir," I said, "do you say this?" "I am telling you," he said, "that this is not a fast which you think you are keeping, but I will teach you what an acceptable and complete fast to the Lord is." "Yes sir," said I, "you will make me happy if I may know that fast acceptable to God." "Listen," said he. 4 "God does not wish such a futile fast as this, for by fasting in this way you do nothing for righteousness. But fast to God in this way: 5 Do nothing evil in your life, but serve the Lord with a clean heart, keeping his commandments and following his orders, and let no evil desire arise in your heart. Believe in God, because, if you do these things and fear him and abstain from every evil deed, you will live to God. And if you do these things, you will complete a fast that is great and acceptable to the Lord."

55 "Listen to the parable which I am going to tell you concerning fasting. 2 A certain man had a field and many slaves, and in a certain part of the field he planted a vineyard. As he was going away on a journey, he selected a certain slave who was reliable and pleasing and called him and said to him, 'Take this vineyard which I have planted and fence it, until I come, and do nothing more to the vineyard. Keep this commandment of mine and you will be a freedman with me.' And the master of the slave went away on a journey. 3 After he departed, the slave took and fenced the vineyard. And when he had finished fencing the vineyard, he saw that the vineyard was full of weeds. 4 So he thought to himself, saying, 'I have completed the commandment of the Lord; in addition, I will cultivate this vineyard, and it will look better after it is cultivated, and with no weeds it will yield more fruit; because it is not choked by the weeds.' He took and cultivated the vineyard and he pulled out all the weeds that were in the vineyard. And that vineyard became very attractive and thriving, for it had no weeds to choke it. 5 After some time the master of the field and the slave came and went into the vineyard. And when he saw the vineyard was attractively fenced and, moreover, was cultivated, and all the weeds were pulled up and the vines were thriving, he rejoiced greatly at the efforts of the slave. 6 So he called his beloved son, who was his heir, and his friends, who were his advisers. He told them what he had commanded his servant to do and what he had found accomplished. And they congratulated the slave on the testimony which the master gave for him. 7 And he said to them, 'I promised freedom to this slave, if he kept my commandment which I gave him. He kept my commandment and added to it good work in the vineyard, and he pleased me greatly. So in return for this work which he has done, I wish to make him a joint heir with my son, because, when he had a good thought he did not neglect it, but carried it out.' 8 The son of the master approved of this decision that the slave should become joint heir with the son. 9 A few days later the master of his house gave a dinner and sent him considerable food from the dinner. When the slave received the food sent him by his master, he took enough for himself and distributed the rest to his fellow slaves. 10 When his fellow slaves received the food they rejoiced, and began to pray for him, that he might find even greater favor with his master, because he treated them in this way. 11 His master heard of all these things which had happened and again was greatly pleased with his conduct. Again the master called together his friends and his son and told them what the slave had done with the food which he had received. They were even more pleased that the slave would be made a joint heir with his son."

56 I said to him, "Sir, I do not understand these parables nor can I comprehend them unless you interpret them to me." 2 "I will interpret everything to you," he said, "and whatever I tell you I will explain. Keep the commandments of the Lord and you will be pleasing to him and be enrolled in the number of those who keep his commandments. 3 If you do something good beyond the commandment of God, you will gain greater glory for yourself and you will be more honored before God than you would have been. If then, while keeping the commandments of God, you add also these services, you will rejoice, if you keep them according to my commandment." 4 I said to him, "Sir, whatever you command me, I will follow it, for I know that you are with me." "I will be with you," he said, "because you have such

zeal for doing good, and I will be with all," said he, "who have the same zeal. 5 This fast," he said, "is very good, if you keep the commandments of the Lord. So observe this fast which you are going to keep in this way: 6 First of all, guard against every evil word and every evil desire, and cleanse your heart of all the vanities of this world. If you observe these things, this fast will be complete. 7 And here is what you will do: when you have finished the above-mentioned, on that day when you are fasting, you will taste nothing except bread and water, and you will be aware of the amount of the cost of your food you would have eaten on that day which you are going to keep. Having set it aside, you will give it to a widow or an orphan or someone else in need, and in this way you will be humble minded, so that from your humility the one who receives may fill his soul and pray to the Lord for you. 8 If, then, you complete the fast in this way, as I command you, your sacrifice will be acceptable before God, and this fast will be recorded, and the service done in this way is good and joyous and acceptable to the Lord. 9 This is the way you shall observe these things, with your children and all your house; if you observe them, you will be blessed and as many as hear them and keep them will be blessed, and whatever they ask from the Lord they will receive."

57 I besought him much to explain to me the parable of the field and the master and the vineyard and the slave who fenced the vineyard, and the fences, and the weeds that were pulled up out of the vineyard, and the son, and the friends who were advisers, for I understood that all these things were a parable. 2 He answered me and said, "You are very arrogant in asking questions. You ought not," said he, "to ask any questions at all, for if it is necessary to have it explained to you, it will be explained." I said to him, "Sir, whatever you show me and do not explain, I will have seen in vain and will not understand what it is. And likewise, if you tell me a parable and do not interpret it to me, I will have heard something from you in vain." 3 Again he answered me and said, "Whoever," he said, "is a servant of God and has his Lord in his heart may ask for understanding from him and receive it, and interpret every parable, and with the help of the Lord those things spoken through parables are made known to him. But as many as," said he, "are weak and careless in prayer, those hesitate to ask of the Lord. 4 But the Lord is very compassionate and gives without hesitating to everyone who asks of him. But since you have been empowered by the glorious angel, and have received from him such a power of intercession and are not careless, why do you not ask for understanding from the Lord and receive it from him?" 5 I said to him, "Sir, since I have you with me, I will, of necessity, ask you and question you, for you show me everything and talk with me. But if I had seen or heard these things without you, I would ask the Lord that it might be explained to me."

58 "I told you just now," he said, "that you were sly and arrogant in asking for the explanations of the parables. But since you are so stubborn, I will explain to you the parable of the field and the rest of all that followed it, so that you can make them known to everyone. Listen now," he said, "and understand them. 2 The field is this world and the Lord of the field is he who created all things, and completed them and gave them power. The son is the holy Spirit. The slave is the Son of God, and the vines are this people which he himself planted. 3 The fences are the holy angels of the Lord who hold his people together. The weeds which were pulled up out of the vineyard are the iniquities of the servants of God. The foods which he sent him from the table are the commandments which he gave to his people through his Son. The friends and advisers are the holy angels who were created first. The absence of the master is the time remaining until his coming." 4 I said to him, "Sir, it is all great and wonderful and it is glorious. So, how," I said, "could I have understood these things? Nor could any other person, even if he were very intelligent, understand these things. Furthermore, sir," I said, "explain to me what I am about to ask you." 5 "Speak," he said, "if you wish anything." "Why, sir," said I, "does the Son of God appear in the guise of a slave in the parable?"

59 "Listen," he said, "the Son of God does not appear in the guise of a slave, but appears with great power and authority." "How, sir?" I said, "I do not understand." 2 "Because God planted the vineyard," he said, "that is, created the people, and he turned it over to his Son. And the Son appointed the angels to protect every one of them, and having worked much and endured many labors, he himself cleansed their sins. For no one is able to cultivate a vineyard without labor and hardship. 3 So when he had cleansed the sins of the people, he showed them the paths of life and gave them the law which he received from his Father. You see, then," said he, "that, since he received all power from his Father, he is Lord of the people. 4 But hear why the Lord took, as a counselor concerning the inheritance of the slave, his Son, and the glorious angels. 5 The preexistent holy Spirit, which created all creation, God caused to dwell in that flesh which he wished. So this flesh, in which the holy Spirit dwelled, served the Spirit well, living in reverence and purity, and did not defile the Spirit in any way. 6 So because it conducted itself appropriately and purely and worked with the Spirit and collaborated in every deed, acting with strength and courage, he chose it as partner with the holy Spirit, for the conduct of this flesh pleased God because it was not defiled while it possessed the holy Spirit on earth. 7 So he took the Son as a counselor, and the glorious angels, that this flesh also, after it served the Spirit blamelessly, should have some place to dwell and not seem to have lost the reward of its servitude. For all flesh in which the holy Spirit has dwelled, when found undefiled and spotless, will receive a reward. 8 You have the explanation of this parable also."

60 "I am glad, sir," I said, "to hear this explanation." "Listen, now," he said, "keep this flesh of yours pure and undefiled, so that the Spirit that dwells in it may bear witness to it and your flesh may be justified. 2 Beware, lest it enter your heart that this flesh of yours is mortal and you misuse it in some defilement. If you defile your flesh, you defile also the holy Spirit; and if you defile your flesh, you will not live." 3 "But if, sir," I said, "there was any previous ignorance, before these words were heard, how will the person who has defiled his flesh be saved?" "Concerning former sins committed in ignorance," he said, "it is possible for God alone to give healing, for all power is his. 4 But now keep these things, and the Lord who is very compassionate will heal them, if henceforth you defile neither your flesh nor the Spirit. For both belong together and neither can be defiled without the other. So keep both clean and you will live to God."

Similitude VI

61 While I was sitting in my house and glorifying the Lord for all that I had seen, and reflecting on the commandments because they were fine and powerful and joyous and glorious and able to save the soul of a person, I said to myself, "I will be blessed if I walk in these commandments, and whoever walks in them will be blessed." 2 While I was saying this to myself, I unexpectedly saw him sitting beside me and saying these things, "Why are you double-minded about the commandments which I have commanded you? They are fine. Be not double-minded at all, but put on the faith of the Lord, and walk in them, for I will strengthen you in them. 3 These commandments are beneficial for those who are going to repent, for if they do not walk in them, their repentance is in vain. 4 So you who repent must put aside the evils of this world which destroy you, and by putting on every virtue of righteousness you will be able to keep these commandments and add no longer to your sins. So by adding nothing you will cut off much of your former sins. So walk in my commandments and you will live to God. All these things have been spoken to you by me." 5 After he had spoken of these things with me, he said to me, "Let us go into the country, and I will show you the shepherds of the sheep." "Let us go, sir," I said. We came to some plain, and he showed me a young shepherd wearing a suit of clothes yellow in color. 6 He was tending very many sheep and these sheep seemed as if they were living luxuriously and indulgently and were joyous as they skipped here and there. And the shepherd himself was most joyful over his flock, and even the appearance of the shepherd was very joyful, and he ran about among the sheep. And I saw in one place other sheep living indulgently and luxuriously, but they were not skipping about.

62 He said to me, "Do you see this shepherd?" he said. "I see, sir," I said. "This," said he, "is the angel of luxury and deception. He destroys the souls of the servants of God who are empty, and turns them away from the truth by deceiving them with evil desires in which they are destroyed. 2 For they forgot the commandments of the living God and walk in deception and vain luxury and are destroyed by this angel, some to death and some to corruption." 3 I said to him, "Sir, I do not know what 'to death' and 'to corruption' mean." "Listen," he said, "the sheep which you see that are very joyful and are skipping about are the ones who have completely withdrawn from God and have given themselves over to the desires of this world. For these, then, there is no repentance unto life, for, in addition, they have blasphemed against the name of the Lord. For such, then, there is death. 4 But the ones that you saw not skipping about, but feeding in one place, are those who have given themselves over to luxury and deceit, but have not blasphemed against the Lord. So these are corrupted from the truth. For them, then, there is hope of repentance, by which they are able to live. So corruption has some hope of renewal, but death has eternal destruction." 5 Again we went on a little farther, and he showed me a large shepherd who seemed wild in appearance, wearing a white goatskin, and he had a bag on his shoulder, and a very hard and knotted staff in his hand, and a great whip. And he had a very bitter look, so that I was afraid of him; such a look had he. 6 This shepherd, then, was receiving from the young shepherd the sheep, those that were living indulgently and luxuriously but not skipping about, and he set them in a certain precipitous place, full of thorns and thistles, so that the sheep were unable to disentangle themselves from the thorns and thistles, but were caught in the thorns and thistles. 7 So they were feeding while entangled in thorns and thistles and, being beaten by him, they were very miserable. And he was driving them about here and there, and he gave them no rest at all, and those sheep had no peace at all.

63 So when I saw them so flogged and miserable, I was distressed on their account because they were so tormented and had no relief at all. 2 I said to the shepherd who was speaking with me, "Sir, who is this shepherd who is so merciless and bitter and has no compassion at all for these sheep?" "This," said he, "is the angel of punishment. He belongs to the righteous angels, but he is in charge of punishment. 3 He receives, then, those who have strayed from God and walked in the desires and deceptions of this world, and he punishes them, as is fitting, with various terrible punishments." 4 "I would like to know, sir," I said, "what these various punishments are like." "Listen," said he, "to the various torments and punishments. The torments befall one during his earthly life, for some are punished with losses, some with deprivations, some with various illnesses, some with total disturbance, some are abused by unworthy persons and suffer many other things. 5 For since many are unsettled in their decisions, they try many things, and nothing at all succeeds for them. And they say that they do not prosper in their affairs, and it does not enter their hearts that they have done evil deeds, but they blame the Lord. 6 So whenever they suffer every kind of affliction, they are turned over to me for good instruction and are strengthened in the faith of the Lord and serve the Lord with pure hearts the rest of the days of their lives. Then whenever they repent, the evil deeds which they did come to their hearts, and then they glorify God because he is a righteous judge and because each one rightly suffered everything for what he had done. From then on they will serve the Lord with their hearts pure, and prosper in all that they do, receiving from the Lord all that they ask. And then they glorify the Lord because they were turned over to me and no longer suffer any evil."

64 I said to him, "Sir, explain something else to me." "What do you want to know?" he said. "Whether, sir," said I, "those who live luxuriously and in self-deception are tormented for the same time as they lived in luxury and self-deception?" He said to me, "They are tormented for the same time." 2 "Sir," said I, "they are tormented too little, for those who live in luxury and forget God ought to be tormented sevenfold." 3 He said to me, "You are foolish and you do not understand the power of torment." "Well, sir," I said, "if I had understood, I would not have asked you to explain it to me." "Listen," said he, "to the power of both. 4 The time of luxury and deception is one hour, but an hour of torment has the power of thirty days. So if anyone lives in luxury and self-deception for

one day, and is tormented for one day, the day of torment has the impact of a whole year. So a man is tormented for as many years as days he lives in luxury. You see, then," he said, "that the time of luxury and deception is very short, while that of punishment and torment is great."

65 "Sir," I said, "since I do not understand at all about the times of deception and luxury and of torment, explain it more clearly to me." 2 He answered and said, "Your foolishness is persistent, and you do not wish to purify your heart and serve God. Be careful," he said, "lest the time be fulfilled and you still be found foolish. Listen then," said he, "so that you understand these things, just as you wish. 3 The one who lives in luxury and self-deception for one day, and does as he pleases, has put on considerable foolishness, and does not know what he is doing. For on the next day he forgets what he has done the day before. For luxury and deception have no memory because of the foolishness in which they are clothed. But when punishment and torment cling to a person for one day, he is punished and tormented for a year, for punishment and torment have long memories. 4 So when a person is tormented and punished for a whole year, then he remembers the luxury and deception, and he knows that he suffers evil because of them. So every person who lives in luxury and self-deception is tormented in this way, for even though they have life, they have given themselves over to death." 5 "Sir," said I, "what sorts of luxury are harmful?" "Everything," he said, "which a person likes to do is a luxury for him. For even the person who is ill-tempered lives in luxury when he satisfies his passion. And the adulterer and the drunkard and the slanderer and the liar and the one who covets and the robber and the one who does such things as these satisfies his own sickness. So he lives in luxury by his own action. 6 All these luxuries are harmful to the servant of God. So because of these deceptions, those who are punished and tormented are suffering. 7 But there are also luxuries which save people. For many live in luxury because they are moved to do good by their own pleasure. So this luxury is advantageous for the servants of God and brings life to such a person. But the harmful luxuries mentioned before bring torments and punishments, and if they persist and do not repent, they bring death on themselves."

Similitude VII

66 A few days later I saw him in the same plain where I had also seen the shepherds, and he said to me, "What do you want to know?" "I am here to ask you, sir," said I, "to command the punishing shepherd to leave my house, for he troubles me very much." "It is necessary for you to be troubled," he said, "for so has the glorious angel given orders concerning you. For he wants you to be tested." "Why, what have I done so evil, sir," said I, "that I should be given over to this angel?" 2 "Listen," he said. "Your sins are many, but not such that you ought to be given over to this angel. But your house has done great sins and iniquities, and the glorious angel has become embittered by their deeds, and for this reason he ordered you to be troubled for a while, that they also might repent and cleanse themselves of all the desires of this world. So whenever they repent and are cleansed, then the angel of punishment will leave you." 3 I said to him, "Sir, even if they have done such things that the glorious angel has become embittered, what have I done?" "There is no other way they can be troubled," said he, "than if you, the head of the house, be troubled. For when you are troubled, they of necessity will also be troubled, but while you prosper, they can have no trouble." 4 "But look, sir," I said, "they have re-pented with all their hearts." "I also know," he said, "that they have repented with all their hearts. Do you think," he said, "the sins of those who repent are immediately forgiven? By no means! But the one who repents must torment his own soul and be extremely humble in everything he does and be troubled with all kinds of tribulations. And if he endures the tribulations that come to him, surely the one who created and enabled all things will have compassion and give him some healing, 5 and this, certainly, if he sees that the heart of the one who repented is clean of every evil deed. But it is beneficial for you and your house to be troubled at this time. But why do I tell you so many things? You must be troubled, just as that angel of the Lord who gave you over to me has ordered. And give thanks to the Lord for this, that he considered you worthy to show you the tribulation beforehand, so that, knowing of it in advance, you may bear it bravely." 6 I said to him, "Sir, you stay with me, and I will be able to endure every tribulation." "I will be with you," he said, "and I will ask the punishing angel to trouble you more lightly. But you will be troubled for a little while and you will be restored again to your place. Only continue to be humble minded and serve the Lord with a pure heart, both your children and your household, and walk in my commandments which I give you, and your repentance can be strong and pure. 7 And if you, with your family, keep these things, all trouble will leave you, and trouble will leave all" he said, "who walk in these my commandments."

The Apocalypse of Peter

Three different apocalypses surviving from ancient Christianity claim to have been written by Peter. The one presented here was discovered in 1887 in the tomb of a Christian monk, along with the *Gospel of Peter* (see that Introduction), and subsequently found in a fuller Ethiopic translation. This apocalypse was well known in early Christianity; some churches counted it among the New Testament Scriptures. Even when it came to be excluded from the canon (in part because Christians realized that it was pseudonymous), the book continued to exercise a significant influence on Christian thought. This is the first Christian writing to describe a journey through hell and heaven, an account that inspired a large number of successors, including, ultimately, Dante's *Divine Comedy*.

The book begins with Peter and the other disciples on the Mount of Olives listening to Jesus deliver his "apocalyptic discourse" (see Mark 13). Peter asks about the end of the world. Jesus responds by describing the terrifying events that will occur when the world is destroyed by fire at the last judgment. He then details the eternal terrors that await those destined for hell and, more briefly (possibly because they are somewhat less interesting, and certainly less graphic), the perpetual blessings of those bound for heaven.

There is some ambiguity over whether Jesus actually takes Peter on a journey through these two abodes of the dead or simply describes them in such vivid detail that it *feels* as if Peter is actually seeing them. There is no ambiguity, however, concerning the respective fates of those destined for one place or the other. In an unsettling way, the horrific punishments of the damned are made to fit their crimes (chaps. 7–12). Those who have followed Christ and kept the commandments of God, however, will be brought into the eternal kingdom, where they will enjoy the blissful life of heaven forever. The book ends with Peter describing firsthand what he saw on the Mount of Transfiguration, possibly in order to validate the legitimacy of the rest of his vision (cf. 2 Pet 1:17–18).

The ultimate goal of this first-hand description of hellish and heavenly realities is reasonably clear. There is one way to escape eternal torment: avoid sin. This message no doubt made a considerable impact on its Christian readers—it was, after all, written by "Peter," the closest disciple to Jesus, who could therefore be expected to know about such things. Moreover, it became an essential element in the Christian missionary proclamation, providing an incentive for pagans and Jews to turn from their false ways to worship the one true God who would reward those who came to accept his truth, but punish for all eternity those who did not.

The following translation follows the more complete and, probably, more accurate Ethiopic version of the text.

1 The Second Coming of Christ and Resurrection of the Dead which Christ revealed through Peter to those who died for their sins, because they did not keep the commandment of God, their creator.

And he (Peter) pondered thereon, that he might perceive the mystery of the Son of God, the merciful and lover of mercy.

And when the Lord was seated upon the Mount of Olives, his disciples came to him.

And we besought and entreated him severally and implored him, saying to him, "Declare to us what are the signs of your coming and of the end of the world, that we may perceive and mark the time of your coming and instruct those who come after us, to whom we preach the word of your gospel, and whom we install in your church, that they, when they hear it, may take heed to themselves and mark the time of your coming."

And our Lord answered us saying, "Take heed that no one deceive you and that you be not doubters and serve other gods. Many shall come in my name saying, 'I am the Christ.' Believe them not, neither draw near to them. For the coming of the Son of God shall not be plain; but as the lightning that shines from the east to the west, so will I come upon the clouds of heaven with a great host in my majesty; with my cross going before my face will I come in my majesty; shining seven times brighter than the sun will I come in my majesty with all my saints, my angels. And my Father shall set a crown upon my head, that I may judge the quick and the dead and recompense every one according to his works.

2 "And you learn a parable from the fig-tree: as soon as its shoots have come forth and the twigs grown, the end of the world shall come."

And I, Peter, answered and said to him, "Interpret the fig-tree to me: how can we understand it? For throughout all its days the fig-tree sends forth shoots and every year it brings forth its fruit for its master? What then does the parable of the fig-tree mean? We do not know."

And the Master answered and said to me, "Do you not understand that the fig-tree is the house of Israel? It is like a man who planted a fig-tree in his garden and it brought forth no fruit. And he sought the fruit many years, and when he did not find it he said to the keeper of his garden, 'Uproot this fig-tree so that it does not make our ground un-fruitful.' And the gardener said to his master, 'Let us rid it of weeds and dig the ground round about it and water it. If then it does not bear fruit, we will straightway uproot it from the garden and plant another in place of it.' Have you not understood that the fig-tree is the house of Israel? Verily I say to you, when its twigs have sprouted forth in the last days, then shall false Christs come and awake expectation, saying 'I am the Christ who has now come into the world.' And when they perceive the wickedness of their deeds they shall turn away and deny him whom our fathers praised, the first Christ whom they crucified and therein sinned a great sin. But this deceiver is not the Christ. And when they reject him, he shall slay them with the sword, and there shall be many martyrs. Then shall the twigs of the fig-tree, that is, the house of Israel, shoot forth: many shall become martyrs at his hand. Enoch and Elijah shall be sent to teach them that this is the deceiver who must come into the world and do signs and wonders in order to deceive. And therefore those who die by his hand shall be martyrs, and shall be reckoned among the good and righteous martyrs who have pleased God in their life."

3 And he showed me in his right hand the souls of all people. And on the palm of his right hand the image of that which shall be accomplished at the last day; and how the righteous and the sinners shall be separated, and how those who are upright in heart will fare, and how the evil-doers shall be rooted out to all eternity. We beheld how the sinners wept in great affliction and sorrow, until all who saw it with their eyes wept, whether righteous or angels, and he himself also.

And I asked him and said to him, "Lord, allow me to speak your word concerning the sinners, 'It were better for them if they had not been created.'" And the Saviour answered and said to me, "Peter, why do you say that not to have been created were better for them? You resist God. You would not have more compassion than he for his image: for he has created them and brought them forth out of not-being. Now because you have seen the lamentation which shall come upon the sinners in the last days, therefore your heart is troubled; but I will show you their works, whereby they have sinned against the Most High.

4 "Behold now what shall come upon them in

the last days, when the day of God and the day of the decision of the judgment of God comes. From the east to the west shall all the children of men be gathered together before my Father who lives for ever. And he shall command hell to open its bars of adamant and give up all that is therein.

"And the wild beasts and the fowls shall he command to restore all the flesh that they have devoured, because he wills that people should appear; for nothing perishes before God and nothing is impossible with him, because all things are his.

"For all things come to pass on the day of decision, on the day of judgment, at the word of God: and as all things were done when he created the world and commanded all that is therein and it was done, even so shall it be in the last days; for all things are possible with God. And therefore he said in the scripture, 'Son of man, prophesy upon the several bones and say to the bones: bone unto bone in joints, sinew, nerves, flesh, and skin and hair thereon.'[1]

"And soul and spirit shall the great Uriel give them at the commandment of God; for God has set him over the resurrection of the dead at the day of judgment.

"Behold and consider the corns of wheat that are sown in the earth. As something dry and without soul do men sow them in the earth: and they live again and bear fruit, and the earth restores them as a pledge entrusted to it.

"And this which dies, that is sown as seed in the earth, and shall become alive and be restored to life, is man.

"How much more shall God raise up on the day of decision those who believe in him and are chosen of him, for whose sake he made the world? And all things shall the earth restore on the day of decision, for it also shall be judged with them, and the heaven with it.

5 "And this shall come at the day of judgment upon those who have fallen away from faith in God and have committed sin. Cataracts of fire shall be let loose; and darkness and obscurity shall come up and clothe and veil the whole world; and the waters shall be changed and turned into coals of fire, and all that is in them shall burn, and the sea shall become fire. Under the heaven there shall be a sharp fire that cannot be quenched, and it flows to fulfil the judgment of wrath. And the stars shall be melted by flames of fire, as if they had not been created, and the firmaments of the heaven shall pass away for lack of water and shall be as though they had not been. And the lightnings of heaven shall be no more, and by their enchantment they shall affright the world. The spirits of the dead bodies shall be like them and shall become fire at the commandment of God.

"And as soon as the whole creation dissolves, the people who are in the east shall flee to the west, [and those who are in the west] to the east; those in the south shall flee to the north, and those who are in the north to the south. And in all places shall the wrath of a fearful fire overtake them; and an unquenchable flame driving them shall bring them to the judgment of wrath, to the stream of unquenchable fire which flows, flaming with fire, and when the waves thereof part themselves one from another, burning, there shall be a great gnashing of teeth among the children of men.

6 "Then shall they all behold me coming upon an eternal cloud of brightness; and the angels of God who are with me shall sit upon the throne of my glory at the right hand of my heavenly Father; and he shall set a crown upon my head. And when the nations behold it, they shall weep, every nation for itself.

"Then shall he command them to enter into the river of fire while the works of every one of them shall stand before them. [Rewards shall be given] to everyone according to his deeds. As for the elect who have done good, they shall come to me and not see death by the devouring fire. But the unrighteous, the sinners, and the hypocrites shall stand in the depths of darkness that shall not pass away, and their chastisement is the fire, and angels bring forward their sins and prepare for them a place wherein they shall be punished for ever, every one according to his transgression.

"Uriel the angel of God shall bring forth the souls of those sinners who perished in the flood, and of all who dwelt in all idols, in every molten image, in every object of love, and in pictures, and of those who dwelt on all hills and in stones and by the wayside, whom people called gods: they shall be burned with them in everlasting fire; and after all of them with their dwelling-

---

[1]Ezek 37:4–6

places are destroyed, they shall be punished eternally.

7 "Then shall men and women come to the place prepared for them. By their tongues wherewith they have blasphemed the way of righteousness shall they be hanged up. There is spread under them unquenchable fire so that they do not escape it.

"Behold another place: there is a pit, great and full. In it are those who have denied righteousness: and angels of punishment chastise them and there they kindle upon them the fire of their torment.

"And again behold two women: they hang them up by their neck and by their hair; they shall cast them into the pit. These are those who plaited their hair, not to make themselves beautiful but to turn them to fornication, that they might ensnare the souls of men to perdition. And the men who lay with them in fornication shall be hung by their loins in that place of fire; and they shall say one to another, 'We did not know that we should come to everlasting punishment.'

"And the murderers and those who have made common cause with them shall they cast into the fire, in a place full of venomous beasts, and they shall be tormented without rest, feeling their pains; and their worms shall be as many in number as a dark cloud. And the angel Ezrael shall bring forth the souls of those who have been slain, and they shall behold the torment of those who slew them and say one to another, 'Righteousness and justice is the judgment of God. For we heard, but we believed not, that we should come into this place of eternal judgment.'

8 "And near this flame there is a pit, great and very deep, and into it flows from above all manner of torment, foulness, and excrement. And women are swallowed up therein up to their necks and tormented with great pain. These are they who have caused their children to be born untimely and have corrupted the work of God who created them. Opposite them shall be another place where children sit alive and cry to God. And flashes of lightning go forth from those children and pierce the eyes of those who for fornication's sake have caused their destruction.

"Other men and women shall stand above them, naked; and their children stand opposite them in a place of delight, and sigh and cry to God because of their parents saying, 'These are they who despised and cursed and transgressed your commandments and delivered us to death: they have cursed the angel that formed us and have hanged us up and begrudged us the light which you have given to all creatures. And the milk of their mothers flowing from their breasts shall congeal and from it shall come beasts devouring flesh, which shall come forth and turn and torment them for ever with their husbands because they forsook the commandments of God and slew their children. As for their children, they shall be delivered to the angel Temlakos. And those who slew them shall be tormented eternally, for God wills it so.

9 "Ezrael the angel of wrath shall bring men and women, with half of their bodies burning, and cast them into a place of darkness, the hell of men; and a spirit of wrath shall chastise them with all manner of torment, and a worm that never sleeps shall devour their entrails; and these are the persecutors and betrayers of my righteous ones.

"And beside those who are there, shall be other men and women, gnawing their tongues; and they shall torment them with red-hot irons and burn their eyes. These are they who slander and doubt my righteousness.

"Other men and women whose works were done in deceitfulness shall have their lips cut off; and fire enters into their mouth and their entrails. These are they who caused the martyrs to die by their lying.

"And beside them, in a place near at hand, upon the stone shall be a pillar of fire, and the pillar is sharper than swords. And there shall be men and women clad in rags and filthy garments, and they shall be cast thereon to suffer the judgment of an unceasing torment; these are the ones who trusted in their riches and despised the widows and the women with fatherless children . . . before God.

10 "And into another place nearby, full of filth, they cast men and women up to the knees. These are they who lent money and took usury.

"And other men and women cast themselves down from a high place and return again and run, and devils drive them. These are the worshippers of idols, and they drive them up to the top of the height and they cast themselves down. And this they do continually and are tormented for ever. These are they who have cut their flesh as apostles of a man: and the women with them . . . and these are the men who defiled themselves together as women.

"And beside them . . . and beneath them shall the angel Ezrael prepare a place of much fire: and all the idols of gold and silver, all idols, the work of human hands, and the semblances of images of cats and lions, of creeping things and wild beasts, and the men and women that have prepared the images thereof, shall be in chains of fire and shall be chastised because of their error before the idols, and this is their judgment for ever.

"And beside them shall be other men and women, burning in the fire of the judgment, and their torment is everlasting. These are they who have forsaken the commandment of God and followed the (persuasions?) of devils.

11 "And there shall be another place, very high . . . The men and women whose feet slip shall go rolling down into a place where is fear. And again while the fire that is prepared flows, they mount up and fall down again and continue to roll down. Thus shall they be tormented for ever. These are they who honored not their father and mother and of their own accord withheld themselves from them. Therefore shall they be chastised eternally.

"Furthermore the angel Ezrael shall bring children and maidens, to show them those who are tormented. They shall be chastised with pains, with hanging up(?) and with a multitude of wounds which flesh-devouring birds shall inflict upon them. These are they who trust in their sins and do not obey their parents and do not follow the instruction of their fathers and do not honor those more aged than they.

"Beside them shall be girls clad in darkness for a garment, and they shall be seriously punished and their flesh shall be torn in pieces. These are they who did not preserve their virginity until they were given in marriage and with these torments shall they be punished and shall feel them.

"And again, other men and women, gnawing their tongues without ceasing, and being tormented with everlasting fire. These are the servants who were not obedient to their masters; and this then is their judgment for ever.

12 "And near by this place of torment shall be men and women who are dumb and blind and whose raiment is white. They shall crowd one upon another, and fall upon coals of unquenchable fire. These are they who give alms and say, 'We are righteous before God', whereas they have not sought after righteousness.

"Ezrael the angel of God shall bring them forth out of this fire and establish a judgment of decision(?). This then is their judgment. A river of fire shall flow, and all those judged shall be drawn down into the middle of the river. And Uriel shall set them there.

"And there are wheels of fire, and men and women hung thereon by the force of the whirling. And those in the pit shall burn; now these are the sorcerers and sorceresses. Those wheels shall be in all decision by fire without number.

13 "Thereafter shall the angels bring my elect and righteous who are perfect in all uprightness and bear them in their hands and clothe them with the raiment of the life that is above. They shall see their desire on those who hated them, when he punishes them and the torment of every one shall be for ever according to his works.

"And all those in torment shall say with one voice, 'Have mercy upon us, for now we know the judgment of God, which he declared to us beforetime and we did not believe.' And the angel Tatirokos shall come and chastise them with even greater torment, and say to them, 'Now do you repent, when it is no longer the time for repentance, and nothing of life remains.' And they shall say, 'Righteous is the judgment of God, for we have heard and perceived that his judgment is good, for we are recompensed according to our deeds.'

14 "Then will I give to my elect and righteous the baptism and the salvation for which they have besought me, in the field of Akrosja (Acherusia) which is called Aneslasleja (Elysium). They shall adorn with flowers the portion of the righteous, and I shall go . . . I shall rejoice with them. I will cause the peoples to enter into my everlasting kingdom, and show them eternal good things to which I have made them set their hope, I and my Father in heaven.

"I have spoke this to you, Peter, and declared it to you. Go forth therefore and go to the city of the west and enter into the vineyard which I shall tell you of, in order that by the sufferings of the Son who is without sin the deeds of corruption may be sanctified. As for you, you are chosen according to

the promise which I have given you. Spread my gospel throughout all the world in peace. Verily people shall rejoice; my words shall be the source of hope and of life, and suddenly shall the world be ravished.

15 And my Lord Jesus Christ, our King, said to me, "Let us go to the holy mountain." And his disciples went with him, praying.

And behold there were two men there, and we could not look upon their faces, for a light came from them, shining more than the sun and their raiment also was shining and cannot be described and nothing is sufficient to be compared to them in this world. And the sweetness of them . . . that no mouth is able to utter the beauty of their appearance, for their aspect was astonishing and wonderful. And the other, great, I say, shines in his aspect above crystal. Like the flower of roses is the appearance of the color of his aspect and of his body . . . his head. And upon his shoulders . . . and on their foreheads was a crown of nard woven from fair flowers. As the rainbow in the water, so was their hair. And such was the comeliness of their countenance, adorned with all manner of ornament.

16 And when we suddenly saw them, we marvelled. And I drew near to God, Jesus Christ, and said to him, "O my Lord, who are these?" And he said to me, "They are Moses and Elijah." And I said to him, "Where then are Abraham and Isaac and Jacob and the rest of the righteous fathers?" And he showed us a great garden, open, full of fair trees and blessed fruits and of the odor of perfumes. The fragrance was pleasant and reached us. And of that tree . . . I saw many fruits. And my Lord and God Jesus Christ said to me, "Have you seen the companies of the fathers?"

"As is their rest, such also is the honor and the glory of those who are persecuted for my righteousness' sake." And I rejoiced and believed and understood that which is written in the book of my Lord Jesus Christ. And I said to him, "O my Lord, do you wish that I make here three tabernacles, one for you, and one for Moses, and one for Elijah?".[2] And he said to me in wrath, "Satan makes war against you, and has veiled your understanding; and the good things of this world prevail against you. Your eyes therefore must be opened and your ears unstopped that you may see a tabernacle, not made with human hands, which my heavenly Father has made for me and for the elect." And we beheld it and were full of gladness.

17 And behold, suddenly there came a voice from heaven, saying, "This is my beloved Son in whom I am well pleased:[3] [he has kept] my commandments." And then came a great and exceedingly white cloud over our heads and bore away our Lord and Moses and Elijah. And I trembled and was afraid; and we looked up, and the heaven opened and we beheld men in the flesh and they came and greeted our Lord and Moses and Elijah and went to another heaven. And the word of the scripture was fulfilled: "This is the generation that seeks him and seeks the face of the God of Jacob."[4] And great fear and commotion took place in heaven, and the angels pressed one upon another that the word of the scripture might be fulfilled which says, "Open the gates, you princes."[5]

Thereafter was the heaven shut, that had been open.

And we prayed and went down from the mountain, glorifying God, who has written the names of the righteous in heaven in the book of life.

---

[2]Matt 17:4; Mark 9:5; Luke 9:33   [3]Matt 17:5   [4]Ps 24:6   [5]Ps 24:7, 9